*Frommer's*

# *Nova Scotia, New Brunswick & Prince Edward Island*

## *6th Edition*

### *by Paul Karr*

Here's what the critics say about Frommer's:

"Amazingly easy to use. Very portable, very complete."

—*Booklist*

"Detailed, accurate, and easy-to-read information for all price ranges."
—*Glamour Magazine*

"Hotel information is close to encyclopedic."

—*Des Moines Sunday Register*

"Frommer's Guides have a way of giving you a real feel for a place."
—*Knight Ridder Newspapers*

WILEY

Wiley Publishing, Inc.

## About the Author

**Paul Karr** has written, coauthored, or edited more than 25 guidebooks, including *Vancouver & Victoria For Dummies* and *Frommer's Canada*. He has also contributed to Discovery Channel/Insight Guides to Montréal, Atlanta, Vienna, Austria, and Switzerland; and *Scandinavia: The Rough Guide*—while writing articles for *Sierra* and *Sports Illustrated,* among other publications. He divides his time among New England, both coasts of Canada, and Europe.

Published by:

## Wiley Publishing, Inc.

111 River St.
Hoboken, NJ 07030-5774

ISBN-13: 978-0-471-78042-7
ISBN-10: 0-471-78042-1

Editor: Jennifer Moore
Production Editor: Michael Brumitt
Cartographer: Andrew Dolan
Photo Editor: Richard Fox
Production by Wiley Indianapolis Composition Services

For information on our other products and services or to obtain technical support, please contact our Customer Care Department within the U.S. at 800/762-2974, outside the U.S. at 317/572-3993 or fax 317/572-4002.

Wiley also publishes its books in a variety of electronic formats. Some content that appears in print may not be available in electronic formats.

Manufactured in the United States of America

5  4  3  2  1

# Contents

**List of Maps**      v

**What's New in the Atlantic Provinces**      1

**1   The Best of the Atlantic Provinces**      2

**1** The Best Active Vacations . . . . . . . . . .2
**2** The Best Spots for Observing Nature . . .2
**3** The Best Scenic Drives . . . . . . . . . . . .4
**4** The Best Hikes & Rambles . . . . . . . .4
**5** The Best Family Activities . . . . . . . . .5
**6** The Best Places for History . . . . . . . . .6
**7** The Most Picturesque Villages . . . . . . .7
**8** The Best Inns . . . . . . . . . . . . . . . . . .7
**9** The Best Bed & Breakfasts . . . . . . . . .8
**10** The Best Local Dining . . . . . . . . . . . . .8

**2   Planning Your Trip to the Atlantic Provinces**      10

**1** The Atlantic Provinces in Brief . . . . . .10
**2** Visitor Information . . . . . . . . . . . . . .11
**3** Entry Requirements & Customs . . . . .12
**4** Money . . . . . . . . . . . . . . . . . . . . . . .13
**5** When to Go . . . . . . . . . . . . . . . . . .16
**6** Travel Insurance . . . . . . . . . . . . . . .17
**7** Health & Safety . . . . . . . . . . . . . . . .19
**8** Tips for Travelers with
Special Needs . . . . . . . . . . . . . . . . .19
**9** Planning Your Trip Online . . . . . . . . .22
*Frommers.com: The Complete
Travel Resource* . . . . . . . . . . . . . . .24
**10** The 21st-Century Traveler . . . . . . . . .24
**11** Getting There . . . . . . . . . . . . . . . . .26
**12** Getting Around . . . . . . . . . . . . . . . .30
**13** Packages for the Independent
Traveler . . . . . . . . . . . . . . . . . . . . .31
**14** Escorted General-Interest Tours . . . . .32
**15** Special-Interest Trips . . . . . . . . . . . .33
**16** Recommended Books,
Films & Music . . . . . . . . . . . . . . . . .34
*Fast Facts: Atlantic Provinces* . . . . . .37

**3   Suggested Itineraries in the Atlantic Provinces**      40

*Lights Out: The Best of Nova Scotia
in 1 Week* . . . . . . . . . . . . . . . . . . . .40
*High Times, High Tides: The Best
of New Brunswick in 1 Week* . . . . . .42
*Reaching the Beach: Prince Edward
Island for Families* . . . . . . . . . . . . . .44
*Rolling Through the Rock: The Best
of Newfoundland in 2 Weeks* . . . . .46

**4   Nova Scotia**      48

**1** Exploring Nova Scotia . . . . . . . . . . . .48
**2** The Great Outdoors . . . . . . . . . . . . .52
**3** Minas Basin & Cobequid Bay . . . . . .54
*A Scenic Drive* . . . . . . . . . . . . . . . .55
**4** Annapolis Royal . . . . . . . . . . . . . . .58
**5** Kejimkujik National Park . . . . . . . . .62

**6** Digby to Yarmouth ..............64

**7** South Shore ..................72

*The Dauntless* Bluenose ..........78

**8** Halifax ......................86

*A Road Trip to Peggy's Cove* .....103

**9** The Eastern Shore ............104

**10** Amherst to Antigonish ..........107

**11** Cape Breton Island ............115

**12** Cape Breton Highlands
National Park ................137

## 5 New Brunswick                          141

**1** Exploring New Brunswick ........141

**2** The Great Outdoors ............143

**3** Passamaquoddy Bay .............145

**4** Grand Manan Island ............155

**5** Saint John ...................158

**6** Fredericton ..................166

**7** Fundy National Park ............176

**8** Moncton ....................181

**9** Kouchibouguac National Park .....185

**10** Acadian Peninsula .............187

**11** Mt. Carleton Provincial Park ......191

## 6 Prince Edward Island                   193

**1** Exploring Prince Edward Island ....194

**2** The Great Outdoors ............196

**3** Queens County ................198

*Family Fun* ...................201

*Lobster Suppers* ..............206

**4** Prince Edward Island
National Park .................208

**5** Charlottetown ................212

**6** Kings County .................221

*An Excursion to the Magdalen
Islands* ......................227

**7** Prince County .................229

## 7 Newfoundland & Labrador              233

**1** Exploring Newfoundland &
Labrador ...................233

**2** The Great Outdoors ............236

**3** Southwestern Newfoundland .....238

**4** Gros Morne National Park .......244

*Journey to the Center
of the Earth* ................246

**5** The Great Northern Peninsula .....250

*Readers Recommend* ..........253

**6** Central Newfoundland .........255

*Iceberg Spotting* ..............259

**7** Terra Nova National Park .......261

**8** The Bonavista Peninsula ......264

**9** The Baccalieu Trail ............270

**10** St. John's ...................274

**11** The Southern Avalon Peninsula ....286

**12** Labrador ....................291

## Index                                    299

# List of Maps

Atlantic Canada   3

Nova Scotia in 1 Week   41

New Brunswick in 1 Week   43

Prince Edward Island for Families   45

Newfoundland in 2 Weeks   46

Nova Scotia   50

Halifax   87

Cape Breton Island   116

Cape Breton Highlands National
   Park   138

New Brunswick   142

Saint John   159

Fredericton   167

Fundy National Park   177

Prince Edward Island   195

Prince Edward Island National
   Park   209

Charlottetown   213

Island of Newfoundland   235

St. John's   275

Labrador   293

## An Invitation to the Reader

In researching this book, we discovered many wonderful places—hotels, restaurants, shops, and more. We're sure you'll find others. Please tell us about them, so we can share the information with your fellow travelers in upcoming editions. If you were disappointed with a recommendation, we'd love to know that, too. Please write to:

*Frommer's Nova Scotia, New Brunswick & Prince Edward Island,* 6th Edition
Wiley Publishing, Inc. • 111 River St. • Hoboken, NJ 07030-5774

## An Additional Note

Please be advised that travel information is subject to change at any time—and this is especially true of prices. We therefore suggest that you write or call ahead for confirmation when making your travel plans. The authors, editors, and publisher cannot be held responsible for the experiences of readers while traveling. Your safety is important to us, however, so we encourage you to stay alert and be aware of your surroundings. Keep a close eye on cameras, purses, and wallets, all favorite targets of thieves and pickpockets.

## Other Great Guides for Your Trip:

*Frommer's Canada*

*Frommer's Toronto*

*Frommer's Vancouver & Victoria*

*Frommer's British Columbia & the Canadian Rockies*

*Vancouver & Victoria For Dummies*

## Frommer's Star Ratings, Icons & Abbreviations

Every hotel, restaurant, and attraction listing in this guide has been ranked for quality, value, service, amenities, and special features using a **star-rating system.** In country, state, and regional guides, we also rate towns and regions to help you narrow down your choices and budget your time accordingly. Hotels and restaurants are rated on a scale of zero (recommended) to three stars (exceptional). Attractions, shopping, nightlife, towns, and regions are rated according to the following scale: zero stars (recommended), one star (highly recommended), two stars (very highly recommended), and three stars (must-see).

In addition to the star-rating system, we also use **seven feature icons** that point you to the great deals, in-the-know advice and unique experiences that separate travelers from tourists. Throughout the book, look for:

| | |
|---|---|
| *Finds* | Special finds—those places only insiders know about |
| *Fun Fact* | Fun facts—details that make travelers more informed and their trips more fun |
| *Kids* | Best bets for kids, and advice for the whole family |
| *Moments* | Special moments–those experiences that memories are made of |
| *Overrated* | Places or experiences not worth your time or money |
| *Tips* | Insider tips—great ways to save time and money |
| *Value* | Great values—where to get the best deals |

The following **abbreviations** are used for credit cards:

| | | | | | |
|---|---|---|---|---|---|
| AE | American Express | DISC | Discover | V | Visa |
| DC | Diners Club | MC | MasterCard | | |

## Frommers.com

Now that you have the guidebook to a great trip, visit our website at **www.frommers.com** for travel information on more than 3,000 destinations. With features updated regularly, we give you instant access to the most current trip-planning information available. At Frommers.com, you'll also find the best prices on airfares, accommodations, and car rentals—and you can even book travel online through our travel booking partners. At Frommers.com, you'll also find the following:

- Online updates to our most popular guidebooks
- Vacation sweepstakes and contest giveaways
- Newsletter highlighting the hottest travel trends
- Online travel message boards with featured travel discussions

# What's New in the Atlantic Provinces

Things change *verrrrry* slowly in Eastern Canada, and sometimes they don't change much at all. Nevertheless, there are a few recent developments to note.

**PLANNING YOUR TRIP** If you prefer an oversea journey to one by air, there's one big change to take note of: Prince of Fundy's *Scotia Prince* cruise line—a popular overnight/daylong cruise ship connecting Portland, Maine with Yarmouth, Nova Scotia—has sadly ceased operations after a protracted dispute with the city of Portland over a marine terminal could not be resolved.

To pick up the slack, the fast **CAT ferry** service ((*C*) **888/249-SAIL;** www.catferry. com) operating out of Bar Harbor, Maine, increased its summertime service schedule in 2005. However, bear in mind that you'll need to plan for 3 extra hours of driving beyond Portland to catch it—and most departures are early in the morning. Check the ferry's website for details of the ferry line's 2006 sailing schedules.

**VIA Rail,** Canada's national rail line ((*C*) **888/842-7245;** www.viarail.com), has added a higher class of service on its overnight run from Montréal to Halifax. Check the website for details of this new Easterly Class service, which is expected to operate from May through October in 2006. Standard overnight sleeper cabin service on the route will continue to be offered year-round.

**EXPLORING NOVA SCOTIA** In the historic waterside town of **Lunenburg,** restoration of the **St. John's Anglican Church,** which burned to the ground in late 2001, has finally been completed. The church was reopened to the public in a stirring ceremony in June 2005, and it may once again be toured daily for free. It is a fine reminder of what had been one of the most beautiful of all wooden churches in North America.

**EXPLORING NEW BRUNSWICK** It's getting easier all the time to reach this province. Where you once had to fly into Saint John if you wanted to visit, **Delta** ((*C*) **888/221-1212;** www.delta.com) now flies twice daily from Boston to Fredericton, and Calgary-based **WestJet** ((*C*) **888/ 937-8538;** www.westjet.com) connects Moncton with Halifax, Toronto, St. John's, and Calgary, which can then be connected onward to Florida, Los Angeles, and Las Vegas without switching airlines.

**EXPLORING PRINCE EDWARD ISLAND** Lady Catherine's, a B&B in Montague, has closed its doors. And Café St. Jean in Oyster Bed Bridge—a fine place to get a Cajun or Creole meal and catch live music—is no longer operating.

**EXPLORING NEWFOUNDLAND & LABRADOR** The most important museum in the city of St. John's has a new home. The **Provincial Museum of Newfoundland and Labrador** relocated to new digs known as The Rooms, at 9 Bonventure Ave., in the summer of 2005.

# The Best of the Atlantic Provinces

**P**lanning a trip to Atlantic Canada can present a bewildering array of choices. I've searched Nova Scotia, New Brunswick, Prince Edward Island, Newfoundland, and Labrador for the best places and experiences. Here are some of my personal and opinionated top choices.

## 1 The Best Active Vacations

- **Sea Kayaking** (Nova Scotia): The twisting, convoluted coastline of this province is custom-made for snooping around by sea kayak. Outfitters are scattered all around the peninsula. For expedition kayaking, contact Coastal Adventures (© **877/404-2774** or 902/772-2774; www.coastaladventures.com), which leads trips throughout Nova Scotia and beyond. See chapter 4.
- **Biking the Cabot Trail** (Nova Scotia): This long and strenuous loop around Cape Breton Highlands National Park is tough on the legs, but you'll come away with a head full of indelible memories. See "Cape Breton Island," in chapter 4.
- **Exploring Fundy National Park & Vicinity** (New Brunswick): You'll find swimming, hiking, and kayaking at this lovely national park. And don't

overlook biking in the hills east of the park, or rappelling and rock climbing at Cape Enrage. See "Fundy National Park," in chapter 5.
- **Bicycling Prince Edward Island:** This island province sometimes seems like it was created specifically for bike touring. Villages are reasonably spaced, the hills virtually nonexistent, coastal roads picturesque in the extreme, and a new island-wide bike path offers detours through marshes and quiet woodlands. See "The Great Outdoors," in chapter 6.
- **Hiking Gros Morne National Park** (Newfoundland): Atlantic Canada's best hiking is found in these rugged hills. You can hike amazing coastal trails, marvel at scenic waterfalls, and stroll alongside landlocked fjords at this exceptional park. See "The Great Outdoors," in chapter 7.

## 2 The Best Spots for Observing Nature

- **Digby Neck** (Nova Scotia): Choose from a dozen whale-watching outfitters located along this narrow peninsula of remote fishing villages. Getting to the tip of the peninsula is half the fun—it requires two ferries.

See "Digby to Yarmouth," in chapter 4.
- **Cape Breton Highlands National Park** (Nova Scotia): The craggy geology of the west coast is impressive, but don't let that overshadow the rest

# Atlantic Canada

GREENLAND
(Denmark)

Resolution I.
(Nunavut)

Akpatok I.
(Nunavut)     C. Chidley

Ungava
Bay

Koksoak R.

L A B R A D O R

Hebron

Nutak

S E A

Baleine R.

George R.

Nain

Davis
Inlet

Caniapiscau
Res.

Postville

Smallwood Res.

Churchill
Falls

Rigolet

Cartwright

L. Melville

Labrador
City

Churchill

Happy Valley-
Goose Bay

Atikunuk L.

Naskaupi

Mécatina R.

Gagnon

Manicouagan
Res.

Red Bay

St. Anthony

Q U É B E C

Port au
Choix

C. St. John

Sept-Îles

Natashquan

Anticosti Island

Corner
Brook

Grand Falls-
Windsor

Gander

Bonavista

Baie-
Comeau

St. Lawrence R.

Gaspé   Gaspé Pen.

Stephenville

Newfoundland

Maelpaeg
Res.

Rimouski

GULF OF
ST. LAWRENCE

ST. JOHN'S

Rivière-
du-Loup

Îles de la
Madeleine
(Que.)

Conception
Bay South

Edmundston

Bathurst

C. Ray

Burgeo

Avalon Pen.

Caribou

Newcastle
NEW
BRUNSWICK

PRINCE
EDWARD
ISLAND

Cabot Strait

Burin Pen.

Trepassey

Houlton

Charlottetown

ST. PIERRE &
MIQUELON
(France)

Fredericton   Moncton

Cape Breton I.   Glace Bay

U.S.A.
MAINE

Saint
John

New-
Glasgow

Sydney

C. Breton

Eastport

Truro

Bangor

Windsor

A T L A N T I C

Bar
Harbor

Bay of
Fundy

Bridgewater

NOVA SCOTIA

HALIFAX

Lunenburg

O C E A N

Yarmouth

Sable I.

C. Sable

| 0 | 200 mi |
| 0 | 200 km |

N

of the park, where you'll find bogs and moose in abundance. See "Cape Breton Highlands National Park," in chapter 4.

- **Grand Manan Island** (New Brunswick): This big, geologically intriguing rock off the New Brunswick coast in the western Bay of Fundy is a great base for learning about coastal ecology. Whale tour operators search out the endangered right whale, and dozens of birds roost and pass through. Boat tours from the island will also take you out to see puffins. See "Grand Manan Island," in chapter 5.

- **Hopewell Rocks** (New Brunswick): The force of Fundy's tremendous tides is the most impressive at Hopewell Rocks, where great rock "sculptures" created by the winds and tides rise from the ocean floor at low tide. See "Fundy National Park," in chapter 5.

- **Avalon Peninsula** (Newfoundland): In 1 busy day you can view a herd of caribou, the largest puffin colony in North America, and an extraordinary gannet colony visible from the mainland cliffs. See "The Southern Avalon Peninsula," in chapter 7.

## 3 The Best Scenic Drives

- **Cape Breton's Cabot Trail** (Nova Scotia): This 300km (185-mile) loop through the uplands of Cape Breton Highlands National Park is one of the world's great excursions. You'll see Acadian fishing ports, pristine valleys, and some of the most picturesque coastline anywhere. See "Cape Breton Island," in chapter 4.

- **Along Cobequid Bay** (Nova Scotia): When it comes to scenery, Cobequid Bay (near Truro) is one of the region's better-kept secrets. The bay is flanked by two roads: Route 2 runs from Parrsboro to Truro; Route 215 from South Maitland to Brooklyn. Take the time to savor the rocky cliffs, muddy flats, and rust-colored bays. See "Minas Basin & Cobequid Bay," in chapter 4.

- **Fundy Trail Parkway** (New Brunswick): East of Saint John, you'll find this 11km (7-mile) parkway winding along the contours of the coast. Get out and stretch your legs at any of the 22 lookouts along the way

for fantastic cliff-side views. Or if the tides are out, clamber down to one of the stretches of sand nestled between the rocks. See p. 165.

- **Prince Edward Island National Park:** Much of the north-central shore of PEI is part of the national park, and a quiet park road tracks along the henna-tinted cliffs and grass-covered dunes. There's no single road, but several shorter segments; all are worth a leisurely drive, with frequent stops to explore the beaches and walkways. See "Prince Edward Island National Park," in chapter 6.

- **Viking Trail** (Newfoundland): Travelers looking to leave the crowds behind needn't look any further. This beautiful drive to Newfoundland's northern tip is wild and solitary, with views of bizarre geology and a windraked coast. And you'll end up at one of the world's great historic sites— L'Anse aux Meadows. See "The Great Northern Peninsula," in chapter 7.

## 4 The Best Hikes & Rambles

- **Point Pleasant Park** (Nova Scotia): Overlooking the entrance to Halifax's harbor, Point Pleasant Park is a wonderful urban oasis, with wide trails

for strolling along the water. You can also crest a wooded rise and visit a stout Martello Tower. See p. 94.

- **Cape Breton Highlands National Park** (Nova Scotia): You'll find bog and woodland walks aplenty at Cape Breton, but the best trails follow rugged cliffs along the open ocean. The Skyline Trail is among the most dramatic pathways in the province. See "Cape Breton Highlands National Park," in chapter 4.

- **Grand Manan Island** (New Brunswick): Grand Manan is laced with informal walking trails, through the forest and along the ocean's edge. This is a place for exploring; ask around locally for suggestions on the best hikes. See "Grand Manan Island," in chapter 5.

- **The Confederation Trail** (Prince Edward Island): This 350km (215-mile) pathway across the island is still being pieced together. But you can already explore 225km (140 miles) along the old rail line that once stitched the province together. It's best for long-distance biking but superb for a quiet stroll. See "Kings County," in chapter 6.

- **Green Gardens Trail** (Gros Morne, Newfoundland): This demanding hike at Gros Morne National Park takes hikers on a 16km (9.5-mile) loop, much of which follows coastal meadows atop fractured cliffs. Demanding, but worth every step of the way. See "Gros Morne National Park," in chapter 7.

- **North Head Trail** (St. John's, Newfoundland): You can walk from downtown St. John's along the harbor, pass through the picturesque Battery neighborhood, and then climb the open bluffs overlooking the Narrows with views out to the open ocean beyond. And where else can you hike from downtown shopping to cliff-side whale-watching? See "St. John's," in chapter 7.

## 5  The Best Family Activities

- **Fossil and Mineral Prospecting** (Nova Scotia): On the Bay of Fundy, Parrsboro is a fossil- and mineral-collector's mecca. You needn't be an expert—a fine, accessible museum and helpful local guides will get you started. The terrain and scenery are the real draw; any finds are icing on the cake. See "Minas Basin & Cobequid Bay," in chapter 4.

- **Upper Clements Park** (Nova Scotia): About 5 minutes south of Annapolis Royal, this wonderfully old-fashioned amusement park is full of low-key amusements and attractions that will especially delight younger kids. Highlights include a flume ride (originally built for Expo '86 in Vancouver) and a wooden roller coaster that twists and winds through trees left standing during the coaster's construction. See "Annapolis Royal," in chapter 4.

- **Waterfront Walk** (Nova Scotia): Halifax's waterfront walk is filled with wonderful distractions, from the province's finest museum to ships for exploring. Look also for buskers, delightful junk food, and sweeping views of the bustling harbor. If you're here in early August for the Busker Festival, it's all your kids will talk about for years. See "Halifax," in chapter 4.

- **Kings Landing** (New Brunswick): History comes alive at this living history museum, where young kids are fascinated by life in early Canada between 1790 and 1910. Ask about the weeklong sessions designed to immerse kids in the past. See p. 171.

- **Prince Edward Island's Beaches:** The red-sand beaches will turn white swim trunks a bit pinkish, but it's hard to beat a day or three splashing around these tepid waters while admiring pastoral island landscapes. See "The Great Outdoors," in chapter 6.

- **Terra Nova National Park** (Newfoundland): This is the less noted of Newfoundland's two national parks,

but the staff has gone the extra mile to make it kid friendly. There's a marine interpretive center with activities for kids, boat tours, hikes just the right length for shorter legs, and campground activities at night. See "Terra Nova National Park," in chapter 7.

## 6 The Best Places for History

- **Annapolis Royal** (Nova Scotia): The cradle of Canadian civilization is found in this broad green valley, where early French settlers first put down roots. Visit Fort Anne and Port Royal, and walk some of the first streets on the continent. See "Annapolis Royal," in chapter 4.

- **Maritime Museum of the Atlantic** (Nova Scotia): Nova Scotia's history is the history of the sea, and no place better depicts that vibrant tradition than this sprawling museum on Halifax's waterfront. See p. 90.

- **Louisbourg** (Nova Scotia): This early-18th-century fort and village was part of an elaborate French effort to establish a foothold in the New World. It failed, and the village ultimately fell to ruin. In the 1960s, the Canadian government reconstructed much of it, and now it's one of the most impressive historic sites in the nation. See "Cape Breton Island," in chapter 4.

- **Village Historique Acadien** (New Brunswick): Around 45 buildings—with the number growing—depict life as it was lived in an Acadian settlement between 1770 and 1890. You'll learn all about the exodus and settlement of the Acadians from costumed guides, who are also adept at skills ranging from letterpress printing to blacksmithing. See p. 189.

- **Province House National Historic Site** (Prince Edward Island): Canadian history took shape in Charlottetown

in 1864, when the idea of joining Britain's North American colonies into an independent confederation was first discussed. Learn about what transpired at this imposing Charlottetown edifice, which has been restored to appear as it did when history was made. See p. 215.

- **Bonavista Peninsula** (Newfoundland): Newfoundland might seem like the edge of the earth today, but in past centuries it was the crossroads of European culture as nations scrapped over fishing rights and settlements. You can learn a lot about how the old world viewed the new during a few days exploring this intriguing peninsula. Base yourself in the perfectly preserved village of Trinity, and spend at least a day exploring up to the town of Bonavista, where you can visit the Ryan's Premises National Historic Site and learn why cod was god. See "The Bonavista Peninsula," in chapter 7.

- **L'Anse aux Meadows National Historic Site** (Newfoundland): This dramatic site on Newfoundland's northern tip celebrated its 1,000th anniversary in 2000—it's been a millennium since the Vikings first landed here and established an encampment. View the intriguing ruins, enter the re-created sod huts, and hear knowledgeable interpreters' theories about why the colony failed. See p. 252.

## 7 The Most Picturesque Villages

- **Lunenburg** (Nova Scotia): Settled by German, Swiss, and French colonists, this tidy town is superbly situated on a hill flanked by two harbors and boasts some of the most unique and quietly extravagant architecture in the Maritimes. See "South Shore," in chapter 4.

- **Victoria** (Prince Edward Island): This wee village west of Charlottetown is surrounded by fields of grain and potatoes, and hasn't changed much in the last 100 years. Try to time your visit to take in an evening show at the town's wonderfully old-fashioned theater. See "Prince County," in chapter 6.

- **Trinity** (Newfoundland): Three centuries ago, Trinity was among the most important ports in the New World, when English merchants controlled the flow of goods in and out of the New World. This compact village has also been among the most aggressive in preserving its past, and the architecture and perfect scale of the village is unmatched in Atlantic Canada. See "The Bonavista Peninsula," in chapter 7.

- **Twillingate** (Newfoundland): This end-of-the-world village on Newfoundland's north-central shore is located on and around the convoluted harbors and inlets. At the mouth of the harbor, high headlands mark the way for incoming ships; walk out here and scan the watery horizon for whales and icebergs. See "Central Newfoundland," in chapter 7.

## 8 The Best Inns

- **Gowrie House** (Sydney Mines, Nova Scotia; © **800/372-1115** or 902/544-1050): The exquisitely decorated Gowrie House is at once resplendent and comfortable, historic and very up-to-date. The smallest guest rooms are more spacious than larger rooms at many other inns. See p. 134.

- **Kingsbrae Arms** (St. Andrews, New Brunswick; © **506/529-1897**): This five-star inn manages the trick of being opulent and comfortable at the same time. This shingled manse is lavishly appointed, beautifully landscaped, and well situated for exploring charming St. Andrews. See p. 152.

- **The Great George** (Charlottetown, PEI; © **800/361-1118** or 902/892-0606): This connected series of restored town houses is historic, central, welcoming, and quite comfortable. Continental breakfast is served in the open-concept lobby, where you can watch the comings and goings without getting in the way; rooms range from spacious doubles to huge, family-sized suites, and most of them have either a fireplace, a whirlpool bath, or both. See p. 216.

- **Inn at Bay Fortune** (Bay Fortune, PEI; © **902/687-3745**, or 860/296-1348 off season): This exceptionally attractive shingled compound was most recently owned by actress Colleen Dewhurst, and current innkeeper David Wilmer pulled out all the stops for his renovations. But the real draw here is the dining room, which is noted for the farm-fresh ingredients grown in the extensive gardens on the property. See p. 225.

## 9 The Best Bed & Breakfasts

- **Duffus House Inn** (Baddeck, Nova Scotia; © **902/295-2172**): A visit to the Duffus House is like a visit to the grandmother's house everyone wished they had. The inn's two adjacent buildings (constructed in 1820 and 1885) overlook Baddeck's channel and are cozy and tastefully furnished with a well-chosen mix of antiques. See p. 129.

- **The Manse at Mahone Bay Country Inn** (Mahone Bay, Nova Scotia; © **902/624-1121**): You won't find a bad room in this four–guest room establishment, built in 1870 and situated on a low hill in the picturesque village of Mahone Bay. Spend the day browsing local shops, and retreat in the evening to the casual luxury of this top-rate lodge. See p. 83.

- **Shipwright Inn** (Charlottetown, PEI; © **888/306-9966** or 902/368-1905): This in-town, seven-room B&B is within easy walking distance of all the city's attractions yet has a settled and pastoral feel. It's informed by a Victorian sensibility without being over-the-top about it. See p. 217.

- **Tickle Inn at Cape Onion** (Cape Onion, Newfoundland; © **709/452-4321** June–Sept, or 709/739-5503 Oct–May): Tickle Inn serves a family-style dinner each night so technically it isn't a B&B at all, but this tiny and remote home has the cordial bonhomie of a well-run bed-and-breakfast. Set on a distant cove at the end of a road near Newfoundland's northernmost point (you can see Labrador across the straits), the Tickle Inn offers a perfect base for visiting L'Anse aux Meadows and walking on the lonesome, windy hills. See p. 254.

- **At Wit's Inn** (St. John's, Newfoundland; © **877/739-7420** or 709/739-7420): This centrally located B&B is bright, cheerful, and whimsical. Opened in 1999 by a restaurateur from Toronto, the inn has managed to preserve the best of the historical elements in this century-old home while graciously updating it for modern tastes. See p. 283.

## 10 The Best Local Dining

- **Digby Scallops** (Nova Scotia): The productive scallop fleet based in Digby, on Nova Scotia's Bay of Fundy coast, hauls back some of the choicest, most succulent scallops in the world. Sample the fare at local restaurants, or cook up a batch on your own. Simple is better: A light sauté in butter brings out their rich flavor. See "Digby to Yarmouth," in chapter 4.

- **Rappie Pie** (Nova Scotia): When traveling between Digby and Yarmouth, watch for shops selling rappie pie—a local Acadian treat made from potatoes plus meat or seafood. See "Digby to Yarmouth," in chapter 4.

- **Fresh Lobster** (Nova Scotia and New Brunswick): Wherever you see the wooden lobster traps piled on a wharf, you'll know a fresh lobster meal isn't far away. Among the most productive lobster fisheries are around Shediac, New Brunswick, and all along Nova Scotia's Atlantic coast. Sunny days are ideal for cracking open a crustacean while sitting at a wharf-side picnic table, preferably with a locally brewed beer close at hand. See chapters 4 and 5.

- **Prince Edward Island Mussels:** PEI has long been known for its wonderful potatoes, but the farmed mussels do more to thrill the taste buds. You'll see the lines of mussel buoys in inlets and harbors. Order up a mess at an island restaurant to share with your whole table. See chapter 6.

- **Newfoundland Berries:** The unforgivingly rocky and boggy soil of this blustery island resists most crops, but produces some of the most delicious berries you can imagine. Look for roadside stands in midsummer, or pick your own blueberries, strawberries, partridgeberries, or bakeapples. Many restaurants serve berries (on cheesecake, in custard) when they're in season. See chapter 7.

# 2

# Planning Your Trip to the Atlantic Provinces

Reading this chapter before you set out can save you money, time, and headaches. Here's where you'll find travel know-how: when to come, the documentation you'll need, and where to get more information. These basics can make the difference between a smooth trip and a bumpy one.

## 1 The Atlantic Provinces in Brief

**NOVA SCOTIA**  This province is the undisputed star of Canada's Atlantic coast: Its capital, Halifax, is a relative financial and cultural powerhouse compared with the rest of the hamlets scattered through Eastern Canada, and the surest bet for an outstanding meal, a world-class musical performance, or a great museum. But there's far more to Nova Scotia besides, including the South Shore, an especially photogenic stretch of fishing villages; the hardscrabble Acadian Coast with is spruce-topped basalt cliffs and miles of sandy beaches; and astonishing Cape Breton, the enormous northerly island dominated by one of Canada's finest parks and lovely, Celtic-influenced music and landscapes.

**NEW BRUNSWICK**  On the other hand, New Brunswick is Canada's Rodney Dangerfield—a strangely shaped province that turns out to possess some of Canada's cutest villages and highest tides. The Bay of Fundy is the place to see huge, twice-daily drops and rises of ocean against cliff and to learn more about the marine ecology that has developed here. Fishing villages such as St. Andrews and Caraquet cry out to be photographed; Fredericton and Moncton each offer more than initially meets the eye; and the city of Saint John contains more culture per square inch than any other place in this book save Halifax.

**PRINCE EDWARD ISLAND**  The island leaves the razzle-dazzle to cities on the mainland, choosing instead to soothe its visitors' souls by offering places for quiet relaxation. A flat island of red sands, potato farms, and purple lupine fields—plus healthy doses of fishing industry, golf, and Acadian culture—Prince Edward Island (PEI) is the sort of province best explored by bicycle, with a good book for company at night. The province's harborside capital city of Charlottetown is genuinely beautiful, historic, and diverse; this was the place where the deal consolidating Canada into one nation, the Confederation, was sealed.

**NEWFOUNDLAND**  This is the province you need to work hardest to reach, but people here are undoubtedly the friendliest in all of Canada. The natural wonders are also rather spectacular, including icebergs, migrating whales, and Viking settlement sites, among others. For good measure, there's a major city (St. John's), fresh fish everywhere, and a hard-to-reach adjacent territory—Labrador—of native culture, fishermen, and absolutely no crowds.

## 2 Visitor Information

It's well worth a toll-free call or postcard in advance of your trip to stock up on the free literature and maps that provincial authorities liberally bestow upon those considering a vacation in their province.

- **Nova Scotia Dept. of Tourism,** P.O. Box 456, Halifax, NS B3J 2R5. © **800/565-0000** or 902/425-5781; explore@gov.ns.ca.
- **Tourism New Brunswick,** P.O. Box 12345, Fredericton, NB E7M 5C3. © **800/561-0123;** info@tourism newbrunswick.ca.
- **Tourism PEI,** P.O. Box 940, Charlottetown, PEI C1A 7M5. © **888/734-7529** or 902/368-4444; peiplay@gov.pe.ca.
- **Newfoundland and Labrador Dept. of Tourism, Culture, & Recreation,** P.O. Box 8700, St. John's, NL A1C 4K2. © **800/563-6353** or 709/729-2830; tourism info@ mail.gov.nl.ca.

**INFORMATION CENTERS** All four provinces staff helpful visitor centers at key access points, including the main roadways into the provinces and the major cities. The best-run centers are in Nova Scotia and Prince Edward Island, which have a cordial staff and exceptionally well-stocked brochure racks overflowing with maps, menus, and booklets. These centers provide a surplus of information on local attractions but can also fill you in on what's happening anywhere in the province so you can plan a few days in advance. If the staffers don't have the information you need at their fingertips, they'll make phone calls and track it down for you. New Brunswick's information centers are also helpful, though not as numerous. Newfoundland's visitor centers—with the exception of the modern information centers near the two main ferry terminals—are typically less polished and sophisticated than in the other provinces, but the authorities have been successful in making improvements over the past couple of years. Look in the regional chapters of this guide for addresses and phone numbers of the main visitor centers in each area.

All four provinces publish free, magazine-size travel guides crammed with routine but often essential information on hotels, inns, campgrounds, and attractions. Nova Scotia's *Doers & Dreamers Guide* sets an international standard for high-quality information, but the others are all excellent and unfailingly helpful. If you haven't obtained a guide in advance by mail, be sure to request one at the first center you come to when entering a province.

**INTERNET RESOURCES** Information on the Web is growing at an explosive rate, with some of the data more reliable than others. Here are a few places to start your search:

- **Nova Scotia:** A tour of accommodations and tourism sites, presented by Nova Scotia Economic Development and Tourism, can be found at www.explorens.com and www.novascotia.com.
- **Nova Scotia Provincial Parks:** The province's website provides basic, up-to-date information about the many excellent parks at www.parks.gov.ns.ca.
- **New Brunswick:** The official tourism site offers a good place to start: www.tourismnewbrunswick.ca.
- **Prince Edward Island:** The official PEI online information center is www.peiplay.com.
- **Newfoundland & Labrador:** The official website is www.gov.nl.ca/tourism.
- **National Parks:** For information about travels in the region's national parks, a good first stop is the Parks Canada official website at www.pc.gc.ca.

## 3 Entry Requirements & Customs

**ENTRY REQUIREMENTS** U.S. citizens or permanent residents of the United States, as well as British, Australian, New Zealand, and Irish nationals, need neither a visa nor a passport to enter Canada. Travelers should, however, carry some identifying papers—such as a passport or birth certificate, baptismal certificate, or voter's certificate—to prove one's citizenship, if only to speed your return to the United States. In some cases, a driver's license is all you're asked to provide going into Canada, but checks have become noticeably tougher in the wake of the September 11, 2001, terrorist attacks on New York and Washington. Permanent U.S. residents who aren't U.S. citizens must have their Alien Registration Cards. Residents of approximately 60 other countries do not need visas to enter Canada; all others do. Inquire about entry requirements at the nearest Canadian embassy or consult the website www.cic.gc.ca/english/offices.

A note for teens traveling alone: If you're under 19, it's helpful to have a letter from a parent or guardian stating the purpose of the trip. If Customs officers are suspicious when you enter the country, they'll notify immigration officers. A letter will go a long way in proving that you're not running away or up to no good. For more information about immigration, browse the website listed above or call © **888/242-2100** (from within Canada only).

**CUSTOMS** Customs regulations allow adult travelers (19 or older) to bring in duty- and tax-free 1.14 liters (40 oz.) of wine or liquor, or 24 bottles of beer; travelers can also bring in 200 cigarettes or 50 cigars without paying duty or tax. If you're bringing gifts for Canadian friends, you're allowed C$60 (US$48) duty-free. An automated phone service will answer most questions about Customs regulations; call © **800/461-9999.** Or check the website www.cbsa-asfc.gc.ca/menu-e.html.

Regulations regarding firearms are complicated and varied. In short, it's best if you don't bring your gun. If you're traveling for hunting and want to bring your rifle into the country, you should be traveling during hunting season and carry proof of your plans to go hunting (a written confirmation from a guide service or hunting lodge should suffice).

**IMPORT RESTRICTIONS** Returning **U.S. citizens** who have been away for at least 48 hours are allowed to bring back, once every 30 days, $800 worth of merchandise duty-free. You'll be charged a flat rate of 4% duty on the next $1,000 worth of purchases. Be sure to keep your receipts handy to expedite the declaration process. On mailed gifts, the duty-free limit is $200. *Note:* If you owe duty, you are required to pay on your arrival in the United States—either by cash, personal check, government or traveler's check, or money order (and, in some locations, a Visa or MasterCard).

To avoid paying duty on foreign-made personal items you owned before your trip, bring along a bill of sale, insurance policy, jeweler's appraisal, or receipts of purchase. Or you can register items that can be readily identified by a permanently affixed serial number or marking—think laptop computers, cameras, and CD players—with Customs before you leave. Take the items to the nearest Customs office or register them with Customs at the airport from which you're departing. You'll receive, at no cost, a Certificate of Registration, which allows duty-free entry for the life of the item.

With some exceptions, you cannot bring fresh fruits and vegetables back into the United States. For specifics on what you can bring back, download the invaluable free pamphlet *Know Before You Go* online at **www.cbp.gov**. (Click on "Travel," and then click on "Know Before You Go! Online Brochure.") Or contact the **U.S. Customs & Border Protection (CBP),** 1300 Pennsylvania Ave., NW, Washington, DC 20229 (© **877/287-8667**) and request the pamphlet.

U.K. citizens returning from **a non-EU country** have a customs allowance of: 200 cigarettes; 50 cigars; 250 grams of smoking tobacco; 2 liters of still table wine; 1 liter of spirits or strong liqueurs (over 22% volume); 2 liters of fortified wine, sparkling wine, or other liqueurs; 60cc (ml) perfume; 250cc (ml) of toilet water; and £145 worth of all other goods, including gifts and souvenirs. People under 17 cannot have the tobacco or alcohol allowance. For more information, contact HM Customs & Excise at © **0845/010-9000** (from outside the U.K., 020/8929-0152), or consult their website at www.hmce.gov.uk.

The duty-free allowance in **Australia** is A$400 or, for those under 18, A$200. Citizens over 18 can bring in 250 cigarettes or 250 grams of loose tobacco, and 1,125 milliliters of alcohol. If you're returning with valuables you already own, such as foreign-made cameras, you should file form B263. A helpful brochure available from Australian consulates or Customs offices is *Know Before You Go*. For more information, call the **Australian Customs Service** at © **1300/363-263,** or log on to www.customs.gov.au.

The duty-free allowance for **New Zealand** is NZ$700. Citizens over 17 can bring in 200 cigarettes, 50 cigars, or 250 grams of tobacco (or a mixture of all three if their combined weight doesn't exceed 250g); plus 4.5 liters of wine and beer, or 1.125 liters of liquor. New Zealand currency does not carry import or export restrictions. Fill out a certificate of export, listing the valuables you are taking out of the country; that way, you can bring them back without paying duty. Most questions are answered in a free pamphlet available at New Zealand consulates and Customs offices: *New Zealand Customs Guide for Travellers, Notice no. 4.* For more information, contact **New Zealand Customs,** The Customhouse, 17–21 Whitmore St., Box 2218, Wellington (© **04/473-6099** or 0800/428-786; www.customs.govt.nz).

## 4 Money

**CURRENCY** Canadian currency, like U.S. currency, is denominated in dollars and cents, though there are some differences. Canada has no $1 bill. It does have a $1 coin (called a "loonie" because it depicts a loon) and a $2 coin (called a "twoonie"). At press time, US$1 was worth approximately C$1.25.

If you're driving into Canada, you needn't worry about stocking up on Canadian dollars before or immediately upon entry into Canada. U.S. currency is widely accepted, especially in border towns, and you'll often see signs at cash registers announcing current exchange rates. These are not always the best rates, however, so it behooves you to visit an ATM (automated teller machine; see below) or cash some traveler's checks as soon as you're able.

You'll avoid lines at airport ATMs by exchanging at least some money—just enough to cover airport incidentals and transportation to your hotel—before you leave home (though don't expect the exchange rate to be ideal). You can exchange money at your local American Express or Thomas Cook office or at your bank. American Express also dispenses traveler's checks and foreign currency via

---

( *Tips* **Small Change**

When you change money, ask for some small bills or loose change. Petty cash will come in handy for tipping and public transportation. Consider keeping the change separate from your larger bills, so that it's readily accessible and you'll be less of a target for theft.

---

www.americanexpress.com or © **800/807-6233,** but they'll charge a $15 order fee and additional shipping costs.

**ATMS**   Obtaining cash is rarely a problem for travelers in Canada. The easiest and best way to get cash away from home is from an ATM, which is widely available in most midsize towns and cities, and the networks are often compatible with U.S. banks, allowing travelers to use their own ATM or credit cards for cash withdrawals. Your bank will convert the currency at the prevailing rate. For example, if you withdraw $100 from a Canadian bank machine, your bank statement will show a withdrawal of around US$80.

**Cirrus** (© **800/424-7787;** www.mastercard.com) and PLUS (© **800/843-7587;** www.visa.com) are the two most popular networks, with PLUS especially well represented in Atlantic Canada. Check the back of your ATM card to see which network your bank belongs to, and then call or check online for ATM locations at your destination. Be sure you know your personal identification number (PIN) and daily withdrawal limit before you depart.

You can use your credit card to receive cash advances at ATMs, too. Keep in mind that credit card companies protect themselves from theft by limiting maximum withdrawals outside their home country, so call your credit card company before you leave home. And keep in mind that you'll pay interest from the moment of your withdrawal, even if you pay your monthly bills on time.

*Note:* Many banks impose a fee every time you use a card at another bank's ATM, and that fee can be higher for international transactions (up to $5 or more) than for domestic ones (where they're rarely more than $2). In addition, the bank from which you withdraw cash may charge its own fee, though in practice many ATMs in Canada still do not charge a transaction fee. To compare banks' ATM fees within the U.S., use **www.bankrate.com**. For international withdrawal fees, ask your bank.

**TRAVELER'S   CHECKS**   Traveler's checks are something of an anachronism from the days before the ATM made cash accessible at any time. Given the fees you'll pay for ATM use at banks other than your own, however, you might be better off with traveler's checks if you're withdrawing money often.

You can get traveler's checks at almost any bank. **American Express** offers denominations of $20, $50, $100, $500, and (for cardholders only) $1,000. You'll pay a service charge ranging from 1% to 4%. You can also get American Express traveler's checks over the phone by calling © **800/221-7282;** Amex gold and platinum cardholders who use this number are exempt from the 1% fee.

**Visa** offers traveler's checks at Citibank locations nationwide, as well as at several other banks. The service charge ranges between 1.5% and 2%; checks come in denominations of $20, $50, $100, $500, and $1,000. Call © **800/732-1322** for information. AAA members can obtain Visa checks for a $9.95 fee (for checks up to $1,500) at most AAA offices or by calling © **866/339-3378. MasterCard** also offers traveler's checks. Call ✆ **800/223-9920** for a location near you.

**Foreign currency traveler's checks** are useful if you're traveling to one country; they're accepted at locations where dollar checks may not be, such as bed-and-breakfasts, and they minimize the currency conversions you'll have to perform while you're on the go. **American Express, Thomas Cook, Visa,** and **MasterCard** offer foreign currency traveler's checks. You'll pay the rate of exchange at the time of your purchase (so it's a good idea to monitor the rate before you buy), and most companies charge a transaction fee per order (and a shipping fee if you order online).

If you do choose to carry traveler's checks, keep a record of their serial numbers separate from your checks in the event that they are stolen or lost. You'll get a refund faster if you know the numbers.

**CREDIT CARDS**    Credit cards are another safe way to carry money. They also provide a convenient record of all your expenses, and they generally offer relatively good exchange rates. You can also withdraw cash advances from your credit cards at banks or ATMs, provided you know your PIN. If you don't know yours, call the number on the back of your credit card and ask the bank to send it to you. It usually takes 5 to 7 business days, though some banks will provide the number over the phone if you tell them your mother's maiden name or some other personal information. Keep in mind that many banks now assess a 1%–3% "transaction fee" on **all** charges you incur abroad (whether you're using the local currency or US dollars). But credit cards still may be the smart way to go when you factor in things like exorbitant ATM fees and the higher exchange rates and service fees you'll pay with traveler's checks.

For tips and telephone numbers to call if your wallet is stolen or lost, go to "Lost & Found" in the "Fast Facts" section of this chapter.

**TAXES**    There's good news and there's bad news on the tax front. The bad news is that high taxes offset some of the price advantage gained when you convert U.S. currency to Canadian. The good news is that foreign visitors can get back many of their taxes if they're careful about retaining and validating receipts, and filling out forms.

In 1997, three of the four Maritime Provinces—New Brunswick, Nova Scotia, and Newfoundland—adopted the **Harmonized Sales Tax,** also known as the HST. This combined the provincial and federal sales into a flat rate of 15%, which is charged on all goods and services. On Prince Edward Island, you'll be charged a Goods and Services Tax of 7%, plus a provincial tax of 10%, on most items except footwear, clothing, books, and groceries.

Non-Canadians can apply for a refund of the entire HST (or the GST only in Prince Edward Island) upon leaving the

---

*Tips*  **Dear Visa: I'm off to Meat Cove!**

Some credit card companies recommend that you notify them of any impending trip abroad so that they don't become suspicious of foreign transactions and block your charges. If you don't call your credit card company in advance, you can still call the card's toll-free emergency number (see "Fast Facts," p. 38) if a charge is refused—provided you remember to carry the phone number with you. Perhaps the most important lesson here is to carry more than one card, so you have a backup.

country. Sometimes you can request this refund at a participating Canadian duty-free shop (a commission applies), but usually you must wait until you get home—and then jump through quite a few hoops.

First, the refund applies primarily to taxes on accommodations and goods bought for use outside the country; it doesn't apply to meals, beverages, tobacco, transportation, gasoline, or professional services. Those leaving Canada by car must stop at the border to have these receipts validated by Canadian Customs, and officials may check to ensure that the goods claimed are actually leaving the country. (Visitors departing by air or boat needn't validate their receipts at the border, but must include a used boarding pass or other documentation to prove they left the country when they file the request.)

To request a refund through the **Visitor Rebate Program,** send the original receipts (copies won't do) along with the proper paperwork. Rebate forms packaged with an instruction booklet are available at most information centers, or by calling ✆ **800/668-4748** (within Canada) or 902/432-5608 outside Canada. (Note that there are two different ways to file: A "quickie" refund can be obtained from private services inside Canada such as Maple Leaf, but they'll hold back a percentage of your rightful refund as a commission. The Canadian government won't charge you anything, but it takes longer to process.) If your application is submitted by mail, refunds are typically sent within 2 or 3 months, with checks issued in U.S. dollars to U.S. citizens.

To obtain the necessary forms, consult the website www.ccra.gc.ca/forms or call ✆ **800/959-2221;** you will need Form GST 176 to get the visitor rebate.

The website www.ccra-adrc.gc.ca/visitors can also answer tax-refund questions.

## 5 When to Go

**THE WEATHER** All the Atlantic Provinces lie within the **Northern Temperate Zone,** which means that they have weather much like neighboring New England in the northeast United States. Spring is damp and cool at the outset, and can be warm and muggy as it eases into summer. Summer's compact high season runs from early July to early September. That's when the great majority of travelers take to the road, enjoying the bright, clear days and warm temperatures. The average high in the southern three provinces is in the upper 70s°F (around 25°C); in Newfoundland, it's more typically in the upper 60s°F (around 20°C). Nights can be cool, even approaching freezing late in the summer.

Be aware that there is no "typical" summer weather in Atlantic Canada. The only thing typical is change, and you're likely to experience balmy, sunny days and howling rainstorms, quite possibly on the same day.

Weather in all four provinces is to a large degree affected by proximity to the ocean. This means frequent fogs, especially on the Fundy Coast of New Brunswick, the Atlantic Coast of Nova Scotia, and Newfoundland's Avalon Peninsula. The ocean also offers an unobstructed corridor for high winds, especially on Prince Edward Island and Newfoundland. Rain is not unusual in summer. Travelers who come well prepared for downpours, both psychologically and equipment-wise, tend to be happier travelers. Note that the ocean also provides some benefits: Prince Edward Island's summer tends to linger into fall thanks to the island's being surrounded by the warm, moderating waters of the Gulf of St. Lawrence.

Finally, a note on winter: Few travelers tackle the Maritimes in the dead of winter, as frequent blustery storms sweep in off the Atlantic. But if you're one of those hardy souls who might, be aware that snow or ice storms are a very real possibility at any time during winter, and they can blow in suddenly; if you're driving, always make sure your car is equipped with good snow tires and special antifreeze windshield wash (you can get it from any gas station). And drive cautiously: Outside the major urban areas, most of this region's high-speed arteries remain two-lane roads without medians, so care must be taken to watch for the other drivers coming your way.

## Halifax Average Monthly Temperatures

|  | Jan | Feb | Mar | Apr | May | June | July | Aug | Sept | Oct | Nov | Dec |
|---|---|---|---|---|---|---|---|---|---|---|---|---|
| High (°F) | 33 | 33 | 39 | 48 | 58 | 67 | 73 | 73 | 67 | 58 | 48 | 37 |
| (°C) | 1 | 1 | 4 | 9 | 14 | 19 | 23 | 23 | 19 | 14 | 9 | 3 |
| Low (°F) | 20 | 19 | 26 | 33 | 41 | 50 | 57 | 58 | 53 | 44 | 36 | 25 |
| (°C) | −7 | −7 | −3 | 1 | 5 | 10 | 14 | 13 | 12 | 7 | 2 | −4 |

**HOLIDAYS** National holidays are celebrated from the Atlantic to the Pacific to the Arctic Oceans, and for the traveler that means that government offices and banks are closed. (Shops remain open on some but not all national holidays.) These holidays include New Year's Day, Good Friday, Easter Monday, Victoria Day (the 3rd Mon in May, always the week before Memorial Day in the United States), Canada Day (July 1), Labour Day (the 1st Mon in Sept, the same as in the United States), Thanksgiving (mid-Oct, the same as Columbus Day weekend in the United States), Remembrance Day (Nov 11), Christmas Day (Dec 25), and Boxing Day (Dec 26).

Locally observed provincial holidays include a civic holiday (Aug 2) in Nova Scotia, and New Brunswick Day (the 1st Mon in Aug). Newfoundland and Labrador celebrate several holidays, including St. George's Day (Apr 26), Discovery Day (the 3rd Mon in June), and Orangeman's Day (July 12).

## 6 Travel Insurance

Check your existing insurance policies and credit-card coverage before you buy travel insurance. You may already be covered for lost luggage, cancelled tickets, or medical expenses.

The cost of travel insurance varies widely, depending on the cost and length of your trip, your age and health, and the type of trip you're taking, but expect to pay between 5% and 8% of the vacation itself. You can get estimates from various providers through **InsureMyTrip.com**. Enter your trip cost and dates, your age, and other information for prices from more than a dozen companies.

**TRIP-CANCELLATION INSURANCE** Trip-cancellation insurance will help retrieve your money if you have to back out of a trip or depart early, or if your travel supplier goes bankrupt. Permissable reasons for trip cancellation can range from sickness to natural disasters to the State Department declaring a destination unsafe for travel. (Insurers usually won't cover vague fears, though, as many travelers discovered when they tried to cancel their trips in October 2001.) In this unstable world, trip-cancellation insurance is a good buy if you're purchasing tickets well in advance—who knows what the state of the world, or of your airline, will be in 9 months? Insurance policy details vary, so read the fine print—and make sure that your airline or cruise line is on the list of carriers covered in case of bankruptcy. A good resource is **"Travel Guard Alerts,"** a list of companies considered high-risk by Travel Guard International (see website below). Protect yourself further by paying for the insurance with a credit card—by law, consumers can get their money back on goods and services not received if they report the loss within 60 days after the charge is listed on their credit card statement.

For more information, contact one of the following recommended insurers: **Access America** (© 866/807-3982; www.accessamerica.com); **Travel Guard International** (© 800/826-4919; www.travelguard.com); **Travel Insured International** (© 800/243-3174; www.travel insured.com); and **Travelex Insurance Services** (© 888/457-4602; www.travelex-insurance.com).

**MEDICAL INSURANCE** For travel outside your country, most health plans (including Medicare and Medicaid) do not provide coverage, and the ones that do often require you to pay for services up front and reimburse you only after you return home. Even if your plan does cover treatment in other countries, Canadian hospitals make you pay your bills up front, and send you a refund only after you've returned home and filed the necessary paperwork with your insurance company. As a safety net, you may want to buy travel medical insurance. If you require additional medical insurance, try **MEDEX Assistance** (© 410/453-6300; www.medexassist.com) or **Travel Assistance International** (© 800/821-2828; www.travelassistance.com; for general information on services, call the company's Worldwide Assistance Services, Inc., at © 800/777-8710).

**LOST-LUGGAGE INSURANCE** On international flights (including U.S. portions of international trips), baggage coverage is limited to approximately $9.07 per pound, up to approximately $635 per checked bag. If you plan to check items more valuable than what's covered by the standard liability, see if your homeowner's policy covers your valuables, get baggage insurance as part of your comprehensive travel-insurance package or buy Travel Guard's "BagTrak" product. Don't buy insurance at the airport, where it's usually overpriced. Be sure to take any valuables or irreplaceable items with you in your carry-on luggage, because many valuables (including books, money, and electronics) aren't covered by airline policies.

If your luggage is lost, immediately file a lost-luggage claim at the airport, detailing the luggage contents. Most airlines require that you report delayed, damaged, or lost baggage within 4 hours of arrival. The airlines are required to deliver luggage, once found, directly to your house or destination free of charge.

**CAR-RENTAL INSURANCE** Ask your insurer if your coverage extends to Canada, and be sure to find out whether your policy covers all persons who will be driving the rental car, how much liability is covered in case an outside party is injured in an accident, and whether the type of vehicle you are renting is included under your contract.

Most major credit cards provide some degree of coverage as well—provided they were used to pay for the rental. Terms vary widely, however, so be sure to call your credit card company directly before you rent. *Note:* If you rely on your credit card for coverage, you may want to bring a second credit card with you, as damages may be charged to the first card, maxing out your limit, and you may find yourself stranded unless you have a backup credit card.

You can buy car-rental insurance from an auto rental agency. The basic insurance coverage offered by most car-rental companies, known as the **Loss/Damage Waiver (LDW)** or **Collision Damage Waiver (CDW),** can cost as much as $20 per day. It usually covers the full value of the vehicle with no deductible if an outside party causes an accident or other damage to the rental car. Liability coverage varies according to the company policy. If you are at fault in an accident, however, you will only be covered for the full replacement value of the car, not for any liability.

Most rental companies will require a police report in order to process any claims you file, but your private insurer will not be notified of the accident.

## 7 Health & Safety

**STAYING HEALTHY**   Although traveling in Canada doesn't pose any particular health threats and food and water are generally safe to consume, you can contact the **International Association for Medical Assistance to Travelers** (IAMAT) (© **716/754-4883** or, in Canada, 416/652-0137; www.iamat.org) for tips on travel and health concerns in your destination, and for lists of local, English-speaking doctors. The United States **Centers for Disease Control and Prevention** (© **800/311-3435;** www.cdc.gov) provides up-to-date information on health hazards by region or country and offers tips on food safety. The website **www.tripprep.com,** sponsored by a consortium of travel medicine practitioners, may also offer helpful advice on traveling abroad. You can find listings of reliable clinics overseas at the **International Society of Travel Medicine** (www.istm.org).

**WHAT TO DO IF YOU GET SICK AWAY FROM HOME**   Any foreign consulate can provide a list of area doctors who speak English. If you get sick, consider asking your hotel concierge to recommend a local doctor—even his or her own. You can also try the emergency room at a local hospital. Many hospitals also have walk-in clinics for emergency cases that are not life-threatening; you may not get immediate attention, but you won't pay the high price of an emergency room visit.

If you suffer from a chronic illness, consult your doctor before your departure. For conditions like epilepsy, diabetes, or heart problems, wear a **MedicAlert identification tag** (© **888/633-4298;** www.medicalert.org), which will immediately alert doctors to your condition and give them access to your records through MedicAlert's 24-hour hotline.

Pack **prescription medications** in your carry-on luggage, and carry prescription medications in their original containers, with pharmacy labels—otherwise, they won't make it through airport security. Also carry copies of your prescriptions in case you lose your pills or run out. Don't forget an extra pair of contact lenses or prescription glasses. Carry the generic name of prescription medicines, in case a local pharmacist is unfamiliar with the brand name.

## 8 Tips for Travelers with Special Needs

**FOR TRAVELERS WITH DISABILITIES**   Most disabilities shouldn't stop anyone from traveling. There are more options and resources out there than ever before.

Canada is making tremendous efforts to eliminate barriers to mobility. City pavements feature curb cuts for wheelchair travel, and larger hotels and airports have wheelchair-accessible washrooms. A growing number of restaurants and tourist attractions are now designed for wheelchair accessibility, although much room for improvement remains.

The **Access-Able Travel Source** (www.access-able.com) is a website featuring an online database with information about hotels, tour operators, and attractions that can accommodate travelers with disabilities in the United States and Canada. The offerings for Atlantic Canada are a bit slim at present, but the site is easy to navigate and has good potential for growth.

The **Canadian Paraplegic Association** (© 800/720-4933 or 613/723-1033; www.canparaplegic.org) offers a range of helpful information of interest to people with disabilities and may be able to answer your questions.

Travelers with disabilities headed for Nova Scotia may ask about transportation or recreational facilities by contacting the **Nova Scotia League for Equal Opportunities,** 5251 Duke St., Suite 1211, Halifax, NS B3J 1P3 (© 866/696-7536 or 902/455-6942; www.nsnet.org/leo).

Many travel agencies offer customized tours and itineraries for travelers with disabilities. **Flying Wheels Travel** (© 507/451-5005; www.flyingwheelstravel.com) offers escorted tours and cruises that emphasize sports and private tours in minivans with lifts. **Access-Able Travel Source** (© 303/232-2979; www.access-able.com) offers extensive access information and advice for traveling around the world with disabilities. **Accessible Journeys** (© 800/846-4537 or 610/521-0339; www.disabilitytravel.com) caters specifically to slow walkers and wheelchair travelers and their families and friends.

**Avis Rent a Car** has an "Avis Access" program that offers such services as a dedicated 24-hour toll-free number (© 888/879-4273) for customers with special travel needs; special car features such as

swivel seats, spinner knobs, and hand controls; and accessible bus service.

Organizations that offer assistance to travelers with disabilities include **Moss-Rehab** (www.mossresourcenet.org), which provides a library of accessible-travel resources online; the **American Foundation for the Blind** (AFB; © 800/232-5463; www.afb.org), a referral resource for the blind or visually impaired that includes information on traveling with Seeing Eye dogs; and **SATH (Society for Accessible Travel & Hospitality;** © 212/447-7284; www.sath.org; annual membership fees: $45 adults, $30 seniors and students), which offers a wealth of travel resources for all types of disabilities and informed recommendations on destinations, access guides, travel agents, tour operators, vehicle rentals, and companion services. **AirAmbulanceCard.com** is now partnered with SATH and allows you to preselect top-notch hospitals in case of an emergency for $195 a year ($295 per family), among other benefits.

**FOR GAY AND LESBIAN TRAVELERS**
The **International Gay and Lesbian Travel Association** (IGLTA; © 800/448-8550 or 954/776-2626; www.iglta.org) is the trade association for the gay and lesbian travel industry, and offers an online directory of gay- and lesbian-friendly travel businesses; go to their website and click on "Members."

Many agencies offer tours and travel itineraries specifically for gay and lesbian travelers. **Above and Beyond Tours** (© 800/397-2681; www.abovebeyondtours.com) is the exclusive gay and lesbian tour operator for United Airlines. **Now, Voyager** (© 800/255-6951; www.nowvoyager.com) is a well-known San Francisco–based, gay-owned and operated travel service. **Olivia Cruises & Resorts** (© 800/631-6277; www.olivia.com) charters entire resorts and ships for exclusive lesbian vacations and offers smaller group experiences for both gay and lesbian travelers.

**Gay.com Travel** (© 800/929-2268 or 415/644-8044; www.gay.com/travel or www.outandabout.com), is an excellent online successor to the popular *Out & About* print magazine. It provides regularly updated information about gay-owned, gay-oriented, and gay-friendly lodging, dining, sightseeing, nightlife, and shopping establishments in every important destination worldwide. It also offers trip-planning information for gay and lesbian travelers for more than 50 destinations, along various themes, ranging from Sex & Travel to Vacations for Couples.

**FOR SENIORS** Few countries in the world are as attentive to the needs of seniors as Canada. Discounts are extended to people over 60 for everything ranging from public transportation to museum and movie admissions. Even many hotels, tour operators, and restaurants offer discounts, so don't be bashful about inquiring, but always carry some kind of identification that shows your date of birth. (It's always best to inquire before checking in or ordering.) The discount varies widely; in general, the gap between senior prices and regular prices seems to have narrowed in the past few years.

Members of **AARP** (formerly known as the American Association of Retired Persons), 601 E St. NW, Washington, DC 20049 (© 888/687-2277; www.aarp.org), get discounts while traveling in Canada at participating hotels, airlines, and car rentals companies. AARP offers members a wide range of benefits, including *AARP: The Magazine* and a monthly newsletter. Anyone over 50 can join.

Many reliable agencies and organizations target the 50-plus market. **Elderhostel** (© 877/426-8056; www.elderhostel.org) arranges study programs for those aged 55 and over (and a spouse or companion of any age) in the U.S. and in more than 80 countries around the world. Most courses outside of the United States last 2 to 4 weeks, and many include airfare, accommodations in university dormitories or modest inns, meals, and tuition. **ElderTreks** (© 800/741-7956; www.eldertreks.com) offers small-group tours to off-the-beaten-path or adventure-travel locations, restricted to travelers 50 and older. **INTRAV** (© 800/456-8100; www.intrav.com) is a high-end tour operator that caters to the mature, discerning traveler (not specifically seniors), with trips around the world that include guided safaris, polar expeditions, private-jet adventures, and small boat cruises down jungle rivers.

**FOR FAMILIES** If you have enough trouble getting your kids out of the house in the morning, dragging them thousands of miles away may seem like an insurmountable challenge. But family travel can be immensely rewarding, giving you new ways of seeing the world through the eyes of children. To locate accommodations, restaurants, and attractions that are particularly kid-friendly, refer to the "Kids" icon throughout this guide.

**Familyhostel** (© 800/733-9753; www.learn.unh.edu/familyhostel) takes the whole family, including kids ages 8 to 15, on moderately priced domestic and international learning vacations. Lectures, field trips, and sightseeing are guided by a team of academics.

Recommended family travel Internet sites include **Family Travel Forum** (www.familytravelforum.com), a comprehensive site that offers customized trip planning; **Family Travel Network** (www.familytravelnetwork.com), an award-winning site that offers travel features, deals, and tips; **Traveling Internationally with Your Kids** (www.travelwithyourkids.com), a comprehensive site offering sound advice for long-distance and international travel with children; and **Family Travel**

**Files** (www.thefamilytravelfiles.com), which offers an online magazine and a directory of off-the-beaten-path tours and tour operators for families.

## 9 Planning Your Trip Online

**SURFING FOR AIRFARES**  The "big three" online travel agencies, **Expedia. com, Travelocity.com,** and **Orbitz.com** sell most of the air tickets bought on the Internet. (Canadian travelers should try expedia.ca and Travelocity.ca; U.K. residents can go for expedia.co.uk and opodo.co.uk.) **Kayak.com** is also gaining popularity and uses a sophisticated search engine (developed at MIT). Each has different business deals with the airlines and may offer different fares on the same flights, so it's wise to shop around. Expedia, Kayak, and Travelocity will also send you **e-mail notification** when a cheap fare becomes available to your favorite destination. Of the smaller travel-agency websites, **SideStep** (www.sidestep.com) has gotten the best reviews from Frommer's authors. The website (with optional browser add-on) purports to "search 140 sites at once," but in reality only beats competitors' fares as often as other sites do.

Also remember to check **airline websites,** especially those for low-fare carriers such as Southwest, JetBlue, AirTran, WestJet, or Ryanair, whose fares are often misreported or simply missing from travel agency websites. Even with major airlines, you can often shave a few bucks from a fare by booking directly through the airline and avoiding a travel agency's transaction fee. But you'll get these discounts only by **booking online:** Most airlines now offer online-only fares that even their phone agents know nothing about. For the websites of airlines that fly to and from your destination, go to "Getting There," p. 26.

Great **last-minute deals** are available through free weekly e-mail services provided directly by the airlines. Most of these are announced on Tuesday or Wednesday and must be purchased

online. Most are only valid for travel that weekend, but some (such as Southwest's) can be booked weeks or months in advance. Sign up for weekly e-mail alerts at airline websites or check mega-sites that compile comprehensive lists of last-minute specials, such as **Smarter Travel** (smartertravel.com). For last-minute trips, **site59.com** and **lastminutetravel. com** in the U.S. and **lastminute.com** in Europe often have better air-and-hotel package deals than the major-label sites.

If you're willing to give up some control over your flight details, use what is called an **"opaque" fare service** like **Priceline** (www.priceline.com; www. priceline.co.uk for Europeans) or its smaller competitor **Hotwire** (www.hot wire.com). Both offer rock-bottom prices in exchange for travel on a "mystery airline" at a mysterious time of day, often with a mysterious change of planes en route. The mystery airlines are all major, well-known carriers—and the possibility of being sent from Philadelphia to Chicago via Tampa is remote; the airlines' routing computers have gotten a lot better than they used to be. Your chances of getting a 6am or 11pm flight, however, are still pretty high. Hotwire tells you flight prices before you buy; Priceline usually has better deals than Hotwire, but you have to play their "name our price" game. If you're new at this, the helpful folks at **BiddingForTravel** (www.bidding fortravel.com) do a good job of demystifying Priceline's prices and strategies. Priceline and Hotwire are great for flights within North America and between the U.S. and Europe. But for flights to other parts of the world, consolidators will almost always beat their fares. *Note:* Priceline also offers a non-opaque service option, with which you can pick exact flights, times, and airlines from a list of offers.

**SURFING FOR HOTELS** Shopping online for hotels is generally done in one of two ways: by booking through the hotel's own website or through an independent booking agency (or a fare-service agency like Priceline; see below). These Internet hotel agencies have multiplied in mind-boggling numbers of late, competing for the business of millions of consumers surfing for accommodations around the world. This competitiveness can be a boon to consumers who have the patience and time to shop and compare the online sites for good deals—but shop they must, for prices can vary considerably from site to site. And keep in mind that hotels at the top of a site's listing may be there for no other reason than that they paid money to get the placement.

Of the "big three" sites, **Expedia** offers a long list of special deals and "virtual tours" or photos of available rooms so you can see what you're paying for (a feature that helps counter the claims that the best rooms are often held back from bargain-booking websites). **Travelocity** posts unvarnished customer reviews and ranks its properties according to the AAA rating system. **Trip Advisor** (www.tripadvisor. com) is another excellent source of unbiased user reviews of hotels around the world. While even the finest hotels can inspire a misleadingly poor review from a picky or crabby traveler, the body of user opinions, when taken as a whole, is usually a reliable indicator.

Other reliable online booking agencies include **Hotels.com** and **Quikbook. com**. An excellent free program, **TravelAxe** (www.travelaxe.net), can help you search multiple hotel sites at once, even ones you may never have heard of—and conveniently lists the total price of the room, including the taxes and service charges. Another booking site, **Travelweb** (www.travelweb.com), is partly owned by the hotels it represents (including the Hilton, Hyatt, and Starwood chains) and is therefore plugged directly into the hotels' reservations systems—unlike independent online agencies, which have to fax or e-mail reservation requests to the hotel, a good portion of which get misplaced in the shuffle. More than once, travelers have arrived at the hotel, only to be told that they have no reservation. To be fair, many of the major sites are undergoing improvements in service and ease of use, and Expedia will soon be able to plug directly into the reservations systems of many hotel chains—none of which can be bad news for consumers. In the meantime, it's a good idea to **get a confirmation number** and **make a printout** of any online booking transaction.

In the opaque website category, **Priceline** and **Hotwire** are even better for hotels than for airfares; through both, you're allowed to pick the neighborhood and quality level of your hotel before paying. Priceline's hotel product even covers Europe and Asia, though it's much better at getting five-star lodging for three-star prices than at finding anything at the

---

**⌐Tips  Finding a B&B via the WWW**

One of the surprising joys of booking travel to Canada via the Internet is the surprisingly good online organization of bed-and-breakfasts. You can research and book a nice B&B from the comfort of your own home. Visit www.bbonline. com/canada.html for very complete listings of Eastern Canadian B&B's. Visit www.canadaselect.com for a listing and rating of most Canadian hotels and inns.

## Frommers.com: The Complete Travel Resource

For an excellent travel-planning resource, we highly recommend **Frommers.com** (www.frommers.com), voted Best Travel Site by *PC Magazine*. We're a little biased, of course, but we guarantee that you'll find the travel tips, reviews, monthly vacation giveaways, bookstore, and online-booking capabilities thoroughly indispensable. Among the special features are our popular **Destinations** section, where you'll get expert travel tips, hotel and dining recommendations, and advice on the sights to see for more than 3,500 destinations around the globe; the **Frommers.com Newsletter,** with the latest deals, travel trends, and money-saving secrets; our **Community** area featuring **Message Boards,** where Frommer's readers post queries and share advice (sometimes even our authors show up to answer questions); and our **Photo Center,** where you can post and share vacation tips. When your research is finished, the **Online Reservations System** (www.frommers.com/book_a_trip) takes you to Frommer's preferred online partners for booking your vacation at affordable prices.

bottom of the scale. On the down side, many hotels stick Priceline guests in their least desirable rooms. Be sure to go to the BiddingforTravel website (see above) before bidding on a hotel room on Priceline; it features a fairly up-to-date list of hotels that Priceline uses in major cities. For both Priceline and Hotwire, you pay up front, and the fee is nonrefundable. *Note:* Some hotels do not provide loyalty program credits or points or other frequent-stay amenities when you book a room through opaque online services.

**SURFING FOR RENTAL CARS** For booking rental cars online, the best deals are usually found at rental-car company websites, although all the major online travel agencies also offer rental-car reservations services. Priceline and Hotwire work well for rental cars, too; the only "mystery" is which major rental company you get, and for most travelers the difference between Hertz, Avis, and Budget is negligible.

## 10 The 21st-Century Traveler

Travelers have any number of ways to check their e-mail and access the Internet on the road. Of course, using your own laptop—or even a PDA (personal digital assistant) or electronic organizer with a modem—gives you the most flexibility. But even if you don't have a computer, you can still access your e-mail and even your office computer from cybercafes.

**TRAVELING WITHOUT YOUR OWN COMPUTER** It's hard nowadays to find a city that *doesn't* have a few cyber-cafes. Although there's no definitive directory for cybercafes—these are independent businesses, after all—three places to start looking are at **www.cybercaptive.com** and **www.cybercafe.com**.

Aside from formal cybercafes, most **youth hostels** have at least one computer with Internet access. And many **public libraries** in Canada offer access free or for a small charge. Avoid **hotel business centers** unless you're willing to pay exorbitant rates or have no other choice.

Most airports now have **Internet kiosks** scattered throughout their gates. These kiosks, which you'll also see in shopping malls, hotel lobbies, and tourist information offices around the world, give you basic Web access for a per-minute fee that's usually higher than cybercafe prices. The kiosks' clunkiness and high price, however, mean you should avoid them whenever possible.

To retrieve your e-mail, ask your **Internet Service Provider (ISP)** if it has a Web-based interface tied to your existing e-mail account. If your ISP doesn't have such an interface, you can use the free **mail2web** service (www.mail2web.com) to view and reply to your home e-mail. For more flexibility, you may want to open a free, Web-based e-mail account with **Yahoo! Mail** (http://mail.yahoo.com). (Microsoft's Hotmail is another popular option, but Hotmail has severe spam problems.) Your home ISP may be able to forward your e-mail to the Web-based account automatically.

If you need to access files on your office computer, look into a service called **GoToMyPC** (www.gotomypc.com). The service provides a Web-based interface for you to access and manipulate a distant PC from anywhere—even a cybercafe—provided your "target" PC is on and has an always-on connection to the Internet (as with Road Runner cable). The service offers top-quality security, but if you're worried about hackers, use your own laptop rather than a cybercafe computer to access the GoToMyPC system.

**TRAVELING WITH YOUR OWN COMPUTER** More and more hotels, cafes, and retailers are signing on as Wi-Fi (wireless fidelity) "hotspots," from where you can get high-speed connection without cable wires, networking hardware, or a phone line (see below). You can get Wi-Fi connection one of several ways. Many laptops sold in the last year have built-in Wi-Fi capability (an 802.11b wireless

Ethernet connection). Mac owners have their own networking technology, Apple AirPort. For those with older computers, you can plug in an 802.11b/**Wi-Fi card** (around $50). You sign up for wireless access service much as you do for cell-phone service, through a plan offered by one of several commercial companies that have made wireless service available in many airports, hotel lobbies, and coffee shops, including some locations in Canada. **Telus** (www.telusmobility.com), a Canadian cellular phone provider, is also slowly spreading its hotspots into eastern Canada, for example. **iPass** providers (see below) also give you access to a few hundred wireless hotel lobby setups. (Pricing policies can be byzantine, but in general you pay around $30 a month for unlimited access, and prices are dropping as Wi-Fi access becomes more common.) To locate other hotspots that provide **free wireless networks** in cities around the world, go to **www.personaltelco.net/index.cgi/Wireless Communities**.

For dial-up access, most business-class hotels in Canada offer dataports for laptop modems, and some even offer free high-speed Internet access using an Ethernet network cable. You can bring your own cables, but most hotels rent them for around $10. Still, **call your hotel in advance** to see what your options are if this is important to you.

In addition, major Internet Service Providers (ISPs) have **local access numbers** around the world, allowing you to go online by placing a local call. Check your ISP's website or call its toll-free number and ask how you can use your current account away from home, and how much it will cost.

The **iPass** network also has dial-up numbers around the world. You'll have to sign up with an iPass provider, who will then tell you how to set up your computer for your destination(s). For a list of iPass providers, go to www.ipass.com and click on "Individuals Buy Now." One solid provider is **i2roam** (www.i2roam. com; ✆ **866/811-6209** or 920/235-0475).

Wherever you go, bring a **connection kit** of the right power and phone adapters, a spare phone cord, and a spare Ethernet network cable—or find out whether your hotel supplies them to guests.

### USING A CELLPHONE IN EAST-ERN CANADA

U.S. cellphones work in Canada, though you'll pay roaming *and* long-distance charges that can push call costs above the $1 per minute level. Fortunately, most U.S. carriers offer Canadian calling plans that may cut into your roaming and long-distance charges while making calls from within Canada. Check with your carrier about switching to one for the duration of your trip.

If your cellphone from another country is on a GSM system, and you have a world-capable multiband phone such as many Sony Ericsson, Motorola, or Samsung models, you can make and receive calls across civilized areas in some parts of Canada. Just call your wireless operator and ask for "international roaming" to be activated on your account. Unfortunately, per-minute charges can be high.

**Renting a Canadian phone** is another option. While you can rent a phone from any number of overseas sites, including kiosks at airports and at car-rental agencies, we suggest renting one before you leave home. That way you can give loved ones and business associates your new number, make sure the phone works, and take the phone wherever you go.

Phone rental isn't cheap. You'll usually pay $40 to $50 per week, plus airtime fees of at least a dollar a minute.

Two good wireless rental companies are **InTouch USA** (✆ **800/872-7626;** www.intouchglobal.com) and **RoadPost** (✆ **888/290-1606** or 905/272-5665; www.roadpost.com). Give them your itinerary, and they'll tell you what wireless products you need.

## 11 Getting There

### BY PLANE

Airports around Atlantic Canada offer access via scheduled flights. Halifax, Nova Scotia, the region's major air hub, has frequent flights in and out of the region, as well as onward connections to local airports. Other major airports include Saint John, New Brunswick; Charlottetown, Prince Edward Island; and Gander and St. John's, Newfoundland. All offer direct flights to and from airports outside of the region.

The main air carriers serving Atlantic Canada are **Air Canada** (✆ **888/247-2262;** www.aircanada.com) and its commuter partner **Jazz** (www.flyjazz.ca), which flies direct from Boston. See the individual "Getting There" sections at the beginning of each chapter for more information.

### GETTING THROUGH THE AIRPORT

With the federalization of airport security, screening procedures at U.S. airports are more stable and consistent than ever. Generally, you'll be fine if you arrive at the airport **1 hour** before a domestic flight and **2 hours** before an international flight; if you show up late, tell an airline employee and he or she will probably whisk you to the front of the line.

Bring a **current, government-issued photo ID** such as a driver's license or passport. Keep your ID at the ready to present at check-in, the security checkpoint, and sometimes even the gate. (Children under 18 do not need government-issued photo IDs for domestic flights, but they do for international flights to most countries.)

In 2003, the TSA phased out **gate check-in** at all U.S. airports. Passengers with e-tickets, which have made paper tickets nearly obsolete, can beat the ticket-counter lines by using airport **electronic kiosks** or even **online check-in** from their home computers. Online check-in involves logging on to your airlines' website, accessing your reservation, and printing out your boarding pass—and the airline may even offer you bonus miles to do so! If you're using a kiosk at the airport, bring the credit card you used to book the ticket or your frequent-flier card. Print out your boarding pass from the kiosk and simply proceed to the security checkpoint with your pass and a photo ID. If you're checking bags or looking to snag an exit-row seat, you will be able to do so using most airline kiosks. Even the smaller airlines are employing the kiosk system, but always call your airline to make sure these alternatives are available. **Curbside check-in** is also a good way to avoid lines, although a few airlines still don't allow it; call for your airline's policy before you go.

Security checkpoint lines are getting shorter than they were during 2001 and 2002, but an orange alert, suspicious passenger, or high passenger volume can still make for a long wait. If you have trouble standing for long periods of time, tell an airline employee; the airline will provide a wheelchair. Speed up security by **not wearing metal objects** such as big belt buckles. If you've got metallic body parts, a note from your doctor can prevent a long chat with the security screeners. Keep in mind that only **ticketed passengers** are allowed past security, except for people escorting passengers or children with disabilities.

Federalization has stabilized **what you can carry on** and **what you can't.** The general rule is that nail clippers and small scissors and tools are okay, and food and beverages must pass through the X-ray machine—but security screeners can't make you drink from your coffee cup. Bring food in your carry-on rather than checking it, as explosive-detection machines used on checked luggage have been known to mistake food (especially chocolate, for some reason) for bombs. Travelers in the U.S. are allowed one carry-on bag, plus a "personal item" such as a purse, briefcase, or laptop bag. Carry-on hoarders can stuff all sorts of things into a laptop bag; as long as it has a laptop in it, it's still considered a personal item. The Transportation Security Administration (TSA) has issued a list of restricted items; check its website (www.tsa.gov/public/index.jsp) for details.

Airport screeners may decide that your checked luggage warrants a hand search. You can now purchase luggage locks that

---

(*Tips* **Don't Stow It—Ship It**

If ease of travel is your main concern, and money is no object, consider shipping your luggage and sports equipment with one of the growing number of luggage-service companies that pick up, track, and deliver travel bags (often through couriers such as Federal Express). Traveling luggage-free, however convenient, isn't cheap: One-way overnight shipping can cost from $100 to $200, depending on what you're sending. Still, for some people, especially the elderly or the infirm, it's a sensible option. Specialists in door-to-door luggage delivery include **Virtual Bellhop** (www.virtualbellhop.com), **SkyCap International** (www.skycapinternational.com), **Luggage Express** (www.usxpluggage express.com), and **Sports Express** (www.sportsexpress.com).

allow screeners to open and relock a checked bag if hand searching is necessary. Look for Travel Sentry–certified locks at luggage or travel shops and Brookstone stores (you can buy them online at www.brookstone.com). Luggage inspectors can open these TSA-approved locks with a special code or key—rather than having to cut them off the suitcase, as they normally do to conduct a hand search. For more information on the locks, visit **www.travelsentry.org**.

## GETTING THE BEST AIRFARE

Passengers sharing the same airplane cabin rarely pay the same fare. Travelers who need to purchase tickets at the last minute, change their itinerary at a moment's notice, or fly one-way often get stuck paying the premium rate. Here are some ways to keep your airfare costs down.

- Passengers who can book their ticket either **long in advance or at the last minute,** or who **fly midweek** or **at less-trafficked hours** may pay a fraction of the full fare. If your schedule is flexible, say so, and ask if you can secure a cheaper fare by changing your flight plans.
- Search **the Internet** for cheap fares (see "Planning Your Trip Online").
- Keep an eye on local newspapers for **promotional specials** or **fare wars,** when airlines lower prices on their most popular routes. You rarely see fare wars offered for peak travel times, but if you can travel in the off-months, you may snag a bargain.
- Try to book a ticket **in its country of origin.** If you're planning a one-way flight from Halifax to Boston, a Canadian–based travel agent will probably have the lowest fares. For multi-leg trips, book in the country of the first leg.
- Join frequent-flier clubs. Frequent-flier membership doesn't cost a cent, but it does entitle you to better seats,

faster response to phone inquiries, and prompter service if your luggage is stolen or your flight is canceled or delayed, or if you want to change your seat. And you don't have to fly to earn points; frequent-flier credit cards can earn you thousands of miles for doing your everyday shopping. With more than 70 mileage awards programs on the market, consumers have never had more options, but the system has never been more complicated—what with major airlines folding, new budget carriers emerging, and alliances forming (allowing you to earn points on partner airlines). Investigate the program details of your favorite airlines before you sink points into any one. Consider which airlines have hubs in the airport nearest you, and, of those carriers, which have the most advantageous alliances, given your most common routes. To play the frequent-flier game to your best advantage, consult Randy Petersen's Inside Flyer (www.inside-flyer.com). Petersen and friends review all the programs in detail and post regular updates on changes in policies and trends. Petersen will also field direct questions (via e-mail) if a partner airline refuses to redeem points, for instance, or if you're still not sure after researching the various programs which one is right for you. It's well worth the $12 online subscription fee, good for 1 year.

## BY CAR & FERRY

Overland access to Atlantic Canada from the United States is through Maine. The most direct route to New Brunswick is to drive to Bangor (about 4½ hr. from Boston), and then head east on Route 9 to Calais, Maine (about 2½ hr.). Here you can cross into St. Stephen, New Brunswick, and pick up Route 1 to Saint John and beyond. If you don't plan to stop until you hit Moncton or points east of Moncton, a slightly faster alternative is to continue northeastward on the Maine Turnpike to Houlton, then cross the border and pick up the Trans-Canada Highway.

Between early May and late October travelers headed to Nova Scotia can save driving time by taking a ferry. Seasonal ferries to Nova Scotia depart from Bar Harbor, Maine, and a year-round ferry serves Saint John, New Brunswick.

**Bay Ferries** (© **888/249-7245;** www.catferry.com) operates the Bar Harbor–Yarmouth ferry aboard *The Cat* (short for catamaran), which claims to be the fastest in North America. Since going into service in 1998, the new ship has cut the crossing time from 6 hours to 2¾ hours, zipping along at up to 50 mph. While exhilarating, some passengers complain that the ship is a bit sterile, more like lingering in an airport lounge than taking a boat excursion. There's an open deck on the rear, but those trying to enjoy the fresh air find it mingled with exhaust fumes. Summer rates are US$58 adult, US$53 senior, US$39 child (ages 6–13), and US$99 and up for vehicles. Off-season and family rates are available. Reservations are vital during the peak summer season.

The year-round ferry from Saint John, New Brunswick, to Digby, Nova Scotia, is 3 hours. Summer fares are C$35 (US$28) for adults, C$25 (US$20) for seniors, C$20 (US$16) for children ages 6 to 13, and C$80 (US$64) and up per vehicle; they drop by about 33% before July and after September. Contact **Bay Ferries** (© **888/249-7245;** www.nfl-bay.com) for schedules and more information.

## BY BUS

Bus service into and out of the region tends to be slow and cumbersome. To get from New York to Halifax, for instance, you'd have to bus to Montréal (8–10 hr.),

and then connect to another bus line to Halifax (18 hr.). A late-spring through early fall alternative from the East Coast of the United States is to bus from New York to Bar Harbor, Maine (about 10 hr.); stay overnight in town; then take the early morning ferry from Bar Harbor to Yarmouth, Nova Scotia (less than 3 hr.). You can catch a connecting bus onward to Halifax (about 4 hr.).

**Greyhound** (© 800/231-2222) offers service from diverse points around the United States to Montréal's bus station (© 514/843-4231), where you can connect to Atlantic Canada–bound buses. **Acadian Lines** (© 800/567-5151; www.smtbus.com), also doing business under the name **SMT,** offers a several-times weekly service from Bangor, Maine, to New Brunswick, and daily services within Nova Scotia, New Brunswick, and Prince Edward Island with connections to Nova Scotia. **DRL Coachlines** (© 888/738-8091 or 902/450-1987; www.drlgroup.com) offers bus service within Newfoundland. It formerly offered service from Halifax to Yarmouth; check the website for updates.

## BY TRAIN

**VIA Rail** (© 888/842-7245) offers train service 6 days a week between Halifax and Montréal, with several stops along the way (see "By Train" in the next section, "Getting Around"). The entire trip takes about 21 hours, and if purchased at least 7 days in advance costs about C$140 to C$210 (US$112–US$168) per person each way, about C$300 to C$400 (US$240–US$320) per person round-trip. The price depends on whether you purchase a seat, lower-bunk berth, upper-berth sleeping bunk, or half of a double cabin with private bathroom. (Don't try to sleep sitting up in a seat.) Check out the website www.viarail.com for more details on routes, schedules, and online booking.

## 12 Getting Around

**BY CAR & FERRY**   Atlantic Canada's road network is extensive and generally well maintained. The Trans-Canada Highway enters the region north of Edmundston, New Brunswick, and continues some 1,800km (1,050 miles) to St. John's, Newfoundland. Numerous feeder roads connect to the Trans-Canada. American travelers expecting to find six-lane highways with high-speed on- and off-ramps will be in for a surprise. With a few exceptions, the highway system is on a far more intimate scale. Many main arteries—such as the inland route from Yarmouth to Halifax and Route 1 across Newfoundland—are just two lanes, albeit with frequent opportunities for passing.

If you're arriving by plane, the usual suspects offer car rentals at major airports. Despite the number of rental outfits, however, it can be difficult to reserve a car during the peak summer season when demand soars. It's best to reserve ahead. Try **Budget** (© 800/527-0700), **Dollar** (© 800/800-4000), **Hertz** (© 800/654-3131), or **National** (© 800/361-5334). See "Car-Rental Insurance," earlier, for information on insuring a rented vehicle while traveling.

**Saving Money on a Rental Car**   Car-rental rates vary even more than airline fares. A few key questions could save you hundreds of dollars.

- Are weekend rates lower than weekday rates?
- Is a weekly rate cheaper than the daily rate?
- Does the agency assess a drop-off charge if you don't return the car to the same location where you picked it up?
- Are special promotional rates available?
- Are discounts available for members of AARP, AAA, frequent-flier programs, or trade unions?

- How much tax will be added to the rental bill?
- What is the cost of adding an additional driver's name to the contract?
- How many free miles are included in the price?
- How much does the rental company charge to refill your gas tank if you return with the tank less than full?

**Maps**   Excellent road maps are available from the provincial tourism authorities (ask at the welcome centers). The maps are free except in Newfoundland, where the province charges C$5 (US$3.55) for them. You can usually obtain a free New-foundland map by calling the visitor information number (© 800/565-0000) before your trip and requesting that information on visiting the province be mailed to you.

**Driving Rules**   As in most of the United States, drivers may make a right turn at a red light, provided that they first stop fully and confirm that no one is coming from the left. At some intersections, signs prohibit such a turn. Radar detectors are prohibited in all the Atlantic Provinces. Drivers and all passengers are required to wear seat belts.

**Gasoline**   Some American drivers get rather excited about the price of gasoline when they first cross the border, thinking it to be very cheap. It is not. Gasoline is priced by the liter, not the gallon, and it is even more expensive than gasoline in the United States.

**BY PLANE**   There's a lack of competition in Eastern Canada, which can mean you'll pay high fares for even a short hop to or around the region. At the moment, **Air Canada** (© 888/AIR-CANA; www.aircanada.com) and its short-hop subsidiary **Jazz** (www.flyjazz.ca) are often your only choices for both domestic and international flights.

The situation is slowly improving, however. **WestJet** (© **888/WEST-JET** or 800/538-5696; www.westjet.com), **Delta** (© **800/221-1212**; www.delta.com), and the new regional airline **Canjet** (© **800/ 809-7777**; www.canjet.com) serve small but growing segments of the Nova Scotia, New Brunswick, and Prince Edward Island air market; check for rates that are competitive with Air Canada's.

Newfoundland is the exception to this rule, with a rather extensive system of small airports stitching together much of the far-flung province—and a smattering of small regional air carriers to match. Contact **Air Labrador** (© **800/563-3042**; www.airlabrador.com) or **Provincial Airlines** (© **800/563-2800** or 709/ 576-1666; www.provincialairlines.ca). Note that smaller airports throughout the region—such as Bathurst, Fredericton, Moncton, Yarmouth, and Sydney—offer connections to the four main provincial hubs of Halifax, Saint John, Charlottetown, and St. John's.

**BY BUS**   Decent bus service is offered between major cities and many smaller towns. For service in Nova Scotia or New Brunswick, contact **Acadian Lines** (© **800/567-5151**), also known as **SMT**; in Newfoundland try **DRL Coachlines** (© **709/738-8091**).

**BY TRAIN**   Interprovincial rail service is a pale shadow of its former self. Prince Edward Island and Newfoundland lack any rail service at all, as does southern New Brunswick (you can't travel by train any longer to Fredericton or Saint John). **VIA Rail** (© **888/842-7245**; www. viarail.com) stops in a handful of towns along its single route between Montréal and Halifax. In New Brunswick, stops are Campbellton, Charlo, Jacquet River, Petit Rocher, Bathurst, Miramichi, Rogersville, Moncton, and Sackville. In Nova Scotia, you can stop at Amherst, Springhill Junction, Truro, or Halifax.

## 13  Packages for the Independent Traveler

Before you start your search for the lowest airfare, you may want to consider booking your flight as part of a travel package. Package tours are not the same as escorted tours. With a package tour, you travel independently but pay a group rate. You can buy airfare, accommodations, and other elements of your trip (such as car rentals, airport transfers, and sometimes even activities) at the same time and often at discounted prices—kind of like one-stop shopping. Packages are sold in bulk to tour operators—who resell them to the public at a cost that usually undercuts standard rates.

One good source of package deals is the airlines themselves, though only a few offer packages to Eastern Canada. Those that do include **Air Canada** (© **888/AIR-CANA**; www.aircanada.ca), **American Airlines Vacations** (© **800/321-2121**; http://aav1. aavacations.com), **Continental Airlines Vacations** (© **800/301-3800**; www.cool vacations.com), and **United Vacations** (© **800/377-1816**; www.unitedvacations. com).

The **United States Tour Operators Association**'s website (www.ustoa.com) has a search engine that allows you to look for operators that offer packages to a specific destination. Travel packages are also listed in the travel section of your local Sunday newspaper.

I've found that **Liberty Travel** (© **888/ 271-1584**; www.libertytravel.com), one of the biggest packagers in the Northeast, offers the best trips to Atlantic Canada. Liberty often runs full-page ads in Sunday papers. Or check ads in the national travel magazines such as *Arthur Frommer's Budget Travel Magazine, Travel + Leisure,*

*National Geographic Traveler,* and *Condé Nast Traveller.*

Several big **online travel agencies**—Expedia, Travelocity, Orbitz, Site59, and Lastminute.com—also do a brisk business in packages. If you're unsure about the pedigree of a smaller packager, check with the Better Business Bureau in the city where the company is based, or go online at www.bbb.org. If a packager won't tell you where they're based, don't fly with them.

Packages have pros and cons, of course. They can save you money while allowing for independent travel. And some even let you add on a few guided excursions or escorted day trips (also at prices lower than if you booked them yourself) without booking an entirely escorted tour.

But you're usually required to make a large payment up front; you may end up on a charter flight; and you have to deal with your own luggage and with transfers between your hotel and the airport, if transfers are not included in the package price. Packages often don't allow for complete flexibility or a wide range of choices. For instance, you may prefer a quiet inn but have to settle for a popular chain hotel instead. Your choice of travel days may be limited as well.

Before you invest in a package tour, get some answers. Ask about the **accommodations choices** and prices for each. Then look up the hotels' reviews in a Frommer's guide and check their rates online for your specific dates of travel. You'll also want to find out what **type of room** you get. If you need a certain type of room, ask for it; don't take whatever is thrown your way. Request a nonsmoking room, a quiet room, a room with a view, or whatever you fancy.

Finally, look for **hidden expenses.** Ask whether airport departure fees and taxes, for example, are included in the total cost.

## 14 Escorted General-Interest Tours

Escorted tours are structured group tours, with a group leader. The price usually includes everything from airfare to hotels, meals, tours, admission costs, and local transportation.

Despite the fact that escorted tours require big deposits and predetermine hotels, restaurants, and itineraries, many people derive security and peace of mind from the structure they offer. Escorted tours—whether they're navigated by bus, motor coach, train, or boat—let travelers sit back and enjoy the trip without having to drive or worry about details. They take you to the maximum number of sights in the minimum amount of time with the least amount of hassle. They're particularly convenient for people with limited mobility and they can be a great way to make new friends.

On the downside, you'll have little opportunity for serendipitous interactions with locals. The tours can be jam-packed with activities, leaving little room for individual sightseeing, whim, or adventure—plus they also often focus on the heavily touristed sites, so you miss out on many a lesser-known gem.

Before you invest in an escorted tour, request a complete **schedule** of the trip to find out how much sightseeing is planned and whether you'll have enough time to relax or have an adventure of your own. Also ask about the **cancellation policy:** Is a deposit required? Can they cancel the trip if enough people don't sign up? Do you get a refund if they cancel? If *you* cancel? How late can you cancel if you are unable to go? When must you pay in full? If you choose an escorted tour, think strongly about purchasing trip-cancellation insurance, especially if the tour operator asks you to pay in advance. See the section on "Travel Insurance," p. 17. If you plan to travel alone, find out if they'll charge a **single supplement** or whether they can pair you with a roommate.

The **size** of the group is also important to know up front. Generally, the smaller the group, the more flexible the itinerary, and the less time you'll spend waiting for people to get on and off the bus. Find out the **demographics** of the group as well. What is the age range? What is the gender breakdown? Is this mostly a trip for couples or singles?

Discuss what is included in the **price.** You may have to pay for transportation to and from the airport. A box lunch may be included in an excursion, but drinks might cost extra. Tips may not be included. Find out if you will be charged if you decide to opt out of certain activities or meals.

Before you invest in a package tour, get some answers. Ask about the **accommodations choices** and prices for each. Then look up the hotels' reviews in a Frommer's guide and check their rates online for your specific dates of travel. You'll also want to find out what **type of room** you get. If you need a certain type of room, ask for it; don't take whatever is thrown your way. Request a nonsmoking room, a quiet room, a room with a view, or whatever you fancy.

These two firms offer escorted tours of Eastern Canada:

- **Collette Vacations,** Pawtucket, Rhode Island (✆ **800/340-5158;** www.collettevacations.com). Collette offers tours that range from fly/drive packages to the escorted everything's-done-for-you variety throughout the Maritimes.

- **Maxxim Vacations,** St. John's, NF (✆ **800/567-6666** or 709/754-6666; www.maxximvacations.com). Newfoundland's largest travel provider has a top-rate reputation and offers a range of trips, including guided and unguided excursions. Call and ask for the extensive and colorful brochure.

## 15 Special-Interest Trips

A growing number of outfitters and entrepreneurs are offering soup-to-nuts adventure tours that take care of all the planning, equipment, accommodations, and meals for a trip. Other specialized vacations available in Eastern Canada include learning vacations, during which you can immerse yourself in local culture, and more traditional sightseeing tours by bus.

**LEARNING VACATIONS** The **Gaelic College of Celtic Arts and Crafts,** St. Ann's, NS (✆ **902/295-3411;** www.gaeliccollege.edu) offers 2-week programs for children and adults that specialize in local culture, such as Highland bagpiping, dancing, drumming, and Cape Breton fiddling. More than 100 students attend classes each session; the school is located on Cape Breton near Baddeck.

At **King's Landing,** near Fredericton NB (✆ **506/363-4999;** www.kings landing.nb.ca), children dress up in period costume and learn about how the early Loyalist settlers lived. The programs range from a few hours to a week, from early June through early October. Admission is charged of all visitors. Adult programs are also offered.

**Sunbury Shores Arts and Nature Centre,** St. Andrews, NB (✆ **506/529-3386;** www.sunburyshores.org) offers day- and week-long trips and classes with topics including plant dyes, printmaking, raku pottery, and watercolor and oil painting. The center is located on the water in St. Andrews; lodging can be arranged.

At **Village Historique Acadien,** near Caraquet, NB (✆ **506/726-2600** or

877/721-2200; www.villagehistorique acadien.com), the lives and arts of early Acadian settlers are the focus of this program, held at a re-created historic village.

**ADVENTURE TRAVEL**   Adventure travel is a growth industry in Atlantic Canada, as it is worldwide. Adventure travel companies are especially helpful for those arriving by air who are interested in outdoor adventures—it's a bit cumbersome to fly with bikes, canoes, and so forth. You can request information on adventure outfitters currently leading trips by calling the toll-free provincial information numbers listed at the beginning of this chapter. The free provincial travel guides also list outfitters, and in each chapter, we've included a "Great Outdoors" section, which offer some pointers based on your interests. Here's a sampling of well-regarded outfitters:

- **Backroads,** Berkeley, CA (© **800/ 462-2848** or 510/527-1555; www. backroads.com). One of North America's largest adventure travel companies offers 6-day walking and biking trips through southeast Nova Scotia. Pick according to your budget and inclination: You can stay at luxury inns, or opt for more rustic camping trips.

- **Coastal Adventures,** Tangier, NS (© **877/404-2774** or 902/772-2774; www.coastaladventures.com). Sea kayak honcho Scott Cunningham and his staff lead trips ranging from 2-day paddles to weeklong adventures throughout the Maritimes and Newfoundland. He also does a range of rentals.

- **Country Walkers,** Waterbury, VT (© **800/464-9255** or 802/244-1387; www.countrywalkers.com). Country Walkers offers van-supported week-long walking trips on Cape Breton Island.

- **Freewheeling Adventures,** Hubbards, NS (© **800/672-0775** or 902/857-3600; www.freewheeling. ca). This popular outfitter based near Halifax offers guided bike tours throughout Nova Scotia, as well as on Prince Edward Island.

## 16  Recommended Books, Films & Music

**BOOKS**   *Anne of Green Gables* by L.M. Montgomery (Oxford University Press, 1997 and Children's Classics, 1998) is a children's book for all time and a lovely evocation of life on Prince Edward Island. Lucy Maud Montgomery's fictional, ever-sunny Anne is the island's most famous export, hands-down; her cycle of novels about the adopted red-haired girl remain enormously popular worldwide, both thanks to her delineation of island characters and Anne's irrepressible optimism. It's less well known that there is an entire series of Anne books; *Anne of Green Gables* only takes Anne's life through age 16. In future installments, Montgomery took her to a school principal job, and through a marriage and childbearing. Montgomery was prolific beyond the Anne cycle as well, writing a series of spinoff novels about the lives of other townspeople in Anne's fictional town of Avonlea; *Chronicles of Avonlea* and *Further Chronicles of Avonlea* are probably best known. She also authored a number of other books and short stories set on the island, not involving Anne at all, though none of these has achieved anywhere near the lasting fame of the Anne stories—works like *Jane of Lantern Hill, Mistress Pat,* and *Along the Shore.*

If you can locate it, the edition of *Anne of Green Gables* by Oxford University Press is annotated with plenty of biographical material, excerpts from the author's girlhood journals, colloquial explanations of cookery, directions to locations featured in the book, and the like—it is perhaps a better choice for adult readers and travelers. The Children's Classic edition is a simple hardcover version of the classic.

No book with adult themes set in the Maritime Provinces is more famous than *The Shipping News* by E. Annie Proulx (Scribner, 1993). Proulx won both a Pulitzer Prize and a National Book Award for her second novel, the tale of a crushed down-and-out New Yorker who moves to the Rock and takes up a job penning articles for a shipping newspaper in the land of his forebears—a position which puts him in intersection with some of the more fascinating characters on (or even just passing through) the island. He must also battle the demons left him by his former wife. Yet somehow he begins to rebuild a life of dignity, hope, and purpose. Though often criticized for its overblown style, there's no denying this novel does capture the combination of isolation and peculiar perkiness and quirkiness of the Newfie.

In *The Bird Artist* by Howard Norman (Farrar, Straus and Giroux, 1994, and Picador, 1998), Norman continues the tradition of Vermont-linked authors (such as E. Annie Proulx, above) heading north and finding literary gold in the Maritimes. This book, about a remote Newfoundland fishing village, was a finalist for the National Book Award, and rightly so. It spins the yarn of a local artist with a tremendous gift for drawing birds who has committed a murder, and seeks some sort of redemption for that through his drawings and a marriage arranged by his parents. His true love, Margaret, is a hoot—a hard-drinking, sexually aware woman—and yet touching, as are many of the assembled minor characters, from the village reverend on down. A heartfelt novel.

Norman was not just a one-trick wonder. His novel *The Museum Guard* (Farrar, Straus and Giroux, 1994, and Picador, 1999) is set in a fictional Halifax art museum, where a downbeat guard's female companion becomes obsessed with a Dutch painting. While not Norman's finest work, the stories of the guard's upbringing, his lady's obsession, and their dreary lives tell much about the often-claustrophobic and hard-bitten lives of Maritimers.

Norman turned to nonfiction for *My Famous Evening* (National Geographic, 2004), recounting both his own personal travels and correspondences in Nova Scotia and sometimes-seemingly-unreal stories of Nova Scotians and the folk tales of the province.

Recently reissued, *A Whale for the Killing* by Farley Mowat (Stackpole Books, 2005) is a true story that became a touchstone for animal rights activists. The famed biologist and activist tells the tale of a huge whale stranded in a Newfoundland cove in the 1970s, and a group of locals bent on killing it; Mowat becomes the whale's protector, but ultimately fails. It is interesting for the clash of ideals between local fisherfolk and an environmentalist from the "outside" (Mowat is from Ontario and Saskatchewan originally). Not a pretty look at the Maritimes, but a slice of life nonetheless.

In *The Boat Who Wouldn't Float* by Mowat (Little, Brown & Co., 1970, and Starfire, 1984), Mowat turned to humor for a change, and the resulting book (now reissued) turns out to be surprisingly raucous and side-splitting at times. Mowat purchases a used schooner in Newfoundland, but it doesn't hold water well, and there are serious doubts he'll ever get out of port. His subsequent misadventures and cruises amongst the ports of Newfoundland and beyond are wonderful fodder. Reading it, you learn about Screech (a famously powerful Newfie liquor) and much more; it's clear Mowat holds great affection for the Newfies, even as he skewers them and himself.

For historical background, try to find *Part of the Main* by Peter Neary and Patrick

O'Flaherty (Breakwater Books, 1983). In it, two of the Maritime Provinces' most prolific historians lay out the history of Newfoundland and Labrador in interesting prose. It was published by a local St. John's publisher; the book is improved by the inclusion of several hundred photographs.

For a look at where the economy of the region is headed lately, *Lament for an Ocean* by Michael Harris (McClelland & Stewart, 1998) is a fine nonfiction work documenting the shockingly sudden decline of the Maritime fisheries—and the consequences both for Newfoundland's way of life and its already-imperiled economy.

**FILMS** Many films have been made in the Maritimes, but precious few have been made *about* them.

*Johnny Belinda* (1948) is one. The film takes place on Cape Breton Island, starring lovely Jane Wyman in a surprisingly sensitive performance as a deaf-mute woman who is sexually assaulted and then turns on her attacker. She won an Oscar for the role.

*The Shipping News* (2001) is an uneven but evocative picture with a stellar cast, based on the novel by E. Annie Proulx. The film was shot in Newfoundland—a condition of Proulx's sale of the screen rights, it's said—and these visuals alone make the film an excellent watch. Kevin Spacey is the news writer Quoyle (he seems to have gained a little weight for the role) and Cate Blanchett is his abusive wife.

**MUSIC** Music in the Maritime Provinces is generally a Celtic-inflected folk, or else a pop music greatly influenced by that sound.

Nova Scotia native Sarah McLachlan is the exception; she has made it bigger around the globe than anyone else from eastern Canada, thanks to a continuing stream of haunting, minor-key pop classics. Among her studio albums, *Fumbling Towards Ecstasy* (Arista Records, 1994)

features the single "Possession" and was her first breakout hit. *Surfacing* (BMG, 1997) features "Sweet Surrender" and "Building a Mystery." The live record *Mirrorball* (Arista Records, 1999) recaps much of McLachlan's best work in a tight live setting, adding the often-heard but little-recorded gem "I Will Remember You."

Among the more folksy bands making headway, the Newfoundland band Great Big Sea have been the standard-bearers of modern Celtic music around the Maritimes for awhile now, graduating from bar band to genuine folk influence in the best tradition of the Chieftains and the like. Of their output, I like *Turn* (Sire/Rhino, 2000) most; tunes such as "Boston and St. John's" speak closely to life in an isolated, seafaring place.

In my humble opinion, the Rankins—a family group from little Mabou, on Cape Breton Island—were sorely underappreciated outside of eastern Canada while they were still together. The band broke up in the late 1990s, and one of its members was subsequently killed in a tragic auto accident on a twisting Cape Breton road; on this magical record, though, their folk roots and chops come together with contemporary production (in the style of Enya or Clannad) in a way that stands the test of time. Although a bit overproduced, there's no denying the mournful power of Jimmy Rankin's ballads, the infectious drive of the late John Morris Rankin's fiddle, and the lovely, sweet harmonies of sisters Cookie, Raylene, and Heather. Among their oeuvre, *North Country* (Angel Records, 1995) is the most fitting legacy to these local kids who made good.

Cape Breton fiddler Natalie MacMaster is probably Canada's finest, drawing very favorable comparisons to American Alison Krauss. *A Compilation* (Rounder, 1998) serves as a nice introduction to her lightning-yet-subtle style. On *Blueprint* (Rounder, 2003), she is joined by American musicians working the same general vein, such as Bela Fleck and Sam Bush.

Finally, any serious discussion of Maritime music must not omit Hank Snow. More than a decade before there was a Bob Dylan, and around the same time Hank Williams Sr. was shooting to prominence, there came Snow, too: born in the small Nova Scotia fishing town of Liverpool (near Lunenburg), a rambling, yodeling ranger of a crooner who made a mark on Nashville and legions of folk and country musicians to come. He's a member of the Country Music Hall of Fame and was a Grand Ole Opry staple for years. *The Essential Hank Snow* (RCA, 1997) includes his still-classic "I'm Movin' On," which he wrote, as well as 19 other cuts.

## FAST FACTS: Atlantic Provinces

*American Express* American Express maintains offices in all four Maritime Provinces, including in Halifax, Truro, and North Sydney. To report lost or stolen American Express traveler's checks while in Canada, call ℂ **800/221-7282.**

*ATM Networks* See "Money," earlier in this chapter.

*Automobile Clubs* CAA (the Canadian Automobile Association) extends member benefits (including maps and road service) to AAA cardholders. If you're a member, bring your membership card. For information about membership in CAA, call ℂ **800/561-8807.** For emergency road service, call ℂ **800/222-4357.**

*Business Hours* Business hours are generally similar to what you'd find in the United States. Most offices are open from 8 or 9am to 5 or 6pm Monday through Friday, and are closed on weekends. Boutiques and souvenir shops typically open up around 10am and stay open until 6pm or so, often later during the peak tourist season. Hours vary widely for general merchandise and grocery stores. In general, you can expect early and late hours in the larger cities (24-hr. groceries are cropping up), but more limited hours in the smaller towns and villages. Most general merchandise stores are closed on Sundays.

*Car Rentals* See "Getting Around," earlier in this chapter.

*Climate* See "When to Go," earlier in this chapter.

*Currency* See "Money," earlier in this chapter.

*Documents* See "Entry Requirements & Customs," earlier in this chapter.

*Driving Rules* See "Getting Around," earlier in this chapter.

*Drugstores* Chain drugstore and independent pharmacies are located throughout Atlantic Canada. Check the phone book under "pharmacy." Stores in larger cities and towns are likely to be open later than those in more remote villages. One of the larger national chains is Pharmasave, with stores in Nova Scotia, New Brunswick, and Prince Edward Island.

*Electricity* Canada uses the same electrical current as the United States: 110–115 volts, 60 cycles.

*Embassies & Consulates* All embassies are in Ottawa, the national capital. The **Australian High Commission** is at 50 O'Connor St., Room 710, Ottawa, ON K1P 6L2 (ℂ **613/236-0841**). The **British High Commission** is at 80 Elgin St., Ottawa, ON K1P 5K7 (ℂ **613/237-1530**). The **Irish Embassy** is at 130 Albert St., Suite 1105, Ottawa, ON K1P 5G4 (ℂ **613/233-6281** or 613/233-1956). The **New**

**Zealand High Commission** is at 99 Bank St., Suite 727, Ottawa, ON K1P 6B9 (© **613/238-5991**). The **South African High Commission** is at 15 Sussex Dr., Ottawa, ON K1M 1M8 (© **613/744-0330**). The **U.S. Embassy** is at 490 Sussex Dr., Ottawa, ON K1N 1G8 (© **613/238-5335**). In the Maritimes, there's a **U.S. Consulate** in Purdy's Wharf Tower 2, Suite 904, 1969 Upper Water St., Halifax, NS B3J 3R7 (© **902/429-2480**); the **British Consulate** is at 1 Canal St., Dartmouth, NS (© **902/461-1381**).

*Emergencies* In life-threatening situations, dial © **911**.

*Holidays* See "When to Go," earlier in this chapter.

*Information* See "Visitor Information," earlier in this chapter.

*Internet Access* See "The 21st-Century Traveler," earlier in this chapter.

*Liquor Laws* The legal drinking age is 19 years of age in all provinces. Restaurants that serve alcoholic beverages are said to be "licensed." If you want to tipple with dinner, look for a sign or ask whether the establishment is licensed. Do not drink and drive. Canadian law takes drunken driving seriously.

*Lost & Found* Be sure to tell all of your credit card companies the minute you discover your wallet has been lost or stolen and file a report at the nearest police precinct. Your credit card company or insurer may require a police report number or record of the loss. Most credit card companies have an emergency toll-free number to call if your card is lost or stolen; they may be able to wire you a cash advance immediately or deliver an emergency credit card in a day or two. Visa's U.S. emergency number is © **800/847-2911** or 410/581-9994. American Express cardholders and traveler's check holders should call © **800/221-7282**. MasterCard holders should call © **800/307-7309** or 636/722-7111. For other credit cards, call the toll-free number directory at © **800/555-1212**.

If you need emergency cash over the weekend when all banks and American Express offices are closed, you can have money wired to you via **Western Union** (© **800/325-6000**; www.westernunion.com).

Identity theft and fraud are potential complications of losing your wallet, especially if you've lost your driver's license along with your cash and credit cards. Notify the major credit-reporting bureaus immediately; placing a fraud alert on your records may protect you against liability for criminal activity. The three major U.S. credit-reporting agencies are **Equifax** (© **800/766-0008**; www.equifax.com), **Experian** (© **888/397-3742**; www.experian.com), and **TransUnion** (© **800/680-7289**; www.transunion.com). Finally, if you've lost all forms of photo ID call your airline and explain the situation; they might allow you to board the plane if you have a copy of your passport or birth certificate and a copy of the police report you've filed.

*Mail* Letters (up to 30g) mailed within Canada are C50¢ (US40¢). Letters up to 30g mailed to the United States cost C85¢ (US68¢). For other international destinations, a letter weighing less than 30g is C$1.45 (US96¢). More detailed information on packages and other options is available at **www.canadapost.ca**.

*Maps* Excellent road maps are available from the provincial tourism authorities (ask at the welcome centers). For more information, see "Getting Around," earlier in this chapter.

*Newspapers & Magazines* Publishers in the major cities of the province—including Halifax, Saint John, Fredericton, Charlottetown, and St. John's—all produce very decent daily newspapers filled with information about goings-on around the town and province. Most also maintain websites on the Internet, so you can scout out happenings before your departure. Canada's two national newspapers—the *Globe and Mail* and the *National Post*—are also widely available in most cities and many larger towns. U.S. papers such as the *Wall Street Journal* and *The New York Times* can be found in larger cities, but you shouldn't count on it. When available, they often sell out early. Newsmagazines such as *Time* and *Newsweek* are not difficult to find on newsstands.

*Pets* Traveling into Canada with your pet dog or cat should pose no difficulties. Be sure to have with you a certificate from your veterinarian certifying that your pet is currently vaccinated against rabies. (Puppies and kittens under 3 months are exempt.)

*Police* For police call © **911.**

*Safety* The cities of Atlantic Canada are relatively small, well policed, and generally safe. Rowdies and drunks sometimes can be threatening, especially late on weekend nights in boisterous downtown neighborhoods, but serious crime is rather rare in this part of Canada. Nonetheless, whenever you're traveling in an unfamiliar place, stay alert and be aware of your immediate surroundings.

*Taxes* See "Money," earlier in this chapter.

*Telephones* Pay phones are located throughout Atlantic Canada and are self explanatory. Local calls are still often C25¢ to C50¢ (US20¢–US40¢). Calls to the United States or elsewhere abroad can be pricey, and you should check in advance whether your calling card works in Canada. (Some do; many don't.) Check at drugstores or convenience stores for prepaid calling cards, which usually offer a better rate than feeding in coins.

The United States and Canada are on the same long-distance system. To make a long-distance call between the United States and Canada (in either direction), simply dial "1" first, then the area code and number. It's no different than calling long distance in the United States.

*Time Zone* Most of Atlantic Canada is on Atlantic Standard Time, 1 hour ahead of Eastern Standard Time (as observed in New England and the U.S. East Coast). The exceptions are Newfoundland and southeast Labrador, which are a half-hour ahead of Atlantic Standard Time.

*Tipping* As in the United States, tips provide a significant portion of the income for waiters, bellhops, and chambermaids. It's standard to leave 15% of the pre-sales-tax total for basic service at a restaurant, more if the service is exceptional. Plan to tip around C$1 (US80¢) per bag for assistance at your hotel and C$1 to C$2 (US80¢–US$1.60) per day to your chambermaid.

*Toilets* Generally called "washrooms" in Canada, public bathrooms are typically abundant and clean. Many towns have a visitor information center, and most of these have washrooms for visitors. In larger cities, washrooms can be found in public buildings, major hotels, some larger shops, and restaurants.

# 3

# Suggested Itineraries in the Atlantic Provinces

The eastern provinces of Canada are big, yet intimate. You drive a long way between major destinations, only to find you're overwhelmed with joy by a small wooden church, a fish stand, a rock outcropping . . . and you end up staying longer than you intended. I've seen it happen, time and again.

So I have two pieces of advice. First, leave a bit of flexibility in your itinerary, because the provinces are full of unexpected surprises. You'd hate to leave Lunenburg without jumping onto a whale-watching boat or the Friday before a weekend fisherman's festival, right? And second, allow yourself time for the long

drives—better yet, bring a companion who can share the load. Except when in Prince Edward Island, you'll log more than a few hours on the road to complete these tours.

The range of possible itineraries in eastern Canada is practically endless (you could even do a kayaking itinerary, or a French-towns itinerary, for instance), but I've focused down to just a few of my favorite places for the purposes of this chapter. So, while even a month is not enough to see all of the Maritime Provinces, realistically most folks simply don't have that long. To help you, I've broken out four itineraries touching on the "greatest hits" of each province.

## LIGHTS OUT   THE BEST OF NOVA SCOTIA IN 1 WEEK

This tour of my favorite Maritime Province takes in lighthouses, quaint villages, a surprisingly vibrant city, and dramatic headlands plunging to the ocean. Begin in Yarmouth, landing point for the ferry from Bar Harbor, Maine.

### Day ❶: The Southernmost Coast
Spend the morning in **Yarmouth,** a compact port city offering a few diversions, such as a **Firefighters' Museum** (p. 70) and a French-speaking region just a short drive to the west. It's worth a half-day— and a stop at **Harris'** Quick-N-Tasty (p. 71), a good takeout stand for a quick bite before pressing onward. I also like to drive the coastline just west of the city, which harbors several relatively unknown (thus empty) beaches.

Drive 100km (62 miles) east along Route 103, exiting the main highway to reach **Shelburne** ❋. This compact little town has a fine, small **historic complex** offering water views, a cooper, boat-builders, and small museums. There's also an attractive main street for a bite to eat, and one of my favorite fish and chips stands in eastern Canada, the aptly named **Mr. Fish.** See p. 74.

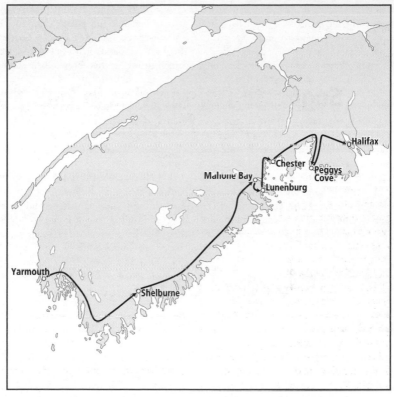

Continue another 120km (73 miles) east along Route 103 to the exit for Route 324; exit and continue about 10km (6 miles) east to

## Days ②–④: Lunenburg 🦉🦉 and Mahone Bay 🦉🦉

These cute twin towns, separated by just a 15-minute drive, are easily worth 2 to 3 nights. (You'll arrive late on the first day anyway.) You can explore remote peninsulas—preferably by bike—shoot some golf, visit a great ocean museum, or book a kayak tour. Some of the province's better bed-and-breakfasts are tucked in these towns, too. I like to time my visit to coincide with one of the summertime fisherman's, arts, or music festivals. See p. 75, 82.

During your 3 days in the region, be sure to follow Route 3 about 10km (6 miles) northeast of Mahone Bay to **Chester** 🦉🦉 (p. 84). This small port town is New England–cute, with a scenic, first-rate golf course, a good little summer theater company, a handful of restaurants, and a ferry service to nearby **Tancook Island.** (If you take the ferry, just be sure to get a schedule so you don't miss the last boat back.) It's surely worth a couple hours.

## Days ⑤–⑦: The Halifax Region

From Lunenburg, Mahone Bay, or Chester, head northeast along Route 3 or route 103 about 24km (15 miles) to the turnoff for Route 333. Take this detour about 24km more (15 miles) down the route to **Peggy's Cove** 🦉🦉🦉. This famously picturesque cove features a lighthouse, surf crashing on rocks, a somber memorial to a passenger plane crash, and more cute souvenirs than you can shake a stick it. Sure, you can take a tour bus from Halifax, but why not just sample it on the way up? It's worth an hour or two. See p. 103.

From Peggy's Cove, backtrack 24km (15 miles) to the main highway; then continue north about 24km (15 miles) along Route 103 to exits for **Halifax** 𝒢𝒢𝒢. This is Nova Scotia's crown jewel, a place where live bands play nightly, buskers perform in the streets, and there's plenty of grog and museum-going to be had. It's not a huge place, and you'll quickly have covered all of it, but the lodging and dining are good enough that it's worth several nights. Be sure to explore the **Maritime Museum of the Atlantic** (Titanic artifacts), and **Pier**

21 (see p. 90, 91) for a look at the immigrant experience in eastern Canada. Or just wander up and down **Spring Garden Road** and back and forth along Barrington Street, hunting for brewpubs, record shops, and old buildings.

Bored with the bright lights? Head for a remote beach down a nearby peninsula, such as **Crystal Crescent Beach;** there are plenty, but you'll need a map to find the way. And roads are a bit rough on the suspension.

From here, rise early and you can speed back down the highway south to Yarmouth in time to catch your ferry back to Maine. Be sure not to dally, though—the 338km (211-mile) drive takes more than 3 hours.

---

| HIGH TIMES, HIGH TIDES | **THE BEST OF NEW BRUNSWICK IN 1 WEEK** |
|---|---|

New Brunswick is strung out; to see some of its best quickly and compactly, this tour takes in the highlights of the southernmost New Brunswick coast, from the province's largest city to its biggest tidal drops. Begin at St. Andrews, the first significant destination beyond the Maine state line (I'm assuming you've driven north from Maine; if you've flown into Saint John, see it first or last and simply switch around the order below).

---

**Days ❶ & ❷: St. Andrews** 𝒢𝒢
This compact little seaside town is the perfect stopping point after rambling through miles of the blessed emptiness that is Downeast Maine. It's worth at least 1 night for shopping and walking, another day and a night if you're intent on taking a whale-watch trip or other excursion from the harbor—or playing the **Algonquin's golf course** (p. 144), which I love.

A day trip to the nearby islands, such as **Deer Island** or **Campobello** (p. 145), is always nice in summer.

From St. Andrews, continue about 19km (12 miles) northeast (do not backtrack) along Route 127 to Route 1, the main road. Then continue 80km (50 miles) along Route 1 to
**Days ❸–❹: Saint John** 𝒢
Saint John (spelled out, please) isn't the capital of New Brunswick, but it's the

province's chief economic engine for sure. The downtown's central square is lovely and worth some time just hanging out; later, you can walk the downtown streets, choosing from gourmet and mid-priced restaurants or a pub with some ale and live music. See p. 158.

The **farmer's market,** also within walking distance, is excellent and a must-visit if you like food.

From Saint John, continue about 90km (56 miles) northeast along Route 1 to Route 114; turn south along Route 114 and continue 15km (9 miles) to its end, which puts you in
**Days ❺–❻: Fundy National Park** 𝒢𝒢
One of the most surprising things you can do in New Brunswick is hightail it to this park, where the world's highest tides slam up the narrowing "V" of the **Bay of**

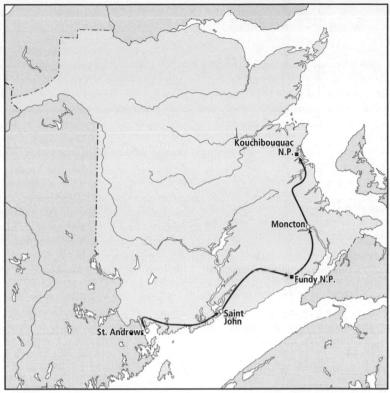

**Fundy.** Any number of tour outfits can take you down to waterside (tide schedules in hand, of course). The weirdly shaped **Hopewell Rocks** make a good trip while here, and there's also an excellent road/hiking path along the bay. This is worth a day or two with the family—you'll have to stay in rustic accommodations, however—and remember to spend time on the bike or on a hike, too. See p. 179.

From the park, continue north along Route 114 80km (50 miles) to

## Day **7**: Moncton 🍴

This city at the crossroads of the Maritimes is showing new signs of life. Stay the night and use the city as base for a day

trip, or else press on to the big park an hour away. See p. 181.

Head 80km (50 miles) north, following routes 115 and 11, passing the big **Dune of Bouctouche** en route, to **Kouchibouguac National Park** 🍴🍴 (p. 185), where you can canoe, bike, or kayak to explore this park, and its flatness makes for easy walking (or picnicking on the beach). Return to Moncton at night, or just stay in the park.

From Moncton, you're just 80km (50 miles) from the bridge to Prince Edward Island (see next itinerary) or a few hours from further coastal exploring. Or return south 266km (166 miles) along Highway 1 to the Maine border, about a 3½-hour trip.

**REACHING THE BEACH** | **PRINCE EDWARD ISLAND FOR FAMILIES**

This tour takes in the trifecta of the island's essential sights, giving each its due: Charlottetown, Anne's Land, and the lovely beaches of Prince Edward Island National Park. Kids will love all three places, and adults will feel a sense of tranquillity they may not have known in years.

### Days ❶–❷: Victoria 🍎🍎 and Charlottetown 🍎

Compact **Victoria** makes a surprise little stop en route to the "big" city. It's all too cute. An hour or two and a cup of tea ought to do it. See p. 229.

Take the Trans-Canada 32km (20 miles) east to **Charlottetown.** The island's capital city is just lovely, with excellent restaurants, inns, a lot of history, and a plain friendly feel. Stay the night for sure. Family activities here include the **Confederation Centre of the Arts** (p. 214), with a constantly changing program of plays and performances (including an annual run of an *Anne of Green Gables* play).

There's also excellent on-street browsing and shopping, and a surfeit of parks in which to push baby strollers—or exercise a pet. See p. 213–214.

From Charlottetown, follow signs west along Route 2 to Route 13, then turn north and follow Route 13 to

### Day ❸: Anne's Land 🍎

The village of **New Glasgow** makes a good stop while heading back to the center of the island. There's a great golf course, nice views from the country roads looping over hillsides, and the **Prince Edward Island Preserve** factory (p. 204), with its factory store and cafe. Kids might enjoy sampling the jams. Give this stop an hour or two.

Continue north along Route 13 to **Cavendish** 🍎 (p. 198), the island's most tourist-friendly and developed (some say overdeveloped) section. The fictional,

red-haired Anne of Green Gables is everywhere in the Cavendish area, and some of the attractions related to her and the book's author really *are* worth seeing—especially for young and teenaged girls and their mothers. If you're just not into children's stories, there are still plenty of other touristy attractions for kids, from the **Ripley's Believe It or Not! Museum** and the **Wax World of the Stars** (check out Lady Di) to amusement parks like the **Sandspit.**

Where to stay? There are numerous "bungalow courts" (small cottage compounds) dotting the area, some with cooking facilities good for frying up a local fish for the little ones, though my first choice might be to pitch a tent in the park (see next entry). This area is definitely worth a day or two with children.

From Cavendish, turn east on Route 6 and travel, through a series of tricky turns, to Prince Edward Island.

### Days ❹–❻: Prince Edward Island National Seashore 🍎🍎🍎 & Souris 🍎

Some of the best beaches in eastern Canada line the northern shores of Prince Edward Island. You'll surely want to spend a few days here with the family walking the beach, snapping photos of glorious sunsets and purple lupines against the red sand, camping among the dunes, hunting down obscure fish and chips shops, and just generally kicking back.

You'll find a wide range of accommodations in these parts, from Victorian resorts to B&Bs to lovely campgrounds—the latter my recommended choice. Any

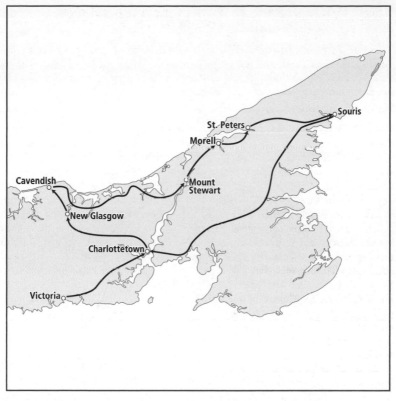

family in the Maritimes should camp together at least 1 night; the quiet and fresh air will do you a world of good. These placid surroundings and warm waters just invite tranquillity, so go ahead; stay a couple nights.

While staying at the park, take some **scenic drives.** From the park, continue east on Route 6 to Route 2, turning east and continuing about 60 scenic kilometers (38 miles) through Mount Stewart, St. Peters, and Morell to Souris.

Some outstanding inns, scenery, and beaches lie near the postage-stamp town of **Souris** (p. 225). If you're an outdoors sort of family, rent yourselves a bike or three and just go exploring. Locals are

unfailingly nice. You can even stay over in the area if you really like, whether in a campground or in your pick of two of the island's most luxurious inns.

**Return 80km (50 miles) along Routes 2, 4, and 5 to**

## Day ❼: Charlottetown ⭐⭐, Once More

I like **Charlottetown** a lot and believe it's worth a repeat visit while making a circuit of PEI. You probably didn't see everything on your first time through, anyway. Why not spend another night? Hit the **Confederation Court Mall,** wander the street snapping photos of the kids and look for souvenirs for friends.

# Newfoundland in 2 Weeks

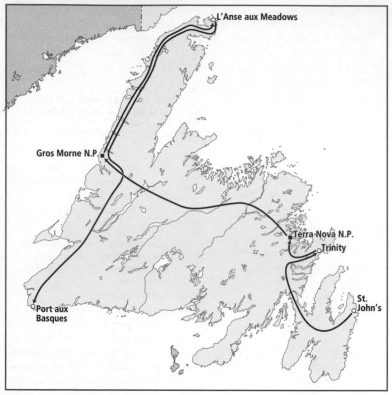

## THE BEST OF NEWFOUNDLAND IN 2 WEEKS

This tour of "the Rock" (a local nickname for Newfoundland) brings you to the capital city, as well as Viking ruins. Be prepared to burn several tanks of gas and plenty of rubber.

### Days ❶–❸: St. John's 😊😊

Few places in North America are more convivial, seafaring, or musical than **St. John's.** You're absolutely required to have a pint (or fake it) in a local pub while trying to catch the next big traditional music act. I'd say it's worth 3 nights of your time if you include some sort of excursion out into the countryside; the area's many outfitters can help. See p. 276.

Drive north along from St. John's about 160km (100 miles) north on the Trans-Canada Highway (Hwy. 1), exiting at Clarenville and continuing 65km (40 miles) east on Route 230 to Route 239. Turn south on Route 239 and continue about 2km (1 mile) to the turnoff for

### Days ❹–❺: Trinity 😊😊: Land of Icebergs

**Trinity** is a lovely town in an inaccessible place—you have to drive 72km (45 miles) down a side road off the already sparse Trans-Canada Highway just to get there, and then do the same in reverse later. There's enough scenery here to eat. If it's iceberg season (that is, late spring), stay a few nights and watch for the big boys (local outfitters will help you). See p. 265.

Retrace your route back along Route 230 to the Trans-Canada Highway at Clarenville (save miles by cutting west on Route 233). Head north on the Trans-Canada, soon passing through

### Day ➏: Terra Nova National Park ✦

This is a convenient stopping point on the way to Gros Morne, with excellent family attractions—more than most anywhere else in the province. See p. 261.

Continue west along the Trans-Canada Highway about 420km (263 miles) to Deer Lake, and then follow Route 430 further west to

### Days ➐–➓: The Grandeur of Gros Morne National Park ✦✦✦

Gros Morne National Park is absolutely the must-see place in Newfoundland, and if you go nowhere else, go here. You'll be tuckered out by the drive, but once here you'll know what the big deal was all about. Stay at least 2 (preferably more) nights in the park, just soaking up atmosphere—not only to take in the stupendous sights (huge cliffs, waterfalls,

beaches, Arctic flowers, snowshoe hares, and the like) but also to rest up for the long drive to your next wonderful destination; a true hiking enthusiast could probably spend a week here happily. See p. 244.

Drive about 338km (211 miles) north along Route 430 to the Route 436 turnoff. Continue about 9km (6 miles) more to

### Days ⑪–⑫: L'Anse aux Meadows ✦✦✦

Eleventh-century Viking artifacts were discovered at Newfoundland's northernmost tip in 1960, and the site is well worth a visit. The artifacts are fascinating. See p. 252.

Return about 400km (250 miles) along Route 430 to Deer Lake, and then continue another 265 km (160 miles) along the Trans-Canada Highway (Hwy. 1) to

### Day ⑬: Port aux Basques

Traveling to Port aux Basques will take you the better part of a day. This town is the docking point for another ferry which carries you back to Cape Breton Island. There's little to do here, and it's best used as a staging area—and last souvenir-grab—before the passage back to Nova Scotia. See p. 238.

# 4

# Nova Scotia

Nova Scotia proves cagey to character-ize. It generally feels more cultured than wild . . . but then you stumble upon those blustery, boggy uplands at Cape Breton Highlands National Park, which seem a good home for druids and trolls. It's a province full of rolling hills and culti-vated farms, especially near the Northumberland Straits on the northern shore . . . but then you find the vibrant, edgy, and lively arts and entertainment scene in Halifax, a city that has more intriguing street life than many cities three times its size. It's a place that earns its name—Nova Scotia is Latin for "New Scotland"—with Highland games and kilts and a touch of a brogue here and there . . . but then suddenly you're amid the enclaves of rich Acadian culture along the coast between Digby and Yarmouth. The place resists characterization at every turn.

This picturesque and historic province is an ideal destination for travelers who are quick to hit the remote control when

parked on the couch back home. There's an extravagant variety of landscapes and low-key attractions, and the scene seems to change kaleidoscopically as you travel along the winding roads: from dense forests to bucolic farmlands, from ragged coast to melancholy bogs, and from his-toric villages to dynamic downtowns. (About the only terrain it doesn't offer is towering mountain peaks.)

Nova Scotia is twice blessed: It's com-pact enough that you needn't spend all your time in a car. Yet it has fewer than a million residents (and one in three are in and around Halifax), making it unpopu-lated enough to provide empty places when you're seeking solitude. Even along the more populated shoreline it's possible to find a sense of remoteness, of being surrounded by big space and a profound history. More than once while traveling here, I've had the fleeting sense that I was traveling in New England, but 60 or 70 years ago, well before anyone referred to tourism as an industry.

## 1 Exploring Nova Scotia

Visitors to Nova Scotia would do well to spend some time poring over a map and this travel guide before leaving home. The hardest chore will be to narrow your options before you set off. Numerous loops and circuits are available, made more complicated by ferry links to the United States, New Brunswick, Prince Edward Island, and New-foundland. Figuring out where to go and how to get there is the hardest part.

The only people I've ever heard complain about Nova Scotia are those who tried to see it all, and to see it within a week. Such an approach will leave you strung out and exhausted. Instead, prioritize your interests and decide accordingly. Looking for those picture-perfect scenes of coastal villages? Focus mostly on the south shore, specifically the trio of Chester, Lunenburg, and Mahone Bay. Drawn to hiking amid rocky coastal scenery? Allow plenty of time at Cape Breton. Looking for more pastoral ocean scenery? Head for the Fundy Coast. Want to spend a quiet day canoeing? Make your stop Kejimkujik National Park. Dying for some gourmet dining and urban buzz? Factor in a few days in Halifax. Above all, schedule plenty of time for simply doing not much of anything. It's the best way to let Nova Scotia's charms unfold at their own unhurried pace.

## ESSENTIALS

**VISITOR INFORMATION**   Every traveler to Nova Scotia should have a copy of the massive (400+ page) official tourism guide, which is the province's best effort to put travel-guide writers like us out of business. This comprehensive, colorful, well-organized, and free guide lists all hotels, campgrounds, and attractions within the province, with brief descriptions and current prices. (Restaurants are given only limited coverage.)

The guide, called the *Nova Scotia Doers & Dreamers Travel Guide,* is available starting each March by phone (© **800/565-0000** or 902/425-5781), fax (902/424-2668), mail (P.O. Box 456, Halifax, NS B3J 2R5), and Internet (www.novascotia.com). If you wait until you arrive in the province before obtaining a copy, ask for one at the numerous visitor information centers, where you can also request the excellent free road map.

The provincial government administers about a dozen official **Visitor Information Centres** throughout the province, as well as in Bar Harbor, Maine, and Wood Islands, Prince Edward Island (PEI). These mostly seasonal centers are amply stocked with brochures and tended by knowledgeable staffers. In addition, virtually every town of any note has a local tourist information center filled with racks of brochures covering the entire province, staffed with local people who know the area. You won't ever be short of information.

In general, the local and provincial visitor information centers are run with cordiality and brisk efficiency. I have yet to come across a single one that wasn't remarkably helpful, although the press of crowds can sometimes require a few minutes' wait to get individual attention at the more popular gateways such as Amherst (outside Halifax) or Port Hawkesbury (entering Cape Breton Island).

For general questions about travel in the province, call **Nova Scotia's information hot line** at © **800/565-0000** (North America) or 902/425-5781 (outside North America).

**GETTING THERE   By Car & Ferry**   Most travelers reach Nova Scotia overland by car from New Brunswick. Plan on at least 4 hours driving from the U.S. border at Calais, Maine, to Amherst (at the New Brunswick–Nova Scotia border). Incorporating ferries into your itinerary can significantly reduce time behind the wheel. Daily seasonal ferries connect both Portland and Bar Harbor, Maine, to Yarmouth, Nova Scotia, at the peninsula's southwest end.

**Bay Ferries** (© **888/249-7245;** www.catferry.com) operates the Bar Harbor–Yarmouth ferry. *The Cat* (short for catamaran) claims to be the fastest ferry in North America and since going into service in 1998 has cut the crossing time from 6 to 2¾ hours, zipping along at up to 50 miles per hour. Summer season rates are C$59 (US$47) adults and children age 13 to 18, C$54 (US$43) seniors, C$39 (US$31) children 6 to 13, and C$99 (US$79) and up per vehicle. Off-season and family rates are available. Reservations are vital during the peak summer season.

To shorten the slog around the Bay of Fundy, a 3-hour ferry (also operated by Bay Ferries) links **Saint John, New Brunswick,** and **Digby, Nova Scotia.** The ferry sails

# Nova Scotia

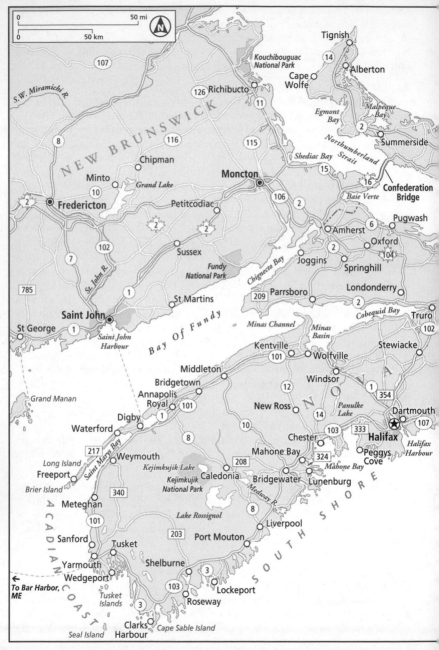

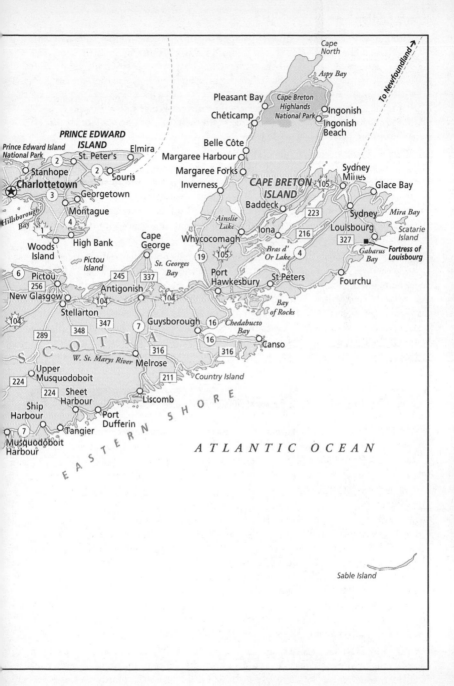

year-round, with as many as three crossings daily in summer. Summer fares are C$35 (US$28) for adults, C$25 (US$20) for seniors, C$20 (US$16) for children, and C$80 (US$64) and up per vehicle; off-season rates are cheaper, but fuel surcharges of C$20 (US$16) or more can add to your tab. Schedules and more information on Bay Ferries can be found at **www.nfl-bay.com**.

For those traveling farther afield, ferries also connect Prince Edward Island to Caribou, Nova Scotia, and Newfoundland to North Sydney, Nova Scotia. See chapters 6 and 7 for more detailed information.

**By Plane**    Halifax is the air hub of the Atlantic Provinces. **Air Canada** (© 888/247-2262; www.aircanada.com) provides direct service from New York and Boston, while its commuter partner **Jazz** (www.flyjazz.ca) uses smaller planes to serve Sydney, Charlottetown, Saint John, and St. John's. Routes that involve connections at Montréal or Toronto can turn a short hop into an all-day excursion, however. The regional airline **Canjet** (© 800/809-7777; www.canjet.com) flies to and from Toronto, Montréal, Ottawa, St. John's, and even Florida (winter only).

**By Train**    VIA Rail (© 888/842-7245; www.viarail.com) offers train service 6 days a week between Halifax and Montréal. The entire trip takes between 18 and 21 hours, depending on direction. The fare is about C$200 (US$160) each way, with discounts for those buying at least 1 week in advance. Sleeping berths and private cabins are available at extra cost. VIA recently added a higher class of service on its overnight run; this new Easterly Class service is expected to operate from May through October in 2006. Standard overnight sleeper cabin service on the route will continue to be offered year-round. Check the company website for updates on routes, schedules, and online booking.

## 2 The Great Outdoors

Nova Scotia's official travel guide (the *Nova Scotia Doers & Dreamers Travel Guide*) has a very helpful "Outdoors" section in the back that lists camping outfitters, bike shops, whale-watching tour operators, and the like. A free brochure that lists adventure outfitters is published by the **Nova Scotia Adventure Tourism Association,** 1099 Marginal Rd., Suite 201, Halifax, NS B3H 4P7 (© **800/948-4267** or 902/423-4480). Write or call for a copy.

**BIKING**    The low hills of Nova Scotia and the gentle, largely empty roads make for wonderful cycling. Cape Breton is the most challenging of destinations; the south coast and Bay of Fundy regions yield wonderful ocean views while making fewer demands on cyclists. A number of bike outfitters can aid in your trip planning. **Freewheeling Adventures** (© **800/672-0775** or 902/857-3600; www.freewheeling.ca) offers guided bike tours throughout Nova Scotia, Prince Edward Island, and Newfoundland. Walter Sienko's guide, *Nova Scotia & the Maritimes by Bike: 21 Tours Geared for Discovery,* is helpful in planning a bike excursion. For an Internet introduction to cycling in Nova Scotia and beyond, point your Web browser to the website of **Atlantic Canada Cycling** (www.atl-canadacycling.com).

**BIRD-WATCHING**    More than 400 species of birds have been spotted in Nova Scotia, ranging from odd and exotic birds blown off course in storms to majestic **bald eagles,** of which some 250 nesting pairs reside in Nova Scotia, mostly on Cape Breton Island. Many whale-watching tours also offer specialized sea bird–spotting tours, including trips to **puffin colonies.**

**CAMPING**    With backcountry options rather limited, Nova Scotia's forte is drive-in camping. The 20 provincial parks with campgrounds are uniformly clean, friendly, well managed, and reasonably priced, and offer some 1,500 campsites among them. For a brochure and map listing all campsites, write to **Nova Scotia Department of Natural Resources, Parks and Recreation Division,** R.R. #1, Belmont, NS B0M 1C0; or call ✆ **902/662-3030.**

Another free and helpful guide is the *Campers Guide,* which includes a directory of private campgrounds that are members of the association. Ask for it at the visitor information centers.

**CANOEING**    Nova Scotia offers an abundance of accessible canoeing on inland lakes and ponds. The premier destination is **Kejimkujik National Park** in the southern interior, which has plenty of backcountry sites accessible by canoe. A number of other fine canoe trails allow paddlers and portagers to venture off for hours or days. General information is available from **Canoe Kayak Nova Scotia,** 5516 Spring Garden Rd., 4th floor, Halifax, NS B3J 1G6 (✆ **902/425-5454, ext. 316**).

**FISHING**    Saltwater fishing tours are easily arranged on charter boats berthed at many of the province's harbors. Inquire locally at the visitor information centers, or consult the "Boat Tours & Charters" section of the *Doers & Dreamers Guide.* No fishing license is needed for those on charters. For saltwater regulations, contact the **Department of Fisheries** at ✆ 902/863-0533 or 902/863-5670.

Committed freshwater anglers come to Nova Scotia in pursuit of the tragically dwindling Atlantic salmon, which requires a license separate from that for other freshwater fish. **Salmon licenses** must be obtained from a provincial office, campground, or licensed outfitter. Other freshwater species popular with anglers are brown trout, shad, smallmouth bass, rainbow trout, and speckled trout. For a copy of the current fishing regulations, contact the **Department of Agricultural and Fisheries** at ✆ **902/424-4560** or go to their website at **www.gov.ns.ca/nsaf**.

**GOLF**    Nova Scotia lays claim to more than 50 golf courses. Among the most memorable: **Highland Links** (✆ **800/441-1118** or 902/285-2600) in Ingonish, which features a dramatic oceanside setting; and **Bell Bay Golf Club** (✆ **800/565-3077** or 902/295-1333) near Baddeck, which is also wonderfully scenic, and was voted "Best New Canadian Golf Course" by *Golf Digest* in 1998.

While the big names are fun, I really enjoy playing some of the less-famous courses around the province, too. The **Bluenose Golf Club** (✆ **902/634-4260**) has been operating on a beautiful tract of land known as Kaulbach Head overlooking Lunenburg's harbor since 1933. (It's visible in the distance from almost any point in the old town.) The short, 5,275-yard track here plays harder than it looks because of numerous slopes and sidehill lies. Views of the ocean and town are stupendous on both the starting and finishing holes; greens fees are C$25 (US$20) for 9 holes, C$40 (US$32) for 18 holes (carts cost extra), and afterward the clubhouse grill serves up some mighty fine burgers and beers on tap. Other nicely scenic tracks open to the public include the **Chester Golf Club** (✆ **902/275-4543**), with amazing ocean views and fine course maintenance, and hilly, beautiful **Osprey Ridge** (✆ **902/543-6666;** www. ospreyridge.ns.ca) near Shelburne; designed by the noted course architect Graham Cooke and opened in 1999.

For one-stop shoppers, **Golf Nova Scotia** (✆ **800/565-0000,** ext. 007; www.golf novascotia.com) represents 27 well-regarded properties around the province and can arrange customized golfing packages at its member courses. A handy directory of

Nova Scotia's golf courses (with phone numbers) is published in the "Outdoors" section of the *Nova Scotia Doers & Dreamers Travel Guide.*

**HIKING & WALKING**    Serious hikers make tracks for Cape Breton Highlands National Park, which is home to the most dramatic terrain in the province. But other options abound—trails are found throughout Nova Scotia, although in many cases they're a matter of local knowledge. (Ask at the visitor information centers.) Published hiking guides are widely available at local bookstores. Especially helpful are the back-pocket-size guides published by **Nimbus Publishing;** call for a catalog (© **800/646-2879** or 902/454-7404; www.nimbus.ns.ca).

**SAILING**    Any area with so much convoluted coastline is clearly inviting to sailors and gunkholers. Tours and charters are available almost everywhere there's a decent-size harbor. Those with the inclination and skills to venture out on their own can rent 5m (16-ft.) Wayfarers, or one of several slightly larger boats, by the hour and maneuver among beautiful islands at **Sail Mahone Bay** (© **902/624-8864**) on the south shore near Lunenburg. The province's premier sailing experience is an excursion aboard the *Bluenose II,* which is virtually an icon for Atlantic Canada. See the "Lunenburg" section later in this chapter.

**SEA KAYAKING**    Nova Scotia is increasingly attracting the attention of kayakers worldwide. Kayakers traveling on their own should be especially cautious on the Bay of Fundy side, since the massive tides create strong currents that overmatch even the fittest of paddlers. Nearly 40 kayak outfitters do business in Nova Scotia, and they offer everything from 1-hour introductory paddles to intensive weeklong trips; consult the directory in *Doers & Dreamers.*

Among the more respected outfitters is **Coastal Adventures,** P.O. Box 77, Tangier, NS B0J 3H0 (© **877/404-2774** or 902/772-2774; www.coastaladventures.com). The company is run by veteran kayaker Scott Cunningham, who leads trips throughout the Maritimes and Newfoundland. For kayaking on the eastern side of Cape Breton, check with **North River Kayak,** R.R. #4, Baddeck, NS B0E 1B0 (© **888/865-2925** or 902/929-2628).

**WHALE-WATCHING**    If you're on the coast, it's likely you're not far from a whale-watching operation. Around two dozen whale-watching outfits offer trips in search of finback, humpback, pilot, and minke whales, among others. The richest waters for whale-watching are found on the Fundy Coast, where the endangered right whale is often seen feeding in summer. Digby Neck (a thin strand extending southwest from the town of Digby) has the highest concentration of whale-watching excursions, but you'll find them in many other coves and harbors. Just ask the staff at visitor information centers to direct you to the whales.

## 3 Minas Basin & Cobequid Bay

If you're not content except off the beaten track, a detour along the Minas Basin and Cobequid Bay will be one of the highlights of your trip. With the exception of Truro, this region is rural, quiet, and full of hidden surprises. You can turn down a dirt road, shut off your car's engine, and not hear much other than the wind and maybe a blackbird or two. You can trek along spectacular hiking trails, or picnic alone on a long stretch of remote and misty coast, literally watching the tides roll in.

There's also a rich history here, but it tends to be hidden and subtle rather than preening and obvious. And don't look for the quaint seaside villages or the surf-washed

## A Scenic Drive

If you're headed from the Truro area southwestward along the Fundy Coast toward Digby, Route 215 offers a wonderful **coastal detour** ★ from Maitland to Windsor. This winding, fast, and rather narrow road (not suggested for bicycling) passes through a number of quiet hamlets, some with handsome early buildings. But the chief appeal comes in the sudden vistas of lush green farmland (often accompanied by the redolent smells of cow by-product) and broad views of expansive Minas Basin beyond. At the town of Walton, there's a handsome lighthouse on a rocky bluff with a nearby picnic area just off the main route (it's well marked). This detour runs 90km (56 miles) from South Maitland to Brooklyn. Few services for tourists are offered along the route, other than a handful of restaurants, B&Bs, and campgrounds. Look for general stores and farm stands if you need a snack. If you don't plan to spend much time in this region, perhaps taking the Trans-Canada and passing through Truro, you can fix up a good picnic for the road by detouring to **The Austrian Smokehaus** (© 902/897-6116; www.austriansmokehaus.com), on Highway 311 in North River (just outside Truro). This operation smokes and sells sandwich meats, sausages, Atlantic salmon, and more by the pound. Owners Hans and Heike Langmann have brought a dozen prizes back to Canada from Austria for their work; they're open March through December only, Tuesday to Saturday from 10am to 5pm. From Highway 102 near Truro, get there by taking exit 14A and heading toward Upper Onslow; then turn onto Highway 311.

rocky coast for which Nova Scotia is famous; that will have to wait until Yarmouth and the South Shore. The natural drama here is pegged to the region's profound remoteness and the powerful but silent tides, among the highest in the world.

## WOLFVILLE ★

The trim and tidy Victorian village of Wolfville (pop. 3,500) has a distinctly New England feel to it, in both its handsome architecture and its layout—a small commercial downtown just 6 blocks long is surrounded by shady neighborhoods of elegant homes. And it's not hard to trace that sensibility to its source. The area was largely populated in the wake of the American Revolution by transplanted New Englanders, who forced off the Acadian settlers who had earlier done so much to tame the wilds.

The town's mainstay these days is handsome **Acadia University,** which has nearly as many full-time students as there are residents of Wolfville. The university's presence gives the small village an edgier, more youthful air. Don't miss the university's Art Gallery at the **Beveridge Arts Centre** ★ (© 902/585-1373), which showcases both contemporary and historic Nova Scotian art; it's open daily from 1 to 4pm and admission is free.

The town has emerged in recent years as a popular destination for weekending Halifax residents, who come to relax at the many fine inns, wander the leafy streets, and explore the countryside. Also a consistent draw is the **Atlantic Theatre Festival** (© 800/337-6661 or 902/542-1515), which has attracted plaudits in the few years it has been presenting shows. Performances are staged throughout the summer season in a comfortable 500-seat theater. Reservations are encouraged; ticket prices are C$10 to C$23 (US$8–US$18). Check upcoming performances on their website (www.atf.ns.ca).

## EXPLORING WOLFVILLE

Strolling the village is the activity of choice. The towering elms and maples that shade the extravagant Victorian architecture provide the dappled light and rustling sounds for an ideal walk. A good place to start is the **Wolfville Tourist Bureau** at Willow Park (© **902/542-7000**) on the north edge of the downtown.

Several **trails** ✦ through rugged landscapes and intriguing geological formations are on **Cape Split,** the hook of land that extends far into the Bay of Fundy north of Wolfville.

At **Blomidon Provincial Park** (© **902/582-7319**), 24km (15 miles) north of Route 101 (Exit 11), some 14km (8.5 miles) of trail at the park take walkers through forest and along the coast. Among the most dramatic trails is the 6km (3.75-mile) **Jodrey Trail** ✦, which follows towering cliffs that offer broad views over the Minas Basin.

For a more demanding adventure, head north of Wolfville about 25 minutes on Route 358, and park off the side of the road near the beginning of the **Cape Split Trail** ✦. This 16km (10-mile) trail offers some of the more breathtaking vistas in Nova Scotia, cresting oceanside cliffs that approach 122m (400 ft.) in height. Allow most of a day to truly enjoy this in-and-back excursion. Basic maps and additional information are available from the Wolfville Tourist Bureau (see above).

One of the more intriguing sights in town occurs each summer day at dusk, in an unprepossessing park surrounded by a parking lot a block off Main Street. At **Robie Swift Park,** a lone chimney (dating from a long-gone dairy plant) rises straight up like a stumpy finger pointed at the heavens. Around sunset, between 25 and 100 chimney swifts flit about and then descend into the chimney for the night. Alas, the swifts have been declining in number in recent years, ever since some predatory merlins started nesting nearby. But you'll learn a lot by browsing the informational plaques posted here, where you can read interesting tidbits such as this: No one knew where swifts migrated in winter until 1943, when explorers in the Peruvian jungle found natives wearing necklaces adorned with small aluminum rings. These, it turned out, were tracking bands placed on swifts by North American ornithologists.

**Grand-Pré National Historic Site** ✦   Long before roving New Englanders arrived in this region, hardworking Acadians had vastly altered the local landscape. They did this in large part by constructing a series of dikes outfitted with ingenious log valves, which allowed farmers to convert the saltwater marshes to productive farmland. At Grand-Pré, a short drive east of Wolfville and just off Route 1, you can learn about these dikes along with the tragic history of the Acadians, who populated the Minas Basin between 1680 and their expulsion in 1755.

More a memorial park than a living history exhibit, Grand-Pré (which means "great meadow") has superbly tended grounds that are excellent for idling, a picnic lunch, or simple contemplation. Among the handful of buildings on the grounds is a graceful stone church, built in 1922 on the presumed site of the original church. Evangeline Bellefontaine, the revered (albeit fictional) heroine of Longfellow's epic poem, was said to have been born here; look for the statue of this tragic heroine in the garden. It was created in 1920 by Canadian sculptor Philippe Hérbert, and the image has been reproduced widely since.

2241 Grand-Pré Rd., Grand-Pré. ⓒ 902/542-3631. www.grand-pre.com. Admission C$6.50 (US$5) adults, C$5.50 (US$4.50) seniors, C$3.25 (US$2.75) children 6–16, C$16 (US$13) families. Daily May–Oct 9am–6pm. Closed Nov–Apr.

## WHERE TO STAY

**Gingerbread House Inn** ☀    The ornate Gingerbread House Inn was originally the carriage house for the building now housing Victoria's Historic Inn (see below). A former owner went wood-shop-wild, adding all manner of swirly accouterments and giving the place a convincingly authentic air. The guest rooms are a modern interpretation of the gingerbread style and are generally quite comfortable, although the two rooms in the back are dark and small. The floral Carriage House Suite features luxe touches like a propane fireplace and two-person Jacuzzi; the Garden House has the most space, plus a spa and a wet bar. The budget choice is the lovely Terrace Room, which is somewhat minuscule but has a lovely private deck on the second floor under a gracefully arching tree. Breakfasts tend toward the elaborate and are served by candlelight.

8 Robie Tufts Dr. (P.O. Box 819), Wolfville, NS B0P 1X0. ⓒ 888/542-1458 or 902/542-1458. Fax 902/542-4718. www.gingerbreadhouse.ca. 9 units. May–Oct C$90–C$129 (US$72–US$103) double, C$149–C$188 (US$119–US$150) suite; Nov–Apr C$85–C$119 (US$68-US$95) double, C$100–C$169 (US$80–US$135) suite. Rates include full breakfast. Ask about golf packages. AE, MC, V. **Amenities:** Dining room. *In room:* A/C, TV.

**Tattingstone Inn** ☀☀    "We sell romance and relaxation," says innkeeper Betsey Harwood. And that pretty well sums it up. This handsome Italianate-Georgian mansion dates from 1874 and overlooks the village's main artery. The inn is furnished with a mix of reproductions and antiques, and traditional and modern art blend well. The attitude isn't over-the-top Victorian as one might guess by looking at the manse, but decorated with a deft touch that mixes informal country antiques and regal Empire pieces. The rooms in the Carriage House are a bit smaller than those in the main house, but they are still pleasant and showcase fine examples of modern Canadian art. The spacious semiformal dining room is rather refined, and diners sup amid white tablecloths and stern Doric columns. Dinner is served nightly in summer from 5:30 to 9pm. Ask for a seat on the enclosed porch, which captures the lambent, early evening light to good effect. House specialties include the rack of lamb and chicken served with pear and ginger sauce; the latter incorporates pears grown right on the property.

434 Main St. (P.O. Box 98), Wolfville, NS B0P 1X0. ⓒ 800/565-7696 or 902/542-7696. www.tattingstone.ns.ca. 10 units. July–Aug C$148–C$185 (US$118–US$140) double; Sept–Oct C$98–C$175 (US$78–US$140) double. AE. MC, V. **Amenities:** Restaurant; outdoor pool; tennis court; steam room. *In room:* A/C, TV/VCR.

**Victoria's Historic Inn** ☀☀    Victoria's Historic Inn was constructed by apple mogul William Chase in 1893 and is architecturally elaborate. This sturdy Queen Anne–style building features bold pediments and massed pavilions, which have been adorned with balusters and ornate Stick Style trim. Inside, the effect seems a bit as if you'd wandered into one of those stereoscopic views of a Victorian parlor. Whereas the nearby Tattingstone Inn resists theme decor, Victoria's Historic Inn embraces it. There's dense mahogany and cherry woodwork throughout, along with exceptionally intricate ceilings. The deluxe Chase Suite features a large sitting room with a gas fireplace and an oak mantle. The less-expensive third-floor rooms are smaller and somewhat less historic in flavor. Four of the inn's suites have fireplaces and Jacuzzis.

600 Main St., Wolfville, NS B4P 1E8. ⓒ 800/556-5744 or 902/542-5744. Fax 902/542-7794. www.victoriashistoric inn.com. 15 units. High season C$108–C$245 (US$86–US$196) double, Nov–Mar C$79–C$130 (US$63–US$104) double. Rates include full breakfast. AE, MC, V. **Amenities:** Laundry service. *In room:* A/C.

## WHERE TO DINE

Coffee strong enough to make the mummified snap bolt upright is available at **The Coffee Merchant and Library Pub,** 472 Main St. (© **902/542-4315**), open from 7am until 9pm most days. The shop also has a selection of pastries and sweets.

In addition to the following restaurant, the dining rooms mentioned above serve some of the more elegant meals in town, but at a price to match.

**Al's Homestyle Café** *Value* DELI    Randy and Linda Davidson now operate this place in the nearby hamlet of Canning (about 16km/10 miles northwest of Wolfville, on Rte. 358), but Al Waddell's popular recipes for sausages live on—choose from Polish, German, hot Italian, and honey garlic. Buy some links to cook later, or order up a quick road meal. You won't find a better cheap lunch: A sausage on a bun with a cup of soup will run you less than C$5 (US$4).

9819 Main St., Canning. © **902/582-7270**. All selections C$2–C$4 (US$1.60–US$3.25). V. Mon–Sat 8am–6pm; Sun 11am–5pm.

## 4 Annapolis Royal ✦✦

Annapolis Royal is arguably Nova Scotia's most historic town—it even bills itself, with justification, as "Canada's birthplace." The nation's first permanent settlement was established at Port Royal, just across the river from the present-day Annapolis Royal, in 1605 by a group of doughty settlers that included Samuel de Champlain. (Champlain called the beautiful Annapolis Basin "one of the finest harbours that I have seen on all these coasts.") The strategic importance of this well-protected harbor was proven in the tumultuous later years, when a series of forts was constructed on the low hills overlooking the water.

Annapolis Royal today is truly a treat to visit. Because the region was largely overlooked by later economic growth (trade and fishing moved to the Atlantic side of the peninsula), it requires little in the way of imagination to see Annapolis Royal as it once was. (The current population is just 700.) The original settlement was rebuilt on the presumed site. Fort Anne overlooks the upper reaches of the basin, much as it did when abandoned in 1854. And the village itself maintains much of its original historic charm, with narrow streets and historic buildings fronting the now-placid waterfront.

Indeed, Annapolis Royal is also considered by many historians to be the birthplace of historic preservation. Starting early in this century, town residents have been unusually active in preserving the character of the place. As testament to their dedication, note that some 150 buildings and homes in town are officially designated heritage sites.

For anyone curious about Canada's early history, Annapolis Royal is one of Nova Scotia's don't-miss destinations.

## ESSENTIALS

**GETTING THERE**    Annapolis is located at Exit 22 of Route 101. It is 200km (124 miles) from Halifax, and 129km (80 miles) from Yarmouth.

**VISITOR INFORMATION**    The **Annapolis District Tourist Bureau** (© **902/532-5769**) is 1km (½ mile) north of the town center (follow Prince Albert Rd. and look for the Annapolis Royal Tidal Generating Station). It's open daily in summer 8am to 8pm, and 10am to 6pm in spring and fall.

## EXPLORING THE TOWN

Start at the tourist bureau, which is located at the **Annapolis Royal Tidal Power Project** (© **902/532-5454**), where the extreme tides have been harnessed to produce electricity in a generating station. It's the only tidal generator in North America, and the world's largest straight-flow turbine. Learn about the generator at the free exhibit center upstairs from the visitor center, open mid-May through mid-October.

Before leaving the center, be sure to request a copy of the free "Footprints with Footnotes" walking-tour brochure. The annotated map provides architectural and historic context for a stroll around the downtown and waterfront. Take a moment to note that as you walk down lower St. George Street, you're walking down the oldest street in Canada.

One of the more entertaining ways to learn about local history is to attend the **Old Burying Ground Walking Tour** ⚜. In past years, these candlelight tours have departed Fort Anne at 9:30pm on Tuesday, Thursday, and Sunday during the summer from mid-June to mid-August. Visitors are given candle lanterns, and then are led on a 1-hour tour of the ancient cemetery next to the fort. You'll learn about fads in headstone art and hear tales of the early inhabitants of Annapolis Royal, including the flamboyant mistress of the Duke of Wellington. There's a small charge for the tours; confirm times and days at Fort Anne National Historic Site (see below).

Children and adults alike adore **Upper Clements Park** ⚜ (© **888/248-4567** or 902/532-7557) on Route 1, 5 minutes south of Annapolis Royal. This is a wonderfully old-fashioned amusement park (you arrive after driving through an old orchard). It's full of low-key amusements and attractions that will especially delight younger kids. Highlights include the flume ride (originally built for Expo '86 in Vancouver) and a wooden roller coaster that twists and winds through trees left standing during the coaster's construction. It's open daily in season from 11am to 7pm; admission to the grounds is C$8 (US$6.50), free for children under 2. The rate includes admission to the adjacent wild animal park. Unlimited rides are C$23 (US$18) per day; individual rides are C$3 (US$2.50) each.

In the evening, there's often entertainment in downtown Annapolis Royal at **King's Theatre,** 209 St. George St. (© **902/532-5466**). Shows range from movies to musical performances to variety shows to touring plays. Stop by or call to find out what's on during your stay.

**Fort Anne National Historic Site** ⚜    What you'll likely remember most from a visit here are the impressive grassy earthworks that cover some 14 hectares (35 acres) of high ground overlooking the confluence of the Annapolis River and Allains Creek. The French built the first fort here around 1643. Since then, dozens of buildings and fortifications have occupied this site. You can visit the 1708 gunpowder magazine (the oldest building of any Canadian National Historic Site), and then peruse the museum located in the 1797 British field officer's quarters. The model of the site as it appeared in 1710 is particularly intriguing. If you find all the history a bit tedious, ask a guide for a croquet set and practice your technique on the lush rolling lawns.

A good strategy for visiting is to come during the day to tour the museum and get a feel for the lay of the land. Then return for the evening sunset, long after the bus tours have departed, to walk the **Perimeter Trail** ⚜ with its river and valley vistas.

Entrance on St. George St. © **902/532-2321.** Free admission to grounds; museum C$4 (US$3.20) adults, C$3.50 (US$2.80) seniors, C$2 (US$1.60) children, C$10 (US$8) families. May 15–Oct 15 9am–6pm; off season by appointment only (grounds open year-round).

**Historic Gardens** 🎖 You don't need to be a flower nut to enjoy an hour or two at these exceptional gardens. The 4-hectare (10-acre) grounds are uncommonly beautiful, with a mix of formal and informal gardens dating from varied epochs. Set on a gentle hill, the plantings overlook a beautiful salt marsh (now diked and farmed), and they include a geometric Victorian garden, a knot garden, a rock garden, and a colorful perennial border garden. Rose fanciers should allow plenty of time—some 2,000 rose bushes track the history of rose cultivation from the earliest days through the Victorian era to the present day. A garden cafe offers an enticing spot for lunch.

441 St. George St. 🕐 **902/532-7018.** www.historicgardens.com. Admission C$8.50 (US$6.80) adults, C$7.50 (US$6) seniors and students, C$23 (US$18) families. July to Aug daily 8am–dusk, spring and fall daily 9am–5pm. Closed Nov–Apr.

**North Hills Museum** On the road to Port Royal, the North Hills Museum occupies a tidy, early shingled home (1764) that's filled with a top-rate collection of Georgian furniture, ceramics, and glassware. This compact museum will be of interest primarily to serious antiques collectors and history buffs, although even they will be frustrated by the limited access to the opulently furnished rooms (you need to be content mostly with views from roped-off doorways).

5065 Granville Rd., Granville Ferry. 🕐 **902/532-2168.** Admission C$3 (US$2.40) adult, C$2 (US$1.60) seniors and children age 6–17, C$7 (US$5.60) family. June to mid-Oct Mon–Sat 9:30am–5:30pm, Sun 1–5:30pm. Closed mid-Oct to May.

**Port-Royal National Historic Site** 🎖 Canada's first permanent settlement, Port-Royal was located on an attractive point with sweeping views of the Annapolis Basin. After spending the dreadful winter of 1604 on an island in the St. Croix River (along the current Maine–New Brunswick border), the survivors moved to this better protected location. Settlers lived here for 8 years in a high style that approached decadent given the harsh surroundings. Many of the handsome, compact, French-style farmhouse buildings were designed by Samuel de Champlain to re-create the comfort they might have enjoyed at home.

Although the original settlement was abandoned and eventually destroyed, this 1939 re-creation is convincing in all the details. You'll find a handful of costumed interpreters engaged in traditional handicrafts like woodworking, and they're happy to fill you in on life in the colony during those difficult early years, an "age of innocence" when the French first forged an alliance with local natives. Allow 1 or 2 hours to wander and explore.

10km (6 miles) south of Rte. 1, Granville Ferry (turn left shortly after passing the tidal generating station). 🕐 **902/ 532-2898.** Admission C$3.50 (US$2.80) adults, C$3 (US$2.40) seniors, C$1.75 (US$1.30) children, C$8.75 (US$7) families. May 15–Oct 15 daily 9am–6pm. Closed Oct 16–May 14.

## OUTDOOR PURSUITS

A short drive from Annapolis Royal and Port Royal are the **Delaps Cove Wilderness Trails,** which provide access to the rugged Fundy coastline. The tricky part is finding the trail head, as signs tend to vanish. Directions and a brochure are usually available from the visitor information center. Otherwise, head to Delaps Cove from Granville Ferry; veer left on the dirt road that cuts steeply downhill at a rightward bend shortly before the cove. (If you get to Tidal Cove Campground and Cabins, you've gone too far.) Follow this dirt road to the end, where you'll find parking and trail maps.

Two trails lead from an overgrown farm road to the rocky coastline. My advice is to take the **Bohaker Trail** 🎖 (2km/1.25 mile) first; then decide whether you want to continue on to **Charlie's Trail** ⚔ (7km/4.25 miles). The Bohaker is a lovely loop through woodlands to a short coastline trail. The highlight is a cobblestone cove piled with driftwood, into which a small waterfall tumbles. This is a fine destination for a picnic. The trails are well marked—once you find them.

## WHERE TO STAY

The closest campground to Annapolis Royal is on a handsome 9-hectare (22-acre) waterfront property across the embayment from the tidal generating station. The privately owned **Dunromin Campsite** ⚔ (℗ **902/532-2808**) has full hookups for trailers and RVs and attractive tenting sites along the water's edge. Sites cost C$22 to C$35 (US$18 US$28).

For more modern, motel-like accommodations near town, try the **Annapolis Royal Inn** (℗ **888/857-8889** or 902/532-2323) on Highway 101, Exit 22 (south of town). Doubles are C$89 to C$148 (US$71–US$118).

**Garrison House Inn** ⚔    The historic Garrison House sits across from Fort Anne in the town center and has bedded and fed guests since it first opened to accommodate officers at Fort Anne in 1854. The rooms are nicely appointed with antiques, some worn, some pristine. There's no air-conditioning, but fans are provided; the top floor can still get a bit stuffy on warm days. Room 2 is appealing, with wide pine floors, braided rug, and settee, though it faces the street and at times can be a bit noisy. Room 7 is tucked in the back of the house, away from the hubbub of St. George Street, and it has two skylights to let in a wonderfully dappled light. In addition to the restaurant (see below), there's a screened-in veranda with food (fish and lobster, mostly) and drink service. Note that there are no TVs or phones, which could be a blessing, and that full breakfast is quirkily only served during the shoulder seasons (mid-May to July 1 and mid-Oct to mid-Nov).

350 St. George St., Annapolis Royal, NS B0S 1A0. ℗ 866/532-5750 or 902/532-5750. Fax 902/532-5501. www. garrisonhouse.ca. 7 units. C$79–C$149 (US$63–US$119) double. AE, MC, V. Street parking. Open May–Nov; call in advance for weekends rest of year. **Amenities:** Restaurant; bar. *In room:* No phone.

**Hillsdale House**    This pale yellow clapboard Italianate home (1849) sits just across the road from the slightly fancier Queen Anne Inn (see below). The first floor features a Georgian-style sitting room with furniture that's both nice to look at and comfortable to sit on. The carpeted guest rooms are handsome if slightly basic, furnished with antiques that aren't overly elaborate. Only the top-floor rooms have air-conditioning. There are now two units with televisions, after years of holding out. Telephones are shared.

519 St. George St. (P.O. Box 148), Annapolis Royal, NS B0S 1A0. ℗ 877/839-2821 or 902/532-2345. Fax 902/532-2345. www.hillsdalehouse.ns.ca. 15 units. May to mid-Oct C$99–C$149 (US$79–US$119) double, rest of the year C$79–C$99 (US$63–US$79). Rates include full breakfast. MC, V. *In room:* A/C (top floor only), TV (2 units), no phone.

**King George Inn** ⚔ *Kids*    The handsome King George Inn was built as a sea captain's mansion in 1868, and served a stint as a rectory before becoming an inn. It's befittingly busy and cluttered for its era; guest rooms are furnished entirely with antiques, most of the country Victorian ilk. (Those who prefer clean lines might find a surplus of decor here.) All rooms have queen-size beds; two family suites have separate bedrooms and a bathroom that's shared between them. The best in the house is Room 7, with a Jacuzzi and a small private deck off the back of the house; a second

Jacuzzi room was added in 2001. The place also features a pump organ and a 19th-century grand piano and provides bikes for guests.

548 Upper St. George St., Annapolis Royal, NS B0S 1A0. ℂ **888/799-5464** or 902/532-5286. Fax 902/532-0144. www.kinggeorgeinn.20m.com. 8 units. C$95–C$189 (US$76–US$151) double. MC, V. Closed mid-Dec to mid-Apr. **Amenities:** Bikes. *In room:* A/C, TV (1 unit), coffeemaker, hair dryer, no phone.

**Queen Anne Inn** ⟡   This Second Empire mansion, built in 1865, looks like the city hall of a small city. You won't miss it driving into town. Like the Hillsdale House across the street, the Queen Anne (built for the sister of the Hillsdale's owner) has benefited from a preservation-minded owner, who restored the Victorian detailing to its former luster. There's a zebra-striped dining-room floor (alternating planks of oak and maple) and a grand central staircase. The guest rooms are quite elegant and furnished appropriately to the Victorian era, although have been updated to include Jacuzzis. With their towering elms, the parklike grounds are shady and inviting. Breakfast is a three-course affair.

494 St. George St., Annapolis Royal, NS B0S 1A0. ℂ **877/536-0403** or 902/532-7850. Fax 902/532-2078. www. queenanneinn.ns.ca. 12 units. May–June C$99–C$169 (US$79–US$135) double, July–Oct C$119–C$209 (US$95–US$167) double. Rates include full breakfast. MC, V. Closed Nov–Apr. *In room:* TV, no phone.

## WHERE TO DINE

**Garrison House** ⟡ ECLECTIC   The Garrison House is the most intimate and attractive of the village's restaurants. The three cozy dining rooms in this historic home each have a different feel, some with colonial colors, some contemporary, most with black Windsor chairs and modern piscine art. (My favorite room is the one with the green floors and the humpback whale.) The menu is also tricky to categorize, with starters such as an Acadian seafood chowder and carrot vichyssoise with coconut and a Thai soup, and entrees ranging from jambalaya, shrimp and chicken in a Vietnamese curry, and jerk chicken to Digby scallops or a simple pasta with garden vegetables. You can get individual-serving pizzas here as well.

In the Garrison House Inn, 350 St. George St. ℂ **902/532-5750.** Reservations recommended in summer. Main courses C$14–C$27 (US$11–US$22). AE, MC, V. Daily 5:30–8:30pm.

**Newman's** ⟡ SEAFOOD   Newman's is an informal spot located in an oddly out-of-place pink Spanish Revival building on Annapolis Royal's historic waterfront. But don't let that confuse you. Inside, you'll find some of the most carefully prepared food in Nova Scotia, with an eye to fresh produce and meats. The place has been run by the same folks for 20 years, and they haven't let standards slip. It's hard to nail down a specialty—the kitchen does so much so very well. The seafood is especially delectable (grilled Atlantic salmon with tarragon sauce, halibut sautéed with sliced almonds), as are the generous, old-fashioned desserts (bananas with chocolate and whipped cream, homemade strawberry shortcake). There's an unexpected bonus here: The wine list is surprisingly creative.

218 St. George St. ℂ **902/532-5502.** Reservations recommended. Main courses C$11–C$19 (US$9–US$15). V. May–Oct Tues–Sun noon–9pm.

## 5 Kejimkujik National Park ⟨★⟩

About 45km (28 miles) southeast of Annapolis Royal is a popular national park that's a world apart from coastal Nova Scotia. Kejimkujik National Park, founded in 1968, is located in the heart of south-central Nova Scotia, and it is to lakes and bogs what the south coast is to fishing villages and fog. Bear and moose are the full-time residents here; park visitors are the transients. The park, which was largely scooped and shaped during the last glacial epoch, is about 20% water, which makes it especially popular with canoeists. A few trails also weave through the park, but hiking is limited; the longest hike in the park can be done in 2 hours. Bird-watchers are also drawn to the park in search of the 205 species that have been seen both here and at the Seaside Adjunct of the park, a 22-sq.-km (14-sq.-mile) coastal holding west of Liverpool. Among the more commonly seen species are pileated woodpeckers and loons, and at night you can listen for the raspy call of the barred owl.

## ESSENTIALS

**GETTING THERE**    Kejimkujik National Park is approximately midway on Kejimkujik Scenic Drive (Rte. 8), which extends 115km (71 miles) between Annapolis Royal and Liverpool. The village of Maitland Bridge (pop. 130) is near the park's entrance. Plan on about 2 hours' drive from Halifax.

**VISITOR INFORMATION**    The park's **visitor center** (© 902/682-2772) is open daily and features slide programs and exhibits about the park's natural history.

**FEES**    Entrance fees are charged from mid-May to mid-October. Daily fees are C$5 (US$4) for adults, C$4.25 (US$3.50) for seniors, C$2.50 (US$2) ages 6 to 16, and C$13 (US$10) for families. Seasonal passes can cut the cost of a longer stay; they cost C$25 (US$20) adults, C$21 (US$17) seniors, C$13 (US$10) children ages 6 to 16, and C$63 (US$50) for families.

## EXPLORING THE PARK

The park's 381 sq. km (237 sq. miles) of forest, lake, and bog are peaceful and remote. Part of what makes the terrain so appealing is the lack of access by car. One short, forked park road from Route 8 gets you partway into the park. Then you need to continue by foot or canoe. A stop at the visitor center is worthwhile, both for the exhibits on the region's natural history and for a preliminary walk on one of the three short trails. The Beech Grove loop (2km/1.5 miles) takes you around a glacial hill called a drumlin. The park has a taped walking tour available for use; ask at the information center.

Canoeing is the optimal means of traversing the park. Bring your own, or rent a canoe at **Jake's Landing** (3km/2 miles along the park access road) for C$6 (US$5) per hour, C$25 (US$20) per day, or C$125 (US$100) per week. Similar rates apply to rentals of bikes, paddleboats, kayaks, and rowboats. Canoeists can cobble together wilderness excursions from one lake to the other, some involving slight portaging. Multiday trips are easily arranged to backcountry campsites and are the best way to get to know the park. Canoe route maps are provided at the visitor center. Rangers also lead short, guided canoe trips for novices.

The park also has 15 **walking trails,** ranging from short, easy strolls to, well, longer, easy strolls. (There's no elevation gain to speak of.) The 6km (4-mile) **Hemlocks and Hardwoods Trail** loops through stately groves of 300-year-old hemlocks; the 3km (1.75-mile) **Merrymakedge Beach Trail** skirts a lakeshore to end at a beach. A free map that describes the trails is available at the visitor center.

Mountain bikers can explore the old **Fire Tower Road,** a round trip of about 20km (12 miles). The road becomes increasingly rugged and ends at a fire tower near an old-growth forest of birch and maple.

## CAMPING

**Backcountry camping** is the park's chief draw. The 44 backcountry sites are so much in demand that they actually cost more than the drive-in campsites. Overnighting on a distant lakeshore is the best way to get to know the park; even if you're planning to car camp, I'd argue that it's worth the extra hassle and expense of renting a canoe and paddling off for a night just for the experience.

The canoe-in and hike-in sites are assigned individually, which means you needn't worry about noisy neighbors playing loud music on their car stereo. Backcountry rangers keep the sites in top shape, and each is stocked with firewood for the night (the wood is included in the campsite fee). Most sites can handle a maximum of six campers. Naturally, there's high demand for the best sites; you're better off here mid-week, when fewer weekenders are down from Halifax. You can also reserve backcountry sites (C$21/US$17 per site) up to 60 days in advance for an additional fee; call the **visitor center** (© **902/682-2772**).

The park's drive-in campground at **Jeremy's Bay** ⚜ offers 360 sites, a few quite close to the water's edge. Campground rates are C$16 to C$23 (US$13–US$18) per night. (During the shoulder seasons in spring and fall, you get a 6th night free after 5 nights; winter camping costs less.) Starting early each April reservations at the drive-in campground may be made for an additional fee by calling © **877/RESERVE** or online at the web site **www.pccamping.ca**.

## 6 Digby to Yarmouth

Two towns serving as gateways to Nova Scotia bracket this 113km (70-mile) stretch of coast. Whereas the South Shore—the stretch between Yarmouth and Halifax—serves to confirm popular conceptions of Nova Scotia (small fishing villages, shingled homes), the Digby-to-Yarmouth route seems determined to confound them. Look for Acadian enclaves, fishing villages with more corrugated steel than weathered shingle, miles of sandy beaches, and spruce-topped basalt cliffs that seem transplanted from Labrador.

The unassuming port town of **Digby** (pop. 2,300) is located on the water at Digby Gap—where the Annapolis River finally forces an egress through the North Mountain coastal range. Set at the south end of the broad watery expanse of the Annapolis Basin, Digby is home to the world's largest inshore scallop fleet, which drags the ocean bottom for tasty and succulent Digby scallops. The town is an active community where life centers around fishing boats, neighborhoods of wood-frame houses, and no-frills seafood restaurants. It also serves as Nova Scotia's gateway for those arriving from Saint John, New Brunswick, via ferry. The ferry terminal is on Route 303 west of Digby.

Aside from the Digby Pines Golf Resort and Spa (see below), the town doesn't have much to draw tourists, and is worth checking out only if you have a few hours to kill before catching your ferry back to Saint John. If you're arriving by ferry and want to visit the town before pushing on, watch for signs directing you downtown from the bypass. Otherwise, you'll end up on Route 101 before you know it.

### DIGBY NECK ⚜

Look at a map of Nova Scotia and you'll see the thin strand of Digby Neck extending southwest from Annapolis Basin. You might guess from its appearance on the map that it's a low, scrubby sand spit. You would be wrong. In fact, it's a long, bony finger of high ridges, spongy bogs, dense forest, and expansive ocean views. The last two knuckles of this narrow peninsula are islands, both of which are connected via 10-minute ferries across straits swept with currents as strong as 9 knots.

Although neither the neck nor the islands have much in the way of services for tourists—just one real lodge, a couple of B&Bs, and a few general stores—it's worth the drive if you're a connoisseur of end-of-the-world remoteness. The town of Sandy Cove on the mainland is picture-perfect, with its three prominent church steeples rising from the forest. Both Tiverton on Long Island and Westport on Brier Island are unadorned fishing villages where pickup trucks are held together with Bondo and bailing wire. You get the distinct feeling that life hasn't changed much in the past few decades—or at least since 1960, when the roads were finally paved on Brier Island.

## ESSENTIALS
**GETTING THERE**    Route 217 runs 72km (45 miles) south from Digby to Brier Island. Two ferries fill in when you run out of mainland. Ferries leave East Ferry on the mainland for Long Island every hour on the half-hour; they depart from Long Island for Brier Island on the hour. Ferries are timed such that you can drive directly from one ferry to the next, provided you don't dawdle. Fares are C$2 (US$1.60) per car round-trip on both ferries; fares are collected on the outbound leg only.

**VISITOR INFORMATION**    A seasonal **information booth** (© **902/839-2853**) is located at the local historical museum in Tiverton on Long Island. It's allegedly open from 9am to 7:30pm in July and August, but hours are more erratic than that. You might be better off collecting information at the Visitor Information Centre located on the harbor in Digby at 110 Montague Row (© **902/245-5714**) before you set off. It's open daily from 8:30am to 8:30pm from May to mid-October, and daily from 9am to 5pm during the spring and fall.

## EXPLORING DIGBY NECK
**BICYCLING**    Brier Island offers an ideal destination for mountain bikers. At just 6.5km (4 miles) long and 2.5km (1½ miles) wide, it's the right scale for spending a slow afternoon poking around dirt roads that lead to the two picturesque lighthouses. Brier Island maps are available free at island stores and lodges. If you park your car on the Long Island side and take your bike over on the ferry, you'll save money; there's no charge for bikes or pedestrians.

Bike rentals are available at **Backstreet Bicycles** in Digby (© **902/245-1989**).

**HIKING**    On Long Island, two short but rewarding woodland hikes take you to open vistas of St. Mary's Bay and the Bay of Fundy.

The trail head for the half-mile hike to **Balancing Rock** is 4km (2½ miles) south of the Tiverton ferry on Route 217; look for the well-marked parking area on the left. The trail crosses through swamp, bog, and forest and is dead straight and flat—until the last 90m (295 ft.). That's when you plummet nearly straight down a sheer bluff to the ocean's edge along some 169 steps. At the base, a series of boardwalks leads you over the surging ocean to get a dead-on view of the tall column of basalt balancing improbably atop another column. For another short hike, return to the parking lot and drive 5km (3 miles) south to the picnic area on the right. From the parking lot atop the hill, a hike of 1km (.5 mile) descends gradually through a forest of moss, ferns, and roots to the remote **Fundy shore.** The coastline here is nearly lunar, with the dark rock marbled with thin streaks of quartz. You're likely to have the coast to yourself, since few venture here.

Farther along, **Brier Island** is laced with **hiking trails** ☞, offering fantastic opportunities for seaside exploration. Pick up one of the maps offered free around the island. A good place to start is the Grand Passage Lighthouse (turn right after disembarking the ferry, and continue until you can't go any farther). Park near the light, and walk through the stunted pines to the open meadows on the western shore, where you can pick up the coastal trail.

**WHALE-WATCHING** ☞   In the Bay of Fundy, ocean currents mingle and the vigorous tides cause upwelling, which brings a rich assortment of plankton to the surface. That makes it an all-you-can-eat buffet for whales, which feed on these minuscule bits of plant and animal. As the fishing industry has declined, the number of fishermen offering whale-watching tours has boomed. Most of these are down-home operations on converted lobster boats—don't expect the gleaming whale-watch ships with comfy seats and full-service cafeterias that you find in larger cities or on the New England coast.

Declining inshore herring stocks means tours need to head farther out into the bay to find whales than in years past, but you'll almost always have sightings of fin, minke, or humpback whales. Right, sperm, blue, and pilot whales, along with the seldom-seen orcas, have also been spotted over the years. Plan on spending around C$35 to C$45 (US$28–US$36) for a 3- to 4-hour cruise.

**Mariner Cruises** (② **800/239-2189** or 902/839-2346) in Westport on Brier Island sails aboard the 14m (45-ft.) *Chad and Sisters Two,* which is equipped with a heated cabin. Both whale- and bird-watching tours are offered. **Pirate's Cove Whale Cruises** (② **888/480-0004** or 902/839-2242), located in Tiverton, has been leading offshore cruises since 1990; three tours are offered daily aboard the 13m (42-ft.) vessels *Fundy Cruiser* and *Fundy Voyager.* **Petite Passage Whale Watch** (② **902/834-2226** or 902/245-6132) sails out of East Ferry aboard a 14m (45-ft.), 45-passenger boat with a partially covered deck.

For a saltier adventure, **Ocean Explorations** (② **877/654-2341** or 902/839-2417) offers tours on rigid-hulled inflatable Zodiacs. The largest boat holds up to a dozen passengers and moves with tremendous speed and dampness through the fast currents and frequent chop around the islands and the open bay. Guests are provided with survival suits for warmth and safety.

## WHERE TO STAY & DINE
**Brier Island Lodge** ☞ *Finds*   Built to jump-start local eco-tourism, the Brier Island Lodge has a rustic-modern motif, with log-cabin construction and soaring glass windows overlooking the Grand Passage 40m (130 ft.) below. The rooms on two floors all have great views, the usual motel amenities, and some unexpected touches (double Jacuzzis in the pricier rooms). A well-regarded dining room serves up traditional favorites, and local fishermen congregate in an airy lounge in the evening to play cards and watch the satellite TV. There's a small but good selection of field guides near the upholstered chairs in the corner of the lounge; hiking trails connect directly from the lodge to the Fundy shore.

Westport, Brier Island. ② **800/662-8355** or 902/839-2300. Fax 902/839-2006. www.brierisland.com. 40 units. C$60–C$139 (US$48–US$111) double. MC, V. **Amenities:** Bike rental; game room. *In room:* A/C, TV. Jacuzzi (4 rooms).

### Digby Pines Golf Resort and Spa ☞☞   Digby Pines is actually located in the town of Digby and is situated on 120 hectares (300 acres) with marvelous views of the

Annapolis Basin. The resort is redolent of an earlier era when old money headed to fashionable resorts for an entire summer. Built in 1929 in a Norman château style, the inn today is owned and operated by the province of Nova Scotia, and it should silence those who believe that government can't do anything right. The imposing building of stucco and stone is surrounded by the eponymous pines, which rustle softly in the wind. Throughout, the emphasis is more on comfort than historical verisimilitude, although the gracious lobby features old-world touches like Corinthian capitals, floral couches, and parquet floors. The guest rooms vary slightly as to size and views (ask for a waterview room; there's no extra charge), and all now have ceiling fans, although air-conditioning is said to be on the way. The cottages have one to three bedrooms and most feature fireplaces and air-conditioning. A new Aveda spa offers a full menu of treatments and services, and an 18-hole Stanley Thompson-designed golf course threads its way through pines and over a babbling brook.

The resort's Annapolis Dining Room is open for all three meals, and the cuisine might best be described as Nova Scotian with a French flair. Look for such entrees as roasted pork tenderloin with apples and a cider sauce, or poached char infused with green Chinese tea. Dinner reservations are advised.

Shore Rd., P.O. Box 70, Digby, NS B0V 1A0. ℂ 800/667-4637 or 902/245-2511. Fax 902/245-6133. www.signature resorts.com. 84 units, 30 cottages. C$154–C$325 (US$123–US$260) double; cottages more expensive. AE, DC, DISC, MC, V. Closed mid-Oct to mid-May. **Amenities:** Restaurant; bar; heated outdoor pool; golf course; 2 tennis courts; health club; spa; sauna; bike rentals; children's center; concierge; tour desk; courtesy car; babysitting; dry cleaning; laundry service. *In room:* A/C (cottages only), TV, dataport, coffeemaker.

## ACADIAN COAST

The Acadian Coast (called the "French Shore" by English-speaking locals) runs roughly from Salmon River to St. Bernard. This hardscrabble coast, where the fields were once littered with glacial rocks and boulders, was one of the few areas where Acadians were allowed to resettle after the 1755 expulsion.

Today, you'll find abundant evidence of the robust Acadian culture, from the frequent sightings of the stella maris (the Acadian tricolor flag with its prominent star) to the towering churches around which each town seems to cluster. The region is more populous and developed than much of the Nova Scotia coast, and thus lacks somewhat the wild aesthetic that travelers often seek. You'll also find few tourist amenities along this stretch.

### ESSENTIAL

**GETTING THERE**   The Acadian Coast is traversed by Route 1. Speedier Route 101 runs parallel and inland some distance; the Acadian Coast is served by Exits 28 to 32.

**VISITOR INFORMATION**   It's best to collect information in the major towns bracketing either end of the Acadian Coast before arriving; that means heading either to the **Yarmouth Visitor Centre** (p. 69) at 228 Main St. or Digby's **information center** (p. 65) on Route 303.

### EXPLORING THE ACADIAN COAST

A drive along this seaside route offers a pleasant detour, in both pace and culture. You can drive the whole length, or pick up segments by exiting from Route 101 and heading shoreward. What follows is a selected sampling of attractions along the coast, from north to south:

- **St. Mary's Church** ⟨⟨, Church Point. Many of the towns along the Acadian coast are proud of their impressive churches, but none is quite as extraordinary as St. Mary's. You can't miss it; it's adjacent to the campus of Université Sainte-Anne, the sole French-speaking university in Nova Scotia. The imposing, gray-shingled church has the stature of a European cathedral made of stone, but St. Mary's, built 1903 to 1905, is made entirely of wood.

   Outside, it's impressive—the fanciful steeple rises some 56m (185 ft.) above the parking lot, with some 40 tons of rock hidden within to provide stability in the high winds. Inside, it's even more extraordinary—all bright and airy and deftly adorned. Whole tree trunks serve as columns, although they're covered in plaster to lend a more traditional appearance. A small museum in the rear offers glimpses of church history. Admission by donation.

- **Rappie Pie.** This Acadian dish is a whole-meal pie typically made with beef or chicken. The main ingredient is grated potatoes, from which the moisture has been extracted and replaced with chicken broth. The full and formal name is "pâté a la rapure," but look for signs for "rapure" or "rappie pie" along Route 1 on the Acadian Coast.

- **Rapure Acadienne Ltd.,** Church Point (© **902/769-2172**). At this unassuming shop on Route 1 just south of Church Point, open daily year-round from 8am to 9pm, you can pick up a freshly baked beef or chicken rappie pie for about C$5 (US$4); it costs about a dollar more for a clam pie. Commandeer an outdoor picnic table to enjoy your meal, or take it to the shady campus of Université Sainte-Anne, a few minutes' drive north.

- **La Vielle Maison** ⟨, Meteghan. This small historical museum displays artifacts of Acadian life in the 19th century. Look for the scrap of original French wallpaper uncovered during restoration of the summer bedroom. Open daily in summer. Admission is free.

- **Smuggler's Cove,** Meteghan. This small provincial picnic area a few minutes south of town has a set of steps running steeply down to a cobblestone cove. From here, you'll have a view of a tidal cave across the way. Rumrunners were said to have used this cave—about 5m (15 ft.) high and 18m (60 ft.) deep—as a hideout during the Prohibition era. Truth or local tourism boosterism? You be the judge. Admission is free.

- **Mavilete Beach** ⟨⟨, Mavilete. This beautiful crescent beach has nearly all the ingredients for a pleasant summer afternoon—lots of sand, grassy dunes, changing-stalls, a nearby snack bar with ice cream, and views across the water to scenic Cape Mary. All that's lacking is an ocean warm enough to actually swim in. It's seriously frigid here, although the courageous appear to be able to splash around for a time without lapsing into immediate cardiac arrest. The beach, managed as a provincial park, is 1km (½ mile) off Route 1, and the turnoff is well marked; admission is free.

- **Port Maitland Beach** ⟨⟨, Port Maitland. Another provincial park beach—and a very long one, at that—Port Maitland Beach is near the breakwater and town wharf. It isn't as scenic or pristine as Mavilete Beach; it's closer to Yarmouth and attracts larger crowds, principally families. But I really enjoy it anyway, because you can walk for miles in solitude here. This makes a good first stroll in the province if you're just off the overnight ferry. Signs direct you to the beach from the village center.

## WHERE TO STAY

Accommodations are thin on the ground here; most consist of small, simple B&B's offering varying degrees of comfort. They are quite affordable, however; you could pay as little as C$50 (US$40) for a night in a double room here. Still, my advice would be to overnight elsewhere: Push onward to the Annapolis Valley if you want a nice inn, to Yarmouth for a motel or hotel if you're leaving the province by ferry or heading for the South Shore, or inland to **Kejimkujik National Park** (p. 62) if you're longing to camp in the woods. The best lodging in these parts is the log lodge **Trout Point Lodge Wilderness Resort** (p. 71), covered below in the Yarmouth section but actually inland from the French Shore.

If you're absolutely stuck, try the **Auberge au Havre du Capitaine** (⟨℅ **902/ 769-2001**) on Route 1 in Meteghan River, with plenty of rooms at C$75 to C$110 (US$53–US$78) per night; two even have air-jetted Jacuzzi tubs.

## YARMOUTH

The constant lament of Yarmouth restaurateurs and shopkeepers is this: The summer tourists who steadily stream off the incoming ferries rarely linger long enough to appreciate the city before they mash the accelerator and speed off to higher-marquee venues along the coast.

There might be a reason for that. Yarmouth is a pleasant burg that offers some note-worthy historic architecture dating from the golden age of seafaring. But the town's not terribly unique, and thus not high on the list of places to spend a few days. It's a bit too big (pop. 7,800) to be charming; too small to generate urban buzz and vital-ity. It has more the flavor of a handy pit stop than a destination, though recent rede-velopment efforts have spruced up the waterfront a bit and added evening entertainment during the summer months, a very welcome sign.

By all means plan to dawdle a few hours while awaiting the ferry (Portland-bound passengers could enjoyably spend the night here before their early morning departure) or to while away an afternoon looping around the coast. Take the time to follow the self-guided walking tour, enjoy a meal, or wander around the newly renovated water-front, where efforts to coax it back from decrepitude have started to take root.

Then: onward.

## ESSENTIALS

**GETTING THERE**   Yarmouth is at the convergence of two of the province's prin-cipal highways, Route 101 and Route 103. It's approximately 300km (180 miles) from Halifax. Yarmouth is the gateway for ferries connecting to Bar Harbor, Maine.

**VISITOR INFORMATION**   The **Yarmouth Visitor Centre** (℅ **902/742-6639** or 902/742-5033) is at 228 Main St., just up the hill from the ferry in a modern, shin-gled building you simply can't miss. Both the provincial and municipal tourist offices are located here; open May through October daily from 8am to 7pm.

## EXPLORING THE AREA

The tourist bureau and the local historical society publish a very informative walking tour brochure covering downtown Yarmouth. It's well worth requesting at the **Yarmouth Visitor Centre.** The guide offers general tips on what to look for in local architectural styles (how do you tell the difference between Georgian and Classic Revival?), as well as brief histories of significant buildings. The whole tour is 4km (2½ miles) long.

The most scenic side trip—and an ideal excursion by bike or car—is to **Cape Forchu** and the **Yarmouth Light** ⚓. Head west on Main Street (Rte. 1) for 2km (1¼ miles) from the visitor center, and then turn left at the horse statue. The road winds picturesquely out to the cape, past seawalls and working lobster wharves, meadows, and old homes.

When the road finally ends, you'll be at the red-and-white-striped concrete lighthouse that marks the harbor's entrance. (This modern lighthouse dates from the early 1960s, when it replaced a much older octagonal light that succumbed to wind and time.) There's a tiny photographic exhibit on the cape's history in the visitor center in the keeper's house.

Leave enough time to ramble around the dramatic rock-and-grass bluffs—part of Leif Eriksson Picnic Park—that surround the lighthouse. Don't miss the short trail out to the point below the light. Bright red picnic tables and benches are scattered about; bring lunch or dinner if the weather is right.

**Firefighters' Museum of Nova Scotia** *(Kids)*    This two-story museum will appeal mostly to confirmed fire buffs, historians, and impressionable young children. The museum is home to a varied collection of early firefighting equipment, with hand-drawn pumpers as the centerpiece of the collection. Also showcased here are uniforms, badges, helmets, and pennants. Look for the photos of notable Nova Scotian fires ("Hot Shots").

451 Main St. ℭ **902/742-5525.** Admission C$3 (US$2.40) adults, C$2.50 (US$2) seniors, C$1.50 (US$1.20) children, C$6 (US$4.80) families. July–Aug Mon–Sat 9am–9pm, Sun 10am–5pm; June and Sept Mon–Sat 9am–5pm; Oct–May Mon–Fri 9am–4pm, Sat 1–4pm.

## WHERE TO STAY

Fifteen kilometers (9 miles) west of town on Route 1 is the **Lake Breeze Campground** (ℭ **902/649-2332**), a privately run spot with the appealingly low-key character of a small municipal campground. It has 32 sites for C$15 to C$20 (US$11–US$14), some right on the shores of tiny **Lake Darling,** and it's well cared for by its owners. It's open mid-May to mid-October.

Yarmouth is home to a number of chain motels. Among them are the **Best Western Mermaid Motel,** 545 Main St. (ℭ **800/772-2774** or 902/742-7821), with rates of C$99 to C$180 (US$79–US$143) double; **Comfort Inn,** 96 Starr's Rd. (ℭ **800/228-5150** or 902/742-1119), at C$75 to C$180 (US$60–US$144) double; and the **Rodd Grand Hotel,** 417 Main St. (ℭ **800/565-7633** or 902/742-2446), C$144 to C$217 (US$115–US$174) double.

**Churchill Mansion Inn**    Between 1891 and 1920, the Churchill Mansion was occupied just 6 weeks a year, when Aaron Flint Churchill, a Yarmouth native who amassed a shipping fortune in landlocked Atlanta, Georgia (go figure), returned to Nova Scotia to summer. This extravagant mansion with its garish furnishings, situated on a low bluff overlooking the highway and a lake, was converted to an inn in 1981 by Bob Benson, who is likely to be found on a ladder or with a hammer in hand when you arrive ("It never ends," he sighs). The mansion boasts some original carpeting, lamps, and woodwork, although it can be a little threadbare, flaky, or water-stained in other spots. The honeymoon suite with a Jacuzzi and lake view is the nicest room.

Rte. 1 (15km/9 miles west of Yarmouth), Yarmouth, NS B5A 4A5. ℭ **888/453-5565** or 902/649-2818. Fax 902/649-2801. www.churchillmansion.com. 8 units. C$69–C$140 (US$55–US$112) double. Meals available. DISC, MC, V. Closed mid-Nov to May. **Amenities:** Bike rental. *In room:* No phone.

**Harbour's Edge B&B**    This exceptionally attractive early Victorian home (1864) sits on 1 leafy hectare (2 acres) and 76m (250 ft.) of harbor frontage. You can lounge on the lawn while watching herons and kingfishers below, making it hard to believe you're right in town and only a few minutes from the ferry terminal. Harbour's Edge opened in 1997 after 3 years of intensive restoration (it had previously been abandoned for 5 years). All the rooms are lightly furnished, which nicely highlights the architectural integrity of the design. The guest rooms have high ceilings and handsome spruce floors. The very attractive Audrey Kenney Room is the largest, but the Ellen Brown Room is my favorite: It has fine oak furniture and a great view of the harbor, although the private bathroom is down the hall.

12 Vancouver St., Yarmouth, NS B5A 2N8. (℃) 902/742-2387. Fax 902/742-4471. www.harboursedge.ns.ca. 4 units. C$125–C$140 (US$100–US$112) double. Rates include full breakfast. MC, V. Head toward Cape Forchu (see above); watch for the inn shortly after turning at the horse statue. *In room:* Iron/ironing board, no phone.

**Lakelawn Motel**    The clean, well-kept Lakelawn Motel offers basic motel rooms done up in freshened bluish colors, newer carpeting, and so forth. It's been a downtown Yarmouth mainstay since the 1950s, when the centerpiece Victorian house (where the office is located) was moved back from the road to make room for the motel wings. Looking for something a bit cozier? The house also has four B&B-style guest rooms upstairs, each furnished simply with antiques.

641 Main St., Yarmouth, NS B5A 1K2. (℃) 877/664-0664 or 902/742-3588. www.lakelawnmotel.com. 35 units. C$59–C$89 (US$47–US$71) double. Meals available. AE, DC, DISC, MC, V. Closed Nov–Apr. *In room:* TV, no phone (some units).

**Trout Point Lodge Wilderness Resort** (✦)    In the late 1990s, Louisiana natives Charles Leary and Vaughn Perret bought property about 25 miles north-northwest of Yarmouth and developed a small rustic property, one that emphasizes the art of cooking. Modeled loosely after an Adirondack hunting lodge, the property was built from scratch using white spruce logs and hand-cut local granite. A simple, natural feeling pervades throughout, from the windows letting in views of forest and river to roaring fireplaces in the public areas. Eight big standard rooms come with log walls, original art, handmade log-and-twig furniture, love seats, and work desks; two add stone fireplaces and decks on the river, while others sport woodstoves, high ceilings, or bay windows. Two suites have canopy beds, sofas, and Jacuzzi tubs, while two cottages with differing amenities are also rented in part or whole; both possess full kitchens. The property offers free canoes, kayaks, and paddleboats for exploring the local system of rivers and lakes (there's a dock and platforms for swimming as well). If you're a serious foodie, ask about the ongoing program of cooking lessons and culinary getaways.

189 Trout Point Rd. off Rte. 203 (P.O. Box 456), E. Kemptville, NS B0W 1Y0. (℃) 902/749-7629. www.troutpoint.com. 12 units. Peak season C$250–C$525 (US$200–US$420) double; off season lower. Meal plans available. Ask about packages. MC, V. No meals late Oct to late May. From Yarmouth or Halifax, take Hwy. 103 to Shelburne-Ohio exit and continue 45 min. to E. Branch Rd. on right. **Amenities:** Restaurant; wood-fired hot tub; water-sports equipment; massage. *In room:* Iron/ironing board, no phone.

## WHERE TO DINE
**Harris' Quick-N-Tasty**    SEAFOOD    The name about says it all. This vintage 1960s restaurant has no pretensions (it's the kind of place that still lists cocktails on the menu) and is hugely popular with locals. The Harrises sold the place a few years ago, but current owner Paul Surette is committed to preserving the place as is. The restaurant is adorned with that sort of paneling that was rather au courant about 30 years

back, and the meals are likewise old-fashioned and generous. The emphasis is on seafood, and you can order your fish either fried or broiled; the "Scarlet O'Harris" lobster club sandwich is notable, as is the seafood casserole. A second, very handy location occupies a converted rail car at 75 Water St., just across the street from the international ferry terminal. Buzz through the drive-through window, or hang at the picnic tables, before tackling the rest of Nova Scotia.

75 Water St., Yarmouth and Rte. 1, Dayton. ℂ 902/742-3467. Sandwiches C$2.95–C$12 (US$2.40–US$9.50); main courses C$7–C$18 (US$5.50–US$15). AE, DC, MC, V. Daily 11am–8pm (winter until 7:30pm). Closed mid-Dec to Feb. Original location just east of Yarmouth on the north side of Rte. 1; 2nd location across from ferry terminal.

**Rudder's Seafood Restaurant & Brewpub** ⟨★ BREWPUB    Yarmouth's first (and Nova Scotia's 4th) brewpub opened in 1997 on the newly spiffed-up waterfront. It occupies an old warehouse dating from the mid-1800s, and you can see the wear and tear of the decades on the battered floor and the stout beams and rafters. The place has been nicely spruced up, and the menu features creative pub fare, with additions including Acadian and Cajun specialties such as rappie pie, and jambalaya, as well as lobster suppers and planked salmon. The steaks are quite good, as is the beer, especially the best bitter. In summer, there's outdoor seating on a deck with a view of the harbor across the parking lot.

96 Water St. ℂ 902/742-7311. Sandwiches C$4–C$11 (US$3.20–US$9); entrees C$10–C$24 (US$8–US$19). AE, DC, MC, V. Mid-Apr to mid-Oct daily 11am–11pm (shorter hours spring and fall). Closed mid-Oct to mid-Apr.

## 7 South Shore ⟨★⟨★

The Atlantic coast between Yarmouth and Halifax is that quaint, Maritime Nova Scotia you see on laminated place mats and calendars. It's all lighthouses and weathered, shingled buildings perched at the rocky edge of the sea, as if tenuously trespassing on the ocean's good graces. But as rustic and beautiful as this area is, you might find it a bit stultifying to visit every quaint village along the entire coastline—involving about 340km (210 miles) of twisting road along the water's edge. If your heart is set on exploring this fabled landscape, be sure to leave enough time to poke in all the nooks and crannies along this stretch of the coast—towns such as Lunenburg, Mahone Bay, and Peggy's Cove are well worth the time.

*Note:* It's sensible to allow more time here for one other reason—fog. When the cool waters of the Arctic currents mix with the warm summer air over land, the results are predictable and soupy. The fog certainly adds atmosphere. It also can slow driving to a crawl.

### SHELBURNE

Shelburne is a historic town with an unimpeachable pedigree. Settled in 1783 by United Empire Loyalists fleeing New England after the unfortunate outcome of the late war, the town swelled with newcomers and by 1784 was believed to have a population of 10,000—larger than Montréal, Halifax, or Québec. With the decline of boat building and fishing in this century, the town edged into that dim economic twilight familiar to other seaside villages (it now has a population of about 3,000), and the waterfront began to deteriorate, despite valiant preservation efforts.

And then Hollywood came calling, hat in hand. In 1992, the film *Mary Silliman's War* was filmed here. The producers found the waterfront to be a reasonable facsimile of Fairfield, Connecticut, around 1776. The crew spruced up the town a bit and buried power lines along the waterfront.

Two years later, director Roland Joffe arrived to film the spectacularly miscast *Scarlet Letter*, starring Demi Moore, Gary Oldman, and Robert Duvall. The film crew buried more power lines, built some 15 "historic" structures near the waterfront (most demolished after filming), dumped tons of rubble to create dirt lanes (since removed), and generally made the place look like 17th-century Boston.

When the crew departed, it left behind three buildings and an impressive shingled steeple you can see from all over town. Among the "new old" buildings is the waterfront cooperage across from the Cooper's Inn. The original structure, clad in asphalt shingles, was generally considered an eyesore and was torn down, replaced by the faux-17th-century building. Today, barrel makers painstakingly make and sell traditional handcrafted wooden barrels in what amounts to a souvenir of a notable Hollywood flop.

## ESSENTIALS

**GETTING THERE**   Shelburne is 216km (134 miles) southwest of Halifax on Route 3. It's a short hop from Route 103 via either Exit 25 (southbound) or Exit 26 (northbound).

**VISITOR INFORMATION**   The **Shelburne Tourist Bureau** (© **902/875-4547**) is located in a tidy waterfront building at the corner of King and Dock streets. It's open daily mid-May to October; hours are 9am to 8pm during peak season, 10am to 6pm off season.

## EXPLORING HISTORIC SHELBURNE

The central historic district runs along the waterfront, where you can see legitimately old buildings, Hollywood fakes (see above), and spectacular views of the harbor from small, grassy parks. (Note that some of the remaining *Scarlet Letter* buildings weren't meant to last and might have been demolished by the time you arrive.) There's a lot more in the district, however, including a helpful little tourist office at the bend in the road (see above), gift shops, a B&B (the Cooper's Inn, reviewed below), a husband-and-wife team of coopers making barrels in an open shop (technically, it's not open to the public, but ask nicely for a look), a kayaking and outdoor adventure center, and the **Sea Dog Saloon** (© **902/875-2862**) at the very end of the road. A block inland from the water is Shelburne's more commercial stretch, where you can find services that include banks, shops, and a wonderful bakery (see "Where to Dine," below).

Flower fanciers should inquire about the self-guided **garden tours** sponsored by the Shelburne County Garden Club. Some 18 gardens are open to the public. Most of the gardens are indeed quite pleasant, but almost as enjoyable is the chance to meet local gardeners and talk about a shared passion. Ask for a brochure at the tourist bureau.

**Shelburne Historic Complex**  *(K) (Kids)*   The historic complex is an association of four local museums located within steps of one another. The most engaging is the **Dory Shop,** right on the waterfront. On the first floor you can admire examples of the simple, elegant craft (said to be invented in Shelburne) and view videos about the late Sidney Mahaney, a master builder who worked in this shop from the time he was 17 until he was 96. Then head upstairs, where all the banging is going on. There you'll meet Sidney's son and grandson, still building the classic boats using traditional methods. "The dory is a simple boat, but there are a lot of things to think about," says the grandson with considerable understatement. While you're there, ask about the difference between a Shelburne dory and a Lunenburg dory.

The **Shelburne County Museum** features a potpourri of locally significant artifacts from the town's Loyalist past. Most intriguing is the 1740 fire pumper; it was made in London and imported here in 1783. Behind the museum is the austerely handsome **Ross-Thomson House** (② 902/875-3219), built in 1784 through 1785. The first floor contains a general store as it might have looked in 1784, with bolts of cloth and cast-iron teakettles. Upstairs is a militia room with displays of antique and reproduction weaponry. The fourth museum, the **Muir-Cox Shipbuilding Interpretive Centre,** was added most recently and features, as you might guess, maritime displays of barks, sailboats, yachts, and more. If you're interested enough in these sorts of things, you could easily spend a half-day here, particularly with children. Plan to have lunch afterward in town

Dock St. (P.O. Box 39), Shelburne, NS B0T 1W0. ② 902/875-3219. Admission to all 4 museums C$8 (US$5.75) adults, free for children under 16; individual museums C$3 (US$2.10) adults, free for children under 16. June to mid-Oct daily 9:30am–5:30pm. Closed mid-Oct to May (Dory Shop closes end of Sept).

## WHERE TO STAY

Just across the harbor from Shelburne is **The Islands Provincial Park** (② 902/875-4304), which offers 64 campsites on 193 hectares (482 acres) from mid-May to early September. Some are right on the water and have great views of the historic village across the way. No hookups for RVs. The sites cost C$18 (US$15) apiece.

**The Cooper's Inn** ⨀ *Finds*    Located facing the harbor in the Dock Street historic area, the impeccably historic Cooper's Inn was originally built by Loyalist merchant George Gracie in 1785. Subsequent additions and updates have been historically sympathetic. The downstairs sitting and dining rooms set the mood nicely, with worn wood floors, muted wall colors (mustard and khaki green), and classical music in the background. The rooms in the main building mostly feature painted wood floors (they're carpeted in the cooper-shop annex), and they are decorated in a comfortably historic-country style. The third-floor suite features wonderful detailing, two sleeping alcoves, and harbor views. It's worth stretching your budget for. The George Gracie Room has a four-poster bed and water view; the small Roderick Morrison Room has a wonderful claw-foot tub perfect for a late-evening soak. The two small, elegant **dining rooms** ⨀ here serve the best meals in town. Dinner is served nightly from 6 to 9pm, and reservations are strongly recommended.

36 Dock St., Shelburne, NS B0T 1W0. ② 800/688-2011 or 902/875-4656. Fax 902/875-4656. www.thecoopersinn. com. 7 units. C$100–C$185 (US$80–US$148) double. Rates include full breakfast. MC, V. **Amenities:** 2 dining rooms. *In room:* TV, kitchenette (1 unit), coffeemaker (most units), hair dryer.

## WHERE TO DINE

For a full dinner out, see the Cooper's Inn, above.

**Mr. Fish** ⨀ *Value* SEAFOOD    You can't miss this little fried-fish stand on the side of busy Route 3, near a shopping center; what the place lacks in location, it more than makes up for in character and good simple seafood. The matronly line cooks fry up messes of haddock, scallops, and shrimp, perfectly jacketed in a light crust, then add great fries and crunchy coleslaw on the side—plus a smile. You eat outside on picnic tables (but watch out for bees); if it's raining, you'll have to eat in your car.

104 King St. (Rte. 3, north of town center). ② 902/875-3474. Meals C$2.60–C$13 (US$2–US$11). V. Mon–Sat 10am–7pm (Fri until 9pm); Sun noon–7pm.

**Shelburne Café** ⨀ *Value* BAKERY/CAFE    When a family of German chefs set about to open the Shelburne Pastry shop in 1995, the idea was to sell fancy pastries.

But everyone who stopped by during the restoration of the Water Street building asked whether they would be selling bread. So they added bread. And today their loaves are among the best you'll taste in the province—especially the delectable Nova Scotian oatmeal brown bread. Though the place is under new ownership, it still offers great pastries (try the pinwheels) as well as satisfying sandwiches and filling meals from an expanding menu that might include seafood entrées such as almond-crusted salmon or poached haddock with a dill-wine sauce, lobster crepes and sandwiches, and seafood pastas. Everything is made from scratch, and everything (except the marked-down day-old goods) is just-baked fresh. You'll find good value for your loonies here.

171 Water St. © **902/875-1164.** Sandwiches C$3.50–C$4.25 (US$3–US$3.50); main courses C$7.99–C$17 (US$6.50–US$14). V. Mon–Sat 8am–8pm, off season closed Sat.

## LUNENBURG 🦆🦆

Lunenburg is one of Nova Scotia's most historic and appealing villages, a fact recognized in 1995 when UNESCO declared the old downtown a World Heritage Site. The town was first settled in 1753, primarily by German, Swiss, and French colonists. It was laid out on the "model town" plan then in vogue (Savannah, Georgia, and Philadelphia, Pennsylvania, were also set out along these lines), which meant seven north-south streets intersected by nine east-west streets. Such a plan worked quite well in the coastal plains. Lunenburg, however, is located on a harbor flanked by steep hills, and implementers of the model town plan saw no reason to bend around these. As a result, some of the streets can be exhausting to walk.

About 70% of the downtown buildings date from the 18th and 19th centuries, and many of these are possessed of a distinctive style and are painted in bright colors. Looming over all is the architecturally unique Lunenburg Academy, with its exaggerated mansard roof, pointy towers, and extravagant use of ornamental brackets. It sets the tone for the town the way the Citadel does for Halifax. The first two floors are still used as a public school (the top floor was deemed a fire hazard some years ago), and the building is open to the public only on special occasions.

What makes Lunenburg so appealing to visitors is its vibrancy. Yes, it's historic, but this is not an ossified village. There's life, including a subtle countercultural tang that dates from the 1960s. Look and you'll see evidence of the tie-dye-and-organic crowd in the scattering of natural food shops and funky boutiques. A growing number of art galleries, crafts shops, and souvenir vendors are moving in, making for rewarding browsing.

### ESSENTIALS

**GETTING THERE**    Lunenburg is 100km (62 miles) southwest of Halifax on Route 3.

**VISITOR INFORMATION**    The **Lunenburg Tourist Bureau** (© **902/634-8100**) is located at the top of Blockhouse Hill Road. It's open from May to October, daily 9am to 8pm. It's not in an obvious place, but the brown "?" signs posted around town will lead you there. The staff here is especially good at helping you find a place to spend the night if you've arrived without reservations. You can also call up local information on the Web at www.town.lunenburg.ns.ca.

### EXPLORING LUNENBURG

Leave plenty of time to explore Lunenburg by foot. An excellent walking tour brochure is available at the tourist office on Blockhouse Hill Road, though supplies are getting limited. If that's gone, contact the **Lunenburg Board of Trade** (© 902/ **634-8100**) for the excellent local and regional map they released in 2001.

**St. John's Anglican Church** 𝕏𝕏 at the corner of Duke and Cumberland streets had been one of the most impressive architectural sights in all of eastern Canada. The original structure was rendered in simple New England meetinghouse style, built in 1754 of oak timbers shipped from Boston; between 1840 and 1880, the church went through a number of additions and was overlaid with ornamentation and shingles to create an amazing example of the "carpenter Gothic" style—one in which many local residents were baptized and attended services throughout their adult lives. All this changed on Halloween night of 2001, however: a fire nearly razed the place, gutting its precious interior and much of the ornate exterior as well. In June of 2005, however, it reopened after a painstaking 3-year restoration project and can be viewed once more.

While exploring the steep streets of the town, note the architectural influence of later European settlers—especially Germans. Some local folks undoubtedly made their fortunes from the sea, but real money was also made by carpenters who specialized in the ornamental brackets that elaborately adorn dozens of homes here. Many of these same homes similarly feature a distinctive architectural element that's known as the "Lunenburg bump"—a five-sided dormer and bay window combo installed directly over an extended front door. Other homes feature the more common Scottish dormer. Also look for the double or triple roofs on some projecting dormers, which serve absolutely no function other than to give the home the vague appearance of a wedding cake.

Guided 1½-hour **walking tours** (© **902/634-3848**) that include lore about local architecture and legends are hosted daily by Eric Croft, a knowledgeable Lunenburg native who's in possession of a sizable store of good stories. Tours depart at 10am, 2pm, and 9pm from Bluenose Drive (across from the parking lot for the Atlantic Fisheries Museum); the cost is C$15 (US$12) adults, C$10 (US$8) children.

Several boat tours operate from the waterfront, most tied up near the Fisheries Museum. **Lunenburg Whale Watching Tours** (© **902/527-7175**) sails in pursuit of several species of whales, along with seals and seabirds on 3-hour excursions. There are four departures daily from mid-March through October, with reservations recommended. **Star Charters** (© **902/634-3535** or 877/247-7075) takes visitors on a mellow 45-minute tour of Lunenburg's inner harbor (no swells!) in a converted fishing boat. The same folks also offer 1½-hour sailing trips on the *Eastern Star,* a 14m (48-ft.) wooden ketch, June through October.

**Fisheries Museum of the Atlantic** 𝕏 *Kids*   The sprawling Fisheries Museum is professionally designed and curated, and it manages to take a topic that some might consider a little, well, dull and make it fun and exciting. It's also been upgraded and expanded recently. You'll find aquarium exhibits on the first floor, including a touchtank for kids. (Look also for the massive 15-lb. lobster, estimated to be 25–30 years old.) Detailed dioramas depict the whys and hows of fishing from dories, colonial schooners, and other historic vessels. You'll also learn a whole bunch about the *Bluenose,* a replica of which ties up in Lunenburg when it's not touring elsewhere (see "The Dauntless *Bluenose*" box, below). Outside, you can tour two other ships—a trawler and a salt-bank schooner—and visit a working boat shop. Allow at least 2 hours to probe all the corners of this engaging waterfront museum.

On the waterfront. ✆ 866/579-4909 or 902/634-4794. Admission C$9 (US$7.20) adults, C$7 (US$5.60) seniors, C$3 (US$2.10) children 6–17, C$22 (US$18) families. May–Oct daily 9:30am–5:30pm; Nov–Apr Mon–Fri 8:30am–4:30pm.

## SHOPPING

Mahone Bay (see later in this chapter) contains a much denser concentration of shops than Lunenburg; nevertheless, there are a few unique places here.

For an eye-opening look at how locals live (and shop), head for the **Scotia Trawler** (✆ **902/634-8218**) at 250 Montague St.—you can pick up run-of-the-mill groceries, but head to the back with the fisherfolk for an impressive assortment of wading boots, rubber gloves, shucking knives, flannels, caps, and off-brand sneakers. It's like L.L. Bean without the pretense. It's open weekdays 8am to 9pm, Saturdays to 6pm.

**Lunenburg Body Care** ✿ *Finds*    This pleasantly old-fashioned operation sells soap made the old-fashioned way: with natural colorings and the highest-quality ingredients. A Frommer's reader from Pennsylvania puts it thus in a letter: "Fabulous soap, nice store, personable shop owner who will give tours of the soap-making process. There's even a 'gentlemen's bench' for the gentlemen to sit and wait while their ladies purchase soap." Especially cool is the shop sign, which blows fragrant soap bubbles (during open hours only) onto the street. 166 Lincoln St. ✆ **902/634-3804**.

## SHORT ROAD TRIPS FROM LUNENBURG

**Blue Rocks** ✿✿ is a tiny, picturesque harbor a short drive from Lunenburg. It's every bit as scenic as Peggy's Cove, but without the tour buses. Head out of town on Pelham Street, and keep driving east. Look for signs indicating either THE POINT or THE LANE and steer in that direction; the winding roadway gets narrower as the homes get more humble. Eventually, you'll reach the tip, where it's just fishing shacks, bright boats and rocks, with views of spruce- and heath-covered islands offshore. The rocks are said to glow in a blue hue in certain light, hence the name. There's a small and friendly bed-and-breakfast, **Blue Rocks Road B&B** (✆ **902/634-8033;** www.bike lunenburg.com), along the road renting rooms at C$75 to C$95 (US$60–US$76) per night; they also rent bikes for exploring the scenic nooks and crannies of the Blue Rocks area.

If you continue on instead of turning toward "the point," you'll soon come to the enclave of **Stonehurst,** another picturesque cluster of homes gathered around a rocky harbor. The road forks along the way; the narrow, winding route to South Stonehurst is somewhat more scenic. This whole area is ideal for exploring by bicycle, with twisting lanes, great vistas, and limited traffic.

Heading eastward along the other side of Lunenburg Harbor, you'll end up eventually at the **Ovens Natural Park** ✿ (✆ **902/766-4621;** www.ovenspark.com) in Riverport, a privately owned campground and day-use park that sits on 1.6km (1 mile) of dramatic coastline. You can follow the seaside trail to view the "ovens" (sea caves, actually) for which the park was named. A closer view can be had on a **Zodiac boat tour** of the caves. The park features a cafe that serves up basic meals and a great view. Entrance fees are C$6 (US$5) adults, C$3 (US$2.40) seniors and children 5 to 11. The park opens from May 15 to October 15.

## WHERE TO STAY

Lunenburg is chock-full of good inns and B&Bs, but the situation is a bit in flux: Some of the properties listed below are up for sale, and as a result, ownership and rates may change in the near future. Call ahead to check.

## The Dauntless *Bluenose*

Take an old Canadian dime—one minted before 2001, that is—out of your pocket and have a close look. That graceful schooner on one side? That's the *Bluenose,* Canada's most-recognized and most-storied ship.

The *Bluenose* was built in Lunenburg in 1921 as a fishing schooner. But it wasn't just any schooner. It was an exceptionally fast schooner.

U.S. and Canadian fishing fleets had raced informally for years. Starting in 1920 the *Halifax Herald* sponsored the International Fisherman's Trophy, which was captured that first year by Americans sailing out of Massachusetts. Peeved, the Nova Scotians set about taking it back. And did they ever. The *Bluenose* retained the trophy for 18 years running, despite the best efforts of Americans to recapture it. The race was shelved as World War II loomed; in the years after the war, fishing schooners were displaced by long-haul, steel-hulled fishing ships, and the schooners sailed into the footnotes of history. The *Bluenose* was sold in 1942 to labor as a freighter in the West Indies. Four years later it foundered and sank off Haiti.

What made the *Bluenose* so unbeatable? A number of theories exist. Some said it was because of last-minute hull design changes. Some said it was frost "setting" the timbers as the ship was being built. Still others claim it was blessed with an unusually talented captain and crew.

The replica *Bluenose II* was built in 1963 from the same plans as the original, in the same shipyard, and even by some of the same workers. It's been owned by the province since 1971, and it sails throughout Canada and beyond as Nova Scotia's seafaring ambassador. The *Bluenose*'s location varies from year to year, and it schedules visits to ports in Canada and the United States. In midsummer, it typically alternates between Lunenburg or Halifax, during which time visitors can sign up for 2-hour harbor sailings (C$20/US$14 adults, C$10/US$7 children 12 and under). To hear about the ship's schedule, call the **Bluenose II Preservation Trust** (© 866/579-4909).

The town's most diverse set of lodgings is that run by the folks at the publike **The Grand Banker Seafood Bar & Grill** (© 902/634-3300) at 82 Montague St. Alan Creaser and company rent out a total of 17 rooms and suites around the old town, including a full-floor apartment with kitchenette, dining room, and laundry in the historic Morash House and a romantic suite with hot tub in the Brigantine Inn above the restaurant. Rates depend on amenities and time of year; check directly with the inn and restaurant for current prices, availability, and to make bookings.

For budget travelers, a great little municipal **campground** is located next to (and managed by) the visitor center (© 902/634-8100) on **Blockhouse Hill.** It has wonderful views and hookups for RVs. Be aware that the 52 sites are packed in tightly, but the location is well situated for exploring the town. Ask about pitching your tent on the less crowded far side of the information center, up on the grassy hill next to the fort's earthworks. The cost to camp is C$18 to C$26 (US$15–US$21). If that campground's full, **Little Lake Emily Campground** (© 902/634-4308) 3km (2 miles) outside town (in the village of Centre) has 85 sites, most with electric hookup and about half with water and sewage lines as well; they go for C$20 to C$29 (US$16–US$23) per night.

Finally, the friendly **Blue Rocks Road Bed & Breakfast** (© **902/634-8033**) outside town is back in business after a hiatus of a few years, and so are the owners' handy bike rentals. The three units run C$80 to C$90 (US$64–US$72) per night. Contact them for the area's best rentals, then strike off and explore some of the remarkable coves, peninsulas, and beaches in the area.

**Boscawen Inn** ⭐   This imposing 1888 mansion occupies a prime hillside site just a block from the heart of town. It's almost worth staying here just to get access to the main-floor deck and its views of the harbor. Most of the rooms are in the main building, which had a newer wing added in 1945. The decor is Victorian, but not aggressively so. Some of the rooms, including two spacious suites, are located in the 1905 MacLachlan House, just below the main house. A few things to know: Room 6 lacks a shower but has a nice tub. Guests on the third floor will need to navigate steep steps. Two rooms have televisions, and in-room phones are available on request; an annex contains five cheaper rooms. The inn's restaurant serves reliable, sometimes imaginative dinners nightly in season from 5:30 to 9pm.

150 Cumberland St., Lunenburg, NS B0J 2C0. © **800/354-5009** or 902/634-3325. Fax 902/634-9293. www.boscawen.ca. 22 units. C$75–C$205 (US$60–US$164) double. Rates include continental breakfast. AE, DISC, MC, V. **Amenities:** 2 restaurants; bar; laundry service. *In room:* Hair dryer, iron, phone available upon request.

**Kaulbach House Historic Inn** ⭐   The in-town Kaulbach House is decorated appropriately for its elaborate architecture: in high Victorian style, although rendered somewhat less oppressive with un-Victorian colors, such as pink and green. The house also reflects the era's prevailing class structure, since the nicest room (the tower room) is on top. It features two sitting areas and a great view. (The least intriguing rooms are the former servants' quarters on street level.) Recent renovations have spruced up the building a good bit, with new rain gutters, windows, mattresses, comforters, and hot water heating all installed in 2000, and the huge breakfast is worth coming for alone. It's a unique property in another regard: This is one of the few small Lunenburg inns in which all the guest rooms have their own private bathrooms.

75 Pelham St., Lunenburg, NS B0J 2C0. © **800/568-8818** or 902/634-8818. Fax 902/634-8818. www.kaulbach house.com. 7 units. C$85–C$163 (US$68–US$130) double. Rates include full breakfast. MC, V. Closed Nov–May. **Amenities:** Laundry service. *In room:* A/C (1 unit), TV, hair dryer, no phone.

**Lennox Inn Bed & Breakfast**   In 1991, this strikingly handsome but simple house in a quiet residential area of Lunenburg was condemned and slated for demolition. Robert Cram didn't want to see it go, so he bought it and spent several years restoring it to its original 1791 appearance, filling it with antiques and period reproduction furniture. It's more rustic than opulent (translation: the wood-floored rooms are pretty spare), but this fine inn should still be high on the list for anyone fond of authentically historic houses. In fact, it claims, quite plausibly, to be the oldest unchanged inn in Canada. Three of the four spacious second-floor rooms have the original plaster, and all four have the original fireplaces (nonworking). A country breakfast is served in the former tavern; be sure to note the ingenious old bar.

69 Fox St. (P.O. Box 254), Lunenburg, NS B0J 2C0. © **888/379-7605** or 902/634-4043. www.lennoxinn.com. 4 units, 2 with private bathroom. C$95–C$120 (US$76–US$96) double. Rates include full breakfast. MC, V. Open year-round; by reservation only mid-Oct to Apr. *In room:* No phone.

**Lunenburg Arms** ✦✦ In a town where nearly all the lodgings consist of converted old seamen's homes, this relatively new hotel (it opened in June 2002)—also converted from a gutted former tavern and boarding house—stands out as a modern alternative, one in which nearly everything you see is new. It's the only accommodation in town where rooms are wheelchair-accessible, there's an elevator, pets are welcomed with open paws, and each unit is wired up for high-speed Internet access at no extra charge. Rooms are furnished in pleasant carpeting and queen and king beds that wouldn't look out of place in a New York boutique hotel, yet there are also thoughtfully homey touches such as wood-laminate floors and a stuffed teddy bear (or two) placed in each room. The smallish bathrooms feature pedestal sinks and all-new fixtures. No two rooms here are laid out exactly like, so examine a few if possible to get the configuration you want—some rooms have Jacuzzis, some feature the town's best harbor views, and there are two bi-level loft suites with beds up small sets of stairs.

94 Pelham St., Lunenburg, NS B0J 2C0. ✆ 800/679-4950 or 902/640-4040. Fax 902/640-4041. www.lunenburg arms.com. 26 units. Peak season C$129–C$299 (US$103–US$239) double; off-peak lower. AE, MC, V. **Amenities:** Dining room; conference room. *In room:* A/C, TV, dataport, coffeemaker, hair dryer.

**The Senator Bed & Breakfast** ✦✦ *Finds* Friendly owner Karen Acton-Bond runs this small B&B out of a large, shipshape house in a serene residential neighborhood within walking distance of Lunenburg's Old Town. It gets raves from Frommer's readers. Surprisingly for the house's size, there are only three rooms here; of the three, two have Jacuzzi-like jetted tubs, and the third—furnished with two twin beds, rather than a double—has a Victorian claw-foot tub. Aperitifs are served at check-in, or later in the evening if you wish, and there's herbal tea to help you sleep. In the morning, you'll tuck into a very full hot breakfast that Acton-Bond says "might keep you from eating lunch." She will also help you book bicycle rentals with a nearby outfit, arrange for valet laundry pickup, and otherwise direct you around the area.

66 Macdonald St., Lunenburg, NS B0J 2C0. ✆ 877/634-9358 or 902/634-9358. www.senatorbb.com. 3 units. C$110–C$200 (US$88–US$160) double; off season from C$85 (US$68) double. Rates include full breakfast. MC, V. **Amenities:** Laundry service. *In room:* No phone.

## WHERE TO DINE

As with Lunenburg's inns, nearly all the prominent restaurants in town also seem to be up for sale at the moment. Check ahead to ensure a given eatery is still open. Note that the Boscawen Inn (see above) also serves well-regarded meals.

**Historic Grounds Coffee House** ✦ *Value* CAFE More than just great coffee drinks, this youthful place in decidedly unhip Lunenburg serves up hearty breakfasts, good chowders, sandwiches, salads, and fish cakes throughout most of the day, and always with a smile (they've been doing it since the mid-1990s, so this isn't one of those flash-in-the-pan, designer java huts). Wash it down with real Italian espresso, something called a frappé (which is not an American-style frappé, but rather more like a frozen espresso), smoothies, or sodas. Ice cream and interesting dessert items are also available. Go for a table on the tiny balcony if you can snag one—they've got the best dining view in town, at a fraction of the cost of what you'd pay for a meal anywhere else. Good choices at lunch include the Caesar salad wrap, the turkey club, and even a lobster sandwich.

100 Montague St. ✆ 902/634-9995. Lunch items C$3.95–C$8.95 (US$3.15–C$7.15). AE, DISC, MC, V. June to mid-Sept Mon–Fri 7:30am–10pm, Sat–Sun 8am–10pm; mid-Sept to May daily 7:30am–6pm.

**The Knot** ✹ (Value) PUB FARE   Good beers on tap and a convivial English atmosphere make this pub a great place to take a break from more upscale eateries in town. Located smack in the center of a tiny commercial district, it serves surprisingly good pub fare—think juicy burgers, fried fish, local sausage, and a warming mussel soup—plus a selection of bitters and ales, some of them brewed locally in Halifax. The crowd is an agreeable mixture of fishermen, local families, and tourists, and bar staff are all too happy to help you decide what's good that day.

4 Dufferin St. ✆ **902/634-3334**. Meals C$6–C$10 (US$4.80–US$8). AE, MC, V. Daily 10am–midnight; kitchen closes 9pm in summer, 8:30pm in winter.

**Magnolia's Grill** ✹ SEAFOOD/ECLECTIC   This is a bright, cheerful, funky storefront with a checkerboard linoleum floor, lively rock playing in the background, and walls adorned with old Elvis and Beatles iconography. It also serves some of the most delectable food in town. Look for rotating seafood specials, chicken tostadas, and sesame-ginger shrimp stir-fry—or whatever else the kitchen feels like scrawling on the blackboard. The restaurant is especially famed for its fish cakes (served with homemade rhubarb chutney) and, for dessert, Mrs. Zinck's Chocolate Sloppy (don't ask; it's terrific). No reservations are accepted, so come at off-peak hours or come expecting a wait.

Yes, that's actress Kathy Bates's picture on the wall. She ate well here while acting in the film *Dolores Claiborne.*

128 Montague St. ✆ **902/634-3287**. Reservations not accepted. Main courses C$6.50–C$14 (US$5–US$11). AE, MC, V. Daily 11:30am–10pm. Closed Nov–Mar.

**Old Fish Factory Restaurant** ✹ SEAFOOD   The Old Fish Factory Restaurant is—no surprise—located in a huge old fish-processing plant, which it shares with the Fisheries Museum. This large and popular restaurant can swallow whole bus tours at once; come early and angle for a window seat or a spot on the patio. Also no surprise: The specialty is seafood, which tends to involve medleys of varied fish. At lunch you might order a fish sandwich or a salmon filet. At dinner, lobster is served four different ways, along with bouillabaisse, snow crab, local haddock and scallops, and a curried mango seafood pasta. There's steak, lamb, and chicken for more terrestrial tastes.

68 Bluenose Dr. (at the Fisheries Museum). ✆ **800/533-9336** or 902/634-3333. www.oldfishfactory.com. Reservations recommended (ask for a window seat). Lunch C$8–C$19 (US$6.50–US$15); dinner C$14–C$35 (US$11–US$28). AE, DC, DISC, MC, V. Daily 11am–9pm. Closed late Oct to early May.

**Rissers** ✹ ECLECTIC   A recent addition to Lunenburg's restaurant menu, Rissers features mostly straight-ahead seafood that's a touch classier than the fried grub that predominates elsewhere around town, and definitely more interesting than it has to be. The kitchen serves grilled steaks, boiled lobsters, house-smoked salmon, and sage-roasted chicken, for example—but also a Nova Scotia lamb chop with osso buco and an onion-risotto cake. The most interesting entrees might be the panko-breaded fried scallops, served with braised Belgian endive, a sauce of Sauvignon Blanc, and hot chile oil; or the cider-brined pork loin steak sided with blackstrap molasses and prunes. Eat inside by the fireplace, at the bar, or out on the stylish terrace opening onto a quiet street. Come on Friday night to catch live entertainment.

94 Pelham St. ✆ **800/679-4950** or 902/640-4040. Reservations accepted. Main courses C$9–C$21 (US$7–US$17). AE, MC, V. Daily 7am–10pm.

## MAHONE BAY 🐦🐦

Mahone Bay, first settled in 1754 by European Protestants, is picture-perfect Nova Scotia. It's tidy and trim with an eclectic Main Street that snakes along the bay and is lined with inviting shops. This is a town that's remarkably well cared for by its 1,100 residents, a growing number of whom live here and commute to work in Halifax. Architecture buffs will find a range of styles to keep them ogling.

A **visitor information center** (℗ **888/624-6151** or 902/624-6151; www.mahonebay. com) is located at 165 Edgewater St., near the three church steeples. It's open daily in summer 9am to 7:30pm, until 5:30pm in shoulder seasons.

Each year in late July, Mahone Bay celebrates the **Wooden Boat Festival** 🐦, where you can see some of the most beautiful craft on the eastern seaboard put through their paces. Entertainment and workshops are offered as well; admission is free.

### EXPLORING THE TOWN

The free **Mahone Bay Settlers Museum,** 578 Main St. (℗ **902/624-6263**), provides historic context for your explorations from June through early September (closed Mon). A good selection of historic decorative arts is on display. Before leaving, be sure to request a copy of "Three Walking Tours of Mahone Bay," a handy brochure that outlines easy historic walks around the compact downtown.

Thanks to the looping waterside routes nearby, this is a popular destination for bikers. And the deep, protected harbor offers superb sea kayaking. If you'd like to give kayaking a go, contact **East Coast Outfitters** (℗ **902/624-0334**), based in the Peggy's Cove area near Halifax. They offer half-day introductory classes and a 5-day coastal tour of the area. Among the more popular adventures is the day-long introductory tour, in which paddlers explore the complex shoreline and learn about kayaking in the process. The price is about C$85 to C$105 (US$60–US$84) per person, including lunch. Rentals are also available, starting at about C$40 (US$32) half day for a single kayak.

### SHOPPING

Mahone Bay serves as a magnet to all manner of creative and crafty types, and Main Street has become a shopping mecca for those who treasure handmade goods. Shops are typically open late spring until Christmas, when Haligonians travel the 55 minutes here for holiday shopping. Among the more interesting options:

**Amos Pewter** Watch pewter come fresh out of the molds at this spacious workshop and gallery located in an 1888 building. The Christmas tree ornament is a popular souvenir. 589 Main St. ℗ **800/565-3369** or 902/624-9547.

**Jo-Ann's Deli, Market & Bake Shop** 🐦 Gourmet and farm-fresh basic fare are sold at this wonderful food shop, where a bag of carrots serves as a counterweight on the screen door. It's the best place for miles around to stock up on local and organic produce, fresh sandwiches, and knockout cookies, sweets, and Cape Breton-influenced oat cakes—the chocolate covered ones blend chocolate, sugar, salt, and oats to perfect effect. If you're in the mood for a picnic, this is your destination. The homemade jams, sold to benefit a local museum, are well priced; and the coffee drinks from the bar are all exceptionally good as well. 9 Edgewater St. ℗ **902/624-6305**.

**Sensational Chocolates** You'll find handmade Belgian chocolates here, many cast in special shapes with local resonance. You can buy samples for C$1 (US70¢). 605 Main St. ℗ **902/624-0323**.

**Suttles & Seawinds**   Vibrant and distinctive clothing designed and made in Nova Scotia is sold at this stylish boutique. (There are others from Halifax to Toronto, but this is the original.) The adjacent shop is crammed with quilts and resplendent bolts of fabric. 466 Main St. ✆ **902/624-6177.**

## WHERE TO STAY

You'll find a clutch of bed-and-breakfast choices in and around Mahone Bay. If those I've listed below are fully booked up, here are three more to consider: **Ocean Trail Retreat** (✆ **888/624-8824** or 902/624-8824; fax 902/624-8899) on Route 3 at Mader's Cove is a relatively new property with 17 airy motel-style rooms and 3 two-bedroom chalets. It's very popular with families, largely because of the heated outdoor swimming pool. This might be the area's best choice if you're bringing children. Rooms go for C$89 to C$109 (US$71–US$87) per night, the one penthouse suite—with a big living room and whirlpool—for C$190 (US$152) per night or C$1,200 (US$960) per week.

Then, right in the center of town, **Mahone Bay Bed & Breakfast** at 558 Main St. (✆ **866/239-6252** or 902/624-6388) is a more Victorian option with four rooms at rates from C$75 to C$125 (US$60–US$100) per night. The restored, bright yellow 1860s-era house was built by one of the town's many former shipbuilders. Finally, there's **Fisherman's Daughter** (97 Edgewater St.; ✆ **902/624-0483**), with its maritime theme and four rooms costing C$100 to C$125 (US$80–US$100) per night.

**The Manse at Mahone Bay Country Inn** ✪   Innkeepers Rose and Allan O'Brien have made a cozy retreat of their 1870 home, tucked off on a side street that's at once removed from and close to the activity in Mahone Bay. All the guest rooms are bright and uncluttered, feature old pine floors, and are tastefully appointed with furniture that's both modern and classic. I'd be happy in any of the rooms, but if it were available, I'd opt for the Loft, a former hayloft on the second floor of the barn. With its whitewashed barn-board walls, large sitting area, small balcony, queen-size bed, and CD player, it's hard to imagine not enjoying a few days hidden away here. The rest of the house is equally attractive, and a morning spent with a cup of coffee in one of the oversize Adirondack chairs on the front deck is a morning well spent indeed. The loft occasionally gets a bit stuffy in the later afternoon, but almost always cools off by evening—and a new fan helps speed the process. Note that this small place is so good and popular that it's always fully booked up for the summer months well in advance, so plan ahead or cross your fingers and hope for a fluke cancellation; they won't have rooms available on short notice.

88 Orchard St. (P.O. Box 475), Mahone Bay, NS B0J 2E0. ✆ **902/624-1121.** Fax 902/624-1182. www.themanse countryinn.ca. 4 units. C$110–C$135 (US$88–US$108) double. Rates include full breakfast. MC, V. **Amenities:** Bar. *In room:* Hair dryer, no phone.

**Nature's Cottage Bed & Breakfast** ✪   Marlene Sabatina's serene B&B is a bit outside town, yet still within hailing distance; it's a nice choice for those who want a quiet experience. The property features a large front porch, great bay views, a private dock on the bay, a lush garden, and an outdoor whirlpool. Guests choose from three themed rooms, each with private bathrooms (stocked with handmade soaps) on the hallway and each possessing various comfort levels; the two-room Safari suite has a television, good view, and pullout sofa bed, while the Bouqet and Rustique rooms are simpler. (An additional loft-style unit above the garage has its own entrance, kitchenette, television, and en suite bathroom.) Full breakfast is served with your stay, and guests also share access to a sauna room.

906 S. Main St., Mahone Bay, NS B0J 2E0. © **877/607-5699** or 902/624-0196. Fax 902/624-0363. 4 units. C$90–C$150 (US$72–US$120) double. **Amenities:** Jacuzzi; sauna. *In room:* No phone.

## WHERE TO DINE

Little Mahone Bay's main street has more than its share of places at which to nosh, though most are priced for tourist dollars.

The seasonally open **Gazebo Cafe** ⚡ at 567 Main St. (© **902/624-6484**) is my favorite—an affable and affordable waterside cafe dishing up filling, healthy sandwiches and thick bowls of seafood chowder. They also do juices, smoothies, and topflight coffee. Fresh desserts are delivered several times weekly. This place is rapidly becoming the arts headquarters of the town, too; check the bulletin board for news of local art shows and musical performances, some of which take place right at the cafe.

**Innlet Café** ⚡⚡ SEAFOOD/GRILL    Former owners Jack and Katherine Sorensen served up great meals here for 2 decades, and new ownership is holding true to the menu they created, which brought back legions of customers. Everything is good, especially the seafood. The menu is all over the place (oven-braised lamb shank to scallop stir-fry), but the smart money hones in on the unadorned seafood. Notable are the "smoked and garlicked mackerel" and the mixed seafood grill. The best seats are on the stone patio, which has a view of the harbor and the famous three-steepled townscape of Mahone Bay. If you end up inside, nothing lost. The clean lines and lack of clutter make it an inviting spot, and the atmosphere is informal and relaxed.

249 Edgewater St. © **902/624-6363**. Reservations recommended for dinner. Main courses C$12–C$21 (US$9.50–US$17). MC, V. Daily 11:30am–9pm.

## CHESTER ⚡⚡

Chester is a short drive off Route 103 and has the feel of an old-money summer colony, perhaps somewhere along the New England coast in the 1920s. It was first settled in 1759 by immigrants from New England and Great Britain, and today it has a population of 1,250. The village is noted for its regal homes and quiet streets, along with the picturesque islands offshore. The atmosphere here is uncrowded, untrammeled, lazy, and slow—the way life used to be in summer resorts throughout the world. Change may be on the horizon: Actors and authors have discovered the place and are snapping up waterfront homes in town and on the islands as private retreats, giving a bit of an edge to the lazy feel of the spot.

The **Chester Visitor Information Centre** (© **902/275-4616;** www.chesterns.com) is in the old train station on Route 3 on the south side of town. It's open daily from 9am to 7pm in July and August, from 10am to 5pm in spring and fall.

### EXPLORING THE AREA

Like so many other towns in Nova Scotia, Chester is best seen out of your car. But unlike other towns, where the center of gravity seems to be in the commercial district, here the focus is on the graceful, shady residential areas that radiate out from the Lilliputian village.

In your rambles, plan to head down Queen Street to the waterfront, and then veer around on South Street, admiring the views out toward the mouth of the harbor. Continue on South Street past the yacht club, past the statue of the veteran (in a kilt), past the sundial in the small square. Then you'll come to a beautiful view of Back Harbour.

At the foot of the small park is a curious municipal saltwater pool, filled at high tide. On warmer days, you'll find what appears to be half the town out splashing and shrieking in the bracing water.

Some creative shops are beginning to find a receptive audience in and around Chester, and there's good browsing for new goods and antiques both downtown and in the outlying areas. One such shop is **Fiasco,** 54 Queen St. (© **902/275-2173**), which has an appealing selection of funky and fun home accessories and clothing. Another good stop is **Juwil By the Sea,** 11 Pleasant St. (© **902/275-4773**), an eclectic store of clothing, antiques, carpets, fine art, woodcarvings, dolls, and pearl jewelry straight from China.

For an even slower pace, plan an excursion out to the Tancook Islands ✪, a pair of lost-in-time islands with 200 year-round residents. The islands, accessible via a short ferry ride, are good for walking the lanes and trails. There's a small cafe on Big Tancook, but little else to cater to travelers. Several ferry trips are scheduled daily between 6am and around 6pm. The ferry ties up on the island, however, so don't count on a last trip back to the mainland. Tickets are C$5 (US$4) round-trip, free for children under 12.

In the evening, the intimate **Chester Playhouse,** 22 Pleasant St. (© **800/363-7529** or 902/275-3933; www.chesterplayhouse.ns.ca), hosts plays, concerts, and other high-quality performances throughout the summer season. Tickets are usually C$21 (US$17) adults. Call for a schedule or reservations.

## WHERE TO STAY

**Graves Island Provincial Park** ✪✪ (© **902/275-4425**) is 3km (1¾ miles) north of the village on Route 3 in East River. The 50-hectare (125-acre) estatelike park is one of the province's more elegant campgrounds, as befits moneyed Chester. The park has 73 sites, many dotting a high grassy bluff with outstanding views out to the spruce-clad islands of Mahone Bay, available mid-May through mid-October. No hookups are available; the camping fee is C$18 (US$15) per night.

**Mecklenburgh Inn** *Value*   This wonderfully funky and appealing inn, built around 1890, is located on a low hill in one of Chester's residential neighborhoods. The building is dominated by broad porches on the first and second floors, which invariably are populated with guests sitting and rocking and watching the town wander by. (Which it does: The post office is just next door.) Innkeeper Suzi Fraser has been running the place with casual bonhomie since the late 1980s, and she's a great breakfast cook to boot. Rooms are modern Victorian and generally quite bright. What's the catch? The four rooms share two hallway bathrooms, but guests often end up feeling like family, so it's usually not much of a bother.

78 Queen St., Chester, NS B0J 1J0. (© 902/275-4638. www.mecklenburghinn.ca. 4 units, 1 with private bathroom. C$85–C$135 (US$68–US$108) double. Rates include full breakfast. AE, V. Closed Jan–Apr. *In room:* Hair dryer, no phone.

## WHERE TO DINE

**Carta** GLOBAL   Carta opened in 1999 in an odd sort of mini-mall hidden away in Chester's mini-downtown, and the proprietors did great and colorful things with their tiny space. They also concocted an appealing menu that's equally colorful and far ranging, with offerings like a bento box, fish and chips, and green Thai curry; for more traditional appetites, they cook big, meaty hamburgers. New owners, of Middle

Eastern descent, have taken over and added their own Mediterranean cuisine as well. It's hard to conceive of any craving that won't be satisfied here.

54 Queen St. (behind Fiasco). © **902/275-5131.** Reservations recommended in summer. Lunch C$5–C$8.50 (US$4–US$6.75); dinner courses C$5.95–C$14 (US$4.75–US$11). DC, MC, V. Tues–Sun 11:30am–10pm. Closed Jan–Apr.

**The Galley Restaurant** SEAFOOD   This local institution is tucked off the main road west of town, and sits on the water next to a marina and boatyard. The decor affects the Ye Olde Crusty Mariner look, but it doesn't go overboard into schlock. You'll find everyone from blazer-wearing, gray-haired yachtspeople to casually dressed 30-somethings who come for the good views and reliable fare. The lunch menu is less oriented toward the sea and specializes in a variety of burgers, including beef, chicken, and haddock burgers. There are also fish cakes and a seafood casserole. Dinner is more elegant; main courses include a daily fresh catch and other seafood options such as jambalaya and lobster linguine. Meats include steaks, rack of lamb, and veal; vegetarian dinners are also available.

Marriott's Cove (3km/1¾ miles west of Chester on Rte. 3). © **902/275-4700.** Reservations recommended (ask for a window). Main courses C$6.50–C$11 (US$5–US$9) at lunch, C$14–C$20 (US$11–US$16) at dinner. AE, DC, MC, V. Daily 11:30am–9pm. Closed Nov–Mar.

**Luigi's Café and Books** ⊛ CAFE   The center of the Chester area's youth culture, Luigi's is the place to go for sandwiches, coffee, good pizza, and to overhear discussions about the latest clear-cutting in British Columbia. The interior is brightly painted and features Canadian books and nature art for sale, of a higher level of quality than you'd expect in a tourist town. The food and drink is quite good, too, for such a casual place; try the popular house pizzas (in 6-in. and 12-in. sizes); haddock chowder; a garden, Caesar, or Mediterranean salad; a daily special such as vegetable soup or linguine with pesto; or just some desserts and coffee, beer, or a smoothie.

19 Pleasant St. © **902/275-5185.** Main courses C$4.50–C$8.50 (US$3.60–US$7). V. Summer daily 9am–8pm; winter hours shorter.

## 8 Halifax ⧏⧏

Halifax's unusually pleasing harborside setting, now home to a city of some 115,000 (about three times as many in the greater metro area), first attracted Europeans in 1749, when Col. Edward Cornwallis established a military outpost here. (The site was named after George Montagu Dunk, second earl of Halifax. Residents tend to agree that it was a great stroke of luck that the city avoided the name Dunk, Nova Scotia.) The city plodded along as a colonial backwater for the better part of a century; one historian wrote that it was generally regarded as "a rather degenerate little seaport town."

But its natural advantages—including that well-protected harbor and its location near major fishing grounds and shipping lanes—eventually allowed it to emerge as a major port and military base. In recent years, the city has grown aggressively (it annexed adjacent suburbs in 1969) and carved out a niche as the vital commercial and financial hub of the Maritimes. The city is also home to a number of colleges and universities, which gives it a youthful, edgy air. Skateboards and bicycles often seem to be the vehicles of choice. In addition to the many attractions, downtown Halifax is home to a number of fine restaurants and hotels.

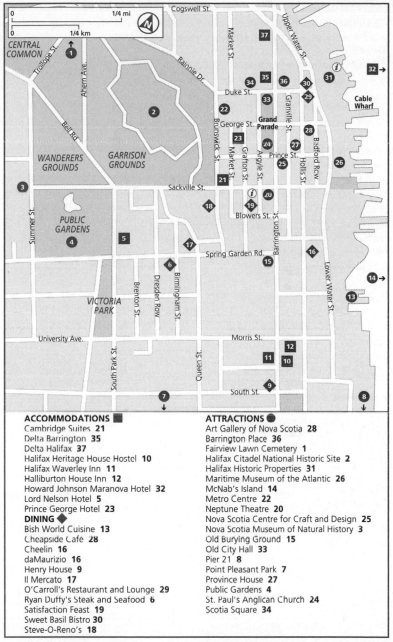

# Halifax

ACCOMMODATIONS
Cambridge Suites **21**
Delta Barrington **35**
Delta Halifax **37**
Halifax Heritage House Hostel **10**
Halifax Waverley Inn **11**
Halliburton House Inn **12**
Howard Johnson Maranova Hotel **32**
Lord Nelson Hotel **5**
Prince George Hotel **23**

DINING
Bish World Cuisine **13**
Cheapside Café **28**
Cheelin **16**
daMaurizio **16**
Henry House **9**
Il Mercato **17**
O'Carroll's Restaurant and Lounge **29**
Ryan Duffy's Steak and Seafood **6**
Satisfaction Feast **19**
Sweet Basil Bistro **30**
Steve-O-Reno's **18**

ATTRACTIONS
Art Gallery of Nova Scotia **28**
Barrington Place **36**
Fairview Lawn Cemetery **1**
Halifax Citadel National Historic Site **2**
Halifax Historic Properties **31**
Maritime Museum of the Atlantic **26**
McNab's Island **14**
Metro Centre **22**
Neptune Theatre **20**
Nova Scotia Centre for Craft and Design **25**
Nova Scotia Museum of Natural History **3**
Old Burying Ground **15**
Old City Hall **33**
Pier 21 **8**
Point Pleasant Park **7**
Province House **27**
Public Gardens **4**
St. Paul's Anglican Church **24**
Scotia Square **34**

## ESSENTIALS

**GETTING THERE**    Coming from New Brunswick and the west, the most direct route is via Route 102 from Truro; allow about 2 to 2½ hours from the provincial border at Amherst.

**Halifax International Airport** (www.hiaa.com) is 34km (21 miles) north of downtown Halifax in Elmsdale; take Route 102 to Exit 6. Nova Scotia's notorious fogs make it advisable to call before heading out to the airport to reconfirm flight times. Airlines serving Halifax include **Air Canada,** Air Canada's commuter airline **Jazz,** and **Canjet.** (See the "Getting There" section of chapter 2 for phone numbers.) The **Airporter** (© 902/873-2091) offers frequent shuttles from the airport to major downtown hotels daily from 6:30am to 11:15pm. The rate is C$14 (US$11) one-way, C$24 (US$19) round-trip.

**VIA Rail** (© 888/842-7245) offers train service 6 days a week between Halifax and Montréal. The entire trip takes between 18 and 21 hours, depending on direction. Stops include Moncton and Campbellton (and bus connections to Québec). Halifax's train station, at Barrington and Cornwallis streets, is within walking distance of downtown attractions.

**VISITOR INFORMATION**    Halifax's main **Visitor Centre** (©902/490-5963) is located downtown at 1598 Argyle St., at the corner of Sackville. It's open daily from 8:30am to 9pm in summer (until 5pm in winter), it's huge, and it's staffed with friendly folks who will point you in the right direction or help you make room reservations. There's another info booth in **Scotia Square** (© 902/490-5963) down by the waterfront, also open year-round, as well as a third located in the domestic arrivals area of the main terminal of the **airport** (© 902/873-1223) open from 9am to 9pm daily. During the summer, travel counselors also cruise the waterfront and boardwalk on Segway scooters. For online information about Halifax, visit **www.halifaxinfo.com**.

**GETTING AROUND**    Parking in Halifax can be problematic. Long-term metered spaces are in high demand downtown, and many of the parking lots and garages fill up fast. If you're headed downtown for a brief visit, you can usually find a 2-hour meter. But if you're looking to spend a day, I'd suggest venturing out early to ensure a spot at a parking lot. The city's most extensive parking (fee charged) is available near Sackville Landing. Or try along Lower Water Street, south of the Maritime Museum of the Atlantic, where you can park all day for around C$6 (US$4).

**Metro Transit** operates buses throughout the city. Route and timetable information is available at the information centers or by phone (© 902/490-4000). Bus fare is C$2 (US$1.60) adults, C$1.40 (US$1.10) seniors and children.

Daily throughout the summer a **bright yellow bus** named Fred (© 902/423-6658 or 902/490-4000) cruises a loop through the downtown, passing each stop about every 30 minutes from 10:30am until 5pm. It's free. Stops include the Maritime Museum, Water Street, the Grand Parade, the Citadel, and Barrington Place. Request a schedule and map at the visitor center.

**EVENTS**    The annual **Nova Scotia International Tattoo** (© 902/420-1114; www.nstattoo.ca) features military and marching bands totaling some 2,000 plus military and civilian performers. This rousing event takes place over the course of a week in early July and is held indoors at the Halifax Metro Center. Tickets are C$18 to C$50 (US$15–US$40).

The annual **Atlantic Jazz Festival** (© 902/492-2225; www.jazzeast.com) has performances ranging from global and avant-garde to local and traditional music each

July. Venues include area nightclubs and outdoor stages, and prices vary considerably; consult the website for the latest details and specifics of performance and price.

In early August, expect to see a profusion of street performers ranging from fire-eaters to comic jugglers. They descend on Halifax each summer for the 10-day **International Busker Festival** (© 902/429-3910; www.buskers.ca). Performances take place along the waterfront walkway all day long and are often quite remarkable. Free, with donations requested.

The **Atlantic Film Festival** (© 902/422-3456; www.atlanticfilm.com) offers screenings of more than 150 films in mid-September. The focus is largely on Canadian filmmaking, with an emphasis on independent productions and shorts. Panel discussions with industry players are also part of the festival. Some films are free, while those with a charge cost about C$5 to C$15 (US$4–US$12) each.

## EXPLORING HALIFAX

Halifax is fairly compact and easily reconnoitered on foot or by mass transportation. The major landmark is the **Citadel**—the stone fortress that looms over downtown from its grassy perch. From the ramparts, you can look into the windows of the tenth floor of downtown skyscrapers. The Citadel is only 9 blocks from the waterfront—albeit 9 sometimes steep blocks—and you can easily see both the downtown and the waterfront areas in 1 day.

A lively neighborhood worth seeking out runs along **Spring Garden Road,** between the Public Gardens and the library (at Grafton St.). You'll find intriguing boutiques, bars, and restaurants along these 6 blocks, set amid a mildly Bohemian street scene. If you have strong legs and a stout constitution, you can start on the waterfront, stroll up and over the Citadel to descend to the Public Gardens, and then return via Spring Garden to downtown, perhaps enjoying a meal or two along the way.

### THE WATERFRONT

Halifax's rehabilitated waterfront is at its most inviting and vibrant between Sackville Landing (at the foot of Sackville St.) and the Sheraton Casino, near Purdy Wharf. (You could keep walking, but north of here the waterfront lapses into an agglomeration of charmless modern towers with sidewalk-level vents that assail passersby with unusual odors.) On sunny summer afternoons, the waterfront is bustling with tourists enjoying the harbor, business folks playing hooky while sneaking an ice-cream cone, and baggy-panted skateboarders striving to stay out of trouble. Plan on about 2 to 3 hours to tour and gawk from end to end.

The city's most extensive parking (fee charged) is available near Sackville Landing, and that's a good place to start a walking tour. Make your first stop the waterfront's crown jewel, the **Maritime Museum of the Atlantic** (see below).

In addition to the other attractions listed below, the waterfront walkway is studded with small diversions, intriguing shops, take-out food emporia, and minor monuments. Think of it as an alfresco scavenger hunt.

Among the treasures, look for **Summit Place,** commemorating the historic gathering of world leaders in 1995, when Halifax hosted the G-7 Economic Summit. There's North America's oldest operating **Naval Clock,** which was built in 1767 and chimed at the Halifax Naval Dockyard from 1772 to 1993. You can visit the **Ferry Terminal,** which is hectic during rush hour with commuters coming and going to Dartmouth across the harbor. (It's also a cheap way to enjoy a sweeping city and harbor view.) The passenger-only ferry runs at least every half-hour, and the fare is C$2 (US$1.60) per adult each way, cheaper for seniors and children age 5 to 15.

The waterfront's shopping core is located in and around the 3-block **Historic Properties,** near the Sheraton. These stout buildings of wood and stone are Canada's oldest surviving warehouses and were once the center of the city's booming shipping industry. Today, the historic architecture is stern enough to provide ballast for the somewhat precious boutiques and restaurants they now house. Especially appealing is the granite-and-ironstone **Privateers' Warehouse,** which dates from 1813.

If you're feeling that a pub crawl might be in order, the Historic Properties area is also a good place to wander around after working hours in the early evening. There's a contagious energy that spills out of the handful of public houses, and you'll find a bustling camaraderie and live music.

**Maritime Museum of the Atlantic** *Kids*    All visitors to Nova Scotia owe themselves a stop at this standout museum on a prime waterfront location. The exhibits are involving and well executed, and you'll be astounded at how fast 2 hours can fly by. Visitors are greeted by a 3m (10-ft.) lighthouse lens from 1906, and then proceed through a parade of shipbuilding and seagoing eras. Visit the deckhouse of a coastal steamer (ca. 1940), or learn the colorful history of Samuel Cunard, a Nova Scotia native (born 1787) who founded the Cunard Steam Ship Co. to carry the royal mail and along the way established an ocean dynasty. Another highlight is the exhibit on the tragic Halifax Explosion of 1917, when two warships collided in Halifax harbor not far from the museum, detonating tons of TNT. More than 1,700 people died, and windows were shattered 100km (60 miles) away. But perhaps the most poignant exhibit is the lone deck chair from the *Titanic*—150 victims of the *Titanic* disaster are buried in Halifax, where rescue efforts were centered. Also memorable are the Age of Steam exhibit, Queen Victoria's barge, and the interesting new Shipwreck Treasures of Nova Scotia section with its stories and artifacts from more than a dozen local shipwrecks.

1675 Lower Water St. (C) **902/424-7490.** www.maritime.museum.gov.ns.ca. Admission C$8 (US$6.50) adults, C$7 (US$5.50) seniors, C$4 (US$3) children 6–17, C$21 (US$17) family. Half-price admission Nov–Apr. May–Oct daily 9:30am–5:30pm (to 8pm Tues), Nov-Apr closed Mon and shorter hours Sun.

## ON THE WATER

A number of boat tours depart from the Halifax waterfront. You can browse the offerings on **Cable Wharf,** near the foot of George Street, where many tour boats are based. On-the-water adventures range from 1-hour harbor tours (about C$12/US$9.60) to 5-hour deep-sea fishing trips (about C$40/US$32).

**Murphy's on the Water** ((C) **902/420-1015**) runs the most extensive tour operation, with three boats and a choice of tours, ranging from a cocktail sailing cruise to whale-watching to tours of historic McNab's Island, located near the mouth of the harbor (see below).

**Peggy's Cove Express** ((C) **902/422-4200**) operates 4-hour scenic boat and bus tours from Cable Wharf to the popular fishing village of Peggy's Cove; a walking tour of the town is included as part of the adventure. The cost is about C$70 (US$56) per adult.

Finally, the **Harbour Hopper** ((C) **902/490-8687**) amphibious craft crosses both land and sea during a tour costing C$23 (US$18) adults, C$20 to C$22 (US$16–US$17) students/seniors, C$14 (US$11) children ages 6 to 13, C$7.95 (US$6.50) children under 5. Families of four can travel for C$66 (US$53).

**C.S.S. Acadia**   This unusually handsome 1913 vessel is part of the Maritime Museum ("our largest artifact"), but it can be viewed independently for a small fee. The *Acadia* was used by the Canadian government to chart the ocean floor for 56 years, until its retirement in 1969. Much of the ship is open for self-guided tours, including the captain's quarters, upper decks, wheelhouse, and oak-paneled chart room. If you want to see more of the ship, ask about the guided half-hour tours (four times daily), which offer access to the engine room and more. You probably wouldn't need more than a half-hour here.

On the water, in front of the Maritime Museum, 1675 Lower Water St. ☎ **902/424-7490**. Free admission with museum ticket, or C$2 (US$1.60) can be applied to museum admission. Mon–Sat 9:30am–5:30pm; Sun 1–5:30pm. Closed mid-Oct to May 1.

**HMCS Sackville**   This blue-and-white corvette (a speedy warship smaller than a destroyer) is tied up along a wood-planked wharf behind a small visitor center. There's a short multimedia presentation to provide some background. The ship is outfitted as it was in 1944, and it is now maintained as a memorial to the Canadians who served in World War II. Plan to spend about a half-hour here.

Sackville Landing (summer), HMC dockyard (winter). ☎ **902/429-2132**. Admission C$3 (US$2.40) adults, C$2 (US$1.60) seniors and students. June–Oct daily 10am–5pm, off-season hours vary.

**Pier 21** ⊛ *Kids*   Between 1928 and 1971 more than one million immigrants arrived in Canada by disembarking at Pier 21, Canada's version of New York's Ellis Island. In 1999, the pier was restored and reopened, filled with engaging interpretive exhibits, which aid visitors in vividly imagining the confusion and anxiety of the immigration experience. The pier is divided roughly into three sections, which recapture the boarding of the ship amid the cacophony of many languages, the crossing of the Atlantic (a 26-min. multimedia show recaptures the voyage in a shiplike theater), and the dispersal of the recent arrivals throughout Canada via passenger train. For those seeking more in-depth information (one in five Canadians today can trace a link back to Pier 21), there's a reference library and computer resources. Plan to spend at least an hour here.

1055 Marginal Rd. (on the waterfront behind the Westin Hotel). ☎ **902/425-7770**. www.pier21.ca. C$8 (US$6.50) adults, C$7 (US$5.50) seniors, C$4.50 (US$3.50) children 6–16, C$20 (US$16) family. May–Nov daily 9:30am–5:30pm; Dec–Apr Tues–Fri 10am–5pm, Sat noon–5pm.

## THE CITADEL & DOWNTOWN

Downtown Halifax cascades 9 blocks down a slope between the imposing stone Citadel and the waterfront. There's no fast-and-ready tour route; don't hesitate to follow your own desultory course, alternately ducking down quiet streets and striding along busy arteries. A good spot to regain your bearings periodically is the **Grand Parade,** where military recruits once practiced their drills. It's a lovely urban landscape—a broad terrace carved into the hill, presided over on either end by St. Paul's (see below) and Halifax's **City Hall.** The sandstone city hall was built between 1887 and 1890, and is exuberantly abristle with the usual Victorian architectural gewgaws, like a prominent clock tower, dormers, pediments, arched windows, pilasters, and Corinthian columns. Alas, there's not much to see inside. If the weather is nice, the Grand Parade is also a prime spot to bring an alfresco lunch and enjoy some people-watching.

**Art Gallery of Nova Scotia**   Located in a pair of sandstone buildings between the waterfront and the Grand Parade, the Art Gallery is arguably the premier gallery in the Maritimes, with a focus on local and regional art. You'll also find a selection of other works by Canadian, British, and European artists, with a well-chosen selection of folk and Inuit art. In 1998, the gallery expanded to include the Provincial Building next door, where the entire house (it's tiny) of Nova Scotian folk artist Maud Lewis has been reassembled and is on display. The museum can be comfortably perused in 60 to 90 minutes; consider a lunch break in the attractive Cheapside Café (later in this chapter).

1723 Hollis St. (at Cheapside). ✆ **902/424-5280.** Admission C$10 (US$8) adults, C$8 (US$6.40) seniors, C$4 (US$3.20) students, C$20 (US$16) families. Daily 10am–5pm (Thurs to 9pm).

## Halifax Citadel National Historic Site ✦✦

Even if the stalwart stone fort weren't here, it would be worth the uphill trek for the astounding views alone. The panoramic sweep across downtown and the harbor finishes up with vistas out toward the broad Atlantic beyond. At any rate, an ascent makes it obvious why this spot was chosen for the harbor's most formidable defenses: There's simply no sneaking up on the place.

Four forts have occupied the summit since Col. Edward Cornwallis was posted to the colony in 1749. The Citadel has been restored to look much as it did in 1856, when the fourth fort was built out of concern over bellicose Americans. The fort has never been attacked.

The site is impressive to say the least: sturdy granite walls topped by grassy embankments form a rough star; in the sprawling gravel and cobblestone courtyard you'll find convincingly costumed interpreters in kilts and bearskin hats marching in unison, playing bagpipes, and firing the noon cannon. The former barracks and other chambers are home to exhibits about life at the fort. If you still have questions, stop a soldier, bagpiper, or washerwoman and ask.

The Citadel is the perfect place to launch an exploration of Halifax: It provides a good geographic context for the city and anchors it historically as well. This National Historic Site is the most heavily visited in Canada, and it's not hard to see why. You won't need more than 45 minutes or an hour here, though.

Citadel Hill. ✆ **902/426-5080.** Admission June to mid-Sept C$10 (US$8) adults, C$8.50 (US$7) seniors, C$5 (US$4) youths (6–16), C$25 (US$20) family. Spring and fall C$6.50 (US$5.50) adults, C$5.50 (US$4) seniors, C$3.25 (US$2.50) youths (6–16), C$16 (US$13) family. Free in winter. July–Aug 9am–6pm; Sept–June 9am–5pm. Visitor center closed, grounds open Oct–Apr; no guides in fall or winter.

## Nova Scotia Centre for Craft and Design

The provincial government runs this center with the idea of encouraging and developing crafts- and design-based industries across the province. Of interest to travelers is the first-floor gallery, where visitors can view oft-changing exhibits of the best of what Nova Scotia craftspeople have produced. Depending on your interest, plan to spend between a half-hour to an hour here.

1683 Barrington St. ✆ **902/492-2522.** Free admission. Gallery Mon 11am–5pm; Tues–Thurs 11am–9pm; Fri 11am–4pm; Sat 10am–4pm; Sun noon–4pm.

## Nova Scotia Museum of Natural History

Situated on the far side of the Citadel from downtown, this modern, midsize museum offers a good introduction to the flora and fauna of Nova Scotia. Galleries include geology, botany, mammals, and birds, plus exhibits of archaeology and Mi'kmaq culture. Especially noteworthy are the extensive collection of lifelike ceramic fungus and the colony of honeybees that freely come and go from their indoor acrylic hive through a tube connected to the outdoors. Allow about 1 hour.

1747 Summer St. ⓒ **902/424-7353**. Admission C$5 (US$4) adults, C$4.50 (US$3.60) seniors, C$3 (US$2.40) children 6–17, C$11–C$15 (US$8.40–US$12) families; free admission Wed nights. June to mid-Oct Mon–Sat 9:30am–5:30pm (Wed until 8pm), Sun 1–5:30pm; mid-Oct to May Tues–Sat 9:30am–5pm (Wed until 8pm), Sun 1–5pm.

**Province House**   Canada's oldest seat of government, Province House has been home to the Nova Scotian legislature since 1819. This exceptional Georgian building is a superb example of the rigorously symmetrical Palladian style. And like a jewel box, its dour stone exterior hides gems of ornamental detailing and artwork inside; note especially the fine plasterwork, rare for a Canadian building of this era. A well-written free booklet is available when you enter, and provides helpful background about the building's history and architecture. If the legislature is in session, you can obtain a visitor's pass and sit up in the gallery and watch the business of the province take place.

Within the building also roost a number of fine stories. My favorite: the headless falcons in several rooms. It's said they were decapitated by an agitated legislator with a free-swinging cane who mistook them for eagles during a period of feverish anti-American sentiment in the 1840s. History buffs should allow an hour for this visit.

1776 Hollis St. (near Prince St.). ⓒ **902/424-4661**. Free admission. July–Aug Mon–Fri 9am–5pm, Sat–Sun and holidays 10am–4pm; rest of year Mon–Fri 9am–4pm.

**St. Paul's Anglican Church** ⓕ   Forming one end of the Grand Parade, St. Paul's was the first Anglican cathedral established outside of England and is Canada's oldest Protestant place of worship. Part of the building, which dates from 1750, was fabricated in Boston and erected in Halifax with the help of a royal endowment from King George II. A classic white Georgian building, St. Paul's has fine stained-glass windows. A piece of flying debris from the explosion of 1917 (see "Maritime Museum of the Atlantic," above) is lodged in the wall over the doors to the nave. Just a quick drop in is enough to get a sense of the place; take one of the summer-only guided tours if you want to see more.

1749 Argyle St. (on the Grand Parade near Barrington St.). ⓒ **902/429-2240**. Mon–Fri 9am–4:30pm; Sun services 8, 9:15, and 11am. Free guided tours June–Aug Mon–Sat.

## GARDENS & OPEN SPACE
**Fairview Lawn Cemetery** ⓕ   When the *Titanic* went down April 15, 1912, nearly 2,000 people died. Ship captains from Halifax were recruited to help retrieve the corpses (you'll learn about this grim episode at the Maritime Museum, described above). Some 121 victims, mostly crewmembers, were buried at this quiet cemetery located a short drive north of downtown Halifax. Some of the simple graves have names; others just numbers. Interpretive signs highlight some of the stories that survived the tragedy. A brochure with driving directions to this and two other *Titanic* cemeteries may be found at the Maritime Museum and visitor information centers. It's definitely worth an hour or more for *Titanic* fans; others might just spend a few minutes here.

Chisholm Ave., off Connaught Ave. ⓒ **902/490-4883**. Daylight hours year-round.

**McNab's Island**   This island wilderness is located within city limits near the mouth of the harbor, and it's a world apart from downtown Halifax. Once part of the city's military defenses and later the site of a popular amusement park, McNab's hasn't had any permanent residents since 1985. You'll find miles of wooded roads and trails to explore, some 200 species of birds, and great views of the city skyline and Point

Pleasant. Fort McNab at the island's south tip dates from 1888, and it was manned during both world wars in this century. All ships visiting the harbor were required to signal the fort. Those that failed to comply were warned with a shot across the bow. Bring a picnic (and a ferry schedule) and plan to spend 2 hours or so.

Halifax Harbor. ℂ 902/465-4563 (ferry service). Admission free; ferry C$18 (US$15) round-trip adult, C$16 (US$13) senior and children 5–17.

**Old Burying Ground**    This was the first burial ground in Halifax, and between 1749 and 1844 some 12,000 people were interred here. (Only 1 in 10 graves is marked with a headstone, however.) You'll find wonderful examples of 18th- and 19th-century gravestone art—especially winged heads and winged skulls. (No rubbings allowed.) Also exceptional is the Welsford-Parker Monument (1855) near the grounds' entrance, which honors Nova Scotians who fought in the Crimean War. This ornate statue features a lion with an unruly Medusa-like mane. The grounds are imbued with a quiet grace a couple of hours before sunset, when the light slants magically through the trees and the traffic seems far away. The cemetery was fully restored in 1991. Cemetery buffs could spend an hour or more; others can easily drop by for 10 minutes en route to downtown attractions or eateries.

Corner of Spring Garden and Barrington. ℂ 902/429-2240. Free admission. June–Sept 9am–5pm; guides until late Aug. Closed rest of year.

**Point Pleasant Park** 🐾    Point Pleasant is one of Canada's finer urban parks, and there's no better place for a walk along the water on a balmy day. This 74-hectare (186-acre) park occupies a wooded peninsular point, and it served for years as one of the linchpins in the city's military defense. You'll find the ruins of early forts and a nicely preserved Martello tower. Halifax has a 999-year lease from Great Britain for the park, for which it pays 1 shilling—about US10¢—per year. You'll also find a lovely gravel carriage road around the point, a small swimming beach, miles of walking trails, and groves of graceful fir trees. The park is located about 2km (1¼ miles) south of the Public Gardens. No bikes are allowed on weekends or holidays.

Point Pleasant Dr. (south end of Halifax). Free admission. Daylight hours. Head south on S. Park St. near Public Gardens and continue on Young.

**Public Gardens** 🐾🐾 *Kids*    The Public Gardens literally took seed in 1753, when they were founded as a private garden. It was acquired by the Nova Scotia Horticultural Society in 1836, and it assumed its present look in 1875, during the peak of the Victorian era. As such, the garden is one of the nation's Victorian masterpieces, more rare and evocative than any mansard-roofed mansion. You'll find wonderful examples of many 19th-century trends in outdoor landscaping, from the "natural" winding walks and ornate fountains to the duck ponds and fussy Victorian bandstand. (Stop by at 2pm on Sun in summer for a free concert.) There are lots of leafy trees, lush lawns, cranky ducks who have long since lost their fear of humans, and tiny ponds. The overseers have been commendably stingy with memorial statues and plaques. You'll usually find dowagers and kids feeding pigeons, and smartly uniformed guards slowly walking the grounds.

Spring Garden and S. Park St. Free admission. Spring to late fall 8am–dusk.

## BOAT TOURS

**Murphy's on the Water** (ℂ 902/420-1015) runs two daily boats from Cable Wharf in downtown Halifax daily in summer for C$16 (US$14) and up round-trip. A faster (and less expensive) route is to drive to Eastern Passage (south of Dartmouth), park free at Government Wharf, and take the **McNab's Island Ferry** (✆ **800/326-4563** or 902/465-4563). For the brief trip, the captain charges C$10 (US$8) adults, C$8 (US$5) ages 4 to 15, free for children under 4, and there's no extra charge for bikes or dogs.

## SHOPPING

Halifax has a pleasing mix of shops, from mainstream retailers to offbeat boutiques. There's no central retail district to speak of; shops are scattered throughout downtown. Two indoor malls are located near the Grand Parade—**Scotia Square Mall** and **Barrington Place Shops,** flanking Barrington Street near the intersection of Duke Street. Another downtown mall, the 85-shop **Park Lane Shopping Centre,** is on Spring Garden Road about 1 block from the Public Gardens.

For souvenir shopping, head to the Historic Properties buildings on the waterfront; for idle browsing, try the shops on and around Spring Garden Road between Brunswick Street and South Park Street.

**Almanac Used Furniture and Antiques**   A classic, old-fashioned antiques shop crammed to the eaves with everything from bureaus to barber chairs, the Almanac is a short drive from downtown. 2810 Windsor St. ✆ **902/455-1141.**

**Ambience Home Accents**   This home furnishings store features neoclassical and faux-Continental items, most with a funky twist. Look for chairs, wrought-iron wall fixtures, lamps, and candle stands. 5431 Doyle St. ✆ **902/423-9200.**

**Art Gallery of Nova Scotia Shop**   The museum's gift shops feature limited but choice selections of local crafts, ranging from creative postcards to birdhouses and tabletop sculptures. There's also work by Mi'kmaq artisans. 1723 Hollis St. ✆ **902/424-1203.**

**Drala Asian Books & Gifts**   This serene shop specializes in Asian imports, including pottery, incense, calligraphy materials, paper screens, chopsticks, and books on Asian design and philosophy. Weekly classes teach meditation and Japanese tea ceremony. 1567 Grafton St. ✆ **902/422-2504.**

**Geddes Furniture and Antiques**   Elegant and formal mahogany reproduction Chippendale and Queen Anne pieces, including dining room chairs and highboys, are the specialty at this shop, which is filled with lovely pieces priced for less than you might expect. Delivery trucks travel to the northeastern United States regularly. 2739 Agricola St. ✆ **902/454-7171.**

**Janet Doble Pottery Studio**   Doble's bright and festive pottery is inspired by European majolica; anything purchased here is certain to brighten a drab kitchen. Note that hours are quirky, as befits a working artist. 2641 Fuller Terrace. ✆ **902/455-6960.**

**Thornbloom, The Inspired Home**   This tidy shop in a small indoor mall on Spring Garden features housewares, knives by Henckels, good bed linens, and intriguing tile "memory blocks" by Vancouver-based Sid Dickens. 5640 Spring Garden Rd. ✆ **902/425-8005.**

**Urban Cottage**   This consignment store in the middle of downtown has an eclectic and sizable selection of stuff, including furniture, housewares, and collectibles, nicely displayed and generally reasonably priced. 1819 Granville St. ✆ **902/423-3010.**

## WHERE TO STAY
### EXPENSIVE
**Cambridge Suites** ☆ 𝕂𝕚𝕕𝕤   The attractive, modern Cambridge Suites is nicely located near the foot of the Citadel and is well positioned for exploring Halifax. It's

perfect for families—40 of the units are two-room suites featuring kitchenettes with microwaves, two phones, coffeemakers, and hair dryers. Expect comfortable, inoffensive decor, and above-average service; everything in the place was freshened up in 2001, too. Dofsky's Grill on the first floor is open for all three meals, which are palatable if not exciting. Look for pasta, blackened haddock, burgers, and jerked chicken.

1583 Brunswick St., Halifax, NS B3J 3P5. (© 888/417-8483 or 902/420-0555. Fax 902/420-9379. www.cambridge-suiteshalifax.com. 200 units. C$139–C$299 (US$111–US$239) suite. Children under 18 stay free in parent's room. AE, DC, MC, V. Parking C$11 (US$9). **Amenities:** Restaurant; health club; Jacuzzi; sauna; concierge; room service; babysitting; coin-op laundry; dry cleaning. *In room:* A/C, TV, dataport, kitchenette (some units), minibar, fridge (some units), coffeemaker, hair dryer, iron.

## Delta Barrington ☆

Convenience and location form the cornerstones of the Delta Barrington, located just 1 block from the waterfront and 1 block from the Grand Parade, and connected to the Metro Centre and much of the rest of downtown by a covered walkway. It's a modern, large hotel, but one that has been designed and furnished with an eye more to comfort than to flash. The guest rooms are decorated with a contemporary country decor, with pine headboards and country-style reproduction furniture. The king rooms are spacious, furnished with sofas and easy chairs. Some rooms face the pedestrian plaza and have been soundproofed to block the noise from the evening rabble, but these windows don't open (most other rooms have opening windows). The quietest rooms face the courtyard but lack a view. The hotel restaurant, the Stone Street Café, serves an attractive upscale menu of rosemary-crusted lamb loin with balsamic-fig reduction, oven-roasted pork tenderloin with an apple compote, lobster spring rolls with Thai dipping sauce, pecan crème brûlée, and the like.

1875 Barrington St., Halifax, NS B3J 3L6. (© 877/814-7706 or 902/429-7410. Fax 902/420-6524. www.delta barrington.com. 200 units. C$129–C$289 (US$103–US$231) double. AE, DC, DISC, MC, V. Valet parking C$16 (US$11). Small pets allowed. **Amenities:** Restaurant; indoor pool; Jacuzzi; sauna; children's programs; concierge; room service; babysitting; laundry service; dry cleaning. *In room:* A/C, TV, dataport, minibar, coffeemaker, hair dryer, iron.

## Delta Halifax ☆

The Delta Halifax (formerly the Hotel Halifax, more formerly the Chateau Halifax) is a slick and modern (built in 1972) downtown hotel that offers premium service. It's located just a block off the waterfront, to which it's connected via skyway, but navigating it involves an annoying labyrinth of parking garages and charmless concrete structures. The lobby is street-side; guests take elevators up above a six-floor parking garage to reach their rooms. The hotel is frequented largely by business travelers during the week. Ask for a room in the so-called "resort wing" near the pool, which feels a bit further away from the chatter of downtown and the press of business. A number of rooms have balconies and many have harbor views; ask when you book. Rooms are in two classes—either 300 or 500 square feet—and all are furnished simply and unexceptionally with standard-issue hotel furniture. The Crown Bistrot restaurant offers informal Continental cuisine, while Sam Slick's Lounge next door is "cigar friendly."

1990 Barrington St., Halifax, NS B3J 1P2. (© 877/814-7706 or 902/425-6700. Fax 902/425-6214. www.deltahalifax. com. 297 units. C$129–C$289 (US$103–US$231) double. AE, MC, V. **Amenities:** Restaurant; bar; indoor pool; health club; Jacuzzi; sauna; concierge; car-rental desk; shopping arcade; limited room service; babysitting; laundry service; dry cleaning. *In room:* A/C, TV, dataport, minibar, coffeemaker, hair dryer, iron.

## Halliburton House Inn ☆

The Halliburton House is a well-appointed, well-run, and elegant country inn located in the heart of downtown. Named after former resident Sir Brenton Halliburton (Nova Scotia's 1st chief justice), the inn is spread among three town house–style buildings, which are connected via gardens and sun decks in the rear but not internally. The main building was constructed in 1809 and was converted to an inn in 1995, when it was modernized without any loss of its native charm. All guest rooms are subtly furnished with fine antiques, but few are so rare that you'd fret about damaging them. The rooms are rich and masculine in tone, and light on frilly stuff. Among my favorites: Room 113, which is relatively small but has a lovely working fireplace and unique skylighted bathroom. Rooms 102 and 109 are both suites with wet bars and fireplaces; there's also one studio apartment. Halliburton is popular with business travelers, but it's also a romantic spot for couples. The intimate **first-floor dining room** ⋇, which serves from 5:30 nightly, is dusky and wonderful with a menu that's small and inventive. The seafood is always reliable.

5184 Morris St., Halifax, NS B3J 1B3. © **902/420-0658.** Fax 902/423-2324. www.halliburton.ns.ca. 29 units. C$145–C$350 (US$116–US$280) double; off-season rates cheaper. All rates include continental breakfast and parking (limited). AE, MC, V. **Amenities:** Restaurant, room service; babysitting; dry cleaning. In room: A/C, TV, coffeemaker, hair dryer.

### The Lord Nelson Hotel and Suites ⋇
The Lord Nelson was built in 1928, and was for years the city's preeminent hostelry. It gradually sank in esteem and eventually ended up as a flophouse. In 1998, it was purchased and received a long-overdue top-to-bottom renovation. It certainly has location going for it: It's right across from the lovely Public Gardens and abuts lively Spring Garden Road. Rooms are furnished with Georgian reproductions. The business-class Flagship Rooms feature desks, ergonomic office chairs, robes, free local calls, and morning newspapers. The hotel charges a premium for a room that faces the street or the gardens, but it's worth it; others face into a rather bleak courtyard filled with service equipment. The Victory Arms is a cozy and convincing English-style pub located off the handsome coffered lobby. There's British pub fare like steak and kidney pie, fish and chips, and liver with bacon and onions, along with a daily roast.

1515 South Park St., Halifax, NS B3J 2L2. © **800/565-2020** or 902/423-6331. Fax 902/491-6148. www.lordnelson hotel.com. 260 units. C$139–C$259 (US$111–US$207) double. AE, DC, DISC, MC, V. Pets allowed with C$100 (US$80) deposit. **Amenities:** Restaurant; bar; health club; sauna; concierge; limited room service; babysitting; laundry; dry cleaning. In room: A/C, TV, coffeemaker, hair dryer, iron.

### Prince George Hotel ⋇
This contemporary and large downtown hotel features understated styling, polished wainscoting, carpeting, and the discreet use of marble; everything was renovated in 2000, though it stills feels a bit sterile and stuffy. In any case, expect modern and comfortably appointed rooms, most with balconies and all with a selection of complimentary tea and coffee, coffeemakers, and hair dryers. This hotel is nicely situated near the Citadel and restaurants and is linked to much of the rest of downtown via underground passageways; parking is beneath the hotel. The hotel's Georgio's restaurant on the first floor features contemporary bistro styling, with a menu to match: Dinners include pasta, pizza, and sandwiches, as well as more upscale offerings, including seared lemon haddock, tile of halibut, and curried maple-glazed chicken.

1725 Market St., Halifax, NS B3J 3N9. © **800/565-1567** or 902/425-1986. Fax 902/429-6048. www.princegeorge-hotel.com. 203 units. C$149–C$299 (US$119–US$239) double. AE, DC, DISC, MC, V. Parking C$14 (US$10). **Amenities:** Restaurant; indoor pool; Jacuzzi; sauna; concierge; business center; limited room service; massage; babysitting; laundry; dry cleaning. In room: A/C, TV, dataport, minibar, coffeemaker, hair dryer, iron.

## MODERATE
### Halifax Waverley Inn ⋇
The Waverley is adorned in high Victorian style, as befits its 1866 provenance. Flamboyant playwright Oscar Wilde was a guest in 1882, and

one suspects he had a hand in the decorating scheme. There's walnut trim, red uphol-stered furniture, and portraits of sourpuss Victorians at every turn. The headboards in the guest rooms are especially elaborate—some look like props from Gothic horror movies. Room 130 has a unique Chinese wedding bed and a Jacuzzi (nine rooms have private Jacuzzis). Newly added is a two-bedroom suite in an annex; with its own kitchen and laundry, it's good for families or extended stays. There's a common deck on which to enjoy sunny afternoons; a first-floor hospitality room stocks complimentary snacks and beverages for guests.

1266 Barrington St., Halifax, NS B3J 1Y5. ☎ 800/565-9346 or 902/423-9346. Fax 902/425-0167. www.waverleyinn. com. 34 units. June–Oct C$119–C$239 (US$95–US$191) double. Rates include continental breakfast, snacks, after-noon tea, and parking. DC, MC, V. *In room:* A/C, TV, hair dryer.

### Howard Johnson Maranova Hotel and Suites *(Value) (Kids)*    Located across the har-bor from Halifax and a 2-minute walk to frequent ferry service to downtown, the Maranova Suites is one of the better options for travelers on a ginger-ale budget. Housed in a modern concrete building, it features rooms that are large and tidy. All guest rooms have sitting areas, kitchenettes, and balconies, and two penthouse suites come with full kitchens. Don't expect anything fancy; the rooms are basic, simple, and clean. Some have wonderful views of the harbor—ask when you book.

65 King St., Dartmouth, NS B2Y 4C2. ☎ 888/561-7666 or 902/463-9520. Fax 902/463-2631. www.maranovasuites. com. 84 units. C$110–C$350 (US$88–US$280) double. AE, DC, MC, V. Underground parking available. **Amenities:** Restaurant; laundry; dry cleaning. *In room:* A/C, TV, kitchenette, coffeemaker, hair dryer, iron.

### INEXPENSIVE
The 75-bed **Halifax Heritage House Hostel** (☎ 902/422-3863) is located at 1253 Barrington St., within walking distance of downtown attractions. You'll usually share rooms with other travelers (several private and family rooms are available); there are lockers in each room, shared bathrooms, and a shared, fully equipped kitchen. Rates are C$19 (US$15) and up per person in dormitories, C$50 (C$40) for a double bed in a private room.

A short way from downtown but convenient to bus lines are university dorm rooms open to travelers during the summer, when school isn't in session. **Dalhousie University** (☎ 902/494-8840) has one-, two-, and three-bedroom units furnished with plain single beds, many with private bathrooms and kitchenettes (you rent the dishes for a small fee). Single rooms begin at C$39 (US$31), double rooms at C$61 (US$49).

## WHERE TO DINE
Coffee emporia have cropped up throughout Halifax in the last couple of years, as they have in urban areas everywhere. Many also stock sandwiches, pastries and light snacks in addition to the java. A few of the best downtown options are **Caffé Ristretto** (☎ 902/425-3087) at 1475 Lower Water St. (Bishop Landing) with its nice harbor views; **Timothy's World Coffee,** which has locations at Spring Garden Road, Barrington Street, and Upper Water Street; **Cabin Coffee** (☎ 902/422-8130) at 1554 Hollis St. with its Bohemian feel and good espresso and cappuccino; and **Amadeus Café** (☎ 902/423-0032) and the dependable chain **Second Cup** (☎ 902/429-0883) on Spring Garden Road.

For chain fast-food meals (if you must), again stick to Spring Garden Road. For a quick snack on the same street, the plastic patio furniture outside belies the good snacks, pastries, coffees, teas, and light meals inside **Annie's Place** (☎ 902/420-0098) at 1513 Birmingham St. (corner of Spring Garden); outstanding bargain lunch specials include changing offerings such as a slab of grilled meat loaf on focaccia. For more upscale fare, explore downtown, or some of the tiny side streets that cross Spring Garden.

**The Brewery** 🎇 complex, on the uphill side of Lower Water Street just above the docks, is perhaps the city's most interesting one-stop shopping and dining experience. Originally the site of the Alexander Keith brewery, North America's oldest, the space was eventually redesigned and renovated to enclose some courtyards from the weather, link up the various structures of the brewery, and create a kind of interior market of shops and restaurants. Today the complex houses the city's finest Italian restaurant, as well as a range of other drinking, dining, and shopping options. While navigating its labyrinthine courtyards to find a particular establishment can be a bit confusing, it's also great fun to see what pops up around the next corner.

The Saturday morning **farmer's market** 🎇 held within the Brewery's walls is a weekly highlight for local Haligonians, rain or shine. It's Canada's oldest—and possibly its most interesting—such market. The market runs between 7am and 1pm each Saturday, but come early in the day for the widest selection of donuts, fruits, vegetables, coffee, baked goods, smoked meats, crafts, Greek pastries, wine and chocolate samples, and dynamite crepes—among many other items.

## EXPENSIVE

**Bish World Cuisine** 🎇 FUSION   Maurizio strikes again! The culinary wizard behind the deservedly popular daMaurizio (see below) in The Brewery Market, has daringly opened a second high-tone eatery—practically across the street from the other one—and, against the odds in a tough economic moment, it's already supplanting his original fine dining establishment as the "in" place to paint this town red. Tucked into a harborside location at the back of the upscale Bishop's Landing development (hence the name—I think), this place combines Asian and Continental influences to fine effect much like a hot young upstart in Manhattan might do. Exhibit A: appetizers and first courses of Thai roasted chicken and coconut soup, dim sum, fish stew, goat cheese salad, duck confit, smoked salmon, foie gras, and the like. Exhibit B: main courses such as a lobster-tasting course, rack of lamb with ratatouille, roasted halibut wrapped in rice paper, basil, and coconut, Serrano ham-crusted tuna, tandoori organic chicken breast with spinach samosa, or a ginger-lacquered barbecued pork tenderloin with shiitake yakisoba and a tempura-style fried apple. Finish it off with ice cream creations, sorbets, pastries, creme caramel, clafouti, a seasonal berry-mint salad, semifreddo, or perhaps a hot milk chocolate pudding with Irish caramel sauce. The water views, professional service, and fine bar and wine list only enhance the experience of having temporarily traded in New Scotland for New York. Dress smartly, expect Halifax's finest to be out in force on the weekends, and reserve early in anticipation of that fact.

1475 Lower Water St. (In Bishop's Landing, entrance at end of Bishop St.). 🕿 **902/425-7993**. Reservations highly recommended. Main courses C$28–C$30 (US$22–US$24). AE, DC, MC, V. Mon–Sat 5–10pm.

**daMaurizio** 🎇 ITALIAN   daMaurizio does everything right. Located in a cleverly adapted former brewery, the vast space has been divided into a complex of hives with columns and exposed brick that add to the atmosphere and heighten the anticipation of the meal. The decor shuns decorative doodads for clean lines and simple class. Much the same might be said of the menu. You could start with an appetizer of squid quick-fried with olive oil, tomato, and chiles or order ravioli with sausage. The main courses tax even the most decisive of diners: there's pasta with lobster, leeks, white wine, cream, and fresh ginger; gnocchi with Bolognese sauce; pumpkin ravioli with citrus and roasted duck sauce; pasta with king crab and mascarpone, drizzled with curry sauce; a variety of scallopine variations; pan-seared scallops with chili and port sauce; or a whole lobster, gratinéed with sweet peppers, onions, brandy, and cream, among many other inspired choices. Desserts run beyond tiramisu and gelati to cake, panna cotta, a fruit, nut, and cheese plate, and tartufo: a molded almond gelato, filled with chocolate and topped with crumbled amaretti and sided with creme anglaise and a chocolate ganache. The kitchen doesn't try to dazzle with outlandish creativity but rather relies instead on the best ingredients and a close eye on perfect preparation.

1496 Lower Water St. (in The Brewery). ℂ 902/423-0859. Reservations highly recommended. Main courses C$28–C$30 (US$22–US$24); pasta dishes C$10–C$16 (US$8–US$13). AE, DC, MC, V. Mon–Sat 5–10pm.

## MODERATE

**O'Carroll's Restaurant and Lounge** SEAFOOD   O'Carroll's is one of the best options for a fulfilling seafood meal in Halifax. It's a dusky, Gaelic-influenced spot on Water Street across from Historic Properties. It's fancier than the average fish house, with white tablecloths, potted plants, and stained-glass lamps on the tables. The kitchen takes a rather creative slant to seafood, with global offerings such as curries and Thai-spiced seafood mingling with more traditional fare including finnan haddie (smoked haddock) and simply prepared salmon. Nonseafood options include duck, filet mignon, and steak-and-kidney pie. There's sometimes live Celtic music in the lounge, and you can order off a lighter bar menu until late.

1860 Upper Water St. ℂ 902/423-4405. Reservations recommended. Main courses C$7.50–C$15 (US$6–US$12) at lunch, C$18–C$29 (US$15–US$23) at dinner. AE, MC, V. Restaurant daily 11am–2:30pm and 5–11pm; pub daily 11am–11pm; weekend hours may vary.

**Ryan Duffy's Steak and Seafood** ℱ STEAKHOUSE   Located on the upper level of a small shopping mall on Spring Garden, Ryan Duffy's may at first strike diners as a knockoff of a middlebrow chain, like T.G.I. Friday's. It's not. It's a couple of notches above. The house specialty is steak, for which the place is justly famous. The beef comes from corn-fed Hereford, Black Angus, and Shorthorn, and it is nicely tender. (When the waiter delivered me an oversize steak knife, he said, "You don't really need this, but it's all part of the show.") Steaks are grilled over a natural wood charcoal and can be prepared with garlic, cilantro butter, or other extras upon request. The more expensive cuts, such as the strip loin, are trimmed right at the table. If you move away from steak on the menu, expect less consistency—the shrimp cocktail is disappointing; the Caesar salad is wonderful. Americans who are disappointed that they can't order rare steak much anymore owing to liability concerns will like it here—you can even order it "blue-rare."

5640 Spring Garden Rd. ℂ 902/421-1116. Reservations recommended. Main courses C$9–C$15 (US$7–US$12) at lunch, C$16–C$28 (US$13–US$23) at dinner. AE, DC, MC, V. Mon–Fri 11:30am–2pm and 5–10pm; Sat–Sun 5–10pm.

**Sweet Basil Bistro** ℱℱ UPMARKET PASTA   If hunger overtakes you while you're snooping around the waterfront's shopping district, this should be your destination. It has the casual feel of a favorite trattoria, but the menu transcends the limited regional offerings that implies. Pastas are well represented, but you'll also find seared scallops with five-spice broth and Asian vegetables, crusted lamb chops with a demi-glace, and a selection of stir-fries. The chef somehow manages to meld Thai cuisine, Italian pasta, cream sauces, and fusion seafood without going overboard, resulting in truly interesting creations such as a seared-tuna salad appetizer of fish, yellow beans, daikon radish, and an egg crepe; a seared pork cutlet entree in sun-dried tomato-and-Calvados sauce, sided with sweetened potatoes and caramelized apples. Desserts such as a maple panna cotta with chocolate spice cake, florentines with vanilla bean custard, or a chocolate fondue pot for two make a perfect conclusion.

1866 Upper Water St. ℂ 902/425-2133. Reservations recommended. Sandwiches C$8–C$15 (US$6.50–US$12); pastas C$9.95–C$11 (US$8–US$9); main courses C$15–C$19 (US$12–US$15). AE, DC, MC, V. Daily 11:30am–9:30pm.

## INEXPENSIVE

**Cheapside Café** *(Value) (Kids)* CAFE    The cheerful and lively Cheapside Café is tucked inside the Provincial Building, one of two structures housing the Art Gallery of Nova Scotia. A whole groaning board of sandwiches and other delectables features choices like chicken breast with avocado and mango chutney, roast beef with fried onions, and smoked salmon served with an egg pancake and asparagus. Other fare includes fish cakes, quiche, and poached salmon with sun-dried tomato chutney. For kids, there's peanut butter and jelly and egg salad with carrot sticks. Desserts are delicious—especially notable is the Cheapside Café Torte.

1723 Hollis St. (inside the Art Gallery of Nova Scotia). ℂ 902/425-4494. Sandwiches and entrees C$8.95–C$11 (US$7–US$9). MC, V. Tues–Sat 10am–5pm; Sun noon–5pm.

**Cheelin** *(Finds)* CHINESE    The city's best Chinese restaurant, Cheelin manages to achieve a seemingly improbable balance between authentic Asian cuisine—as evidenced in such normally hard-to-find dishes as *mapo* tofu (spicy tofu, cubed and stir-fried, often mixed with ground pork or beef) and *yu xiang* pork (pork with Szechwan sauce, usually made from some combination of ginger, garlic, sesame, vinegar, or fish flavoring)—and a funkier, Haligonian vibe (the brightly painted interior, hip young staff and crowd, and dishes such as scallops paired with mango sauce). Despite the low prices, this is definitely not a hole-in-the-wall Chinese eatery. Go for Hunan haddock, the excellent vegetable spring rolls, orange beef, shredded pork with bitter melon, or a daily special such as peppery mala shrimp with sautéed bok choy and squash. They also deliver to the downtown area—good to know when you're hungry late at night.

1496 Lower Water St. (inside The Brewery). ℂ 902/422-2252. Main courses C$7.50–C$12 (US$6–US$9.50). AE, MC, V. Mon 11am–2:30pm; Tues–Sat 11am–2:30pm and 5:30–10pm; Sun 5:30–10pm.

**Henry House** *(Finds)* BREWPUB    Eastern Canada's pioneer brewpub—this was the first—is housed in an austere building far down Barrington Street. The starkly handsome 1834 stone building has a medium-fancy dining room upstairs with red tablecloths and captains' chairs. (The pub downstairs is more boisterous and informal.) You can order off the same menu at either spot, and it's what you'd expect at a brewpub, only better-tasting: Entrees include beer-battered fish, steak sandwiches, an excellent smoked salmon club sandwich, burgers, beef-and-beer stew, salads, and meatloaf. The beer here is fresh and good; they also do Sunday brunches.

1222 Barrington St. ℂ 902/423-5660. Main courses C$7–C$14 (US$5.50–US$11). AE, DC, MC, V. Mon–Sat 11:30am–12:30am; Sun noon–11pm.

**Il Mercato** *(Finds)* NORTHERN ITALIAN    Light-colored Tuscan sponged walls and big rustic terra-cotta tiles on the floor set an appropriate mood at this popular spot amid the clamor of Spring Garden. Come early or late or expect to wait a bit (no reservations accepted), but it's worth making the effort. You'll find a great selection of meals at prices that approach bargain level. Start by selecting antipasti from the deli counter in the front (you point; the waitstaff will bring them to your table). The focaccias are superb and come with a pleasing salad, while the ravioli with roast chicken and wild mushrooms is sublime. Non-Italian entrees include a seafood medley and grilled strip loin with wild mushroom sauce. For dessert, repeat the antipasto routine: Head to the counter and ogle the luscious offerings under glass, then point and sit, awaiting a fine gelato finale. Just passing by? Order a cone or dish to go.

5560 Spring Garden Rd. (C) 902/422-2866. Reservations not accepted. Main courses C$10–C$17 (US$8–US$14). AE, DC, MC, V. Mon–Sat 11am–11pm.

**Satisfaction Feast** VEGETARIAN  Located along the newly cool stretch of Grafton Street, Satisfaction Feast, Halifax's original vegetarian restaurant (it turns 25 in 2006), has been voted one of the top 10 veggie restaurants in Canada by the *Globe and Mail*. It's funky and fun, with a certain spare grace inside and a canopy and sidewalk tables for summer lounging. Entrees include lasagna, bean burritos, pesto pasta, veggie burgers, and a macrobiotic rice casserole. There's also "neatloaf" and tofu-and-rice based "peace burgers" for those who like their food with cute names. The vegan fruit crisp is the dessert to hold out for. They also do takeout; consider a hummus-and-pita picnic atop nearby Citadel Hill.

1581 Grafton St. (C) 902/422-3540. Main courses C$5–C$12 (US$4–US$9.50). AE, DC, MC, V. Daily 11am–10pm (winter until 8:30 or 9pm).

**Steve-O-Reno's** *Value* CAFE  Tucked off Spring Garden, this coffee shop is also a popular lunch stop for locals. You'll have your choice of potent coffee and coffeelike beverages (such as chai tea latte), along with inventive fruit smoothies, a small selection of sandwiches and salads, and a pleasantly relaxed atmosphere. They do everything well and inexpensively, and the hip young staff is as friendly and cheerful as can be. There's now a second location on Robie Street as well.

1536 Brunswick St. (C) 902/429-3034. Meals C$4–C$6 (US$3.20–US$5). No credit cards. Mon–Sat 7:30am–6pm; Sun 8am–6pm.

## HALIFAX BY NIGHT

For starters, stop by the visitor center or the front desk of your hotel and ask for a copy of *Where Halifax,* a comprehensive monthly guide to the city's entertainment. Among the city's premier venues for shows are the downtown **Halifax Metro Centre,** 1800 Argyle St. ((C) **902/451-1221** or 902/451-8000), which hosts sporting events and concerts by a wide variety of artists.

### PERFORMING ARTS

**Shakespeare by the Sea** ((C) **902/422-0295**) stages a whole line of Bardic and non-Bardic productions July through August at several alfresco venues around the city. Most are held at Point Pleasant Park, where the ruins of old forts and buildings are used as the stage settings for delightful performances, with the audience sprawled on the grass, many enjoying picnic dinners. Most shows ask for a suggested donation of C$10 (US$7). The more elaborate productions (past shows have included *King Lear* at the Citadel and *Titus Andronicus* at the park's Martello Tower) have limited seating, with tickets ranging up to C$30 (US$21).

   **The Neptune Theatre,** 1593 Argyle St. ((C) **902/429-7070**), benefited from a C$13.5 million (US$10.8 million) renovation and now also includes an intimate

## A Road Trip to Peggy's Cove

About 42km (26 miles) southwest of Halifax is the picturesque fishing village of **Peggy's Cove** 🎣🎣 (pop. 120). The village offers a postcard-perfect tableau: an octagonal lighthouse (surely one of the most photographed in the world), tiny fishing shacks, and graceful fishing boats bobbing in the postage stamp–size harbor. The bonsai-like perfection hasn't gone unnoticed by the big tour operators, however, so it's a rare summer day when you're not sharing the experience with a few hundred of your close, personal bus-tour friends. The village is home to a handful of B&Bs and a gallery, but scenic values draw the day-trippers with cameras and lots of film. While there, make sure to check out the touching **Swissair Flight 111 Memorial** 🎣 among the rocks just before the turnoff to the cove; this site memorializes the passengers of that flight, which crashed into the Atlantic just off this coast. Want to stay awhile? One good lodging choice in the area is **Peggy's Cove B&B** (📞 800/SALT-SEA or 902/423-1102; www.nsinns.com), a three-bedroom restored fisherman's home close to the lighthouse. If it's full, **West Dover Seaside Cottages** (same phone numbers and website), less than 3km (2 miles) away, consists of a red boathouse on stilts plus cottages with kitchens, barbeques, and picnic tables. Rooms at both go for C$85 to C$205 (US$68–US$164) per night.

---

200-seat studio theater. Top-notch dramatic productions are offered throughout the year. (The main season runs September through May, with a summer season filling in the gap with eclectic performances.) Main-stage tickets range from C$15 to C$46 (US$12–US$37).

For a more informal dramatic night out, there's the **Grafton Street Dinner Theater,** 1741 Grafton St. (📞 **902/425-1961**), which typically offers light musicals and mysteries with a three-course dinner (choice of prime rib, salmon, or chicken).

### CLUB & BAR SCENE

The young and restless tend to congregate in pubs, in nightclubs, and at street corners along two axes that converge at the public library: Grafton Street and Spring Garden Road. If you're thirsty, wander the neighborhoods around here, and you're likely to find a spot that could serve as a temporary home for the evening. One of the coolest places to hang out is **Economy Shoe Shop** (📞 **902/423-7463**) at 1663 Argyle St., not a shop but rather a cafe-bar where many of Halifax's pretty people show up sooner or later. In the evening (and late afternoons on Sat), you'll also find lively maritime music and good beer at the **Lower Deck** (📞 **902/425-1501**), one of the popular restaurants in the Historic Properties complex on the waterfront. There's music nightly, and often on Saturday afternoons. Among the clubs offering local rock, ska, and the like are the **Marquee Club,** 2041 Gottingen St. (📞 **902/423-2072**) and **The Attic,** 1741 Grafton St. (📞 **902/423-0909**). **Maxwell's Plum** at 1600 Grafton St. (📞 **902/423-5090**) is a free-for-all English pub where peanut shells litter the floor and there are dozens upon dozens of selections of import and Canadian draft and bottled beers. Happy-hour specials run about C$2.50 (US$2) a bottle for a selected import each night.

Check *The Coast,* Halifax's free weekly newspaper (widely available), for listings of upcoming performances.

## 9 The Eastern Shore

Heading from Halifax toward Cape Breton Island (or vice versa), you have to choose between two basic routes. If you're burning to get to your destination, take the main roads of Route 102 connecting to Route 104 (the Trans-Canada Hwy.). If you're in no particular hurry and are most content venturing down narrow lanes, destination unknown, by all means allow a couple of days to wind along the Eastern Shore, mostly along Route 7. Along the way you'll be rewarded with glimpses of a rugged coastline that's wilder and more remote than the coast south of Halifax. Communities tend to be farther apart, less genteel, and those that you come upon have fewer services and fewer tourists. With its rugged terrain and remote locales, this region is a good bet for those drawn to the outdoors and seeking coastal solitude.

Be forewarned that the Eastern Shore isn't always breathtakingly scenic if you limit yourself to the main road. You'll drive through cutover woodlands and past scrappy towns. To get the most out of the Eastern Shore, you should be committed to making periodic detours, the more impetuous the better. Wander down dead-end roads to coastal peninsulas, where you might come upon wild roses blooming madly in the fog, or inland to the persistent forest, home of moose and sudden dusk.

### ESSENTIALS

**GETTING THERE**    Route 107 and Route 7 run along or near the coast from Dartmouth to Stillwater (near Sherbrooke). A patchwork of other routes—including 211, 316, 16, and 344—continues onward along the coast to the causeway to Cape Breton. (It's all pretty obvious on a map.) An excursion along the entire coastal route—from Dartmouth to Cape Breton Island with a detour to Canso—is 407km (253 miles).

**VISITOR INFORMATION**    Several tourist information centers are staffed along the route. You'll find the best-stocked and most-helpful centers at **Sheet Harbour** (next to the waterfall; © **902/885-2595;** open daily in summer 10am–7pm); **Sherbrooke Village** (at the museum; © **902/522-2400;** open daily in summer 9:30am–5:30pm), and **Canso** (1297 Union St.; © **902/366-2170;** open daily in summer 9am–6pm).

### A DRIVING TOUR OF THE EASTERN SHORE

This section assumes travel northeastward from Halifax toward Cape Breton. If you're traveling the opposite direction, hold this book upside down (just kidding).

Between Halifax and Sheet Harbour the route plays hide-and-seek with the coast, touching the water periodically before veering inland. The most scenic areas are around wild and open **Ship Harbour,** as well as **Spry Harbour,** noted for its attractive older homes and islands looming offshore.

At the **Fisherman's Life Museum** (© **902/889-2053**) in Jeddore Oyster Pond you'll get a glimpse of life on the Eastern Shore a century ago. The humble white-shingle-and-green-trim cottage was built by James Myers in the 1850s; early in this century it became the property of his youngest son, Ervin. Ervin and his wife raised a dozen daughters here ("This was quite a popular spot among the young men in the area," reported the laconic guide), and the home and grounds have been restored to look as they might around 1900 or 1920. A walk through the house and barn and down to the fishing dock won't take much more than 20 minutes or so. Open June to mid-October, Monday through Saturday 9:30am to 5:30pm, Sunday 1 to 5:30pm. Admission is C$3 (US$2.40) adults, C$2 (US$1.60) seniors and children age 6 to 17, C$7 (US$5.60) family. It's located on Route 7 and is well marked.

At the town of Lake Charlotte you can opt for a side road that weaves along the coast (look for signs for Clam Harbour). The road alternately follows wooded coves and passes through inland forests; about midway you'll see signs for a turn to **Clam Harbour Beach Provincial Park.** A broad crescent beach attracts sunbathers and swimmers from Halifax and beyond, with lifeguard-supervised swimming on weekends. A picnic area is set amid a spruce grove on a bluff overlooking the beach. No admission charge; gates close at 8pm. Continue on up the coast from the park and you'll reemerge on Route 7 in Ship Harbour.

Between Ship and Spry Harbours is the town of Tangier, home to **Coastal Adventures** (© 877/404-2774 or 902/772-2774), which specializes in kayak tours. It's run by Scott Cunningham, who literally wrote the book on Nova Scotia kayaking (he's the author of the definitive guide to paddling the coast). This well-run operation is situated on a beautiful island-dotted part of the coast, but it specializes in multiday trips throughout Atlantic Canada. You're best off writing (P.O. Box 77, Tangier, NS B0J 3H0) or calling for a brochure well in advance of your trip.

There's also a terrific little fish-smoking business just outside Tangier, **Willie Krauch & Sons Smokehouse** (© 800/758-4412 or 902/772-2188). Krauch (pronounced "craw") and family sell wood-smoked Atlantic salmon, mackerel, and eel in an unpretentious little store; they'll also give you a tour of the premises, if you like, where you can check out the old-style smoking process in action. Take some to go for a picnic.

**Sheet Harbour** (pop. 900) is a pleasant, small town with a campground open May through September, a couple of small grocery stores, two motels, and a **visitor information center** (© 902/885-2595), behind which is a short nature trail and boardwalk that descends along low, rocky cascades. Inland from Sheet Harbour on Route 374 is the **Liscomb Game Sanctuary,** a popular destination for hearty, self-contained explorers equipped with map, compass, canoe, and fishing rod. There are no services to speak of for casual travelers. Continuing eastward from Sheet Harbour, you'll pass through the wee village of **Ecum Secum,** which has little to attract the tourist but is unusually gratifying to say out loud to others in the car.

Adjacent to the well-marked Liscombe Lodge (see below), and just over the main bridge, is the **Liscomb River Trail** system. Trails follow the river both north and south of Route 7. The main hiking trail follows the river upstream for 5km (3 miles), crosses it on a suspension bridge, and then returns on the other side. The Mayflower Point Trail follows the river southward toward the coast, then loops back inland.

Continuing on Route 211 beyond historic Sherbrooke Village (see description below), you'll drive through a wonderful landscape of lakes, ocean inlets, and upland bogs and soon come to the scenic **Country Harbour Ferry.** The 12-car cable ferry crosses each direction every half-hour when open; it's a picturesque crossing of a broad river encased by rounded and wooded bluffs. The fare is about C$2 (US$1.60) per car, which includes driver and passengers. The ferry isn't always running, in which case you'll have to turn right around and head back, so it's wise to check at the Canso or Sherbrooke visitor centers before detouring this way.

Further along (you'll be on Rte. 316 after the ferry), you'll come to **Tor Bay Provincial Park.** It's 4km (2½ miles) off the main road, but well worth the detour on a sunny day. The park features three sandy crescent beaches backed by grassy dunes and small ponds that are slowly being taken over by bog and spruce forest. The short boardwalk loop is especially picturesque.

Way out on the eastern tip of Nova Scotia's mainland is the end-of-the-world town of Canso (pop. 1,200). It's a rough-edged fishing and oil-shipping town, often windswept and foggy. (If you're coming to Canso in summer, watch out for the annual folk music festival created to honor Nova Scotia's own Stan Rogers.) The chief attraction here is the **Grassy Island National Historic Site** (© **902/295-2069**). First stop by the small interpretive center on the waterfront and ask about the boat schedule. A park-run boat will take you out to the island, which once housed a bustling community of fishermen and traders from New England. (The interpretive center features artifacts recovered from the island.) A trail links several historic sites on this island, which tends to be a bit melancholy whether foggy or not. The boat serves the island June to September from 10am to 6pm daily. Fares are C$2.50 (US$2) adults, C$2 (US$1.60) seniors, and C$1.25 (US$1) children 6 to 16.

Route 16 between the intersection of Route 316 and Guysborough is an uncommonly **scenic drive.** The road runs high and low along brawny hills, affording soaring views of Chedabucto Bay and grassy hills across the way. Also pleasant, although not quite as distinguished, is Route 344 from Guysborough to the Canso causeway. The road twists, turns, and drops through woodlands with some nice views of the strait. It will make you wish you were riding a large and powerful motorcycle.

**Sherbrooke Village** 🞧 *Kids*    About half of the town of Sherbrooke comprises Sherbrooke Village, a historic section surrounded by low fences, water, and fields. (It's managed as part of the Nova Scotia Museum.) You'll have to pay admission to wander around, but the price is well worth it. This is the largest restored village in Nova Scotia, and it's unique in several respects. For one, almost all of the buildings are on their original sites (only two have been moved). Also, many homes are still occupied by local residents, and private homes are interspersed with the buildings open to visitors. The church is still used for services on Sundays, and you can order a meal at the old Sherbrooke Hotel. (I recommend the fish cakes and oven-baked beans.)

Some 25 buildings have been restored and opened to the public, ranging from a convincing general store to the operating blacksmith shop and post office. Look also for the temperance hall, courthouse, printery, boat-building shop, drugstore, and schoolhouse. These are staffed by genial, costumed interpreters, who can tell you about life in the 1860s. Be sure to ask about the source of the town's early prosperity. Plan to spend up to a half-day, depending on your (and your kids') interest level.

Rte. 7, Sherbrooke. © **902/522-2400.** Admission C$9 (US$7) adults, C$7.25 (US$5.75) seniors, C$3.75 (US$3) children, C$25 (US$20) families. June to mid-Oct 9:30am–5:30pm.

## WHERE TO STAY & DINE

Other than a handful of motels and B&Bs, few accommodations are available on the Eastern Shore.

**Liscombe Lodge** 🞧🞧 *Kids*    This modern complex, owned and operated by the province, consists of a central lodge and a series of smaller cottages and outbuildings.

It's situated in a remote part of the coast, adjacent to hiking trails and a popular boating area at the mouth of the Liscomb River. The lodge bills itself as "the nature lover's resort," and indeed it offers good access to both forest and water. But it's not exactly rustic, with well-tended lawns, bland modern architecture, shuffleboard, a marina, and even an oversize outdoor chessboard. In addition, plenty of kid-friendly offerings (table tennis, horseshoe pitches, and so forth) make this a good choice for vacationing families. The rooms are modern and motel-like; the cottages and chalets have multiple bedrooms and are good for families. The dining room is open to the public and serves resort fare.

Rte. 7, Liscomb Mills, NS B0J 2A0. (℃) **800/665-6343** or 902/779-2307. Fax 902/779-2700. www.signatureresorts. com. 68 units. C$130–C$350 (US$104–US$280) double. Inquire about packages. AE, DISC, MC, V. Closed mid-Oct to early May. Pets allowed in chalets. **Amenities:** Restaurant; indoor pool; tennis court; fitness center; free bikes; coin-op washers and dryers; shuffleboard. *In room:* TV w/VCR (some units), fridge (some units), hair dryer, iron, no phone.

## SeaWind Landing Country Inn 𝄢

What to do when your boat-building business plummets as the fisheries decline? How about opening an inn? That's what Lorraine and Jim Colvin did, and their 8-hectare (20-acre) oceanfront compound is delightful and inviting. Half of the guest rooms are in the 130-year-old main house, which has been tastefully modernized and updated. The others are in a more recent outbuilding—what you lose in historic charm, you make up for in brightness, ocean views, and double Jacuzzis. The innkeepers are especially knowledgeable about local artists (much of the work on display here was produced nearby), and they have compiled an unusually literate and helpful guide to the region for guests to peruse. The property has three private sand beaches, and coastal boat tours and picnic lunches can be easily arranged. The inn also serves dinner nightly (inn guests only), featuring local products prepared in a country-French style and wines from the inn's own wine cellar.

1 Wharf Rd., Charlos Cove, NS B0H 1T0. (℃) **800/563-4667** or 902/525-2108. Fax 902/525-2108. www.seawind landing.com. 14 units. C$95–C$169 (US$82–US$147) double. AE, MC, V. Closed mid-Oct to mid-May. **Amenities:** Dining room; laundry service. *In room:* Hair dryer, no phone.

## 10 Amherst to Antigonish

The north shore of Nova Scotia—dubbed the Sunrise Trail at visitor information centers and in provincial tourism publications—is chock-full of rolling hills and pastoral landscapes that rarely fail to enchant. Driving along Route 6, you pass through farmlands along the western reaches from Amherst to Pugwash and beyond; around Tatamagouche the landscape at times mirrors that found on the other side of the straits on Prince Edward Island—softly rolling fields of grain punctuated with a well-tended farmhouse and barn, and rust-red soil appearing where the ground cover has been scraped off. Cows will dominate one field, and in the next are those massive bull's-eyes of rolled hay. The Amherst to Pictou drive is especially scenic early or late on a clear day, when the low sun highlights the fields and forests. After Pictou, back on the Trans-Canada Highway, you'll see more forest and hills as you make your way toward Cape Breton Island.

## AMHERST

Amherst is best known for the busy and bustling information center staffed by the province just off the Trans-Canada (see below). But it's a lovely small town perched on a low hill at the edge of the sweeping Amherst Marsh that demarcates the border between Nova Scotia and New Brunswick. It's worth slowing and taking a detour through town just to appreciate the historic streetscapes.

## ESSENTIALS
**GETTING THERE**    Amherst is the first Nova Scotia town you'll encounter heading east on the Trans-Canada highway. Amherst is the terminus for both Route 6 (to the north) and Route 2 (to the south). It's about 40 minutes east of Moncton, and a stop on the **VIA Rail** (© 888/842-7245) train between Montréal and Halifax.

**VISITOR INFORMATION**    The huge **Nova Scotia Visitor Information Centre** (© 902/667-8429) is on Amherst's western edge, just off Exit 1 of the Trans-Canada Highway. In addition to the usual vast library of brochures and pamphlets, there's an ice-cream stand, videos, helpful staff, extraordinary views across the usually windy marsh, and often a bagpiper providing the appropriate mood out in front. It's open year-round: daily from 8am to 9pm during the summer, and the same hours but weekdays only during the rest of the year. A portion of the center that includes washrooms, vending machines, and payphones is open 24 hours a day in summer.

Just east of the provincial visitor center is the **Amherst Visitor Information Centre** (© 902/667-0696), housed in a handsome 1905 rail car. It's a good bet for more detailed information on activities in the immediate area. It's open late May to early September daily from 10am to 6pm.

## EXPLORING AMHERST
Downtown Amherst is compact (just a few blocks, really) but uncommonly attractive in a brick and sandstone way best appreciated by those who were dour Scots in a previous life. A half-dozen or so buildings are rough gems of classical architecture, and are nicely offset by the town's trees, including a few elms that continue to soldier on despite Dutch elm disease. Note especially the elaborately pedimented 1888 courthouse on the corner of Victoria and Church; a short stroll north is the sandstone Amherst First Baptist Church with its pair of prominent turrets. Farther north are the stoutly proportioned Doric columns on the 1935 Dominion Public Building, the front of which has apparently attracted the attention of local teens. ("No loitering. No skateboarding.")

Driving east on Route 6 you'll go through a residential area of large and beautiful historic homes dating from the last century and a half that display an eclectic range of architectural styles and materials.

Those seeking more information on Amherst's history can visit the **Cumberland County Museum,** 150 Church St. (© 902/667-2561), located in the 1836 home of R. B. Dickey, one of the Fathers of Canadian Confederation. (Historical note: Four of the Fathers of Confederation were from Amherst.) The museum is especially strong in documenting details of local industry and labor; it's open Tuesday through Saturday from 9am to 5pm. Admission costs C$3 (US$2.40) adult, C$5 (US$4) family.

## PUGWASH & TATAMAGOUCHE
If you're in the planning phase of your trip, note that it takes roughly the same amount of time—about 2 hours—to drive from Amherst to New Glasgow via the Trans-Canada Highway (which dips southward through Truro) or via Route 6 along the northern shore. On the Trans-Canada the driving is typically steady and fast, but you'll likely glaze over and find yourself punching the radio's scan button for entertainment.

Route 6 has far more visual interest, and you'll speed along sprawling farms, fields of wheat and corn, azure ocean inlets, and verdant coastal marshes. You'll spot the wide straits dotted with sails, with Prince Edward Island in the distance. The landscape changes frequently enough to prevent it from ever growing repetitious. *One caveat:* Both routes require the same amount of time—assuming you don't stop. But traveling on Route 6 you most likely will stop—to walk on beaches, to order up a mess of french fries and vinegar, or to shop at one of the handful of specialized crafts stores. It's worth the sacrifice in time.

## ESSENTIALS
**GETTING THERE**   Both towns are located on Route 6; you can't miss them from either direction.

**VISITOR INFORMATION**   The **Tatamagouche Visitor Information Center** (© 902/657-3285) is in the Fraser Cultural Center at 362 Main St.

## EXPLORING THE REGION
This region is home to a number of picnic parks, as well as local and provincial beaches. Signs along Route 6 point the way; most require a detour of a few miles. Pack a picnic and make an afternoon of it.

Pugwash, which comes from the Mi'kmaq word *Pagweak* meaning deep waters, today has a slightly industrial feel, with its factory and a midsize cargo port on the Pugwash River. **Seagull Pewter,** Route 6 (© 902/243-3850), is well known throughout the province, and is made in a factory on the east side of town; look for the retail store (which also stocks antiques) on the other side of town, just west of the Pugwash River bridge on Route 6. It's open 7 days a week in the summer.

Between Pugwash and Tatamagouche you'll drive through the scenic village Wallace (motto: "A Friendly Place"), where the road winds along the water and you'll take in fine views of the forested shores on the far side of Wallace Bay. East of Wallace, watch for the remains of ancient Acadian dikes in the marshes, built to reclaim the land for farming (signs point these out).

Near Malagash look for the signs crafted of casks along the road; these direct you to the **Jost Vineyards** ⚓ (© 800/565-4567 or 902/257-2636), which produces wines you may have sipped in Nova Scotia's better restaurants. You can take a free tour of the winery, enjoy a picnic (a deli opens on the premises during the summer), or sample the wines produced here and stock up on those that impress you. The vineyard is open Monday through Saturday 9am to 6pm, noon to 6pm on Sunday. Tours are offered twice daily, at noon and 3pm.

Tatamagouche is a pleasant fishing village with a surprisingly large annual Oktoberfest, and it's also home to the **Fraser Cultural Centre** (362 Main St.; © 902/657-3285), which strives to preserve the region's cultural heritage through ongoing exhibits, as well as to promote activities that encourage greater involvement in the arts and crafts. It's open daily June through August from 10am to 5pm (1–4pm in Sept), and admission is free.

Also in Tatamagouche is the shop of **Sara Bonnyman Pottery** (© 902/657-3215), where you'll find rustic, country-style plates, mugs, and more in a speckled pattern embellished with blueberries and other country motifs. The shop is on Route 246, 1 mile from the post office.

## WHERE TO STAY

**Train Station Inn** *(Finds)*    This is among the more unique inns in the province. Located down a side street in and around a weedy rail yard, the inn offers rooms in the lovely, century-old brick station and in six Canadian National cabooses that have been refurbished as guest rooms. Go for the cabooses, where you don't have to sacrifice comfort for character. All have been nicely done over, and vary in style, decor, and layout. Among my favorites: no. 7, which is decorated in a regal Edwardian parlor motif with natural beadboard paneling and striped wallpaper, and has a very excellent bathroom in the rear, just off that area where traveling politicians used to give speeches; and no. 10, one of two later model cars outfitted with hardwood floors, gas woodstove, kitchenette, and private little elevated sitting area (for one). The other, more modern car is no. 11. All cabooses have TVs; inn rooms do not. Rates include a continental breakfast served in the men's waiting room, which is lined with lanterns and other railway memorabilia and doubles as a cafe. The reception and gift shop is located in the ladies' waiting room; pick up an engineer's cap if you like.

21 Station Rd., Tatamagouche, NS B0K 1V0. (© **888/724-5233** or 902/657-3222. Fax 902/657-9091. www.trainstation. ca. 10 units. Apr–Oct C$69–C$169 (US$55–US$135) double. Rates include light breakfast. Closed Nov–Mar. AE, DC, MC, V. Pets allowed with advance notice. **Amenities:** Restaurant; kitchenette; coin-op washer and dryer. *In room (caboose only):* A/C, TV, kitchenette (2 units), fridge, coffeemaker.

## PICTOU

Pictou was established as part of a development scheme hatched by speculators from Philadelphia in 1760. Under the terms of their land grant, they needed to place some 250 settlers at the harbor. That was a problem. Few Philadelphians wanted to live there. So the company sent a ship called the *Hector* to Scotland in 1773 to drum up some impoverished souls who might be more amenable to starting life over in North America.

This worked out rather better, and the ship returned with some 200 passengers, mostly Gaelic-speaking Highlanders. The stormy voyage was brutal, and the passengers were threatened with starvation. But they eventually arrived at Pictou, and they disembarked wearing tartans and playing bagpipes.

The anniversary of the settlers' arrival is celebrated mid-August each year with the **Hector Festival** (© **800/353-5338**), when you might spot members of the clans wearing kilts and dining out in high style in memory of their ancestors; tickets cost around C$14 to C$18 (US$11–US$15). Pictou is Scottish enough that you might find yourself a bit wary that locals will try to slip some haggis into your meal while you're not paying attention.

## ESSENTIALS

**GETTING THERE**    Pictou is located on Route 106, which is just north of Exit 22 off Route 104 (the south branch of the Trans-Canada Hwy.). The **Prince Edward Island ferry** is several kilometers north of town at the coast near Caribou. (See chapter 6 for details on the ferry.)

**VISITOR INFORMATION**    The **Tourist Information Centre** (© **902/485-6213**) is located just off the rotary at the junction of Route 106 and Route 6. It's open daily 8am to 10pm in summer, 9am to 6pm in fall, and 9am to 5pm the rest of the year.

## EXPLORING PICTOU

Pictou is a pleasant and historic harborside town with an abundance of interesting architecture. There's a surfeit of dour sandstone buildings adorned with five-sided dormers, and at times you might think you've wandered down an Edinburgh side street. Water Street is especially attractive, and it offers an above-average selection of boutiques, casual restaurants, and pubs. Look for the headquarters and factory outlet of **Grohmann Knives,** 116 Water St. (*©* **888/756-4837** or 902/485-4224). At Grohmann's, located in a 1950s-mod building with a large knife piercing one corner, you'll find a good selection of quality knives (each with a lifetime guarantee) at marked-down prices. It's open daily; free factory tours are offered Monday through Friday from 9am to 7pm, Saturday until 6pm, and Sunday from noon to 6pm.

The harbor is well protected and suitable for novices who want to explore by sea kayak or canoe. Check with **Harbourtown Canoe and Kayak,** which rents canoes and kayaks from the **Hector Visitors Marina** on the waterfront at 37 Caladh Ave.

### Hector Heritage Quay

Learn about the hardships endured on the 1773 voyage of the singularly unseaworthy *Hector*—which brought Scottish settlers to the region—at this modern, small museum on the waterfront in downtown Pictou. You'll pass by intriguing exhibits en route to the museum's centerpiece: a full-size replica of the 33m (110-ft.) *Hector* at the water's edge. Stop by the blacksmith and carpentry shops to get a picture of life in the colonies in the early days.

33 Caladh Ave. *©* 902/485-4371. Admission C$5 (US$4) adults, C$4 (US$3.20) seniors, C$2 (US$1.60) children 6–12. Mid-May to mid-Oct Mon–Sat 9am–5pm, Sun noon–5pm; longer hours July-Aug.

## WHERE TO STAY

### Auberge Walker Inn ✷

This handsome downtown inn is located in a brick town house–style building dating to 1865 and overlooking one of Pictou's more active intersections. The innkeepers have done a commendable job of giving the place a comfortable feel while retaining its historic sensibility. Some rooms (such as Room 10 on the 3rd floor) have nice harbor views. A first-floor suite has a small kitchen, Jacuzzi, and dark bedroom in the back. All rooms have private bathrooms, but the conversions have come at some sacrifice. (The upstairs rooms have showers only, and one Frommer's reader wrote that his was so small he couldn't bend over to wash his legs.) On the upside: The inn is perfectly situated to enjoy Pictou's restaurants and attractions.

34 Coleraine St. (P.O. Box 629), Pictou, NS B0K 1H0. *©* 800/370-5553 or 902/485-1433. Fax 902/485-1222. walk-erinn@ns.sympatico.ca. 11 units. C$75–C$85 (US$60–US$68) double; C$149 (US$119) suite. Rates include breakfast. AE, MC, V. Parking on street, at rear of building, and in lot 1 block away. *In room:* Kitchenette (1 unit).

### Braeside Inn ✷

This three-story hotel at the edge of downtown was built in 1938 as an inn, and it has been one of the town's more enduring hostelries. The public rooms are done up in pinks and greens; the TV room has a large herd of wingback chairs and is a good spot to settle in with a book or to catch up on the news before dinner. The guest rooms are all carpeted and comfortable, if a bit small. The dining room has hardwood floors and views down a lawn and across the gravel lot to the harbor. Meals aren't terribly exciting but are well prepared, with selections including prime rib, fresh salmon, and rack of lamb. Dinner reservations suggested.

126 Front St., Pictou, NS B0K 1H0. *©* 800/613-7701 or 902/485-5046. Fax 902/485-1701. www.braesideinn.com. 18 units. C$65–C$155 (US$52–US$124) double. AE, DC, MC, V. At the end of Water St., make a right on Coleraine St., then left on Front St. **Amenities:** Dining room; TV lounge. *In room:* Fridge (some units), hair dryer.

### Consulate Inn ✷

No surprise: This doughty 1810 historic home of sandstone and ivy was originally a consulate. Three guest rooms are upstairs in the main building and share a handsome sitting area; seven larger and more modern rooms are located next door. The decor tends more toward the cute than the elegant, with innkeepers

Debbie and Garry Jardine striving to impart a romantic mood to appeal to couples. Two newer rooms are located in a walk-in basement and are a tad claustrophobic, but feature nice touches such as Jacuzzis and mood lighting; three other suites also have Jacuzzis, VCRs, and luxury touches. The PEI ferry is just a 10-minute drive away, and the inn is well situated for exploring Pictou. The first-floor restaurant is dim and intimate, with a Continental menu.

157 Water St., Pictou, NS B0K 1H0. ℂ 800/424-8283 or 902/485-4554. Fax 902/485-1532. www.consulateinn.com. 11 units. C$75–C$159 (US$60–US$119) double. Rates include continental breakfast. AE, DC, MC, V. **Amenities:** Restaurant; laundry service. *In room:* A/C (some units), TV (some units w/VCR), fridge (some units).

**Customs House Inn** ❀❀    This hulking brick and sandstone building with heroic arches and dentils was built in 1872 and thoroughly renovated in 1997. The former office building today is home to some of the more spacious and dramatic guest rooms in the province, each with high ceilings, lustrous maple floors, and a certain Spartan grace. The innkeepers have been reserved in their decorating, letting the architectural space speak for itself. Three of the rooms have kitchenettes with refrigerators; all have whirlpool tubs. Many are also adorned with the moody and notable nautical paintings of contemporary local painter Dave Macintosh. Among the best rooms is no. 2F, a bright corner room with kitchenette and water views. In the basement is the Old Stone Pub, a wonderfully renovated space with an informal menu (lots of seafood and pasta), 16 beers on tap, and live Celtic music some evenings.

38 Depot St., Pictou, NS B0K 1H0. ℂ 902/485-4546. Fax 902/485-2546. www.customshouseinn.ca. 8 units. Summer C$119–C$169 (US$95–US$135) double; off season C$79–C$119 (US$63–US$95) double. AE, DC, MC, V. **Amenities:** Bar. *In room:* A/C, TV, dataport, kitchenette (some units).

**Pictou Lodge Resort** ❀    The original rustic log lodge and a handful of log outbuildings have gone through a number of owners—including the Canadian National Railway—since entrepreneurs built the compound on a far-off grassy bluff overlooking a pristine beach early in the 20th century. It's now owned by Maritime Inns and Resorts, and has been modestly upgraded and improved with two new family suites. The older log rooms, most of which have kitchenettes, have considerably more character, but some still regard them as a bit dowdy. The newer rooms, alas, have the bland sameness of modern motel rooms everywhere. The lodge is located about 10 minutes' drive from downtown but has a wonderfully remote feel. Lunch and dinner are served in the Adirondack-style lodge, with its soaring spaces hammered together with time-burnished logs. Dinner entrees might be termed "creative traditional," and feature dishes such as wild blueberry chicken, seafood linguine, and cedar-planked salmon.

Shore Rd. (P.O. Box 1539), Pictou, NS B0K 1H0. ℂ 888/662-7484 or 902/485-4322. Fax 902/485-4945. www. maritimeinns.com. 51 units. C$125–C$265 (US$100–US$212) double. AE, DC, DISC, MC, V. Closed mid-Oct to mid-May. Follow Shore Rd. from downtown toward PEI ferry; watch for signs. **Amenities:** Restaurant; outdoor pool; free boats and bikes; playground; game room; room service. *In room:* A/C, kitchenette (some units), TV (some units).

## WHERE TO DINE

For an unhurried, relaxed meal in unstuffy environs, try the **Stone House Cafe & Pizzeria,** 13 Water St. (ℂ **902/485-6885**). There's a decent selection of pizza (including a lobster, scallop, and haddock pizza) and basic meals including smoked pork chops, lasagna, croquettes, and roast chicken. Most entrees are around C$10 to C$15 (US$8–US$12); it's open daily from 11am until midnight, weekends until 1am.

**Fougere's** 𝒱𝒶𝑙𝓊𝑒 UPSCALE TRADITIONAL    Fougere's is situated in a bright, simply furnished dining room right downtown that's as appealing as it is tidy. This local institution was run for years by Ben Fougere; it was taken over in 1998 by Stefan and Giovanna Sieber, who have impressed regular diners with their broadly appealing menu and their deftness in the kitchen. The couple moved to Nova Scotia after 12 years in Switzerland, and some Swiss dishes appear from time to time. But the menu is mostly anchored by traditional dishes like surf and turf, seafood casserole, and smoked haddock. Nonseafood dishes include T-bone steak, roast turkey dinner, and jaegerschnitzel.

91 Water St. ℂ **902/485-1575.** Reservations recommended. Main courses C$6–C$9 (US$5–US$7) at lunch, C$14–C$22 (US$11–US$18) at dinner. AE, MC, V. May–Oct daily 11:30am–9pm. Call for off-season hours.

**Piper's Landing** UPSCALE TRADITIONAL   This contemporary, attractive dining room on a stretch of residential road outside of Pictou remains a local favorite and your best bet in the area for a sophisticated meal, despite sometimes frustrating service. The interior is sparely decorated and understated. Likewise, the menu looks simple— entrees include grilled beef tenderloin, pork schnitzel, and a filling seafood platter—but you'll be impressed by the flair in preparation. The wine list, alas, is small and tired.

Rte. 376, Lyons Brook. ℂ **902/485-1200.** Reservations recommended. Main courses C$11–C$15 (US$9–US$12) at lunch, C$16–C$25 (US$13–US$20) at dinner. AE, MC, V. Mon–Sat 11:30am–2:30pm and 4:30–9pm; Sun 11am–9pm. From the Pictou Rotary take Rte. 376 toward Lyons Brook; it's 3km (1¾ miles) on your left.

## ANTIGONISH

Antigonish traces its European roots back to the 1650s, when the French arrived, only to be driven off by the Mi'kmaq. The French returned a century later, only to be driven off by Irish Loyalists. These Irish settlers established the first permanent settlement, and today there thrives a handsome town of 5,500 residents with a bustling main street and the respected St. Francis Xavier University, which was founded in 1853.

The town has a bustling commercial center (be prepared for some traffic midsummer) and is a good spot to stock up on groceries or get a bite for lunch. There are several cafes on and around Main Street, and a shop or two that merit browsing. For mild outdoor adventure, drive 9km (5½ miles) northeast of town on Route 337 and look for the **Fairmont Ridge Trail** ⚘. Here you'll find 12km (7.5 miles) of hiking that will take you through ravines and into forests with old-growth trees. Nearby is the home base of **Shoreline Adventures** (ℂ **902/863-5958**), which offers sea kayaking tours in the Antigonish Harbor area. For self-motivated travelers, sea kayak rentals with instructions on where to go are also available. Advance reservations are requested.

> *Fun Fact* **The Name Game**
>
> The name Antigonish (pronounced "an-tee-gun-ish") creates some contention among linguists. In the original native dialect it means either "five-forked rivers of fish" or "place where the branches are torn off by bears gathering beechnuts." There's no consensus.

## ESSENTIALS

**GETTING THERE**   Antigonish is on Route 104 (Trans-Canada Hwy.) 53km (33 miles) west of the Canso Causeway (the connection to Cape Breton Island).

**VISITOR INFORMATION**   The **Nova Scotia Tourist Office** (ℂ **902/863-4921**) is located at 56 West Rd. (Exit 32 on the Trans-Canada Hwy.). It's open daily from 9:30am to 8pm in summer, 9am to 6pm in June, September, and October.

**SPECIAL EVENTS**   The **Highland Games** ✿ have been staged in mid-July annually since 1861. What started as a community diversion has become an international event—and these are now the oldest continuously played highland games in North America. This is the place for everything Scottish, from piping to dancing to tossing the caber. Contact the **Antigonish Highland Society** (© 902/863-4275) for dates and details. Rooms are scarce during the 3-day games (Fri–Sun), so if you plan to attend, be sure to book well ahead. You can buy daily tickets or a 3-day pass.

**Festival Antigonish** ✿ (© 800/563-7529 or 902/867-3333) features a variety of plays and live performances held on the campus of St. Francis Xavier University from late June to late August. Shows range from locally written productions to Agatha Christie tales and *Rumpelstiltskin*. Tickets for children's productions are usually under C$10 (US$8); tickets for adult performances usually range from C$10 to C$20 (US$8–US$16).

## WHERE TO STAY

Antigonish is conveniently located just off the Trans-Canada Highway and is the last mainland town of any consequence before Cape Breton Island. As such it's home to a number of chain motels, both in town and on the strip outside of town. If nightfall is overtaking you and you're pushing for Cape Breton, I'd suggest overnighting here and pushing onward early the next morning. Port Hastings and Port Hawkesbury—the first towns on Cape Breton—also have a slew of chain motels, but both towns tend toward the sprawling and charmless. Antigonish is the better choice for staging an assault on the island, and has better restaurants to boot.

Budget travelers can book a no-frills dorm room at **St. Francis Xavier University** (© 902/867-2855) between mid-May and mid-August. Rooms are simple and share hallway washrooms, but they include all the basics: linen, pillows, towels, and soap. Rates are about C$50 (US$40) for two, including tax, with apartments going for around C$115 to C$145 (US$92–US$116). All-you-can-eat meals are also available at Morrison Dining Hall; figure about C$5 (US$4) for breakfast and C$10 (US$8) for dinner. If you're looking for a room after business hours, head to the Security Office in the basement of MacKinnon Hall.

At the west edge of town on the Trans-Canada, you'll find the **Chateau Motel,** 112 Post Rd. (© 877/339-8544 or 902/863-4842), which is unexciting, but in a good way. It has 17 rooms and cottages and a laundromat on the premises. Rates are C$69 to C$99 (US$55–US$79) for two.

**Maritime Inn Antigonish**   The basic, modern Maritime Inn Antigonish has benefited from new management and renovations. The rooms are comfortable and clean if unexceptional. The best thing about the place? Its location on Antigonish's Main Street, where you can easily walk to the city's best restaurant (Sunshine on Main; see below), and take care of basic shopping needs without getting back in that car you've been caged up in for the past 2 days. A restaurant on the premises—Main Street Café—serves three meals daily.

158 Main St., Antigonish, NS B2G 2B7. © 888/662-7484 or 902/863-4001. Fax 902/863-2672. www.maritimeinns. com/antigonish. 32 units. C$88–C$170 (US$70–US$136) double. AE, DC, DISC, MC, V. Take Exit 33 off the Trans-Canada; follow Church St. to Main St. and turn right. **Amenities:** Restaurant. *In room:* A/C, TV, dataport (some units), coffeemaker.

## WHERE TO DINE

**Lobster Treat** ✿ *Kids*   SEAFOOD   Housed in a red-shingled former schoolhouse (note the original hanging lamps) just west of town on the Trans-Canada Highway,

Lobster Treat has been doing seafood justice for the past quarter-century. It's not too fancy and features the usual family restaurant decor (potted plants, mauve carpeting). But the seafood is fresh and well prepared, the service both friendly and professional. The menu ranges from the traditional boiled lobster dinner to surf and turf combos to several spicy seafood concoctions served in curry. You can get haddock just about anywhere in the Maritimes, but here it's in lemon and lime juice and olive oil, and seasoned with oregano before being pan-fried or broiled (your choice). Complete meals for kids are available for under C$5 (US$3.35), and they serve pasta, chicken, and steaks for landlubbers.

241 Post Rd. (Rte. 104), Antigonish. ℭ 902/863-5465. Reservations not necessary. Main courses C$7.95–C$30 (US$6.50–US$24) at dinner; most dishes under C$20 (US$16). AE, DC, MC, V. Daily 11am–10pm. Closed late Dec to mid-Apr.

**Sunshine on Main Café & Bistro** ECLECTIC    You'll need to detour a bit off the Trans-Canada Highway and venture downtown, but it's worth it if you're in the mood for simple but creative bistro fare offered at attractive prices. The interior is dominated by a large and lovely wall mural, the other walls painted a cool lemon-sherbet yellow. The creative lunch menu includes a good selection of sandwiches and salads, including a spicy Thai chicken salad. Come evening, the selections expand and get fancier, with an emphasis on pastas (such as fettuccine mixed with six varieties of fish, or linguine with roasted veggies and baby clams). There's also a good selection of grilled entrees, ranging from salmon to lamb chops.

332 Main St., Antigonish. ℭ **902/863-5851.** Reservations recommended. Main courses C$6.50–C$12 (US$5–US$9.50) at lunch, C$9.95–C$22 (US$8–US$18) at dinner. AE, DC, MC, V. Sun–Thurs 7am–9:30pm; Fri–Sat 7.30am–10pm.

## 11 Cape Breton Island ★★★

Isolated and craggy Cape Breton Island—Nova Scotia's northernmost land mass— should be high on the list of don't-miss destinations for travelers, especially those with an adventurous bent. The island's chief draw is **Cape Breton Highlands National Park,** far north on the island's western lobe. But there's also the **historic fort at Louisbourg** and scenic **Bras d'Or Lake,** the inland saltwater lake that nearly cleaves the island in two. Above all, there are the picturesque drives. It's hard to find a road that's not a scenic route in Cape Breton. By turns the vistas are wild and dramatic, then settled and pastoral.

When traveling on the island, be alert to the cultural richness. Just as southern Nova Scotia was largely settled by English Loyalists fleeing the United States after they lost the War of Independence, Cape Breton was principally settled by Highland Scots whose families came out on the wrong side of rebellions against the Crown. You can still see that heritage in the accents of elders in some of the more remote villages, and in the great popularity of Scottish-style folk music.

You'll often hear references to the **Cabot Trail** ★★★ when on the island. This is the official designation for the 300km (185-mile) roadway around the northwest part of the island, which encompasses the national park. It's named after John Cabot, who many believe first set foot on North American soil near Cape North. (However, many disagree, especially in Newfoundland.)

If you're in a hurry, you might do well to base yourself in Baddeck, which is centrally located, offers the best accommodations and restaurants, and is well positioned for day excursions to the island's two best attractions: the national park and the reconstructed

# Cape Breton Island

QUÉBEC
PRINCE EDWARD ISLAND
MAINE
NEW BRUNS-WICK
NOVA SCOTIA
CAPE BRETON ISLAND

CT Cabot Trail
TransCanada Highway

0        40 mi
0        40 km

Cape North
Meat Cove
Bay St. Lawrence
Aspy Bay
Dingwall
Cape North
CT
Pleasant Bay
Neils Harbour
CAPE BRETON HIGHLANDS NATIONAL PARK
Presqu'île
Ingonish
Ingonish Beach
Chéticamp
CT
Wreck Cove
Cap Le-Moine
CT
Belle Cote
Breton Cove
Margaree Harbour
Chimney Corner
219
Margaree Valley
Indian Brook
St. Ann's Bay
Dunvegan
Margaree Centre
Englishtown
Sydney Mines
New Waterford
Inverness
Finlayson
St. Anns
105
North Sydney
28
Glace Bay
19
Lake Ainslie
CT
Boularderie
125
SYDNEY
4
225
Baddeck
St. Andrew's Channel
Mabou
105
Albert Bridge
Mira
Mira Bay
Scaterie Island
Port Hood
Whycocomagh
Christmas Island
Ben Eoin
Marion Bridge
Cape Breton
Orangedale
Iona
Grand Narrows
4
Big Pond
327
Louisbourg
Judique
Bras d'Or Lake
Louisbourg National Historical Site
19
Glendale
Johnstown
Gabarus Bay
St. Georges Bay
Craigmore
Kingsville
Loch Lomond
Canso Causeway
105
Dundee
Fourchu
Port Hastings
4
St. Peter's
4
Mulgrave
104
Port Hawkesbury
L'Archeveque
ATLANTIC OCEAN
Arichat
Isle Madame

ferry to Port aux Basques, Newfoundland
Ferry to Argentia, Newfoundland

historic settlement of Louisbourg. The southeastern portion of the island—near Isle Madame and Port Hawkesbury—can be picturesque in parts, but it isn't nearly as inviting as the rest of the island. I encourage travelers to focus more on the west and central sections.

*Note:* I've divided Cape Breton into two sections: Cape Breton Island and Cape Breton Highlands National Park. For information on adventures in the park itself, jump ahead to the next section.

## ESSENTIALS

**GETTING THERE** Cape Breton is connected to the mainland via the Canso Causeway, a 24m-wide (80-ft.), 65m-deep (217-ft.), 1,290m-long (4,300-ft.) stone causeway built in 1955 with 10 million tons of rock. (You can see a half-mountain, the other half of which was sacrificed for the cause, as you approach the island on the

Trans-Canada Hwy.) The causeway is 262km (163 miles) from the New Brunswick border at Amherst, 272km (169 miles) from Halifax.

**VISITOR INFORMATION** Nine tourist information centers dot the island. The best stocked (and a much recommended 1st stop) is the bustling **Port Hastings Info Centre** (© **902/625-4201**), located on your right just after crossing the Canso Causeway. It's open daily from 8am to 8:30pm most of the year, although closed from January through late April.

**SPECIAL EVENTS** Celtic Colours (© **877/285-2321** or 902/562-6700; www. celtic-colours.com) is a big annual music shindig timed to approximate the peak of the lovely highland foliage. Few tourists know about it—well, until now, that is—and the concentration of local Celtic musicians getting together for good times and music is simply astounding if you're into that sort of thing. It usually begins around the second week of October and lasts a full foot-stompin', pennywhistlin', fiddle-playin' week.

## MABOU & VICINITY ⊛

Mabou (pop. 400) is situated on a deep and protected inlet along the island's picturesque west shore. Scenic drives and bike rides are a dime a dozen hereabouts; few roads fail to yield opportunities to break out the camera or just lean against your vehicle and enjoy the panorama. The residents are strongly oriented toward music in their activities, unusually so even for musical Cape Breton Island.

Evening entertainment tends to revolve around fiddle playing, square dancing, or a traditional gathering of musicians and storytellers called a **ceilidh** ⊛ (pronounced *kay*-lee). To find out where things are going on, stop by the village grocery store or **The Mull** across the road (see below) and scope out the bulletin boards.

In a handsome valley between Mabou and Inverness is the distinctive post-and-beam **Glenora Distillery** ⊛ (© **800/839-0491** or 902/258-2662). This modern distillery began producing single-malt whisky from a pure local stream in 1990 and began selling it in 2000. (The owner can't call it Scotch, because it isn't made in Scotland.) He has modified the process slightly to use Kentucky bourbon casks, which the distillers here believe imparts a mellower taste to the spirit than traditional sherry casks. Production runs take place later in the fall, but tours of the facility are offered throughout the summer. Tours cost about C$5 (US$4) and last about a half-hour (offered daily 9am–5pm from May–Oct); they conveniently end near the gift shop, where you can buy local music CDs, gift glasses, and even bottles of the whisky itself for about C$80 (US$64) a pop. Swing by and savor this new contribution to local highland lore.

The distillery has an adjoining restaurant and nine-room hotel, plus some spiffy chalets with knockout views (see below); traditional music is often scheduled for weekends or evenings in the contemporary pub.

### WHERE TO STAY

**Duncreigan Country Inn** The Duncreigan occupies a quiet wooded bluff just across the bridge from the village. Modern and airy, it was built in 1991 by two wayward Connecticut Yankees and manages to meld contemporary and traditional stylings. Guest rooms are located in the main lodge and an outbuilding (connected via boardwalk), decorated in soothing dark, burgundy tones. Many rooms are furnished with Nova Scotian antiques, with headboards creatively designed by a local artisan to match the furnishings. There's no charge to use the inn's bikes or canoe, and dinners are served nightly.

Rte. 19, Mabou, NS B0E 1X0. ℂ **800/840-2207** or 902/945-2207. Fax 902/945-2206. www.duncreigan.ca. 8 units. C$110–C$195 (US$88–US$156) double. Rates include continental breakfast. MC, V. **Amenities:** 2 restaurants; free bikes and canoes. *In room:* A/C, TV, fridge (2 units).

**Glenora Inn & Distillery Resort** 🐄🐄    So, when was the last time you spent the night at a distillery? This distiller of single-malt whiskey added nine modern rooms in a building next to the pub, which in turn is located next to the actual distillery. The contemporary yet rustic architecture has a pleasant feel to it, but the real attraction is easy access to the pub and restaurant on the premises, which often features live performers from the area. The distillery has the feel of being in a remote vale in the Scottish highlands. Honeymooners will appreciate the half-dozen modern chalets, located on the hills overlooking the distillery: each has a Jacuzzi, satellite TV, and a wonderful view of the mist-covered valley below. (Do be prepared for a bone-rattling ride up the hill on a gravel road.) These chalets are available in one-, two-, or three-bedroom configurations.

Rte. 19, Glenville, NS B0E 1X0. ℂ **800/839-0491** or 902/258-2662. Fax 902/258-3572. www.glenoradistillery.com. 15 units. C$120–C$145 (US$96–US$116) double, C$175-C$240 (US$140–US$192) chalet. AE, MC, V. Closed mid-Oct to mid-May. **Amenities:** Restaurant; bar. *In room:* TV.

**Haus Treuburg**    Located a few miles from Mabou in the undistinguished oceanside village of Port Hood, Haus Treuburg is a handsome Queen Anne–style home dating from 1914. The three guest rooms in the main building (one is a suite) are nicely furnished in a spare style. As nice as they are, though, the better deals are the cottages behind the house, each with a private deck, an ocean view, and a gas barbecue. These are usually booked by the week (C$720/US$480), but it can't hurt to ask whether they're open for the night. German and Italian specialties are featured in the two downstairs dining rooms. Dinner is served at one seating, and it might include beef stroganoff with spaetzle, or lobster bordelaise on homemade fettuccine. Four-course meals are about C$30 to C$34 (US$24–US$27) prix fixe. The German "Sunday morning breakfast" is available every morning.

175 Main St. (P.O. Box 92), Port Hood, NS B0E 2W0. ℂ **902/787-2116.** Fax 902/787-3216. www.haustreuburg.com. 6 units. C$95–C$115 (US$76–US$87) double, C$135 (US$108) cottage. Breakfast about C$10 (US$8) extra. AE, DC, MC, V. **Amenities:** 2 dining rooms; babysitting. *In room:* TV/VCR.

**Mabou River Inn** 🐄 *Finds*    Located not far from the river and adjacent to the Mother of Sorrows Pioneer Shrine, this former bunkhouse has been converted into a homey little inn just off the main road with private bathrooms in some rooms and a kitchen and dining room for guests; there are also three two-bedroom suites. Hosts Donna and David Cameron keep things running smoothly, dispense great advice, and trot out an included continental breakfast. Nature lovers will appreciate the opportunity to hike, kayak, fish, and mountain bike on the scenic Ceilidh Trail, while night owls can stroll a few minutes across the bridge and into the village to check out some of the local traditional music offerings that fill Mabou on summer nights.

19 Mabou Ridge Rd., Mabou, NS B0E 1X0. ℂ **888/627-9744** or 902/945-2356. www.mabouriverinn.com. 12 units. C$99–C$155 (US$79–US$124) double. MC, V. **Amenities:** Restaurant; bike and sea kayak rentals; game room. *In room:* No phone (some units).

## WHERE TO DINE

**The Mull** CAFE    The Mull is a simple country deli that serves simple food. Lunches include such basics as seafood chowder, fish and chips, and deli-style sandwiches. After 5pm, the dinner menu kicks in, with such entrees as grilled halibut, T-bone steak, and scallops in a light wine sauce. Don't expect to be wowed by fancy food; do expect a filling meal and good company. One bonus for nonsmokers: The dining is completely nonsmoking, a marked contrast with the other eating places in Mabou.

Rte. 19 (north of village), Mabou. ℂ **902/945-2244**. Reservations accepted for parties of 6 or more. Sandwiches C$4–C$7 (US$3–US$5.50); main courses C$12–C$16 (US$9.50–US$13). AE, MC, V. Daily 11am–9pm (closes an hour or 2 earlier in the off season).

**The Red Shoe Pub** *(Finds* PUB FARE   You won't find a more local pub than "the Shoe," yet a constant stream of summer tourists keeps the mix interesting. The menu here features basic pub fare such as buffalo wings, fried fish, salads, and burgers; there are a few beers on tap, plus all the obvious bottles. The real highlight, though, is the frequent musical performances in the pub—the next area Celtic music star might be playing for peanuts on the night you swing by. Be aware that the place is small and, when crowded, can get quite claustrophobic and smoky. Also, the kitchen closes promptly at 8pm.

Main Street (Hwy. 19), Mabou. ℂ **902/945-2996**. Meals C$5–C$12 (US$4–US$9.50). MC, V. July–Sept daily noon–1am; shorter hours rest of the year.

**Shining Waters Bakery** CAFE   This bakery, smack in the center of what passes for downtown, is a locals-only kind of place all the way, with a simple menu of breakfast items and sandwiches and a cooler full of canned and bottled drinks. Don't come expecting atmosphere or service here; instead, you'll get a slightly hectic (and smoky) meal, elbow-to-elbow with the real Mabou.

11497 Main St., Mabou. ℂ **902/945-2728**. Meals C$2.25–C$8 (US$2–US$6.50). MC, V. June to mid-Oct Mon–Sat 6:30am–8pm, Sun 9am–8pm; shorter hours off season.

## MARGAREE VALLEY ⚓

West of Baddeck and south of Chéticamp, the Margaree Valley region loosely consists of the area from the village of Margaree Valley near the headwaters of the Margaree River, down the river to Margaree Harbor on Cape Breton's west coast. Some seven small communities are clustered in along the valley floor, and it's a world apart from the rugged drama of the surf-battered coast; it's vaguely reminiscent of the farm country of upstate New York. The Cabot Trail gently rises and falls on the shoulders of the gently rounded hills flanking the valley, offering views of the farmed floodplains and glimpses of the river. In autumn, the foliage here is often among Eastern Canada's best.

The **Margaree River** has been accorded celebrity status in fishing circles—it's widely regarded as one of the most productive Atlantic salmon rivers in North America, and salmon have continued to return to spawn here in recent years, which is unfortunately not the case in many other waterways of Atlantic Canada. The river has been closed to all types of fishing except fly-fishing since the 1880s, and in 1991 it was designated a Canadian Heritage River.

Learn about the river's heritage at the **Margaree Salmon Museum** ⚓ ((ℂ **902/248-2848**) in North East Margaree. The handsome building features a brief video about the life cycle of the salmon, and exhibits include fisherman photos by the score as well as antique rods (including one impressive 5m/18-footer), examples of poaching equipment, and hundreds of hand-tied salmon flies. Museum docents can help you find a guide to try your hand on the water. (Mid-June to mid-July and Sept and early Oct are the best times.) The museum is open mid-June to mid-October daily from 9am to 5pm. Admission is C$1 (US80¢) adult, C25¢ (US20¢) child.

The whole area is best explored by slow and aimless driving, or better yet, by bike or canoe. **Margaree River Canoe Rentals** (© **800/565-9993** or 902/235-2658), based at the Duck Cove Inn in Margaree Harbour, can arrange for a lazy paddle down the river.

When prowling around, watch for **Cape Breton Clay** ⭐⭐ (© **902/248-2860;** www.capebretonclay.com), in the Margaree Valley, northeast of the salmon museum. One of the occupational hazards of being a guidebook writer is the requirement that I look at a lot of pottery, much of it bad and almost all of it claiming to be "unique." This work, by Margaree Valley native Bell Fraser, actually is unique. And quite wonderful. Crab, lobster, fish, shellfish, and ears of corn are worked into her platters and bowls in ways that are both whimsical and elegant. It's definitely worth a stop.

## WHERE TO STAY

**Normaway Inn** ⭐ From the moment you turn down the drive lined with tall Scotch pines, you'll feel you're in another world. The lodge is located on some 200 hectares (500 acres), was built in 1928, and has been run by the MacDonald family since the 1940s. While it's the sort of place you might imagine running into gentlemen anglers dressed in tweed, it's not a true fishing resort. It appeals to both families and honeymooners, and is spread out enough to accommodate all. Nine of the rooms are in the main lodge and have a timeless quality, with a vague 1920s character. I'd opt for one of the three first-floor rooms, which are larger and have corner windows for better ventilation. The cottages are spread around the property an easy walk to the main lodge, and have hardwood floors and a clean, almost Scandinavian quality. The older cottages were built in the 1940s and are a bit smaller and more spare. Eight newer cottages have Jacuzzis, all but two have woodstoves, and some have two bedrooms. The dining room, decorated in pleasingly simple country farm style, is known for its Atlantic salmon and its lamb, which is raised for the inn about 16km (10 miles) away. (Don't fret: The sheep wandering the property are breed stock and won't appear on your dinner plate.)

The inn's strong card is evening entertainment, with events ranging from films to live performances, including Acadian music, storytelling, and local fiddling. The weekly square dance here (small charge), held in the inn's barn, attracts hundreds of locals and tourists.

P.O. Box 121, Margaree Valley, NS B0E 2C0. © **800/565-9463** or 902/248-2987. Fax 902/248-2600. www. normaway.com. 9 units, 17 cottages. C$99–C$249 (US$79–US$199) double and cottage. Late-afternoon same-day booking discounts. Breakfast about C$11 (US$9) extra. DC, MC, V. Closed late Oct to May. Pets allowed in cottages only. **Amenities:** Dining room; tennis court; free bikes. *In room:* No phone.

## CHÉTICAMP ⭐

The Acadian town of Chéticamp (pop. 1,000) is the western gateway to Cape Breton Highlands National Park and the center for French-speaking culture on Cape Breton. The change is striking as you drive northward from Margaree Harbour—the family names suddenly go from MacDonald to Doucet, and the whole culture and cuisine change.

The town itself consists of an assortment of restaurants, boutiques, and tourist establishments spread along Main Street, which closely hugs the harbor. A winding boardwalk follows the harbor's edge through much of town, and offers a good spot to stretch your legs and get your bearings. (That's Chéticamp Island just across the water; the tall coastal hills of the national park are visible up the coast.) Chéticamp is a good stop for provisioning, topping off the gas tank, and finding shelter.

My, what an inefficient way to fish.

Ring toss, good. Horseshoes, bad.

Faster! Faster! Faster!

We take care of the fiddly bits, from providing over 43,000 customer reviews of hotels, to helping you find our best fares, to giving you 24/7 customer service. So you can focus on the only thing that matters. Goofing off.

**travelocity**
You'll never roam alone.

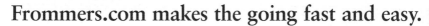

Chéticamp is noted worldwide for its hooked rugs, a craft perfected by early Acadian settlers. Those curious about the craft should allow time for a stop at Les Trois Pignons, which houses the **Elizabeth LeFort Gallery and Museum.** It is located on Main Street in the north end of town (© **902/224-2642;** www.lestroispignons.com) and displays some of the 300 fine tapestries, many created by Elizabeth LeFort, who was Canada's premier rug-hooking artist for many decades until she passed away in 2005. It's open daily from 8am to 7pm in July and August; 9am to 5pm spring and fall; and 8:30am to 4:30pm in winter. Admission is C$4.50 (US$3.50) adult, C$4 (US$3) seniors, C$3.50 (US$3) students, C$15 (US$12) family, free for ages 12 and under.

In the 1930s artisans formed the **Co-operative Artisanale de Chéticamp,** located at 5067 Main St. (© **902/224-2170**). A selection of hooked rugs—from the size of a drink coaster on up—are sold here, along with other trinkets and souvenirs. There's often a weaver or other craftsperson at work in the shop. A small museum downstairs (admission is free) chronicles the life and times of the early Acadian settlers and their descendants. It's closed from mid-October to May.

Several boat tour operators are based in Chéticamp Harbour. **Seaside Whale and Nature Cruises** (© **800/959-4253** or 902/224-2400) sets out in search of whales, seals, and scenery, and has hydrophones on board for listening to any whales you may encounter.

The most pleasing drive or bike ride in the area is out to Chéticamp Island, connected to the mainland by road. Look for the turn south of town; the side road is just north of Flora's gift shop on the Cabot Trail.

## WHERE TO STAY

A handful of motels service the thousands of travelers who pass through each summer. **Laurie's Motor Inn,** Main Street (© **800/959-4253** or 902/224-2400), has more than 50 motel rooms in three buildings well situated right in town, with rates of C$95 to C$155 (US$76–US$124) double. The inn also manages nicer suites and apartments scattered throughout the town; inquire if you're interested in something larger, or with cooking facilities.

**Parkview Motel** The basic yet comfortable Parkview's best claim is its location—within walking distance of the national park's visitor center, and away from the hubbub of town. Don't expect anything fancy and you won't be disappointed; at least it has cable television and recently upgraded bathrooms. There's a dining room and lounge in a separate building across the street.

Cabot Trail, Chéticamp, NS B0E 1H0. © 902/224-3232. Fax 902/224-2596. www.parkviewresort.com. 17 units. C$75–C$109 (US$60–US$87) double. AE, MC, V. Closed mid-Oct to early May. **Amenities:** Dining room; bar; bike rentals. *In room:* A/C (some units), TV, coffeemaker (some units).

**Pilot Whale Chalets** ❀ These spare, modern cottages (constructed in 1997) each have two bedrooms and full housekeeping facilities, including microwaves. They may have a bit of an antiseptic, condo air, but they are well equipped with TVs and VCRs, gas barbecues, coffeemakers, decks, and woodstoves; some even have Jacuzzis and fireplaces, as well. The best feature, though, is the grand view northward toward the coastal mountains. (Cottages 1, 2, 4, and 5 have the best vistas.) The lodge added apartments to the walk-out basements beneath two of the cottages in 1999, which impinges slightly on the privacy of those both upstairs and down.

Rte. 19, Chéticamp, NS B0E 1H0. (✆ **902/224-1040.** Fax 902/224-1540. www.pilotwhales.com. 12 units. C$90–C$189 (US$72–US$151) double. AE, MC, V. *In room:* TV/VCR, kitchenette (some units), no phone.

## WHERE TO DINE

**La Boulangerie Aucoin** (✆ **902/224-3220**) has been a staple of Chéticamp life since 1959. Located just off the Cabot Trail between town and the national park (look for signs), the bakery is constantly restocking its shelves with fresh-baked goods; ask what's still warm when you order at the counter. Among the options: croissants, scones, loaves of fresh bread, and berry pies. This is a recommended last stop for snack food before setting off into the park.

For an informal and quick lunch in town, there's **L&M Chéticamp Seafoods,** Ltd. (✆ **902/224-1688**), located on Main Street just north of the Harbour restaurant. It's a take-out spot with a few picnic tables inside and outside. It's best known for its fish and chips, but also offers hamburgers and chicken fingers. If you're camping in the park, this is also the spot for fresh fish for the grill. Open from 8am to 8pm daily May to mid-September.

**Harbour Restaurant and Bar** ⨁ SEAFOOD    The Harbour is Chéticamp's sleekest restaurant, located in an easy-to-pass-by building on the waterfront. The water views are excellent, and the food well above average for the region. The light fare menu consists of pub favorites (hamburgers, club sandwiches, fish and chips), along with an Acadian specialty or two. The dinner menu favors seafood, with options like an East Coast casserole (scallops, lobster, shrimp, and haddock in a cheese sauce), broiled salmon, and farm-raised Margaree trout, served charbroiled and finished with a tarragon butter; there's also Alberta beef. The bar, which serves a good selection of single-malt Scotches, stays open until midnight.

15299 Cabot Trail (Main St.). (✆ 902/224-2042. Reservations recommended in peak season. Light fare C$6–C$12 (US$5–US$9.50); dinner entrees C$9.95–C$19 (US$8–US$15). AE, MC, V. Daily 11am–10pm. Closed mid-Oct to mid-May.

**Restaurant Acadien** ACADIAN    This restaurant is attached to a crafts shop on the south side of town and has the uncluttered feel of a cafeteria. The servers wear costumes inspired by traditional Acadian dress, and the menu also draws on local Acadian traditions. Look for fricot (a kind of chicken-potato soup), stewed potatoes, and the meat pies for which the region is renowned. Also on the menu: blood pudding and butterscotch pie, for the brave and carefree.

15067 Main St. (✆ 902/224-3207. Reservations recommended. Breakfast C$3.50–C$5 (US$2.80–US$4); lunch and dinner C$1.95–C$17 (US$1.60–US$14). AE, MC, V. Daily 7am–9pm. Closed Nov to mid-May.

## PLEASANT BAY ⨁

At the north end of the Cabot Trail's exhilarating run along the western cliffs, the road turns inland at the village of Pleasant Bay. The attractive, active fishing harbor, protected by a man-made jetty, is a short walk off the Cabot Trail, and sits at the base of rounded, forested mountains that plunge down to the sea.

The newly opened **whale interpretive center** (✆ **902/224-1411**), built on a rise overlooking the harbor, features exhibits to help explain why the waters offshore are so rich with marine life. It's open June through mid-October from 9am to 5pm; admission is C$4.50 (US$3.60) adults, C$3.50 (US$2.80) children and seniors, C$14 (US$11) family.

Whale-watching tours are offered daily June through mid-October from the harbor by Capt. Mark Timmons of **Capt. Mark's Whale and Sea Cruise** (✆ **888/754-5112** or 902/224-1316). The 2½-hour cruise on the 42-ft. *Bay Hookup* provides unrivaled glimpses at the rugged coast both north and south, and often a close-up look at whales (almost always pilot whales, frequently finbacks and minkes, occasionally humpbacks). The boat has a hydrophone on board, so you can hear the plaintive whale calls underwater. Trips are C$25 (US$20) per adult, C$12 (US$9.50) children, and reservations are encouraged. The outfit runs three to five tours daily during the season.

As you entered town you may have noticed the **Timmons Folk Art Studio** (© **902/224-3575**) near the "Y" in the road. Inside and out you'll find the colorful, whimsical folk art by Reed Timmons (Capt. Mark Timmons's cousin). Reed carves fish, cows, seagulls, and sailors that are rustic and visually arresting.

If you bear right at the "Y" and continue northward, the road wraps around the coastal hills and turns to gravel after 5km (3 miles). Keep going another 4km (2½ miles). Here you'll come to a spectacular **coastal hiking trail** 𝆏𝆏, which runs to **Pollett's Cove,** about 10km (6 miles) up the coast. A dozen families once lived here, and two cemeteries remain. The cove and the trail are on private land, but hiking and other quiet recreation are allowed.

## CAPE NORTH 𝆏

Cape North is a much-recommended detour for adventurous travelers hoping to get off the trafficked Cabot Trail. Folks say that Cape North is much like the Cabot Trail used to be 20 or 30 years ago, before the travel magazines started trumpeting its glories and large numbers of tourists started showing up. It's worth the extra driving and backtracking.

Cape North is reached via a turnoff at the northern tip of the Cabot Trail, after you descend into the Aspy Valley. You'll soon come to Cabot Landing Provincial Park, where local lore claims that John Cabot first made landfall in North America in 1497. You can debate the issue near the Cabot statue or take a long walk on the lovely 3km (2-mile) ocher sand beach fronting Aspy Bay. The views of the remote coast are noteworthy.

The road winds onward to the north; at a prominent fork, you can veer right to Bay St. Lawrence, where you can sign up for a whale-watching trip. Try **Captain Cox's Whale Watch** (© **888/346-5556** or 902/383-2981) or **Oshan Whale Cruise** (© **877/383-2883** or 902/383-2882). Both offer 2½-hour whale-watching cruises for C$25 (US$20) adults and C$12 (US$9.50) children; Oshan will also take you deep-sea fishing and even clean your fish for cooking.

Turn left at the fork and continue along a remarkable cliff-side road to Meat Cove. The last 5km (3 miles) track along a dirt road that runs high on the shoulders of coastal mountains and then drops into shady ravines to cross brooks and rivers. The road ends at Meat Cove, a rough-hewn settlement that's been home to fishermen, mostly named McClellan, for generations.

There's a rustic private campground here, **Meat Cove Campground** 𝆏 (© **902/383-2379**), which is open June through October, with 25 campsites that might have the most dramatic ocean views of any campground in Nova Scotia; they start at about C$18 (US$15) apiece. Ask owner Kenneth McClellan about the hiking trails in the hills above the campground (there's a day-use fee for noncampers).

### WHERE TO STAY
**Four Mile Beach Inn** *Value*    This handsome inn (which opened in 1998) has quickly become one of the more interesting on Cape Breton. Located in an old inn

and general store dating from 1898, the inn is run by John Cuthbert and Janet Conner, who have done a superb job fixing the place up, making it feel comfortable and historic yet not cloying. The old general store has been spruced up and stocked with (not-for-sale) items that turned up in the basement and attic; two parlors are perfect for evening reading or card playing; and there's often traditional Maritime music piped throughout the downstairs. The breakfast is all you can eat, and tasty. Two of the regular rooms share a bathroom, while another has a private bathroom across the hall; the best of the lot is no. 2, a snug spot with low eaves and a ceiling fan, and a great bathroom with wainscoting and a tub fit for serious relaxing. The innkeepers recently opened a small cafe that serves meals summer and fall, and they rent kayaks, canoes, and bikes; you can paddle North Bay after a short stroll down a dirt road through their backyard. This place offers good value for the money.

> ### *Moments* Baywatch
>
> The 8km (5-mile) trip from Bay St. Lawrence to Meat Cove is ideal by mountain bike if you've brought one along. This is one of the few places you can pedal your bike and whale-watch simultaneously.

RR No. 1, Cape North, NS B0C 1G0. © **888/503-5551** or 902/383-2282. www.fourmilebeachinn.com. 8 units. C$75–C$129 (US$60–US$103) double. Rates include full breakfast. MC, V. Closed mid-Oct to mid-June. Pets in efficiency only. **Amenities:** Canoe, kayak, and bike rentals. *In room:* Kitchenette (some units), coffeemaker (some units), safe (some units), no phone.

**Markland Coastal Resort** 𝓡 The Markland may have the best location of any resort on the island. It's sited on 28 hectares (70 acres) where a meandering river meets a long sand beach fronting spectacular Aspy Bay. It's hard to imagine a more idyllic spot, especially on clear mornings when the sun illuminates the coastal range to the north. The resort features two kinds of accommodations, both furnished in an uncluttered style: One- and two-bedroom cottages have kitchens, sitting areas, and porches—most with views of the bay. The motel units are narrow and a bit dark, though air-conditioning was recently added. Canoes are available to explore the river, or you can linger on the shore and beachcomb. The resort **dining room** 𝓡 offers a nice contrast of modern furniture in a rustic setting with ocean views; three meals daily are served, including the best dinners in northern Cape Breton. The Markland also hosts cultural performances at the Octagon, a performance building on the grounds. Friday nights typically feature Cape Breton music and other traditional tunes; on Sunday, there's a chamber music series.

Cabot Trail, Dingwall, NS B0C 1G0. © **800/872-6084** or 902/383-2246. Fax 902/484-5762. www.marklandresort. com. 12 units, 13 cottages. In rooms C$99–C$139 (US$79–US$111) double; log cabins C$169–C$289 (US$155–US$231). Ask about packages. Children 16 and under stay free in parent's room. AE, DC, DISC, MC, V. Closed mid-Oct to mid-June. "Well-behaved pets" allowed. **Amenities:** Outdoor pool; bike rentals; game room; babysitting; canoes. *In room:* A/C (some units).

## WHERE TO DINE

For upscale dining, see the Markland Coastal Resort, above.

**Morrison's Restaurant** 𝓡 *(Value)* SEAFOOD/INFORMAL Morrison's is a favorite with locals and travelers, and with good reason. It serves good food at a good price. It's a comfortable, rustic spot, with old wood floors, wood-splint baskets hanging from the ceiling, and moose antlers on the wall. The menu tends toward comfort food, with such selections as fettuccine with pesto, and beer-battered haddock (recommended).

Other options include braised halibut in a dill cream sauce, and a sinful "Cape Islander"—consisting of scallops and lobster in a velouté sauce sandwiched between halibut and salmon and served with hollandaise. Desserts are traditional: cheesecake, gingerbread, and a tart bumbleberry pie. Bus tours often stop here, and when they do the service can sometimes be aggravating.

Cabot Trail, Dingwall. ℂ 902/383-2051. Main courses C$5.95–C$11 (US$5–US$9) at lunch, C$11–C$17 (US$9–US$14) at dinner. AE, MC, V. Daily 8am–9pm. Closed late Nov to mid-May.

## WHITE POINT & NEIL'S HARBOUR

From South Harbor (near Dingwall) you can drive on the speedy Cabot Trail inland to Ingonish, or stick to the coast on an alternate route that arcs past White Point, continues onward to Neil's Harbor, then links back up with the Cabot Trail. If the weather's agreeable, the coast road is a recommended detour. Initially, the road climbs upward along abrupt and jagged cliffs with sweeping views of Aspy Bay; at White Point, you can veer out to the tip for even more expansive views of this remote section of coast. The road then tracks inland before emerging at Neil's Harbour, a postcard-perfect fishing village. On a rocky knob located on the far side of the fishing fleet is a squarish red-and-white lighthouse (now an ice-cream parlor). Just beyond that is the **Chowder House** (ℂ **902/336-2463**), a low-key, pine-paneled take-out restaurant that specializes in, well, chowder, along with platters of deep-fried seafood and crab cakes (C$4.50–C$16/US$3–US$11). There's a grassy area outside the restaurant for picnicking as you admire the panorama of the rocky shoreline shaded with pink-orange rock. Consider yourself warned, though: It's a popular spot with bus tours. From Neil's Harbour it's just a 2-minute drive back to the Cabot Trail.

## INGONISH 👫

This area includes a number of similarly named towns (Ingonish Centre, Ingonish Ferry, South Ingonish Harbor), which together have a population of about 1,300. Like Chéticamp on the peninsula's east side, Ingonish serves as a gateway to the national park and is home to a park visitor information center and a handful of motels and restaurants. Oddly, there's really no critical mass here—the services are spread along a lengthy stretch of the Cabot Trail, and there's never any sense of arrival. You pass a liquor store, some shops, a bank, a post office, and a handful of cottages. Then you're suddenly in the park.

Highlights in the area include a sandy beach (near Keltic Lodge), good for chilly splashing around, and a number of shorter hiking trails. (See "Cape Breton Highlands National Park," later in this chapter.) For golfers, windswept **Highland Links course** 👫 (ℂ **800/441-1118** or 902/285-2600), located adjacent to the Keltic Lodge (see below) but under separate management, is considered one of the best in Nova Scotia, if not all of Atlantic Canada. Ask about packages whenever booking a room in the area, and be sure to reserve tee times well in advance.

South of Ingonish the **Cabot Trail** 👫👫 climbs and descends the hairy 300m-high (1,000-ft.) promontory of Cape Smokey, which explodes into panoramic views from the top. At the highest point, there's a provincial park where you can cool your engine and admire the views. An 11km (7-mile) hiking trail leads to the tip of the cape along the high bluffs, studded with unforgettable viewpoints along the way.

Sea kayak tours are offered in protected Ingonish Harbor by burly and gregarious raconteur Mike Crimp of **Cape Breton SeaCoast Adventures** (ℂ **877/929-2800** or 902/929-2800). Both full-day (about C$89/US$71 per person) and half-day (about

C$49/US$39) tours are offered from June through October, and both are designed for novices who've never set bottom in a kayak. You'll look for whales, but are more likely to spot bald eagles or blue herons. The landscape hereabouts is dramatic, with Cape Smokey rising powerfully to the south, Middle Head to the north, and marsh grasses serving as home to a mix of shorebirds.

## WHERE TO STAY

A number of serviceable cottage courts and motels are located in this area. The recently expanded **Glenghorm Beach Resort** in Ingonish (© **800/565-5660** or 902/286-2049) has 90 units on a spacious property that fronts a sand beach. Some rooms feature painted cinder-block walls, and the decorating is a bit dated, with avocado and gold hues that recall a bygone era. Options include motel rooms and efficiencies, along with 10 cottages and 10 elaborate suites. Prices are C$89 to C$129 (US$71–US$103) for the motel rooms, C$130 to C$190 (US$104–US$152) for the cottages, and C$299–C$399 (US$239–US$319) for the suites.

**Castle Rock Country Inn**    The recently built Castle Rock Inn sits boldly on a high hill overlooking Ingonish Harbor—a little too boldly, say some of the locals, who note that the inn's bulldozers greatly altered the pristine view of the hillside flanking Cape Smokey, and that no landscaping has been added to soften the impact. The inn opened in 1997 and is a squarish two-story lodge clad in wood shingles. The dozen rooms and one suite are surprisingly basic—furnished the way you might expect in a midrange chain hotel. Rooms facing north have outstanding ocean views and cost extra. The inn's dining room has—no surprise—stunning water views and features a menu with what might be called "new traditional cuisine." Entrees include maple-glazed salmon, mussels with pasta, and cheese crepes with salad.

39339 Cabot Trail, Ingonish Ferry, NS B0C 1L0. © **888/884-7625** or 902/285-2700. Fax 902/285-2525. www.ingonish.com/castlerock. 15 units. C$92–C$142 (US$73–US$114) double. AE, MC, V. **Amenities:** Restaurant; bar; laundry service. *In room:* TV, hair dryer, iron, no phone.

**Keltic Lodge**    The Keltic Lodge is reached after a series of dramatic flourishes: You pass through a grove of white birches, cross an isthmus atop angular cliffs, and then arrive at the stunning, vaguely Tudor resort that dominates the narrow peninsula. The views are extraordinary. Owned and operated by the province, the resort is comfortable without being slick, nicely worn without being threadbare. Some of the guest rooms are painted in that soothing mint green that was popular in the 1940s; most are furnished rather plainly with run-of-the-mill motel furniture. (You might expect more for the price.) The cottages are set amid birches and have three bedrooms each; you rent just one bedroom and share a common living room with other guests. Be aware that some of the guest rooms are located at the more modern Inn at the Keltic building a few hundred meters away, which has better views but a more sterile character. One Frommer's reader wrote to lament the inadequate soundproofing in the modern annex, and recommended an upstairs room here to avoid hearing heavy footfalls.

The food in the main dining room is among the best on the island; the excellent fixed-price dinner menu (included in room rates) offers several selections, with prime rib and lemon-pepper salmon filet among the favorites. A less formal option is the new Atlantic Restaurant, specializing in lighter fare like grilled salmon and pasta.

Middle Head Peninsula, Ingonish Beach, NS B0C 1L0. © **800/565-0444** or 902/285-2880. Fax 902/285-2859. www.signatureresorts.com. 72 standard units, 30 cottage units. C$152–C$352 (US$122–US$282) double and cottage unit. Rates include breakfast and dinner. AE, DC, DISC, MC, V. Closed late Oct to late May. **Amenities:** 2 restaurants;

outdoor pool; golf course; game room; laundry service. *In room:* A/C (2 units), TV (most units), fridge (some units), hair dryer, iron, no phone.

## ST. ANN'S

Traveling clockwise around the Cabot Trail, you'll face a choice when you come to the juncture of Route 312. One option is to take the side road to the Englishtown ferry and cross over St. Ann's Harbor in slow but picturesque fashion. The crossing of the fjordlike bay is very scenic, and takes just about 2 minutes (when there's no line). The ferry runs around the clock, and the fare is nominal.

In Englishtown, one of Nova Scotia's more unique museums is the **Giant MacAskill Museum,** Route 312 (© **902/929-2925**). This honors the memory of Angus MacAskill, who lived from 1825 to 1863. He was a big man, standing 7 feet 9 inches, and weighing 425 pounds. At the museum you can see many of his personal effects, including oversize boots, walking stick, and clothing, along with his bed and chair. (If you'd care to pay your respects to the man, he's buried at the Englishtown cemetery.) The museum is open daily mid-June to mid-September from 9am to 6pm. Admission is C$1 (US75¢) adults, C75¢ (US60¢) seniors and youth, C50¢ (US40¢) under 12.

Your second option is not to cross via ferry, but to stay on the Cabot Trail, heading down the western shore of St. Ann's Harbor. A good launching point for exploring the waters is North River, where kayak guide Angelo Spinazzola offers tours through his **North River Kayak Tours** (© **888/865-2925** or 902/929-2628) from mid-May through mid-October. The full-day tour (C$99/US$79 per person) includes a steamed mussel lunch on a beach; there's also a gold-panning tour. Most every trip includes sightings of a bald eagle or two. Kayaks may also be rented.

In the village of St. Ann's you'll pass the **Gaelic College of Celtic Arts and Crafts** ℛ (© **902/295-3411**), located 1km (½ mile) off the Trans-Canada Highway at Exit 11. The school was founded informally in 1938, when a group of area citizens began offering instruction in Gaelic language in a one-room log cabin. Today, both the campus and the curriculum have expanded significantly, with classes now offered in bagpiping, fiddle, Highland dance, weaving, spinning, and Scottish history.

The 140-hectare (350-acre) campus is home to the Great Hall of Clans, where visitors can get a quick lesson in Scottish culture. A number of exhibits provide answers to many questions, such as, what is the deal with tartan plaid, how did Scotsmen get reputations as fierce warriors, and what do Scotsmen really wear under a kilt? (Alas, the question "Is bagpiping really music?" is not addressed.) Robbie Burns's walking stick is on display, and you can buy intriguing clan histories as well. The Hall of Clans is open daily June through September from 8:30am to 5pm; admission is about C$2.50 (US$2) per person, free for children under 12. A campus crafts shop has shelves full of Gaelic items, including bolts of tartan plaid and tapes of traditional music. Live performances are also offered throughout the summer; call ahead or ask at the crafts shop for a schedule.

### WHERE TO STAY

**Luckenbooth Bed & Breakfast**    Built in 1999, this modern, log-accented B&B has three bedrooms and is nicely located on 305m (1,000 ft.) of wooded shore frontage. (There's a trail down to the water.) Guests have the run of several common areas, including the main living room with its cozy fireplace and soaring cathedral ceiling and a yellow-tartan-themed basement room with satellite television, a VCR, and games. (It's decorated in the clan tartans of proprietors Frances and Wayne McClure;

Frances is also a bagpiper.) The guest rooms each have modern furnishings. The best of the lot is no. 3, upstairs with hardwood floors, views of the bay, and a sitting area just outside the door. The other two rooms are in the walk-out basement, and feature cork floors. The inn has a no-shoes-inside policy, and slippers are furnished to guests.

R.R. 4, Baddeck, St. Ann's, Cabot Trail, NS B0E 1B0. © 877/654-2357 or 902/929-2722. Fax 902/929-2503. luckenbooth@ns.sympatico.ca. 3 units. C$120–C$145 (US$96–US$116) double. Rates include breakfast. MC, V. *In room:* No phone.

## BADDECK

Although Baddeck (pronounced *Bah*-deck) is at a distance from the national park, it's often considered the de facto "capital" of the Cabot Trail. The town offers the widest selection of hotels and accommodations along the whole loop, an assortment of restaurants, and a handful of useful services like grocery stores and laundromats. Baddeck is also famed as the summer home of revered inventor Alexander Graham Bell, who is memorialized at a national historic site. It's also compact and easy to reconnoiter by foot, scenically located on the shores of Bras d'Or Lake, and within striking distance of the Fortress at Louisbourg. That makes it the most practical base for those with limited vacation time who are planning to drive the Cabot Trail in 1 day (figure on 6–8 hr.).

If, however, your intention is to spend a few days exploring the hiking trails, bold headlands, and remote coves of the national park (which I'd recommend!), you're better off finding a base farther north; the town's single street, frankly, can get claustrophobically packed with tourists and tour buses, and beyond Bell's home there's little of lingering interest here.

The useful **Baddeck Welcome Center** (© **902/295-1911**) is located just south of the village at the intersection of Route 105 and Route 205. It's open daily in season (June to mid-Oct) from 9am to 7pm.

### EXPLORING THE TOWN

Baddeck is much like a modern New England village, skinny and centered around a single commercial boulevard (Chebucto St.) just off the lake. Ask for a free walking tour brochure at the welcome center. A complete tour of the village's architectural highlights won't take much more than 15 or 20 minutes.

Government Wharf (head down Jones St. from the Yellow Cello restaurant) is home to three boat tours, which offer the best way to experience **Bras d'Or Lake. Fan-A-Sea** (© **902/295-1900**) runs charter fishing trips from Baddeck May through mid-October, and with some luck you may land cod, haddock, or trout. Bait and rods are supplied; the rate is about C$40 (US$32) per person, and a minimum of two people is required per tour. Also in Baddeck, **Loch Bhreagh Boat Tours** (© **902/295-2016**) offers thrice-daily motorboat tours that pass Alexander Graham Bell's palatial former estate and other attractions at this end of the lake from May through October.

About 180m (600 ft.) offshore from the downtown wharf is Kidston Island, owned by the town. It has a wonderful sand beach with lifeguards and an old lighthouse to explore. The Lion's Club offers frequent pontoon boat shuttles between 10am and 6pm (noon–6pm on weekends) across St. Patrick's Channel; the crossing is free, but donations are encouraged.

### Alexander Graham Bell National Historic Site ⊛ ⟨Kids⟩    Each summer for much of his life, noted inventor Alexander Graham Bell fled the heat of Washington, D.C., for a hillside retreat high above Bras d'Or Lake. The mansion, which is still owned and

occupied by the Bell family, is visible across the harbor from various spots around town. But to learn more about Bell's career and restless mind, you should visit this modern exhibit center, perched on a grassy hillside at the north edge of the village. You'll find extensive exhibits about Bell's invention of the telephone at age 29, as well as considerable information about Bell's less-lauded contraptions, like his ingenious kites, hydrofoils, and airplanes. There's an extensive discovery area, where kids are encouraged to apply their intuition and creativity in solving problems.

Chebucto St., Baddeck. (C) **902/295-2069**. Admission C$6.50 (US$5.20) adults, C$5.50 (US$4.40) seniors, C$3.25 (US$2.60) youth age 6–16, C$16 (US$13) family. June daily 9am–6pm; July to mid-Oct daily 8:30am–6pm; mid-Oct to May daily 9am–5pm.

## WHERE TO STAY

If the places below are booked, try **Auberge Gisele's,** 387 Shore Rd. ((C) **800/304-0466** or 902/295-2849), a modern 75-room hotel that's open May to late October and popular with bus tours; rooms cost C$135 to C$175 (US$108–US$140). Or try the **Cabot Trail Motel,** Route 105, 1.6km (1 mile) west of Baddeck ((C) **902/295-2580**), with about 40 rooms and four chalets overlooking the lake and a heated outdoor pool. Doubles run around C$95 to C$115 (US$76–US$92).

**Duffus House Inn** *(F)*  A visit to the Duffus House is like a visit to the grandmother's house everyone wished they had. These two adjacent buildings, constructed in 1820 and 1885, overlook the channel and are cozy and very tastefully furnished with a mix of antiques (the Cunard Room is decorated with memorabilia from the cruise line of the same name). The Duffus House is located far enough from Baddeck's downtown to keep the commotion at arm's length, yet you can still walk everywhere in a few minutes' time. (The inn also has its own dock, recently fixed up, where you can swim or just sit peacefully.) The several cozy common areas are comfortably furnished and offer great places to chat with the other guests, as does the intimate garden. The inn doesn't charge bargain room rates, but delivers fair value for the cost.

108 Water St. (P.O. Box 427), Baddeck, NS B0E 1B0. (C) **902/295-2172**. www.baddeck.com/duffushouse. 7 units. C$125–C$165 (US$100–US$132) double. Rates include continental breakfast. V. Closed mid-Oct to June. *In room:* No phone.

**Green Highlander Lodge**  The Green Highlander is located atop the Yellow Cello, a popular in-town eatery. The three rooms are nicely decorated in a sort of Abercrombie & Fitch gentleman's fishing camp motif. (Rooms are named after Atlantic salmon flies.) Blue Charm has a private sitting room. Rosie Dawn and Lady Amherst have private decks that look out to Kidston Island. Ask about the moonlight paddle trips, kayak rentals, and the private beach located a mile away.

525 Chebucto St., Baddeck, NS B0E 1B0. (C) **902/295-2303** or 902/295-2240. Fax 902/295-1592. www.greenhighlanderlodge.com. 3 units. C$90–C$120 (US$72–US$96) double. Rates include full breakfast. AE, MC, V. Closed Nov to mid-May. **Amenities:** Kayak rentals. *In room:* Hair dryer, no phone.

**Inverary Resort**  This sprawling resort, located on 5 lakeside hectares (12 acres) within walking distance of town, is a good choice for families with active kids. The slew of activities runs the gamut from fishing and paddleboats to nightly bonfires on the beach. Sports fans will love the volleyball, tennis, and shuffleboard courts. Guest rooms and facilities are spread all over the well-maintained grounds, mostly in buildings painted dark-chocolate brown with white trim and green roofs. The rooms vary in size and style, but all are quite comfortable, even the snug motel-style units in the cottages; five two-bedroom units are offered, and four units have kitchens. The resort has two dining rooms: a café overlooking the resort's small marina serves informal fare like penne with pesto and vegetable lasagna; the more formal dining room in the main lodge serves classier food in a sun-porch setting.

Shore Rd. (P.O. Box 190), Baddeck, NS B0E 1B0. ⓒ **800/565-5660** or 902/295-3500. Fax 902/295-3527. www.inverary resort.com. 138 units. C$90–C$175 (US$72–US$160) double, C$130–C$390 (US$104–US$312) suite. AE, DC, MC, V. Closed Dec–May. **Amenities:** 2 restaurants; pub; indoor pool; 3 tennis courts; spa; Jacuzzi; sauna; watersports equipment; bike; playground; room service. *In room:* A/C, TV (w/VCR in some units), no phone.

**Telegraph House**　The rooms in this 1861 hotel right on Baddeck's bustling main street are divided between the original inn and two motel units on a rise behind the inn. This is where Alexander Graham Bell stayed when he first visited Baddeck, and the rooms are still rooming-house small. Four rooms on the top floor share two bathrooms between them, an arrangement that works well with families. Guests can linger on the front or side porch (there are several sitting nooks) and watch commerce happen on the main drag. I actually prefer the larger if unexciting motel rooms in back; ask for rooms 22 to 32, which have small sitting decks outside their front doors with glimpses of the lake. The dining room serves traditional favorites for both lunch and dinner. Expect shepherd's pie, ham plate, meatloaf, roast turkey, fish cakes—and big, sloppy, wonderfully nasty desserts.

Chebucto St. (P.O. Box 8), Baddeck, NS B0E 1B0. ⓒ **902/295-1100.** Fax 902/295-1136. www.baddeck.com/ telegraph. 41 units. C$70–C$119 (US$56–US$95) double, C$89–C$115 (US$71–US$92) cabin. AE, MC, V. **Amenities:** Restaurant. *In room:* A/C (1 unit), TV, no phone.

## WHERE TO DINE

Many of Baddeck's larger hotels have dining rooms, where you'll find some of the town's more refined fare. **Auberge Gisele's** dining room (see above) features Continental cuisine, although try to come later in the evening after the bus tours have finished feeding. At the Inverary Resort (see above), the aptly named **Lakeside Cafe** is a popular spot, with a view of the marina and a moderately priced menu with pastas and stir-fries. The resort's main dining room, Flora's, features more creative (and more expensive) fare. At the **Silver Dart Lodge,** Shore Road (ⓒ **902/295-2340**), there's informal McCurdy's Dining Room, which has a good reputation for seafood.

**Baddeck Lobster Suppers** *(Overrated)* SEAFOOD　This no-frills restaurant has the charm of a Legion Hall and charges an arm and a leg, but tourist crowds contentedly and noisily chow down here every summer nonetheless. The lobster dinner—which virtually everyone orders—includes one smallish steamed crustacean, plus all-you-can-eat mussels (recommended), chowder, biscuits, dessert, and soda. Beer and wine costs extra, and can push the bill for a family into the "unexpectedly expensive" category. Not in the mood for lobster? There's also planked salmon here—which is cooked out back by a chef happy to talk about the process; if you've never eaten it, though, it might taste dry in the mouth—and a cold ham plate that nobody orders. A kids' menu is available.

Ross St. ⓒ **902/295-3307.** Reservations accepted for groups of 10 or more. Lobster dinner around C$27 (US$22); lunch items C$3–C$7 (US$2.40–US$5.60). MC, V. Daily 11:30am–1:30pm and 4–9pm. Closed mid-Oct to mid-June.

**Yellow Cello Café** PUB FARE　If you don't set your culinary expectations too high, this is a convivial spot to while away an afternoon or evening. Angle for a seat outdoors under the awning facing Chebucto Street. The menu will be familiar to those who watch a lot of sports on TV: pizza, nachos, chili, lasagna, sandwiches, and the like.

525 Chebucto St. ✆ 902/295-2303. Reservations suggested during peak season. Main courses C$7–C$12 (US$5.60–US$9.50). AE, MC, V. May–Oct daily 8am–11pm.

## BRAS D'OR LAKE

"Yeah, this is gorgeous, but how much gorgeous can you take?" That was the comment I overheard at a high overlook with a stunning panoramic view of Bras d'Or Lake, the vast inland sea that nearly cleaves Cape Breton Island in two. The man uttered the comment to his family, which then trudged back to their car and set off for the Cape Breton coast.

It was actually a telling comment. With so much beauty around the island's perimeter, the lake hardly gets noticed. This in itself is remarkable. Almost anywhere else in the world, Bras d'Or Lake (pronounced bra door) would be a major attraction, ringed by motels, lodges, boat tour operators, and chain restaurants. But today, along the twisting shoreline of this 114km-long (71-mile) saltwater lake, you'll find . . . nothing. Granted, roads circumnavigate the whole lake, but you'll generally find few services for tourists. Is that good or bad? Depends on your outlook.

Bras d'Or is a difficult lake to characterize, since it changes dramatically from one area to the next—near wilderness here, rolling farmland there, a summer home colony at another location. Wherever you go around the lake, watch for the regal silhouettes of bald eagles soaring high above, or that telltale spot of vivid white among the verdant trees indicating a perched eagle. Dozens of pairs of bald eagles nest along the shores or nearby, making this one of the best areas in the Maritimes for eagle sightings.

### EXPLORING BRAS D'OR LAKE

What's a good strategy for touring the lake? For starters, I would caution against trying to drive around it in 1 day—or even over 2 days. There's no equivalent to the Cabot Trail around the lake's perimeter. The road serves up breathtaking views from time to time, but for much of the route it's dull and uninteresting, running at a distance from the lakeshore and offering mostly views of scrappy woods. It's better to select one or two portions of the lake, and focus your travels there.

For **scenic drives,** three segments lend themselves nicely to touring by car. One is the quiet shore near Iona and along the St. Andrew's Channel on Route 223. Another is the hump between St. Peters and Dundee, which winds high and low and in recent years has become the area of choice for the summer homes of vacationing Germans. And a third segment is Route 4 from East Bay to St. Peters, where you'll get the most uninterrupted views of the lake, and best sense of its vast size.

Off-the-beaten-track explorers would do well to roam the road that snakes along western shore backwaters between the towns of Marble Mountain through Orangedale to Estmere, although a decent map is essential. This is a good area to explore by canoe or mountain bike; bring your own or rent in one of the larger towns, because you won't find outfitters (or any other service providers) around this part of the lake. Several boat tours are offered from **Baddeck** (see above), however.

On the southeastern shore is the town of St. Peters, where the lake comes within 800m (2,624 ft.) of breaking through to the Atlantic Ocean and splitting Cape Breton into two islands. Nature didn't, but humans did when they built **St. Peter's Canal** in 1854. The canal still operates, and if you linger long enough, you may see some impressive pleasure craft making their way up to the lake. The pathway along the canal makes for good strolling.

The village of **Marble Mountain,** on the southwestern shore, offers an intriguing glimpse into history. The town was once a bustling metropolis of sorts. In 1868 a lustrous seam of marble was located here, and by the early part of this century a full-scale mining operation was in effect, supplying builders worldwide. At its peak, the quarry employed 750, and the town was home to more than 1,000. Today, it's reverted to a sleepy backwater. The free **Marble Mountain Museum and Library** (✆ **902/756-3289**), in a former schoolhouse, is open daily July to September from 10am to 5pm; it provides a glimpse at the former prosperity of the area.

Afterward, drive north of town to the overlook high above the island-dotted lake. On the uphill side, look for the gravel lane across the road that angles upward to the right. It's just a 5- or 10-minute walk up to the quarry, a hulking and melancholy hole encroached upon by thistles and Queen Anne's lace. There's an even better view of the lake from here.

Hot and bothered? You can cool off down at the lake, and in style. The **town beach,** which looks from above to be of white sand, really isn't. It's marble chips from the old quarrying operation. You can scramble down from the overlook, or drive into the village and make your way to the lakeshore.

Also worth a quick detour is **Isle Madame** (actually a group of small islands), just south of the lake off Route 4 between St. Peter's and Port Hawkesbury; it's almost entirely French-speaking. Drop by a local bakery or restaurant for a croissant or other French treat. Near the village of Arichat, the **Duke of York Cranberry Meadow** (✆ **902/226-0001;** www.dukeofyork.ca) has been cultivating the sour berry since 1894. The proprietors operate tours, sell berries, drinks, and other products, and even rent out the central farmhouse on a daily and weekly basis.

**Nova Scotia Highland Village Museum** ☆ *Kids*   The Highland Village is located near Iona, on a grassy hillside with sweeping views over the lake. When you finally turn your back on the panorama, you'll be at a living history museum—a 17-hectare (43-acre) village featuring 10 buildings that reflect the region's Gaelic heritage, including historic structures moved here from locations around the island and exacting replicas. These range from the Black House (ca. 1790), a stone and sod hut of the sort an immigrant would have lived in prior to departing Scotland, to a schoolhouse and general store from the 1920s. Staffers dressed in historical costume will answer any questions you may have about early island life, and happily answer kid-size questions, too. Ask about Living History Tours (daylong events allowing visitors to immerse themselves in daily life) and candlelight tours after-hours (summer only); drop by the genealogy center, too, if you suspect your family has local roots. It's worth spending at least an hour here.

Rte. 223, Iona. ✆ 902/725-2272. http://museum.gov.ns.ca/hv. Admission C$8 (US$5.60) adults, C$6 (US$5) seniors, C$3 (US$2.40) children 5–18, C$19 (US$15) families. Mid-May to mid-Oct daily 9am–6pm. Closed mid-Oct to mid-May.

## WHERE TO STAY
**Highland Heights Inn** ☆ *Value*   The Highland Heights is a well-managed motel with clean, well-maintained rooms, but it's different from other well-run motels in one critical way: the views! Every room has a view of the lake. The second-floor rooms cost a bit more, but are worth the splurge just for the balconies from which you can monitor the lake's shifting moods. (The 2nd-floor rooms are also a bit bigger and brighter.) All rooms have fans and windows that open. The motel's dining room is cheerful and sunny in a 1970s sort of way (the inn was built in 1972), with lake views

from the tables along the windows. It's open for three meals daily, and features home-style cooking.

Rte. 223 (P.O. Box 19), Iona, NS B0A 1L0. © **800/565-5660** or 902/725-2360. Fax 902/725-2800. www.highland heightsinn.com. 32 units. C$72–C$119 (US$58–US$95) double. Ask about multinight packages. DISC, MC, V. Closed mid-Oct to mid-May. **Amenities:** Dining room. *In room:* No phone.

## WHERE TO DINE

**Rita's Tea Room** ☆ *(Finds* LIGHT FARE    Singer-songwriter Rita MacNeil grew up in Big Pond, and she never forgot her roots during her rise to fame. She always told audiences to stop by for a cup of tea if they were in the neighborhood. Problem was, they did. So Rita opened a tearoom for her fans, housing it in a converted 1939 schoolhouse. Today it contains a thriving gift shop (offering the music of Rita and others), with a comfortable and homey dining room where you can get baked goods, sandwiches, and soup. The tea for two is perfect on a drizzly Cape Breton day.

Rte. 4, Big Pond (about 40km/25 miles southwest of Sydney). © **902/828-2667**. Snacks and sandwiches C$3.95–C$7.95 (US$3.15–US$6); tea for two, C$13 (US$11). V. Mid-June to mid-Oct daily 10am–6pm. Closed mid-Oct to mid-June.

## SYDNEY

Nova Scotia's third-largest city (pop. 30,000) was northern Nova Scotia's industrial hub for decades, and to this day three out of four Cape Breton Islanders live in and around Sydney. Recent economic trends have not been kind to the area, though, and once-thriving steel mills and coal mines have not exactly prospered. This gritty port city has been striving to reinvent itself as a tourist destination, but success has been elusive—in part because Cape Breton's other charms offer such tough competition.

Although the commercial downtown is a bit gnarly, the historic residential areas will appeal to architecture and history aficionados. Three early buildings are open to the public in summer and are within easy walking distance of one another. They don't get a lot of traffic; as a result, the costumed attendants don't display that wearied fatigue so often present in other guides, and their fresh enthusiasm is appealing and infectious.

The **Cossit House Museum,** 75 Charlotte St. (© **902/539-7973**), is Sydney's oldest house, built in 1785. It's been lovingly restored and furnished with a fine collection of 18th-century antiques. There's a small charge to visit. The **Jost Heritage House,** 54 Charlotte St. (© **902/539-0366**), was built in 1787 and had a number of incarnations in the intervening years, including service as a store. It's open June through August Monday through Saturday from 9:30am to 5:30pm, Sunday from 1pm; hours are shorter during the fall. Highlights of the home include an early apothecary, and again there's a small entry fee to view it. **St. Patrick's Church Museum,** 87 Esplanade (© **902/539-1572**), is in Cape Breton's oldest Roman Catholic church (it dates to 1828) and opens to the public daily in summer from 9:30am to 5:30pm (opens at 1pm Sun). There's an old burying ground and a collection of local artifacts. It's free. Plan to spend a few hours visiting this trifecta.

## PUFFIN TOURS

Thirty minutes west of Sydney (just off the Trans-Canada Hwy. en route to St. Ann's or Baddeck) is the home port of **Bird Island Boat Tours** (© **800/661-6680** or 902/674-2384; www.birdisland.net). On a 2½-hour narrated cruise you'll head out to the Bird Islands, home to a colony of around 300 nesting puffins. You'll get within about 18m (60 ft.) of the colorful birds (they nest in grassy burrows above rocky cliffs), and you may also see razorbills, guillemots, and the occasional bald eagle. Three tours are offered daily from mid-May through mid-September; the fare is C$32 (US$23) adults, C$15 (US$11) children 6 to 12; free for children under 5. Reservations are suggested. The outfit also maintains rental cottages in the area.

## AN UNDERGROUND TOUR

Northeast of Sydney is the town of Glace Bay, a former coal-mining center. The mines have slipped into a long economic twilight of late, but the province has made lemonade from lemons by inaugurating the surprisingly intriguing **Cape Breton Miners' Museum** ☙☙, 42 Birkley St. (© **902/849-4522;** www.minersmuseum.com). The museum provides background on the rich geology of the area and offers insight into the region's sometimes rough labor history.

But the highlight of the trip is a 20-minute descent into the mine itself, with damp walls and cool temperatures (it's always 50°F/10°C). Retired miners, who can convey what it was like to be working in the mines better than anyone else, lead the tours. One Frommer's reader reported that her two teenage sons were all groans and eye rolls when she announced their destination, but the two came away in awe of the place. Altogether, plan to spend at least an hour here.

Admission is C$5 (US$4) adults, C$4 (US$3.20) children for either the museum or the mine tour. Open daily in summer from 10am to 6pm (Tuesdays until 7pm); open weekdays in winter from 9am to 4pm.

## WHERE TO STAY & DINE

**Gowrie House** ☙☙    This is a standout inn, easily among the best in Nova Scotia. Located across the harbor from Sydney and a few minutes' drive north of the Newfoundland ferry, Gowrie House is at once resplendent and comfortable, historic and very up-to-date. Portions of the gray-shingled house on 4 hectares (10 acres) were originally built in 1820, and the building has been expanded and decorated with Oriental carpets, Asian ceramics, stout Regency furniture, and splashes of modern art. The smallest guest rooms are more spacious than the largest rooms at some other inns. Especially nice is the separate Caretaker's Cottage, lavishly furnished and accompanied by its own small deck and garden. Four rooms are in the more modern Garden House; these are carpeted and airy and have microwaves and refrigerators. Five rooms have kitchenettes, nine have fireplaces, and three have Jacuzzis. The only problem? Getting a room. The whole summer season is often booked up by mid-June, so call as far in advance as you can.

The inn's well-regarded **dining room** ☙ features regional cuisine and local ingredients, such as grilled halibut with mango chutney and marinated lamb. There's one seating nightly at 7:30pm; the price is about C$40 (US$32) per person for four courses. Houseguests receive a carafe of wine; for outside guests, who should try to reserve a table at least 3 or 4 days in advance, it's BYOB.

840 Shore Rd., Sydney Mines, NS B1V 1A6. © **800/372-1115** or 902/544-1050. Fax 902/736-0077. www.gowriehouse.com. 11 units. C$145–C$175 (US$116–US$140) double, C$265 (US$212) cottage. Rates include continental breakfast. AE, MC, V. Closed Jan–Mar. Pets allowed with advance notice. **Amenities:** Dining room. *In room:* A/C, hair dryer.

## LOUISBOURG ☙☙

In the early 18th century, **Louisbourg on Cape,** Breton's remote and windswept easternmost coast was home to an ambitious French fortress and settlement. Despite its brief prosperity and durable construction of rock, it virtually disappeared after the

British finally forced the French out (for the 2nd time) in 1760. Through the miracle of archaeology and historic reconstruction, much of the imposing settlement has been re-created, and today Louisbourg is among Canada's most ambitious national historic parks. It's an attraction everyone coming to Cape Breton Island should make an effort to visit.

And a visit does require some effort. The site, 36km (22 miles) east of Sydney, isn't on the way to anyplace else, and it's an inconvenient detour from Cape Breton Highlands National Park. As such, it's far too easy to justify not going—it's too out of the way, it's not conveniently on a loop, and so on. By employing such excuses you're only cheating yourself. Commit yourself to going, then go. A few hours spent wandering this wondrous rebuilt town, then walking amid ruins and out along the coastal trail, will be one of the highlights of your trip to Atlantic Canada.

## EXPLORING THE VILLAGE

The hamlet of Louisbourg—which you'll pass through en route to the historic park— is pleasantly low-key, still scouting for ways to rebound from one devastating economic loss after another, including the cessation of the railway, the decline in boat building, and the loss of the fisheries. Louisbourg is now striving to gear its economy more toward tourism, and you can see the progress year by year.

A short **boardwalk** with interpretive signs fronts the town's tiny waterfront. (You'll get a glimpse of the national historic site across the water.) Nearby is a faux-Elizabethan theater, the **Louisbourg Playhouse** (© 902/733-2996; www.louisbourgplayhouse. com), at 11 Aberdeen St. This was originally built near the old town by Disney for filming the movie *Squanto*. After the production wrapped up, Disney donated it to the village, which dismantled it and moved it to a side street near the harbor. Various performances and concerts are staged here throughout the summer.

As you come into town on Route 22 you'll pass the **Sydney and Louisbourg Railway Museum** (© 902/733-2720), which shares the gabled railway depot with the local **visitor information center** (© 902/733-2720). The museum commemorates the former railway, which shipped coal from the mines to Louisbourg harbor between 1895 and 1968. You can visit some of the old rolling stock (including an 1881 passenger car), and view the Roundhouse. Open daily mid-May to mid-October; hours in July and August are 8am to 8pm; in spring and fall 9am to 5pm. Admission is free.

Leave enough time during your trip for the detour a couple of miles out to the **Lighthouse Point,** the site of the first Canadian lighthouse. (The current lighthouse is a replacement.) The rocky coastline is dramatic and undeveloped, and it's a perfect spot for a picnic or to just idle away a late afternoon. The road, which is partly gravel, departs from the main road near the visitor information center.

**Fortress of Louisbourg National Historic Site** 𝕽𝕽 𝓚𝓲𝓭𝓼 The historic French village of Louisbourg has had three lives. The first was early in the 18th century, when the French first colonized this area—aggressively—in a bid to stake their claim in the New World. They built an imposing fortress of stone. Imposing but not impregnable, as the British were to prove when they captured the fort in 1745. The fortress had a second, if short-lived, heyday after it was returned to the French following negotiations in Europe. War soon broke out again, however, and the British recaptured it in 1758; this time they blew it up for good measure. The final resurrection came during the 1960s, when the Canadian government decided to rebuild one-fourth of the stone-walled town—virtually creating from whole cloth a settlement from some grass hummocks and a few scattered documents about what once had been. The park was built to re-create life as it looked in 1744, when this was an important French military capital and seaport; visitors today arrive at the site after walking through an interpretive center and boarding a bus for the short ride to the site. (Keeping cars at a distance does much to enhance the historic flavor.)

You will wander through the impressive gatehouse—perhaps being challenged by a costumed guard on the lookout for English spies—and then begin wandering the narrow lanes and poking around the faux-historic buildings, some of which contain informative exhibits, others of which are restored and furnished with convincingly worn reproductions. Chicken, geese, and other barnyard animals peck and cluck as vendors hawk freshly baked bread out of wood-fired ovens.

To make the most of your visit, ask about the free guided tours. And don't hesitate to question the costumed interpreters, who are as knowledgeable as they are friendly. Allow at least 4 hours to explore. It's an extraordinary destination, as picturesque as it is historic.

Louisbourg, NS. © 902/733-2280 or 902/733-3546. Admission C$15 (US$12) adults, C$13 (US$10) seniors, C$7.50 (US$6) children, C$38 (US$30) family. July–Aug daily 9am–5pm; May–June and Sept–Oct daily 9:30am–5pm. Costumed interpreters limited in off season. Closed Nov–Apr.

## WHERE TO STAY

**Cranberry Cove Inn** 🦋    You won't miss this attractive, in-town inn when en route to the fortress—it's a three-story Victorian farmhouse painted a boisterous cranberry red with cranberry-tinged meals to match. Inside it's decorated with a light Victorian motif. The upstairs rooms are carpeted and furnished around themes—Anne's Hideaway is the smallest but has a nice old tub and butterfly collection; Isle Royale is done up in Cape Breton tartan. My favorite room is also the quirkiest: *Field and Stream,* with a twig headboard, and mounted deer head and pheasant. Breakfast includes cran-apple sauce and "cran-bran" muffins; dinner is served nightly from 5 to 8:30pm in the handsome first-floor dining room, which has a polished wood floor and cherrywood tables and chairs. Entrees range from charbroiled Atlantic salmon to (you guessed it) cranberry-marinated breast of chicken. A "cranberry cottage" is said to be coming in the near future. *Note:* Due to the three-story open staircase, this inn is not suitable for toddlers.

12 Wolfe St., Louisbourg, NS B1C 2J2. © 800/929-0222 or 902/733-2171. www.louisbourg.com/cranberrycove. 7 units. C$105–C$160 (US$84–US$128) double. Rates include breakfast. MC, V. Closed Nov–Apr. **Amenities:** Dining room. *In room:* TV (some units), hair dryer, no phone (some units).

**Louisbourg Harbour Inn** 🦋    This golden-yellow, century-old clapboard home is conveniently located in the village, a block off the main street and overlooking fishing wharves, the blue waters of the harbor, and, across the way, the Fortress of Louisbourg. The inn's lustrous pine floors have been nicely restored, and all the guest rooms are tidy and attractive, with some fussier than others. The best rooms are on the third floor, requiring a bit of a trek; Room 6 is bright and cheerful; Room 7 is very spacious and boasts an in-room Jacuzzi and a pair of rockers from which to monitor the happenings at the fish pier. A nice touch: All rooms facing the harbor have Jacuzzis. Room 1 and Room 3 also have private balconies. Dinner is occasionally available by advance reservations to guests in the first-floor dining room. A three-course meal (entree choices typically include steak, lobster, or crab) runs C$20 to C$30 (US$13–US$20), depending on what's being offered.

9 Lower Warren St., Louisbourg, NS B1C 1G6. © 888/888-8466 or 902/733-3222. www.louisbourg.com/louisbourg harbourinn. 8 units. C$115–C$180 (US$92–US$144) double. Rates include breakfast. MC, V. Closed mid-Oct to mid-June. *In room:* Fridge (some units), no phone.

## WHERE TO DINE

Louisbourg has a handful of informal, family-style restaurants, plus upscale dining at Cranberry Cove. My choice for more casual eating out would be **The Grubstake** ✪, 7499 Main St. (✆ **902/733-2308**), open mid-June to early October from noon to about 9pm. The place was founded by a few friends in 1972, and ever since it has embraced the philosophy that food should be fresh and honest. Expect good food at good prices and served with a winning attitude. The seafood is especially tasty.

## 12  Cape Breton Highlands National Park ✪✪✪

Cape Breton Highlands National Park is one of the two crown-jewel national parks in Atlantic Canada (Gros Morne in Newfoundland is the other). Covering some 950 sq. km (365 sq. miles) and stretching across a rugged peninsula from the Atlantic to the Gulf of St. Lawrence, the park is famous for its starkly beautiful terrain. It also features one of the most dramatic coastal drives east of Big Sur, California. One of the great pleasures of the park is that it holds something for everyone, from tourists who prefer to sightsee from the comfort of their car, to those who prefer backcountry hiking in the company of bear and moose.

The mountains of Cape Breton are probably unlike those you're familiar with elsewhere. The heart of the park is fundamentally a huge plateau. In the vast interior, you'll find a flat and melancholy landscape of wind-stunted evergreens, bogs, and barrens. This is called the taiga, a name that refers to the zone between tundra and the northernmost forest. In this largely untracked area (which is also Nova Scotia's largest remaining wilderness), you might find 150-year-old trees that are only knee-high.

But it's the park's edges that capture the attention. On the western side of the peninsula, the tableland has eroded into the sea, creating a dramatic landscape of ravines and ragged, rust-colored cliffs pounded by the ocean. The Cabot Trail, a paved road built in 1939, winds dramatically along the flanks of the mountains, offering extraordinary vistas at every turn. On the park's other coastal flank—the eastern, Atlantic side—the terrain is less dramatic, with a coastal plain interposed between mountains and sea. But the lush green hills still offer a backdrop that's exceptionally picturesque.

Note that this section focuses only on the park proper, which offers no lodging or services other than camping. You will find limited lodging and restaurants in the handful of villages that ring the park. See "Cape Breton Island," earlier in this chapter.

## ESSENTIALS

**GETTING THERE**   Access to the park is via the Cabot Trail, one of several tourist routes well marked by provincial authorities. The entire loop is 300km (185 miles). The distance from the park entrance at Chéticamp to the park entrance at Ingonish is 105km (65 miles). Although the loop can be done in either direction, I would encourage visitors to drive it in a clockwise direction solely because the visitor center in Chéticamp offers a far more detailed introduction to the park.

**VISITOR INFORMATION**   **Visitor information centers** are located at both Chéticamp and Ingonish and are open daily summers from 8am to 8pm. The Chéticamp center has more extensive information about the park, including a 10-minute slide presentation, natural history exhibits, a large-scale relief map, and a very good bookstore specializing in natural and cultural history. The park's main phone number is ✆ **902/224-2306**.

# Cape Breton Highlands National Park

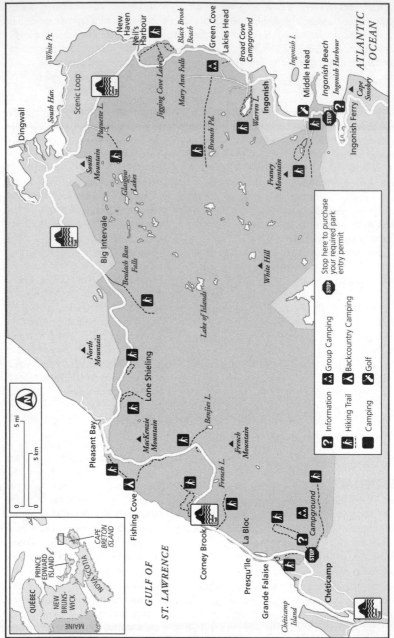

**FEES**    Entrance permits are required from mid-May through mid-October and can be purchased either at information centers or at tollhouses at the two main park entrances. Permits are required for any activity along the route, even stopping to admire the view. Daily fees are C$6 (US$5) adults, C$5 (US$4) seniors, C$3 (US$2.40) children age 6 to 16, and C$15 (US$12) family.

## EXPLORING THE PARK
### SCENIC DRIVES

Cape Breton Highlands National Park offers basically one drive, and with few lapses it's scenic along the entire route. The most breathtaking stretch is the 43km (27-mile) **jaunt** 🎔🎔🎔 from Chéticamp to Pleasant Bay along the western coast. Double the time you figure you'll need to drive this route, because you'll want to spend time at the pullouts admiring the views and perusing informational signboards. If it's foggy, save yourself the entrance fee and gas money. Without the views, there's little reason to travel and you'd be well advised to wait until the fog lifts. Until then, you could hike in the foggy forest or across the upland bogs, or explore some of the nearby villages in the atmospheric mist.

For an excellent detour at the northern apex of the loop, consider a side trip to Meat Cove (see the "Cape North" section, earlier in this chapter).

### HIKING

The park has 27 hiking trails departing from the Cabot Trail. Many excursions are quite short and have the feel of a casual stroll rather than a vigorous tromp, but those determined to be challenged will find suitable destinations. All trails are listed with brief descriptions on the reverse side of the map you'll receive when you pay your entry fee.

The **Skyline Trail** 🎔🎔🎔 offers all the altitude with none of the climbing. You ascend the tableland from Chéticamp by car, and then follow a 7km (4.25-mile) hiking loop out along dramatic bluffs and through wind-stunted spruce and fir. A spur trail descends to a high, exposed point overlooking the surf; it's capped with blueberry bushes. Moose are often spotted along this trail. Downside: It's a very popular trek and often crowded.

Further along the Cabot Trail, the .8km (.5-mile) **Bog Trail** 🎔 offers a glimpse of the tableland's unique bogs from a dry boardwalk. **Lone Shieling** 🎔 is an easy .8km (.5-mile) loop through a verdant hardwood forest in a lush valley that includes 350-year-old sugar maples. A re-creation of a hut of a Scottish crofter (shepherd) is a feature along this trail.

If you're looking to leave the crowds behind, the **Glasgow Lake Lookoff** 🎔 is a relatively gentle 8km (5-mile) round-trip hike that takes you through barrens and scrub forest to a rocky bald overlooking a series of pristine highland lakes with distant views of the ocean. The trail is alternately swampy and rocky, so rugged footwear is advised.

On the eastern shore, try the superb 4km (2.5-mile) **hike to Middle Head** 🎔🎔, beyond the Keltic Lodge resort. This dramatic, rocky peninsula thrusts well out into the Atlantic. The trail is wide and relatively flat, you'll cross open meadows with wonderful views north and south. The tip is grassy and open, and it offers a fine spot to scan for whales or watch the waves crash in following a storm. Allow about 2 hours for a relaxed excursion out and back.

> ⓘ **Tips  Check Your Brakes**
>
> You'll want to be very confident in your car's brakes before setting out on the Cabot Trail. The road rises and falls with considerable drama, and when cresting some ridges you might feel mildly afflicted with vertigo. Especially stressful on the brakes (when traveling the Cabot Trail clockwise) are the descents to Pleasant Bay, into the Aspy Valley, and off Cape Smokey.

## BIKING

The 282km (175-mile) **Cabot Trail loop** ⋇⋇⋇ is the ironman tour for bike trekkers, both arduous and rewarding. The route twists up ravines and plummets back down toward the coast. One breathtaking vista after another unfolds, and the plunging, brake-smoking descent from Mt. MacKenzie to Pleasant Bay will be one you're not likely to forget. Campgrounds and motels are well spaced for a 3- or 4-day excursion. As for disadvantages, the road is uniformly narrow and almost universally without shoulders, and bikers often get the sense that motor-home drivers don't always know where the far side of their rig is located. This can be a bit harrowing.

If you're not inclined to pedal the whole loop, pick and choose. Especially scenic stretches for fit bikers include **Chéticamp to Pleasant Bay** ⋇⋇ and back, and **the climb and descent** ⋇⋇ from Lone Shieling eastward into the Aspy Valley. See also the "Cape North" section, earlier in this chapter.

**Mountain bikes** are allowed on just four trails within the park—check with the visitor center when you arrive for details. The longest backcountry trail is the 13km (8-mile) route into the **Lake of Islands** ⋇, which doesn't appear on all maps. Ask at one of the two park visitor centers.

## CAMPING

The park has five drive-in campgrounds. The largest are at **Chéticamp** (on the west side) and **Broad Cove** (on the east), both of which have the commendable policy of never turning campers away. Even if all regular sites are full, they'll find a place for you to pitch a tent or park an RV at an overflow area. All the national park campgrounds are well run and well maintained. Chéticamp and Broad Cove offer three-way hookups for RVs. Rates run from C$18 to C$34 (US$15–US$28) per night. Remember that you're also required to buy a day-use permit when camping at Cape Breton, and take note that you can only make advance reservations at Chéticamp, where half the sites are set aside for advance bookings, using the website **www.pccamping.ca**. At the other campgrounds, it's first-come, first-served.

Cape Breton also has some backcountry campsites at **Fishing Cove** ⋇ that are especially attractive, set on a pristine cove; just remember to plan for an 8km (5-mile) hike in from the Cabot Trail and your car. Once there, however, you can watch for pilot whales at sunset from the cliffs. The fee is C$9 (US$7) per person per night; make arrangements at one of the visitor information centers.

# 5

# New Brunswick

Think of New Brunswick as the Rodney Dangerfield of Atlantic Canada—it just gets no respect. It is probably better known for pulp mills, industrial forests, cargo ports, and oil refineries (the huge Irving Oil conglomerate is based here) than for its quaint villages and charming byways, which is a shame. Travelers tend to view New Brunswick as a place you need to drive through—preferably really fast—en route from Québec or Maine to the rest of Atlantic Canada.

Granted, there's a grain of truth behind the province's reputation. But rest assured, New Brunswick has pockets of wilderness and scenic beauty that are unrivaled anywhere in eastern Canada. You'll find sandy beaches on warm ocean waters that hold their own to anything on Prince Edward Island. Not to mention rocky, surf-pounded headlands that could be in the farthest reaches of Newfoundland. The province's appeal tends to be more hidden than that of other locales. But with a little bit of homework, you can quite easily cobble together memorable excursions through an exquisite landscape.

Culturally, New Brunswick is Canada in microcosm. It's split between Anglophone and Francophone populations (about one-third of the residents speak French). Its heritage is both proudly Acadian and proudly pro-British—in fact, New Brunswick is sometimes called the "Loyalist Province" since so many Loyalists fleeing the United States settled here after the American Revolution.

But the cultural divide is less contentious here than in Québec. Interestingly, French-speaking New Brunswick residents share few cultural roots with French-speaking Québecois. (New Brunswick's French ancestors came mostly from central and western France; Québecois trace their ancestry to Brittany and Normandy.) Acadians celebrate the Feast of the Assumption as their national holiday, though in Québec it's the day of St. Jean Baptiste that's biggest. With its unusually harmonious détente between two cultures, New Brunswick likes to offer itself as a model for Québec, but Québec tends to ignore New Brunswick. Too bad; they're missing a national treasure.

## 1 Exploring New Brunswick

Visitors drawn to rugged beauty should plan to focus on the Fundy Coast with its stupendous tides, rocky cliffs, and boreal landscape. (The south coast actually feels more remote and northerly than the more densely settled northeast coast.) Those interested in Acadian history or sandy beaches should veer toward the Gulf of St. Lawrence. Those interested in hurrying through the province to get to Prince Edward Island or Nova Scotia . . . well, you should at least detour down through Fundy National Park and visit Cape Enrage and Hopewell Rocks, which number among eastern Canada's more dramatic attractions.

# New Brunswick

## ESSENTIALS

**VISITOR INFORMATION**    New Brunswick publishes several free annual directories and guides that are helpful in planning a trip to the province, including *Experience New Brunswick,* with listings of attractions, accommodations, campgrounds, and multi-day and daylong adventure packages, as well as an official *New Brunswick Travel Map.* Contact **New Brunswick Department of Tourism and Parks,** P.O. Box 12345, Campbellton, NB E3N 3T6 (© **800/561-0123;** www.tourismnewbrunswick.ca).

The province staffs a series of visitor information centers; most cities and larger towns also have their own municipal information centers. A complete listing of phone numbers for these centers can be found in the Travel Planner guide, or look for "?" direction signs on the highway. Phone numbers and addresses for the appropriate visitor information centers are provided in each section of this chapter.

**GETTING THERE**    The Trans-Canada Highway bisects the province, entering from Québec at St. Jacques. It follows the Saint John River Valley before veering through Moncton and exiting into Nova Scotia at Aulac. The entire distance is about 530km (330 miles).

The fastest route from New England to southwestern New Brunswick is to take the Maine turnpike to Bangor, and then head east on Route 9 to connect to Route 1 into Calais, which is just across the river from St. Stephen, New Brunswick. A more scenic variation is to drive to Campobello Island across the bridge from Lubec, Maine (see the "Passamaquoddy Bay" section, below), then take a ferry to Deer Island, drive the length of the island, and board a second ferry to the mainland. Those headed to Fredericton or Moncton will speed their trip somewhat by following U.S. I-95 to Houlton, and then connecting with the Trans-Canada after crossing the border.

**By Ferry**    **Bay Ferries** (© **888/249-7245;** www.nfl-bay.com) operates a 3-hour ferry that links Saint John with Digby, Nova Scotia. The ferry sails year-round, with as many as three crossings daily each way in summer. Summer fares are C$35 (US$28) for adults, C$25 (US$20) for seniors, C$20 (US$16) for children ages 6 to 17, and C$75 (US$60) and up per vehicle; all are cheaper in the off season. Reservations are advised.

**By Air**    The province's main airports are at Fredericton (the provincial capital), Saint John, and Moncton, all of which are chiefly served by **Air Canada** (© **888/AIR-CANA;** www.aircanada.com) and the major car-rental companies.

**By Train**    **VIA Rail** (© **888/842-7245;** www.viarail.com) offers train service through the province (en route from Montréal to Halifax) 6 days per week. The train follows a northerly route, with stops in Campbellton, Miramichi, and Moncton. Check out the website www.viarail.ca for more details on routes, schedules, and online booking.

## 2 The Great Outdoors

The province has put together a well-conceived campaign called **"Experience New Brunswick"** to encourage visitors of all budgets to explore its outdoor attractions and activities. The travel guide also outlines dozens of multi-day and day adventures ranging from a C$10 (US$8) guided hike at Fundy National Park to C$276 (US$221) biking packages that include inn accommodations and gourmet dinners. For more information on the program, call © **800/561-0123.**

I'd recommend that readers with an adventurous bent look closely at the outdoor center at **Cape Enrage** (see the "Fundy National Park" section, later in this chapter), where you can canoe, rappel, rock climb, and kayak in a dramatic coastal setting.

**BACKPACKING**    Among the best destinations for a backcountry tromp are **Mount Carleton Provincial Park** and **Fundy National Park,** both of which maintain backcountry sites. See the appropriate sections later in this chapter for more information.

**BICYCLING**    The islands and peninsulas of **Passamaquoddy Bay** lend themselves nicely to cruising in the slow lane—especially Campobello, which also has good dirt roads for mountain biking. **Grand Manan** holds appeal for cyclists, although the main road (Rte. 776) has narrow shoulders and fast cars. Some of the best coastal biking is around **Fundy National Park**—especially the back roads to Cape Enrage, and the **Fundy Trail Parkway,** an 11km (6.75-mile) multiuse trail that hugs the coast west of the national park. Along the Acadian Coast, **Kouchibouguac National Park** has limited but unusually nice biking trails through mixed terrain (rentals available).

A handy guide is *Biking to Blissville,* by Kent Thompson. It covers 35 rides in the Maritimes, and costs C$15 (US$12). Contact Goose Lane Editions, 469 King St., Fredericton, NB E3B 1E5 (© **888/926-8377** or 506/450-4251).

**BIRD-WATCHING**    **Grand Manan** is among the province's most noted destinations for birders, located smack on the Atlantic flyway. (John James Audubon lodged here when studying local bird life more than 150 years ago.) Over the course of a year, as many as 275 species are observed on the island, with September typically the best month for sightings. It's not hard to swap information with other birders. On the ferry, look for excitable folks with binoculars and Tilley hats dashing from port to starboard and back, and talk to them. Boat tours from Grand Manan will bring you to Machias Seal Island, with its colonies of puffins, Arctic terns, and razorbills.

On **Campobello Island,** the mixed terrain also attracts a good mix of birds, including sharp-shinned hawk, common eider, and black guillemot. Ask for a checklist and map at the visitor center. Shorebird enthusiasts flock to **Shepody Bay National Wildlife Area,** which maintains preserves in the mud flats between Alma (near Fundy National Park) and Hopewell Cape. Also offering excellent birding is the marsh that surrounds **Sackville,** near the Nova Scotia border.

**CANOEING** New Brunswick has 3,500km (2,200 miles) of inland waterways, plus lakes and protected bays. Canoeists can find everything from glass-smooth waters to daunting rapids. In Kouchibouguac National Park, for example, there is a rental and tour concession based at **Ryans Recreational Equipment Rental Centre** (© 506/876-8918) from mid-May to mid-September. More experienced canoeists looking for a longer expedition should head to the **St. Croix River** on the U.S. border, where you can embark on a multi-day paddle trip and get lost in the woods, spiritually if not in fact.

**FISHING** The **Miramichi River** has long attracted anglers both famous and obscure, lured by the wily Atlantic salmon. In some considered opinions, this ranks among the best salmon rivers in the world, although diminished runs have plagued this river in recent years as they have all rivers in the Maritimes. Salmon must be caught on flies, and nonresidents need to hire a guide to go after salmon. For other freshwater species, including bass, and saltwater angling, the restrictions are less onerous. Get up to date on the rules and regulations by requesting copies of two brochures: "Sport Fishing Summary" and "Atlantic Salmon Angling." These are available from **Fish and Wildlife,** P.O. Box 6000, Fredericton, NB E3B 5H1.

**GOLF** In St. Andrews, the **Algonquin Hotel**'s newly expanded golf course is a beauty—easily among Eastern Canada's top 10, right behind the bigger-name stars on Cape Breton Island and Prince Edward Island. It features nine newer inland holes (the front nine), and then nine older seaside holes that become increasingly spectacular as you approach the point of land separating New Brunswick from Maine. (All 18 of them are challenging, so bring your "A" game.) Service and upkeep are impeccable here, and there's both a snack bar on premises and a roving club car with sandwiches and drinks. Greens fees are C$105 to C$125 (US$84–US$100) for 18 holes, lessons are offered, and there's a short-game practice area in addition to a driving range; call © 888/460-8999 or 506/529-8165 for tee times. In Fredericton, **Kingswood** (© 800/423-5969 or 506/443-3333; www.nbgolf.ca/golf.php) was recognized by *Golf Digest* as the best new Canadian golf course in 2003. It features 27 holes, a par-3 course, and a double-ended driving range.

**HIKING** The province's highest point is in the center of the woodlands region, at **Mount Carleton Provincial Park.** Several demanding hikes in the park yield glorious views. There's also superb hiking at **Fundy National Park,** with a mix of coastal and woodland hikes on well-marked trails. The multiuse, 11km (6.75-mile) **Fundy Trail Parkway** has terrific views of the coast and is wheelchair accessible. **Grand**

**Manan** is a good destination for independent-minded hikers who enjoy the challenge of finding the trail as much as the hike itself.

An excellent resource is *A Hiking Guide to New Brunswick,* published by Goose Lane Editions. It's C$15 (US$12) and available in bookstores around the province, or directly from the publisher (469 King St., Fredericton, NB E3B 1E5; © **888/926-8377** or 506/450-4251).

**SEA KAYAKING**   The huge tides that make kayaking so fascinating along the **Bay of Fundy** also make it exceptionally dangerous—even the strongest kayakers are no match for a fierce ebb tide if they're in the wrong place. Fortunately, the number of skilled sea-kayaking guides has boomed in recent years.

Among the most extraordinary places to explore is **Hopewell Rocks.** The rocks stand like Brancusi statues on the ocean floor at low tide but offer sea caves and narrow channels to explore at high tide. **Baymount Outdoor Adventures** (© **877/601-2660** or 506/734-2660) offers 90-minute sea kayak tours of Hopewell Rocks for C$55 (US$44) adults, C$45 (US$36) children. Other kayak outfitters along the Fundy Coast include **FreshAir Adventure** (© **800/545-0020** or 506/887-2249) in Alma, and **Seascape** (© **866/747-1884** or 506/747-1884) in **Deer Island.**

**SWIMMING**   Parts of New Brunswick offer wonderful ocean swimming. The best beaches are along the **Acadian Coast,** especially near Shediac and in Kouchibouguac National Park. The water is much warmer and the terrain more forgiving along the Gulf of St. Lawrence than the Bay of Fundy.

**WHALE-WATCHING**   The **Bay of Fundy** is rich with plankton, and therefore rich with whales. Some 15 types of whales can be spotted in the bay, including finback, minke, humpback, the infrequent orca, and the endangered right whale. Whale-watching expeditions sail throughout the summer from Campobello Island, Deer Island, Grand Manan, St. Andrews, and St. George. Any visitor information center can point you in the right direction; the province's travel guide also lists many of the tours, which typically cost around C$40 to C$50 (US$32–US$40) for 2 to 4 hours of whale-watching.

## 3 Passamaquoddy Bay

The Passamaquoddy Bay region is often the first point of entry for those arriving overland from the United States. The deeply indented bay is wracked with massive tides that produce currents powerful enough to stymie even doughty fishing boats. It's a place of lasting fogs, spruce-clad islands, bald eagles, and widely scattered development. It's also home to a grand old summer colony and a peninsula that boasts two five-star inns and a rambling turn-of-the-20th-century resort.

## CAMPOBELLO ISLAND ⊛

Campobello is a compact island (about 16km/10 miles long and 5km/3 miles wide) at the mouth of Passamaquoddy Bay. Among its other distinctions, it's connected by a graceful modern bridge to Lubec, Maine, and is thus easier to get to from the United States than from Canada. To get here from the Canadian mainland without driving through the United States requires two ferries, one of which operates only during the summer.

Campobello has been home to both humble fishermen and wealthy families over the years, and both have coexisted quite nicely. (Locals approved when summer folks built golf courses earlier this century, since it gave them a place to graze their sheep.) Today, the island is a mix of elegant summer homes and less interesting tract homes of a more recent vintage.

The island offers excellent shoreline **walks** at both **Roosevelt Campobello International Park** (see below) and **Herring Cove Provincial Park** (© 506/752-7010), which opens from mid-May to mid-October. The landscapes are extraordinarily diverse. On some trails you'll enjoy a Currier and Ives tableau of white houses and church spires across the channel in Lubec and Eastport; 10 minutes later you'll be walking along a wild, rocky coast pummeled by surging waves. Herring Cove has a 1.6km-long (1-mile) beach that's perfect for a slow stroll in the fog. Camping and golf are also offered at the park.

## ESSENTIALS

**GETTING THERE**   Campobello Island is accessible year-round from the United States. From Route 1 in Whiting, Maine, take Route 189 to Lubec, where a bridge links Lubec with Campobello. In the summer, there's another option. From the Canadian mainland, take the free ferry to Deer Island, drive the length of the island, and then board the small seasonal ferry to Campobello. The ferry is operated by **East Coast Ferries** (© **506/747-2159**) and runs from late June to early September. The fare is C$14 (US$11) for car and driver, C$3 (US$2.40) for each additional passenger.

**VISITOR INFORMATION**   The **Campobello Welcome Center,** 44 Route 774, Welshpool, NB E5E 1A3 (© **506/752-7043**), is on the right side just after you cross the bridge from Lubec. It's open mid-May to early September from 9am to 7pm, and from 10am to 6pm until mid-October.

**Roosevelt Campobello International Park** 🐾🐾   Like a number of other affluent Americans, the family of Franklin Delano Roosevelt made an annual trek to the prosperous summer colony at Campobello Island. The island lured folks from the sultry cities with a promise of cool air and a salubrious effect on the circulatory system. ("The extensive forests of balsamic firs seem to affect the atmosphere of this region, causing a quiet of the nervous system and inviting sleep," read an 1890 real-estate brochure.) The future U.S. president came to this island every summer between 1883, the year after he was born, and 1921, when he was stricken with polio. Franklin and his siblings spent those summers exploring the coves and sailing around the bay, and he always recalled his time here fondly. (It was his "beloved island," he said, coining a phrase that gets no rest in local brochures.)

You'll learn much about Roosevelt and his early life at the visitor center, where you can watch a brief film, and during a self-guided tour of the elaborate mansion, covered in cranberry-colored shingles. For a "cottage" this huge, it's surprisingly comfortable and intimate. The park is truly international; run by a commission with representatives from both the United States and Canada, it's like none other in the world.

Be sure to save some time to explore farther afield in the 1,120 hectares (2,800-acre) park, which offers scenic coastline and 14km (8.75 miles) of walking trails. While the Park's Visitor Centre closes on Canada's Thanksgiving Day in late October, these extensive grounds and parklands remain open to the public year-round. Maps and walk suggestions are available at the visitor center. The park, should you find your way here, is easily worth a half-day.

459 Rte. 774, Welshpool. ℰ **506/752-2922.** www.fdr.net. Free admission. Daily 10am–6pm; last tour at 5:45pm. Closed mid-Oct to mid-May.

## WHERE TO STAY & DINE

There is camping at **Herring Cove Provincial Park** (ℰ **506/752-7010**) for C$22 to C$24 (US$17–US$19), with discounts for seniors.

**Lupine Lodge** *Value*    In 1915, cousins of the Roosevelts built this handsome compound of log buildings not far from the Roosevelt cottage. A busy road runs between the lodge and the water, but the buildings are located on a slight rise and have the feel of being removed from the traffic. Guest rooms are in two long lodges adjacent to the main building and restaurant. The rooms with bay views cost a bit more but are worth it—they're slightly bigger and better furnished in a log-rustic style. All guests have access to a deck that overlooks the bay. The lodge's attractive restaurant exudes rustic summer ease with log walls, a double stone fireplace, bay views, and mounted moose head and swordfish. Three meals are served daily. Dinner entrees include favorites such as shrimp, haddock, salmon, and T-bones.

610 Rte. 774, Welshpool, Campobello Island, NB E5E 1A5. ℰ **888/912-8880** or 506/752-2555. www.lupinelodge. com. 11 units. C$65–C$125 (US$52–US$100) double. MC, V. Closed Nov–Apr. Pets accepted for an additional C$15 (US$11). **Amenities:** Restaurant. *In room:* No phone.

**Owen House, A Country Inn & Gallery**    This three-story clapboard captain's house dates from 1835 and sits on 4 tree-filled hectares (10 acres) at the edge of the bay. The first-floor common rooms are nicely decorated in a busy Victorian manner with Persian and braided carpets and mahogany furniture. The guest rooms are a mixed lot, furnished with an eclectic mélange of antique and modern furniture that sometimes blends nicely. Likewise, some rooms are bright and airy and filled with the smell of salty air (Room 1 is the largest, with waterfront views on two sides); others, like Room 5, are tucked under stairs and rather dark, but the Owens are slowly renovating the old house with bigger bathrooms and new showers. The third-floor rooms share a single bathroom but also have excellent views. A filling breakfast served family-style is included in the room rates.

11 Welshpool St., Welshpool, Campobello, NB E5E 1G3. ℰ **506/752-2977.** www.owenhouse.ca. 9 units, 5 with private bathroom. C$112–C$207 (US$90–US$166) double. Rates include full breakfast. AE, MC, V. Closed Nov–Apr. No children under 6 in Aug. *In room:* No phone.

## ST. STEPHEN

St. Stephen is the gateway to Canada for many travelers arriving from the United States. It's directly across the tidal St. Croix River from Calais, Maine, and the two towns share a symbiotic relationship—it's a local call across the international border from one town to the other, fire engines from one country will often respond to fires in the other, and during the annual summer parade the bands and floats have traditionally marched right through customs without stopping.

## ESSENTIALS

**VISITOR INFORMATION**    The **Provincial Visitor Information Centre** (ℰ **506/466-7390**) is open daily from 10am to 6pm mid-May to mid-October. It's in the old train station on Milltown Boulevard, about a mile from Canadian customs; turn right after crossing the border (following signs for St. Andrews and Saint John), and watch for the information center at the light where the road turns left.

## EXPLORING ST. STEPHEN

St. Stephen is a town in transition. The lumber industry and wood trade that were responsible for the handsome brick and stone buildings that line the main street have by and large dried up. The town now depends on a paper mill and the large Ganong chocolate factory as its economic mainstays. (For the truly cocoa bean–obsessed, there's also a small Chocolate Festival in mid-Aug.) As a regional commercial center, it has a gritty, lived-in feel to it, and not much in the way of stylish boutiques or upscale restaurants.

You can learn about the region's history with a brief stop at the **Charlotte County Museum,** 443 Milltown Blvd. (© **506/466-3295**), open June through September.

### The Chocolate Museum (Kids)

St. Stephen's claim to fame is that it's the home of the chocolate bar—the first place (1910) where somebody thought to wrap chocolate pieces in foil and sell them individually. At least that's according to local lore. Chocolate is still big around here—not quite like Hershey, Pennsylvania, but still a part of the local psyche and economy. The Ganong brothers started selling chocolate from their general store here in 1873, and from this an empire was built, employing some 700 people by the 1930s. Ganong was also the first to package chocolates in heart-shaped boxes for Valentine's Day, and still holds 30% of the Canadian market for heart-box chocolates.

Ganong's modern new plant is on the outskirts of town and isn't open for tours, but in 1999 the nonprofit Chocolate Museum was opened in one of Ganong's early factories, a large brick structure on the town's main street. Here you'll view an 11-minute video about the history of local chocolates, and then see the displays and exhibits, including 19th-century chocolate boxes, interactive multimedia displays about the making of candy, and games for young children (my favorite: "Guess the Centers"). A highlight of a visit is watching one of the expert hand-dippers make chocolates the old fashioned way; samples are available afterward.

Want more? Ganong's Chocolatier, an old-fashioned candy shop, is located in the storefront adjacent to the museum. Don't miss the budget bags of factory seconds. There's also a Heritage Chocolate Walk offered, which combines a factory tour with a walk through the downtown's historic areas. Plan to spend about an hour here altogether.

73 Milltown Blvd. © **506/466-7848.** www.chocolatemuseum.ca. Admission C$5 (US$4) adults, C$4 (US$3.20) students, C$3 (US$2.40) children under 6, C$10 (US$8) families. Mid-June to Aug Mon–Sat 9am–6:30pm, Sun 1–5pm; Mar to mid-June and Sept–Nov Mon–Fri 9am–5pm. Closed Dec–Feb.

## ST. ANDREWS ★★

The lovely village of St. Andrews—or St. Andrews By-The-Sea, as the chamber of commerce likes to call it—traces its roots back to the days of the Loyalists. After the American Revolution, New Englanders who supported the British in the struggle were made to feel unwelcome. They decamped first to Castine, Maine, which they presumed was safely on British soil. It wasn't; the St. Croix River was later determined to be the border between Canada and the United States. Uprooted again, the Loyalists dismantled their houses, loaded the pieces aboard ships, and rebuilt them on the welcoming peninsula of St. Andrews. Some of these saltbox houses still stand today.

This historic community later emerged as a fashionable summer resort in the late 19th century, when many of Canada's affluent and well-connected nabobs built homes and gathered annually here for an active social season. Around this time, the Tudor-style

Algonquin Hotel was built on a low rise overlooking the town in 1889, and it quickly became the town's social hub and defining landmark.

St. Andrews is beautifully sited at the tip of a long, wedge-shaped peninsula. Thanks to its location off the beaten track, the village hasn't been spoiled much by modern development, and walking the wide, shady streets—especially those around the Algonquin—invokes a more genteel era. Some 250 homes around the village are more than a century old. A number of appealing boutiques and shops are spread along Water Street, which stretches for some distance along the town's shoreline. Also don't miss the weekly farmer's market, held Thursdays in summer from 9am to about 1pm on the waterfront.

## ESSENTIALS

**GETTING THERE**   St. Andrews is located at the apex of Route 127, which dips southward from Route 1 between St. Stephen and St. George. The turnoff is well marked from either direction. **SMT bus lines** (© 800/567-5151; www.smtbus.com) run daily bus service between St. Andrews and Saint John; the one-way fare is C$20 (US$16) adult.

**VISITOR INFORMATION**   St. Andrews' **Welcome Centre** (© 506/529-3556), is located at 46 Reed Ave., on your left as you enter the village. It's in a handsome 1914 home overarched by broad-crowned trees. It's open daily from 9am to 6pm in May, September, and October, to 8pm from June to August. The rest of the year, contact the **Chamber of Commerce** in the same building (© 800/563-7397 or 506/529-3555) by writing P.O. Box 89, St. Andrews, NB E0G 2X0.

## EXPLORING ST. ANDREWS

The chamber of commerce produces two brochures, the *Town Map and Directory* and the *St. Andrews by-the-Sea Historic Guide,* both of which are free and can be found at the two visitor information centers. Also look for *A Guide to Historic St. Andrews,* produced by the St. Andrews Civic Trust. With these in hand you'll be able to launch an informed exploration. To make it even easier, many of the private dwellings in St. Andrews feature plaques with information on their origins. Look in particular for the saltbox-style homes, some of which are thought to be the original Loyalist structures that traveled here by barge.

For a guided tour, contact **Heritage Discovery Tours** (© 506/529-4011). Elaine Bruff's "Magical History Tour" is recommended; prices start at C$11 (US$9) per person. She gives one tour daily from May 15 to October 15, starting at 10am. If she's booked full (it happens), another outfit in town, **HMS Transportation** (© 800/254-5466 or 506/529-3371), offers a similar tour at similar prices, but normally only does so for groups of six travelers or more.

The village's compact and handsome downtown flanks Water Street, a lengthy commercial street that parallels the bay. You'll find low, understated commercial architecture, much of it from the turn of the 20th century, that encompasses a gamut of styles. Allow an hour or so for browsing at boutiques and art galleries. There's also a mix of restaurants and inns.

Two blocks inland on King Street, you'll get a dose of local history at the **Ross Memorial Museum,** 188 Montague St. (© 506/529-5124). The historic home was built in 1824; in 1945 the home was left to the town by Rev. Henry Phipps Ross and Sarah Juliette Ross, complete with their eclectic and intriguing collection of period furniture, carpets, and paintings. The museum is open June to early October, Monday through Saturday from 10am to 4:30pm. Admission is by donation.

Walk up the hill to the head of King Street, and you'll eventually come to the **Kingsbrae Garden** (see below).

On the west end of Water Street, you'll come to Joe's Point Road at the foot of Harriet Street. The stout wooden **blockhouse** that sits just off the water behind low grass-covered earthworks was built by townspeople during the War of 1812, when the British colonials anticipated a U.S. attack that never came. This structure is all that remains of the scattered fortifications created around town during that war.

Across the street from the blockhouse is the peaceful Centennial Gardens, established in 1967 to mark the centenary of Canadian confederation. The compact, tidy park has views of the bay and makes a pleasant spot for a picnic.

To the east of the blockhouse is the **Niger Reef Tea House,** 1 Joe's Point Rd. (© 506/529-8007), built in 1926 as the chapter house of the Imperial Order of the Daughters of the Empire. Tea was served summer afternoons, with the proceeds going to support the group's charitable endeavors. In 1999, the building was restored by the St. Andrews Civic Trust, with profits going to support the Trust's preservation efforts. Notable are the dreamy, evocative landscape murals on the walls, painted in 1926 by American artist Lucille Douglass. A very limited selection of light meals is served here, along with excellent tea and coffee drinks (including espresso and cappuccino). Afternoon tea is served from 3 to 5pm (about C$8/US$6.50), and includes cakes, sweets, and finger sandwiches. If the weather's right, it's hard to top afternoon tea on the outside deck.

At the other end of Water Street, headed east from downtown, is the open space of Indian Point and the Passamaquoddy Ocean Park Campground. The views of the bay are panoramic; somehow it's even dramatic on foggy days, and swimming in these icy waters will earn you bragging rights.

Look for history at your feet when exploring the park's rocky beaches. You'll sometimes turn up worn and rounded flint and coral that washed ashore. It's not native, but imported. Early traders sailing here loaded their holds with flint from Dover, England, and coral from the Caribbean to serve as ballast on the crossing. When they arrived, the ballast was dumped offshore, and today it still churns up from the depths.

For a more protected swimming spot, wander down **Acadia Drive,** which runs downhill behind the Algonquin Hotel. You'll come to popular Katy's Cove, where floating docks form a sort of natural swimming saltwater pool along a lovely inlet. You'll find a snack bar, a playground, and an affable sense of gracious ease here, and it's a fine place for families to while away an afternoon. There's a small fee.

## BOAT TOURS

St. Andrews is an excellent spot to launch an exploration of the bay, which is very much alive, biologically speaking. On the water you'll look for whales, porpoises, seals, and bald eagles, no matter which trip you select.

**Quoddy Link Marine** (© 877/688-2600 or 506/529-2600) offers whale-watch tours on a 16.7m (55-ft.) power catamaran, and the tour includes seafood snacks and use of binoculars. Whale-watch and sunset tours are offered aboard the *Seafox* (© 506/636-0130), a 12m (40-ft.) Cape Islander boat with viewing from two decks. Two-hour tours in search of wildlife aboard 7.2m (24-ft.) rigid-hull Zodiacs are offered by **Fundy Tide Runners** (© 506/529-4481); passengers wear flotation suits as they zip around the bay. For a more traditional experience, sign up for a trip aboard the *Tallship Cory* (© 506/529-8116), which offers 3-hour tours under sail, with music and storytelling on board.

**Seascape Kayak Tours** (© 866/747-1884 or 506/747-1884), in nearby Deer Island (see "Getting There," in the Campobello Island section, earlier), offers an up-close and personal view of the bay on full- and half-day tours, with lunch provided on full-day trips, and snacks on the half-day (2½-hr.) tour. No kayaking experience is needed. The daylong trip costs C$115 to C$125 (US$92–US$100); the half-day trip runs C$59 (US$47).

**Atlantic Salmon Interpretive Centre**    The splashy visitor center of the Atlantic Salmon Federation, sometimes called Salar's World after the main exhibit, is dedicated to educating the public about the increasingly rare and surprisingly intriguing Atlantic salmon. Located in a bright and airy post and beam facility, the center allows visitors to get oriented through exhibits and presentations and viewing salmon through underwater windows or strolling the outdoor walkways along Chamcook Stream. Plan to spend about a half-hour here.

24 Chamcook Rd. (6.5km/4 miles from St. Andrews via Rte. 127). © 506/529-1384. Admission C$4 (US$3.20) adults, C$3.50 (US$2.80) seniors and college students, C$2.50 (US$2) children, C$10 (US$8) families. Daily 9am–5pm. Closed mid-Oct to mid-May.

**Kingsbrae Garden** *(Kids*    This 11-hectare (27-acre) public garden opened in 1998, using the former grounds of a long-gone estate. The designers incorporated the existing high hedges and trees, and have ambitiously planted open space around the mature plants. The entire project is very promising, and as the plantings take root and mature it's certain to become a noted stop for garden lovers. The grounds include almost 2,000 varieties of trees (including old-growth forest), shrubs, and plants. Among the notable features: a day lily collection, an extensive rose garden, a small maze, a fully functional Dutch windmill that circulates water through the two duck ponds, and a children's garden with an elaborate Victorian-mansion playhouse.

With views over the lush lawns to the bay below, the on-site Garden Cafe is a pleasant place to stop for lunch. Try the thick, creamy seafood chowder and one of the focaccia bread sandwiches. Those with a horticultural bend should plan to spend at least a few hours here.

220 King St. (© 866/566-8687 or 506/529-3335. Admission C$8.50 (US$6.80) adults, C$7 (US$5.60) students and seniors, C$23 (US$18) family, free for children under 6. Daily 9am–6pm. Closed early Oct to late May.

**Ministers Island Historic Site/Covenhoven** *ϾϾ*    This rugged, 200-plus-hectare (500-acre) island is linked to the mainland by a sandbar at low tide, and the 2-hour tours are scheduled around the tides. (Call for upcoming times.) You'll meet your tour guide on the mainland side, and then drive your car out convoy-style across the ocean floor to the magical island estate created in 1890 by Sir William Van Horne.

Van Horne was president of the Canadian Pacific Railway, and the person behind the extension of the rail line to St. Andrews. He then built a sandstone mansion (Covenhoven) with some 50 rooms (including 17 bedrooms), a circular bathhouse (where he indulged his passion for landscape painting), and one of Canada's largest and most impressive barns. The estate also features heated greenhouses, which produced grapes and mushrooms, along with peaches that weighed up to 2 pounds each. When Van Horne was home in Montréal, he had fresh dairy products and vegetables shipped daily (by rail, of course) so that he could enjoy fresh produce year-round.

Rte. 127 (northeast of St. Andrews), Chamcook. (☎ 506/529-5081 for recorded tour schedule. Admission C$5 (US$4) adults, C$2.50 (US$2) children 13–18, free for children 12 and under. Closed mid-Oct to May 31.

## WHERE TO STAY

St. Andrews offers an abundance of fine B&Bs and inns. Those traveling on a budget should head for the **Picket Fence Motel,** 102 Reed Ave. (☎ **506/529-8985**). This trim and tidy motel is near the handsome, newly expanded Algonquin golf course (see "Golf," earlier in this chapter) and within walking distance of the village center. Rooms cost C$60 to C$85 (US$48–US$68) in peak season.

**The Fairmont Algonquin** 🎔🎔   The Algonquin's distinguished pedigree dates from 1889, when it first opened its doors to wealthy vacationers seeking respite from city heat. The original structure was destroyed by fire in 1914, but the surviving annexes were rebuilt in sumptuous Tudor style; in 1993 an architecturally sympathetic addition was built across the road, linked by a gatehouse-inspired bridge.

The red-tile–roofed resort commands one's attention through its sheer size and aristocratic bearing (not to mention through its kilt-wearing, bagpipe-playing staff). The inn is several long blocks from the water's edge, but it perches on the brow of a hill and affords panoramic bay views from the second-floor roof garden and many guest rooms. The rooms were recently redecorated and are comfortable and tasteful. In addition to the outstanding seaside golf course (see "Golf," earlier), there's also a spa at the hotel featuring a full card of treatments ranging from facials and nail services to body wraps and massage. *One caveat:* The hotel happily markets itself to bus tours and conferences, and if your timing is unfortunate you might feel a bit overwhelmed and small. The resort's main dining room is one of the more enjoyable spots in town—it's often bustling (great people-watching) and the kitchen produces some surprisingly creative meals. Informal dining options include The Library (just off the main lobby) and the downstairs lounge. Further afield, the Italian bistro food at the Algonquin Clubhouse on the resort's golf course is well worth the drive—try the seared salmon with cilantro corn salsa served over pasta.

184 Adolphus St., St. Andrews, NB E5B 1T7. (☎ **800/441-1414** or 506/529-8823. Fax 506/529-7162. www.fairmont. com. 234 units. C$129–C$459 (US$103–US$367) double, C$289–C$729 (US$231–C$583) suite. Rates include continental breakfast. AE, DC, DISC, MC, V. Valet parking. Small cats and dogs $25 per night. **Amenities:** 2 restaurants; 2 bars; outdoor heated pool; golf course; 2 tennis courts; health club; spa; Jacuzzi; sauna; bike rentals; children's programs; game room; concierge; salon; massage; babysitting; laundry service; dry cleaning. *In room:* TV, dataport, minibar, coffeemaker, hair dryer, iron.

**Kingsbrae Arms Relais & Châteaux** 🎔🎔🎔   Kingsbrae Arms, part of the upscale Relais & Châteaux network, is a five-star inn informed by an upscale European elegance. Kingsbrae brings to mind a rustic elegance—a bit of Tuscany, perhaps, melded with a genteel London town house. Located atop King Street, this intimate inn occupies an 1897 manor house, where the furnishings—from the gracefully worn leather chesterfield to the Delft-tiled fireplace—all seem to have a story to tell. The grand, shingled home, built by prosperous jade merchants, occupies .4 hectares (1 acre), all of which has been well employed. A heated pool sits amid rose gardens at the foot of a lawn, and immediately next door is the 11-hectare (27-acre) Kingsbrae Horticultural Gardens (some guest rooms have wonderful views of the gardens, others a panoramic sweep of the bay; one has both). Guests will feel pampered here, with luxurious amenities including 325-thread-count sheets, plush robes, and a complete guest-services suite stocked with complimentary snacks and refreshments. Five rooms have

Jacuzzis; all have gas fireplaces. Guests can also enjoy a four-course meal around a stately table in the dining room during peak season. (This dining room is not open to the public.) One meal is offered nightly, and the new Canadian-style cuisine is ever-changing and scrumptious. Entrees might include Fundy salmon, PEI mussels, New Zealand rack of lamb, or Alberta steaks; high-quality wines are carefully paired with these meals.

219 King St., St. Andrews, NB E5B 1Y1. ℂ **506/529-1897**. Fax 506/529-1197. www.kingsbrae.com. 8 units. C$300–C$1,700 (US$240–US$1,360) double. 2-night minimum; 3-night minimum July–Aug weekends. 5% room service charge additional. AE, MC, V. Closed Nov–Apr. Pets allowed with advance permission. **Amenities:** Babysitting; laundry service; dry cleaning. *In room:* A/C, TV, coffeemaker, hair dryer, iron.

**Salty Towers**    Behind this somewhat staid Queen Anne home on Water Street lurks the soul of a wild eccentric. Salty Towers is equal parts turn-of-the-20th-century home, 1940s boarding house, and 1960s commune. Overseen with great affability by artist-naturalist Jamie Steel, this is a world of wondrous clutter—from the early European landscapes with overly wrought gilt frames to exuberant modern pieces. Think *Addams Family* meets Timothy Leary.

The guest rooms lack the visual chaos of the public spaces and are nicely done up, furnished with eclectic antiques and old magazines. (Especially nice is Room 2, with hand-sponged walls and a private sitting area surrounded by windows.) The top floor is largely given over to single rooms; these are a bargain at C$30 (US$24) with shared bathroom. Guests have full run of the large if sometimes confused kitchen. Don't be surprised to find musicians strumming on the porch, artists lounging in the living room, and others of uncertain provenance swapping jokes around the stove. If that sounds pretty good to you, this is your place.

340 Water St., St. Andrews, NB E5B 2R3. ℂ **506/529-4585**. www.salty-towers.com. 15 units, some with private bathroom. C$55–C$75 (US$44–US$60) double. V. **Amenities:** Bar; babysitting. *In room:* Kitchenette (some units), no phone.

**The Windsor House** ⧓    Located in the middle of the village on busy Water Street, the lovely Windsor House offers guests a quiet retreat amid lustrous antiques in a top-rate restoration. The three-story home was originally built in 1798 by a ship captain. It's served almost every purpose since then, including stagecoach stop, oil company office, and family home, before reopening its doors as a luxury inn in 1999. The new owners—Jay Remer and Greg Cohane—spent more than 2 years and C$2 million (US$1.3 million) renovating the home, and their attention to detail shows. The rooms are furnished with antiques (no reproductions) far above what one normally expects at an inn; Remer spent 5 years at Sotheby's in New York and knows what he's looking for. All of the rooms are superbly appointed, most with detailed etchings of animals adorning the walls; four have working fireplaces. The best two are the suites on the third floor, with peaceful sitting areas, exposed beams, Oriental carpets, handsome armoires, and limited views of the bay. (Both also have claw-foot tubs and glass shower stalls.) The basement features an appealing terra-cotta-floored billiard room. The hotel's restaurant (see below) can be found on the first floor, and the adjacent pub is the perfect spot for an early evening libation or after-dinner drink.

132 Water St., St. Andrews, NB E5B 1A8. ℂ **888/890-9463** or 506/529-3330. Fax 506/529-4063. www.windsorhouse inn.com. 6 units. Summer C$225–C$300 (US$180–US$240) double, off-season C$125–C$200 (US$100–US$160) double. Rates include full breakfast. AE, DC, MC, V. Restaurant closed Jan–Apr. **Amenities:** Restaurant; bar. *In room:* TV (some units), no phone.

## WHERE TO DINE

**The Gables** SEAFOOD/PUB FARE   This informal eatery is located in a trim home with prominent gables fronting Water Street, but you enter down a narrow alley where sky and water views suddenly blossom through a soaring window from a spacious outside deck. Inside, expect a bright and lively spot with a casual maritime decor; outside there's a plastic-porch–furniture informality. Breakfast is served during peak season, with homemade baked goods and rosemary potatoes. Lunch and dinner options include burgers, steaks, and such seafood entrees as breaded haddock, daily specials, and a lobster clubhouse—a chopped lobster salad served with cheese, cucumber, lettuce, and tomato; there's a kid's menu as well. Margaritas and sangria are available by the pitcher. The view here tends to outclass the menu, but those ordering simpler fare will be satisfied.

143 Water St. © 506/529-3440. Main courses C$3.95–C$6.95 (US$3.15–US$5.55) at breakfast, C$7.50–C$25 (US$6–US$20) at lunch and dinner. MC, V. July–Aug daily 8am–11pm; Sept–June daily 11am–9pm.

**L'Europe** ®® CONTINENTAL   In an intriguing yellow building that once housed a movie theater and dance hall, Bavarian husband-and-wife transplants Markus and Simone Ritter whip up fine French-, Swiss- and German-accented Continental cuisine for a 35-seat room. Starters include smoked salmon with rosti and capers; scallops in Mornay sauce, baked with cheese; French onion soup; and escargots. Main courses run to haddock in Champagne sauce, scallops fried Provencal-style, Zurich-style chicken in cream sauce, loin of lamb, pork cordon bleu, tenderloin steak with béarnaise sauce, and (as a nod to Canada) venison in a red-currant sauce—though it's sided with spaetzle. All are prepared with skill and restraint. Finish with chocolate mousse or homemade almond parfait. The wine list is also surprisingly strong given that this is such a small, out-of-the-way place in a small, out-of-the-way town.

48 King St. © 506/529-3818. Reservations recommended. Main courses C$19–C$28 (US$15–US$22). MC, V. Mid-May to Sept daily 5–9pm; Oct Tues–Sat 5–9pm; Nov to mid-Feb Thurs–Sat 5–9pm. Closed mid-Feb to mid-May.

**Lighthouse Restaurant** SEAFOOD   Located on the water at the eastern edge of the village, this spot rewards diners with a great view while they enjoy fresh-from-the-boat seafood. It's a bustling, popular place that seems to attract families and those who crave lobster. Look for a good selection of fish and lobster served with little fanfare or pomp. The menu includes sautéed scallops, seafood pasta, and lobster prepared any number of ways. The surf-and-turf specials (including filet mignon and lobster tail for C$34/US$23) are especially popular, and children's meals are offered at both lunch and dinner. The owners also rent out three suites on nearby Queen Street under the name Harry's Hatch B&B for C$95 (US$63). If you're in a pinch for a room, inquire about them.

Patrick St. (drive eastward on Water St. toward Indian Point; look for signs). © 506/529-3082. Reservations recommended. Lunch C$5.50–C$11 (US$4.40–US$9); dinner main courses C$15–C$36 (US$12–US$29); most C$18–C$24 (US$15–US$19). AE, DC, MC, V. Mid-May to Labor Day daily 11:30am–2pm and 5–9pm. Closed Labor Day to mid-May.

**The Windsor House** ®®   Guests are seated in one of two intimate dining rooms on the first floor of this historic home (see "Where to Stay," above), which serves only dinner on weekdays. The setting is formal, the guests are dressed with a bit more starch than you'll find elsewhere in town, and the service is excellent. Weekend brunches are somewhat less formal and quite delectable, including cornmeal-crusted salmon cakes and eggs served various ways. Dinner offerings might include strip loin or cedar-planked salmon. Watch for theme nights such as a Texas grill night.

132 Water St., St. Andrews, NB E5B 1A8. (📞 **888/890-9463** or 506/529-3330. Reservations recommended. Brunch Sat-Sun C$4–C$12 (US$3–US$9.60); dinner C$26–C$35 (US$21–US$28). AE, DC, MC, V. Mon–Sat 5:30–9:30pm; Sun 11am–2pm and 5:30–9:30pm. Spring and fall closed Mon-Tues; closed Jan–Apr.

## 4 Grand Manan Island (★)

Geologically rugged, profoundly peaceable, and indisputably remote, this handsome island of 2,800 year-round residents is a 90-minute ferry ride from Blacks Harbour, southeast of St. George. For adventurous travelers Grand Manan is a much-prized destination and a highlight of their vacation. Yet the island remains a mystifying puzzle for others who fail to be smitten by its rough-edged charm. "Either this is your kind of place, or it isn't," said one island resident. "There's no in between." The only way to find out is to visit.

Grand Manan is a special favorite among serious birders and enthusiasts of novelist Willa Cather. Hiking the island's noted trails, don't be surprised to come across knots of very quiet people peering intently through binoculars. These are the birders. Nearly 300 different species of birds either nest here or stop by the island during their long migrations, and it's a good place to add to one's life list, with birds ranging from bald eagles to puffins (you'll need to sign up for a boat tour for the latter).

Willa Cather kept a cottage here and wrote many of her most beloved books while living on the island. Her fans are as easy to spot as the birders, say locals. In fact, islanders are still talking about a Willa Cather conference some summers ago, when 40 participants wrapped themselves in sheets and danced around a bonfire during the summer solstice. "Cather people, they're a wild breed," one innkeeper intoned gravely to me.

### ESSENTIALS

**GETTING THERE**    Grand Manan is connected to Blacks Harbour on the mainland via frequent ferry service in summer. **Coastal Transport ferries** (📞 **506/642-0520;** www.coastaltransport.ca), each capable of hauling 60 cars, depart from the mainland and the island every 2 hours between 7:30am and 5:30pm during July and August; a ferry makes three to four daily trips the rest of the year. The round-trip fare is C$10 (US$8) per passenger (C$5/US$4 ages 5–12), C$30 (US$24) per car. Boarding the ferry on the mainland is free; you purchase tickets when you leave the island.

Reserve your return trip at least a day ahead to avoid getting stranded on the island, and get in line early to secure a spot. A good strategy for departing from Blacks Harbour is to bring a picnic lunch, arrive an hour or two early, put your car in line, and head to the grassy waterfront park adjacent to the wharf. It's an attractive spot; there's even an island to explore at low tide.

**VISITOR INFORMATION**    The island's **Visitor Information Centre,** Route 776, Grand Manan, NB E5G 1A3 (📞 **888/525-1655** or 506/662-3442) is open Monday to Friday in summer (8am–5pm except Sun, when it's open 9am–1pm) in the town of Grand Harbour. If the center is closed, ask at island stores or inns for a free island map published by the **Grand Manan Tourism Association** (📞 **888/525-1655;** www.grandmanannb.com), which has a listing of key island phone numbers.

### EXPLORING THE ISLAND

Start your explorations before you arrive. As you come abreast of the island aboard the ferry, head to the starboard side. You'll soon see **Seven Day's Work** in the rocky cliffs of Whale's Cove, where seven layers of hardened lava and sill (intrusive igneous rock) have come together in a sort of geological Dagwood sandwich.

You can begin to open the puzzle box that is local geology at the **Grand Manan Museum** (② **506/662-3424**) in Grand Harbour, one of three villages on the island's eastern shore. The museum's geology exhibit, located in the basement, offers pointers about what to look for as you roam the island. Birders will enjoy the Allan Moses collection upstairs, which features 230 stuffed and mounted birds in glass cases. The museum also has an impressive lighthouse lens from the Gannet Rock Lighthouse, and a collection of stuff that's washed ashore from the frequent shipwrecks. The museum is open mid-June to mid-September Monday through Friday 9am to 5:30pm; it's also open Saturdays (same hours) in July and August. Admission is C$4 (US$3.20) adults, C$2 (US$1.60) seniors and students, and free for children under 12.

This relatively flat and compact island is perfect for exploring by bike; the only stretches to avoid are some of the faster, less scenic segments of Route 776. All the side roads offer **superb biking.** Especially nice is the **cross-island road** ☞☞ (paved) to **Dark Harbour,** where you'll find a few cabins, dories, and salmon pens. The route is wild and hilly at times but offers a memorable descent to the ocean on the island's west side.

Bike rentals are available at **Adventure High** (② **800/732-5492** or 506/662-3563) in North Head, not far from the ferry. (Day-trippers might consider leaving their cars at **Blacks Harbour** and exploring by bike before returning on the last ferry.) **Adventure High** also offers sea kayak tours of the island's shores for those who prefer a **cormorant's-eye view** ☞ of the impressive cliffs. Bikes rent for C$22 (US$18) per day, C$16 (US$13) for a half-day. Kayak tours run from C$39 (US$31) for a 2-hour sunset tour to C$99 (US$79) for a full-day excursion.

If Grand Manan seems too crowded and hectic (unlikely, that), you can find more solitude at **White Head Island.** Drive to Ingalls Head (follow Ingalls Head Road from Grand Harbour) to catch the half-hour ferry to this rocky island, home to about 200 people. On the island, you can walk along the shore to the lighthouse between Battle Beach and Sandy Cove. The ferry holds 10 cars, is free of charge, and sails up to 10 times daily in summer.

## HIKING

Numerous hiking trails lace the island, and they offer a popular diversion throughout the summer. Trails can be found just about everywhere, but most are a matter of local knowledge. Don't hesitate to ask at your inn or the tourist information center, or to ask anyone you might meet on the street. *A Hiking Guide to New Brunswick* (Goose Lane Editions; ② **506/450-4251**) lists 12 hikes with maps; this handy book is often sold on the ferry.

The most accessible clusters of trails are at the island's northern and southern tips. Head north up Whistle Road to Whistle Beach, and you'll find both the **Northwestern Coastal Trail** ☞ and the **Seven Day's Work Trail** ☞, both of which track along the rocky shoreline. Near the low lighthouse and towering radio antennae at Southwest Head (follow Rte. 776 to the end), trails radiate out along cliffs topped with scrappy forest; the views are remarkable when the fog's not in.

## WHALE-WATCHING & BOAT TOURS

A fine way to experience island ecology is to mosey offshore. Several outfitters offer complete nature tours, providing a nice sampling of the world above and beneath the sea. On an excursion you might see minke, finback, or humpback whales, along with exotic birds including puffins and phalaropes. **Sea Watch Tours** (© 506/662-8552) runs 5-hour excursions from July to late September, with whale sightings guaranteed, aboard a 13m (42-ft.) vessel with canopy. The rate is C$55 (US$44) adults, and C$30 (US$24) per child.

## WHERE TO STAY

**Anchorage Provincial Park** ⚞ (© 506/662-7022) has about 100 campsites scattered about forest and field. There's a small beach and a hiking trail on the property, and it's well situated for exploring the southern part of the island. It's very popular midsummer; call before you board the ferry to ask about campsite availability. Sites are C$24 (US$19) with hookups for RVs, C$22 (US$17) for a tent.

**Inn at Whale Cove Cottages** ⚞    The Inn at Whale Cove is a delightful, family-run compound set in a grassy meadow overlooking a quiet and picturesque cove. The original building is a cozy farmhouse that dates to 1816. It's been restored rustically with a nice selection of simple country antiques. The three guest rooms in the main house are comfortable (Sally's Attic has a small deck and a large view); the living room has a couple years' worth of good reading and a welcoming fireplace. Five cottages are scattered about the property, and they vary in size from one to four bedrooms; some only rent by the week, others daily as well. The 4-hectare (10-acre) grounds, especially the path down to the quiet cove-side beach, are wonderful to explore. Innkeeper Laura Buckley received her culinary training in Toronto, and she demonstrates a deft touch with local ingredients. The menu might include bouillabaisse, seafood risotto, salmon in phyllo, or pork tenderloin with a green peppercorn sauce. Dinner is served nightly from 6 to 8:30pm; on Saturday night a full dinner is served with one seating at 7pm.

Whistle Rd. (P.O. Box 233), North Head, Grand Manan, NB E0G 2M0. © 506/662-3181. 3 rooms, 5 cottages (some only rented by week). C$120–C$150 (US$96–US$120) double or C$800 (US$640) weekly. Rates include full breakfast. MC, V. Closed late Oct to Apr. Pets accepted. **Amenities:** Dining room. *In room:* TV (2 units), kitchenette (2 units).

**Shorecrest Lodge** ⚞ *(Value) (Kids)*    This century-old inn is a fine place to put your feet up and unwind. Located just a few hundred yards from the ferry, the inn is nicely decorated with a mix of modern furniture and eclectic country antiques. Most of the guest rooms have private bathrooms (a rarity for Grand Manan). The best is Room 8 with burgundy leather chairs and a great harbor view. Kids like the spacious TV room in the back, which also has games and a library that's strong in local natural history. The homey country-style dining room has a fireplace and hardwood floors, and a menu that includes local fresh seafood and filet mignon. It's open daily from 5 to 9pm during peak season; hours are limited during the shoulder season.

100 Rte. 776, North Head, Grand Manan, NB E5G 1A1. © 506/662-3216. www.shorecrestlodge.com. 10 units, 8 with private bathroom. C$75–C$119 (US$60–US$95) double. Rates include continental breakfast. MC, V. Closed Nov–May. **Amenities:** Restaurant; fitness room. *In room:* No phone.

## WHERE TO DINE

Options for dining out aren't exactly extravagant on Grand Manan. The three inns listed above offer appetizing meals and decent value.

In the mood for a dare? Try walking into **North Head Bakery** ⚞⚞ (© 506/662-8862) and walking out without buying anything. It cannot be done. This superb bakery (open Tues–Sat 6am–6pm) has used traditional baking methods and whole grains since it opened in 1990. Breads made daily include a crusty, seven-grain Saint John

Valley bread and a delightful egg-and-butter bread. Nor should the chocolate-chip cookies be overlooked. The bakery is on Route 776 on the left when you're heading south from the ferry.

## 5 Saint John ⟨★⟩

Centered on a sizable commercial harbor, Saint John is New Brunswick's largest city, and the center of much of the province's industry. Spread over a low hill, the downtown boasts wonderfully elaborate Victorian flourishes on the rows of commercial buildings. (Be sure to look high along the cornices to appreciate the intricate brickwork.) A handful of impressive mansions lord over side streets, their interiors a forest of intricate wood carving—appropriate for the timber barons who built them.

There's a certain industrial grittiness to Saint John; some find this raw and unappealing, and others find in it a certain ragged raffishness. It all depends on your outlook. Just don't expect a tidy garden city with lots of neat homes. Saint John has a surfeit of brick architecture in various states of repair, and from throughout the downtown you'll get glimpses of industry: large shipping terminals, oil storage facilities, and paper mills, of the sort that was so popular with the Ashcan artists. (A 1978 book on New Brunswick put it diplomatically: "Saint John's heavy industries ensure that the city is not famed for beauty, but the setting is magnificent.")

Don't let this put you off—make the effort to detour from the highway to downtown. And it does take some effort—the traffic engineers have been very mischievous here. When you finally arrive, you'll discover an intriguing place to stroll around for an afternoon while awaiting the ferry to Digby, to grab a delicious bite to eat, or to break up village-hopping with an urban overnight. The streets often bustle with everyone from skateboarders sporting nose rings to impeccably coifed dowagers shopping at the public market.

*One final note:* Saint John is always spelled out, just like that. It's never abbreviated as St. John. That's to keep mail aimed for St. John's in Newfoundland from ending up here, and vice versa. Locals will be quick to correct you if you err.

### ESSENTIALS

**GETTING THERE**   Saint John is located on Route 1. It's 106km (66 miles) from the U.S. border at St. Stephens, and 427km (265 miles) from Halifax, Nova Scotia.

Year-round ferry service connects Saint John to Digby, Nova Scotia. See "Exploring New Brunswick" at the beginning of this chapter for information. Saint John's airport has regular flights to Toronto, Halifax, and other Canadian points; contact **Air Canada** (© **888/AIR-CANA;** www.aircanada.com) for more information. The airport folds a C$15 (US$12) fee into the tickets of all departing passengers to help finance improvements.

**VISITOR INFORMATION**   Saint John has three **visitor information centers.** Arriving from the west, look for a contemporary triangular building just off the Route 1 West off-ramp (open mid-May to mid-Oct), where you'll find a trove of information and brochures (© **506/658-2940;** www.tourismsaintjohn.com). A smaller **seasonal information center,** reached by exits 119A and 119B, is located inside the observation building overlooking the Reversing Falls on Route 100 (© **506/658-2937**).

If you've already made your way downtown, look for the **City Centre Tourist Information Centre** (© **886/GO-FUNDY** or 506/658-2855) inside Market Square,

"The Inside Connection"

**ACCOMMODATIONS ■**
Dufferin Inn **2**
Earle of Leinster "Inn Style" B&B **13**
Hilton Saint John **6**
Homeport Historic B&B **4**
Inn on the Cove **1**

**ATTRACTIONS ●**
Canada Games
Aquatic Centre **5**
Loyalist House **7**
New Brunswick Museum **3**
Old City Market **8**

**DINING ◆**
Beatty and the Bistro **12**
Billy's Seafood Co. **9**
D'Amico **10**
Taco Pica **11**

a downtown shopping mall just off the waterfront reached via Exit 22. Find the info center by entering the square at street level at the corner of St. Patrick and Water Streets. During peak season (mid-June to mid-Sept) the center is open daily from 9am to 8pm. The rest of the year it's open daily 9am to 6pm.

## EXPLORING SAINT JOHN

If the weather's cooperative, start by wandering around near the **waterfront.** Tourism Saint John has published three walking tour brochures that offer plenty of history and architectural trivia. Saint John is noted for the odd and interesting gargoyles and sculpted heads that adorn the brick and stone 19th-century buildings downtown. If you have time for only one tour, I'd opt for **"Prince William's Walk,"** an hour-long, self-guided tour of the impressive commercial buildings. Obtain the tour brochures at the **Market Square information center.**

Try to end your walk at the **Old Burial Ground** (across from King's Square), which is an especially attractive spot to wander while reading the old headstones, or simply to sit and rest your feet. The cemetery dates from 1784 but was recently renovated—note the new beaver fountain, symbolic of the town's hardworking citizens.

If the weather's disagreeable, head indoors. Over the past two decades, Saint John has been busy linking its downtown malls and shops with an elaborate network of underground and overhead pedestrian walkways, dubbed **"The Inside Connection."**

It's not just for shopping—two major hotels, the provincial museum, the city library, the city market, the sports arena, and the aquatic center are all part of the network.

**Canada Games Aquatic Centre**    The gleaming and modern Aquatic Centre was built smack downtown in 1985 for the Canada Games. It remains a remarkably popular destination for exercise and recreation, and it's open to the public most hours all week long. Facilities include an eight-lane Olympic-size pool, warm-up and leisure pools, water slides, rope swings, whirlpools, and saunas. Also available are weight and exercise rooms (extra charge).

50 Union St. ℰ **506/658-4715.** Admission C$7.50 (US$6) adults, C$5 (US$4) children, C$20 (US$16) families. Summer Mon–Thurs 6am–9pm, Fri 6am–8pm; rest of year Mon–Thurs 6am–10pm, Fri 6am–9pm.

**Loyalist House**    A mandatory destination for serious antique buffs, this stately Georgian home was built in 1817 for the Merritt family, who were wealthy Loyalists from Rye, New York. Inside is an extraordinary collection of furniture dating from before 1833, most pieces of which were original to the house and have never left. Especially notable are the extensive holdings of Duncan Phyfe Sheraton furniture and a rare piano-organ combination. Other unusual detailing includes the doors steamed and bent to fit into the curved sweep of the stairway, and the carvings on the wooden chair rails. Tours last 30 to 45 minutes, depending on the number of questions you ask.

120 Union St. ℰ **506/652-3590.** C$3 (US$2.40) adults, C$1 (US80¢) children, C$7 (US$5.60) families. July–mid-Sept daily 10am–5pm; May–June Mon–Fri 10am–5pm; mid-Sept to Apr by appointment only.

**New Brunswick Museum**    The New Brunswick Museum is an excellent stop for anyone in the least bit curious about the province's natural or cultural history. The collections are displayed on three open floors, and they offer a nice mix of traditional artifacts and quirky objects. (Among the more memorable items is a frightful looking "permanent wave" machine from a 1930s beauty parlor.) The exhaustive exhibits include the complete interior of Sullivan's Bar (where longshoremen used to slake their thirst a few blocks away), a massive section of a ship frame, a wonderful geological exhibit, and even a sporty white Bricklin from a failed New Brunswick automobile manufacturing venture in the mid-1970s. The Wind, Wood and Sail exhibit describes 19th-century shipbuilding in the province. Allow at least 2 hours to enjoy these eclectic and uncommonly well-displayed exhibits.

1 Market Sq. ℰ **506/643-2300.** Admission C$6 (US$5) adults, C$4.75 (US$3.80) seniors, C$3.25 (US$2.60) students and children 4–18, C$13 (US$10) families. Mon–Fri 9am–5pm (Thurs until 9pm), Sat 10am–5pm, Sun noon–5pm.

**Old City Market**    Hungry travelers venture here at their peril! This spacious, bustling, and bright marketplace is crammed with vendors hawking meat, fresh seafood, cheeses, flowers, baked goods, and bountiful fresh produce. You can even sample dulse, a snack of dried seaweed from the Bay of Fundy. (One traveler has compared the experience to licking a wharf.) The market was built in 1876, and it has been a center of commerce for the city ever since. Note the construction of the roof—local lore says it resembles an inverted ship because it was made by boat builders who didn't know how to build anything else. And watch for the small, enduring traces of tradition: The handsome iron gates at either end have been in place since 1880, and the loud bell is rung daily by the Deputy Market Clerk, who signals the opening and closing of the market. A number of vendors offer meals to go, and there's a bright seating area in an enclosed terrace on the market's south side. It's worth an hour or two (including a stop to eat, of course).

47 Charlotte St. ℭ **506/658-2820.** Mon–Thurs 7:30am–6pm, Fri 7:30am–7pm, Sat 7:30am–5pm. Closed Sun and holidays.

## OUTDOOR PURSUITS

**Irving Nature Park**   Located along the coast across the Saint John River (take Exit 119A off Rte. 1 and follow Bleury St. to Sand Cove Rd.), the Irving Nature Park consists of 240 dramatic coastal hectares (600 acres), where as many as 240 species of birds have been spotted. Soft wood-chipped trails and marsh boardwalks provide access to a lovely forest and wild, salty seascapes. The observation tower on the "Squirrel Trail" gives a fine vantage of the park and its mud flats, where migrating sandpipers devour shrimp for a week to double their weight before flying 4 days nonstop to Surinam. Seals throng the park in mid-June and mid-October and are so thick on the rocks that they've been described as "a great gray noisy carpet." Irving Nature Park can get very busy—there are some 125,000 visitors a year—and Sundays are the most popular. Call beforehand to ask about the excellent tours; otherwise, you can see everything in an hour.

Sand Cove Rd. ℭ **506/653-7367.** Free admission and tours. Daylight hours; early May to mid-Nov information booth staffed daily.

**Reversing Falls** *(Overrated*   Just west of downtown is Reversing Falls, located within an impressive, rocky gorge. Owing to the massive tide hereabouts, rapids, low waterfalls, and large, slurping whirlpools flow one-way through the gorge during one tide, then reverse during the opposite tide. It's a sometimes-dramatic sight in a dramatic location, but few publicity photos or descriptions include one important caveat: The gorge is all but overwhelmed by a huge paper mill just yards upriver. There's also an active train trestle and a busy highway spanning the gorge directly over the falls, which are drowned out by the constant clang and hum of industry and trade. If you don't come expecting wild and brutish nature, you're less likely to be disappointed.

There are several ways of observing this natural spectacle. You can scramble down the wooden steps to a park along the river's edge, or climb up atop a rooftop viewing platform (free).

More sedentary souls can try **The Falls Restaurant** (ℭ **506/635-1999**), which is peaceful in that chirpy, elevator-music kind of way. Just remember that you're paying a premium for the view—not the unexciting seafood. My recommendation: If you can't get a table overlooking the falls, take a look out the full-length windows and move on. At least it's open year-round.

Across the river is **Fallsview Park** (turn left on Douglas Ave., then left again on Fallsview Ave.). Here you'll get a duck's-eye view of the river from this small park directly across from the paper mill.

Departing from a narrow cove at Fallsview Park are the **Reversing Falls Jet Boat Rides** (ℭ **888/634-8987** or 506/634-8987), which offer fun, fast boat trips through the falls at all tides. The always-breezy, sometimes-damp trip takes 20 minutes and costs C$30 (US$24) adults, C$25 (US$20) children, C$100 (US$80) family, all of which include use of raincoats. Two specially designed boats—one offering a more heart-pounding "thrill ride"—depart several times daily from the park. Reservations are recommended during peak season.

Rte. 100. ℃ 506/658-2937. Free admission to viewing platform; explanatory film C$2.50 (US$2). Early June to mid-Oct daylight hours, but best at low or high tide. Call for tidal schedule.

**Rockwood Park**   The footpaths attract walkers and joggers to this 880 hectare (2,200-acre) urban preserve of lakes, forest, and rocky hills. But there is also swimming at sandy lake beaches, golf at the 18-hole municipal course (℃ 506/634-0090; C$18–C$35/US$15–US$28 greens fees), picnic areas, a campground, and a small zoo with 38 species of exotic animals (including six species of monkeys, all on the endangered species list). Boat rentals at Fisher Lakes include canoes and kayaks (from around C$5/US$4 per half-hour). There's also an aquatic driving range, where duffers practice their swings by hitting floating golf balls into a lake (about C$6/US$5 for a large bucket of balls), which are later harvested by boat. The park, located just 5 minutes' drive north of downtown, is especially popular on weekends.

Lake Dr. S. ℃ 506/658-2883. Free admission; fees charged for various activities. Interpretation Centre late May to early Sept daily 8am–dusk.

## WHERE TO STAY

Budget travelers should head to Manawagonish Road for lower-priced motels. Unlike many other motel strips, which tend to be notably unlovely, Manawagonish Road is reasonably attractive. It winds along a high ridge of residential homes west of town, with views out to the Bay of Fundy. It's about a 10-minute drive into downtown. Rates at most Manawagonish motels are approximately C$50 to C$60 (US$40–US$48) peak season. The **Econo Lodge,** 1441 Manawagonish Rd. (℃ 800/55ECONO or 506/635-8700), is somewhat more expensive but a bit more comfortable, and the rooms have sweeping views.

In-town camping is available summers at **Rockwood Park** (℃ 506/652-4050). Some 80 sites are spread across a rocky hill; many overlook downtown, the highway, and a rail yard (expect nighttime noise). RVs requesting full hookups are directed to an area resembling a parking lot, but it's quite serviceable. Other sites vary widely in privacy and scenic attributes. Rates range from C$18 (US$15) for a tent site to C$24 (US$19) for hookups. Follow signs to the park from either Exit 122 or Exit 125 off Route 1.

### EXPENSIVE
**Hilton Saint John** ⚘   This 12-story waterfront hotel was built in 1984 and has the amenities one would expect from an upscale chain hotel. Rooms on the top two Plaza Floors were repainted, redecorated, and upgraded to include perks such as electronic safes, cordless phones, bigger desks, and terry-cloth robes. This property boasts the best location in Saint John, overlooking the harbor yet just steps from the rest of downtown by street or indoor walkway. Windows in all guest rooms open, a nice touch when the breeze is coming from the sea. The Hilton is connected to the convention center and attracts major events; ask whether anything's scheduled before you book if you don't want to be overwhelmed by conventioneers.

The hotel's lounge offers light meals from 11:30am to 1am daily. For more refined fare, head for the main dining room, which serves three meals daily in an understated and classical harborside setting. Entrees include creatively prepared steaks, pheasant, and salmon.

1 Market Sq., Saint John, NB E2L 4Z6. ℃ 800/561-8282 in Canada, 800/445-8667 in the U.S., or 506/693-8484. Fax 509/657-6610. www.hiltonsaintjohn.com. 197 units. C$119–C$219 (US$95–US$175) double. AE, DC, DISC, MC, V. Parking C$15 (US$12) per day. Pets allowed. **Amenities:** 2 restaurants; bar; indoor pool; fitness room; Jacuzzi; sauna;

game room; concierge; car-rental desk; business center; salon; 24-hr. room service; babysitting; laundry service. *In room:* A/C, TV, dataport, minibar, coffeemaker, hair dryer, iron, safe.

**Homeport Historic Bed & Breakfast** 🌟🌟 *Kids*    This architecturally impressive Italianate home built by a prominent shipbuilding family sits high atop a rocky ridge on the north side of Route 1, overlooking downtown and the harbor. Built around 1858, the home is one of Saint John's more gracious options for staying overnight. Rooms are furnished eclectically with furniture gleaned from area auctions and shops; all have individually controlled heat. Ask for the Veranda Room; it's spacious, has fine harbor views, and gets superb afternoon sun. (I'm also partial to the pink-tiled bathroom.) The Harbour Master Suite has a small separate sitting room, which is ideal for those traveling with a child. Five more rooms were recently added in the twin house next door. "Come-hungry" breakfasts are served family-style around a long antique table in the formal dining room.

80 Douglas Ave., Saint John, NB E2K 1E4. (C) 888/678-7678 or 506/672-7255. Fax 506/672-7250. www.homeport. nb.ca. 10 units. C$90–C$165 (US$72–US$132) double. Rates include full breakfast. AE, MC, V. *In room:* A/C, TV, dataport.

**Inn on the Cove** 🌟🌟    Inns like to tout celebrity connections, but the Inn on the Cove has the thinnest link to fame I've yet found: It was built by Alexander Graham Bell's gardener. Nevertheless, it's in a lovely setting, on a quiet road overlooking the water about 15 minutes' drive from downtown. The Irving Nature Park is next door; guests can hike right from the inn to dramatic Sheldon's Point. The house was once a classic late Victorian, built in 1910. In the 1950s it suffered from "improvements." Architectural preservationists will wince, but the changes did make for bright, spacious rooms that take advantage of the views. Meals here are excellent, and there's a day spa as well offering mud wraps, facials, and more for an extra charge.

Room 3 is the most expensive and has a Jacuzzi with perhaps the best bathtub view in the Maritimes. On the other hand, the least-expensive room—Room 2—has a detached private bathroom down the hall with the same view. The new apartment suite is good for families, with its private laundry and kitchen. All rooms have complimentary high-speed Internet. Ownership is so accommodating here, they'll even allow you to make short long-distance calls within North America for free.

1371 Sand Cove Rd. (mailing address: P.O. Box 3113, Station B, Saint John, NB E2M 4X7). (C) 877/257-8080 or 506/ 672-7799. Fax 506/635-5455. www.innonthecove.com. 6 units. Mid-June to mid-Oct C$149–C$225 (US$119– US$180) double, off-season rates lower. Rates include full breakfast. MC, V. Small dogs allowed in kennels. Children 12 and up welcome. **Amenities:** Restaurant; day spa; salon. *In room:* A/C, TV/DVD, kitchenette (1 unit), coffeemaker, hair dryer.

## MODERATE
**Dufferin Inn** 🌟🌟 *Finds*    This handsome Queen Anne house, across the harbor from downtown near the Digby ferry, was once home to a former premier of New Brunswick, and it has fine architectural touches like a wood-lined library and splashes of stained glass. The place has a wonderfully settled air, with oak furniture and overstuffed chairs, and recent renovations have updated all four rooms—all with complimentary high-speed Internet—to include both a whirlpool tub and a fireplace; one has a separate bedroom and living room as well.

Guests often stay here for access to the excellent **dining room** 🌟🌟, which is open to the public as well as guests. (Reservations encouraged.) Chef/owner Axel Begner has a deft hand in the kitchen, and he produces fine Continental dishes along the lines of rack of lamb in a Parmesan crust and maple crème brûlées. Meals are available a la carte or prix fixe; the four-course fixed-price dinner runs around C$60 (US$48) per person.

357 Dufferin Row, Saint John, NB E2M 2J7. ℂ **506/635-5968.** Fax 506/674-2396. www.dufferininn.com. 4 units. C$135–C$265 (US$108–US$212) double. Rates include breakfast. AE, DC, MC, V. **Amenities:** Dining room. *In room:* TV, hair dryer, iron.

**Earle of Leinster "Inn Style" Bed & Breakfast**     For more than a decade, Lauree and Stephen Savoie have operated the Earle of Leinster, a handsome Victorian row house in a working-class neighborhood a 5-minute walk from King's Square. It's a welcoming and casual place, nothing fancy, with a kitchen for guests to make themselves at home, and a pool table and TV in the basement. The Fitzgerald and Lord Edward rooms in the main house are the most historic, with high ceilings and regal furniture. Most of the remaining rooms are in the carriage house and are a bit more motel-like, although the second-floor loft is quite spacious. (Some rooms can be musty after a rainy spell.) The bathrooms are private, but they're also small. Added bonus: There's a free self-serve washer and dryer, plus VCRs in all rooms and a small library of films to select from. Recently the owner has expanded some of the smaller rooms, making them into minisuites with small kitchenette facilities.

96 Leinster St., Saint John, NB E2L 1J3. ℂ **506/652-3275.** http://earleofleinster.tripod.com. 7 units. C$70–C$100 (US$56–US$80) double. Rates include breakfast. AE, DC, MC, V. Pets allowed. **Amenities:** Laundry service. *In room:* TV/VCR, fridge, hair dryer, no phone.

## WHERE TO DINE

For lunch, don't overlook the Old City Market, mentioned above. With a little snooping you can turn up tasty light meals and fresh juices in the market, and then enjoy your finds in the alley atrium.

**Beatty and the Beastro**     BISTRO/CONTINENTAL     The small, simple, and attractive interior of this large-windowed establishment fronting King's Square features a mild European-moderne look, and is the most handsome eatery in Saint John. The service is cordial and efficient, and the meals are among the best in the city, always good, sometimes excellent. Lunch includes soups, salads, omelets, curry wraps, and elaborate sandwiches. At dinner the restaurant is noted for its lamb, the preparation of which varies nightly according to the chef's desire; the curry dish is also recommended, as is chicken parmigiana and almost anything else. When dessert time rolls around, be aware that both the butterscotch pie and the lemon chess pie have large local followings.

60 Charlotte St. (on King's Sq.). ℂ **506/652-3888.** Reservations recommended weekends and when shows are slated at the Imperial Theatre. Main courses C$5.95–C$9.95 (US$5–US$8) at lunch, C$20–C$23 (US$16–US$19) at dinner. AE, DC, MC, V. Mon–Fri 11:30am–3pm; Mon–Sat 5:30–9pm (Fri–Sat until 10pm). Sept–July closed Sun.

**Billy's Seafood Co.**     SEAFOOD     Billy Grant's restaurant off King's Square boasts a congenial staff, exceptionally fresh seafood (they sell to City Market customers by day), and slightly better prices than the more tourist-oriented waterfront seafood restaurants. The chef at this classy-yet-casual eatery knows how to prepare fish without overcooking. Specialties include cedar-planked salmon, and Billy's bouillabaisse is also quite good. Lunch entrees are surprisingly versatile, too, including Thai curried mussels and seafood crepes among other choices. Offerings of beef, veal, and pasta fill out the menu for those not in the mood for fish.

49–51 Charlotte St. (at City Market). ℂ **506/672-3474.** Reservations suggested. Light meals C$5.95–C$11 (US$5–US$9); dinner entrees C$16–C$29 (US$13–US$23). AE, DC, MC, V. Mon–Thurs 11am–10pm; Fri–Sat 11am–11pm; Sun 4–10pm.

**D'Amico** ITALIAN   Owner Paul Grannan has done a nice job converting an old printing office into a dramatic setting for reliable Italian fare. It's housed in a soaring, two-story space, anchored downstairs by a beautiful bar topped with polished red granite. Guests sit in austerely handsome chairs around lustrous wooden tabletops. You can "build your own" pasta by picking shape and sauce, along with add-ins. The same's true for the wood-fired pizza. Or select from a handful of traditional entrees including salmon and chicken Asiago.

33 Canterbury St. (C) **506/648-2377.** Reservations recommended. Lunch C$7–C$15 (US$5.50–US$12); dinner C$10–C$22 (US$7–US$16); pizzas C$9–C$15 (US$7–US$12). AE, DC, MC, V. Mon–Thurs 11:30am–11pm; Fri–Sat 11:30am–midnight; Sun 4–10pm.

**Taco Pica** LATIN AMERICAN   This cooperative is owned and run by a group of Guatemalans and their friends. It's bright, festive, and just a short stroll off King Street. The restaurant has developed a devoted local following since it opened in 1994, and features a menu that's a notch above the usually dreary Canadian adaptations of Mexican or Latin American fare. Among the most reliably popular dishes are *pepian* (a spicy beef stew with chayote), garlic shrimp, and shrimp taco with potatoes, peppers, and cheese. Vegetarian offerings are available as well. There's also a good selection of fresh juices, and the restaurant now possesses a liquor license—which means you can quaff any of a variety of fruit margaritas.

96 Germain St. (C) **506/633-8492.** Reservations recommended on weekends. Main courses C$7.95–C$17 (US$6.50–US$14). AE, MC, V. Mon–Sat 10am–10pm. Closed Sun and holidays.

## SAINT JOHN AFTER DARK

The best entertainment destination in town is the **Imperial Theatre** ✦ ((C) **506/ 674-4100**) on Kings Square; not always because of the acts that appear here, but because the performances are in what the *Toronto Globe and Mail* called the "most beautifully restored theatre in Canada." The theater originally opened in 1913 and hosted performances by such luminaries as Edgar Bergen, Al Jolson, and Walter Pidgeon (the latter a Saint John native). After being driven out of business by movie houses, then serving a long interim as home to a Pentecostal church, the theater was threatened with demolition in the early 1980s. That's when concerned citizens stepped in, raising funds to ensure that the theater would survive.

The Imperial reopened to much fanfare in 1994, and it has since hosted a wide range of performances from Broadway road shows to local theatrical productions and concerts. Even if nothing is slated during your stay, in the summer a guide is stationed on the premises to give you a tour, during which you can admire the intricate plasterwork and the 2.7m (9-ft.) chandelier. Thirty-minute tours are offered Monday through Saturday between 9am and 5pm, by appointment only; there's a small charge of about C$2 (US$1.60) per person, less for children.

Nightlife revolves around the seemingly innumerable pubs, most featuring live music, concentrated in the city's central downtown district. If you're looking to catch a big-time recording act, though, **Harbour Station** ((C) **506/632-6103**) at 99 Station St. is the place to go; acts might range anywhere from Motley Crue (we'll pass) to Willie Nelson (we're in).

## ROAD TRIP TO FUNDY TRAIL PARKWAY

**Fundy Trail Parkway** ✦ *(Kids)*   The parkway is an ambitious project that will eventually extend some 50km (31 miles) up the coast (it's currently 11km/6.75 miles) and link up with the Trans Canada Trail. This multiuse trail is nicely integrated with the natural environment, and makes the Fundy Coast accessible without despoiling its beauty. The trail is wide and easy to hike or bike and it has wheelchair-accessible pull-outs with spectacular coastal views. Additional hiking trails lead to various beaches, some of which can only be reached at low tide. If you don't have the time or energy to walk, you can drive the paved road that parallels the trail, or catch the shuttle (free with paid admission, runs noon–6pm weekends and holidays) that stops at each of the parkway's eight parking lots. To make life even simpler, there are judiciously placed water stations and covered picnic tables at various locations along the way—and families traveling with children will appreciate these resting stops. The interpretive center has some interesting displays and a short film on the logging history of the area; guided tours of the parkway are also offered. A 2-hour tour costs C$2 (US$1.60), a half-day excursion C$25 (US$20) for adults and C$12 (US$9.50) per child.

© **866/386-3987** or 506/833-2019. www.fundytrailparkway.com. Day pass C$3 (US$2.40) adult, C$2 (US$1.60) child, C$10 (US$8) family. Mid-May to mid-Oct trail gates daily 6am–8pm, interpretive center opens at 8am. Take Rte. 111 east; entrance is 10km (6½ miles) east of St. Martins (watch for signs). Leashed dogs allowed.

## 6 Fredericton

New Brunswick's provincial capital is a compact and historic city of brick and concrete that unfolds lazily along the banks of the wide St. John River. The handsome buildings, broad streets, and wide sidewalks make the place feel more like a big, tidy village than a small city. Keep an eye out for the two icons that mark Fredericton: the stately, stubborn elm trees that have resisted Dutch elm disease and still shade the occasional park and byway, and the Union Jack, which you'll occasionally see fluttering from various buildings, attesting to long-standing historic ties with the Loyalists who shaped the city.

For travelers, the city can be seen as divided into three zones: the malls and motels atop the hills and near the link to the Trans-Canada Highway; the impressive, Georgian-style University of New Brunswick on the hillside just south of downtown; and the downtown proper, with its casual blend of modern and historic buildings.

Most visitors focus on downtown. The main artery—where you'll find the majority of the attractions and many restaurants—is Queen Street, which parallels the river between 1 and 2 blocks inland. An ill-considered limited-access four-lane bypass separates much of downtown from the river, but you can still reach the water's edge via the Green or by crossing a pedestrian bridge at the foot of Carleton Street.

Fredericton, with a population of about 80,000, is low-key and appealing in a quiet and understated way. There's really not a must-see attraction here, but the collective impact of strolling the streets adds up to a full sense of history and place. (Surprisingly, it has also been selected as one of the most "wired" cities in North America; this rating must have been per-capita, but it's still worth using your laptop to hunt for hot spots.) My advice: If eastern Canada's allure for you is the shimmering sea, deep woods, and wide open spaces, you won't miss much by bypassing Fredericton. If your passions include history—especially the history of British settlement in North America—then it's well worth the detour.

## ESSENTIALS

**GETTING THERE**　A major relocation and widening of the Trans-Canada Highway near Fredericton has relieved traffic congestion somewhat. Look for signs directing you to downtown; from the west, follow Woodstock Road, which tracks along the

# Fredericton

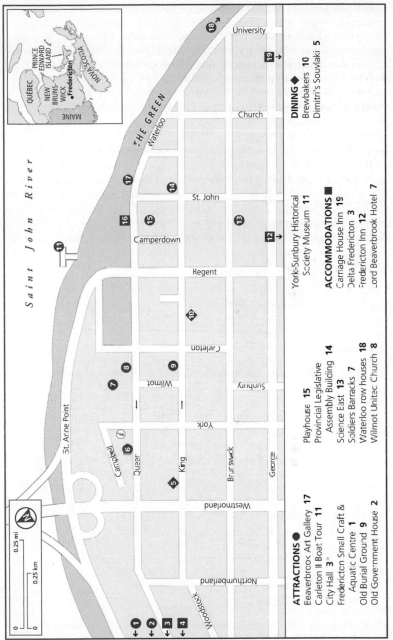

Saint John River

THE GREEN

University
Church
Waterloo
St. John
Camperdown
Regent
Carleton
Wilmot
Sunbury
York
King
Brunswick
George
Westmorland
Northumberland
Woodstock

St. Anne Point
Campbell
Queen

0.25 mi
0.25 km

**ATTRACTIONS** ●
Beaverbrook Art Gallery **17**
Carleton II Boat Tour **11**
City Hall **3**
Fredericton Small Craft &
    Aquatic Centre **1**
Old Burial Ground **9**
Old Government House **2**

Playhouse **15**
Provincial Legislative
    Assembly Building **14**
Science East **13**
Soldiers Barracks **7**
Waterloo row houses **18**
Wilmot United Church **8**

York-Sunbury Historical
    Society Museum **11**

**ACCOMMODATIONS** ■
Carriage House Inn **19**
Delta Fredericton **3**
Fredericton Inn **12**
Lord Beaverbrook Hotel **7**

**DINING** ◆
Brewbakers **10**
Dimitri's Souvlaki **5**

river to downtown. From Saint John, look for Route 7 to Regent Street, and then turn right down the hill.

The **Fredericton Airport** (© **506/444-6100**) is located 10 minutes southeast of downtown on Route 102 and is served by cab and rental car companies. For flight information, contact **Air Canada** (© **888/AIR-CANA;** www.aircanada.com). There's also a new direct **Delta Connection** (© **800/221-1212;** www.delta.com) shuttle service from Boston.

**VISITOR INFORMATION**    Always careful to cater to visitors, Fredericton maintains no less than two center-city visitor information centers: the original in **City Hall** at 397 Queen St., open May through October, and a second, newer one at **11 Carleton St.** which has racks of information year-round (it's the central office). Call © **888/888-4768** or 506/460-2129 to reach either. Then there's a third information center at **King's Landing** (© **506/460-2191**), just west of town, open approximately May through October as well. No matter which one you find first, ask for a Visitor Parking Pass, which allows visitors from outside the province to park free at city lots and meters in town for up to 3 days without penalty. You can also request travel information in advance by visiting the city's website at **www.city.fredericton.nb.ca**.

## EXPLORING FREDERICTON

The free *Fredericton Visitor Guide,* available at the information centers and many hotels around town, contains a well-written and informative **walking tour** of the downtown. It's worth tracking down before launching an exploration of the city.

City Hall, 397 Queen St., is an elaborate Victorian building with a prominent brick tower and 2.4m (8-ft.) clock dial. The second-floor City Council Chamber occupies what was the opera house until the 1940s. Small, folksy tapestries adorn the **visitor's gallery** and tell the town's history. Learn about these and the rest of the building during the free building tours, which are offered twice daily from mid-May to mid-October (both in English and French). In the off season, call © **506/460-2120** to schedule a tour.

Officers' Square, on Queen Street between Carleton and Regent, is now a handsome city park. In 1785, the park was the center of military activity and used for drills, first as part of the British garrison, and later (until 1914) by the Canadian Army. Today, the only soldiers are local actors who put on a show for the tourists. Look also for music and dramatic events staged at the square in the warmer months. The handsome colonnaded stone building facing the parade grounds is the former officer's quarters, now the **York-Sunbury Historical Society Museum** (see below).

In the center of the square the prominent statue of the robed figure is Lord Beaverbrook. That's a name you'll hear a lot of in Fredericton: a street, a museum, and a hotel bear his name. Lord Beaverbrook was Max Aitken, a native of Newcastle, New Brunswick, who amassed a significant fortune as a press baron and through other business endeavors. Although he lived much of his life in Britain (he was made a lord in 1917, taking the name after a stream near Newcastle where he had fished as a young man), he maintained close ties to Canada. He donated an art collection and modern building to house it (the Beaverbrook Art Gallery), along with a modern playhouse, which now is home to **Theatre New Brunswick.** The playhouse was built in 1964, the same year Lord Beaverbrook died.

Two blocks upriver of Officers' Square are the Soldiers' Barracks, housed in a similarly grand stone building. Check your watch against the sundial high on the end of the barracks, a replica of the original timepiece. A small exhibit shows the life of the enlisted man in the 18th century. Along the ground floor, local craftspeople sell their wares from small shops carved out of former barracks.

Fredericton is well noted for its distinctive architecture, especially the fine Victorian and Queen Anne residential architecture. Particularly attractive is **Waterloo Row,** a group of privately owned historic homes—some grand, some less so—just downriver of downtown.

One entertaining and enlightening way to learn about the city's history is to sign up for a walking tour with the **Calithumpians of Fredericton's Outdoor Summer Theatre.** Costumed guides offer free tours daily in July and August, pointing out highlights with anecdotes and dramatic tales. Recommended is the evening "Haunted Hike" tour, which runs 5 nights each week. The evening tour is about 2 hours and costs about C$13 (US$11) for adults, C$8 (US$6.40) for children; call © **506/457-1975** for more information.

If you happen to be in town on a Saturday, a worthy detour is to the **Boyce Farmers' Market** (© **506/451-1815**), located on George Street, behind the old jail at 668 Brunswick St. The market, which runs from about 6am until about 1pm, has existed here in one form or another since the late 18th century. The current building was constructed in 1951 and expanded in 1990. More than 200 vendors offer everything fresh, from seasonal vegetables to meats, baked goods, and crafts. The market is adjacent to **Science East** (see below).

## OUTDOOR PURSUITS

Fredericton recently expanded its trail system for walkers and bikers. The centerpiece of the system is **The Green,** a 5km (3-mile) pathway that follows the river from the Sheraton hotel to near the Princess Margaret Bridge. It's a lovely walk, and you'll pass the **Old Government House** (see below), downtown, and the open parklands near Waterloo Row.

Connecting with The Green is a well-used pedestrian bridge that crosses an abandoned railroad trestle just east of downtown. From this vantage point you'll get wonderful views of the downtown and river valley. If you continue onward, the **Nashwaak/Marysville Trail** follows an abandoned rail bed along the attractive Nashwaak River; after about 4km (2.5 miles) you can cross the Nashwaak at Bridge Street and loop back to the pedestrian rail-bridge via the **Gibson Trail.**

A number of other trails link up to this expanding network, which stretches more than 60km (37 miles). A free trail guide brochure is available at the information centers, or contact the **New Brunswick Trails Council** at © **506/459-1931.**

Bikes may be rented by the hour or the day at the Fredericton Lighthouse at the **Lighthouse Adventure Centre** (© **506/460-2939**) near **Regent St. Wharf,** or at **Radical Edge,** 386 Queen St. (© **506/459-3478**). Rentals are around C$35 (US$28) per day or C$5/US$4 per hour.

The *Carleton II* (© **506/454-2628**) offers 1-hour excursions on the river aboard a ship with a capacity of 100 passengers. You'll learn about local history, view the city from the scenic river, and perhaps spot a bald eagle flying along the shoreline. The tours depart several times daily in summer from the wharf near the **Fredericton Lighthouse** (at the foot of Regent St.). Rates are about C$7 (US$5.60) adults, C$3 (US$2.40) children.

Another option for getting on the water is the **Small Craft Aquatic Centre,** on Woodstock Road (behind the Victoria Health Centre and near the Old Government House; © **506/460-2260**). It's open daily from the middle of May to early October, and rents rowing shells, canoes, and kayaks. Ask also about naturalist-guided tours of the river.

Finally, the **Kingswood** golf course (© **800/423-5969** or 506/443-3333; www. nbgolf.ca/golf.php) was recognized by *Golf Digest* as the best new Canadian course in 2003. It features 27 holes, a par-3 course, and a double-ended driving range.

## ATTRACTIONS DOWNTOWN

**Beaverbrook Art Gallery** *Value*    This surprisingly good museum overlooks the waterfront and is home to an impressive collection of British paintings, including works by Reynolds, Gainsborough, Constable, and Turner. Antiques buffs gravitate to the rooms with period furnishings and early decorative arts. Most visitors find themselves drawn to Salvador Dalí's massive *Santiago El Grande,* and studies for an ill-fated portrait of Winston Churchill. A new curator has brought in more controversial modern art exhibits of late; one focused on nudity, featuring various artistic perceptions of the unclothed human form, for example. But other shows have touched on more conventional ground, such as 19th-century French realism and a show on the cities of Canada drawn from the Seagram Collection. Stop by to find out what's currently on display.

703 Queen St. © **506/458-2028.** www.beaverbrookartgallery.org. Admission C$5 (US$4) adults, C$4 (US$3.20) seniors, C$2 (US$1.60) students, free for children under 6; Thurs evenings pay what you wish. Daily 9am–5:30pm (Thurs until 9pm).

**Old Government House**    The wonderfully severe Government House was built in 1828, when it was created as the official residence of the lieutenant governor, who was the official representative of the British Crown. It was built of locally quarried sandstone in a rigorously classical style, featuring Palladian symmetry, intricate plasterwork, and other haute touches. It served as the official residence until 1890, after which it served variously as a school and home to a detachment of Mounties. Recently spared from the wrecking ball, the home underwent an exhaustive restoration and reopened in 1999. It once again is the official residence of the lieutenant governor, who has an apartment on the third floor and an office on the second floor.

The bilingual tours begin in a basement interpretive center, and last about 45 minutes. You'll hike up sweeping staircases and view the extraordinarily high-ceilinged ground-floor reception rooms, and have a chance to peruse art displayed in the second floor art gallery. Guides are loaded with stories and anecdotes. The tour will be of special interest to those who number historic architecture among their passions, and those attracted to the grandeur of bygone days.

51 Woodstock Rd. (next to the Sheraton hotel). © **506/453-2505.** Free admission. June–Sept tours daily 10am–5pm; off season by appointment. Tours leave on the hour; last tour at 5pm.

**Provincial Legislative Assembly Building**    The Legislative Assembly Building, constructed starting in 1880, boasts an exterior designed in that bulbous, extravagant Second Empire style. But that's just the prelude. Inside, it's even more dressed up and fancy. Entering takes a bit of courage if the doors are closed; they're heavy and intimidating, with slits of beveled glass for peering out. (They're reminiscent of the gates of Oz.) Inside, it's creaky and wooden and comfortable, in contrast to the cold, unyielding stone of many seats of power. In the small rotunda, look for the razor-sharp prints from John James Audubon's elephant folio, on display in a special case.

The assembly chamber nearly takes the breath away, especially when viewed from the heights of the visitor gallery on the upper floors. (You ascend via a graceful wood spiral stairway housed in its own rotunda.) The chamber is ornate and draperied in that fussy Victorian way, which is quite a feat given the vast scale of the room. Note all the regal trappings, including the portrait of the young Queen Elizabeth. This place just feels like a setting for high drama, whether or not it actually delivers when the chamber is in session. Half-hour long tours are available; plan to spend at least an hour here.

706 Queen St. (across from the Beaverbrook Art Gallery). © 506/453-2527. Free admission. June to mid-Aug daily 9am–7pm (last tour at 6:30pm); off season Mon–Fri 9am–4pm.

**Science East** ✪ *(Value* *(Kids*    Children enjoy a visit to this newish (1999) science center for two reasons. First, it's located in the old county jail, a sturdy stone structure built in the 1840s. (It was still being used as a jail as late as 1996.) And then there are the great exhibits—more than 100 interactive displays indoor and out, including a huge kaleidoscope, a periscope for people-watching, a solar-powered water fountain, and a minitornado. It's an ideal destination for a family on a chilly or rainy day, and there's plenty to do in the outdoors portion on nice days too. If you have kids, this place is easily worth up to 2 hours of your time.

668 Brunswick St. © 506/457-2340. www.scienceeast.nb.ca. Admission C$5 (US$4) adults, C$3 (US$2.40) students and seniors, C$14 (US$11) families. June–Aug Mon–Sat 10am–5pm, Sun 1–4pm; rest of year Tues–Fri noon–5pm, Sat 10am–5pm.

**York-Sunbury Historical Society Museum** *(Kids*    This well-done small museum lures visitors with the promise of a stuffed 42-pound frog. It was said to belong to Fred Coleman, who in the late 19th century fed it a nasty concoction of June bugs, cornmeal, buttermilk, and whiskey to give it Rubenesque proportions. After it perished at the hands of some miscreants, the famous frog was displayed at the Burke House Hotel until 1959, when it traveled with little ceremony to the museum. It's displayed on the top floor to ensure that you wander through all the exhibits looking for it—a clever trick on the part of the curator.

Actually, the frog is a disappointment. (Not to mention suspect—it looks like it's made of bad papier-mâché.)

Still, the rest of the museum is nicely done. Displays feature the usual artifacts of life gone by, but several exhibits rise well above the clutter, including a fine display on Loyalist settlers. Kids will love the claustrophobic re-creation of a German World War II trench on the second floor—and likely will end up talking more about that on the way home than Fred's portly frog. Plan to spend about a half-hour here.

Off Queen St. near Regent St. © 506/455-6041. Admission C$3 (US$2.40) adults, C$2 (US$1.60) seniors, C$1 (US80¢) students, C$6 (US$4) families. July–Aug daily 10am–5pm; spring and fall Tues–Sat 1–4pm. Closed Nov–May.

## ATTRACTIONS OUTSIDE OF TOWN

**Kings Landing Historical Settlement** ✪    Kings Landing, on the bank of the St. John River, is 34km (21 miles) and about 150 years from Fredericton. The authentic re-creation brings to life New Brunswick from 1790 to 1910, with 10 historic houses and nine other buildings relocated here and saved from destruction by the flooding during the Mactaquac hydro project. The aroma of freshly baked bread mixes with the smell of horses and livestock, and the sound of the blacksmith's hammer alternates with that of the church bell. More than 160 costumed "early settlers" chat about their lives.

You could easily spend a day exploring the 120 hectare (300 acres), but if you haven't that much time, focus on the Hagerman House (with furniture by Victorian cabinetmaker John Warren Moore), the Ingraham House with its fine New Brunswick furniture and formal English garden, the Morehouse House (where you'll see a clock Benedict Arnold left behind), and the Victorian Perley House. The Ross Sash and Door Factory will demonstrate the work and times of a turn-of-the-20th-century manufacturing plant.

Afterward, hitch a ride on the sloven wagon, or relax at the Kings Head Inn, which served up grub and grog to hardy travelers along the St. John River a century or more ago. Today it serves lemonade, chicken pie, and corn chowder, along with other traditional dishes. Lunch prices are around C$8 to C$13 (US$6.40–US$11), and dinner is about C$13 to C$19 (US$11–US$15).

Exit 253 off the Trans-Canada Hwy. (Rte. 2 west). ℂ 506/363-4999. www.kingslanding.nb.ca. Admission C$15 (US$12) adults, C$13 (US$11) seniors, C$12 (US$9.60) students over 16, C$10 (US$8) children 6–16, C$36 (US$29) families. June to mid-Oct daily 10am–5pm. Closed mid-Oct to May.

## SHOPPING

Fredericton is home to a growing number of artists and artisans, as well as entrepreneurs who have launched a handful of offbeat shops. It's worth setting aside an hour or two for browsing.

**Aitkens Pewter**   This well-known shop sells classically designed pewter dishes and mugs based on historic patterns, as well as modern adaptations and jewelry. 408 Queen St. ℂ 800/567-4416 or 506/453-9474.

**Cultures Boutique**   This is one of a chain of YMCA-run shops that promote alternative trade to benefit craftspeople in the Third World. Look for goods from foreign lands as well as North American native cultures, mostly from community-based cooperatives. 383 Mazzucca's Lane (off York St. between King and Queen). ℂ 506/462-3088.

**Gallery Connexion**   Expect vibrant modern artwork, much of it experimental and in all sorts of media, at this lively nonprofit gallery run by area artists. Studios are within the same building, and you may have a chance to see the artists at work. 453 Queen St. (behind the Justice Building). ℂ 506/454-1433.

**Gallery 78**   An exceptionally solid and handsome Queen Anne–style mansion is home to the province's oldest private art gallery. Sunny spaces upstairs and down showcase a range of local art, much of it sold at affordable prices. 796 Queen St. (near the Beaverbrook Art Gallery). ℂ 506/454-5192.

## WHERE TO STAY

A handful of motels and chain hotels are located in the bustling mall zone on the hill above town, mostly along Regent and Prospect Streets. Allow about 10 minutes to drive downtown from here.

Among the classiest of the bunch is the **Fredericton Inn,** 1315 Regent St. (ℂ 800/561-8777 or 506/455-1430), situated between two malls. It's a soothing-music-and-floral-carpeting kind of place that does a brisk business in the convention trade. But with its indoor pool and classically appointed rooms, it's a comfortable spot for vacation travelers as well. Peak season rates are C$109 to C$149 (US$87–US$119) and up to C$189 (US$151) for suites.

Also near the malls are the **Comfort Inn,** 797 Prospect St. (ℂ 506/453-0800), at C$105 to C$199 (US$84–US$159) double; **City Motel,** 1216 Regent St. (ℂ 800/268-2858 or 506/459-9900), with rooms for C$95 (US$76); and the **Lakeview Inn and Suites,** 655 Prospect St. (ℂ 877/355-3500 or 506/459-0035), C$107 (US$86).

**Carriage House Inn**   Fredericton's premier bed-and-breakfast is located a short stroll from the riverfront pathway in a quiet residential neighborhood. A former mayor built this imposing three-story Victorian manse in 1875. Inside, it's a bit somber in that heavy Victorian way, with dark wood trim and deep colors, and feels solid enough to resist glaciers. Rooms are eclectically furnished and comfortable without being opulent. High-speed wireless Internet is available throughout the inn. Delicious and elaborate breakfasts are served in a sunny room in the rear of the house.

Dinner is available at the inn with 48-hour advance notice; ask about the menu when you book. A complete dinner runs around C$25 (US$20) per person.

230 University Ave., Fredericton, NB E3B 4H7. (C) **800/267-6068** or 506/452-9924. Fax 506/452-2770. www.carriage house-inn.net. 10 units. C$90–C$125 (US$72–US$100) double. Rates include full breakfast. AE, MC, V. "Small, well-trained pets" allowed. **Amenities:** Restaurant. *In room:* A/C, TV, hair dryer.

**Crowne Plaza Federickton–Lord Beaverbrook Hotel** ✦ *Kids*   This stern and hulking 1947 waterfront hotel is severe and boxy in an early deco kind of way, a look that may at first suggest that it houses the Ministry of Dourness. Inside, the mood lightens considerably, with composite stone floors, Georgian pilasters, and chandeliers. The downstairs indoor pool and recreation area are positively whimsical, a sort of Tiki-room grotto that kids adore. The guest rooms are nicely appointed with traditional reproduction furniture in dark wood. Standard rooms can be somewhat dim, and most of the windows don't open (ask for a room with opening windows when you book). The suites are spacious and many have excellent river views. This is the best accommodation for those who want the convenience of a downtown location and who enjoy the solid architectural touches of an old-fashioned hotel. Those looking for a modern polish may be more content at the Delta.

You've got three choices for dining. The Terrace Room is the main dining area, with an indoor gazebo and a seasonal outdoor deck overlooking the river. The menu corrals resort standards, starting with relish trays and puffy white dinner rolls. Main courses range from Asian shrimp stir-fry to chicken fettuccine Alfredo. The more intimate Governor's Room has higher aspirations, with such dinner entrees as duck breast with a raspberry and Grand Marnier coulis. The James Joyce Irish Pub is the spot for a pint and a snack.

659 Queen St., Fredericton, NB E3B 5A6. (C) **866/444-1946** or 506/455-3371. Fax 506/455-1441. www.cpfredericton. com. 165 units. C$110–C$255 (US$88–US$204) double. AE, DC, MC, V. **Amenities:** 3 restaurants; pub; indoor pool; Jacuzzi; sauna; business center; babysitting; laundry service; dry cleaning. *In room:* A/C, TV, dataport, coffeemaker; hair dryer; iron.

**Delta Fredericton** ✦   This modern resort hotel, built in 1992, occupies a prime location along the river about 10 minutes' walk from downtown via the riverfront pathway. Much of summer life revolves around the outdoor pool (with poolside bar) on the deck overlooking the river, and on Sunday the lobby is surrendered to an over-the-top breakfast buffet. Although decidedly up to date, the interior is done with classical styling and is comfortable and well appointed. The hotel lounge is an active and popular spot on many nights, especially weekends. Across the lobby is Bruno's Fredericton Restaurant, which offers a good alternative to the restaurants downtown. Look for seasonal and regional specialties, including fiddleheads in early summer.

225 Woodstock Rd., Fredericton, NB E3B 2H8. (C) **800/325-3535** or 506/457-7000. Fax 506/457-4000. www.delta fredericton.com. 222 units. C$109–C$229 (US$87–US$183) double. AE, DC, MC, V. Free parking. Pets accepted. **Amenities:** Restaurant; 2 bars; heated indoor pool and heated outdoor pool; fitness room; Jacuzzi; sauna; salon; room service; babysitting. *In room:* A/C, TV, minibar, coffeemaker, hair dryer, iron.

**On the Pond Lodge** ✿ *Finds*   In 1999, Donna Evans opened On the Pond, about 15 minutes west of Fredericton, with the idea of creating a comfortable retreat where guests could be pampered with spa treatments after indulging in soft adventure at the adjacent provincial park and surrounding countryside. The lodge is lovely, constructed in a strong sort of William Morris–inspired style with dark wood trim, slate floors in the entryways, and fieldstone fireplaces. The two downstairs common rooms—one with wood fireplace and one lined with bookshelves—invite lingering and chatting with the other guests. The upstairs guest rooms each feature a queen and a double bed, and are slightly larger than the average hotel room with nice extras like bathrobes and duvets. The basement spa includes two massage rooms, a hot tub, a sauna, an aesthetics room (offering manicures, pedicures, and facials), and a fitness center. Keeping with the theme, heart-healthy dinners are also served on request if ordered in advance or as part of a package; the cost is approximately C$40 (US$32) for a four-course meal.

The lodge is on "The Arm"—an impoundment of the St. John River behind the nearby hydroelectric dam—in a marshy setting that's better for bird-watching than swimming. There's a small wharf here, with canoes, kayaks and bikes that guests may use for free. Also nearby are a golf course and King's Landing Historical Settlement (see above). Beach swimming is available across the road at the provincial park.

20 Rte. 615, Mactaquac, NB E6L 1M2. ✆ 506/363-3420. Fax 506/363-3479. www.onthepond.com. 8 units. C$145–C$150 (US$116–US$120) double. MC, V. Drive west of Fredericton on Woodstock Rd.; cross the Mactaquac Dam and continue to the Esso station; turn right and look for sign on right. No children. **Amenities:** Dining room; spa; Jacuzzi; sauna; watersports equipment. *In room:* A/C, TV/VCR, dataport, hair dryer.

## WHERE TO DINE

**Brewbakers** ✿ ITALIAN/PUB FARE   Brewbakers is a convivial pub, cafe, and restaurant, located on three levels in a cleverly adapted downtown building. It's a bustling and informal spot, creatively cluttered with artifacts and artworks, and does boomtown business during lunch hours and early evenings. The cafe section is quieter, as is the mezzanine dining room above the cafe. The third floor bustles, with an open kitchen and folks lined up for the popular build-your-own pasta buffet. And pasta is the main attraction here, served up with the usual array of sauces. Also good are the personal pizzas, the roasted chicken, the grilled strip loin, and the herb-crusted tenderloin. The lunch buffet is one of the better deals in town—bring a large appetite. For a meal on the go, the cafe offers a creative selection of boxed lunches.

546 King St. ✆ 506/459-0067. Reservations recommended. Main courses C$6–C$10 (US$5–US$8) at lunch, C$12–C$26 (US$9.60–US$21) at dinner. AE, DC, MC, V. Mon–Wed 11:30am–10pm; Thurs–Fri 11:30am–midnight; Sat 4pm–midnight; Sun 4–10pm.

**Dimitri's Souvlaki** *Value* GREEK   Dimitri's is hard to find, and easy to keep walking past once you've found it. But the generic, chain-restaurant interior with its hide-the-crumbs paisley carpeting belies better-than-average cooking that will appeal especially to budget-conscious diners. You'll get a big plate of food here for not a lot of money. The Greek specialties include moussaka (with and without meat), souvlakia, and dolmades, and all are quite good. (Avoid the mystery-meat donairs.) Deluxe dinner plates are served with delicious potatoes—hearty wedges that are cooked crispy on the outside and remain hot and soft on the inside. The meats are sometimes on the tough side, but most diners will find this a good value.

349 King St. (in Piper's Lane area). ✆ 506/452-8882. Main courses C$8.25–C$18 (US$6.50–US$15). AE, DC, MC, V. Mon–Wed 11am–11pm; Thurs–Sat 11am–11:30pm.

## FREDERICTON AFTER DARK

Fredericton's downtown is often lively with university students and young profession-als after-hours. **Lunar Rogue,** 625 King St. (© **506/450-2065**), features more than 50 whiskeys and 14 draft beers in a comfortable, pubby atmosphere. Tuesday is nacho night, which lures out the local folks in droves.

Finally, **Dolan's Pub,** 349 King St. (© **506/454-7474**), is your best bet for live maritime music, which is on tap every Thursday through Saturday. Also on tap is the city's largest selection of microbrews. Don't miss the barrel of free peanuts.

## ROAD TRIP TO GAGETOWN

About 55km (34 miles) southeast of Fredericton is the untroubled, unassuming vil-lage of Gagetown. (The village can be visited via a scenic driving detour en route to or from Saint John.) It's been largely unchanged over the years—backed by farm fields on one side and a placid inlet off the St. John River known as Gagetown Creek. The peaceable surroundings and simple vernacular country architecture have attracted the attention of craftspeople and artists, who have settled here and slowly made it a quiet arts colony—quaint and creative, but not annoyingly so. Look for a handful of low-key enterprises, including art galleries, a cafe, a decoy carver, a bookstore, a cider press, a crafts cooperative, and several potters.

Things to do, besides wander around: You can **bird-watch** and explore—the region is noted for its avian life, with a wide range of birds enjoying the mixed terrain that includes marsh grass, forest, and field. Some 144 species have been reliably identified in and around Gagetown. Gagetown Island is just offshore (easily accessible by kayak or canoe, which inn guests may borrow; see below). The island is 400 hectare (1,000 acres) and features a glacial deposit that rises some 23m (75 ft.), the ruins of a stone house that dates from the early 19th century, and an osprey-viewing platform.

You can visit the **Queens County Museum** (no phone), birthplace of Sir Samuel Leonard Tilley, one of the fathers of confederation. (The 1786 home is located across from the Steamers Stop Inn, and is open to the public in summer.)

### WHERE TO STAY & DINE

**Steamers Stop Inn**     Most of the riverside Steamer Stop Inn was built around 1910, with a harmonious addition completed in the 1930s. It's a rustic, homey spot, though the downstairs common rooms are furnished more with an eye to comfort—some modern velour-upholstered, some Victorian—than to attract any design awards. His-toric touches add a nice patina, with lots of oak woodwork and old pine paneling. The guest rooms vary in size. Rooms 4 and 5 both face the road; the latter is the smallest, the former the largest and brightest in the inn. Room 3 has nice river views and the original bathroom with hulking old tub; Room 6 is a corner room with a view up the river, a pair of wicker chairs, and a relatively large bathroom in the former linen closet. The inn has two kayaks and a canoe for guests to use; there's also river swimming from the wharf and an outdoor hot tub.

As for chow, the inn's dining room is about the only game in town. Dinners are by reservation only, and guests are seated in several pleasant dining areas; request a table on the screened porch if the weather's warm. The well-regarded menu features such favorites as filet mignon, scallops, and halibut.

74 Front St., Village of Gagetown, NB E5M 1A1. © **506/488-2903.** Fax 506/488-1116. 7 units. C$95–C$125 (US$76–US$100) double. Rates include continental breakfast. AE, MC, V. Closed mid-Oct to May. Pets allowed only if kept in kennel. **Amenities:** Restaurant; Jacuzzi; watersports equipment. *In room:* Hair dryer, no phone.

## 7 Fundy National Park ⋆⋆

The Fundy Coast between Saint John and Alma is for the most part wild, remote, and unpopulated. It's plumbed by few roads other than the new Fundy Drive (see "Saint John," earlier in this chapter), making it difficult to explore unless you have a boat. The best access to the wild coast is through Fundy National Park, a gem of a destination that's hugely popular with travelers with an outdoor bent. Families often settle in here for a week or so, filling their days with activities in and around the park that include hiking, sea kayaking, biking, and splashing around a seaside pool. Nearby are lovely drives and an innovative adventure center at Cape Enrage. If a muffling fog moves in to smother the coast, head inland for a hike to a waterfall or through lush forest. If it's a day of brilliant sunshine, venture along the rocky shores by foot or boat.

## ESSENTIALS

**GETTING THERE**   Route 114 runs through the center of Fundy National Park. If you're coming from the west, follow the prominent national park signs just east of Sussex. If you're coming from Prince Edward Island or Nova Scotia, head southward on Route 114 from Moncton.

One word of warning for travel from Moncton: Beware the signs at the Route 15 rotary directing you to Fundy National Park. Moncton's traffic czars send tourists on a silly Mr. Toad's Wild Ride around the city's outskirts, apparently to avoid downtown traffic; after 16km (10 miles) of driving you'll end up within sight of the rotary again, just across the river. It's far more sensible to head downtown via Main Street, cross the river on the first steel bridge (you can see it from about everywhere), and then turn left on Route 114.

**VISITOR INFORMATION**   The park's main **Visitor Centre** (© 506/887-6000) is located just inside the Alma (eastern) entrance to the park. The stone building is open daily during peak season from 8am to 10pm (to 4:30pm in the off season). You can watch a video presentation, peruse a handful of exhibits on wildlife and tides, and shop at the nicely stocked nature bookstore.

The smaller **Wolfe Lake Information Centre** (© 506/432-6026) is at the park's western entrance and is open daily in summer from 10am to 6pm.

**FEES**   Park entry fees are charged from mid-May to mid-October. The fee is C$6 (US$5) adults, C$5 (US$4) seniors, C$3 (US$2.40) children ages 6 to 16, and C$15 (US$12) families. Seasonal passes are also available.

## EXPLORING FUNDY NATIONAL PARK

Most national park activities are centered around the Alma (east) side of the park, where the park entrance has a cultivated and manicured air, as if part of a landed estate. Here you'll find stone walls, well-tended lawns, and attractive landscaping, along with a golf course, amphitheater, lawn bowling, and tennis.

Also in this area is a **heated saltwater pool,** set near the bay with a sweeping ocean view. There's a lifeguard on duty, and it's a popular destination for families. The pool is open late June to August. The cost is C$3 (US$2.40) adults, C$2.50 (US$2) seniors, C$1.50 (US$1.20) children, and C$7.50 (US$6) families.

Also unique to the park are two **auto trails**—basically overgrown dirt roads that you can explore with the family car. **Hastings Auto Trail** is one-way so you needn't worry about oncoming vehicles. It's a good way to see some of the great outdoors

# Fundy National Park

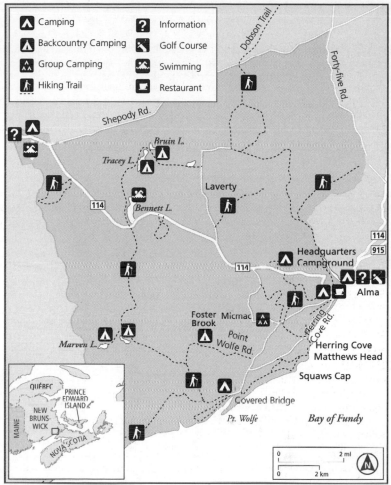

**Legend:**
- Camping
- Backcountry Camping
- Group Camping
- Hiking Trail
- Information
- Golf Course
- Swimming
- Restaurant

Dobson Trail
Forty-five Rd.
Shepody Rd.
Bruin L.
Tracey L.
Laverty
Bennett L.
114
Headquarters
Campground
114
915
Alma
Foster Brook
Micmac
Point Wolfe Rd.
Herring Cove Rd.
Marven L.
Herring Cove
Matthews Head
Squaws Cap
Covered Bridge
Pt. Wolfe
Bay of Fundy

QUÉBEC
PRINCE EDWARD ISLAND
MAINE
NEW BRUNS-WICK
NOVA SCOTIA

0        2 mi
0        2 km

without suffering the indignities that often result from actual encounters with nature (rain, bugs, blisters, and so on).

Sea kayaking tours are a way to get a good, close look at the ocean landscape and the tides. **FreshAir Adventure** (© **800/545-0020**) in Alma offers tours that range from 2 hours to several days. The half-day tours explore marsh and coastline (C$40–C$52/US$32–US$42 including lunch); the full-day adventure includes a hot meal and 6 hours of exploring the wild shores (C$65–C$95/US$52–US$76).

## HIKING

The park maintains 105km (65 miles) of trails for hikers and walkers. These range from a 20-minute loop to a 4-hour trek, and they pass through varied terrain. The trails are arranged such that several can be linked into a 48km (30-mile) backpacker's loop, dubbed the **Fundy Circuit,** which typically requires 3 nights in the backcountry. Preregistration is required for the overnight trek, so ask at the visitor center.

Among the most accessible hikes is the **Caribou Plain Trail** ✿, a 3km (2-mile) loop that provides a wonderful introduction to the local terrain. You'll hike along a beaver pond, on a boardwalk across a raised peat bog, and through lovely temperate forest. Read the interpretive signs to learn about deadly "flarks," which lurk in bogs and can kill a moose.

The **Third Vault Falls Trail** ✿✿ is a 7.5km (4.5-mile) in-and-back hike that takes you to the park's highest waterfall, about 14m (45 ft.) high. The trail is largely a flat stroll through leafy woodlands until you begin a steady descent into a mossy gorge. You round a corner and there you are, suddenly facing the cataract.

All the park's trails are covered in the pullout trail guide you'll find in "Salt & Fir," the booklet you'll receive when you pay your entry fee.

## BIKING

The roads east of Alma offer superb bicycling terrain, at least if you get off busy Route 114. Especially appealing is **Route 915** ✿ from Riverside-Albert to Alma, along with a detour to Cape Enrage. Along this scenic road you'll pedal through rolling farmland and scattered settlements, past vistas of salt marshes and the wonderfully named Ha Ha Cemetery. The hills are low but can be steep and require a serious grind, so you should be in reasonable shape. Route 915 runs 27km (17 miles), with the spur to Cape Enrage an additional 6.5km (4 miles) each way.

Bike rentals have not been available in Alma in recent years, but check with the **Alma visitor information center** (✆ **506/887-6127**) to see if the situation has changed. Otherwise, bikes may be rented in Saint John or Moncton.

## CAMPING

The national park maintains four drive-in campgrounds and 15 backcountry sites. The two main campgrounds are near the Alma entrance. **Headquarters Campground** ✿ is within walking distance of Alma, the saltwater pool, and numerous other attractions. Since it overlooks the bay, this campground tends to be cool and subject to fogs. **Chignecto North Campground** ✿ is higher on the hillside, sunnier, and warmer. You can hike down to Alma on an attractive hiking trail in 1 to 2 hours. Both campgrounds have hookups for RVs, flush toilets, and showers, and sites can be reserved in advance (✆ **877/737-3783;** www.pccamping.ca); sites cost C$23 to C$30 (US$19-US$24) per night.

The **Point Wolfe** and **Wolfe Lake** campgrounds lack RV hookups and are slightly more primitive (Wolfe Lake lacks showers), but they are the preferred destinations for campers seeking a quieter camping experience. Rates at most sites are C$14 to C$30 (US$11–US$24), depending on services required; Wolfe Lake has pit toilets only and is C$14 (US$8.50) per night.

Backcountry sites are scattered throughout the park, with only one located directly on the coast (at the confluence of the coast and Goose River). Ask at the visitor centers for more information or to reserve a site (mandatory). Backcountry camping fees are C$9 (US$7) per person per night.

## ROAD TRIP TO CAPE ENRAGE

Cape Enrage is a blustery and bold cape that juts impertinently out into Chignecto Bay. It's also home to a wonderful adventure center that could be a model for similar centers worldwide.

Cape Enrage Adventures ⭐ traces its roots to 1993, when a group of Harrison Trimble High School students in Moncton decided to do something about the decay of the cape's historic lighthouse, which had been abandoned in 1988. They put together a plan to restore the light and keeper's quarters and establish an adventure center. It worked. Today, with the help of experts in kayaking, rock climbing, rappelling, and other rugged sports, a couple dozen high-school students staff and run this program throughout the summer months. The program closes in late August, when the student-managers head back to school.

Part of what makes the program so notable is its flexibility. Day adventures are scheduled throughout the summer, from which you can pick and choose, as if from a menu. These include **rappelling workshops, rock-climbing lessons, kayak trips,** and **canoeing excursions.** Prices are about C$50 (US$40) per person for a 2-hour rock climbing or rappelling workshop, about C$55 (US$44) for a half-day kayak trip. (*Note to parents:* This is an ideal spot to drop off restless teens while you indulge in scenic drives or a trip to Hopewell Rocks.)

Families looking to endure outdoor hardships together should inquire about **custom adventures.** For about C$180 to C$300 (US$144–US$240) per person, the center can organize a 2- to 5-night adventure vacation that includes equipment, instruction, food, and lodging. You pick your own activities—maybe a sea kayak trip early one morning, followed by an afternoon of rappelling. It's entirely up to you.

As if running the center didn't keep the students busy enough, they also operate a restaurant (open to the public), called the **Keepers' Lunchroom.** Light but tasty meals include a notable fish chowder made with fresh haddock from a recipe provided by a local fisherman's wife, served with hot biscuits. A few other selections are offered—like grilled cheese and cheesecake—but the smart money gets the chowder.

For more information about the program, which runs May through September, contact **Cape Enrage Adventures** (© **888/280-7273** or 506/887-2273; www.capenrage.com).

## ROAD TRIP TO THE HOPEWELL ROCKS

There's no better place to witness the extraordinary power of the Fundy tides than at **Hopewell Rocks** ⭐ (© **877/734-3429;** www.thehopewellrocks.ca), located about 40km (24 miles) northeast of Fundy National Park on Route 114. Think of it as a natural sculpture garden. At low tide (the best time to visit), eroded columns as high as 15m (50 ft.) tower above the ocean floor. They're sometimes called the "flowerpots," on account of the trees and plants that still flourish on their narrowing summits.

You park at the new visitor center and restaurant and wander down to the shore. (There's also a shuttle service that runs from the interpretive center to the rocks for a small fee.) Signboards fill you in on the natural history. If you're here at the bottom half of the tide, you can descend the steel staircase to the sea floor and admire these wondrous free-standing rock sculptures, chiseled by waves and tides.

The visitor center is a pleasant place to spend some time. It not only has intriguing exhibits (in particular look for the satellite photos of the area, and the time-lapse video of the tides) but the cafeteria-style restaurant has terrific views from its floor-to-ceiling windows and serves good, simple food. Salads and various sandwiches (salmon burgers, steak hoagies, lobster rolls, and so on) are satisfying, and the soup of the day, a harvest vegetable bisque, is the perfect antidote to the often chilly, damp weather. There's also a children's menu.

The site can be crowded, but that's understandable. If your schedule allows it, come early in the day when the sun is fresh over Nova Scotia across the bay, the dew is still on the ground, and most travelers are still sacked out in bed. The park charges an entry fee of C$8 (US$6.40) adults, C$6.75 (US$5.40) seniors, C$5.75 (US$4.60) children ages 5 to 18, and C$20 (US$16) families.

If you arrive at the top half of the tide, consider a sea kayak tour around the islands and caves. **Baymount Outdoor Adventures** (© 877/601-2660 or 506/734-2660) runs 90-minute tours daily for C$55 (US$44) adults, C$45 (US$36) youths. (Caving tours at nearby caverns are also offered; inquire for details.)

## WHERE TO STAY

**Broadleaf Guest Ranch** ⚘ *Kids*    The two-bedroom cottages at this homey, family-operated ranch are a great choice for families or couples traveling together, particularly those with an interest in horses: The ranch offers trail rides of varying duration, cattle checks, and some basic spa packages. Think of it as a dude ranch without the rattlesnakes and extreme weather of the West.

The cottages feature full kitchens, a small sitting area with gas stove, TV and VCR, and lovely, sweeping views of the ranch's 600 hectare (1,500 acres) and the bay. Bedrooms are furnished with bunk beds (a single over a double) plus a single bed. You won't mistake these lodgings for a five-star luxury experience, but staying here is like sinking into a favorite armchair at the end of the day: supremely comforting and satisfying. The same could be said of the hearty, simple home-cooking Broadleaf dishes up in their large, cafeteria-style dining area. There's also a campground and some mountain chalets available.

5526 Rte. 114, Hopewell Hill, Fundy, Albert County, NB E4H 3N5. © **800/226-5405** or 506/882-2349. Fax 506/882-2075. www.broadleafranch.com. 7 units. $150 (US$120) double, many packages. MC, V. **Amenities:** Restaurant; spa; watersports equipment; bike rentals; business center; room service; laundry service. *In room:* TV/VCR (some units), kitchenette (some units), no phone.

**Fundy Park Chalets**    These storybook-like cabins are set amid birch and pines just inside the park's eastern entrance and will have immediate appeal to fans of classic motor courts. The steeply gabled white clapboard cabins have interiors that will bring to mind a national park vacation from the 1950s—painted wood floors, pine paneling, metal shower stalls, and small kitchenettes. Two beds are located in the main rooms, separated by a hospital-style track curtain that pulls around one bed. What the cabins lack in privacy they more than make up for in convenience and an unironic retro charm. The golf course, playground, tennis courts, lawn bowling, and saltwater pool are all within walking distance.

23 Fundy Chalet Rd. (P.O. Box 72), Alma, NB E4H 4Y8. © **506/887-2808.** www.fundyparkchalets.com. 29 cabins. Summer C$90 (US$72) double, off-season C$60–C$85 (US$48–US$68) double. Discounts in spring and fall. MC, V. Closed Dec–Apr. Pets accepted. *In room:* Kitchenette, no phone.

**Parkland Village Inn** *Value* *Kids*    The Parkland opened the same day as the park in 1948. It's an old-fashioned seaside hotel in the village of Alma, with five two-room suites that have been modernized and thinly furnished in a sort of budget-motel modern style. Some rooms have been set up as two-bedroom units, others with a sitting room and bedroom. All have fine views of the bay. It's not deluxe by any means, but it's handy to the park and offers good value for families. The downstairs dining room specializes in seafood, prepared with little fuss or flair. It's open for breakfast in July and August only.

8601 Main St. (Rte. 114), Alma, NB E4H 1N6. ℂ 877/887-2808 or 506/887-2313. Fax 506/887-2315. www.parkland villageinn.com. 5 units. C$75–C$125 (US$60–US$100) double. Discounts in off season. MC, V. Closed Dec–Apr. **Amenities:** Restaurant. *In room:* TV, Jacuzzi (some units), no phone.

## WHERE TO DINE
**Seawinds Dining Room** PUB FARE/CANADIAN   Seawinds overlooks the park golf course, and it serves as a de facto clubhouse for hungry duffers. The handsome and open dining room has hardwood floors, a flagstone fireplace, and wrought-iron chandeliers. The menu offers enough variations to please most anyone. Lunches include a variety of hamburgers, fish and chips, and bacon and cheese dogs. Dinner is somewhat more refined, with main courses like grilled trout, roast beef, and fried clams.

47 Fundy Park Chalet Rd. (near park headquarters), Fundy National Park, NB E4H 4Y8. ℂ 506/887-2808. Reservations recommended. Sandwiches C$3–C$7 (US$2.40–US$5.60); main courses C$9–C$16 (US$7–US$13). AE, MC, V. Summer daily 8am–9:30pm. Closed Oct–May.

## 8 Moncton

Moncton makes the plausible claim that it's at the crossroads of the Maritimes, and it hasn't been bashful about using its geographic advantage to promote itself as a business hub. As such, much of the hotel and restaurant trade caters to people in suits, at least on weekdays. But walk along Main Street in the evening or on weekends, and you're likely to spot spiked hair, grunge flannel, skateboards, and other youthful fashion statements from current and lapsed eras. There's life here.

For families, Moncton offers a good stopover if you're traveling with kids. Magnetic Hill and Crystal Palace both offer entertaining (albeit somewhat pricey) ways to fill an afternoon.

### ESSENTIALS
**GETTING THERE**   Moncton is at the crossroads of several major routes through New Brunswick, including Route 2 (the Trans-Canada Hwy.) and Route 15. The airport is about 10 minutes from downtown on Route 132 (head northeast on Main St. from Moncton and keep driving). **Air Canada** (ℂ 888/AIR-CANA; www.aircanada. com) has traditionally served the city, but the upstart carrier **WestJet** (ℂ 888/937-8538; www.westjet.com) now connects Moncton with Halifax, Toronto, St. John's, and Calgary, and **Continental** (ℂ 800/525-0280; www.continental.com) offers daily direct service from Newark, NJ.

**VIA Rail**'s (ℂ 888/842-7245; www.viarail.com) train from Montréal to Halifax stops in Moncton 6 days a week. The rail station is downtown on Main Street, next to Highfield Square.

**VISITOR INFORMATION**   Moncton's primary visitor information center is at **Magnetic Hill,** Exit 488 off the Trans-Canada Highway (ℂ 506/855-8622). It's located in the Wharf Village section and isn't particularly convenient—you're required to walk from the parking lot through the faux "village" of shops and boutiques to reach the center. It's open 8am to 8pm daily, late May to early September; weekdays 9am to 5pm, weekends 10am to 6pm through mid-October (closed the rest of the year). A downtown visitor information center is located in **Bore Park,** just off Main Street at 10 Bendview Ct. (ℂ 506/853-3540). It's open daily from 8:30am to 8pm from the end of May to early September, and closes at 4:30pm on weekdays the rest of the year. A third visitor information center can be found at 655 Main St. in the lobby of the modern **City Hall,** but it's only open in the off season. The city's website is www.gomoncton.com.

## EXPLORING MONCTON

Moncton's downtown can be easily reconnoitered on foot—once you find parking, which can be vexing. (Look for the paid lots a block or so north and south of Main St.) **Downtown Moncton Inc.** (© **506/857-2991**) publishes a nicely designed "Historic Walking Tour" brochure that touches on some of the more locally significant buildings; ask for it at either visitor center.

The most active stretch of Main Street is the few blocks between City Hall and the train underpass. Here you'll find cafes, newsstands, hotels, and restaurants, along with a handful of intriguing shops. Note the sometimes-jarring mix of architectural styles, the earlier examples of which testify to Moncton's historic prosperity as a commercial center.

**Exploring by bike** offers some wonderful dividends, especially when pedaling along Riverfront Park or through popular 120-hectare (300-acre) Centennial Park. A local nonprofit called Hub City Wheelers schedules group bike rides nearly every day throughout the summer, and nonmembers are welcome; it's a good way to meet some of the local bikers and find the best routes. Ask at the visitor information center for a brochure with a schedule.

**Crystal Palace** *(Kids)*   The indoor amusement park at Crystal Palace will make an otherwise endless rainy day go by quickly. The spacious enclosed park includes a four-screen cinema, shooting arcades, numerous games (ranging from old-fashioned Skee-Ball to cutting-edge video games), a medium-size roller coaster, a carousel, a swing ride, laser tag, bumper cars, miniairplane and miniature semitruck rides, minigolf, batting cages, and a virtual-reality ride. From late June to early September, outdoor activities include go-karts and bumper boats. The park will particularly appeal to kids under the age of 12, although teens will likely find a video game to occupy them. To really wear the kids down, you can stay virtually inside the park by booking a room at the adjoining Ramada Plaza Crystal Palace Hotel (see below).

At Champlain Place Shopping Centre (Trans-Canada Hwy. Exit 504-A W), Dieppe. © 877/856-4386 or 506/859-4386. www.crystalpalace.ca. Free admission. Rides are 1–4 tickets each (book of 25 for C$20/US$16). Unlimited ride bracelets C$16–C$20 (US$12–US$16) adults, C$17 (US$14) children, C$62 (US$50) families. July and Aug daily 10am–10pm; rest of year Mon–Thurs noon–8pm, Fri noon–9pm, Sat 10am–9pm, Sun 10am–8pm.

**Magnetic Hill** *(Overrated)* *(Kids)*   Magnetic Hill, located on Moncton's northwest outskirts a few miles from downtown, began as a simple quirk of geography. Cars that stopped at the bottom of a short stretch of downhill started to roll back uphill! Or at least what appeared to be uphill. It's a nifty illusion—not to pull back the curtain, but it works because the slope is on the side of a far larger hill, which tilts the whole countryside and effectively skews one's perspective. Starting in the 1930s, locals capitalized on the phenomenon by opening canteens and gift shops nearby. By the 1950s, the hill boasted the largest souvenir shop in the Maritimes.

This mysterious stretch of country road was preserved for posterity when a bypass was built around it, and today you can still experience the mystery. The atmosphere is a bit more glossy than a half-century ago, however. You enter a well-marked drive with magnet-themed road signs and streetlights, pay a toll at a gatehouse, and wind around a comically twisting road to wait your turn before being directed to the hill.

Young kids often find the "uphill roll" entertaining—for a few meters. Then their attention is riveted by the two amusement complexes that have sprouted in the fields on either side of the road. Attractions within a few hundred yards of the hill include Wharf Village (a collection of souvenir shops and snack bars designed to look like a seaside village), a minigolf course, a zoo, video arcades, go-kart racing, batting cages, a driving range, a kiddie train, and bumper boats. But the chief attraction is the Magic Mountain Water Park, which features wave pools and numerous slides, including the towering Kamikaze Slide, where daredevils can reach speeds of 40 miles per hour.

Despite—or perhaps because of—the unrepentant cheesiness, Magnetic Hill is actually a great destination for families weary of beaches, hikes, and the dreary natural world. Just be aware that nothing's cheap after you fork over that C$5 (US$4) to roll up the hill; an afternoon here can put a serious hurt on your wallet.

Trans-Canada Hwy. (Exit 488), Moncton. 🕾 506/853-3516. Admission Magnetic Hill C$5 (US$3.55) per car; Magic Mountain Water Park C$20 (US$14) full day age 12 or older, C$15 (US$11) children 4–11, C$65 (US$46) families; Magnetic Hill Zoo C$8 (US$5.70) adults, C$7 (US$5) seniors and children 12–18, C$5 (US$3.55) children 4–11, C$22 (US$16) families. June–Oct daily 10am–8pm; off season some attractions closed; call for info.

## WHERE TO STAY

Several chain hotels have set up shop near the attraction known as Magnetic Hill (Trans-Canada Hwy. Exit 488). These include **Comfort Inn,** 2495 Mountain Rd. (🕾 800/228-5150 or 506/384-3175); **Country Inn & Suites,** 2475 Mountain Rd. (🕾 800/456-4000 or 506/852-7000); and **Holiday Inn Express,** also just off the exit at 2515 Mountain Rd. (🕾 800/561-7666 or 506/384-1050). At these clean, convenient hotels, rooms range from C$85 to C$199 (US$68–US$159).

**Delta Beauséjour** 🕰  The downtown Delta Beauséjour, constructed in 1972, is boxy, bland, and concrete, and the entrance courtyard is sterile and off-putting in a Cold War Berlin sort of way. But inside, the decor is inviting in a spare, International Modern manner. The property is well maintained, with rooms and public areas recently renovated. The third-floor indoor pool offers year-round swimming. (There's also a pleasant outdoor deck overlooking the distant marshes of the Petitcodiac River.) The hotel is a favorite among business travelers, but in summer and on weekends, leisure travelers largely have it to themselves. In addition to the elegant Windjammer (see below), the hotel has a basic cafe/snack bar, a piano bar and lounge, and a rustic, informal restaurant that serves three meals a day.

750 Main St., Moncton, NB E1C 1E6. 🕾 800/268-1133 or 506/854-4344. Fax 506/858-0957. www.deltahotels.com. 310 units. C$129–C$199 (US$83–US$159) double. Rates include continental breakfast. AE, DC, MC, V. **Amenities:** 3 restaurants; bar; indoor heated pool; fitness center; business center; shopping arcade; salon; 24-hr. room service; babysitting; laundry service; dry cleaning. *In room:* A/C, TV, fax (some units), dataport, minibar, coffeemaker, iron.

**Ramada Plaza Crystal Palace Hotel** *(Overrated*  This modern, three-story chain hotel (built in 1990) adjoins the Crystal Palace amusement park and is a short walk from the region's largest mall. As such, it's surrounded by acres of asphalt and has little in the way of native charm. Most rooms are modern but unexceptional—not counting the 12 fantasy suites that go over the top with themes like "Deserted Island" (sleep in a thatched hut) or "Rock 'n' Roll" (sleep in a 1959 replica pink Cadillac bed). Some rooms face the indoor pool, others, the vast parking lot. For entertainment nearby, there's the amusement park, obviously. Also within the amusement complex is the hotel's restaurant, McGinnis Landing, which offers basic pub fare. Prices are high for what you get for main dinner courses; but specials are always available, and the restaurant caters well to younger appetites.

499 Paul St., Dieppe, NB E1A 6S5. (𝘊 **800/528-1234** or 506/858-8584. Fax 506/858-5486. 115 units. www.crystal palacehotel.com. C$90–C$275 (US$72–US$220) double. Ask about value packages, which include amusement-park passes. AE, DC, DISC, MC, V. **Amenities:** Restaurant; bar; indoor pool; Jacuzzi; sauna; limited room service; babysitting; dry cleaning. *In room:* A/C, TV, minibar, coffeemaker.

## WHERE TO DINE

**Boomerang's Steakhouse** STEAK    Boomerang's is likely to remind diners of the Aussie-themed Outback Steakhouse chain, right down to the oversize knives. But since this is the only Boomerang's (it's not a chain), the service is rather more personal, and the Aussie-whimsical decor is done with a lighter hand. It's a handsome spot with three dining rooms, all quite dim with slatted dividers, drawn shades, and ceiling fans, which create the impression that it's blazingly hot outside. (That's a real trick in Feb in New Brunswick.) The menu features the usual stuff from the barbie, including grilled chicken breasts and ribs. The steak selection is grand, ranging from an 8-ounce bacon-wrapped tenderloin to a 14-ounce porterhouse. The burgers are also excellent.

130 Westmoreland St. (𝘊 **506/857-8325.** Call-ahead seating in lieu of reservations. Hamburgers and grilled sandwiches C$9–C$11 (US$7–US$9); dinners C$14–C$20 (US$11–US$16). AE, DC, DISC, MC, V. Sun–Wed 4–10pm; Thurs–Sat 4–11:30pm.

**The Windjammer** 🕮🕮 CONTINENTAL    Tucked off the lobby of Moncton's best hotel is The Windjammer, an intimate dining room that serves the city's best meals. With its heavy wood and nautical theme, it resembles the private officer's mess of an exclusive ship. The menu is ambitious, and the dining room has garnered an excellent reputation for its seafood dishes, including an appetizer of scallops served with a truffle jus, and entree of pan-fried salmon marinated in molasses and ginger. Despite the seafaring decor, the chef also serves up treats for carnivores, including tournedos of caribou with jus and blueberries, served with a fricassee of wild mushrooms.

750 Main St. (in the Delta Beauséjour). (𝘊 **506/854-4344.** Reservations recommended. Main courses C$25–C$37 (US$20–US$30). AE, DC, MC, V. Mon–Sat 5:30–11pm.

## EN ROUTE TO KOUCHIBOUGUAC NATIONAL PARK

If you decide to head directly to Kouchibouguac from Moncton, **La Dune de Bouctouche** makes for a good stop along the way. To reach the dune, take Route 15 east out of Moncton; then go north on Route 11 at its intersection with Shediac. The drive takes about an hour.

This striking, white sand dune stretches an impressive 12km (7¼ miles) across Bouctouche Bay, and is home to the endangered piping plover, a unique butterfly species, and some rare plants. The sensitive dune area itself can be viewed from a wheelchair-accessible, 2km (1¼-mile) boardwalk that snakes along its length. On a sunny day, the sand beach is a lovely spot to while away a couple hours, or even to take a dip in the warm seawater. The visitor center is fairly straightforward in its explanations of the flora and fauna indigenous to the dune; kids will probably be most amused by the larger than life, baby plover puppet that can be removed from its just-hatched "egg." Admission is free; the boardwalk is open year-round in "good weather" and the visitor center is open daily from 10am to 8pm (until 5pm in the off season).

If you're interested in spending the night in the area, or grabbing a bite to eat, stop by the **Dune View Inn** 🕮, 589 Route 875 ((𝘊 **506/743-9993;** www.aubergevuedela dune.com), where the new owners (one's a trained chef who previously cooked in Montréal) serve up French-inflected local seafood. The rooms feature TVs, telephones, and private bathrooms; they're pretty and light, but rather cramped. A double with breakfast costs from C$90 to C$135 (US$72–US$108); open year-round. They can also arrange golf and kayaking packages to combine a little local sightseeing with your stay.

## 9 Kouchibouguac National Park (★

Much is made of the fact that this sprawling park has all sorts of ecosystems worth studying, from sandy barrier islands to ancient peat bogs. But that's a little bit like saying Disney World has nice lakes. It causes one's eyes to glaze over, and it entirely misses the point. In fact, this artfully designed national park is a wonderful destination for relaxing biking, hiking, and beach going. If you can, plan to spend a couple of days here doing a whole lot of nothing. The varied ecosystems (which, incidentally, are spectacular) are just an added attraction.

Kouchibouguac is, above all, a place for bikers and families. The park is laced with well-groomed bike trails made of finely crushed cinders that traverse forest and field, and meander along rivers and lagoons. Where bikes aren't permitted (such as on boardwalks and beaches), there are usually clusters of bike racks for locking them up while you continue on foot. If you camp here and bring a bike, there's no need ever to use your car.

The only contingent the park might disappoint is gung ho hikers. This isn't for serious hiking, but rather for walking and strolling. The pathways are wide and flat and invite a leisurely pace. Most trails are very short—on the order of 1 or 2 kilometers—and seem more like detours than destinations. In fact, approaching the park as a sort of desultory tour with intriguing detours might be the best way to go about a visit here.

Although the park is ideal for campers, day-trippers also find it a worthwhile destination. *One tip:* Plan to remain here until sunset. The trails tend to empty out, and the dunes, bogs, and boreal forest take on a rich, almost iridescent hue as the sun sinks over the spruce.

Be aware that this is a fair-weather destination. If it's blustery and rainy, there's little to do except take damp and melancholy strolls on the beach. It's best to save a visit here for more cooperative days.

By the way, the ungainly name is a Mi'kmaq Indian word meaning "River of the Long Tides." It's pronounced "Koosh-uh-*boog*-oo-whack." If you don't get it right, don't worry. Few do.

## ESSENTIALS

**GETTING THERE**   Kouchibouguac National Park is between Moncton and Miramichi. The exit for the park off Route 11 is well marked.

**VISITOR INFORMATION**   The park is open from mid-May to mid-October. The **Visitors Centre** ((© **506/876-2443**) is just off Route 134, a short drive past the park entrance. It's open from 8am to 8pm during peak season, with shorter hours in the off season. There's a slide show to introduce you to the park's attractions, and a small collection of field guides to peruse.

**FEES**   A daily pass is C$6 (US$4.80) adults, C$5 (US$4) seniors, C$3 (US$2.40) children 6 to 16, and C$13 (US$11) families. (From Apr to June and in Oct and Nov, rates are discounted.) Four-day passes are also available. You should have permits for everyone in your car when you enter the park; though there are no formal checkpoints, occasional roadblocks during the summer ensure compliance. Note that, for a small extra charge, you can also get a helpful map of the park at the information center.

## CAMPING

**Kouchibouguac** is at heart a camper's park, best enjoyed by those who plan to spend at least a night. **South Kouchibouguac** ✿, the main campground, is centrally located and very nicely laid out with 311 sites, most rather large and private. The 46 sites with electricity are nearer the river and somewhat more open. The newest sites (1–35) lack grassy areas for pitching a tent, and campers have to pitch tents on gravel pads. It's best to bring a good sleeping pad or ask for another site. Sites are C$19 to C$28 (US$15–US$23) per night. Reservations are accepted for about half of the campsites; call ✆ 506/876-2443 starting in late April. The remaining sites are doled out first-come, first-served.

Other camping options within the park: Across the river on Kouchibouguac Lagoon is the more remote, semiprimitive **Côte-à-Fabien.** It lacks showers and some sites require a short walk, but it's more appealing for tenters. The cost is C$14 (US$10) per night. The park also maintains three backcountry sites. **Sipu** is on the Kouchibouguac River and is accessible by canoe or foot; **Petit Large** by foot or bike; **Pointe-à-Maxime** by canoe only. Backcountry sites cost C$9 (US$7.20) per night, including firewood.

## BEACHES

The park features some 15km (9 miles) of sandy beaches, mostly along barrier islands of sandy dunes, delicate grasses and flowers, and nesting plovers and sandpipers. **Kellys** is the principal beach, and it's one of the best-designed and best-executed recreation areas I've come across in Eastern Canada. At the forest's edge, a short walk from the main parking area, you'll find showers, changing rooms, a snack bar, and some interpretive exhibits. From here, you walk some 540m (1,800 ft.) across a winding boardwalk that's plenty fascinating on its own. It crosses a salt marsh, lagoons, and some of the best-preserved dunes in the province.

The long, sandy beach features water that's comfortably warm, with the waves that are usually quite mellow—they lap rather than roar, unless a storm's offshore. Lifeguards oversee a roped-off section of about 90m (300 ft.); elsewhere, you're on your own. For very young children who still equate waves with certain death, there's supervised swimming on a sandy stretch of the quiet lagoon.

## BOATING & BIKING

**Ryans** (✆ 506/876-8918)—a cluster of buildings between the campground and Kellys Beach—is the place for renting bikes, kayaks, paddleboats, and canoes seasonally. Bikes rent for C$4.60 (US$3.70) per hour. Most of the watersports equipment (including canoes and pedal boats) rent for about C$7 (US$5.60) per hour, with double kayaks at C$12 (US$9.60) per hour. Canoes may be rented for longer excursions; it's around C$30 (US$24) daily, around C$45 (US$36) for 2 days. Ryans is located on the lagoon, so you can explore up toward the dunes or upstream on the winding river.

The park offers a **Voyageur Canoe Marine Adventure** in summer, with a crew paddling a sizable canoe from the mainland to offshore sandbars, where the naturalist-guide will help identify the wildlife encountered. Expect to see osprey and bald eagles. The 3-hour excursion is C$30 (US$24) adults, C$14 (US$11) children 6 to 16. Inquire about the trip at the park's information center.

# HIKING

The hiking and biking trails are as short and undemanding as they are appealing. The one hiking trail that requires slightly more fortitude is the **Kouchibouguac River Trail,** which runs for some 13km (8 miles) along the banks of the river.

The **Bog Trail** is just 2km (1.25 miles) each way, but it opens the door to a wonderfully alien world. The 4,500-year-old bog is a classic domed bog, made of peat from decaying shrubs and other plants. At the bog's edge you'll find a wooden tower ascended by a spiral staircase that affords a panoramic view of this eerie habitat.

The boardwalk crosses to the thickest, middle part of the bog. Where the boardwalk stops, you can feel the bouncy surface of the bog—you're actually standing on a mat of thick vegetation that's floating atop water. Look for the pitcher plant, a carnivorous species that lures flies into its bell-shaped leaves, where downward-pointed hairs prevent them from fleeing. Eventually, the plant's enzymes digest the insect, providing nutrients for growth in this hostile environment.

**Callanders Beach** and **Cedar Trail** are at the end of a short dirt road. There's an open field with picnic tables, a small protected beach on the lagoon (there are fine views of dunes across the way), and a 1km (.5-mile) hiking trail on a boardwalk that passes through a cedar forest, past a salt marsh, and through a mixed forest. This is a good alternative for those who'd prefer to avoid the larger crowds at Kellys Beach.

# WHERE TO STAY & DINE

**Habitant Motel and Restaurant**    At about 15km (9 miles) from the park entrance, the Habitant is the best choice for overnighting if you're exploring Kouchibouguac by day. It's a modern, mansard-roofed, Tudor-style complex—well, let's just say "architecturally mystifying"—with a restaurant and small campground on the premises. The rooms are decorated in a contemporary motel style and are very clean. The motel features a distinctive indoor pool, along with a fitness center and sauna. The restaurant next door serves three meals a day and is informal, comfortable, and reasonably priced. Seafood dinners are the specialty, including a heaping "fisherman's feast" for about C$25 (US$20). One nice touch: There's a self-serve wine cellar, where wines are sold at liquor-store prices, many under C$20 (US$16).

Rte. 134 (RR No. 1, Box 2, Site 30), Richibucto, NB E4W 4E6. (©) **888/442-7222** or 506/523-4421. Fax 506/523-9155. www.habitant.nb.ca. 29 units. C$85–C$110 (US$60–US$00) double. AE, DC, DISC, MC, V. "Small, well trained pote" allowed. **Amenities:** Restaurant; indoor pool; sauna. *In room:* A/C, TV.

## 10 Acadian Peninsula

The Acadian Peninsula is that bulge on the northeast corner of New Brunswick, forming one of the arms of the Baie des Chaleurs (Québec's Gaspé Peninsula forms the other). It's a land of tidy if generally nondescript houses, miles of shoreline (much of it beaches), modern concrete harbors filled with commercial fishing boats, and residents proud of their Acadian heritage. (You'll see everywhere the stella maris flag—the French tricolor with a single gold star in the field of blue.)

On a map it looks like much of the coastline would be wild and remote here. It's not. Although a number of picturesque farmhouses dot the route and you'll come upon brilliant meadows of hawkweed and lupine, the coast is more defined by manufactured housing that's been erected on squarish lots between the sea and fast two-lane highways.

Other than the superb Acadian Village historical museum near Caraquet, there are few organized attractions in the region. It's more a place to unwind while walking on a beach, or sitting along harbors while watching fishing boats come and go.

## ESSENTIALS

**VISITOR INFORMATION**   Each of the areas mentioned below maintains a visitor information center. **Caraquet Tourism Information** is at 51 Blvd. St-Pierre Est (© **506/726-2676**). This seasonal (June to mid-Sept) office offers convenient access to other activities in the harbor (see below), and there's plenty of parking. Shippagan dispenses information from a wooden lighthouse near the Marine Centre.

**GETTING THERE**   Route 11 is the main highway serving the Acadian Peninsula.

## SHIPPAGAN & MISCOU ISLAND

Both of these destinations require a detour off Route 11 but are worthwhile if you're interested in glimpsing Acadian New Brunswick in the slow lane. As an added bonus, Miscou Island boasts some fine beaches.

Shippagan is a quiet, leafy village that's home to a sizable crabbing fleet. It's also home to the modern **Aquarium and Marine Centre,** 100 Aquarium St. (© **506/336-3013**). The center is on the water near the harbor (prominently posted signs around town will direct you there) and is a good destination if you're the least bit curious about local marine life. You'll learn about the 125 species of native fish hereabouts, many of which are on display. Kids are drawn to the seal tank outside, where trainers prompt the sleek beasts to show off their acrobatic skills. Admission is C$7 (US$5.60) adults, C$5.25 (US$4.20) seniors, C$4.35 (US$3.50) children, and C$12 (US$8.50) families. The center is open May to October from 10am to 6pm daily; seal feedings are at 11am and 4pm.

Keep driving north on Route 113 and you'll soon cross a low drawbridge to Lamèque Island. If you're traveling through in mid-July, don't be surprised to hear fine baroque music wafting from the Ste-Cecile Church. Since 1975, the island has hosted the **Lamèque International Baroque Music Festival** (© **506/344-5846,** or 800/320-2276 from Canada only). For about 10 days each summer, talented musicians perform an ambitious series of concerts, held in an architecturally striking, acoustically wonderful church in a small village on the island's north coast. Tickets often sell out well in advance, and most are priced at C$25 to C$35 (US$20–US$28) per adult.

North of Lamèque is Miscou Island, which for decades was served by a modest ferry. That era ended in the mid-1990s, when a shiny, arched bridge spanned the strait. The bridge made some islanders a bit grumpy, but happily the island still retains a sense of remoteness, especially north of the village of **Miscou Centre,** where you get into bog territory. The extraordinary view of the islands and ocean from the crest of the bridge serves as some consolation for the breach of isolation.

Drive northward on Route 113 until you run out of road, and you'll come to New Brunswick's oldest lighthouse. **Point Miscou Lighthouse** marks the confluence of the Gulf of St. Lawrence and the Baie des Chaleurs.

The dominant natural feature of Miscou is the bog. The **bog landscape** is as distinctive as that of the Canadian Rockies and the buttes of the desert Southwest. It's flat and green and can stretch for miles. You'll see much of this on northern **Miscou Island** (some of the bogs have been harvested for peat).

A finely constructed **interpretive nature trail** is on Route 113 north of Miscou Centre. A boardwalk loops through the bog around an open pond. Learn about the orchids and lilies that thrive in the vast and spongy mat of shrubs and roots. Look for the fascinating carnivorous plants (the pitcher plants are relatively easy to spot). The loop takes about 20 minutes, and it's free.

## WHERE TO STAY

**Miscou Beach Cottage & Camping**   Far up Miscou Island are these simple, unpretentious cottages right on the beach. Six cottages sit side by side facing the dunes and the ocean beyond; small decks front each cottage and invite idleness. All considered, the place has an English caravan park feel, with camp trailers crowded in a field behind the cottages. There's also a no-frills family restaurant on the premises. Not much else goes on here (unless you consider the bare-bones minigolf course), so plan to spend most of your day exploring the long sandy strand out front. *A warning:* Beware of the voracious mosquito population, which descends at dusk early in the season.

Rte. 113 (mailing address 118 Paradis du Campeur Lane), Miscou, NB E8T 2A2. *C* **506/344-1015** or 506/344-8463. 6 units. C$50–C$90 (US$40–US$72). MC, V. Closed Sept 15–June 15. **Amenities:** Restaurant. *In room:* Kitchenette, no phone.

## CARAQUET  &

The historic beach town of Caraquet—widely regarded as the spiritual capital of Acadian New Brunswick—just keeps on going and going, geographically speaking. It's spread thinly along a commercial boulevard parallel to the beach. Caraquet once claimed the honorific "longest village in the world" when it ran to some 21km (13 miles) long. As a result of its length, Caraquet lacks a well-defined downtown or any sort of urban center of gravity; there's one stoplight, and that's where Boulevard St-Pierre Est changes to Boulevard St-Pierre Ouest. (Most establishments mentioned below are somewhere along this boulevard.)

A good place to start a tour is the **Callefour de la Mer** (51 Blvd. St-Pierre Est), a modern complex overlooking the man-made harbor. It has a spare, Scandinavian feel to it, and you'll find the tourist information office (see above), a seafood restaurant, a snack bar, a children's playground, and two short strolls that lead to picnic tables on jetties with fine harbor views.

While you're here you can consider your options for viewing the bay. Half-hour boat tours aboard the *Ile Caramer* (*C* **506/727-0813**) cost about C$17 (US$14) adults, C$15 (US$12) seniors, C$10 (US$8) children 12 and under.

**Village Historique Acadien**  &   New Brunswick sometimes seems awash in Acadian museums and historic villages. If you're interested in visiting just one such site, this is the place to hold out for. Some 45 buildings—most of which were dismantled and transported here from other villages on the peninsula—depict life as it was lived in an Acadian settlement between the years 1770 and 1890. The historic buildings are set throughout 183 hectares (458 acres) of woodland, marsh, and field. You'll learn all about the exodus and settlement of the Acadians from costumed guides, who are also adept at skills ranging from letterpress printing to blacksmithing. Plan on spending at least 2 to 3 hours exploring the village.

In June 2002, the village opened a major addition, which focuses on a more recent era. Some 26 buildings (all but one are replicas) are devoted to continuing the saga, showing Acadian life from 1890 to 1939, with a special focus on industry. The attractive yellow Chateau Albert Hotel, which mostly houses students enrolled in multiday workshops in traditional Acadian arts and crafts, was part of this new construction project; the simple rooms lack phones and televisions, but there is a convivial bar area and a thrown-back-in-time vibe. Rooms run about C$100 to C$125 (US$80–US$100).

Rte. 11 (10km/6 miles west of Caraquet). © **506/726-2600**. www.villagehistoriqueacadien.com. Admission C$15 (US$12) adults, C$13 (US$10) seniors, C$9.50–C$12 (US$7.50–US$9) children, C$35 (US$28) family. Early June to Aug daily 10am–6pm, Sept to mid-Oct 10am–5pm. Closed mid-Oct to early June.

## WHERE TO STAY

**Auberge de la Baie**   The Auberge de la Baie is your basic motel that has dressed itself up nicely with a modern lobby and dining room. The rooms are cheerless but adequate (some have cinder-block walls, some have bay views). Particularly inviting is the broad lawn that descends toward the water; stake your claim to a lawn chair and dive into a book. There's a small beach for swimming. The oaky, Scandinavian modern-style restaurant is open for all three meals but specializes in seafood dinners. There's salmon with beurre blanc sauce, English-style fish and chips, and the ever-present fried clams with tartar sauce.

139 Blvd. St-Pierre Ouest, Caraquet, NB E1W 1B7. © **506/727-3485**. 54 units. C$79–C$159 (US$63–US$143) double. AE, MC, V. **Amenities:** Dining room; bar. *In room:* A/C, no phone.

**Hôtel Paulin** ❀❀   This attractive Victorian hotel, built in 1891, has been operated by the Paulin family for the past three generations and has recently gone more upscale with added units and rising prices. It's a three-story red clapboard building with a green-shingled mansard roof, located just off the main boulevard and overlooking the bay. (Some of the charm has been compromised by encroaching buildings nearby.) The lobby puts one immediately in mind of summer relaxation, with royal blue wainscoting, canary yellow walls, and stuffed furniture upholstered in white with blue piping. Expect rooms, including four suites, comfortably but sparely furnished with antiques; only one suite has an ocean view. The hotel's first floor also houses a handsome, well-regarded **restaurant** ❀. Specialties include a delectable crab mousse and a cure for the sweet tooth: brown-sugar pie.

143 Blvd. St-Pierre Ouest, Caraquet, NB E1W 1B6. © **506/727-9981** or 506/727-3165. www.hotelpaulin.com. 12 units. Mid-June to mid-Sept C$195–C$315 (US$159–US$252) double, mid-Sept to mid-June C$179–C$235 (US$143–US$188). MC, V. **Amenities:** Restaurant, massage. *In room:* A/C, TV, hair dryer, iron, no phone.

## WHERE TO DINE

Caraquet is a good place for seafood, naturally. My preference is still with the Hotel Paulin's restaurant for its charm, but the several inexpensive-to-moderate spots along the main drag all serve fresh seafood nicely if simply prepared.

For a delicious and sophisticated snack, head to **Les Blancs d'Arcadie** ❀, 340-A Blvd. St-Pierre Est (© **506/727-5952**), a handsome compound of yellow farm buildings hard against the forest just east of town. The specialties here are cheese and yogurt from the milk of a Swiss breed of goats called Saanen. The goats are raised indoors year-round; you can learn about the goats and the cheese- and yogurt-making process on a tour of the operation, which includes tastings. The 90-minute tour costs about C$6 (US$4.80). There's also a small shop to buy fresh cheeses and milk. (I recommend both the peppercorn and the garlic soft cheeses.) Les Blancs d'Arcadia is en route to Bas Caraquet on Route 145; watch for the goat sign on the right shortly after you pass the road to St-Simon. Reservations for tours are appreciated.

## GRANDE-ANSE

Grande-Anse is a wide-spot-in-the-road village of low, modern homes near bluffs overlooking the bay. The town is lorded over by the stern, stone Saint Jude church. The best view of the village, and a good spot for a picnic, is along the bluffs just below the church. (Look for the sign indicating QUAI 45m/150 ft. west of the church.) Here you'll find a small man-made harbor with a fleet of fishing boats, a tiny sand beach, and some grassy bluffs where you can park overlooking the bay.

If you'd prefer picnic tables, head a few miles westward to **Pokeshaw Park.** Just off-shore is a large kettle-shaped island ringed with ragged cliffs that rise from the waves, long ago separated from the cliffs on which you're now standing. An active cormorant rookery thrives among the eerie skeletons of trees, lending the whole affair a somewhat haunted and melancholy air. There's a small picnic shelter for inclement weather. It's open daily from 9am to 9pm; a small admission fee is charged.

For the full-blown ocean swimming experience, head to **Plage Grande-Anse,** located 2km (1¼ miles) east of town. This handsome beach has a snack bar near the parking area and is open from 10am to 9pm daily. There's a small entrance fee for adults.

**Pope Museum** *(Finds)*   Deep vermilion hues and liturgical strains piped into all the rooms mark the modern Pope Museum, founded in 1985—the year after the pope visited Moncton. The devout will enjoy the portrait gallery featuring portraits of all 264 popes. But all will be fascinated by the intricate model of the Vatican, which occupies much of the central hall (the top of the dome stands about 6 ft. high). Other models of houses of worship include a smaller Florence Cathedral, Bourges Cathedral, Cheops pyramid, and the Great El Hakim Mosque. Head upstairs for displays of various Roman Catholic artifacts and contemporary religious accouterment, including vestments and chalices. Most descriptions are bilingual, but a handful are in French only. The devoted should plan to spend a half-hour here.

184 Acadie St., Grande-Anse. (C) **506/732-3003.** Admission C$7 (US$5.60) adults, less for seniors and children. Daily July–Aug 10am–6pm (tickets sold until 5pm). Closed Sept–June.

## 11 Mt. Carleton Provincial Park (★

In 1969, New Brunswick carved out some of the choicest land and set it aside as a wilderness park. Mt. Carleton Provincial Park contains 2,821 hectares (7,052 acres) of azure lakes, pure streams, thick boreal forest, and gently rounded mountains, the largest of which afford excellent views. When visiting, look for moose, black bear, coyotes, bobcat, and more than 100 species of birds. And, of course, black flies.

## ESSENTIALS

**GETTING THERE**   Mt. Carleton Provincial Park is 42km (26 miles) east of Saint-Quentin on Route 180. Be aware that Saint-Quentin is the nearest community for supplies; there are no convenient general stores just outside the park gates. The park is also accessible from Bathurst to the east, but it's a 111km (69-mile) drive on a road that's mostly paved but gravel in spots. There are no services along the road and frequent logging trucks.

**VISITOR INFORMATION**   The park's gates are open daily in summer from 7am to 10pm (8am–8pm in spring and fall). A small **interpretive center** (© **506/ 235-0793**), located at the entrance gate, offers background on the park's natural and cultural history from mid-May through early September. The park is open but unstaffed the rest of the year.

## CAMPING

**Armstrong Brook** 🐾🐾 is the principal destination for visiting campers. It has 88 sites split between the forest near Lake Nictau's shore (no lakeside sites) and an open, grassy field. Campers can avail themselves of hot showers and a bathhouse for washing up. A path leads to the lake's edge; there's a spit of small, flat pebbles that's wonderful for swimming and sunbathing. Camping fees are C$11 (US$9) weekdays, C$14 (US$11) weekends.

Four backcountry sites are located high on the slopes of Mt. Carleton (preregistration required). The sites, which require a 4km (2.5-mile) hike, offer views into a rugged valley and a great sense of remoteness. Water is available but should be treated (beavers are nearby). No fires are permitted, so bring a stove. The fee is C$5 (US$4) per night. Two other remote campsites on the shores of Lake Nictau are accessible by either canoe or a moderate walk. Register in advance; the fee is C$9 (US$7) per night. *Note:* At press time these backcountry sites were all scheduled to be closed for all of 2006. Check with the park in advance to learn their status for 2007.

## HIKING & BIKING

The park has 10 hiking trails that total 68km (42 miles). The helpful park staff at the gatehouse will be happy to direct you to a hike that suits your experience and mood.

The park's premier hike is to the summit of **Mount Carleton,** the province's highest point at 820m (2,697 ft.). Although that elevation is not going to impress those who've hiked in the Canadian Rockies, size is relative here, and the views seem endless. A craggy comb of rocks with a 360-degree view of the lower mountains and the sprawling lakes marks the summit. The trail head is about a 25-minute drive from the gatehouse; allow about 4 hours for a round-trip hike of about 10km (6 miles). Overlooking Nictau Lake is **Mount Sagamook,** at an altitude of 777m (2,555 ft.). It's a steep and demanding hike of about 3km (1.75 miles) to the summit, where you're rewarded with spectacular views of the northern park.

For the truly gung-ho, there's the ridge walk that connects Sagamook and Carleton via **Mount Head.** The views from high above are unforgettable; you'll need to set up a shuttle with two cars to do the whole ridge in 1 day.

If you have a mountain bike, bring it. The gravel roads are perfect for exploring. Motor vehicles have been banned from two of the roads, which take you deep into the woods past clear lakes and rushing streams.

# 6

# Prince Edward Island

Prince Edward Island (PEI) might not be the world's leading manufacturer of relaxation and repose, but it's certainly a major distribution center.

Visitors soon suspect there's something about the richly colored landscape of azure seas and henna-tinged cliffs capped with lush farm fields that triggers an obscure relaxation hormone, resulting in a pleasant ennui. It's hard to conceive that verdant PEI and boggy, blustery Newfoundland share a planet, never mind the same gulf.

The north coast is lined with red-sand beaches, washed with the warmish waters of the Gulf of St. Lawrence. Swimming here isn't quite like taking a tepid dip in North Carolina, but it's quite a bit warmer than in Maine or New Hampshire, farther down the eastern seaboard. Away from the beaches you'll find low, rolling hills blanketed in trees and crops, especially potatoes, for which the island is justly famous. Small farms make up the island's backbone—one-quarter of the island is dedicated to agriculture, with that land cultivated by more than 2,300 individual farms.

The island was first explored in 1534 by Jacques Cartier, who discovered the Mi'kmaq living here. Over the next 2 centuries, dominion over the island bounced between Great Britain and France (who called the island Isle-St-Jean). Great Britain was awarded the island in 1763 as part of the Treaty of Paris; just over a century later, the first Canadian Confederation was held at Charlottetown and resulted in the creation of Canada in 1867 (PEI didn't join the confederation until 1873). The island is named for Edward Augustus (1767–1820), who was the son of George III of England.

The island is compact and its roads are unusually well marked. It's difficult to become disoriented and confused. But do try. I can think of few joys in life as simple and pleasurable as getting lost on some of PEI's back roads.

PEI is steeped in the slower pace of an earlier era; milkmen still make their quiet rounds, and you return soda pop bottles for refilling, not just recycling. Indeed, the population has grown only from 109,000 in 1891 to about 140,000 today. You should take your cue from this comforting cadence and do yourself this favor: Schedule 1 or 2 extra days into your vacation, and make absolutely no plans. You will not regret this.

This chapter is divided into the counties that neatly trisect the province. It's easy to remember: They rise in order of royal hierarchy—Prince to Queens to Kings—in the direction of England.

One final note: The island has, somewhat remarkably, managed to retain its bucolic flavor of a century ago, and pockets of kitsch and sprawl are still happily few. But the handwriting is on the wall, especially in the central part of the island. The handwriting reads COTTAGE LOTS FOR SALE. Such signs have been springing up in greater number in alfalfa and potato fields, and in coming years more and more of the island is certain to be claimed by subdivisions and shopping plazas.

The sooner you can visit, the better.

## 1 Exploring Prince Edward Island

PEI is Canada's smallest province—just about 193km (120 miles) at its greatest length—which keeps the scuttling about down to a minimum and makes it very manageable for day explorations from one or two bases. However, take note: Island roads tend to be slower than you would expect elsewhere, so don't count on speedy travel despite the short distances.

In recent years a number of PEI hotels and attractions have banded together to market some 80 different vacation packages that offer discounts ranging from moderate to generous. There are some good values hidden within. Call © **888/734-7529** or 902/368-4444 to request information on discount packages.

## ESSENTIALS

**VISITOR INFORMATION**    Tourism PEI publishes a comprehensive free guide to island attractions and lodgings that's well worth picking up. The **Visitors Guide** is available at all information centers on the island, or in advance by calling © **888/734-7529** or 902/368-4444. You can also request it by fax (© 902/368-4438), e-mail (peiplay@gov.pe.ca), or mail (P.O. Box 940, Charlottetown, PEI C1A 7M5). The official PEI website is located at www.peiplay.com.

PEI's splashy information center is located at **Gateway Village** (© **902/437-8570**), just as you arrive on the island via the Confederation Bridge. It's a good spot for gathering brochures and asking last-minute questions. There's also a well-laid-out interpretive center featuring nicely designed exhibits about island history and culture. After zipping across the bridge, the exhibits on venturing to the mainland by iceboat in winters past are especially intriguing.

Yet the whole 12-hectare (29-acre) Gateway development, which features a number of retail shops selling island products, is a little odd. As the promoters put it, "Gateway Village portrays a turn-of-the-century PEI streetscape encompassing an exposition pavilion, food and retail services, liquor store, visitor information center and the Festivals at Gateway." My suggestion: Stop for brochures, maps, and a quick walk through the interpretive center. But then push on. Why not experience the real thing rather than this fussy, faux version?

**WHEN TO GO**    PEI's tourism season is rather brief, running for 6 or 7 weeks from early **July to mid-to-late August.** Most attractions don't open fully until July and a few even close before August is done.

Officials and more serious entrepreneurs are striving to convince shops and attractions to maintain more regular hours during the shoulder seasons, but they still have a way to go. If you do plan to visit in June or September, expect to be disappointed when some restaurants and attractions are closed. It may also behoove you to base out of Charlottetown for much of your shoulder-season visit, since the city's restaurants keep year-round hours.

**GETTING THERE**    If you're coming from the west by car, you'll arrive via the Confederation Bridge, which opened with great fanfare in June 1997.

Sometimes you'll hear it referred to as the "fixed link," a reference to the guarantee Canada made in 1873 to provide a permanent link from the mainland. The dramatic 13km (8-mile) bridge is open 24 hours a day and takes about 10 to 12 minutes to cross. Unless you're high up in a van, a truck, or an RV, the views are mostly obstructed by the concrete Jersey barriers that form the guardrails along the sides.

# Prince Edward Island

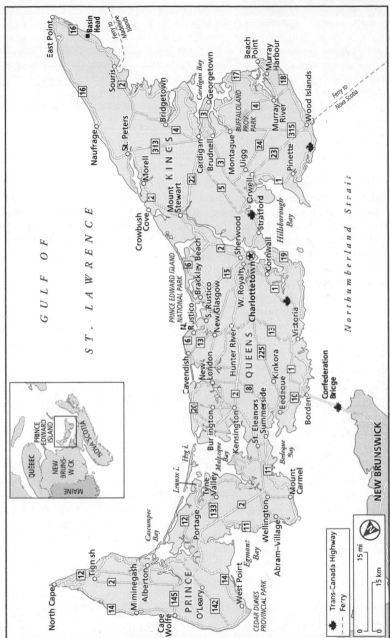

195

The bridge toll is C$40 (US$32) round-trip for cars, C$45 (US$36) for campers and RVs. No fare is paid when you travel to the island; the entire toll is collected when you leave. Credit cards are accepted. Call ℂ **888/437-6565** for more information.

PEI Express Shuttle (ℂ **877/877-1771**) offers transportation via seven-person vans 4 days weekly between Charlottetown and Halifax for C$45 to C$50 (US$36–US$40) one-way, C$90 to C$95 (US$72–US$76) round-trip. Square One Shuttle (ℂ **877/675-3830** or 902/436-3830) also makes runs from Charlottetown to Moncton and Halifax for C$50 (US$40) per person, C$45 (US$36) seniors and students.

**By Ferry**　For those arriving from Cape Breton Island or other points east, Northumberland Ferries Limited (ℂ **888/249-7245**; www.nfl-bay.com) provides seasonal service between Caribou, NS (just north of Pictou), and Woods Island, PEI. Ferries with a 250-car capacity run from May to mid-December. During peak season (June to mid-Oct), ferries depart each port approximately every 90 minutes throughout the day, with the last ferry departing at 8pm. The crossing takes about 75 minutes.

No reservations are accepted; it's best to arrive at least an hour before departure to boost your odds of securing a berth on the next boat. Early morning ferries tend to be less crowded. Fares are C$55 (US$44) for a car and all its passengers. Major credit cards are honored. As with the bridge, fares are paid upon exiting the island; the ferry to the island is free.

**By Air**　The island's main airport (www.flypei.com) is a few miles north of Charlottetown. **Air Canada Jazz** (ℂ **888/247-2262**; www.flyjazz.com) commuter flights to Halifax take just a half-hour, and Jazz also flies to Toronto and Montréal. Calgary-based **WestJet** (ℂ **888/937-8538**; www.westjet.com) almost daily connects Charlottetown with Toronto, which can then be connected onward to Florida, Los Angeles, and Las Vegas without switching airlines; **Northwest** (ℂ **800/447-4747**; www.nwa.com) flies from Detroit daily in summer.

## 2 The Great Outdoors

Prince Edward Island doesn't have any wilderness or even much wildness to speak of. It's all about cultivated landscapes that have long ago been tamed by farmers. That doesn't mean you can't find outdoor adventure.

Here are some places to start.

**BICYCLING**　There's perhaps no finer destination in Atlantic Canada for relaxed road biking than Prince Edward Island. The modest size of the island, the gentleness of the hills (the island's high point is just 142m/465 ft.), and the loveliness of the landscapes all conspire to provide a memorable biking trip. Although you won't find much rugged mountain biking here, you will find a surfeit of idyllic excursions, especially in the northern and eastern portions of the island. Avoid the Trans-Canada Highway on the south coast and main arterials like Route 2, and you'll find superb biking throughout the secondary road network.

The main off-road bike trail is the **Confederation Trail** ⚑. Eventually, the trail will cover some 350km (215 miles) along the old path of the ill-fated provincial railway from Tignish to Souris.

At present, about half the trail has been completed, mostly in Prince and Kings Counties; Queens County is still largely under development. The pathway is covered mostly in rolled stone dust, which makes for good travel with a mountain bike or hybrid. Services are slowly developing along the route, with bike rentals and inns cropping up.

Ask at the local tourist bureaus for updated information on completed segments. An excellent place to base for exploring the trail is the **Trailside Café** (p. 228) in Mount Stewart, where several spurs of the trail converge. The cafe can arrange for return shuttles if you'd prefer one-way cycling.

**MacQueen's Island Tours & Bike Shop** (© 800/969-2822 or 902/368-2453), at 430 Queen St. in Charlottetown, organizes bicycle tour packages, with prices including bike rentals, accommodations, route cards, maps, luggage transfers, and emergency road repair service. Seven-night tours start at C$1,300 (US$1,040) double occupancy. Rentals are also available for C$20 (US$16) and up per day, C$125 (US$100) and up per week. MacQueen's can be reached via e-mail at biketour@macqueens.com.

For rentals and repairs, you might also try **Cycle Smooth** (© 800/310-6550 or 902/566-5530) at 172 Prince St. in Charlottetown. Rentals include helmet, water bottle, and a lock and cost C$25 (US$18) per day.

**FISHING**    For a taste of deep-sea fishing, head to the north coast, where you'll find plenty of outfitters happy to take you out on the big swells. The greatest concentrations of services are at North Rustico and Covehead Bay; see the "Queens County" section, below. Rates are quite reasonable, generally about C$20 (US$16) for 3 hours or so.

Trout fishing holes attract inland anglers, although, as always, the best spots are a matter of local knowledge. A good place to start your inquiries is at **Island Rods and Flies,** 18 Birch Hill Dr., Charlottetown (© 902/566-4157), which specializes in fly-fishing equipment. Information on required fishing licenses can be had from any visitor information center, or by contacting the **Department of Fisheries, Aquaculture, and Environment,** P.O. Box 2000, Charlottetown, PEI C1A 7N8 (© 902/368-4820; www.gov.pe.ca/af).

**GOLF**    PEI's reputation for golf has soared in the last few years. That's due in part to a slew of new and expanded courses and in part because the greens fees haven't followed the same sharply upward trajectory that has afflicted many courses in the United States. As a result, you can golf along the ocean at fees just a fraction of what you'd expect in similarly dramatic settings elsewhere. One of the best-regarded courses is the **Links at Crowbush Cove** ✿✿ (© 800/235-8909 or 902/961-7300). Sand dunes and persistent winds off the gulf add to the challenge at this relatively young course, which is on the northeastern coast. Another perennial favorite is the **Brudenell River Golf Course** (© 800/235-8909 or 902/652-8965) near Montague along the eastern shore; in the late 1990s the course added a second 18-holer, this designed by Michael Hurdzan, who has also created well-regarded courses in Toronto and Vancouver. As part of its expansion, the course also launched the **Canadian Golf Academy** (© 888/698-4653). Programs take place on the two golf courses as well as at the 475-yard double-ended driving range, and on the 1.6 hectare (4 acres) of tee decks.

Golf PEI publishes a booklet outlining the essentials of the 25 island courses. Request a copy from island information centers or from the provincial tourist information number (© 902/368-4653), or write 565 N. River Rd., Charlottetown, PEI C1E 1J7. The information is also available online at **www.golfpei.com.**

**SEA KAYAKING**    PEI has 1,260km (783 miles) of attractive coastline and relatively warm water, making for excellent sea kayaking.

Paddlers can vary the scene from broad tidal inlets ringed with marsh to rusty-red coastline topped with swaying waves of marran grass. **Outside Expeditions** (© **800/ 207-3899** or **902/963-3366**; www.getoutside.com) hosts half-day excursions daily at the national park for C$50 to C$55 (US$40–US$44). More ambitious paddlers can sign up for 1- to 7-day trips departing throughout the summer. Excursions are also available from Peake's Wharf in Charlottetown and at Brudenell River Provincial Park in eastern PEI.

**SWIMMING**    Among PEI's chief attractions are its red-sand beaches. You'll find them all around the island, tucked in among dunes and crumbling cliffs. Thanks to the moderating influence of the Gulf of St. Lawrence, the water temperature is more humane here than elsewhere in Atlantic Canada, and it usually doesn't result in unbridled shrieking among bathers. The most popular beaches are at Prince Edward Island National Park along the north coast, but you can easily find other beaches with great swimming.

Among my favorites: Cedar Dunes Provincial Park on the southwest coast, Red Point Provincial Park on the northeast coast, and Panmure Island Provincial Park on the southeast coast.

## 3 Queens County

Queens county occupies the center of the province, is home to the island's largest city, and hosts the greatest concentration of traveler services.

The county is neatly cleaved by the Hillsborough River, which is spanned by bridge at Charlottetown. Cavendish on the north shore is the most tourist-oriented part of the entire province; if the phrase "Ripley's Believe It or Not Museum" lacks positive associations for you, you might consider avoiding this area, which has built a vigorous tourist industry around a fictional character, Anne of Green Gables. On the other hand, much of the rest of the county—not including Charlottetown—is quite pastoral and untrammeled.

Two parts of Queens County merit their own sections within this chapter: the capital city of Charlottetown on the south shore, and Prince Edward Island National Park on the north shore. Flip ahead for more detailed information on these destinations.

### ESSENTIALS

**GETTING THERE**    Route 2 is the fastest way to travel east-west through the county, although it lacks charm. Route 6 is the main route along the county's north coast; following the highway involves a number of turns at intersections, so keep a sharp eye on the directional signs.

The **Shuttle** (© **902/566-3243**) provides daily service between Charlottetown and several points in Cavendish from June through September. The rate is C$18 (US$15) round-trip, C$10 (US$8) one-way.

**VISITOR INFORMATION**    The snazzy, well-stocked little **Cavendish Visitor Information Centre** (© **902/963-7830**) is open daily from 8am to 9pm mid-June to the middle of October (only until 4:30pm in shoulder seasons) and is located just north of the intersection of Route 13 and Route 6.

### CAVENDISH

Cavendish is the home of the fictional character Anne of Green Gables. If you mentally screen out the tourist traps constructed over the past couple of decades, you'll find the area a bucolic mix of woodlands and fields, rolling hills, and sandy dunes—a fine setting for a series of pastoral novels.

However, the tremendous and enduring popularity of the novels has attracted droves of curious tourists, who in turn have attracted droves of entrepreneurs who've constructed new buildings and attractions. The bucolic character of the area has thus become somewhat compromised. There are wax museums and loud amusements, all of which would probably alarm Anne, along with a surfeit of motels and cottage courts. The new developments don't approach the garishness quotient of, say, Niagara Falls, but they're quite unavoidable, especially along Route 6 west of Route 13. Happily, most attractions are set off the road and spread well apart from one another. I wouldn't go so far as to say that the new developments harmonize with the landscape, but the collateral damage has been slight compared to what might have occurred. And the development is rather limited—you need only head east or west of Cavendish on Route 6 for a few miles to be back into the lovely landscapes of rolling farm fields that made the region famous in the first place.

Of the village of Cavendish, you should be aware that there's no *there* there, to steal from Gertrude Stein. There's no discernible village center; everything is sprawled out along the approach roads. A new commercial development called Avonlea (see below) is seeking to manufacture a new village center, but, well, it's just not quite the same. Those who like their villages quaint and are not terribly interested in the cult of Anne are better off steering for North or South Rustico, among other villages in the area.

## EVERYTHING ANNE

All visitors to Prince Edward Island owe it to themselves to read *Anne of Green Gables* at some point. Not that you won't enjoy your stay here without doing this, but if you don't, you might feel a bit out of touch, unable to understand the inside references that seep into many aspects of PEI culture. (Even some gas stations in Cavendish sell Anne dolls.) In fact, Anne has become so omnipresent and popular on the island that a licensing authority was created in 1994 to control the crushing glacier of Anne-related products.

Some background: Lucy Maud Montgomery wrote *Anne of Green Gables* in 1908. It's a fictional account of Anne Shirley, a precocious and bright 11-year-old who's mistakenly sent from Nova Scotia to the farm of the taciturn and dour Matthew and Marilla Cuthbert. (The mistake? The Cuthberts had requested a boy orphan to help with farm chores.) Anne's vivid imagination and outsized vocabulary get her into a series of pickles, from which she generally emerges beloved by everyone who encounters her. It's a bright, bittersweet story, and it went on to huge popular success, spawning a number of sequels.

### Anne of Green Gables Museum at Silver Bush
About 20km (12 miles) west of Cavendish near the intersection of Route 6 and Route 20 is the Anne of Green Gables Museum at Silver Bush. It's located in the home of Montgomery's aunt and uncle; the author was married here in 1911. The building still holds some of Montgomery's furniture, linens, photos, and other personal effects. For the best view of the "Lake of Shining Waters," take the wagon ride. It's hardly essential, but a half-hour visit might be in order if you're ticking off Anne destinations.

Rte. 20, Park Corner. ℂ **800/665-2663** or 902/886-2884 (weekends only). Admission C$2.75 (US$2.20) adults, C75¢ (US60¢) children under 16, C$6 (US$4.80) families. May and Oct daily 11am–4pm; June and Sept daily 9am–5pm; July–Aug daily 9am–6pm.

*Anne of Green Gables—The Musical*    This sprightly, professional musical has been playing for years at the downtown arts center, and brings to the stage many of Montgomery's stories and characters from late June through September. The 2-hour show takes place twice daily, at 2 and 7:30pm.

Confederation Centre of the Arts, 145 Richmond St., Charlottetown. ℂ 800/565-0278 or 902/566-1267. Tickets C$13–C$28 (US$10–US$23).

**Avonlea** *Kids*    This development of faux historic buildings was opened in the summer of 1999 with the idea of creating the sort of a village center you might find in reading the Anne novels. It's located on a large lot amid amusement parks and motels, and the new buildings have been constructed with an eye to historical accuracy. Several Anne-related buildings and artifacts are located on the site, including the schoolhouse in which Montgomery taught (moved here from Belmont), and a Presbyterian church (moved from Long River), which Montgomery occasionally attended. There's also a variety show, hayrides, staff in period dress, a restaurant, several stores (including an art gallery and music shop), and a spot for ice cream and candy. It's a bit overpriced, however, to my eye.

Rte. 6, Cavendish. ℂ 902/963-3050. www.avonlea.ca. Admission C$17 (US$14) adults, C$15 (US$12) seniors, C$10 (US$8) children 6–16. Musical variety show C$3 (US$2.10) extra. Mid-June to Aug daily 9am–5pm; Sept daily 10am–4pm. Closed Oct to mid-June.

**Cavendish Cemetery**    This historic cemetery was founded in 1835, but it's best known now as the final resting spot for author Lucy Maud Montgomery. It's not hard to find her gravesite: Follow the pavement blocks from the arched entryway, which is across from the Anne Shirley Motel.

Intersection of Rte. 13 and Rte. 6, Cavendish. Daily.

**Green Gables Heritage Site** *Overrated*    The best place to start an Anne tour is at Green Gables itself. The house is operated by Parks Canada, which also operates a helpful visitor center on the site. You can watch a 7-minute video presentation about Montgomery, view a handful of exhibits, and then head out to explore the farm and trails. The farmhouse dates from the mid–19th century and belonged to cousins of Montgomery's grandfather. It was the inspiration for the Cuthbert farm, and it has been furnished according to descriptions in the books.

If you're a diehard Anne fan, you'll delight in the settings where characters ventured, such as the Haunted Woods and Lover's Lane. But you might need as active an imagination as Anne's to edit out the golf carts puttering through the landscape at the adjacent Green Gables Golf Course, or the busloads of tourists crowding through the house and moving herdlike down the pathways. Come very early or very late in the day to avoid the largest crowds, and plan to spend 45 minutes or so. (*One last note:* Rumors still persist that Green Gables burned down a few years ago. It didn't. These tenacious fictions evidently stem from news reports of a minor fire in 1997.)

2 Palmers Lane (just off Rte. 6), Cavendish (just west of intersection with Rte. 13). ℂ 902/963-7874. Admission C$6.50 (US$5) adults, C$5.50 (US$4.40) seniors, C$3.25 (US$2.50) children, C$16 (US$13) families. Discounted rates spring and fall. May–Oct daily 9am–8pm (off season Wed 10am–4pm only).

**Lucy Maud Montgomery Birthplace**    Very near the Anne of Green Gables Museum is the Lucy Maud Montgomery Birthplace, where the author was born in 1874. The house is decorated in the Victorian style of the era, and it includes

## Kids  Family Fun

Cavendish has capitalized on its tourist allure with a handful of "museums" and theme parks to appeal to younger kids. All are located along Route 6 westward from the intersection with Route 13. The small, manageable **Sandspit** (© 902/963-2626) has "Indy" go-kart racing, an 18m (60-ft.) Ferris wheel, a roller coaster, bumper cars, and the like. There's no admission charge to visit the grounds; you can pay as you go (the roller coaster is about C$2/US$1.60) or buy a bracelet that covers all rides. Open daily mid-June to Labor Day.

Rainy-day diversions include **Ripley's Believe It or Not! Museum** (© 902/963-2242), which is about what you'd expect it to be, and **Wax World of the Stars** (© 902/963-4444), which renders Hollywood stars like Julia Roberts, Jim Carrey (who's Canadian, of course), and Tom Cruise forever in wax. One, er, interesting scene features John Travolta dancing with Lady Di. Both of these attractions are located near the intersection of Route 6 and Route 13 in Cavendish.

Montgomery mementos like her wedding dress and scrapbook. It's worth 45 minutes, but only for die-hard Anne fans.

Intersection of Rte. 6 and Rte. 20, New London. © **902/886-2099** or 902/436-7329. Admission C$2.50 (US$2) adults, C50¢ (US40¢) children 6–12. Mid-May to mid-Oct daily 9am–5pm (July and Aug to 6pm). Closed mid-Oct to mid-May.

### Site of Lucy Maud Montgomery's Cavendish Home    Montgomery lived with her grandparents, Alexander and Lucy Macneill, from 1876 (when she was just 21 months old) to 1911. Montgomery wrote *Anne of Green Gables,* among other books, while living in their farmhouse. Alas, the building is no longer standing, but visitors can roam the grounds and read interpretive signs about the property's literary history. There's also a small bookshop featuring books by and about Lucy Montgomery. Again, the site will be mainly of interest to true Anne buffs.

Rte. 6. Cavendish (just east of Rte. 13 intersection.) © **902/963-2231.** Admission C$3 (US$2.40) adults, C$1 (US80¢) children, C$8 (US$6.40) family. Mid-May to mid-Oct daily 9am–5pm (July and Aug to 6pm). Closed mid-Oct to mid-May.

## WHERE TO STAY

Cottage courts are to Cavendish what 19th-century inns are to Vermont—they're everywhere, and vary tremendously as to quality. Be aware that many of the cottage courts and motels are more interested in high volume and rapid turnover than personal attention to guests. A number also believe that hanging a straw hat or two on a door allows them to boast of "country charm," when they have anything but.

If you arrive in town without reservations, check the board at the visitor information centre (see above), which lists up-to-the-minute vacancies.

Also, you might ask around among local residents about under-the-table rentals. One fine writer I know rented a handsome three-bedroom Cavendish farmhouse built in 1910 and set in a barley field. The way he tells it, it was a lovely 10-minute stroll to the beach down a dirt lane, and the cost of paradise was just C$100 (US$80) per night. How did he learn about it? Why, from a scrap of paper tacked to the wall of the local laundromat, of course. So keep your eyes open.

**Cavendish Beach Cottages**    Location, location, location. This compound of 13 cottages is located on a grassy rise within the national park, just past the gatehouse into the park. The pine-paneled cottages are available in one-, two-, or three-bedroom configurations, and all feature ocean views, kitchenettes with microwaves, and outdoor propane barbecue grills. Some of the better-equipped cottages have dishwashers, and all are a 2-minute walk from the beach. There's also easy access to Gulf Shore Drive, where you'll find some of the island's premier biking.

Gulf Shore Dr., Cavendish (mailing address 166 York Lane, Charlottetown, PEI C1A 7W5). ⓒ **902/963-2025.** Fax 902/963-2025. www.cavendishbeachcottages.com. 13 units. C$150–C$200 (US$120–US$160) double. MC, V. Closed early Oct to late May. **Amenities:** Laundry. *In room:* A/C, TV, kitchenette, no phone.

**Green Gables Bungalow Court**    Located next to the Green Gables house, this pleasant cluster of one- and two-bedroom cottages began as a government make-work project promoting tourism in the 1940s. As a result, they're quite sturdily built, and nicely arrayed among lawn and pines. All have kitchens with refrigerators and coffeemakers, and many have outdoor gas grills for an evening barbecue. The linoleum floors and spartan furnishings take on a certain retro charm after a few hours of settling in. Some cabins were trimmed with cheap sheet paneling, others have the original pine paneling; ask for one with the latter. The beach is about 1km (½ mile) away, and there's a small heated outdoor pool on the premises.

Rte. 6 (Hunter River RR no. 2), Cavendish, PEI C0A 1N0. ⓒ **800/965-3334** or 902/963-2722. www.greengables bungalowcourt.com. 40 cottages. C$94–C$130 (US$75–US$104) up to 4 people. AE, MC, V. Closed Oct–June. **Amenities:** Outdoor heated pool. *In room:* TV, kitchenette, fridge, no phone.

**Red Road Country Inn** 🦆    Located 20 minutes west of Cavendish, this cream-colored inn sits on 13 hectares (33 acres) atop a lovely knoll. Rooms have unobstructed views down a long and rustling hayfield to Harding Creek, which widens and flows into the gulf. (Rowboats are tied up at a dock for guests.) The inn, which doesn't promise much from outside, was built in 1994 and 1995, but adopts a more historic character inside thanks to pine floors, large beams, and the handiwork of the owner, who is also a furniture maker—the guest rooms are each tastefully furnished with his Shaker reproductions and Windsor chairs. (One also even has its own balcony and a Jacuzzi bath.) A buffet-style breakfast featuring homemade breads is included in the rates; on pleasant days guests like to take their meals to the porch and enjoy the morning sun coming across the gently rounded hills that surround the inn.

Rte. 6, Clinton, PEI C0B 1M0. ⓒ **800/249-1344** or 902/886-3154. Fax 902/886-2267. www.redroadinn.com. 9 units. C$115–C$175 (US$92–US$140) double, lower in off season. Rates include full breakfast. MC, V. *In room:* TV (upon request), no phone.

## WHERE TO DINE

Cavendish itself offers limited opportunities for creative dining, although it's well stocked with restaurants offering hamburgers, fried clams, and the like. Both places mentioned below require a 10- to 15-minute drive from Cavendish proper, but they're worth it. See also the "Lobster Suppers" box, below.

**Café on the Clyde**    LIGHT FARE    This cafe is part of the noted Prince Edward Island Preserve Co, itself a worthwhile stop for the delicious homemade preserves. Light meals are served in the bright and modern dining room just off the preserve showroom. In this popular and often crowded spot, you can order from a menu that has a small but appealing selection; the smoked fish platter and lobster chowder are just the ticket on a drizzly afternoon. Just be prepared for the tour bus crowd: Buses get their own parking lot here, closer to the door, while cars park on gravel farther away.

Intersection of Rte. 224 and Rte. 258 (6.5km/4 miles south of Rte. 6 on Rte. 13), New Glasgow. (C) 902/964-4300. Main courses C$2–C$9 (US$1.60–US$7) at breakfast and lunch, C$9–C$16 (US$7–US$13) at dinner. AE, DC, MC, V. July–Aug daily 9am–9pm; June and Sept limited hours. Closed Oct–May.

**Olde Glasgow Mill Restaurant** ☆ REGIONAL/CANADIAN  This casual restaurant, formerly a 19th-century feed mill in twee little New Glasgow, is nicely shielded from the tourist throngs at Cavendish. The place overlooks a small pond and features an eclectic assortment of regional food. Appetizers include seafood chowder and a chilled strawberry and wine soup along with salads and PEI mussels. Lunch entrees are uncomplicated, with seafood crepes and Cajun chicken pizza being typical, but dinner is more serious: Besides Atlantic salmon and scallops, you'll find rack of lamb swabbed in Dijon mustard and rosemary herb crust served with a rosemary peppercorn sauce, or chicken breast served with a cranberry confit. There's a leisurely brunch on the weekends.

Rte. 13, New Glasgow. (C) 902/964-3313. Reservations recommended. Lunch C$4.95–C$11 (US$4–US$9); dinner C$15–C$30 (US$12–US$24). AE, MC, V. June–Oct Mon–Sat noon–10pm, Sun 10am–10pm; shorter hours in winter.

## NORTH & SOUTH RUSTICO TO BRACKLEY BEACH

A few miles east of Cavendish are the Rusticos, of which there are five: North Rustico, South Rustico, Rusticoville, Rustico Harbour, and Anglo Rustico. The region was settled by Acadians in 1790 and many residents are descendants of the original settlers. North and South Rustico are both attractive villages that have fewer tourist traps and are more amenable to exploring by foot or bike than Cavendish. Although out of the hubbub, they still provide easy access to the national park and Anne-land, with beaches virtually at your doorstep.

North Rustico clusters around a scenic harbor with views out toward Rustico Bay. Plan to park and walk around, perusing the deep-sea fishing opportunities (see below) and peeking in the shops. The village curves around Rustico Bay to end at North Rustico Harbour, a sand spit with fishing wharves, summer cottages, and a couple of informal restaurants. A wood-decked promenade follows the water's edge from the town to the harbor, and is a worthy destination for a quiet afternoon ramble or a picnic. Also here in the bright yellow wharf building is **Outside Expeditions** ((C) 800/ 207-3899 or 902/963-3366; www.getoutside.com), which offers sea kayak excursions of the harbor and surrounding area (see "Sea Kayaking," earlier in this chapter).

In **South Rustico** ☆, turn off Route 6 and ascend the low hill overlooking the bay. Here you'll find a handsome cluster of buildings that were home to some of the more prosperous Acadian settlers. Among the structures is the sandstone **Farmers' Bank of Rustico** ((C) 902/963-3168 or 902/963-2304), established with the help of a visionary local cleric in 1864 to help farmers get ahead of the hand-to-mouth cycle. Renovations have been ongoing for several years; it is open for tours June to October Monday through Saturday 10am to 5pm, Sunday 1 to 5pm. Next door is handsome St. Augustine's Parish Church (1838) and a cemetery beyond. If the church's door is open, head in for a look at this graceful structure.

**Brackley Beach** is the gateway to the eastern section of the national park and has the fewest services of all. It's a quiet area with no village center to speak of; it will be best appreciated by those who prefer their beach vacations unadulterated.

## DEEP-SEA FISHING

PEI's north shore is home to the island's greatest concentration of deep-sea fishing boats. For about C$20 (US$16) per person, you'll get 3 hours out on the seas in search of mackerel, cod, and flounder. Don't worry about lack of prior experience: Equipment is supplied, crewmembers are very helpful, and most will even clean and fillet your catch for you.

In North Rustico, about a half-dozen captains offer fishing trips. Among them are: Aiden's Deep Sea Fishing (© **866/510-3474** or 902/963-3522), Bob's Deep-Sea Fishing (© **902/963-2666**), and Bearded Skipper's Deep-Sea Fishing (© **902/963-2334**). A 20-minute drive east of North Rustico, at Covehead Harbour (within the national park), try Richard's Deep-Sea Fishing (© **902/672-2376**) or Salty Seas Deep-Sea Fishing (© **902/672-3246**).

## SHOPPING

Between Cavendish and Brackley Beach you'll find a number of shops offering unique island crafts and products. Browsing is a good option for a rainy or overcast day that keeps you off the beach.

**Cheeselady's Gouda** *Finds*   This is a short detour off Route 6, but well worth it. Watch a brief video about the making of Gouda cheese, and then get down to business: buying some of the excellent cheeses produced here. If you don't want to stick with the traditional aged Gouda, try the flavored varieties, including peppercorn, garlic, and herb. Sizes ranging from a wedge to a wheel are available. Rte. 223, Winsloe North southeast of Oyster Bed Bridge. © 902/368-1506.

**The Dunes Studio Gallery and Café**   This architecturally striking, modern gallery on the way to the eastern section of PEI National Park is among the best spots on the island to browse the fine works produced by island artisans and craftspeople. Situated on two open levels, the gallery features pottery, furniture, lamps, woodworking, sculpture, and paintings, along with more accessible crafts including handmade soaps and jewelry. The gallery is also home to an appealing cafe open May through October, a good spot for a coffee, a lunch break, or even a fancy, full-blown dinner of lamb, steak, or seafood. Rte. 15, Brackley Beach. © 902/672-2586.

**Gaudreau Fine Woodworking** *&*   All woodworking sold here is made on the premises. Items range from elegantly timeless sushi trays to modern wrist rests for computer keyboards crafted from birds-eye maple. Also sold are crafts and paintings from selected island artisans. The recent expansion here allows better viewing of the woodworkers, and a new gallery space displays the work of maritime craftspeople. Rte. 6, South Rustico. © 902/963-2273.

**Prince Edward Island Preserve Co.**   PEI Preserve Co. sells accessible luxury. The firm makes a variety of exceptionally tasty preserves at this small factory in a lovely valley. You can sample those that are currently available, and watch the process through a glass window. It's pricey for a jar of jam (about C$7/US$5.60 at last visit), but that never deters me from stocking up on raspberry and champagne jam and sour cherry marmalade—two good choices. There's also a cafe on the site, which opens from mid-May through mid-October. (See "Café on the Clyde" in the Cavendish section, above.) Intersection of Rte. 224 and Rte. 258 (just off Rte. 13), New Glasgow. ☎ 902/964-4300.

**Seasway Hammock Shop** The sturdy, attractive hammocks at this shop are crafted on the premises during the winter months by retired fisherman Keith Smith, and then sold in the summer tourist season. They not only look good, they're made to last. Churchill Avenue, North Rustico. ☎ 902/963-2846.

## WHERE TO STAY

**Barachois Inn** ☆☆ *Finds* The proudly Victorian Barachois Inn was built in 1870, and it is a soothing retreat for road-weary travelers. It's topped with a lovely mansard roof adorned with pedimented dormers, and it boasts a fine garden and historic fur nishings throughout. Innkeepers Judy and Gary MacDonald bought the place as derelict property in 1982, and have done an outstanding job bringing it back from the brink, adding modern art along the way to soften the staid Victorian architecture. The main house is furnished with high-quality period antiques; the two rooms on the third floor are a bit cozier than the spacious second-floor suites, but guests feel far away from the world when tucked under the slanted eaves. Room 1 has a canopy bed dating from the 1840s and an unusually large bathroom. Room 3 on the top floor has both a claw-foot tub and a stall shower. There's a second, newer building next door with four additional executive-style rooms and perks like a sauna, exercise bike, and a meeting room.

The inn is located amid a cluster of other historic buildings on a gentle rise overlooking Rustico Bay. Factor in some time to just stroll around and enjoy both the village and the inn's tidy garden. Ask about the special occasions package, which includes an Anne of Green Gables–themed carriage ride and picnic lunch.

2193 Church Rd., Rustico (mailing address: Hunter River RR no. 3, PEI C0A 1N0). ☎ 902/963-2194. Fax 902/963-2906. www.barachoisinn.com. 8 units, 1 with private bathroom in hallway. June–Sept C$160–C$250 (US$128–US$200) double, Oct–May C$140–C$200 (US$112–US$160). Rates include full breakfast. Ask about packages. AE, MC, V. Closed Nov–Mar. **Amenities:** Sauna; laundry service. *In room:* A/C, VCR, kitchenette, hair dryer, iron, no phone.

**Shaw's Hotel** ☆ Shaw's is a delightfully old-fashioned compound located down a tree-lined dirt road along a marsh-edged inlet. It's been in the same family since 1860, and even with its regimen of modernization—new in 1999 were a sun deck, a bar, and a dining room addition that accommodates 40 more people—the place still has the feel of a farm-stay vacation in the 19th century. It remains the kind of place where ripply and worn carpeting in the hallways adds to the charm rather than detracts. (*One caveat:* A new subdivision across the river is starting to encroach on the pastoral environment.)

The hotel's centerpiece is the Victorian farmhouse with its lipstick-red mansard roof. Fifteen guest rooms are located upstairs; they are "boarding-house style," which is to say, small. The cottages vary in size and vintage. None are lavish, but most have the essentials (some with kitchenettes, some just with cube refrigerators) and some are downright comfy (double Jacuzzis have recently been installed in some of them). While the new cottages are perfectly fine, the older ones—like my favorite, no. 6 with its dark beadboard paneling and brick fireplace—have a creaky, summer home charm all their own. This is still the kind of place where you walk down a sandy lane to get to the beach, and where signs admonish you, "Don't let Chase (the dog) follow you to the beach." (As the beach is just .5km/¼ mile away, he might do so anyway.) The spare but handsome main dining room serves breakfast and dinner daily. The dinner

## Lobster Suppers

The north shore of Prince Edward Island is home to famous lobster suppers, which are a good bet if you have a craving for one of the succulent local crustaceans. These suppers took root years ago as events held in church basements, in which parishioners would bring a covered hot dish to share and the church would provide a lobster. Everyone would contribute some money, and the church netted a few dollars. Outsiders discovered these good deals, the fame of the dinners spread, and today several establishments offer the bountiful lobster dinners, although few are raising money for charity these days.

Expect a large and impersonal dining experience (Fisherman's Wharf can accommodate 500 diners at a time), especially if you have the misfortune to pull up after a couple of bus tours have unloaded. Lobster is naturally the main feature, although you'll usually find roast beef, ham, or other alternatives. These are typically accompanied by an all-you-can-eat buffet with a button-bursting selection of rolls, salads, chowder, mussels, desserts, and more. The cost? Figure on C$20 to C$30 (US$16–US$24) per person, depending on the options.

**St. Ann's Church Lobster Suppers** (© **902/621-0635**) remains a charitable organization, as it was 3 decades ago when it was the first and only lobster supper on PEI. Located in a modern church hall in the small town of St. Ann, just off Route 224 between Routes 6 and 13, St. Ann's has a full liquor license and the home-cooked food is served at your table (no buffet lines). Lobster dinners are served mid-June to late September Monday through Saturday from noon to 2pm and from 4 to 8:30pm. (As befits a church, it's closed Sun.)

**Fisherman's Wharf Lobster Suppers** (© **902/963-2669**) in North Rustico boasts an 18m (60-ft.) salad bar to go with its lobster; it's open daily from noon to 9pm, mid-June to mid-October, from 4pm mid-May to mid-June. And near the PEI Preserve Company in New Glasgow is the barnlike **New Glasgow Lobster Suppers** (© **902/964-2870**). Meals here include unlimited mussels and chowder; it's on Route 258 (just off Rte. 13) and is open June to mid-October daily from 4 to 8:30pm.

menu changes frequently, but typical entrees are filet mignon au poivre, poached halibut with béarnaise, or penne with smoked salmon in a vodka cream sauce. The Lobster Trap Lounge, located in a nearby outbuilding, is open until 1am daily, and it offers more casual fare like chicken potpie, nachos, and steamed island mussels.

Rte. 15, Brackley Beach, C1E 1Z3. © **902/672-2022.** Fax 902/672-3000. www.shawshotel.ca. 41 units. Inn rooms, July–Aug C$220–C$400 (US$176–US$320) double, rest of the year C$110–C$230 (US$88–US$184). Cottages more expensive. Inn rates include breakfast and dinner. AE, MC, V. Closed Nov to late May. Pets allowed in cottages only. **Amenities:** 2 restaurants; canoes, kayaks, and bike rental; secretarial services; babysitting; laundry. *In room:* TV (some units), kitchenette, no phone.

## WHERE TO DINE

See also **Shaw's Hotel,** above, and **Dalvay-by-the-Sea** 🦆🦆, listed under "Prince Edward Island National Park," below.

**Sea Side Fish and Chips** *(Value)* *(Kids)* SEAFOOD   This little shack overlooking Rustico Bay is the place to go when you don't have the time for a sit-down dinner. The menu's simple—fried fish and scallops, basically—and not particularly healthy. But portions are huge and tasty, and a bottle of cola washes it down nicely. Here's a tip: Take a seat on the back deck, both to be shielded from the persistent winds and to get a nice view of the water.

Rte. 6, Rusticoville, at bridge over Hunter River. No phone. Meals C$5–C$11 (US$3.50–US$8). No credit cards. Hours vary according to weather, but often daily 11am–sundown. Closed Sept to mid-June.

## ORWELL

In southeastern Queens County, the village of Orwell offers a historic detour off speedy Route 1 between Charlottetown and the Wood Islands ferry. Both sites mentioned below are near one another on a side road; there are few landmarks other than simple signs directing you here, so keep a sharp eye out.

The **Orwell Corner Historic Village** 🦆 (© **902/651-8510**) is one of the most aesthetically pleasing historic villages in the province. Set on a gentle slope amid a profusion of leafy trees, the village re-creates life in a small agricultural town in the 1890s. You can visit the general store, stop by the blacksmith shop, or wander the lush gardens. If it works out, plan to visit around lunchtime and pick up a picnic from the community hall to enjoy under a shady tree on the grounds. Ask about the lively ceilidhs (Scottish concerts) with traditional music, held Wednesday evenings in the community hall (extra charge). The village is one of several sites island-wide managed by the **Prince Edward Island Museum and Heritage Foundation.** It's open 9am to 4:30pm daily in July and August, the same hours but weekdays only in May and June, and Sunday to Thursday from September to mid-October. Admission is C$7.50 (US$6) for adults, C$3 (US$2.40) for children 6 to 18, free for children under 6.

A few minutes' drive from the village is the modest, white-shingled home of **Sir Andrew Macphail,** a gifted polymath born here in 1864. Macphail found renown as a medical doctor, pathologist, professor, writer, editor, and agricultural tinkerer. You'll learn about his exceptional career while walking through the house, which includes a handful of exhibits and period furniture. (There's also a restaurant; see below.) But the real allure of the site is a stroll through the 56-hectare (140-acre) farm grounds, which are accessible via several **trails.** It's lush and pastoral, filled with the summer sounds of crickets and songbirds.

Admission to this national historic site (© **902/651-2789**) is free, with donations happily accepted. It's open daily in summer 10am to 8:30pm, except on Monday, Tuesday, and Saturday, when it closes at 5pm.

## WHERE TO DINE

**Sir Andrew Macphail Homestead** 🦆 *(Value)* TRADITIONAL   The simple, sparely decorated restaurant is located in the Macphail homestead (see above) and features a limited menu of classic dishes. Arrive early enough for a leisurely walk through the grounds, and then request a table on the sun porch, which is always bright and summery. The menu includes the Macphail haggis, a modern adaptation of the traditional Scottish meal ("There are no sheep stomachs involved," the hostess assured me).

## Impressions

*"The man who farms only for the money . . . is a fool, because one who can make money out of farming can make a good deal more out of something else. But for the man who would live a quiet, interesting, reasonable, and useful life there is no other occupation which affords so favorable an opportunity. It demands the exercise of every facility. Every movement of the day is full of surprise, and every effort has its immediate reward either in success or failure. For the finest minds it affords an outlet for activity; for the poorest it affords a living without the sordid accompaniment of poverty. And Prince Edward Island presents a field the freest for all who would live this life."*

—Sir Andrew Macphail, 1912.

Other dishes range from roast lamb to sole amandine, and the menu always includes a vegetarian selection. Lunches feature soups, sandwiches, and salads.

Off Rte. 1, Orwell. ℂ 902/651-2789. Reservations requested for dinner. Main courses C$3–C$10 (US$2.40–US$8) at lunch, C$12–C$16 (US$9.60–US$13) at dinner. V. Daily 11:30am–3:30pm; Sun–Fri 5–8:30pm. Closed early Oct to late June.

## 4  Prince Edward Island National Park ⭑⭑

Prince Edward Island National Park encompasses a 40km (24-mile) swath of red-sand beaches, wind-sculpted dunes topped with marran grass, vast salt marshes, and placid inlets. The park is located along the island's sandy north-central coast, which is broached in several spots by broad inlets that connect to harbors. As a result, you can't drive along the entire park's length in one shot. The coastal road is disrupted by inlets, requiring backtracking to drive the entire length. And, actually, there's little point in trying to tour the whole length. It's a better use of your time to pick one spot, then settle in and enjoy your surroundings.

The reddish sand and abstract dunes define the park for many. But also look for woods and meadows nearby, as well as wildlife. You might spot the tracks of red fox, mink, or muskrat. In the marshes and tidal flats, dozens of great blue heron stalk their aquatic prey near sunset. Where beach and dune meet, watch for the piping plover, a small and endangered beach bird.

The national park also oversees the Green Gables house and grounds; see "Cavendish," earlier in this chapter.

## ESSENTIALS

**GETTING THERE**    From Charlottetown, Route 15 offers the most direct route to the eastern segments of the park. To head to the Cavendish area, take Route 2 to Hunter River, and then head north on Route 13.

**VISITOR INFORMATION**    Two visitor centers provide information on park destinations and activities between June and October. The **Cavendish Visitor Information Centre** (ℂ 902/963-7830) is near the intersection of Routes 6 and 13; it's open daily from 9am to 10pm in the peak summer season (it closes earlier during the shoulder seasons).

The **Brackley Visitor Information Centre** (ℂ 902/672-7474) is at the intersection of Routes 6 and 15; it's open daily in July and August from 9am to 9pm

# Prince Edward Island National Park

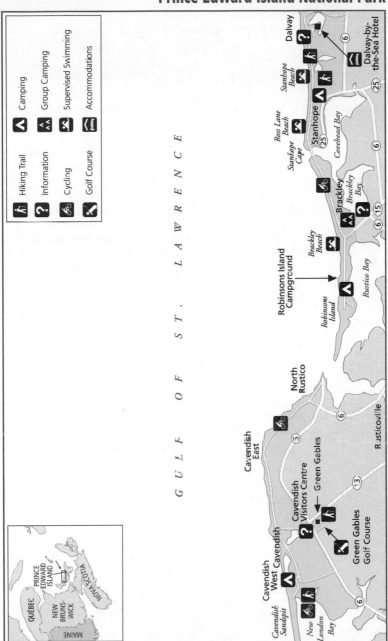

**Legend:**
- Hiking Trail
- Information
- Cycling
- Golf Course
- Camping
- Group Camping
- Supervised Swimming
- Accommodations

GULF OF ST. LAWRENCE

Dalvay
Dalvay-by-the-Sea Hotel
Stanhope Beach
Stanhope
Ross Lane Beach
Stanhope Cape
Covehead Bay
Brackley
Brackley Bay
Brackley Beach
Rustico Bay
Robinsons Island Campground
Robinsons Island
North Rustico
Cavendish East
Cavendish Visitors Centre
Green Gables
Green Gables Golf Course
Rusticoville
Cavendish
West Cavendish
Cavendish Sandspit
New London Bay

QUÉBEC
PRINCE EDWARD ISLAND
NOVA SCOTIA
NEW BRUNSWICK
MAINE

(9am–4:30pm in June and Sept–Oct). In the off season, contact the **park administration office** (© **902/672-6350**) near the Dalvay Hotel.

**FEES**    Between May and October, visitors to the national park must stop at one of the tollhouses to pay entry fees. Daily rates are C$6 (US$5) adults, C$5 (US$4) seniors, C$3 (US$2.40) children 6 to 16, C$15 (US$12) family. Ask about multiday passes if you plan to visit for more than 3 days.

## BEACHES

PEI National Park is nearly synonymous with its beaches. The park is home to two kinds of sandy strands: popular and sometimes crowded beaches with changing rooms, lifeguards, snack bars, and other amenities; and all the other beaches. Where you go depends on your temperament. If it's not a day at the beach without the aroma of other people's coconut tanning oil, head to Brackley Beach or Cavendish Beach. The latter is within walking distance of the Green Gables house and many other amusements (see "Cavendish," earlier in this chapter) and makes a good destination for families.

If you'd just as soon be left alone with the waves, sun, and sand, you'll need to head a bit farther afield, or just keep walking down the beaches until you leave the crowds behind. I won't reveal the best spots here for fear of crowding. But suffice it to say, they're out there.

## HIKING & BIKING

Hiking is limited here compared to that at Atlantic Canada's other national parks, but you will find a handful of pleasant strolls. And, of course, there's the beach, which is perfect for long walks.

The park maintains eight trails for a total of 20km (12 miles). Among the most appealing is the **Homestead Trail** ⚘, which departs from the Cavendish campground. The trail offers a 5.2km (3.25-mile) loop and an 8km (4.75-mile) loop. The trail skirts wheat fields, woodlands, and estuaries, with frequent views of the distinctively lumpy dunes at the west end of the park. Mountain bikes are allowed on this trail, and it's a busy destination on sunny days. The two **short trails** ⚘ at the Green Gables house— Balsam Hollow and Haunted Wood—are lovely but invariably crowded. Avoid them if you're looking for a relaxing walk in the woods.

**Biking** along the shoreline roads in the park is sublime. The traffic is light, and it's easy to make frequent stops to explore beaches, woodlands, or the marshy edges of inlets. The two shoreline drives within the national park—between Dalvay and Rustico Island, and from Cavendish to North Rustico Harbour—are especially beautiful on a clear evening as sunset edges into twilight. Snack bars are located at Brackley Beach and Covehead Bay.

Your safest bet for bike rentals is in **Charlottetown.** Try **Cycle Smooth,** 308 Queen St. (© **800/310-6550** or 902/566-5530), open daily from 9am to 5:30pm and renting bikes for C$25 (US$20) per day. You can often find rentals closer to the beach as well. In Brackley Beach, a good option is **Northshore Rentals** (© **902/672-2022**), located at Shaw's Hotel; their rentals cost C$7 (US$5.60) per hour, C$20 (US$16) per day.

## CAMPING

Prince Edward Island National Park has three campgrounds. Reservations are not accepted, so plan to arrive early in the day for the best selection of sites. Campground fees start at C$23 (US$19) per night (slightly less at Robinson's Island), with serviced sites costing up to C$30 (US$24). For more information, contact the **Cavendish Visitors Centre** (© 902/963-7830).

The most popular (and first to fill) is **Cavendish,** located just off Route 6 west of Green Gables. It has more than 300 sites spread among piney forest and open, sandy bluffs; the sites at the edge of the dunes overlooking the beach are the most popular. The sites aren't especially private or scenic. A limited number of two-way hookups are available for RVs, and the campground has free showers, kitchen shelters, and evening programs.

The **Stanhope** ✹ campground lies just across the park road from lovely Stanhope Beach, which is on the eastern segment of the park (enter through Brackley Beach). The road isn't heavily traveled, so you don't feel much removed from the water's edge. Most sites are forested, and you're afforded more privacy here than at Cavendish. Two-way hookups, free showers, and kitchen shelters are offered.

To my mind, the best campground is **Rustico Island** ✹✹✹. It's down a dead-end sand spit, with a number of sites overlooking a placid cove and the rolling countryside beyond. It lacks hookups for RVs, which might explain why sites are usually available here after the other campgrounds fill up. The sites are mostly wooded, very large, and quite private. Supervised swimming is 4km (2½ miles) away at Brackley Beach. If you'd rather have quiet than a lifeguard, turn left out at the campground gate and walk or bike along the gated dirt road to the pleasant (and often deserted) narrow beach at the mouth of Rustico Bay.

## WHERE TO STAY & DINE

Also see listings for "Cavendish" and "North & South Rustico to Brackley Beach," earlier in this chapter.

**Dalvay-by-the-Sea** ✹✹  This imposing Tudor mansion was built in 1895 by Alexander MacDonald, a partner of John D. Rockefeller. The place is unusually large for a private home, but it's rather intimate for a luxury inn. There are glimpses of the ocean across the road from the upper floors, even as the landscaping largely focuses on a beautiful freshwater pond out front. Inside, you'll be taken aback by the extraordinary cedar woodwork in the main entryway, and by the grand stone fireplace. The guest rooms are elegantly appointed and wonderfully solid and quiet; in the evening you'll hear mostly the roar of the sea. (The inn is just across the road from one of the park's better beaches; there are also plenty of walking trails nearby.)

Dalvay added a new pavilion-style dining room to the main inn in 1999. Not to worry—it's been constructed in a classic style that blends nicely with the original architecture. The net result has been to add some much-needed seats, along with improved views of the gardens and pond. The well-regarded kitchen features dishes such as tea-smoked Atlantic salmon with artichoke salad and crème fraîche. For dessert, try the sticky date pudding with toffee sauce, which was featured in *Gourmet* magazine. Those not on the hotel's meal plan will pay extra for these meals, but they're worth it.

The hotel serves afternoon tea each day from 2 to 4pm.

Off Rte. 6, Grand Tracadie (mailing address P.O. Box 8, Little York, PEI C0A 1P0). © **902/672-2048.** Fax (summer only) 902/672-2741. www.dalvaybythesea.com. 34 units. June to early Oct C$250–C$370 (US$200–US$296) double, cottages C$500 (US$400). Rates include breakfast and dinner. National park entrance fees also charged. 2-night minimum in summer. AE, DC, MC, V. Closed mid-Oct to early June. **Amenities:** Tennis court; bike rentals; croquet; lawn bowling; horseshoes; canoeing. *In room:* Minibar (cottage only), fridge (cottage only), coffeemaker (cottage only), no phone.

## 5 Charlottetown ★

It's not hard to figure out why early settlers put the province's political and cultural capital where they did: It's on a point of land between two rivers and within a large protected harbor. For ship captains plying the seas, this quiet harbor with ample anchorage and wharf space must have been a welcome sight. Of course, travelers rarely arrive by water these days (unless a cruise ship is in port), but the city's harborside location translates into a lovely setting for one of Atlantic Canada's most graceful and relaxed cities.

Named after Queen Charlotte, consort of King George III, Charlottetown is home to some 40,000 people—nearly one of every three islanders. Within Canada, the city is famous for hosting the 1864 conference that 3 years later led to the creation of the independent Dominion of Canada. For this reason, you're never far from the word *confederation,* which graces buildings, malls, and bridges. (In a historic twist, PEI itself actually declined to join the new confederation until 1873.)

Today, the downtown has a brisk and busy feel to it, with a pleasing mix of modern and Victorian commercial buildings, as well as government and cultural centers. Outside the business core, you'll find leafy streets and large, elegant homes dating from various eras, with the most dramatic from the late 19th century. Charlottetown is also blessed with a number of pocket parks, which provide a quiet respite amid the gentle clamor. Charlottetown's only charmless place? The outlying suburbs off Route 2, where you'll find traffic and strip malls of the sort that seem to be proliferating throughout North America.

Charlottetown is centrally located and serves admirably as a base for exploring the rest of the island (only the far western coast is a bit distant for relaxed day tripping). You can be touring Green Gables, relaxing on a north shore beach, or teeing off at Brudenell Provincial Park within 45 minutes of leaving Charlottetown. The capital has the island's best selection of inns and hotels, and a fine assortment of restaurants that ensure you can dine out every night for a week and still be pleasantly surprised. As for scheduling time for exploring the city itself—I'd suggest saving it for a rainy day. And you don't really need much more than a day to take in all the highlights.

### ESSENTIALS

**GETTING THERE**   Both Route 1 (the Trans-Canada Hwy.) and Route 2 pass through or near Charlottetown. For information on arriving by air, see "Exploring Prince Edward Island" at the beginning of this chapter. **Square One Shuttle** (© 877/ 675-3830 or 902/436-3830) runs seven-person vans 4 days a week from Moncton and Halifax for C$45 to C$50 (US$36–US$40) one-way. **PEI Express Shuttle** (© 877/877-1771) offers a similar van service from Halifax for almost exactly the same cost.

**VISITOR INFORMATION**   The city's main **Visitor Information Centre** (© 902/ 368-7795) is at 178 Water St. (across from 169 Water St. and next to Confederation Landing Park). Look for the brown "?" sign to direct you to a brick building with helpful staffers, an interactive computer kiosk, and an ample supply of brochures. There's also a vacancy board to let you know where rooms are currently available. The center is open daily in July and August from 8am to 10pm; weekdays only in the off season from 8am to 5pm. There's a second information center at **City Hall** on Queen Street (© 902/566-5548) that's open daily in summer from 8am to 5pm; in the off season, weekdays only, 8:30am to 5pm.

# Charlottetown

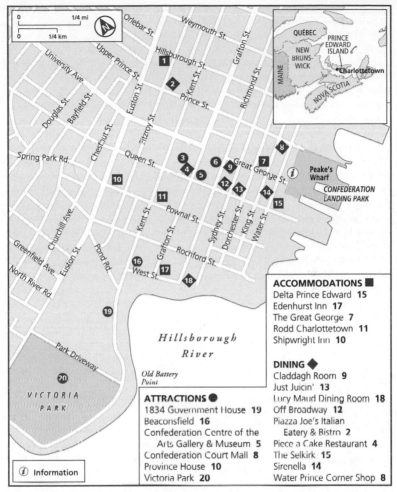

**ACCOMMODATIONS** ■
Delta Prince Edward **15**
Edenhurst Inn **17**
The Great George **7**
Rodd Charlottetown **11**
Shipwright Inn **10**

**DINING** ◆
Claddagh Room **9**
Just Juicin' **13**
Lucy Maud Dining Room **18**
Off Broadway **12**
Piazza Joe's Italian
   Eatery & Bistro **2**
Piece a Cake Restaurant **4**
The Selkirk **15**
Sirenella **14**
Water Prince Corner Shop **8**

**ATTRACTIONS** ●
1834 Government House **19**
Beaconsfield **16**
Confederation Centre of the
   Arts Gallery & Museum **5**
Confederation Court Mall **8**
Province House **10**
Victoria Park **20**

ⓘ Information

## EXPLORING CHARLOTTETOWN

Charlottetown is a compact city that's easy to reconnoiter once you park your car. Three main areas merit exploration: the waterfront, the downtown area near Province House and the Confederation Court Mall, and parks and residential areas near Victoria Park.

You're best off first heading to the main **Visitor Information Centre** (see above), and then starting your tour from the waterfront. Parking is generally scarce downtown, but it's relatively abundant near the visitor center, both on the street and in free and paid lots. At the visitor center, be sure to ask for a map and one of the free walking tour brochures, "The First Five Hundred: Heritage and History Walks."

The **waterfront** has been spruced up in recent years with the addition of **Peake's Wharf,** a collection of touristy boutiques and restaurants that attracts hordes in summer. The complex is attractive and offers good people-watching, but it has a somewhat formulaic "festival marketplace" feel to it and is rather lacking in local character. To see the city from the water, sign up with **Peake's Wharf Boat Tours** (© **902/ 566-4458**), which offers three tours daily for about C$16 to C$22 (US$13–US$18).

Next to the wharf is **Confederation Landing Park** 𝒢, an open, modern park with a boardwalk along the water's edge, lush lawns, and benches nicely situated for indolence. There's also a 220-boat marina, where you can scope out newly arrived pleasure craft.

From Peake's Wharf, you can stroll up **Great George Street** 𝒢𝒢𝒢. This is surely one of the most handsome streets in all of Canada, with leafy trees, perfectly scaled Georgian row houses, and stately churches.

At the top of Great George Street stop by the **Province House** and **Confederation Centre of the Arts** (see below); then explore the shops and restaurants of downtown Charlottetown. Watch for historical characters: Students dressed in period costume lead free 1-hour walking tours; others portray the Fathers of the Confederation, the politicians who were the key players in the confederation conference. Check with the visitor center for times.

For a pleasant walk affording fine water views, head southwest on Kent Street (just north of the Confederation Mall). At 2 Kent St., you'll see **Beaconsfield** (© **902/368- 6603**), a mansard-roofed mansion designed in 1877 by locally prominent architect William Harris for a prosperous shipbuilder. The architecture boasts an elegant mix of Georgian symmetry and Victorian exuberance, and the rooms are furnished in high Victorian style. The home, which is part of the Prince Edward Island Museum and Heritage Foundation, hosts lectures and events throughout the year, or you can just stop in and look around. It's open daily in summer from noon to 4pm; admission is C$4.25 (US$3.50) adults, C$3.25 (US$2.60) students, C$14 (US$11) family, free for children under 12.

From Beaconsfield, look for the boardwalk that follows the edge of the harbor for 1.6km (1 mile) into **Victoria Park** 𝒢𝒢, which is home to ball fields and grassy picnic areas. The walk along the water has unobstructed views of the harbor and Northumberland Strait beyond.

Along the way look for the **1834 Government House** 𝒢, also known as Fanningbank. This sturdy, white-shingled residence with Ionic columns is set back on a broad lawn and is home to the lieutenant governor. Only the gatehouse is open to the public, but you're welcome to explore the grounds, and there are tours of the gardens. The famous picture of the Fathers of the Confederation (you'll see it most everywhere around town) was taken on the front portico.

**Confederation Centre of the Arts Gallery and Museum**    Part of the Confederation Centre of the Arts (which includes three theaters; see "Charlottetown After Dark," later in this chapter), this is the largest art gallery in Atlantic Canada. The center is housed in a bland and boxy modern complex of glass and rough sandstone; about the best that can be said of it is that it doesn't detract too much from the stylishly classical Province House next door. (Canadian writer Will Ferguson has referred to the building as "one of the greatest unprosecuted crimes of urban planning in Canadian history.") Inside, however, the gallery is spacious and nicely arranged on two levels, and it features displays from the permanent collection as well as imaginatively curated changing exhibits. Shows might range from an exhibit on Canadian legal history to Uruguayan paintings, but mostly it focuses on the work of up-and-coming Canadian artists. Spend an hour if you like.

145 Richmond St. © 902/628-6112. www.confederationcentre.com. Summer daily 9am–5pm; off season Wed–Sat 11am–5pm, Sun 1–5pm.

**Province House National Historic Site** ⭐ This neoclassical downtown landmark was built in 1847 in an area set aside by town fathers for colonial administration and church buildings. When it served as a colonial legislature, the massive building rose up from vacant lots of dust and mud; today, as the provincial legislature, it's ringed by handsome trees, an inviting lawn, and a bustling downtown just beyond. This stern and imposing sandstone edifice occupies a special spot in Canadian history as the place where the details of the Confederation were hammered out in 1864. In the early 1980s, the building was restored to appear as it would have looked in that year.

Start your tour by viewing a well-made 17-minute film that documents the process of confederation. Afterward, wander the halls and view the Legislative Assembly, where legislators have been meeting since 1847. It's surprisingly tiny, but perhaps appropriate given that PEI's legislature has just 27 members, making it the smallest in Canada. Especially impressive is the second-floor Confederation Chamber, where a staffer is usually on hand to explain what took place and to answer that burning question: Why did PEI wait 9 years to join Canada? Plan to spend about an hour here.

2 Palmer's Lane. © 902/566-7626. Free admission (donations requested). July–Aug daily 8:30am–6pm; June and Sept to mid-Oct 8:30am–5pm; rest of year Mon–Fri 9am–5pm.

## SHOPPING

Charlottetown has a number of shops and boutiques, but few are all that impressive, with some notable exceptions. Better quality and more creative crafts can be found in outposts elsewhere on the island, especially along the north shore.

**Peake's Wharf** on the waterfront has an abundance of shops, most of which are tourist-oriented. This is a good destination if you're in search of a souvenir emblazoned with PRINCE EDWARD ISLAND. You'll also find casual dining, ice cream, and harbor cruises here.

The **Confederation Court Mall** (© 902/894-9505) is located downtown across from the Province House. Architecturally, this 90-store mall blends in nicely with its neighbors. Inside, however, the place is less distinctive, and the food courts, escalators, and chain stores (RadioShack, The Body Shop) might give you a shudder of déjà vu.

**Anne of Green Gables Store** Everything Anne, from dolls to commemorative plates. 110 Queen St. © 902/368-2663.

**The Bookman** Located across from the mall, this small shop has the city's best selection of used books, with a strong inventory of PEI and Canadian titles. 177 Queen St. © 902/892-8872.

**Cows** PEI's answer to Ben & Jerry's. It's as much a clothing store as an ice-cream shop; fans of the premium ice cream scoop up T-shirts and other bovine whimsy. Ice-cream flavors include Wowie Cowie Coffee Toffee Crunch and Cotton Candy Bunny Tails. 150 Queen St. © 902/892-6969.

**Great Northern Knitters** This shop recently moved and expanded its retail operations. It sells a diverse line of unusually well-made sweaters handcrafted on PEI. Every sweater is guaranteed for life. 133 Queen St. © 800/565-9665.

**The Kitchen Store** Serious amateur cooks trek here to buy the elegant stainless-steel Paderno brand cookware made with heat-conducting pads; these high-quality pots and pans, which come with a 25-year warranty, are made right on PEI. The store also sells other high-quality kitchen items as well. There's a smaller shop in the Charlottetown Mall. (If you want even more Paderno, there are a half-dozen outlet stores scattered across the island.) Confederation Court Mall (Grafton St.). ℂ **800/263-9768** or 902/629-2217.

**PEI Company Store** This is a great place to pick up locally made PEI products in one fell swoop. If you didn't get out to the factory in New Glasgow to pick up Prince Edward Island Preserve Co.'s great preserves, for example, stop here to stock up: The products are priced the same here as at the factory, so you're not saving anything by making a special trip to the source. Confederation Court Mall (Grafton St.). ℂ **902/566-5267.**

## WHERE TO STAY

For those traveling on a tight budget, several moderately priced motels are situated along the city's main access roads and across from the airport a few miles from downtown. Two with rooms under C$100 (US$80) are **Royalty Maples Cottages and Motel,** Route 2 (ℂ **800/831-7829** or 902/368-1030) and the **Winfield Motel,** Route 1 (ℂ **800/267-5525** or 902/566-2675). Two motels are situated within easy walking distance of downtown attractions. The **Islander Motor Lodge,** 146–148 Pownal St. (ℂ **800/268-6261** or 902/892-1217), has 49 rooms and is a few minutes' walk from Province House. Rates are around C$150 (US$120) double. The **Best Western,** 238 Grafton St. (ℂ **800/528-1234** or 902/892-2461), has 146 rooms and suites in two buildings a couple blocks east of the Confederation Court Mall. Rooms and suites range from about C$99 to C$259 (US$79–US$207).

### EXPENSIVE
**Delta Prince Edward** 𝕗𝕗 A modern, boxy, 10-story hotel overlooking the harbor, the Prince Edward Hotel is part of the Canadian Pacific chain and has all the amenities expected by business travelers and upscale tourists, including coffeemakers, hair dryers, free exercise bikes delivered to your room, and even cordless phones (in about half the rooms). You enter the hotel to a two-story atrium, home to a very well-regarded restaurant, and then head up to the guest rooms. The better rooms are furnished with reproduction Georgian-style furniture; others have those oak and beige-laminate furnishings that are virtually invisible. Higher rooms have better views; there's a premium for water views, but the city views are actually nicer and you can usually still glimpse the water. The in-hotel Selkirk restaurant (see below) might be the city's best, with upscale service and presentation to complement a fine menu. Summers only, a more informal restaurant serves tasty lunches on a patio near the harbor. For fun, try out the golf simulator.

18 Queen St., Charlottetown, PEI C1A 8B9. ℂ **800/268-1133** or 902/566-2222. Fax 902/566-2282. www.deltaprince edward.com. 211 units. Peak season C$169–C$370 (US$135–US$296) double, C$219–C$879 (US$175–US$703) suite; call for off-season rates. AE, DC, DISC, MC, V. Off-site parking C$9 (US$6) per day. Pets allowed. **Amenities:** 2 restaurants; indoor pool; fitness room; Jacuzzi; sauna; concierge; business center; shopping arcade; salon; room service; babysitting; laundry; dry cleaning; golf simulator. *In room:* A/C, TV, minibar, coffeemaker, hair dryer, iron.

**The Great George** 𝕗𝕗𝕗 The Great George opened in 1997 and has since established itself as one of Charlottetown's very classiest addresses. The inns encompass a collection of striking buildings on and near historic Great George Street, most of which were jacked up and renovated from states of former disrepair. (You can learn the story from a series of black-and-white photographs in the attractive lobby.)

Twenty-four rooms are located in the old (1846) Pavilion Hotel; others are in smaller, brightly painted town houses and homes nearby. All rooms have been thoroughly updated and refurbished with antiques, down duvets, and early black-and-white prints; all but two rooms are carpeted. The more expensive rooms have fireplaces and Jacuzzis, but many of the others have claw-foot tubs, perfect for soaking in after a day of roaming the city. Room 403 has buttery pine floors, a wonderful tub, and lots of light. Room 308 has a Shaker-style canopy bed, an in-room two-person Jacuzzi, and a gas fireplace. Families or couples traveling together should ask about Room 662, an attractive three-bedroom suite, or one of a number of other renovated suites. The recent addition of a garden space out back only makes this place more desirable.

58 Great George St., Charlottetown, PEI C1A 4K3. (C) **800/361-1118** or 902/892-0606. Fax 902/628-2079. www.inns ongreatgeorge.com. 53 units. C$184–C$499 (US$147–US$399) double, C$299–C$899 (US$239–US$719) suite. Rates include continental breakfast. AE, DC, MC, V. Free parking. **Amenities:** Fitness room; limited room service; babysitting; laundry service; dry cleaning. *In room:* A/C, TV (some units), hair dryer, iron.

**Shipwright Inn** 🦊🦊 This understated Victorian home was built by a shipbuilder, and expertly renovated and refurbished. It's decorated with period furniture and with a deft touch—no over-the-top Victoriana here. All rooms have lovely wood floors (some with original ship planking floors), and three are in a recent addition, which was built with a number of nice touches. Among the best rooms are those with extras: the Ward Room, a suite with a private deck; the Purser's State Room, which shares a lovely deck with another room; and the Crow's Nest luxury apartment. The business center, with its computer and fax machine, is a nice bonus, and innkeepers Judy and Trevor Pye and their staff are very helpful. This inn is located right in the city, yet has a settled, pastoral farmhouse feel to it.

51 Fitzroy St., Charlottetown, PEI C1A 1R4. (C) **888/306-9966** or 902/368-1905. Fax 902/628-1905. www.shipwright inn.com. 8 units. C$135–C$279 (US$108–US$223) double. Rates include full breakfast. AE, DC, MC, V. Free parking. **Amenities:** Dining room; business center. *In room:* A/C, TV/VCR, minibar, hair dryer, iron.

## MODERATE

**Edenhurst Inn** 🦊 James Eden was a prosperous wine merchant on the island, and in 1897 he built this regal Queen Anne Revival mansion in one of the city's better neighborhoods—looking west toward the sunset over the water. It's three floors tall, and the exterior bustles with turrets, gables, and covered porches. The innkeepers have done a fine job restoring this historic property to its former splendor, and the rooms are furnished with the appropriate period antiques. When booking, ask about rooms with deluxe touches, such as fireplaces and Jacuzzis.

12 West St., Charlottetown, PEI C1A 3S4. (C) **877/766-6439** or 902/368-8323. Fax 902/894-3707. 7 units. www.pe island.com/edenhurst. C$120–C$205 (US$96–US$164). Rates include full breakfast. AE, MC, V. Closed Nov–Apr. Not suitable for children under 8. *In room:* A/C, VCR (some units), coffeemaker (some units), hair dryer, no phone (some units).

**Hillhurst Inn** Another fine mansion built in 1897 in another fine neighborhood (3 blocks northeast of Province House), Hillhurst features a raft of nice touches, not the least of which is the extraordinarily detailed woodworking carved by some of the city's shipbuilders. When built, locals called it "the crystal palace" because of its profusion of windows. The rooms are varied in size and style. As is often the case, the third floor rooms require a bit of a hike, and are smaller and cozier than the rooms on the second floor. The drawbacks? Many of the bathrooms are quite small (often shoehorned into closets), and the furnishings are less historic and creative compared to other comparably priced inns, including Edenhurst and the Shipwright Inn.

181 Fitzroy St., Charlottetown, PEI C1A 1S3. (℗ **877/994-8004** or 902/894-8004. Fax 902/892-7679. www.hillhurst. com. 9 units. Peak season C$125–C$225 (US$100–US$180) double; off season cheaper. Rates include full breakfast. AE, DISC, MC, V. *In room:* A/C, TV, dataport, hair dryer, no phone.

**Rodd Charlottetown**   This 1940s-era hotel—part of the Rodd Hotel chain—is located in a five-story brick building next to a shady park and is just a few minutes' walk to most downtown attractions. The hotel features Georgian flourishes inside and out, and it has been updated and remodeled with a nod to its heritage. The dusky lobby has the feel of a prewar New York City apartment building, with a vaulted ceiling and echoey composite floors. The rooms, which have opening windows, were tastefully remodeled in the mid-1990s with reproduction-period furniture. Five suites were added in 1999. The hotel will certainly appeal to travelers drawn to the solid construction and understated styling of yore, although some of the public areas are growing weary with age and are overdue for remodeling. A low-ceilinged indoor pool is open to guests on the ground floor.

The in-hotel Carvery restaurant is open daily for dinner and features hotel favorites including prime rib, jumbo shrimp, Atlantic salmon, and a popular shellfish buffet. Across the lobby, a dinner theater performs nightly in July and August.

Kent and Pownal sts. (P.O. Box 159), Charlottetown, PEI C1A 7K4. (℗ **800/565-7633** or 902/894-7371. Fax 902/368-2178. www.rodd-hotels.ca. 115 units. C$158–C$237 (US$128–US$190) double, C$255–C$388 (US$204–US$310) suite. AE, DC, DISC, MC, V. Free parking. Pets accepted with C$10 (US$8) charge. **Amenities:** Indoor pool; Jacuzzi; sauna; limited room service; babysitting; laundry service; dry cleaning. *In room:* A/C, TV, dataport, coffeemaker, hair dryer, iron.

## WHERE TO DINE

For a late afternoon pick-me-up, try **Beanz,** 38 University Ave. (℗ **902/892-8797**), for its industrial-strength cappuccino. They also sell pastries and offer light lunches.

A locally popular spot for inexpensive meals is **Cedar's Eatery** at 81 University between Fitzroy and Kent (℗ **902/892-7377**). Lebanese dishes are the specialty here, such as *yabrak* (stuffed vine leaves) and *kibbee* (ground beef with crushed wheat and spices). There are also sandwiches and burgers. Specials start at C$4.95 (US$4), both lunch and dinner.

The **Harbour House** (℗ **902/367-9999**) at 45 Water St. is run by the former chef of the Dunes; expect mussels, crepes, and other good things.

**Claddagh Room**   SEAFOOD   Despite the Irish name and the Dublin Pub located downstairs, the Claddagh Room isn't the place for corned beef. It's the place for seafood, the house specialty. The seafood chowder is very tasty, as is the bouillabaisse. You can also order lobster from the tank, surf and turf, and a variety of other selections. There's no harbor view, as there is at other seafood places in town, but the preparation and service here are a notch above. Live Irish entertainment is often featured downstairs in the pub during the summer months.

131 Sydney St. (℗ **902/892-9661**. Reservations recommended. Main courses C$6–C$10 (US$5–US$8) at lunch, C$15–C$25 (US$12–US$20) at dinner. AE, DISC, MC, V. Mon–Fri 11:30am–2pm; Sun–Thurs 5–10pm; Fri–Sat 5–10:30pm.

**Just Juicin'**   Value   Kids   CAFE   This place has been a downtown Charlottetown fixture for a while now, but new ownership is taking it to a new level. Originally a smoothie and juice bar whizzing up incredibly tasty and healthy drinks, it has since added pita sandwiches, homemade chocolate cake, and other delicious treats. It's a three-generation family operation, too—the owner, her daughter, and her mother have all been spotted working the counter simultaneously during busy summer-vacation times.

62 Queen St. ℂ **902/894-3104.** Reservations not accepted. Juices and sandwiches C$2–C$6 (US$1.60–US$5). June–Aug Mon–Sat 8am–8pm, Sun noon–5pm; rest of year Mon–Fri 8am–5:30pm, Sat 10am–5pm.

**Lucy Maud Dining Room** 🎯🎯 REGIONAL   The Lucy Maud Dining Room is located within the Culinary Institute of Canada's campus. The building itself is a bit institutional and charmless, and the 80-seat dining room has much the feel of a hotel restaurant. But plenty of nice touches offset the lack of personality. Among them: custom china and a beautiful view of the bay and Victoria Park from oversize windows. Best of all, diners get to sample some of the best of island cuisine, prepared and served by Institute students eager to please. The lunch and dinner menus change each semester, but typical dinner entrees might include duck breast with a sour cherry sauce, or venison loin with a blueberry peppercorn sauce (the kitchen is noted for its venison). There's always salmon on the menu, and often the curried seafood chowder with fresh tarragon, a local favorite. A short wine list is available as well.

4 Sydney St. ℂ **902/894-6868.** Reservations recommended June–Sept for lunch and dinner. Main courses C$8–C$13 (US$6.40–US$11) at lunch, C$15–C$28 (US$12–US$23) at dinner. AE, MC, V. Tues–Fri 11.30am–1:30pm; Tues–Sat 6–8pm. Closed holiday weekends.

**Off Broadway** 🎯 UPSCALE CANADIAN   Affiliated with the Great George (see above), this friendly upscale restaurant has the feel of an intimate, wood-paneled English eating house. At dinner, its dimness can be downright romantic, though the proximity of other diners might be a slight deterrent to popping the question then and there. It's known for an unusually wide selection of crepes (some filled with seafood), as well as steaks, salmon, island shellfish, and the like; the bar upstairs is quite nice as well.

125 Sydney St. ℂ **902/566-4620.** Reservations recommended. Lunch C$6–C$12 (US$5–US$9.60); dinner C$14–C$22 (US$11–US$18). AE, DISC, MC, V. Mon–Thurs 11:30am–10pm; Fri–Sat 11:30am–11pm; Sun 11am–10pm.

**Piazza Joe's Italian Eatery and Bistro** PIZZA/ITALIAN   Piazza Joe's, located in a handsome, historic building 1 long block from the Confederation Mall, has gone a bit overboard with the Tuscan-style washed tones and fake ivy climbing fake trellises. But it works in a comic-book kind of way. The place is pleasantly casual and can be loud on weekends, but it offers friendly service, a long menu, and lots of comic-book-type mixed drinks to match the decor. (It's the best spot for a late night meal if you get into town late.) The wood-fired pizza is consistently quite good; take your chances on the rest of the selections, such as five-vegetable lasagna or veal a la limone. There's also a bistro menu, with items that include burgers, chicken wings, and fish and chips.

189 Kent St. ℂ **902/894-4291.** Reservations accepted. Main courses C$9.95–C$15 (US$8–US$12); individual pizzas C$7 (US$5.50) and up. AE, DC, MC, V. Mon–Thurs 11am–midnight; Fri–Sat 11am–1am; Sun 10am–midnight.

**Piece a Cake Restaurant** 🎯🎯 ECLECTIC   This very modern, very handsome restaurant occupies the second floor of a building that's part of the Confederation Court Mall. With hardwood floors, high ceilings, rich custard-colored walls, and window frames suspended whimsically from the ceiling, there's a welcoming, airy grace to the spot. It's the kind of place where friends who don't see each other very often like to get together and relax over a lively meal. The menu is wonderfully far-ranging, and it's hard to imagine someone not finding something appealing—lunches range from a teriyaki salmon wrap to Thai scallop salad to Tuscan grilled chicken sandwiches. Dinners are similarly eclectic and include a range of adventurous pastas. (A personal favorite: "penne on fire," with charred onions, grilled zucchini, toasted pecans, and a tangerine relish.) Other dinner options include Thai seafood medley, blackened salmon, and pecan-crusted pork loin. Only the unimaginative wine list is a bit of a disappointment. Also ask about the gourmet brown bag lunches—eight choices are offered (C$9.95/US$6.65 to C$14/US$9.30 with dessert and beverage), including a lobster salad croissant and a jerk chicken pasta salad.

119 Grafton St. (upstairs in the Confederation Court Mall). ✆ 902/894-4585. Reservations recommended. Main courses C$6–C$12 (US$5–US$10) at lunch, C$9–C$18 (US$7–US$15) at dinner. AE, DC, MC, V. Mon–Sat 11am–10pm.

**The Selkirk** ✦✦✦ NEW CANADIAN   Charlottetown's most stylish restaurant is smack in the middle of the lobby of the high-end Prince Edward Hotel. Yet it has a more informal character than many upscale hotel restaurants, with an eclectic mix of chairs and a piano player providing the live soundtrack. The menu is also more ambitious and creative than you'll find elsewhere in the city. The signature appetizer is lobster and prawns served with a three-melon salsa, or you might opt for pheasant confit. Main courses could include sashimi of salmon, oysters, and scallops with a sauce of lime, ginger, and garlic; or a Maritime jambalaya with lobster, mussels, shrimp, scallops, and salmon. Carnivores aren't ignored, with a selection that includes duck breast with a raspberry and green peppercorn vinaigrette, or beef tenderloin with a shiitake ragout. A downside: The lobby location can get clamorous at times, especially when conferees are milling about. Ask for one of the tables under the mezzanine, near the piano.

In the Delta Prince Edward, 18 Queen St. ✆ 902/566-2222. Reservations recommended. Main courses C$6–C$12 (US$5–US$10) at breakfast, C$8–C$15 (US$6.50–US$12) at lunch, C$15–C$32 (US$12–US$26) at dinner. AE, DC, DISC, MC, V. Daily 7:30am–1pm and 5:30–9:30pm.

**Sirenella** ITALIAN   Sirenella is a locally popular spot that offers good value when the service staff and kitchen are both operating smoothly, which, alas, is not all the time. When it's missing the mark, expect slipshod service and indifferent meals. When all systems are go, it's another story. You'll understand why the place has diehard fans who swear by its most popular dishes, including the grilled calamari, and ravioli with ricotta, spinach, and prosciutto. Sirenella is tucked on a quiet side street and could be considered either romantically intimate or claustrophobic, depending on your mood.

83 Water St. ✆ 902/628-2271. Reservations recommended. Main courses C$8–C$12 (US$6.50–US$9.50) at lunch, C$12–C$18 (US$9.50–US$15) at dinner. AE, MC, V. Mon–Fri 11:30am–2pm and 5–10pm; Sat 5–10pm.

**Water Prince Corner Shop** ✦✦ *Finds* SEAFOOD   This place is a real find, tucked into an attractive corner building at Water and Prince streets (hence the name) that looks at first glance like a simple newsstand or convenience store. Inside, though, you'll find one of the city's most convivial seafood joints, serving lobster dinners, superb seafood chowder, cooked mussels, and even lobster rolls to an appreciative mixture of tourists and locals. There's a liquor license if you want to tip a few (and you might).

If the weather's good, try to get a seat on the street near sundown. You can see the waterfront from some tables.

141 Water St. ✆ 902/368-3212. Reservations recommended. Lunch C$4.95–C$11 (US$4–US$9); dinner C$6.95–C$25 (US$5.55–US$20). AE, DISC, DC, MC, V. May, June, Sept, and Oct daily 9am–8pm; July–Aug daily 9am–10pm.

## CHARLOTTETOWN AFTER DARK

A good resource for evening adventure is *Buzz*, a free monthly newspaper that details ongoing and special events around the island with an emphasis on Charlottetown. It's widely available; look at visitor centers or area bars and restaurants.

For high culture, check out the **Confederation Centre of the Arts Gallery and Museum** (*©* 800/565-0278 or 902/628-1864; see earlier), where three stages bustle with activity in the warm-weather months. The musical *Anne of Green Gables,* a perennial favorite, is performed here throughout the summer, as are revivals and new shows.

For low culture, head to the **Charlottetown Driving Park** (*©* 902/892-6823), located at Kensington Road on the Hillsborough River at the northeast edge of downtown. Harness racing is slated every few days in afternoons and evenings from June to September; call for the current schedule. Parimutuel betting is offered, and there's a club on the upper level for enjoying snacks and drinks while handicapping the ponies.

The art-house **City Cinema,** 64 King St. (*©* 902/368-3669), has an excellent lineup of domestic and foreign films throughout the year; typically, there's a choice of two films each evening.

Outdoor libations are on tap at **Victoria Row,** on pedestrian-only Richmond Street behind the Confederation Centre. Several restaurants and pubs cluster here and serve meals and drinks on street-side patios; some offer live music. The row is a popular destination for university students and younger locals.

For live Celtic-flavored music and occasional roast beef buffet dinners, head no farther than the fun and popular **Olde Dublin Pub,** above the Claddagh Room (see above) at 131 Sydney St. (*©* 902/892-6992). **Myron's,** at 151 Kent St. (*©* 902/892-4375), features a dance club and cabaret located on two floors with a robust 22,000 square feet of entertainment space; performers range from country to rock.

## 6 Kings County

After a visit to Charlottetown and the island's central towns, Kings County comes as a bit of a surprise. It's far more tranquil and uncluttered than Queens County (Anne's reach is much diminished here), and the landscapes feature woodlots alternating with corn, grain, and potato fields. Although much is made of the county's two great commercial centers on the coast—Souris and Montague—it's good to keep in mind that each of these has a population of around 1,500. In some parts of North America, that wouldn't even rate a dot on the map.

Don't arrive here expecting county attractions to go out of their way to amuse and entertain you. You'll have to do that yourself. It's prime biking territory, and walks on the empty beaches are a good tonic if you suffer from a hectic schedule in your non-vacation life. Long drives in the country with occasional stops are likewise relaxing.

If you're headed to southeastern Kings County from Charlottetown, you'll pass Orwell and its historic sites. See the listing earlier in this chapter, in Queens County.

### ESSENTIALS

**GETTING THERE**    Several main roads—including Highways 1, 2, 3, and 4—connect eastern PEI with Charlottetown and western points. The ferry to Nova Scotia sails from Woods Island on the south coast. See "Exploring Prince Edward Island," earlier in this chapter, for more information.

**VISITOR INFORMATION**    There's a provincial **Visitor Information Centre** (© **902/687-7030**) at 95 Main St. in Souris, open daily (hours vary) from mid-June to mid-October.

## MURRAY RIVER & MURRAY HARBOUR

It's not especially hard to guess the name of the family that originally settled this area—it seems that "Murray" is appended to every natural landmark of note. These two small and tidy villages offer little drama, but lots of repose. It's hard to imagine a better place to listen to the crickets and the wind in the trees. As you drive, watch for the tight lines of buoys in the coastal waterways: The noted blue mussels are cultivated in mesh bags suspended from ropes attached to these buoys, and then shipped world-wide to great acclaim.

### EXPLORING THE MURRAYS

Seals are practically as common as crows in this part of PEI. You just have to know where to look. The best way to view these sleek creatures is close-up, from the water. Visit the island's largest **seal colony** 𝔾𝔾 with **Marine Adventures Seal Watching** (© **800/496-2494** or 902/962-2494; www.sealwatching.com), based in Murray River. You'll travel in enclosed boats (tours offered rain or shine) and see seals, mussel farms, herons, and, with luck, bald eagles. Tours are offered daily in summer; the cost is C$18 (US$14) adults, C$15 (US$12) students and seniors, C$12 (US$9.50) children and students. Allow at least 2 hours for the entire trip.

Younger children rarely fail to enjoy **King's Castle Provincial Park** 𝔾 (© **902/ 962-7422**), an old-fashioned kiddy wonderland of the sort that was popular in the 1950s and 1960s. This pleasant picnic park, on the shores of the Murray River (there's swimming at a small beach), features life-size storybook characters scattered about field and woodlands. Kids can visit with Goldilocks or the Three Little Pigs, then scamper about the array of playground equipment or get an ice cream at the park's canteen. It's open daily from 9am to 9pm from mid-June to mid-October; admission is free. The park is on Route 348 just east of the town of Murray River, on the south bank of the river.

A couple of beaches are worthy of note: A short drive from Murray River along the north bank of the river is remote and peaceful **Poverty Beach** 𝔾𝔾. Dunes back this long strand of eastward-facing beach. You can park at the end of the road and walk along the beach watching for bird life. Swimming is problematic; the beach is pebbly at low tide, and the currents can sometimes be troublesome. But it's a great getaway: I spent an hour here on a glorious August afternoon and didn't see another soul. North of Poverty Beach is **Panmure Island Provincial Park.** The island is connected to the mainland via a sand-dune isthmus. The contrast between the white sand on the ocean side and the red-sand beach on the inside cove is striking. It's a lovely spot, with swimming on the ocean side and views northward to a striking lighthouse.

### WHERE TO STAY

**Forest and Stream Cottages**    These five cottages are located on 8 hectares (20 acres) of peaceful woodlands near a narrow lake and the site of an old gristmill. The grounds are shady, lovely, and laced with nature trails; you can also swim in the lake or use the rowboats and life jackets for free. The cottages, however, are fairly basic, with 1950s-style kitchenettes and linoleum floors, TVs, screened-in porches with picnic tables and gas grills outside.

Fox River Rd. (off Rte. 18), Murray Harbour, PEI C0A 1V0. (✆ **800/227-9943** or 902/962-3537. Fax 902/962-2130. www. forestandsteamcottages.com. 5 cottages (3 1-bedroom, 2 2-bedroom). Mid-June to mid-Sept C$85–C$125 (US$68–US$100), slightly lower May to mid-June and mid-Sept to Oct. MC, V. Closed Nov–Apr. Small pets allowed. **Amenities:** Bike rentals; laundry facility. *In room:* TV, kitchenette, no phone.

**Fox River Cottages**   These modern two-bedroom cottages with kitchenettes are beautifully situated on 5.2 hectares (13 acres) down a winding dirt road at the edge of a field overlooking the islands of Murray Bay. The cottages are tidy and furnished with televisions and VCRs. The cabins are near one another, but staggered to create a sense of privacy. You can relax on the screened porches, or wander to the river beach and dabble around in the canoe. One unit has a woodstove, and all have electric heat and gas barbecues for evening grilling. If you have a croquet set, by all means bring it. The cottages rent by the week for C$550–C$615 (US$440–US$492) per week, double occupancy.

Machon Point Rd., Murray Harbour, PEI C0A 1V0. (✆ **902/962-2881.** www.foxriver.ca. 5 units. C$85–C$95 (US$68–US$76). Off-season rates available. V. Closed Nov–May. **Amenities:** Laundry facility. *In room:* TV/VCR, kitchenette, coffeemaker, no phone.

# MONTAGUE

Montague is the region's main commercial hub, but it's a hub in low gear. It's compact and attractive, with a handsome business district on a pair of flanking hills sloping down to a bridge across the Montague River. (A century and a half ago, the town was called Montague Bridge.) Shipbuilding was the economic mainstay in the 19th century; today, it's dairy and tobacco.

## EXPLORING THE OUTDOORS

**Cruise Manada** ((✆ **800/986-3444** or 902/838-3444; www.tourpei.ca/seals) offers seal- and bird-watching tours daily during peak season aboard restored fishing boats; the cost is C$21 (US$17) adults, C$19 (US$15) seniors and students, C$11 (US$8.40) children under 13. Trips depart from the marina on the Montague River, just below the visitor center in the old railway depot; four daily depart in July and August, fewer from mid-May to June and in September. Reservations are advised. Allow at least 2 hours.

Southeast of Montague (en route to Murray River) is the **Buffaloland Provincial Park** ((✆ **902/652-8950**), where you'll spot a small herd of buffalo. These were a gift to PEI from the province of Alberta, and they now number about 25. Walk down the 90m (300-ft.) fenced-in corridor into the paddock and ascend the wooden platform for the best view of the shaggy beasts. Often they're hunkered down at the far end of the meadow, but they sometimes wander near. The park is right off Route 4; watch for signs. Open year-round.

A few minutes north of Buffaloland on Route 4, between Route 216 and Route 317, is the **Harvey Moore Wildlife Management Area** ((✆ **902/838-4834**), a delightful place for a stroll. Named after a revered local naturalist (1916–60) who created this sanctuary in 1949, the park's centerpiece is a 45-minute trail that loops around a pond and through varied ecosystems. A well-written nature guide is available free at the signboard. Watch especially for the waterfowl, with which Moore had an unusually close rapport. Avian visitors include black duck, blue-winged teal, ring-necked duck, pintail, and an abundance of Canada geese. Open daylight hours June to mid-September. Free admission.

**Brudenell River Provincial Park** (© **902/652-8966**) is one of the province's better-bred parks, and a great spot to work up an athletic glow on a sunny afternoon. On its 600 riverfront hectares (1,500 acres) you'll find two well-regarded golf courses, a golf academy, a full-blown resort (see below), tennis, lawn bowling, a wildflower garden, a playground, a campground, and nature trails. Kids' programs—including Frisbee golf, shoreline scavenger hunts, and crafts workshops—are scheduled daily in summer. You can also rent canoes, kayaks, and jet skis from private operators located within the park. The park is open daily mid-May to mid-October from 9am to 9pm; free admission. Head north of Montague on Route 4; then east on Route 3 to the park signs.

## WHERE TO STAY

**Rodd Brudenell River Resort** 🌟 *Kids*    The attractive Brudenell River Resort was built in 1991, and its sleek, open, and vaguely Frank Lloyd Wright–esque design reflects its recent vintage. It's an especially popular destination with golfers—it's set amid two golf courses that have been garnering plaudits from serious duffers in recent years. Guests choose between three types of rooms. The hotel proper has 51 well-appointed guest rooms, each with balcony or terrace. The upmarket Echelon Gold Cottages each have two bedrooms, cathedral ceilings, fireplaces, and large-screen TVs. The more basic Countryside Cabins are the best bet for those traveling on a budget; just beware that the detailing isn't of the highest quality, and the units are clustered together a bit oddly, like pavilions left over from some forgotten world exposition. In addition to the two excellent golf courses (one hosts a Golf Academy offering extensive lessons), the resort has indoor and outdoor pools. The dining room on the first level overlooks one of the golf courses. It's rather cavernous, but the high-backed chairs carve out a sense of intimacy. Breakfast and dinner are served; you'll enjoy what might be described as creative country-club cuisine, with entrees including charbroiled steak, sole in a puff pastry, and pasta primavera.

Rte. 3 (P.O. Box 67), Cardigan, PEI C0A 1G0. © **800/565-7633** or 902/652-2332. Fax 902/652-2886. www.rodd-hotels.ca. 165 units. C$188–C$331 (US$150–US$265) double, C$120–C$169 (US$96–US$162) cabin, C$233–C$504 (US$186–US$403) cottage. AE, DC, MC, V. Closed mid-Oct to mid-May. Pets allowed with C$10 (US$7) fee per pet per night. **Amenities:** 2 restaurants; 2 bars; indoor and outdoor pools; golf course (with academy); 2 tennis courts; fitness center; Jacuzzi; sauna; canoe/kayak/bike rental; children's center; babysitting; dry cleaning. *In room:* A/C, TV, dataport, minibar (some units), kitchenette (some units), fridge (some units), coffeemaker, hair dryer, iron.

**Rodd Marina Inn & Suites** 🌟    The Marina Inn has the casually modern feel of the sort of midsize chain hotel you'd expect to find on a strip at the edge of a midsize town. With this difference: It boasts a great location tucked off Montague's main street, right along the Montague River (boat tours available), and smack on a spur of the Confederation Trail. The hotel's rooms are mostly standard-size and equipped with the usual amenities. A dozen "studio-suites" (their term) offer a small sitting area along with microwave, refrigerator, and Jacuzzi. Be sure to request a room on the riverside for the view.

115 Sackville St. (P.O. Box 1540), Montague, PEI C0A 1R0. © **800/565-7633** or 902/838-4075. Fax 902/838-4180. www.rodd-hotels.ca. 52 units. C$115–C$183 (US$90–US$146) double. Rates include continental breakfast. AE, DC, MC, V. **Amenities:** Small exercise room. *In room:* A/C, TV/VCR, coffeemaker, hair dryer.

## WHERE TO DINE

**Windows on the Water Café** 🌟 SEAFOOD    If you haven't yet dined on PEI mussels, this is the place to let loose. The blue mussels are steamed in a root *mirepoix* (soup base), with sesame, ginger, and garlic. It's a winner. Main courses include sole stuffed with crab and scallop and topped with hollandaise, and the chef's peppered steak—a filet mignon served with sweet peppers, red onion, and mushrooms in a peppercorn sauce. Lunches are lighter, with choices that include grilled chicken and mandarin salad, and homemade fish cakes. The appealing and open dining room features press-back chairs and a lively buzz, but if the weather's agreeable, angle for a seat under the canopy on the deck.

106 Sackville St. (corner of Main St.), Montague. ✆ 902/838-2080. Reservations recommended. Main courses C$7.50–C$9.95 (US$6–US$8) at lunch, C$15–C$21 (US$12–US$17) at dinner. AE, DC, MC, V. June–Oct daily 11:30am–9:30pm. Closed Nov–May.

## SOURIS & NORTHEAST PEI

Some 42km (26 miles) northeast of Montague is the town of Souris, an active fishing town attractively set on a gentle hill overlooking the harbor. Souris (pronounced Soo-ree) is French for "mouse"—so named because early settlers were beset by voracious field mice, which destroyed their crops. The town is the launching point for an excursion to the Magdalen Islands, and it makes a good base for exploring northeastern PEI, which is considered by more urban residents as the island's outback—remote and sparsely populated. You'll also find it somewhat less agricultural and more forested, especially away from the coast, than the rest of the island.

### EXPLORING THE AREA

Several good beaches can be found ringing this wedge-shaped peninsula that points like an accusing finger toward Nova Scotia's Cape Breton Island. **Red Point Provincial Park** ((✆ **902/357-3075**) is 13km (8 miles) northeast of Souris. Open from June until mid-September, it offers a handsome beach and supervised swimming, along with a campground that's popular with families; sites cost C$19 to C$25 (US$15–US$20). Another inviting and often empty **beach** 𝒢 is a short distance northeast at Basin Head, which features a "singing sands" beach that allegedly sings (actually, it's more like squeak) when you walk on it. The dunes here are especially appealing. Look also for the nearby **Basin Head Fisheries Museum** 𝒢 ((✆ **902/357-7233**), a provincially operated museum that offers insight into the life of the inshore fisherman. Admission is C$3.50 (US$2.50), free for under 12. Open daily in peak season from 9am to 7pm, to 5pm in spring and fall; closed October through May.

At the island's far eastern tip is the aptly named **East Point Lighthouse** 𝒢 ((✆ **902/357-2106**). You can simply enjoy the dramatic setting or take a tour of the building (mid-June to Aug only). Ask for your East Point ribbon while you're here. If you make it to the North Cape Lighthouse on the western shore, you'll receive a Traveller's Award documenting that you've traveled PEI tip-to-tip. Admission to the lighthouse is C$3 (US$2.40) adults, C$2 (US$1.60) seniors and students, C$1 (US80¢) children. Closed September to mid-June.

A spur of the Confederation Trail ends in Souris, making this a good spot from which to launch a bike excursion of the area. One suggested day trip would be to link to the main trunk trail, and then venture northeast to East Point Lighthouse.

### WHERE TO STAY

**Inn at Bay Fortune** 𝒢𝒢   This exceptionally attractive, shingled compound on 18 hectares (46 acres) was built by playwright Elmer Harris in 1910 as a summer home, and it quickly became the nucleus for a colony of artists, actors, and writers. (Most recently the home was owned by Canadian actress Colleen Dewhurst, who sold it to current innkeeper David Wilmer in 1988.) Wilmer pulled out the stops in renovating, bringing it back from the brink of decay. In 1998 he added a wing with six new rooms (two with Jacuzzis), including the wonderful North Tower Room 4, with a high ceiling and a balcony overlooking the lodge and bay beyond. (My favorite room remains South Tower Room 4, which requires a schlep up a narrow staircase, but once you're in this high lair it feels a world removed.) The newer rooms are larger than the older ones, but all are quite cozy with a mix of antiques and custom-made furniture. Eight of the rooms have wood-burning fireplaces, and six have propane fireplaces. The inn is also home to one of PEI's best restaurants (see below).

Rte. 310 (off Rte. 2), Bay Fortune, PEI C0A 2B0. © **902/687-3745** or off season 860/296-1348. Fax 902/687-3540. www.innatbayfortune.com. 18 units. C$150–C$335 (US$120–US$268) double. Rates include full breakfast. DC, MC, V. Closed mid-Oct to mid-May. **Amenities:** Restaurant.

**Inn at Spry Point** ✰✰ *Finds*    This inn was originally founded in the 1970s on remote Spry Point as a United Nations–funded prototype of a self-sufficient community affiliated with the New Alchemy Institute—think windmills, solar power, greenhouses, trout ponds, the whole shooting match. But oil prices dropped, interest in conservation waned, and the experiment failed. Enter David Wilmer, owner of Inn at Bay Fortune (see above). He bought the 32-hectare (80-acre) property and has undertaken the monumental task of bringing it up to date. All 15 rooms have canopied king-size beds and are tastefully appointed with comfortable sitting areas. Most have their own private balconies, and four have a garden terrace. Outside, the location is top-rate—2,440m (8,000 ft.) of undeveloped shorefront that invite exploration—and you can walk along trails that traverse red-clay cliffs with views of the Northumberland Strait. Later, dine in the outstanding contemporary **dining room** ✰✰ featuring locally grown organic vegetables and island seafood; prix-fixe meals cost about C$45 (US$36) per person, and you can also order a la carte.

Souris RR no. 4, Little Pond, PEI C0A 2B0. © **902/583-2400**. Fax 902/583-2176. www.innatsprypoint.com. 15 units. C$185–C$335 (US$148–US$268) double. Rates include full breakfast. DC, MC, V. Closed Oct to late May. **Amenities:** Restaurant. *In room:* A/C.

**The Matthew House Inn** ✰    Kimberly and Franco Olivieri came to PEI on vacation from Italy in 1995. They fell in love with the island's grand old homes, and before their holiday had ended they found themselves owners of this fine B&B. ("My husband is very impulsive by nature," says Kimberly.) Located atop a pleasant lawn overlooking the harbor and ferry to the Magdalen Islands, this stately Victorian dates from 1885 and maintains many of the original flourishes inside and out. Eastlake-style furnishings and William Morris touches give the place an architectural richness without seeming too grandmotherly about it; for big families, a two-bedroom cottage adjacent to the inn rents by the week, sleeps up to seven, and is equipped with a kitchen and laundry. This place will be appreciated by those passionate about historic architecture.

15 Breakwater St. (P.O. Box 151), Souris, PEI C0A 2B0. © **902/687-3461**. Fax 902/687-3461. www.matthewhouse inn.com. 6 units. C$95–C$210 (US$76–US$168) double. Rates include full breakfast. AE, MC, V. Closed early Sept to mid-June. Children over 10 welcome. **Amenities:** Dining room; laundry service. *In room:* TV/VCR, hair dryer.

## WHERE TO DINE
**Inn at Bay Fortune** ✰✰✰ CREATIVE CONTEMPORARY    To fully appreciate a meal at the Inn at Bay Fortune, arrive early enough to wander the gardens behind the inn. The herbs and edible flowers are a short walk from the kitchen; a little further beyond is the 1.2 hectare (3-acre) vegetable garden. This is good introduction to the local products emphasized on the menu. Young executive chef Renée Lavallée worked

## An Excursion to the Magdalen Islands

The **Magdalen Islands (Les Isles de la Madeleine),** located a 5-hour ferry ride north of PEI, consist of a dozen low, sandy islands, linked to one another by sand spits. About 14,000 people live here, and the islands are dotted with peaceful fishing villages and farming communities. The islands, part of the province of Québec, also boast some 299km (186 miles) of beaches, a fact that has not gone unnoticed by urban Québecois in search of leisure. (The island is linked by air and a 2-day ferry from Québec.) It's also famous for its persistent winds, which rake across the Gulf and find little resistance here.

Advance planning is needed for a trip to the islands, since the demand for accommodations often outstrips supply. A free island tourist guide is available by calling © 877/624-4437. On the Web, head to www.tourismeilesde lamadeleine.com.

Ferry service from Souris to Cap-aux-Meules is provided by the **Coopérative de Transport Maritime** (© 888/986-3278 or 418/986-3278; www.ctma.ca), also known as the CTMA. The *Lucy Maud Montgomery* holds 95 cars and 400 passengers. Boats sail 10 times weekly in summer; the schedule is limited to six weekly boats in the off season, so call for information. One-way summer rates are C$41 (US$33) adults, C$34 (US$27) seniors, C$20 (US$16) children 5 to 12, and C$77 (US$62) for a normal automobile. Those rates plunge 30 to 50 percent in the off season.

with founding chef Michael Smith to develop the inn's regional cuisine and its vaunted openness—how many restaurants feature a KITCHEN—WELCOME sign inviting diners to stop in for a visit? The place is wildly successful, with an always-shifting menu that rarely fails to produce a winning meal.

For those with a serious interest in cooking, ask about the coveted chef's table (a glass-enclosed booth within the kitchen in which dinner is served just once nightly; parties dine on seven courses) and the five course tasting menu.

Rte. 310 (off Rte. 2), Bay Fortune, PEI C0A 2B0. © 902/687-3745. Reservations strongly recommended. Main courses C$24–C$32 (US$19–US$26); tasting menu about C$70 (US$56); chef's table about C$95 (US$76). AE, MC, V. Daily 5–9pm. Closed mid-Oct to late May.

## ST. PETER'S BAY & ENVIRONS

Eastern Kings County attracts few tourists—other than those speeding through en route to East Point. Few commercial services are located here, and it's easy to zip right through without much of a second glance. Yet it's well worth slowing down—the pastoral landscapes are sublime, and the best vistas are found off the paved roads. It's also an area blessed with a number of appealing bike routes, and what may be the island's best golf course. This region has few prominent natural landmarks, with the exception of St. Peter's Bay—a narrow and attractive inlet that twists eastward from the coast. As such, impatient travelers may grow irritated, wishing for more clearly defined destinations. The only cure is to avoid hurrying, take a more desultory path, and welcome the opportunity to get lost.

## EXPLORING THE AREA

Follow Route 313 along the north shore of St. Peter's Bay to its tip, and you'll come to the **Greenwich Dunes** ⚅, a stunning area of migrating sand dunes capped with grasses. You'll find unique, wind-carved dunes here. This remarkable region was slated for vacation home development up until 1997, when it was acquired by Parks Canada and added as an extension to Prince Edward Island National Park.

The town of **Mount Stewart** (on Rte. 2 just over the county line in Queens County) is located near the confluence of several spurs of the **Confederation Trail,** the island-wide recreation trail that's being carved from an abandoned rail line. The Mount Stewart area is home to some of the better-developed and better-maintained segments of the trail.

The trail's popularity and potential didn't go unnoticed by a father-and-son team, who opened **Trailside Café & Inn** (✆ **888/704-6595** or 902/676-3130; www.trailside. ca) and set up a bike rental operation a few years ago (see below for a review of the restaurant and hotel). Today, they rent a fleet of some 80 mountain bikes, at rates of C$15 (US$12) per half day, C$20 (US$16) per full day, and C$80 (US$64) per week. The staff is very helpful with suggestions and directions, and they can arrange for a van shuttle to pick you up at your destination if you'd prefer a one-way trip. Among the most popular trips is the northeast ride toward **East Point** (64km/40 miles), which takes you over a few low train trestles retrofitted for bikes, and along St. Peter's Bay.

**Greenwich Interpretation Centre** ⚅    An annex of the island's National Park, this interpretive center offers a look at the unique dune formations adjacent to St. Peter's Bay. In addition to programs and displays, there are guided tours for individuals and groups. You can also take a cool break by making use of the beach, where supervised swimming is allowed from late June to the end of August. There are also bathrooms, changing facilities, showers, and an observation tower here. A visit here is worth at least 20 minutes of your time.

Rte. 313, Greenwich, Prince Edward Island National Park. ✆ **902/961-2514.** Call for rates. Late May to Oct daily, summer 9am–7pm, spring and fall 10am–4pm.

## WHERE TO STAY & DINE

**Trailside Café & Inn**    The Trailside Café is housed in a 1937 grocery store that's been converted to an inn, cafe, and outdoor adventure center (see "Exploring the

---

### ⟨Finds⟩ Golf along the Gulf

Hidden away in this quiet part of the island is the **Links at Crowbush Cove** ⚅⚅⚅ (✆ **800/235-8909** or 902/368-5761), considered by many to be the island's best golf course for both its aesthetics and its subtle challenges. (It captured 5 stars from *Golf Digest*.) The 6,901-yard, par 72 course, built in 1994, is located along the Gulf of St. Lawrence; it has nine water holes and eight that run next to the dunes. (Talk about your sand trap!) The 11th tee tends to be a bottleneck, as golfers are momentarily distracted from their game by the sweeping views up and down the coast. Reserved tee times are available. The course is located west of the village of Morell; take Route 2 to Route 350 and drive northwest to the course. For more information, call or write P.O. Box 204, Morell, PEI C0A 1S0.

Area," above, regarding bike rentals). There's nothing fancy here, but the four rooms (each with private bathroom) are comfortable and simply furnished and have nice touches like radiant heat under hardwood floors. Few guests spend much time lingering in their rooms. The clientele consists primarily of bicyclists, who migrate here for its location smack on the Confederation Trail, but everyone benefits from the live local music: thrice-weekly shows of Celtic or gospel music.

The funky, informal cafe on the first floor is a fine spot for hanging out, especially when there's live music. Dinner and entertainment packages invariably sell out; reservations are strongly suggested. The cafe serves lunch and dinner daily in summer. The menu is basic, but everything is homemade and tasty. Soups and chowders are perfect for drizzly or blustery days; there's also a smoked salmon plate, lobster rolls, broiled scallops, pizza, and linguine with vegetables.

109 Main St., Mount Stewart, PEI C0A 1T0. (℃ 888/704-6595 or 902/676-3130. www.trailside.ca. 4 units. C$80 (US$64) double. MC, V. Closed late Sept to mid-June. **Amenities:** Restaurant, bike rentals. *In room:* TV, no phone.

## 7 Prince County

Prince County encompasses the western end of PEI and offers a varied mix of lush agricultural land, rugged coastline, and unpopulated sandy beaches. This is Prince Edward Island with calluses. With a few exceptions, the region is a bit more ragged around the edges in a working-farm, working-waterfront kind of way. It typically lacks the pristine-village charm of Kings County or much of Queens County.

Within this unrefined landscape, however, you'll find pockets of considerable charm, such as the village of Victoria on the south coast at the county line, and in Tyne Valley near the north coast, which is reminiscent of a Cotswold hamlet.

In addition, the **Confederation Trail** offers quiet access to the rolling countryside throughout much of northwest Prince County. Several provincial parks here rank among the most inviting on the island.

### ESSENTIALS

**GETTING THERE**    Route 2 is the main highway connecting Prince County with the rest of the island. Feeder roads typically lead from or to Route 2. The Confederation Bridge from the mainland connects to Prince County at Borden Point, southeast of Summerside.

**VISITOR INFORMATION**    The best source of travel information for the county is **Gateway Village** (℃ 902/437-8570) at the end of the Confederation Bridge. It's open daily year-round.

### VICTORIA 🕸🕸

The town of Victoria—located a short detour off Route 1 between the Confederation Bridge and Charlottetown—is a tiny and unusually scenic village that has attracted a number of artists, boutique owners, and craftspeople. The village is perfect for strolling—parking is near the wharf and off the streets, keeping the narrow lanes free for foot traffic. Wander the short, shady lanes while admiring the architecture, much of which is in elemental farmhouse style, clad in clapboard or shingle and constructed with sharply creased gables. (Some elaborate Victorians break the mold.) What makes the place so singular is that the village, which was first settled in 1767, has utterly escaped the creeping sprawl that has plagued so many otherwise attractive places. The entire village consists of 4 square blocks, which are surrounded by potato fields and the Northumberland Strait. It's not hard to imagine that the village looked much the same a century ago.

## EXPLORING VICTORIA

The **Victoria Seaport Museum** (no phone) is located in a shingled, square lighthouse near the town parking lot. (You can't miss it.) You'll find a rustic local history museum with the usual assortment of artifacts from the past century or so. In summer, it's open daily except Monday from noon to 5pm; admission is by donation.

In the middle of town is the well-regarded **Victoria Playhouse** (© 902/658-2025). Built in 1913 as a community hall, the building has a unique raked stage (it drops 18cm/7 in. over 6.5m/21 ft.) to create the illusion of space, four beautiful stained-glass lamps, and a proscenium arch (also unusual for a community hall). Plays staged here from late June through September attract folks out from Charlottetown for the night. It's hard to say what is more enjoyable: the high quality of the acting or the wonderful big-night-out air of a professional play in a small town where nothing else is going on. There's also a Monday-night concert series, with performers offering up everything from traditional folk to Latin jazz. Most tickets are C$22 (US$18) adults, C$20 (US$16) seniors, and C$18 (US$15) students, though some are priced higher; matinees cost about C$16 (US$13).

Among the two dozen or so businesses in the village, the most intriguing is **Island Chocolates** (© 800/565-2320 or 902/658-2320), where delicious Belgian-style chocolates are made; the shop is open most days from June through September. You'll also find a quilt maker, a candle maker, a used-book store, art galleries, and an antiques shop.

## WHERE TO STAY

**Orient Hotel**   You have to book an entire week to stay at the Orient, but it's worth it if you like peace and quiet. The hotel has been a Victoria mainstay for years—a 1926 guide notes that the inn had 20 rooms at C$2.50 (US$1.65) per night (of course, back then a trip to the bathroom required a walk to the carriage house). It has been modernized in recent years (all rooms now have private bathrooms), but it retains much of its antique charm. The century-old building with its yellow shingles and maroon trim is at the edge of the village overlooking potato fields lurid with purple blooms in late summer. Rooms are painted in warm pastel tones and furnished eclectically with flea-market antiques. Although some of the updating has diminished the charm—such as the velour furniture in the lobby and the industrial carpeting—the place has a friendly low-key demeanor, much like the village itself. The enthusiastic owners have also added a combination television/game room set up for cribbage and crokinole (an old-fashioned maritime game), and ceilidhs (Celtic folk dances) have been known to happen, too.

Mrs. Proffit's Tea Shop, on the first floor, serves lunch and afternoon tea (open daily noon–5pm) and also has a growing reputation for its scones; the light lunches are appropriate to a tearoom, and they include tea sandwiches, lobster rolls, and soups and salads.

34 Main St. (mailing address P.O. Box 55, Victoria, PEI C0A 2G0). © 800/565-6743 or 902/658-2503. Fax 902/658-2078. 6 units. C$79–C$119 (US$63–US$95) double. Rates include full breakfast. AE, MC, V. Closed mid-Oct to mid-May. Not suitable for children under 12. **Amenities:** Tearoom. *In room:* TV.

## WHERE TO DINE

**Landmark Café** CAFE   Located across from the Victoria Playhouse, the Landmark Café occupies a small, cozy storefront teeming with shelves filled with crockery, pots, jars, and more, some of which is for sale. But the effect is more funky than Ye Olde Quainte, and the limited menu is very inviting. The steamed mussels and vine leaves with feta cheese are a favorite of regulars. Other offerings include salads, lasagna, meat pie, and tarragon-steamed salmon.

12 Main St. © **902/658-2286.** Reservations recommended. Sandwiches around C$5.50 (US$4.50); main courses C$11–C$16 (US$9–US$13). MC, V. Daily 11am–9:30pm. Closed mid-Sept to late June.

## TYNE VALLEY ☞

The village of Tyne Valley is just off Malpeque Bay and is one of the most attractive and pastoral areas of western PEI. There's little to do here, but much to admire. Verdant barley and potato fields surround the village of gingerbread homes, and azure inlets encroach here and there; these are the arms of the bay, which is famous for its succulent Malpeque oysters. A former 19th-century shipbuilding center, the village now attracts artisans and others in search of a quiet lifestyle. A handful of good restaurants, inns, and shops caters to visitors.

### EXPLORING TYNE VALLEY

Just north of the village on Route 12 is the lovely **Green Park Provincial Park** ☞ (© **902/831-7912**), open from mid-June through early September. Once the site of an active shipyard, the 88-hectare (219-acre) park is now a lush riverside destination with emerald lawns and leafy trees, and it has the feel of a turn-of-the-20th-century estate, which, in fact, it was. In the heart of the park is the extravagant gingerbread mansion (1865) once owned by James Yeo, a merchant, shipbuilder, and landowner who in his time was the island's wealthiest and most powerful man.

The historic Yeo House and the **Green Park Shipbuilding Museum** (© **902/831-7947**), open June through September, are now the park's centerpieces. Managed by the Prince Edward Island Museum and Heritage Foundation, exhibits in two buildings provide a good view of the prosperous life of a shipbuilder and the golden age of PEI shipbuilding. The museum and house are open daily in summer 10am to 5pm. Admission is C$5 (US$4) plus tax adults; free for children under 12.

Frequent musical and stage performances are held summers at the 125-seat **Brittania Hall Theatre** (© **902/831-2191**), on Route 178. Prices are reasonable, usually under C$10 (US$8) for both plays and concerts. Call for information on upcoming shows.

When leaving the area, consider taking the highly scenic drive along the bay on Route 12 from Tyne Valley to MacDougall.

### WHERE TO STAY

**Green Park Provincial Park** ☞☞ (© **902/831-7912**) may be the most gracious and lovely park on the island, and offers camping on 58 grassy sites overlooking an arm of Malpeque Bay. Cost is C$19 to C$25 (US$15–US$20) per night.

**Caernarvon Cottages, B&B, and Gardens** 𝘒𝘪𝘥𝘴    The sense of quiet and the views over Malpeque Bay across the road are the lure at this attractive, well-maintained cottage compound on 2 hectares (5 acres) a few minutes' drive from Tyne Valley. The four modern (ca. 1990) knotty pine cottages are furnished simply but comfortably. Each has two bedrooms and a sleeping loft, outdoor gas barbecue, cathedral ceiling, and porch with a bay view. This is a good choice if you're looking to get away, but it's also popular with families—there's a playground out back, so it may not be the best option for a romantic escape, even with the pretty 10m (34-ft.) high gazebo on the lawn just steps from the bay. (The gazebo is encircled by three large flower beds filled with peonies, lilies, and hardy roses.) Three simply furnished rooms are available in the main house; breakfast is included in those rates.

4697 Hwy. 12, Bayside, PEI (mailing address: Richmond RR1, C0B 1Y0). © **800/514-9170** or 902/854-3418. www. cottagelink.com/caernarvon. 7 units. C$80–C$100 (US$64–US$80) double, cottages C$500 (US$400) weekly. Rates include full breakfast (inn only). V. Cottages closed mid-Sept to mid-June. Pets in cottages only. *In room:* TV/VCR (some units), hair dryer, iron, no phone.

**Doctor's Inn** ⭐ *Value*    A stay at the Doctor's Inn is a bit like visiting relatives you didn't know you had. Upstairs in this handsome in-town farmhouse are just two guest rooms, which share a bathroom. (Note that you could rent both for less than the cost of a room at some other inns.) There's an upstairs sitting area, and the extensive organic gardens out back to peruse. It's a pleasant retreat, and innkeepers Jean and Paul Offer do a fine job of making guests feel relaxed and at home. There's also one cottage available for rent; the rate ranges from C$360 to C$450 (US$288–US$360) per week.

The Offers also serve up one of Atlantic Canada's most memorable dining experiences. They cater to a maximum of six people on any night at a single sitting. You first gather for appetizers and wine in the sitting room, then move to the large oval dining-room table. The extraordinary salads feature produce from the Offers' famous garden (they grow more than two dozen kinds of lettuce), and you'll have a choice of entrees, which are cooked on the woodstove in an old-fashioned kitchen. Look for scallops, arctic char, salmon, veal, or whatever else is fresh. Desserts are fresh-baked and wonderful. Reservations are requested at least 24 hours in advance; dinner is served at 7pm, a four-course meal with wine for about C$40 (US$32) per person.

Rte. 167, Tyne Valley, PEI C0B 2C0. © **902/831-3057.** www.peisland.com/doctorsinn. 2 units, neither with private bathroom. C$60–C$75 (US$48–US$60) double. All rates include breakfast. MC, V. "Well-mannered" pets allowed. **Amenities:** Dining room. *In room:* No phone.

## WHERE TO DINE

Also see the "Doctor's Inn," above.

**The Shipwright's Café** REGIONAL    This locally popular restaurant moved to the village of Margate in the summer of 2001. It's elegant yet informal, and you'd be comfortable here in either neat jeans or pre-dinner sport clothes. Expect good service, a modest but useful wine list, and salads with greens from the Offers's organic gardens, just down the street (see Doctor's Inn above). Justly popular dishes include the local oysters broiled with spinach and cheese, and the seafood chowder, which is rich and loaded with plump mussels.

11869 Rte. 6, Margate, PEI C0B 1M0. © **902/836-3403.** Reservations recommended in summer. Lunch C$9.95–C$17 (US$8–US$14); dinner C$15–C$20 (US$12–US$16), more for lobster. MC, V. June–Sept daily 11:30am–8:30pm. Closed Oct–May.

# 7

# Newfoundland & Labrador

If you have but one atom of adventure in you, you'll know it after a few minutes poring over a map of Newfoundland and Labrador. Your electrons begin to pulse madly. Your heart races. All those isolated harbors! All those miles of remote lakes! And those extraordinary names that dot the map: Jerry's Nose, Snook's Arm, Leading Tickles, Heart's Delight, Happy Adventure, Chapel Island, St. Bride's, Mistaken Point, Misery Hill, Breakheart Point, Cape Pine, Shuffle Board.

Newfoundland and Labrador might be the Eastern seaboard's last best place. (These two distinct geographic areas are administered as one province, so sometimes the phrase "Newfoundland and Labrador" refers to a single place, sometimes to two places.) Wild, windswept, and isolated, the province often reveals a powerful paradox. Although the landscape is rocky and raw—at times it looks as if the glaciers had receded only a year or two ago—the residents often display a genuine warmth that makes visitors feel right at home. Tourists only recently started arriving here in any number, and long-time residents more often than not like to chat, offer advice, and hear your impressions of their home. Travelers who are usually reluctant to ask questions of locals for fear of embarrassment usually drop their hesitation after an encounter or two.

An excursion to The Rock—as the island of Newfoundland is commonly called—is magical in many ways. Not only in the extraordinary northern landscape and the gracious people, but also in the rich history that catches many first-time visitors off guard. This is where European civilization made landfall in the New World—by both the Vikings and the later fishermen and settlers in the wake of John Cabot's arrival here in 1497—and you'll find traces of that rich legacy at almost every turn. Although other parts of North America might claim an equally historic lineage, there are few places in the New World where one feels as if not a whole lot has transpired since the first settlers sailed into the harbor some centuries ago. History isn't buried here; it's right on the surface.

One last note: There's some to-and-fro among travelers about how to accent *Newfoundland*. Correctly done, there's a little bit of emphasis on the final syllable, but it's subtle. Here's a trick. Recite this bit of doggerel: "You just won't understand, 'Til you've been to Newfoundland." Now drop everything but the last word.

## 1 Exploring Newfoundland & Labrador

Don't let the maps of the Atlantic Provinces fool you. Newfoundland (and sometimes Labrador) is commonly published as an inset map alongside Nova Scotia, Prince Edward Island, and New Brunswick. Carefully note the scale. Whereas an inch might equal 30km (19 miles) in Nova Scotia, it may be 60 or 70km (37 or 43 miles) in Newfoundland. The amount of time to travel anywhere on the island goes up accordingly.

The island has about the same landmass as Pennsylvania, but that's misleading because the island is twisted and pulled as if made of taffy, and thus it seems bigger when you're traveling from one end to another. One example: that peninsula that extends northward along the west coast? It takes about 8 or 9 hours to drive from Port aux Basques (where the ferry from Nova Scotia docks) to the tip at St. Anthony's.

A couple of weeks is enough for a bare-bones tour of the whole island, although you'll be frustrated by all that gets left out. You're better off selecting a few regions and focusing on those.

For those arriving by ferry: If you've got less than a week, you should probably come and go via Port aux Basques and focus on Gros Morne National Park, which is commonly the highlight of a stay here, especially for outdoor-oriented travelers. If you're planning on at least 2 weeks, you should consider arriving and leaving the island at opposite ports (see below), completing a traverse of the island.

For those arriving by air: St. John's is well situated for exploring the wonderful Avalon Peninsula, and the intriguing Bonavista Peninsula isn't too distant. If you have your heart set on venturing to Gros Morne or beyond, plan to spend a couple of weeks, or be prepared for some hours behind the wheel. It's about 7 to 8 hours straight driving from St. John's to the national park. The best option in this case would be to fly in to St. John's, and depart via Deer Lake.

## ESSENTIALS

**WEATHER & TIME**   The weather in Newfoundland might charitably be called "mercurial." You might very well experience all four seasons during a 1-week trip to the island—from relatively warm and sunny days (the average high temperature in summer is about 70°F/21°C) to the downright frigid (it often dips into the range of 40°F/4°C or lower on summer evenings). If you have a rain suit, bring it. When the rain pairs up with the high winds, the results can be, well, less than comforting.

Note that Newfoundland keeps its own clock, and "Newfoundland time" is a half-hour ahead of Atlantic time.

**VISITOR INFORMATION**   Visitor information centers aren't as numerous or well organized in Newfoundland as they are in Nova Scotia or Prince Edward Island, where almost every small community has a place to load up on brochures and ask questions. In Newfoundland, you're better off stocking up on maps and information either in St. John's or just after you disembark from the ferries, where excellent centers are maintained.

*The Newfoundland and Labrador Travel Guide,* published by the province's department of tourism, is hefty and helpful, with listings of all attractions and accommodations. Request a free copy before arriving by calling © **800/563-6353** or 709/729-2830. You can also request it by fax (709/729-1965), e-mail (tourisminfo@mail.gov.nf.ca), or mail (P.O. Box 8700, St. John's, NL A1B 4J6). The guide is available on the ferries and at the province's information centers.

Newfoundland is also better wired than you might expect when it comes to the Internet, and many residents and businesses maintain websites.

**GETTING THERE**   Air transportation to Newfoundland is typically through Gander or St. John's, although scheduled flights are also available to Deer Lake and St. Anthony. Flights originate in Montréal, Toronto, Halifax, and London, England. Airlines serving the island include **Air Canada** (© **888/AIR-CANA;** www.aircanada.com), **Air Labrador** (© **800/563-3042** or 709/6730; www.airlabrador.com), and

# Island of Newfoundland

**Provincial Airlines** (© **800/563-2800** or 709/576-1666; www.provair.com). Flight time from Toronto to St. John's is about 3 hours. Calgary-based **WestJet** (© **888/937-8538**; www.westjet.com) connects St. John's with Halifax, which can then be connected onward to Toronto and Calgary without switching airlines.

**Marine Atlantic** (© **800/341-7981**; www.marine-atlantic.ca) operates a year-round ferry service from North Sydney, Nova Scotia to Port aux Basques, with as many as three sailings each way daily during the peak summer season. The crossing is about 5 hours; one-way fares are C$27 (US$22) adults, plus C$77 (US$61) for an automobile. A seasonal ferry (summers only) also connects North Sydney with Argentia on the southwest tip of the Avalon Peninsula. This crossing is offered three times weekly in summer and takes 14 to 15 hours. The one-way fare is C$80 (US$64) adults, C$157 (US$128) for cars. On both ferries, children 5 to 12 years old ride for half-price (free for children under 5). Reserved reclining seats, sleeping berths, and private cabins are available.

Marine Atlantic also runs ferries to Argentia, Newfoundland, usually three times daily in summer, one to two times daily in the off season. One-way fares are C$157 (US$126) for cars, and C$76 (US$60) adults, C$68 (US$55) seniors, and C$38 (US$30) children 5 to 12. The ferry operates year-round, and the trip takes about 14 hours.

A much shorter ride on the M/V *Apollo* connects Blanc-Sablon, Labrador with St. Barbe, Newfoundland. The ride takes 20 minutes and costs C$22 (US$17) one-way for autos, C$11 (US$8.50) adults, C$8.75 (US$7) seniors, and C$5.50 (US$4.50) children ages 5 to 12. Call © **866/535-2567** for more information.

For all ferries, advance reservations are strongly advised during the peak travel season. As many as 100 cars have been backed up at Port aux Basques awaiting the next berth off the island. The reservation policy is quite fair: When you reserve over the phone with a credit card, you pay a C$25 (US$18) deposit. You can cancel or change your reservations up to 48 hours before departure for a full refund of your deposit. The balance is due at the terminal; you're required to check in at least 1 hour before sailing to hold your reservation. The terminals all have snack bars, restrooms with free showers, television lounges, and up-to-date facilities.

**GETTING AROUND**    Newfoundland has no rail service, but several bus lines connect the major ports and cities. **DRL Coachlines** (© **709/738-8088**) has one bus daily from Port aux Basques to St. John's. The trip takes 10 to 13½ hours, and the one-way fare is C$107 (US$86) adults, C$96 (US$77) seniors, and C$53 (US$42) for children.

To explore the countryside, you'll need a car. Major rental companies with fleets in Newfoundland include **Avis** (© **800/230-4898**), **Budget** (© **800/472-3325**), **Thrifty** (© **800/367-2277**), **National** (© **800/227-7368**), **Enterprise** (© **800/261-7331**), and **Rent-A-Wreck** (© **800/535-1391**).

Sock away some extra cash for gasoline when traveling the island. The price of fuel on Newfoundland tends to be a bit higher than in other Atlantic provinces.

## 2 The Great Outdoors

**BIKING**    Bike touring in Newfoundland is for the hearty. It's not that the hills are necessarily brutal (although many are). But the weather can be downright demoralizing. Expect more than a handful of blustery days, complete with horizontal rains that seem to swirl around from every direction. The happiest bike tourists seem to be those who allow themselves frequent stays in motels or inns, where they can find hot showers and places to dry their gear. **Aspenwood Tours,** P.O. Box 622, Springdale, NF A0J 1T0 (© **709/673-4453**), arranges mountain biking trips in and around central Newfoundland; **Freewheeling Adventures,** R.R. 1, Hubbards, NS B0J 1T0 (© **800/672-0775** or 902/857-3600), runs van-supported trips based in hotels and B&Bs. Its Viking Tour is a week of pure pleasure.

**BIRD-WATCHING**    If you're from a temperate climate, bird-watching doesn't get much more interesting or exotic than in Newfoundland and Labrador. Seabirds typically attract the most attention, and eastern Newfoundland and the Avalon Peninsula are especially rich in bird life. Just south of St. John's is the **Witless Bay Ecological Reserve,** where several islands host the largest colony of breeding puffins and kittiwakes in the western Atlantic. On the southern Avalon Peninsula, **Cape St. Mary's** features a remarkable sea stack just yards from easily accessible cliffs that's home to a cacophonous colony of northern gannets. (See the section on the Avalon Peninsula later in this chapter.)

**CAMPING**    In addition to the two national parks, Newfoundland maintains a number of provincial parks open for car camping. (About a dozen of these were "privatized" in 1997 and are now run as commercial enterprises, although many still appear on maps as provincial parks.) These are listed in the provincial travel guide, as are most privately run campgrounds.

If you're properly equipped, you might want to take part in a traditional activity in Newfoundland called "gravel-pit camping." Basically, that means pulling over to the side of the road (typically in a gravel pit) and spending the night away from organized campgrounds. You'll see gravel-pit campers all over the island, often in beautiful and dramatic spots overlooking coves or ponds. Although there's no law guaranteeing public access as there is in some Scandinavian countries, it's a hallowed tradition, and as long as you don't pitch your tent or park your RV in someone's driveway, you usually won't be hassled.

**CANOEING**    A glance at a map shows that rivers and lakes abound in Newfoundland and Labrador. Canoe trips can range from placid puttering around a pond near St. John's to world-class descents of Labrador rivers hundreds of miles long. The Department of Tourism produces a free brochure outlining several canoe trips; call ℂ **800/563-6353.** A popular guide—*Canyons, Coves and Coastal Waters*—is sold in bookstores around the province, or it can be ordered by mail from **Newfoundland Canoe Association,** 13 Brett Place, Mount Pearl NF A1N 3B4 (ℂ **709/729-0365**).

**FISHING**    Newfoundland and Labrador are legendary among serious anglers, especially those stalking the cagey Atlantic salmon, which can weigh up to 18kg (40 lbs.). Other prized species include landlocked salmon, lake trout, brook trout, and northern pike. More than 100 fishing-guide services on the island and mainland can provide everything from simple advice to complete packages that include bush-plane transportation, lodging, and personal guides. One fishing license is needed for Atlantic salmon, one for other fish, so be sure to read the current *Newfoundland & Labrador Hunting and Fishing Guide* closely for current regulations. It's available at most visitor centers, or by calling ℂ **800/563-6353** or 709/729-2830. To request it by mail, write the provincial tourism office at P.O. Box 8700, St. John's, NL A1B 4J6.

**HIKING & WALKING**    Newfoundland has an abundance of trails, but you'll have to work a bit harder to find them here than in the provinces to the south. The most obvious hiking trails tend to be centered around national parks and historic sites, where they are often fairly short—good for a half-day's hike, rarely more. But Newfoundland has hundreds of trails, many along the coast leading to abandoned communities. Some places are finally realizing the recreational potential for these trails and are now publishing maps and brochures directing you to them. The Bonavista Peninsula and the Eastport Peninsula, both on Newfoundland's east coast, are two areas that are attracting attention for world-class trails that were all but overlooked until recently.

The best-maintained trails are at **Gros Morne National Park,** which has around 100km (60 miles) of trails. In addition to these, there's also off-track hiking on the dramatic Long Range for backpackers equipped to set out for a couple of days. Ask at the park visitor center for more information.

More adventurous hikers will find enjoyment by just pulling over and setting off across one of the island's vast and intriguing bogs, following a compass heading out and back. These areas are spongy, but you'll rarely sink through the peat. Waterproof shoes will increase your enjoyment, and the phrase "bogged down" will be rather more evocative for you in the future.

**SEA KAYAKING**    With all its protected bays and inlets, Newfoundland is ideal for exploring by sea kayak. But there's a catch: the frigid water. There's a reason you'll see icebergs offshore, and it's called the Labrador Current. You'll need to be well prepared in the event you end up in the drink, because you won't have a lot of time for a rescue before the cold gets you in its grip. Experts traveling with their own gear can pick and choose their destinations. I would suggest that the area northeast of **Terra Nova National Park,** with its archipelago centering around St. Brendan's Island, would hold up well under close scrutiny.

Novices should stick to guided tours. **Eastern Edge Outfitters** (© **709/782-5925**) offers a variety of tours, mostly on the Avalon Peninsula. Rates start at C$60 (US$48) for a half-day tour and C$110 (US$88) for a 1-day tour, and go up to C$540 (US$432) for a 6-day South Coast tour with meals and equipment included. **Sea Kayaking with Whitecap Adventures** (© **709/726-9283**) is based in St. John's and leads paddling tours at Witless Bay, Cape Broyle, and Conception Bay, with prices starting at about C$40 (US$32) for a 2-hour sunset paddle. Extended tours and customized trips may be arranged. **Coastal Safari** (© **877/888-3020** or 709/579-3977), also based in St. John's, is a similar outfitter.

At **Terra Nova National Park,** 2-hour sea kayak tours leave from the Marine Interpretation Centre and explore protected Newman's Cove. (See the "Terra Nova National Park" section, later in this chapter.)

## 3 Southwestern Newfoundland

For most travelers arriving by ferry, this region is the first introduction to The Rock. And it's like starting the symphony without a prelude, jumping right to the crescendo. There's instant drama in the brawny, verdant Long Range Mountains that run parallel to the Trans-Canada Highway en route to Corner Brook. There are also the towering seaside cliffs of the Port au Port Peninsula, and intriguing coastal villages that await exploration. You might also be surprised that winds can blow with such intensity hereabouts, yet not attract any comment from the locals.

### PORT AUX BASQUES

Port aux Basques is a major gateway for travelers arriving in Newfoundland, with ferries connecting to Nova Scotia year-round. It's a good way station for those arriving late on a ferry or departing early in the morning. Otherwise, it can easily be viewed in a couple of hours when either coming or going.

This appealing harborside village is situated on treeless emerald hills that define the terrain around the harbor. "Downtown" consists of brightly colored, boxy homes set on the hills around a compact commercial zone. A narrow boardwalk snakes along the water's edge and links the ferry terminal and the town; it's worth the walk if you've got an hour or two to kill before your ferry, especially at sunset, which brings out the supple contours of the surrounding hills. At the edge of town are a tiny mall and newer residential neighborhoods. The town also has a one-screen movie theater and a few family-style restaurants.

#### ESSENTIALS

**GETTING THERE**    Port aux Basques is commonly reached via ferry from Nova Scotia. See "Exploring Newfoundland & Labrador," earlier, for ferry information. The Trans-Canada Highway (Rte. 1) links the major communities of southwestern Canada. Port aux Basques is 874km (543 miles) from St. John's via the Trans-Canada Highway.

**VISITOR INFORMATION**    In Port aux Basques, the **Provincial Interpretation and Information Centre** (© **709/695-2262**) is located on the Trans-Canada Highway about 3km (2 miles) from the ferry terminal. You can't miss it: It's the modern, ecclesiastical-looking building on the right. Inside are displays to orient you regarding the island's regions, and racks aflutter with great forests of brochures. It's open from mid-May to the middle of October daily from 6am to 11pm.

## EXPLORING PORT AUX BASQUES

**The Gulf Museum,** 118 Main St. (© **709/695-7560**), across from the Town Hall, has a quirky assortment of artifacts related to local history. The museum's centerpiece is a Portuguese astrolabe dating from 1628, which was recovered from local waters in 1981. Also intriguing is a display about the Caribou, a ferry torpedoed by a German U-boat in 1942; 137 people died in the tragedy. The museum is open daily in summer from 9am to 7pm; admission is C$3.50 (US$2.80) adults, C$1 (US80¢) children, C$5 (US$4) family.

On the way out of town you'll pass the **Port aux Basques Railway Heritage Center,** Route 1 (© **709/695-7560**), dedicated to the memory of the Newfie Bullet, the much-maligned, much-reminisced-about passenger train that ran between Port aux Basques and St. John's from 1898 to 1969. (The highway across the island opened in 1966, dooming the train.) The train required 27 hours to make the trip (at an average speed of 48kmph/30 mph), and during a tour of several restored rail cars you'll learn how the train made the run through deep snows of winter, how the passengers slept at night (very cozily, it turns out), and life aboard the mail car and caboose. Tours last just 15 minutes and cost C$3.50 (US$2.50) adults, free for students, C$5 (US$3.50) family.

Departing from the edge of Railway Heritage Center is the **T'Railway,** a coast-to-coast pathway being converted from the old train line. It's used by pedestrians, bikers, and ATVers, and in this stretch it runs through marsh and along the ocean to Cheeseman Park (see below) and beyond. It's a good spot to get your mountain bike limbered up for further adventures.

**J. T. Cheeseman Provincial Park** ✶ (© **709/695-2222**) is 15km (9 miles) west of town on Route 1 (confusingly, you follow Rte. 1 East out of town). Much of the park lies along sandy dunes, which are home to the piping plover, an endangered species. An observation platform offers a view of the plover's habitat; bring binoculars and patience (they're present here from early May to mid-Aug). The park has 102 campsites, along with a section of the T'Railway, which is good for walking or mountain biking.

## WHERE TO STAY

About a half-dozen hotels and B&Bs offer no-frills shelter to travelers at Port aux Basques. The two largest are **Hotel Port aux Basques,** Route 1 (© **877/695-2171** or 709/695-2171), and **St. Christopher's Hotel,** Caribou Road (© **800/563-4779** or 709/695-7034). Both might be described as "budget modern," with clean, basic rooms in architecturally undistinguished buildings. I'd give St. Christopher's the edge since it's located on a high bluff with views of the town and the harbor. Both have around 50 rooms and charge from C$69 to C$140 (US$55–US$112) for a double.

## WHERE TO DINE

Dining opportunities are limited. Both hotels mentioned above have dining rooms, serving basic, filling meals. A short walk from the ferry terminal on the boardwalk is the **Harbour Restaurant,** 1 Main St. (✆ **709/695-3238**), a family-style restaurant that serves budget-friendly meals (entrees C$4.95–C$14/US$3.50–US$10, with most under C$10/US$7). Expect fried fish, fried chicken, fish cakes, sandwiches, and the like. Most tables have good views of the harbor.

## CORNER BROOK

With a population of about 35,000, Corner Brook is Newfoundland's second-largest city. Like St. John's, it's also dramatically sited—in this case, on the banks of the glimmering Humber River, which winds down through verdant mountains from beyond Deer Lake, then turns the corner to flow into Humber Arm. The hills on the south shore of the Humber are nearly as tall as those in **Gros Morne National Park,** making a great backdrop for the town, which has gradually expanded up the shoulders of the hills.

Corner Brook is a young city with a long history. The area was first explored and charted in 1767 by Capt. James Cook, who spent 23 days mapping the islands at the mouth of the bay. But it wasn't until early in the 20th century that the city started to take its present shape. Copper mines and the railroad brought in workers; in the early 1920s the paper mill, which still dominates downtown, was constructed. By 1945 it was the largest paper mill in the world.

The city has grown beyond its stature as a mill town and has a more vibrant feel than other spots anchored by heavy industry. This is no doubt aided in large part by the energy from two institutions of higher learning: **Sir Wilfred Grenfell College of Memorial University of Newfoundland,** and the **College of the North Atlantic.** You'll also find well-developed services and suppliers, including grocery stores, banks, hotels, and restaurants. This is your last chance to stock up and indulge if you're headed to Gros Morne—from here on out, you'll be dependent on small grocery stores and mom-and-pop restaurants.

## ESSENTIALS

**GETTING THERE**   Corner Brook is on the Trans-Canada Highway 217km (135 miles) north of Port aux Basque. Air access is via the **Deer Lake Regional Airport** (✆ **709/635-3601**).

**VISITOR INFORMATION**   The **Corner Brook Tourist Chalet** (✆ **709/639-9792**) is up the hill, just off the Trans-Canada Highway at the intersection of West Valley Road and Confederation Drive (near the Best Western Mamateek). It's open daily, mid-June to September, from 9am to 9pm, and also weekdays from 9am to 5pm during the spring and fall.

## EXPLORING CORNER BROOK

Downtown Corner Brook looks promising on your approach—it's located on the hill-flanked Humber Arm, a well-protected ocean inlet and famed salmon fishing area. With the residential areas stacked neatly on the hills around the commercial center in the valley, it's got great topographical interest.

Alas, downtown is likely to disappoint sightseers. The city center consists of a large paper mill and two small malls. The enclosed malls offer basic goods but little charm. The mill offers an interesting olfactory experience when the wind is right.

It's still worth the detour: Tree-lined **West Street** is fun to explore, where you'll find coffee shops, restaurants, and pharmacies. The **Corner Brook Museum and Archive,** 2 West St. (✆ **709/634-2518**), is housed in a solid 1920s-era building that once was home to customs offices, the court, and the post and telegraph offices. A visit here offers a quick way to learn just how young the city really is (grainy black-and-white photos show empty hills surrounding the paper mill as late as the 1920s), and how civilized it has become. An assortment of locally significant artifacts (a prominent doctor's desk, ship models) rounds out the collection. The museum is open daily from 9am to 8pm in summer, weekdays only from 9am to 5pm in winter; admission is C$4 (US$3.20) adults, C$2 (US$1.60) students; children under age 12 enter free.

Nearby, at Glynmill Inn, you can follow a connector trail to the **Corner Brook Stream Trail,** which runs through the heart of the city. The trail is being developed along the 19km (12-mile) length of the stream (formerly the city's water supply), but for now it offers access to a narrow and pleasantly green sanctuary within the city. From Glynmill Inn you'll round a man-made pond; from here you can head upstream to **Margaret Bowater Park** (a locally popular spot with swimming pool and playground), or downstream toward Main Street and City Hall.

The **Newfoundland Emporium,** 7 Broadway (© **709/634-9376**), is a traditional downtown stop for travelers. It's an eclectic shop with a mix of antiques, crafts, books, and—in the owner's words—"flotsam and jetsam." It's the city's best destination for souvenirs.

## OUTDOOR PURSUITS

For outdoor enthusiasts, Corner Brook makes an excellent base for exploring outlying mountains and waters.

Mountain bikers should plan a stop by **TNT Professional Bicycles,** 8 Maple Valley Rd. (© **709/634-6799**). These guys know their business; ask for suggestions on where to go, and for the free map of backcountry bike routes. Didn't bring your bike? You can also rent one here.

Some of the region's best **hiking** is found along Route 450 toward Bottle Cove (see "A Road Trip from Corner Brook," below). But other hikes will get you quickly up into the hills around Corner Brook. At Marble Mountain ski area (head east on the Trans-Canada Hwy.), you can park at the ski lodge parking lot and follow a 1km (.5-mile) trail up to **Steady Brook Falls,** which is especially impressive after a summer rain. More extensive hikes are outlined in the "Corner Brook Hiking Guide and Map," available free at the visitor information center.

Anglers in search of the noted Atlantic salmon that spawn in the Humber have a wide selection of outfitters who provide an all-inclusive **fishing** experience; one price covers transportation from the airport, accommodations, meals, and a guide. Try the **Strawberry Hill Resort** in Little Rapids (© **877/434-0066** or 709/634-0066), or **Upper Humber Tours** in Deer Lake (© **709/635-5351**). Other outfitters are listed in the province's "Hunting and Fishing Guide," available at provincial information centers or in advance by calling © **800/563-6353.**

Atlantic Canada has just one downhill ski area that I'd classify as a destination resort, and that's **Marble Mountain** ✦, just a 10-minute drive from Corner Brook. You can eye the steep hills just north of the city. With a location near the Gulf of St. Lawrence and in the path of persistent northwest winds, it gets plenty of powder dumps in the winter, and the 480m (1,600-ft.) vertical drop is respectable. Many skiers take advantage of packages that include airfare, lodging, lift tickets, and a rental car; ask for a brochure by calling © **888/462-7253** or 709/637-7600, or pointing your browser at www.skimarble.com.

## WHERE TO STAY

Corner Brook is home to several convenient chain motels. Among others, you'll find the **Mamateek Inn,** 64 Maple Valley Rd. (© **709/639-8901**), near the tourist information booth, and the **Holiday Inn,** 47 West St. (© **800/399-5381** or 709/634-5381), which is within walking distance of the city's best restaurant (see below). Rooms go for C$80 to C$110 (US$64–US$88) for a double at either place.

Camping is offered on the north banks of the Humber at **Prince Edward Park** 🙀🙀 (© **709/637-1580**), with 80 sites spread along a bluff from which you can often spot osprey and bald eagles. Both fully serviced (C$20/US$16) and unserviced sites (C$15/US$12) are available. Exit the Trans-Canada Highway at Marble Mountain and follow Route 440 until you see the signs. It's about 10 minutes' drive from downtown. The campground is open June to mid-September.

**Glynmill Inn** 🙀 *Value*    This Tudor inn is set in a quiet, parklike setting—an easy stroll to the services and shops of West Street. Built in 1924 and extensively renovated in 1994, the four-story hotel's appealing detailing will charm you. (The place was designated a Registered Heritage Structure in 2001.) Rooms are tastefully decorated with colonial reproductions; the popular Tudor Suite has a private Jacuzzi. You'll get far more character here than at the chain motels in town, and for about the same price. The inn's two dining rooms are quite popular among local diners; the setting can feel a bit institutional (they do a rousing business with conventions and banquets), but the food is nevertheless pretty good.

1 Cobb Lane (near West St.), Corner Brook, NF A2H 6E6. © **800/563-4400** or 709/634-5181. Fax 709/634-5106. glynmill.inn@nf.sympatico.ca. 81 units. C$79–C$155 (US$63–US$124) double. AE, DC, MC, V. **Amenities:** 2 dining rooms; bar; business center; laundry service. *In room:* A/C, fridge (some units), coffeemaker, hair dryer, iron.

## WHERE TO DINE

**Thirteen West** 🙀🙀 GLOBAL    Western Newfoundland's best restaurant can easily compete with the better restaurants of St. John's in both the quality of the food and the casual but professional attitude. Tucked along shady West Street in an unobtrusive building (there's a patio fronting the street for the rare balmy night), the kitchen does an outstanding job preparing top-notch meals, and the staff knows how to make good service seem easy. At lunchtime look for offerings like grilled strip loin spiced Montréal-style, salmon salad, and a warm seafood salad of mussels, shrimp, scallops, and bacon. In the evening, you'll find a menu with items such as grilled salmon with a dill pesto, roasted rack of lamb, barbecued chicken with Cajun shrimp and black pepper sauce, and a seafood platter. Don't leave without sampling at least one of the delightful desserts, which have usually included such standards as crème caramel and profiteroles along with more inventive selections such as sautéed bananas with a rum pecan caramel sauce and vanilla ice cream.

13 West St. © **709/634-1300.** Reservations recommended. Main courses C$6–C$13 (US$5–US$11) at lunch, C$16–C$28 (US$13–US$23) at dinner. AE, DC, MC, V. Mon–Fri 11:30am–2:30pm and 5:30–9:30pm (Fri until 10:30pm); Sat 5:30–10:30pm; Sun 5:30–9:30pm (summer until 10:30pm).

## A ROAD TRIP FROM CORNER BROOK

One of western Newfoundland's most scenic drives is between Corner Brook and Bottle Cove, driving west on Route 450, also known as Captain Cook's Trail. It takes about 45 minutes to an hour to drive to the end of the road at Bottle Cove if you don't make any stops. But you should. The region stands up well to a leisurely excursion.

The road is winding and dramatic, running between the looming Blow Me Down Mountains and the dark and dappled waters of Humber Arm. Near Lark Harbour is **Blow Me Down Provincial Park** ✵ (✆ **709/681-2430**), a fine destination for a hike and a picnic. Start off with the 1km (.5-mile) hike to the lookout tower. Along the way you can view the Governor's Staircase, a unique rock formation some 450 million years old. Continue along the up-and-down trail for 3km (2 miles) one-way to Tortoise Point, with its exceptional views of the Bay of Islands. The park is open daylight hours and there's no admission charged. They also have a campground (see below).

On the way back to Corner Brook is the **Blow Me Down Nature Trail** ✵✵, west of the village of Frenchman's Cove and about 500m (1,640 ft.) west of the bridge over the brook. This is an especially appealing walk on a warm day, since this easy 1km (.5-mile) trail leads to great swimming holes in Blow Me Down Brook. Bring towels!

## DEER LAKE

Deer Lake is an unassuming crossroads town near the head of the Humber River where travelers coming from the south either continue on the Trans-Canada Highway toward St. John's, or veer northwest to Gros Morne National Park, some 69km (43 miles) distant. Deer Lake is the gateway for those coming by air directly to western Newfoundland. There's little to detain a visitor here; it's a good spot to buy gas, peruse the brochures at the provincial information center, and then push on.

Deer Lake is located 48km (30 miles) north of Corner Brook on the Trans-Canada Highway. **Deer Lake Regional Airport** (✆ **709/635-3601**) serves western Newfoundland with scheduled flights both within the island and to Halifax. Car rentals are available.

### EXPLORING DEER LAKE

Lucky is the traveler who arrives here during the short strawberry season (mid- to late July some years, early Aug in others). If you're here at the right time, do yourself a favor and stop at one of the several seasonal roadside stands for a pint or two. They're plump, they're cheap, and they're sinfully sweet and flavorful—nothing at all like the tasteless commercial berries that invade grocery stores in the United States and elsewhere.

**The Newfoundland Insectarium** (✆ **866/635-5454** or 709/635-4545; www.nf insectarium.com) opened in 1999 on Route 440, half a kilometer from the Trans-Canada Highway. Funded privately and operated as a for-profit venture, the insectarium will appeal to impressionable children and anyone fascinated with bugs. It's housed in a retrofitted dairy farm framed in red cedar, with most of the exhibits on a spacious second floor. These include more than 4,000 mounted actual insects (no faux bugs are displayed here), and 28 terrariums with live insects, including tiger beetles, American cockroaches, and honeybees. A walking trail and bug-themed gift shop (chocolate-coated crickets!) round out the experience. It's open daily in summers 9am to 8pm, mid-May through June and September through mid-October weekdays 9am to 5pm, weekends 10am to 5pm. Admission is C$6.50 (US$5.20) adults, C$5.50 (US$4.40) seniors, C$4.50 (US$3.60) children 5 to 14, C$22 (US$18) family. You could spend the better part of an hour here—but only if you *really* dig bugs.

### WHERE TO STAY & DINE

**Blow Me Down Provincial Park** ✵ (✆ **709/681-2430**) has camping for C$13 (US$11) per site.

**Deer Lake Motel**    This serviceable motel is located right on the Trans-Canada Highway and has clean, basic rooms. On the premises are a coffee shop, lounge, and restaurant. It's a good place to lay your head if you're arriving late en route to Gros Morne or points north or east; otherwise, there's little call to remain overnight in Deer Lake.

Trans-Canada Hwy, Deer Lake, NF A0K 2E0. ( 800/563-2144 in Newfoundland, or 709/635-2108. Fax 709/635-3842. www.deerlakemotel.com. 56 units. C$85–C$129 (US$68–US$103) double. AE, DC, MC, V. **Amenities:** 2 restaurants; bar. *In room:* A/C, TV, coffeemaker, hair dryer, iron.

## 4 Gros Morne National Park (★(★(★

"Gros Morne" translates roughly from the French as "big gloomy," and if you arrive on a day when ghostly bits of fog blow across the road and scud clouds hover in the glacial valleys, you'll get a pretty good idea how this area got its name. Even on brilliantly sunny days there's something about the stark mountains, lonely fjords cut off from the ocean, and miles of tangled spruce forest that can trigger mild melancholia.

**Gros Morne National Park** is one of Canada's true treasures, and few who visit here fail to come away awed. In fact, it's been officially designated as one of the world's treasures. In 1987, the park was declared a **UNESCO World Heritage Site,** which in large part reflected the importance of an area called the **Tablelands.** This geological quirk formed eons ago, when a portion of the earth's mantle broke loose during the continental drift and was forced to the surface, creating an eerie, rust-colored tableau. (See "Journey to the Center of the Earth," below, for more information.)

The park is divided into two sections, north and south, riven by the multiarmed Bonne Bay (locally pronounced like "Bombay"). Alas, a ferry connecting the two areas has not operated for years, so exploring both sections by car requires backtracking. The park's visitor center and most tourist services are found in the village of Rocky Harbour in the north section. But you'd be shortchanging yourself to miss a detour through the dramatic southern section, a place that looks to have had a rough birth, geologically speaking.

The dramatic terrain throughout the park is of a scale large enough to be appreciated if you prefer to tour by car. But to really get a sense of the place, plan to get out often on foot, by bike, or in a boat. Excellent hikes and awe-inspiring boat rides take you right into the heart of the park's wild character. To do the park justice, plan on spending at least 3 days here. A week would not be too much if you're an ardent hiker.

If you'd prefer to let someone else do the planning for you, contact **Gros Morne Adventures** (( 800/685-4624 or 709/458-2722; www.grosmorneadventures.com), which organizes guided sea kayaking and hiking excursions around the park.

### ESSENTIALS

**GETTING THERE**    From the Trans-Canada Highway in Deer Lake, turn west on Route 430 (the Viking Trail). This runs through the northern section of the park; it's 71km (44 miles) from Deer Lake to Rocky Harbour. For the southern section, turn left (south) on Route 431 in Wiltondale; from the turn, it's 27km (17 miles) to Woody Point.

**VISITOR INFORMATION**    The main **national park visitor information center** (( 709/458-2417) is just south of Rocky Harbour on Route 430. It's open daily from 9am to 10pm in summer, from 9am to 4:30pm the rest of the year. The center features exhibits on park geology and wildlife; there's also a short film about the park that's picturesque but not terribly informative. Interactive media kiosks are exceptionally well done; you can view video clips depicting highlights of all hiking trails and other attractions simply by touching a video screen. The center is also the place to stock up on field guides, as well as to request backcountry camping permits.

Across the bay just outside of Woody Point on Route 431 en route to Trout River is the new **Discovery Centre.** This building is an enlightening stop, with interactive exhibits, a fossil room, and a multimedia theater to help make sense of the Gros Morne landscape. More information is available at the visitor center.

**FEES** All visitors must obtain a permit for any activity within the park. May through October, daily fees are C$8 (US$6.40) adults, C$7 (US$5.60) seniors, C$4 (US$3) children 6 to 18, and C$16 (US$13) family; in the off season, fees are somewhat lower. Annual passes are available for C$40 (US$32) per adult or C$80 (US$64) per family.

## GROS MORNE'S SOUTHERN SECTION

The road through the southern section dead-ends at Trout River, and accordingly it seems to discourage convenience-minded visitors who prefer loops and through-routes. That's too bad, because the south contains some of the park's most dramatic terrain. Granted, you can glimpse the rust-colored Tablelands from north of Bonne Bay near Rocky Harbour, thereby saving the 48km (30-mile) detour. But without actually walking through the desolate landscape, you miss much of the impact. The south also contains several lost-in-time fishing villages that predate the park's creation in 1973, and a new Discovery Centre (see above) with exhibits about the park's natural history.

The region's scenic centerpiece is **Trout River Pond,** a landlocked fjord some 15km (9 miles) long. You can hike along the north shore to get a great view of the Narrows, where cliffs nearly pinch the pond in two. For a more relaxed view, sign up for a boat tour, which surrounds you with breathtaking panoramic views. From mid-June through mid-October, **Trout River Pond Boat Tours** (© 709/451-7500) offers excursions aboard a 40-passenger tour boat. Two-and-a-half-hour trips are offered daily at 10am, 1pm, and 4pm in July and August (1pm only in June and Sept). The cost is about C$25 (US$20) adults, about C$9.25 (US$7.50) children ages 6 to 16. Tickets are sold at a gift shop between the village of Trout River and the pond; watch for signs.

### HIKES & WALKS

For a superb panorama encompassing ocean and mountains, watch for the **Lookout Trail** just outside of Woody Point en route to Trout River. This steep trail is about 5km (3 miles) round-trip.

The **Tablelands Trail** departs from barren Trout River gulch and follows an old gravel road up to Winterhouse Brook Canyon. You can bushwhack along the rocky river a bit farther upstream, or turn back. It's about 2km (1.25 miles) each way, depending on how adventurous you feel. This is a good trail to get a feel for the unique ecology of the Tablelands. Look for the signboards that explain the geology at the trail head, and at the roadside pull-off on your left before reaching the trail head.

Experienced hikers looking for a challenge should seek out the **Green Gardens Trail**. There are two trail heads to this loop; I'd recommend the second one (closer to Trout River). You'll start by trekking through a rolling, infertile landscape,

## Journey to the Center of the Earth

If you see folks walking around the **Tablelands** ✦ looking twitchy and excited, they're probably amateur geologists. The Tablelands are one of the world's great geological celebrities, and a popular destination among pilgrims who love the study of rock.

To the uninitiated, the Tablelands area—south of Woody Point and the south arm of Bonne Bay—will seem rather bleak and barren. From a distance, the muscular hills rise up all rounded and rust-colored, devoid of trees or even that pale green furze that seems to blanket all other hills. Up close, you discover just how barren they are—little plant life seems to have established a toehold.

There's a reason for that. Some 570 million years ago, this rock was part of the earth's mantle, that part of the earth just under the crust. Riding on continental plates, two landmasses collided forcefully hereabouts, and a piece of the mantle was driven up and over the crust, rather than being forced under, as is usually the case. Years of erosion followed, and what's left is a rare glimpse of the earth's skeleton. The rock is so laced with magnesium that few plants can live here, giving it a barrenness that seems more appropriate for a desert landscape in the American Southwest than the rainy mountains of Newfoundland.

and then the plunge begins as you descend down, down, down wooden steps and a steep trail toward the sea. The landscape grows more lush by the moment, and soon you'll be walking through extraordinary coastal meadows on crumbling bluffs high above the surf.

The trail follows the shore northward for about 4 or 5km (2.5–3 miles), and it's one of the most picturesque coastal trails I've hiked anywhere in the world. In July, the irises and a whole symphony of other wildflowers bloom wildly. The entire loop is about 16km (9.5 miles) and is rugged and very hilly; allow about 5 or 6 hours. An abbreviated version involves walking clockwise on the loop to the shore's edge, and then retracing one's steps back uphill. That's about 9km (5.5 miles).

### CAMPING

The two **drive-in campsites** in the southern section—**Trout River Pond** and **Lomond**—both offer showers and nearby hiking trails. Of the two, Trout River Pond is more dramatic, located on a plateau overlooking the pond; a short stroll brings you to the pond's edge with wonderful views up the fjord. Lomond is near the site of an old lumber town and is popular with anglers. Camping is C$17 to C$23 (US$14–US$19) per site.

Three exceptional **backcountry campsites** are located along the Green Garden Trail (registration required at the park Visitor Centre; C$14/US$11 per night). The northernmost site is near the coast in a ravine where Wallace Brook meets the ocean. The two southern sites are on grassy bluffs above pebble beaches, and both have outstanding coastal views.

## WHERE TO STAY

**Victorian Manor B&B**   This 1920s home is one of the most impressive in the village, but that doesn't mean it's extravagant. It's more solid than flamboyant, set in a residential neighborhood near the town center and a few minutes' walk to the harbor. The attractive guesthouse has its own whirlpool. If that's booked, ask for one of the efficiencies, which cost about the same as the rooms but afford much greater convenience, especially considering the slim dining choices in town.

Main Rd. (P.O. Box 165), Woody Point, NF A0K 1P0. ✆ **866/453-2485** or 709/453-2485. www.grosmorne.com/victorianmanor. 3 units. C$70–C$95 (US$56–US$76) double. Rates include continental breakfast. AE, MC, V. **Amenities:** Jacuzzi; coin-op washers and dryers. *In room:* TV, kitchenette, fridge, coffeemaker, no phone.

## WHERE TO DINE

**Seaside Restaurant** ⸎ SEAFOOD   The Seaside has been a Trout River institution for years, and it's clearly a notch above the tired fare you often find in tiny coastal villages, but the service can be slow when the place fills up. The restaurant is nicely polished without being swank, and it features magnificent harbor views. The pan-fried cod is superb, as are a number of other seafood dishes. (Sandwiches and burgers are at hand for those who don't care for seafood.) Desserts, such as the partridgeberry parfait, are quite good.

Main St., Trout River. ✆ **709/451-3461.** Main courses C$10–C$19 (US$8–US$15). MC, V. Daily noon–8pm. Closed mid-Oct to June.

# GROS MORNE'S NORTHERN SECTION

Gros Morne's northern section flanks Route 430 for some 72km (45 miles) between Wiltondale and St. Paul's. The road winds through the abrupt, forested hills south of Rocky Harbour; beyond these, the road levels out, following a broad coastal plain covered mostly with bog and tuckamore. East of the plain rises the extraordinarily dramatic monoliths of the Long Range. This section contains the park's visitor center as well as the park's one must-see attraction: **Western Brook Pond.**

The hardscrabble fishing village of Rocky Harbour is your best bet for tourist services, including motels, B&Bs, laundromats, and small grocery stores. One caveat, however: Rocky Harbour and the surrounding area lack a well-lighted, well-stocked grocery store of the sort one might expect near a national park of international importance. What you'll find are modest-size grocery stores—the sorts of places where you'll want to check the dates on bread and milk very carefully.

## EXPLORING THE NORTHERN SECTION

If you have time for only one activity in Gros Morne—and heaven forbid that's the case—make it the **BonTours** boat trip up **Western Brook Pond** ⸎⸎. The trip begins with a 20-minute drive north of Rocky Harbour. Park at the Western Brook Pond trail head; then set off on an easy 45-minute hike across the northern coastal plain, with interpretive signs explaining the wildlife and bog ecology you'll see along the way. (Keep an eye out for moose.) Always ahead, the mighty monoliths of the Long Range rise high above, inviting and mystical, more like a 19th-century scene from the Rockies than the Atlantic seaboard.

You'll soon arrive at the pond's edge, where there's a small collection of outbuildings near a wharf, where the tour boats dock. Once aboard one of the vessels (there are two), you'll set off into the maw of the mountains, winding between the sheer rock faces that define this landlocked fjord. The spiel on the boat is recorded, but even that unfortunate bit of cheese fails to detract from the grandeur of the scene. You'll learn about the glacial geology and the remarkable quality of the water, which is considered among the purest in the world. Bring lots of film and a wide-angle lens. The trip lasts about 2½ hours. The cost is C$38 (US$30) adults, C$16 (US$13) students 12 to 16 (must be accompanied by an adult), C$10 (US$9) children under 11, C$78 (US$62) family. For reservations, contact the **Ocean View Motel** (② **800/563-9887** or 709/458-2730) in Rocky Harbour.

If rain or heavy fog puts a damper on outdoor activities, there's a modern indoor pool at the **Gros Morne Recreation Centre** (② **709/458-2350**), on Route 430 high above Rocky Harbour in summer. The view of Bonne Bay from the outdoor terrace is great, and the pool is inviting. This is also a good spot for a shower if you're staying at the park's one showerless campground. Tickets good for a 1-hour swim cost about C$3 (US$2.40) for adults, C$2 (US$1.60) for children.

If you're looking for diversion that requires minimal physical effort, both the **SS Ethie** shipwreck 🎯🎯 and **Broom Point** 🎯 (both near Western Brook Pond) are worth stopping for. The coastal steamer *Ethie* met its fate during a storm in 1919; all passengers were saved, including an infant shuttled to shore in a mailbag. The wreck has long been prominent in song and story, but the years have taken their toll on the rusting scrap. The hull is all but gone, leaving only the massive boiler and some other stray parts. But the cobbles nearby are beautiful.

Broom Point is an easy stroll out to a picturesque and rocky peninsula, where active fishing operations take place. The views from the point are outstanding; don't miss the superb sand beach down a side trail to your left as you walk toward the point.

**HIKES & WALKS**    The summit of **Gros Morne Mountain** is the Mount Everest of this national park—at 793m (2,644 ft.) it's the highest peak in the park, and the most demanding. What makes it especially challenging isn't so much the height or the length (about 16km/10 miles round-trip). It's the terrain. You expend considerable energy scrambling over loose scree on the upper reaches. But the views of the bay and beyond to the Gulf of St. Lawrence are well worth it if the weather cooperates. Allow about 7 or 8 hours for the whole excursion, and bring plenty of water and food. Pick up a trail brochure at the information center. (If you're traveling with a pet, note that this is the one trail on which dogs aren't allowed.)

Even if you're not planning on signing up for the Western Brook Pond boat tour (reconsider!), you owe yourself a walk up to the pond's wharf and possibly beyond. The 45-minute one-way trek from the parking lot north of Sally's Cove follows well-trod trail and boardwalk through bog and boreal forest. When you arrive at the wharf, the view to the mouth of the fjord will take your breath away. A very well executed outdoor exhibit explains how glaciers shaped the landscape in front of you.

Two spur trails continue on either side of the pond for a short distance. The **Snug Harbour Trail** 🎯🎯, which follows the northern shore to a primitive campsite (registration required), is especially appealing. After crossing a seasonal bridge at the pond outlet, you'll pass through scrubby woods before emerging on a long and wonderful sand and pebble beach; this is a great destination for a relaxed afternoon picnic and requisite nap. The hike all the way to Snug Harbour is about 8km (5 miles) one-way.

Three easy but enjoyable strolls depart from the **Berry Hill Campground** just north of Rocky Harbour. Berry Hill Pond is a perfect place for walking off your meal in the evening; it's a loop just 2km (1.25 miles) long. The equally short 1.5km (1-mile) round-trip hike up **Berry Hill** 🎯 is a saunter except for a demanding set of steps at the end; a short loop trail around the summit affords excellent views. Departing from the same parking area is the somewhat more demanding **Baker Brook Falls Trail** ⟨. This level trail runs 10km (6.25 miles) round-trip, ending at a wooden platform overlooking tumultuous, wild cascades. The trail crosses large amounts of bog on boardwalks.

**CAMPING**    The northern section has three campgrounds open to car campers. The main campground is **Berry Hill,** which is just north of Rocky Harbour. There are 146 drive-in sites, plus six walk-in sites on the shores of the pond itself. It's just 10 minutes' drive from the visitor center, where evening activities and presentations are held.

**Shallow Bay** ⟨ has 50 campsites and is near the park's northern border and an appealing 4km (2.5-mile) sand beach. Both of these campgrounds have showers and flush toilets.

**Green Point** ⟨⟨ is an intimate, popular campground with just 18 sites divided between two areas. The upper area is more open and has views of the gulf; the lower area is set amid evergreen and offers more privacy and shelter from the wind. Green Point has pit toilets and no showers. In midsummer, the northern section campgrounds tend to fill up readily; it's best to arrive soon after the 2pm checkout time to secure a site. Rates at Berry Hill and Shallow Bay are C$17 to C$23 (US$14–US$19) per site (C$14/US$11 for Green Point). Reservations are very helpful during peak season; call ⟨ **800/563-6353.**

**BACKPACKING**    Backcountry camping is available only at **Snug Harbour** on Western Brook Pond. This requires an 8km (5-mile) hike from the road. Register for a site at the visitor center; the cost is C$15 (US$12).

For an unforgettable but exceedingly demanding adventure, inquire at the center about the backpack trips along the **Long Range** ⟨⟨ and the **North Rim** ⟨⟨. On both of these, you strike out cross-country, bushwhacking through the high subarctic terrain. These traverses require 2 or 3 nights to complete. You also need to be in good physical condition and well versed in a range of backcountry skills, including proficiency with map and compass. A brief pretrip orientation at the visitor center is mandatory, as is the rental of a small (pager-size) locator beacon to help pinpoint your location should you become disoriented. A one-time backcountry fee of C$30 to C$35 (US$20–US$23) per person is charged (including locator rental) for these trips.

## WHERE TO STAY

Rocky Harbour has more tourist services than any other village in or around the park, but it still has trouble handling the influx of travelers in July and August. Two or three bus tours can pretty well fill up the town. One B&B owner told me she turned away 20 people seeking a room one night in July. It's an unwise traveler who arrives without a reservation.

The largest motel in town is the **Ocean View Motel** (⟨ **800/563-9887** or 709/458-2730), located on the harbor. It has 48 basic rooms (some have small balconies with bay views), but everything feels a bit chintzy, from the carpeting to the walls to the furnishings. The motel is popular with bus tours, and it often fills up early in the day. Rooms are C$85 to C$160 (US$68–US$128) double in season.

**Gros Morne Cabins**    My favorite thing about the Gros Morne Cabins? Pulling up and seeing the long lines of freshly laundered sheets billowing in the sea breeze, like a Christo installation. The trim and tidy log cabins are clustered tightly along a grassy rise overlooking Rocky Harbour, and all have outstanding views toward the Lobster

Cove Head Lighthouse. Inside they're new and clean, more antiseptically modern than quaintly worn. Each cabin is equipped with a kitchenette, and gas barbecues are scattered about the property. The complex also includes a store and a laundromat. There's a pizza place just across the street for relaxed sunset dining at your own picnic table.

Main St. (P.O. Box 151), Rocky Harbour, NF A0K 4N0. (C) **888/603-2020** or 709/458-2020. Fax 709/458-2882. 22 units. C$99–C$149 (US$79–US$119) double. AE, DC, MC, V. Pets allowed. *In room:* Kitchenette.

**Sugar Hill Inn** *&* This appealing green-shingled inn opened in 1991 on the road between Rocky Harbour and Norris Point. The six rooms are quite comfortable, although some guests have found them a bit condolike and sterile. Nice touches abound, like hardwood floors in all rooms, plenty of natural wood trim, well-selected furnishings, and a shared sauna and hot tub in a cedar-lined room. The upstairs sitting room is spacious and bright, with a fireplace and modern furnishings; it's a good spot to swap local adventure ideas with other guests. The inn's dining room serves breakfast and dinner daily, although breakfast isn't included in the room rates.

115–129 Sexton Rd. (P.O. Box 100), Norris Point, NF A0K 3V0. (C) **888/299-2147** or 709/458-2147. Fax 709/458-2166. www.sugarhillinn.nf.ca. 6 units. C$96–C$225 (US$77–US$180). AE, MC, V. Closed mid-Oct to mid-Jan. **Amenities:** Restaurant; bar; Jacuzzi; sauna. *In room:* Fridge.

**Wildflowers Country Inn** This 1930s home near the village center was modernized and updated before its opening as a B&B in 1997, giving it a casual country look inside. The rooms are tastefully appointed if a bit small, although two newer rooms have private bathrooms and are a bit larger. The neighborhood isn't especially scenic (there's an auto repair shop across the way), but the house is very peaceful, the innkeepers are exceptionally friendly, and this is a great choice for those seeking reasonably priced lodging with a comfortable, homey feel.

Main St. N (P.O. Box 291), Rocky Harbour, NF A0K 4N0. (C) **888/811-7378** or 709/458-3000. wildflowers@nf.aibn. com. 6 units. C$89–C$119 (US$71–US$95) double. Rates include full breakfast. MC, V. **Amenities:** Restaurant; bar; laundry service. *In room:* TV, no phone.

## WHERE TO DINE

**Fisherman's Landing** SEAFOOD With its industrial carpeting and generic chain-restaurant chairs and tables, Fisherman's Landing is lacking in homespun character. But it does offer efficient service and dependable meals, with specialties including fish and chips, cod tongues, and squid rings. For breakfast, there's the traditional Newfie fisherman's breakfast of a mug of tea, served with homemade bread and molasses. Meals are quite reasonably priced, and you can get in and out faster than at most other joints. There's also a glimpse of the harbor from a few tables, provided that not too many RVs park out front.

Main St., Rocky Harbour. (C) **709/458-2711.** Sandwiches C$3–C$7 (US$2.40–US$5.60); main courses C$7–C$17 (US$5.60–US$14). MC, V. Late June to early Sept 6am–11pm; limited hours off season.

## 5 The Great Northern Peninsula

On a map, the Great Northern Peninsula looks like a stout cudgel threatening the shores of Labrador. If Newfoundland can even be said to have a beaten track, rest assured that the peninsula is well off it. It's not as mountainous or starkly dramatic as Gros Morne, but the road unspools for kilometer after kilometer through tuckamore and evergreen forest, along restless coast and the base of geologically striking hills. There are few services, and even fewer organized diversions. But it has early history in spades, a handful of fishing villages clustering along the rocky coast, and some of the most unspoiled terrain anywhere. The road is in good repair, with the chief hazard being a stray moose or caribou. In the spring the infrequent polar bear might wander through a village, often hungry after a long trip south on ice floes.

How nice is it? On one camping vacation I drove down a rocky road one evening to make dinner and watch the sun sink over the Labrador hills across the straits. I came upon a waterfall that tumbled into a magical cobblestone cove, where driftwood was piled chest-high for firewood. A beautiful grassy plateau—perfect for a tent— overlooked the sea. I had recently stocked up on food, and I had a milk crate full of books I wanted to read.

To make a long story short, it was 3 days before I was finally able to extricate myself from this idyllic spot. And this might be the place I recall most fondly when I think back on travels in Newfoundland.

## ESSENTIALS

**GETTING THERE**   Route 430, which is also called the Viking Trail, runs from Deer Lake (at the Trans-Canada Hwy.) to St. Anthony, a 419km (260-mile) jaunt. Scheduled flights on **Air Labrador** (© 800/563-3042 or 709/896-6730; www.air labrador.com) and **Provincial Airlines** (© 800/563-2800 or 709/576-1666; www. provair.com) stop at St. Anthony, where rental cars are available. The airport is on Route 430 approximately 30km (18 miles) west of St. Anthony.

**VISITOR INFORMATION**   For information about the Great Northern Peninsula and the Viking Trail, contact the **Viking Trail Tourism Association,** P.O. Box 251, St. Anthony, NF A0K 4T0 (© 877/778-4546 or 709/454-8888). Visitor centers are located at **St. Anthony** (© 709/454-8898) and **Hawke's Bay** (© 709/248-5344).

## PORT AU CHOIX

A visit to Port au Choix (pronounced *port a shwaw*) requires a 13km (8-mile) detour off the Viking Trail, out to a knobby peninsula that's home to a sizable fishing fleet. The windswept lands overlooking the sea are low, predominantly flat, and lush with grasses. Simple homes speckle the landscape; most are of recent vintage.

The town's chief attraction is the historic site (see below). But be sure to visit the archaeological excavations at **Philip's Garden** ★★. (Ask for directions at the historic site's visitor center.) Getting here requires a 20-minute hike over low coastal cliffs of fissured slabs splashed with rust-orange lichens. And although there's little here other than a placard or two to mark the site of the millenniums-old native settlement, it doesn't take much to imagine an ancient community taking root here. If you hunker down behind a rock to find solace from the howling winds, look carefully in the grass for the unusually tasty wild strawberries, which are no bigger than blueberries.

**Port au Choix National Historic Site** ★ *Kids*   Back in 1967 a local businessman began digging the foundation for a new movie theater in town. He came upon some bones. A lot of bones. In fact, what he stumbled upon turned out to be a remarkable burying ground for what are now called the Maritime Archaic Indians.

This group of hunters populated parts of Atlantic Canada starting 7,500 years ago, predating the Inuit, who only arrived around 4,000 years ago. These early natives relied chiefly on the sea, and among artifacts recovered here are slate spears and antler harpoon tips, which featured an ingenious toggle that extended after being thrust into flesh. One of the enduring historical mysteries is the disappearance of the Maritime Archaic Indians from the province about 3,500 years ago; to this day no one can explain their sudden departure.

You'll learn about this fascinating historic episode at the modern visitor center. From here, staffers will be able to direct you to various nearby sites, including the original burial ground, now surrounded by village homes. (Don't miss Philip's Garden; see above.) You can also visit the nearby lighthouse, scenically located on a blustery point thrusting into the Gulf of St. Lawrence. Plan to spend about 90 minutes exploring this area.

Point Riche Rd., Port au Choix. ℂ 709/861-3522. Admission C$6.50 (US$5) adults, C$5.50 (US$4.40) seniors, C$3.25 (US$2.60) children 6–16, C$16 (US$13) families. Visitor center mid-June to mid-Oct daily 9am–5pm (summer until 8pm).

## L'ANSE AUX MEADOWS 🎖🎖🎖

Newfoundland's northernmost tip is not only exceptionally remote and dramatic, but is also one of the most historically significant spots in the world. A Viking encampment dating from A.D. 1,000 was discovered here in 1960, and it has been thoroughly documented by archaeologists in the decades since. An unusually well conceived and well managed national historic site (see below) probes this earliest chapter in European expansion, and an afternoon spent here piques the imagination.

Another fine way to fire up your fantasies is to sign up for a tour on the Viking Saga, a replica of one of the early ships run by **Viking Boat Tours.** Based in Noddy Bay (about 1.5km/1 mile south of L'Anse aux Meadows), this handsome knaar (a type of work boat) was built after extensive study of a Viking ship recovered from the bottom of a fjord near Roskilde, Denmark. This boat has been upgraded to meet current safety standards (this includes the addition of an engine), but it's prohibited from carrying passengers under sail. You'll get a good sense of life aboard these compact boats as you motor along the remote coast, and you might see whales and icebergs in the bargain.

Tours are offered three times daily from June to late September. They take about 2½ hours and the fare is C$40 (US$32) adults, C$25 (US$20) children 5 to 12, C$10 (US$8) for children under 5. Call for reservations at ℂ **709/623-2100.**

**L'Anse aux Meadows National Historic Site** 🎖🎖🎖 *Kids* *Value*   In the late 1950s a pair of determined archaeologists named Helge Ingstad and Anne Stine Ingstad pored over 13th-century Norse sagas searching for clues about where the Vikings might have landed on the shores of North America. With just a few scraps of description, the Ingstads began cruising the coastlines of Newfoundland and Labrador, asking locals about unusual hummocks and mounds.

At L'Anse aux Meadows, they struck gold. In a remote cove noted for its low, grassy hills, they found the remains of an ancient Norse encampment that included three large halls, along with a forge where nails were made from locally mined pig iron. As many as 100 people lived here for a time, including some women. The Vikings abandoned the settlement after a few years to return to Greenland and Denmark, thus ending the first experiment in the colonization of North America by Europeans. It's telling that no graves have ever been discovered here.

Start your visit by viewing the recovered artifacts in the visitor center and watching the half-hour video about the site's discovery. Then I suggest signing up for one of the free, guided tours of the site. The guides offer considerably more information than the simple markers around the grounds. Near the original encampment are several re-created sod-and-timber buildings, depicting how life was lived 1,000 years ago. These are tended by costumed interpreters, who have a wonderful knack of staying in character without making you feel like a dork when you ask them questions. If you time it right, you might be rewarded with a bit of flat bread cooked old-style over an open fire. This is one of Eastern Canada's major attractions, and I'd recommend sticking around for a couple hours to soak it all up.

Rte. 436, L'Anse aux Meadows. © **709/623-2608.** Admission C$9 (US$7) adults, C$7.50 (US$6) seniors, C$4.50 (US$3.60) children 6–16, C$23 (US$18) families. Peak season daily 9am–8pm; off season daily 9am–5pm. Closed mid-Oct to early June.

## ST. ANTHONY 🕀

The seaport town of St. Anthony—named by explorer Jacques Cartier in 1534—was first visited by 16th-century French and Basque fishermen. Today, with its 3,200 residents, St. Anthony is the northern peninsula's largest town, and its undisputed commercial center. It's a good place to restock on basic supplies or secure a motel room for day trips to L'Anse aux Meadows, about 50km (30 miles) north of town.

Be sure to visit **Fishing Point Park** 🕀, at the end of a dirt road at the mouth of the harbor. With propitious timing and some luck, you'll be able to view icebergs and whales from the rugged, rocky bluffs. A series of short trails and wooden platforms makes life easy for the casual explorer.

In the evening, there's live entertainment at the **Great Viking Feast at Leifsburdur** (© **877/454-4900** or 709/454-4900). In a replica sod hut, up to 85 diners can feast on local fare such as Jigg's dinner (boiled meat and potatoes), moose stew, cod tongues, and baked cod, while being amused by a crew of Vikings. The show is staged daily at 7:30pm from July to early September (reservations required), and costs about C$35 (US$28), which includes dinner.

**Grenfell House Museum and Interpretation Centre** 🕀🕀    Dr. Wilfred Grenfell is more or less the patron saint of St. Anthony. A devout Christian, Grenfell was born in England and as a young man became active in providing medical care to North Sea fishermen. In 1892, he visited Newfoundland and Labrador. Appalled by the conditions, he founded the first hospital; he was to spend much of the rest of his life ministering to residents of remote outports and agitating for better services from the government. In 1912, he established the International Grenfell Association, which established hospitals and nursing homes throughout the region. Grenfell was restless in trying to improve the lot of the northland's residents, and to improve the delivery of medicines and services. One example: In 1909, he experimented using reindeer rather than sled dogs for winter travel, having observed that the dogs had the unfortunate habit of savaging the driver if he fell helpless in deep snow.

An interpretive center features two floors of exhibits that nicely fill visitors in on the Grenfell's history. There's also a 14-minute video that's worth watching. Afterwards, you can tour the handsome house the grateful town built for Grenfell and his devoted wife, Anne, in 1910. It's furnished with numerous artifacts and interesting exhibits about Grenfell's life and works. You'll also learn about Grenfell cloth, a versatile fabric made of Egyptian cotton and invented in 1922 specifically to withstand the rigors of severe winter travel. Garments made of Grenfell cloth are available at **Grenfell Handicrafts,** in the interpretation center. Plan to spend about an hour here.

West St., St. Anthony (across from the hospital). ℂ **709/454-4010.** Admission C$6 (US$5) adults, C$5 (US$4) seniors, C$2.75 (US$2.25) children 6–16, C$12 (US$9.50) families. May–Sept daily 9am–8pm (Sept until 5pm).

## WHERE TO STAY & DINE
### The Lightkeepers' Cafe ✵ SEAFOOD    Located at scenic Fishing Point Park, this cafe is housed in a simple but handsome white building with fire-engine-red trim overlooking the ocean. Inside, it's sparely decorated and flooded with natural light. The proprietors have placed binoculars on windowsills for you to scope out the whales and icebergs while awaiting your meal. The daily specials are fresh and tasty. Perennial favorites include butter-fried cod, steaks, burgers, ribs, and seafood chowder. The truly famished can order the Commissioner's Feast, which includes samples of "all the seafood in the house" plus lobster or crab.

Fishing Point Park. ℂ **877/454-4900** or 709/454-4900. Reservations not accepted. Main courses C$8–C$22 (US$6.50–US$18), feast more. AE, MC, V. Daily 11:30am–9pm. Closed Nov–May.

### Tickle Inn at Cape Onion ✵ ℱⁱⁿᵈˢ    If you're seeking that end-of-the-world flavor, you'll be more than a little content here. Set on a remote cove at the end of a road near Newfoundland's northernmost point (you can see Labrador across the straits), the Tickle Inn occupies a solid fisherman's home built around 1890 by the great-grandfather of the current innkeeper, David Adams. (He's a retired school counselor from St. John's.) After lapsing into decrepitude, the home was expertly restored in 1990, and it has recaptured much of the charm of a Victorian outport home. The guest rooms are small but comfortable, and they share two bathrooms. Before dinner, guests often gather in the parlor and enjoy snacks and complimentary cocktails; afterward, there's often music or some other form of entertainment. One of the highlights of a stay here is exploring the small but superb network of hiking trails maintained by Adams, which ascend open bluffs to painfully beautiful views of the Labrador Straits. The inn is about a 40-minute drive from L'Anse aux Meadows. Meals are served family-style at 7:30pm each evening. (Your only other option for a meal is to drive a considerable distance to the nearest restaurant.) The food here is excellent, featuring local cuisine. You might have Cape Onion soup with a touch of Newman's port, or the "Polaris paella," with squid, scallops, and shrimp. Time your visit for berry season and you can expect such delights as the northern berry flan for dessert.

RR no. 1 (Box 62), Cape Onion, NF A0K 4J0. © **709/452-4321** or 709/739-5503. Fax 709/452-2030. www.tickleinn. net. 4 units, none with private bathroom. C$50–C$70 (US$40–US$56) double. Rates include deluxe continental breakfast. MC, V. Closed Oct–May. **Amenities:** Dining room. *In room:* No phone.

# 6 Central Newfoundland

Spruce. Larch. Spruce. Bog. Spruce. Lake. Spruce. Bog.

You get the idea. This 350km (215-mile) stretch of the Trans-Canada Highway is long and, if you're in a grumpy mood, awfully tedious. Travelers crossing the interior typically spend more of their time cursing slow-moving RVs and wishing for passing lanes than admiring the scenery. The vast forest is certainly monumental, and along the way you'll crest some hills and take in panoramic views of lakes or ocean inlets that finger their way down from the north. You can also detour to some appealing fishing villages on the north coast. These notwithstanding, Newfoundland's interior is widely regarded as an area you pass through to more inviting areas, not one in which you linger. If you've been saving a book-on-tape in the trunk, this is the time to rummage around and get it out.

Grand Falls–Windsor and Gander are both regional service centers and offer reasonable destinations to stretch your legs at one of the attractions, gas up, get a bite to eat, perhaps spend a night if evening is encroaching. But neither offers much as destinations for travelers, with the exception of hunters, fishermen, canoeists, and backpackers who might choose to employ the towns as bases from which to explore the woody, boggy, lake-filled interior. The area around Twillingate is a distinct exception—it's well worth the northward detour off the Trans-Canada and could easily occupy a traveler who enjoys low-key, off-the-beaten-path destinations.

## GRAND FALLS–WINDSOR

The settlement of Grand Falls dates from 1903, when British tycoons Lord Northcliffe and Lord Rothermere grew concerned that a restless Germany might disrupt the supply of newsprint from the Continent. They liked what they found at Grand Falls, where the Exploits River rushed over cascades amid a seemingly endless supply of timber. An ambitious paper mill was constructed on the banks of the river; it cost C$7.5 million (US$5.25 million) to build and employed 15,000 mill and woods workers when it was finally completed in 1909. The mill took root and expanded over the decades. Today, it's a major regional employer owned and operated by Abitibi-Price.

The once-independent towns of Grand Falls and Windsor were joined as a single municipality in 1991, resulting in the ungainly name. It's also a bit cumbersome to get from one town to the other because the Trans-Canada Highway neatly bisects the two. There's really little need to venture to Windsor, however; focus your attention on Grand Falls, which is south of the highway.

The **visitor information center** (© **709/489-6332**) is just off the Trans-Canada Highway on the west side of town. It's well marked from the highway.

### EXPLORING GRAND FALLS–WINDSOR

You'll find a worthwhile detour to the **Salmonid Interpretation Centre** (© **709/489-7350**), across the river from the mill. Finding the place is a bit of a trick; you should stop at the visitor information center on the Trans-Canada Highway west of town and ask for a map, which the staff will happily supply.

The interpretation center is more intriguing than you might think. Not only will you get a good view of the rocky gorge through which the river tumbles lustily, but you also will be able to watch the Atlantic salmon laboring their way up the fish ladder, which opened in 1992. A series of concrete pools linked by short waterfalls leads to a main holding tank, where the fish are counted before a final gate is opened and they continue their upstream journey.

Inside the exhibit center you can descend to an observation area below ground and see the impatient salmon through aquarium-like walls. The fish are surprisingly majestic, though the exhibits themselves are scattered and a bit dull. The staff is happy to answer your questions. If you're passing through town around lunch or dinner, the cozy restaurant, located at the interpretation center, offers basic, reasonably priced meals.

The center is open mid-June to mid-September daily from 8am to dusk. Admission is about C$3 (US$2.40) adults, C$2 (US$1.60) seniors and children.

Back across the river in Grand Falls is the **Mary March Regional Museum,** 16 St. Catherine St. (© **709/292-4522**). It honors a Beothuk Indian who was captured in 1819 at Red Indian Lake; she died of tuberculosis after a year in captivity. The museum covers Newfoundland's 5,000-year history of inhabitation, from the early Maritime Archaic Indians on through the Paleo-Eskimo, Beothuk, Mi'kmaq, and, eventually, Europeans. Intriguing artifacts such as ancient stone gouges and the geometrically incised game pieces and pendants of the Beothuk are displayed. The museum also offers a perspective on the local pulp and paper industry, and the coming of the railway. Hours are May 1 to late October daily from 9am to 5pm. Admission is C$2.50 (US$2) adults, C$2 (US$1.60) students and seniors, free for under 18.

The area around Grand Falls–Windsor is great for backcountry exploring, although you need guidance owing to the extensive logging operations to feed the mill. **Red Indian Adventures** (© **709/486-0892**) is located 18km (11 miles) west of Grand Falls–Windsor in Aspen Brook, right off the Trans-Canada Highway. Proprietors Paul and Joy Rose offer a full range of excursions and classes, ranging from white-water kayak courses (the rapids on the Exploits River are vigorous and challenging) to day-long sea kayaking trips in Notre Dame Bay. Rates for day tours are C$69 to C$99 (US$55–US$79) per person. Overnight trips cost C$175 to C$215 (US$140–US$172) per person.

## WHERE TO STAY & DINE

The **Mount Peyton Hotel** (© **800/563-4894** or 709/489-2251) is the town's largest hotel and motel (Take your pick: The seasonal motel is on the north side of the Trans-Canada Hwy., the year-round hotel on the south). It has 102 hotel rooms and 48 motel and housekeeping units; all the hotel rooms are air-conditioned. I prefer the slower pace of the **Robin Hood** (below); the Mount Peyton can be noisy with highway sounds and is often bustling with meetings or conference attendees. Doubles range from C$87 all the way to C$250 (US$70–US$200).

**Hotel Robin Hood**   This modern, basic, comfortable hotel is in a quiet area between the residential and commercial neighborhoods of Grand Falls. The building was constructed in 1997 and has been well maintained; all the rooms are larger than standard-issue motel rooms. (Note that rooms on the 2nd floor are slightly bigger than those on the 1st.) It's the hotel closest to the salmon interpretation center. With its beadboard wainscoting, the in-house restaurant Friar Tuck's is more pleasantly intimate than one might expect from a hotel restaurant. The restaurant is open for dinner and lunch; the menu includes traditional favorites along the lines of fish and chips, lamb chops, fresh salmon, and pepper steak.

78 Lincoln Rd., Grand Falls–Windsor, NF A2A 1N2. © **709/489-5324**. Fax 709/489-6191. robin.hood@nf.sympatico. ca. 22 units. C$80–C$100 (US$64–US$80) double. Rates include continental breakfast. AE, DC, MC, V. Pets allowed. **Amenities:** Restaurant; room service. *In room:* A/C, TV.

## TWILLINGATE  ✦✦

North and South Twillingate Islands are a photographer's dream. You'll find a bit of everything here—historic fishing harbors, gently rolling forested ridges, jagged cliffs washed by the surf, and open rocky barrens that roll down to the sea. There's also a good chance of spotting whales and icebergs—a good many of the Greenland icebergs seem to drift into Notre Dame bay to the west of Twillingate, where they can be spotted in late spring and early summer.

Twillingate was named by early French fishermen, who noted a striking resemblance between the rocky cliffs of this region and the stone shores of their hometown of Toulinguet, near Brest, France. The spelling was subsequently Anglicized. The region around Twillingate is actually an archipelago linked by a series of causeways, and the drive northward on Route 340 from Boyd's Cove is extremely picturesque, with views of inlets and harbors cropping up between the low, green, forested hills. Twillingate (pop. 5,000) itself is a surprisingly active commercial center, with a number of bustling stores lining the road down to the old harbor. It's been connected to the mainland by causeway since 1972.

The communities around Twillingate have shown more entrepreneurial drive in offering services for travelers than you typically find in Newfoundland's villages. A number of homes have been converted to B&Bs, and the route on to the two Twillingate Islands is lined with homemade billboards touting boat tours, B&Bs, and restaurants.

### ESSENTIALS

**GETTING THERE**   Twillingate is 142km (88 miles) northeast of Grand Falls–Windsor. Coming from the west, turn north on Route 340 approximately 50km (31 miles) east of Grand Falls–Windsor. From the east, head north on Route 330 at Gander; then take Route 331 to connect with Route 340 at Boyd's Cove. Gander to Twillingate is 101km (63 miles).

**VISITOR INFORMATION**   The **regional visitor information center** (© 709/628-7454) is located on Route 340 in Newville. It's open late June to early September, Monday through Friday from 8:30am to 6:30pm, and weekends from 10:30am to 6:30pm.

### EXPLORING TWILLINGATE

As you reach Twillingate's harbor on Route 340 you'll arrive at a "T" intersection at Main Street. You can go right or left; both directions merit exploration.

Turning left leads to **Long Point** and the region's most prominent lighthouse. Along the way you'll pass the **Twillingate Museum and Crafts Shop** (© 709/884-2825, off season 709/884-2044) housed in a 1914 white clapboard building that was formerly the rectory for St. Peter's Anglican Church. Inside the handsome home you'll find displays of goods that might have been found in this outport community late in the 19th century, including hooked rugs, cranberry glass, dolls, and fashions. There's also a display of local artifacts from the Maritime Indian culture, and a display about Georgina Stirling, a soprano from town who was once the toast of European opera houses, performing as Madame Toulinguet (she's buried at St. Peter's).

The museum also houses an inviting gift shop, with hand-knit sweaters, jams, and a selection of local history books. It's open daily May to early October from 9am to 8pm. Admission is C$1 (US80¢) adults, C50¢ (US40¢) children.

Continuing on, the road to Long Point passes through small communities before entering undeveloped barrens riven with coves and cliffs. You'll soon pass **Seabreeze Municipal Park** ✵ (C$2/US$1.60 admission in summer), with picnic tables and dramatic hiking trails along the cliffs. The rusted equipment in the meadows is from a short-lived copper mine, which operated here between 1908 and 1917. The area is not only unusually beautiful; it's also of interest to geologists owing to the ancient lava flows exposed in the cliff faces.

A few minutes' drive beyond the park is the **Long Point Lighthouse** ✵, Twillingate's one must-see destination. The red-and-white milk-bottle–shaped lighthouse, built in 1876, isn't open to the public, but you can park along the cliffs and enjoy the sweeping views from these high headlands. (Photographer's curse: Antennae and microwave towers share the headland with the light.) Whales and icebergs are often spotted from here.

On the other side of the parking lot is the **Long Point Interpretation Centre** (℃ 709/884-5755), owned and operated by Suzanne Carter and Garry Troake. Inside you'll find a well-stocked gift shop and tearoom serving local specialties (occasionally including seal flipper), and downstairs is a free display on local natural history. The park grounds adjacent to the lighthouse are open year-round from 9am to 9pm daily; the center is only open May to mid-October, however.

Turning right at Twillingate's main intersection takes you on a winding road through clustered homes along the harbor's edge. In 2km (1¼ miles) you'll come to **Weil Winery** (℃ 709/884-2707), which has produced Notre Dame fruit wines since 1998. Among the varieties available here are dogberry, partridgeberry, blueberry, and rhubarb wines. You're probably thinking they taste like Kool-Aid, but some of the wines are far drier than you might imagine. You can learn about the process and pick up a few bottles at the retail store; there's a small charge for a winery tour, but call ahead if you're thinking of taking it, as there's no set schedule.

Continue along the road until you reach the CAUTION: ONE LANE traffic sign. Park here and continue on by foot to find some wonderful **hiking trails** ✵✵. The lane leads to a summer cottage and private property, but foot traffic is permitted. To the left is a broad cobblestone beach; to the right are rocky, open hills and headlands laced by a network of informal hiking trails (look for cairns) that lead to oceanside cliffs and spectacular views. In mid- to late summer, bring containers so you can return with a bountiful crop of the raspberries and blueberries that grow in such profusion here. These berries are also among the plumpest and sweetest I've found on the island. None of the trails are very long or demanding; allow about 2 hours or so.

## WHERE TO STAY

Camping is available in season at **Dildo Run Provincial Park** ✵ (℃ 709/629-3350) on Route 340 in Virgin Arm, about 20 minutes south of Twillingate. The park has 55 sites, many along the water. A nicely maintained hiking trail winds along the remote coastline to Black Head, a hike of about an hour. Rates are C$13 (US$11) per night.

One of Atlantic Canada's most dramatically sited campgrounds is at **Seabreeze Municipal Park** ✵✵ near the Long Point Lighthouse. It offers primitive camping (no showers or washrooms) from June through mid-October, with sites that are grassy and

## Iceberg Spotting

Twillingate is famous for the number of icebergs that float into the area, then often run aground, providing a theatrical backdrop. That's not to say you'll be guaranteed icebergs if you arrive in midsummer. Some years are good for sighting icebergs; some are not. Numerous factors conspire to determine when and if icebergs will show up; these range from the thickness of sea ice to the direction of ocean currents to the summer temperature in the Arctic the previous year, when glaciers in Greenland calved to produce the icebergs.

If icebergs are in the area, you should be able to spot them from the Long Point lighthouse—or any of the other headlands or bays around Twillingate. (As anyone who's seen *Titanic* knows, icebergs tend not to be subtle or elusive.) Your best bet is to arrive in June or July, although I once saw a solitary iceberg in the distance on a trip in mid-August.

Speaking of the *Titanic,* you can get a closer view of icebergs via boat tours, two of which are offered from Twillingate harbor. **Twillingate Island Boat Tours** (© **800/611-2374** or 709/884-2242) has been operating since 1985 and offers iceberg and whale-watching tours from the Iceberg Shop, painted with colorful murals of icebergs. (Turn right on Main St. when you enter Twillingate.) Also offering tours is **Twillingate Adventure Tours** (© **888/ 447-8687** or 709/884-5999; www.daybreaktours.com), with a 40-passenger vessel. These 2-hour tours typically run about C$30 (US$24) per adult, while children's fares are half-price; they run from mid-May to Labor Day.

perched at the edge of soaring cliffs. The sunsets can't be beat, and the price is a deal at C$4 (US$3) per night.

**Anchor Inn Motel**    The Anchor Inn is a well-maintained, relatively modern (1973) hotel just off the harbor. It was extensively updated in 1995, and has been kept up nicely since. Don't expect fancy: It's boxy and bland with beige siding, and the rooms are standard motel units with durable furniture. The better deals by far are the efficiency units in a separate building on a rise above the motel. They are larger and have small kitchens (you can buy fresh seafood in town and cook it yourself). Ask for a room with a harbor view. If you can't snag a room with a kitchen, there's a restaurant on the premises.

Main St. (P.O. Box 550), Twillingate, NF A0G 4M0. © **800/450-3950** or 709/884-2777. Fax 709/884-2326. 22 units. C$77 (US$54) double. AE, MC, V. **Amenities:** Restaurant.

**Harbour Lights Inn** *Value*    This attractive home on a hill and across the road from the harbor was built in the 19th century for a British customs collector. It's been thoroughly updated with vinyl siding and some furniture that was imported from the suburbs, from around 1978. Guest rooms are located on the upper two floors. The best are the higher-priced nos. 4 and 5, which have burnished pine floors, in-room Jacuzzis, and wonderful views of the harbor. They're worth the extra few dollars.

189 Main St. (P.O. Box 729), Twillingate, NF A0G 4M0. © **877/884-2763** or 709/884-2763. Fax 709/884-2763. www.harbourlightsinn.com. 9 units. C$60–C$109 (US$48–US$87) double. MC, V. *In room:* TV, hair dryer, no phone.

## WHERE TO DINE

Options for dinner out are limited in Twillingate, despite the growing influx of travelers. The **Anchor Inn Motel** dining room (see above) and **R&J Restaurant,** Main Street (℃ **709/884-2212**), remain the local favorites. Both serve family fare; at R&J you'll find burgers, sandwiches, pizza, fried chicken, and the like.

## GANDER

Gander (pop. 13,000) has historic resonance for aviation buffs. In the 1930s, when the island was still a British colony, the British Air Ministry developed a new airfield here. As the nearest fog-free spot to England, Gander was envisioned as a key link in transcontinental air traffic. World War II erupted less than a decade later, and the air base took on an outsized importance as a staging area and refueling depot for troops and supplies heading overseas. After the war, the airstrip became a familiar sight to a generation of groggy tourists headed to Europe, since planes had to stop here to refuel before or after the leap across the Atlantic.

The Boeing 707—which could leap the Atlantic from New York to Europe in a single bound—diminished Gander's importance, and today the airfield is a shadow of its former self. The airport still exists and still gets a fair amount of commercial traffic (especially when St. John's is fogged in), but Gander's Trans-Canada Highway is now a more familiar sight to motorists refueling before continuing their way east or west.

The **visitor information center** (℃ **709/256-7110**), open from 9am to 9pm in summer and 9am to 5pm the rest of the year, is well marked on the south side of the Trans-Canada Highway (next to the Aviation Museum and across from the Albatross Motel) as you drive through town.

### EXPLORING GANDER

The Trans-Canada Highway skirts the southern edge of downtown, which isn't really worth a detour. The town was developed after the advent of the automobile, and as a result you'll find a handful of cheerless shopping plazas and fast-food joints. It's mostly a good place to stock up on supplies if you're headed for Twillingate or Terra Nova National Park. I will admit, however, that I saw something in Gander I'd never seen before. On an otherwise quiet Sunday, an evangelical rock group had set up on one of the covered shopping plaza walkways, facing a parking lot. They played for two dozen or so appreciative listeners, who sat in their cars facing the band, parked covered-wagon-style in a large semicircle.

A handful of hotels, restaurants, and gas stations are on the Trans-Canada Highway. You'll also find the **North Atlantic Aviation Museum** (℃ **709/256-2923**), which is identified by the butt-end of a plane jutting out of the hangarlike building. A couple of historic planes can be viewed on the grounds, including a very handsome fire-fighting plane. With its emphasis on aviation arcana, the museum itself will be of interest chiefly to confirmed airplane addicts. It's open from 9am to 9pm daily in summer; fall through spring it's open Monday through Friday from 9am to 4pm. The cost is C$3 (US$2.40) adults, C$2 (US$1.60) seniors and children 6 to 16.

Just east of town, look for a sign directing you to the **Silent Witness Memorial.** This memorial marks the site where a plane carrying members of the U.S. 101st Airborne mysteriously went down shortly after takeoff in 1985. The plane was returning from a peacekeeping mission in the Middle East; all 259 on board were killed, marking it as the worst aviation disaster on Canadian soil. The breathtaking view of Gander Lake from the crash site makes visiting the memorial a bittersweet experience.

## WHERE TO STAY & DINE

Two largish hotels right on the Trans-Canada Highway offer the best accommodations in town, although neither will win personality awards. The **Albatross Hotel** (*©* **800/ 563-4900** in Canada, or 709/256-3956) has 97 modern rooms and a ground-floor restaurant and cocktail lounge. Prices range from C$75 to C$150 (US$60–US$120). Nearby is the **Hotel Gander** (*©* **800/563-2988** in Canada, or 709/256-3931) with 152 rooms, an aviation theme, a small indoor pool, modest fitness facilities, and a chain-hotel–style restaurant that offers many traditional Newfoundland specialties. Room rates are C$84 to C$169 (US$67–US$135). Both are popular with bus tours, conference planners, and wedding parties. Another option is **Sinbad's Hotel,** Bennett Drive (*©* **800/563-8330** or 709/651-2678), a 112-room hotel/motel with suites off the highway that has an above-average dining room. Rates are C$79 to C$156 (US$63–US$125).

## 7 Terra Nova National Park

You may have heard other travelers rave about Gros Morne National Park as you discussed your impending trip to Newfoundland. At the same time, you might have heard a deafening silence upon mention of the island's other national park, Terra Nova, on the island's eastern shore.

There's a reason for that. Words like *dramatic* and *grandeur* don't get tossed around here much. This is an exceedingly pleasant spot with lots of boreal forest and coastal landscape, along with a surplus of low, rolling hills. Within its boundaries forest and shoreline are preserved for wildlife and recreation, and make for excellent exploration. But the terra, however nova, isn't likely to take your breath away. (With one possible exception: the cliffy hills at the mouth of Newman Sound.) More than likely, a visit here will leave you soothed and relaxed, your nerves unjangled.

Activities and facilities at Terra Nova have mostly been designed with families in mind. There's always something going on, from playing with starfish at the interpretation center to games and movies at the main campground. The park has a junior naturalist program, many of the hikes are just the right duration for younger kids, and there's a fine (and relatively warm) swimming area at Sandy Pond.

If your goal is to put some distance between yourself and the noisy masses, plan to head into the backcountry. A number of campsites are accessible by foot, canoe, or ferry. Out here, you'll be able to scout for bald eagles and shooting stars in silence.

## ESSENTIALS

**GETTING THERE**    Terra Nova is located on the Trans-Canada Highway. It's about 232km (144 miles) from St. John's, and 609km (378 miles) from Port aux Basques.

**VISITOR INFORMATION**    Visitor information is available at the **Marine Interpretation Centre** (*©* **709/533-2801**) at the Saltons Day-Use Area, about 5km (3 miles) north of the Newman Sound Campground. It's open daily June to mid-October from 9am to 9pm (limited hours after Labor Day).

**FEES**    A park entry fee is required of all visitors, even those just overnighting at a park campground. Fees are C$5 (US$4) per day for adults, C$4.25 (US$3.50) seniors, C$2.50 (US$2) children 6 to 16, C$13 (US$10) family. Annual passes are available for C$25 (US$20) per adult or C$63 (US$50) per family. Fees may be paid at the Marine Interpretation Centre.

## EXPLORING THE PARK

A trip to the park should begin with a visit to the spiffy, modern **Marine Interpreta-tion Centre** (see above). It's located on a scenic part of the sound, encased in verdant hills, and from here the sound looks suspiciously like a lake. Oceangoing sailboats tied up at the wharf will suggest otherwise, however.

The center has a handful of exhibits focusing on local marine life, and many are geared toward kids. There's a touch tank where you can scoop up starfish and other aquatic denizens, and informative displays on life underwater. Especially nifty is an underwater video monitor that allows you to check out the action under the adjacent wharf with a joystick and zoom controls. There's also a **Wet Lab,** where you can con-duct your own experiments under the guidance of a park naturalist. The center is free with your paid park admission. You'll also find a snack bar and gift shop here.

While here, check with the ranger on duty for all your options in exploring the park. They're good at pointing you in the right direction, whether your interests are soft adventure or going mano a mano with nature in the backcountry.

## HIKING & BOATING

The park has 77km (48 miles) of maintained **hiking trails.** Many of these are fairly easy treks of an hour or so through undemanding woodlands. The booklet you'll receive when you pay your entrance fee offers descriptions of the various trails. Among the more popular is the 4.4km (2.75-mile) **Coastal Trail** 🦀🦀, which runs between Newman Sound Campground and the Marine Interpretation Centre. You get great views of the sound, and en route you pass the wonderfully named **Pissing Mare Falls.**

The most demanding is probably the **Outport Trail,** a 32km (20-mile) round-trip that winds in and around the south shore of Newman Sound past abandoned settle-ments. It's possible to overnight at two backcountry sites along the way. Each direction can be completed in about 6 hours, but with camping layovers the whole trip typically takes 2 to 3 days, with the going sometimes slowed by bogs and wet trail sections.

*Note:* Maps and advice on hiking options are available at the Marine Interpretation Centre.

For **canoeing,** head to either Sandy Pond or Southwest Arm. Canoes are available for rent at Sandy Pond by the hour or day. You can cobble together a very attractive 10km (6-mile) one-way trip from Sandy Pond by paddling to Beachy Pond (this requires a 400m/1,320-ft. portage), and then continuing onward to Dunphy's Pond.

The park also lends itself quite nicely to **sea kayaking.** If you've brought your own boat, ask for route suggestions at the information center. (Overnight trips to Minchin and South Broad coves are good options, as are day trips to Swale Island.) If you're a paddling novice, sign up with **Terra Nova Adventures** (✆ **888/533-8687** or 709/533-9797), located at the Marine Interpretation Centre. The crew leads guided tours of the sound three times daily, when you're likely to spot eagles and maybe even a whale. The tours last between 2½ and 4 hours and cost around C$45 to C$60 (US$36–US$48) adults, C$35 to C$45 (US$28–US$36) youths. Reservations are recommended.

For a more passive view from the water, consider a tour with **Ocean Watch Tours** (✆ **709/533-6024**), which sails in a converted fishing boat four times daily from the wharf at the Marine Interpretation Centre. You're all but certain to see bald eagles and old outports, and, with some luck, whales and icebergs. The tours cost around C$35 (US$28; 2 hr.) and C$45 (US$36; 3 hr.), half-price for children. Reservations are rec-ommended during peak season, when the tours take place three times daily.

## CAMPING

Terra Nova's main campground is at **Newman Sound.** It has 355 campsites (mostly of the gravel-pad variety) set in and around spruce forest and sheep laurel clearings. Amenities include free showers, limited electrical hookups, grocery store and snack bar, evening programs, laundromat, and hiking trails. Be aware that the campground can be quite noisy and bustling in peak season. Fees are C$17 to C$26 (US$14–US$21).

At the park's northern border is the somewhat more rustic **Malady Head** 🦌 camping area. This is the better destination for those looking for quiet. It has 99 campsites, along with showers and access to a popular hiking trail. If you want your own campfire, head here; at Newman Sound fires are restricted to community fire pits. The fee is C$14 to C$17 (US$10–US$14) per site.

The park also maintains five backcountry campsites. Between four and eight parties can camp at each site, and all but Beachy Pond allow open fires. Dunphy's Island is accessible by canoe only and involves a 400m (1,320-ft.) portage; on the shore across from the island site is another site, which is also accessible via a 5km (3-mile) footpath.

For a more coastal backcountry experience, head for either **Minchin Cove** or **South Broad Cove.** Both can be reached via demanding hikes (11km/6.75 miles and 16km/10 miles, respectively) on the **Outport Trail** 🦌, which departs from Newman Sound Campground (see above). You can also arrange to be dropped off by boat, and then picked up later; ask at the visitor center for details. Backcountry campers need to register in advance and pay a fee of C$8 (US$6) per site.

## WHERE TO STAY & DINE

Campgrounds are the only option within the park itself. At the north end of the park, the town of Eastport (see "Nearby Excursions," below) is 16km (10 miles) from the Trans-Canada Highway on Route 310, and offers several places to stay overnight. From May through the end of October, try **The Doctor's Inn Bed & Breakfast,** 5 Burden's Rd., Eastport, NF A0G 1Z0 (© 877/677-3539 or 709/677-3539), with six rooms priced at C$65 to C$90 (US$52–US$72); there's a large patio here and breakfast is included. Right on a sandy beach is **Seaview Cottages,** 325 Beach Rd., Eastport, NF A0G 1Z0 (© 709/677-2271), open May through September with 23 basic cottages and a small indoor heated pool. Rates are C$55 to C$70 (US$44–US$56).

At the southern edge of the park you'll find:

**Terra Nova Park Lodge** 🦌 *(Kids)*    This modern three-story resort is a short drive off Route 1 about 2km (1¼ miles) south of the park's southern entrance. Most notably, it's adjacent to the well-regarded, 5,850m (6,500-yd.) Twin River Golf Course, one of Atlantic Canada's more scenic and better-regarded links. The hotel isn't lavish and lacks a certain personality. It feels rather inexpensively built (pray that you don't have heavy-footed children staying overhead), and it features bland, cookie-cutter rooms. On the other hand, it's clean, comfortable, and well located for a golfing holiday or exploring the park. It's a popular spot with families, since kids can roam the grounds, splash around the pool, and congregate at the downstairs video games. The Clode Sound Dining Room is open daily for all three meals. It offers standard resort fare with an emphasis on chicken and beef with some seafood; dinners include fried cod, filet mignon, pork chops and applesauce, and surf and turf. There's also a pub downstairs.

Rte. 1, Port Blandford, NF A0C 2G0. (C) **709/543-2525**. Fax 709/543-2201. www.terranovagolf.com. 94 units. C$101–C$157 (US$81–US$126) double. AE, DC, DISC, MC, V. **Amenities:** 2 restaurants; bar; outdoor pool; 2 tennis courts; Jacuzzi; sauna; game room. *In room:* A/C, TV, kitchenette (some units).

## NEARBY EXCURSIONS

Route 310 runs along the northern edge of Terra Nova National Park and winds along inlets and hillsides to the Eastport peninsula. Around the town of Eastport are a number of fine **sandy beaches** both hidden in coves and laid out in long strands edging the road. Notable beaches are located along Route 310 between Eastport and Salvage, and in the aptly named village of **Sandy Cove** (follow signs to the right when you enter Eastport).

Across from the Sandy Cove beach is the start of **The Old Trails** ✦. The main trail winds along a wooded ridge and past remote ponds approximately 8km (5 miles) to the village of Salvage. The trail is still under development and hiking may be a bit rugged. Bring lunch, sturdy hiking boots, and a compass, and plan to make an adventure of it. Brochures with general trail descriptions are sometimes available at area visitor information centers.

From Eastport, continue on toward the picturesque fishing village of Salvage, about 10km (6 miles) farther. The drive follows along the water with the periodic detour up into the hills. The village itself is tucked in and around several coves, and everywhere great slabs of rock protrude from the earth, lending a sort of cinematic drama. More about the region's history can be found at the **Salvage Fisherman's Museum** ✦, set on a low hill overlooking the harbor ((C) **709/677-2414**). It's housed in the oldest building in the area—an 1860 home that's now filled with displays on the whys and hows of fishing. It's open daily mid-June to early September from 9:30am to 7:30pm (sometimes shorter hours), and there's a small admission charge.

A longer excursion is a ferry trip that winds through a beautiful archipelago to remote **St. Brendan's Island** ✦. From Burnside, just north of Eastport, the hour-long ferries ((C) **709/466-4121** or 709/677-2204) run several times daily in summer, with each-way fares of C$9.75 (US$7.80) for a car and driver, C$6.50 (US$5.20) for additional passengers (C$3.50/US$2.80 for seniors and students). Pay when leaving the island. The island is home to several small communities located along some 9km (5½ miles) of unpaved road, but St. Brendan's offers little in the way of services for travelers—just a few general stores, and no restaurants or overnight accommodations.

There are no services—or even buildings, for that matter—at the island's ferry landing. This makes a good destination for adventurous mountain bikers; otherwise, you might consider just taking the ferry out and back as a low-budget boat tour. The islands between Burnside and St. Brendan's are uninhabited, wild, and beautiful: you might spot bald eagles perched along the shore during the 45-minute crossing.

## 8 The Bonavista Peninsula ✦

The Bonavista Peninsula juts northeast into the sea from just south of Terra Nova National Park. It's a worthy side trip for travelers fascinated by the island's past. You'll find a historic village, a wonderfully curated historic site, and one of the province's most intriguing lighthouses. It's also a good spot to see whales, puffins, and icebergs.

Along the south shore of the peninsula is Trinity, an impeccably maintained old village. (It's the only village in Newfoundland where the historic society has say over what can and can't be built.) Some long-time visitors grouse that it's becoming overly popular and a bit dandified with too many B&Bs and traffic restrictions. That might be. But there's still a palpable sense of tradition to this profoundly historic spot. And anyway, it's the region's only destination to find good shelter and a decent meal.

From Trinity it's about 40km (24 miles) out to the tip of the peninsula. Somewhere along the route, which isn't always picturesque, you'll wonder whether it's worth it. Yes, it is. Keep going. Plan to spend at least a couple of hours exploring the dramatic, ocean-carved point and the fine fishing village of Bonavista with its three excellent historic properties.

Note that there's little in the way of interesting accommodations or restaurants this far out, so it's better to plan this as a day trip (perhaps from Trinity) rather than an overnight. The one sight possibly worth seeing is the **Bonavista North Regional Museum** (© 709/536-2110), open daily from 10am to 6pm July through September. It features displays on fishermen and the local fishing industry, as well as some items depicting community life here during the early 20th century.

## ESSENTIALS

**GETTING THERE**    Depending on the direction you're coming from, the Bonavista Peninsula can be reached from the Trans-Canada Highway via Route 233, Route 230, or Route 230A. Route 230 runs all the way to the tip of the cape; Route 235 forms a partial loop back and offers some splendid water views along the way. The round-trip from Clarenville to the tip is approximately 232km (144 miles).

**VISITOR INFORMATION**    The **Southern Bonavista Bay Tourist Chalet** is on Route 230 just west of the intersection with Route 235. It's open daily from 8:30am to 8:30pm in summer. The region maintains a website, as well: **www.trinitybight.com**.

## TRINITY ⚘

The tiny coastal hamlet of Trinity, with a year-round population of just 200, once had more residents than St. John's. For more than 3 centuries, from its first visit by Portuguese fishermen in the 1500s until well into the 19th century, Trinity benefited from a long and steady tenure as a hub for traders, primarily from England, who supplied the booming fishing economy of Trinity Bay and eastern Newfoundland.

Technological advances (including the railroad) doomed Trinity's merchant class, and the town lapsed into an extended economic slumber. But even today, you can see lingering traces of the town's former affluence, from the attractive flourishes in much of the architecture to the rows of white picket fences all around the village.

In recent years, the provincial government and concerned individuals have taken a keen interest in preserving Trinity, and it's clearly benefiting from a revival in which many homes have been preserved, and a good number made over as bed-and-breakfasts. Several buildings (see below) are open to the public as provincial historic sites, two others as local historical museums. Most are open mid-June to early October, then shuttered the remainder of the year. Allow about 3 hours to wander about and explore.

Days on which the popular historic pageant is held (see "Tours & Shows," below) bring a flood tide of visitors to Trinity, making parking and rooms scarce, and meals sometimes difficult to obtain. The village is also well worth seeing on non-pageant days, when a great quiet settles in.

Start your voyage into the past at the **Trinity Interpretation Centre** (© 709/464-2042) at the Tibbs House, open 10am to 5:30pm daily. (It's a bit tricky to find, since signs don't seem to be a priority. Follow the one-way road around the village and continue straight past the parish hall. Look on the left for the pale green home with the prominent gable.) Here you can purchase tickets, pick up a walking-tour map, and get oriented with a handful of history exhibits.

Several ticket options exist; if you want to visit just one or two of the places listed below, buy individual tickets, which cost C$2.50 (US$2) and up per adult. For a full day, the better bet is the C$7 (US$5.50) ticket, which admits you to six buildings. Most maintain the same hours as the interpretation center.

A minute's walk away is the brick **Lester-Garland Premises** (© 709/464-2042), usually the first stop on a Trinity itinerary, where you can learn about the traders and their times. This handsome Georgian-style building is a convincing replica (built in 1997) of one of the earlier structures, built in 1819. The original was occupied until 1847, when it was abandoned and began to deteriorate. It was torn down (much to the horror of local historians) in the 1960s, but parts of the building hardware, including some doors and windows, were salvaged and warehoused until the rebuilding.

Next door is the **Ryan Building,** where a succession of the town's most prominent merchants kept shop. The grassy lots between these buildings and the water were once filled with warehouses, none of which survived. The new Rising Tide theater, built in 1999, approximates one of the warehouses; a good imagination is helpful in envisioning the others.

A short walk away, just past the parish house, is the **Hiscock House** (© 709/464-2042), a handsome home where Emma Hiscock raised her children and kept a shop after the untimely death of her husband in a boating accident at age 39. The home has been restored to appear as it might have been in 1910, and helpful guides fill in the details.

The **Trinity Historical Society Museum** on Church Road (© 709/464-3599) contains a selection of everyday artifacts that one might have seen in Trinity a century or more ago; the nearby **Green Family Forge Blacksmith Museum** will leave you well informed about one of the essential local industries.

## TOURS & SHOWS

An entertaining way to learn about the village's history is through the **Trinity Pageant** (© 888/464-3777 or 709/464-3232). On Wednesdays, Saturdays, and Sundays at 2pm, actors lead a peripatetic audience through the streets, acting out episodes from Trinity's past. Tickets are C$10 (US$8) adults, free for children under 14. In the evenings, the innovative **Rising Tide Theatre** (same phone as the pageant) offers a number of performances throughout the summer, most depicting island episodes or themes. In the past the cast staged their shows at impromptu venues around town (upstairs at the parish hall, in a field at the water's edge, on the front porch of a B&B, and the like). In 2000, they opened a 255-seat theater in a newly constructed building architecturally styled after a historic waterfront warehouse. The performances are top-rate, and well worth the money (about C$14–C$30/US$11–US$24).

Also recommended is the 2-hour historical walking tour of Trinity led daily at 10am by **Kevin Toope** (© 709/464-3723). Toope's family has been in the area for generations, and Kevin (a schoolteacher in St. John's most of the year) has put together an informed and entertaining tour of the village he knows so well. After a tutored loop around the winding streets, you'll come away with lots of fascinating facts and bits of color that help bring the town to life. One example: What happened to the family of one of the town's merchant princes, who owned practically everything and treated his employees with contempt? Historians have traced only one descendent: a derelict in London.

## OUTDOOR PURSUITS

A trail system on the Bonavista Peninsula is being created through woodlands and over headlands. The **Discovery Trail Tourism Association** (© 709/466-3845; www.thediscoverytrail.org) has been working with other groups to develop and promote hiking trails on the Bonavista peninsula. A trail guide is now available at visitor centers. To date, 10 trails in the area have been opened to public use; more may be opened in the future.

A superb hike is found 15 minutes' drive south of Trinity outside the fishing village of New Bonaventure. The **Kerley's Harbour Trail** 𝕮 departs from the end of the parking area adjacent to St. John's Anglican Church (make the 1st right as you enter New Bonaventure and drive uphill to the end of the road). The 2km (1.25-mile) trail—a grassy lane that winds over rolling hills and past a pristine pond—requires about 35 minutes, and ends at the abandoned outport of Kerley's Harbour. This well-protected cove is flanked with rocky hills and open meadows dotted with fallen homes. Along the waters are remnants of fishing stages, and a new extension trail leads to a resettled community—in the early 1900s the government moved remote communities to a more central area in order to provide them with better services—which is no longer inhabited but can still be visited on foot. It's all as melancholy as it is beautiful.

## WHERE TO STAY

All three properties mentioned below are in the heart of Trinity's historic area. Reservations are essential during the peak summer season, especially on Wednesdays, Saturdays, and Sundays when the pageant is scheduled. Those who come unprepared risk a drive to Clarenville to find a room.

**Lockston Path Provincial Park** (© 709/464-3553) is a 15-minute drive from Trinity in Port Rexton. From mid-May to mid-September, the park maintains 56 campsites, along with a modern comfort station with free hot showers. Sites are C$13 (US$11).

**Bishop White Manor Bed & Breakfast**    This historic house with early woodwork and tin ceilings was home to Newfoundland's first native-born bishop, and is convenient to just about everything in Trinity. It's more serviceable than elegant, and the small rooms are very small. The extra cost for a larger room is worth it, especially if it's a rainy day. There's limited common space on the first floor, although the rear deck is a nice spot to unwind if the weather's sunny.

Gallavan's Lane (P.O. Box 58), Trinity, NF A0C 2S0. © 877/464-3698 or 709/464-3299. Fax 709/464-2104. www.trinityexperience.com. 9 units. C$80–C$90 (US$64–US$72) double. Rates include full breakfast. AE, MC, V. Closed mid-Oct to mid-May. *In room:* No phone.

**Campbell House Bed & Breakfast Inn** 𝕮 *Finds*    This handsome 1840 home and two nearby cottages are set amid lovely gardens on a twisting lane overlooking Fisher Cove. Two rooms are on the second floor of the main house, and these have a nice historic flair, even to the point that they'll require some stooping under beams if you're over 5 feet, 10 inches tall. Two rooms are located in a lovely and simple pine-paneled house just beyond the gardens, and they feature an adjacent waterfront deck and a full kitchen on the first floor; the Twine Loft (home to a restaurant) also overlooks the water. An affiliated property, the **Artisan Inn,** offers similar simple rooms at C$115 to C$135 (US$92–US$108), double occupancy. Innkeeper Tineke Gow also recently added a third property on Fisher Cove, the **Kelly House,** dating from the 1940s.

Cottages here are rented to just one party at a time who can use one, two, or three bedrooms (priced accordingly). Gow is a great source of information on local adventures and maintains a wine cellar on the premises. Reserve well in advance for July and August when the inn only rarely has a free room.

High St., Trinity, Trinity Bay, NF A0C 2S0. ℰ 877/464-7700 or 709/464-3377. www.trinityvacations.com. 3 units. C$109–C$229 (US$87–US$183). Rates include full breakfast. AE, DC, MC, V. Closed Nov–May. *In room:* Kitchenette, hair dryer, iron, no phone.

**Hangashore Bed & Breakfast**    The rooms in this historic 1860 home are cozy (read: tiny), just as they would have been in, well, 1860. But they're utterly uncluttered in a modern Scandinavian sort of way, and painted with bold, welcoming colors. There's a parlor with television and telephone downstairs, and relaxed breakfasts are served around a pine picnic-style table in a cheerful ground-floor room; recent renovations have freshened the interior decor, bathrooms, and veranda.

1 Ash's Lane, Trinity, Trinity Bay, NF A0C 2S0. ℰ 866/464-3807 or 709/464-2060. 4 units (2 with shared bath). C$59–C$79 (US$47–US$63) double. Rates include full breakfast. MC, V. Closed Nov–May. Pets allowed with C$5 (US$4) charge. *In room:* No phone.

**Village Inn**    The eight rooms in this handsome old inn, located on what passes for a busy street in Trinity (busy with pedestrians, that is), has a pleasantly lived-in feel, with eclectic but leaning-toward-Victorian furniture, a newly replaced front porch for relaxing, and a small dining room that feels as if it hasn't changed a whit in 75 years. Innkeepers Christine and Peter Beamish do a fine job of making guests feel at home; they also run Ocean Contact, a whale-watch operation that uses an 8m (26-ft.) rigid-hull inflatable. Ask about tour availability when you book your room.

Taverner's Path (P.O. Box 10), Trinity, Trinity Bay, NF A0C 2S0. ℰ 709/464-3269. Fax 709/464-3700. www.ocean contact.com. 7 units. C$75 (US$60) and up double. MC, V. Open by advance arrangement Nov–Apr. "Small, well-behaved pets" allowed. **Amenities:** 2 dining rooms; pub. *In room:* No phone.

## WHERE TO DINE
**Eriksen Premises** ℰ TRADITIONAL    Despite some inelegant touches (like butter served in those pesky plastic tubs with the peel-off tops), this is Trinity's best restaurant, and it offers good value. The restaurant shares the first floor of a B&B with a gift shop, and has a homey feel with oak floors, beadboard ceiling, and Victorian accents. (There's also dining on an outside deck, which is especially inviting at lunchtime.) The meals are mostly traditional: cod tongue, broiled halibut, scallops, liver and onion, and chicken. The service and food quality are consistently a notch above the expected. Desserts, like the cheesecake with fresh berry toppings, are especially good.

*Note:* If you're stuck for a room, the restaurant also maintains and rents out six well-appointed suites with TV and VCR (one also has a Jacuzzi); they run from C$80 to C$110 (US$57–US$78) per night.

West St. ℰ 877/464-3698 or 709/464-3698. Reservations recommended during peak season. Main courses C$4.95–C$6.95 (US$4–US$5.50) at lunch, C$9.95–C$19 (US$8–US$15) at dinner. MC, V. Daily 8am–9:30pm. Closed Nov–May.

**Village Inn** ℰ *Finds* TRADITIONAL/VEGETARIAN    The pleasantly old-fashioned dining room at the Village Inn (see "Where to Stay," above) has a good reputation for its vegetarian meals (something of a rarity in Newfoundland), with options including a lentil shepherd's pie and a rice and nut casserole. But those looking for comfort food are also well served here, with options like chowder, meatloaf, fried cod, liver and onions, a ham plate, and a seafood platter. This is country cooking at its finest; everything is made from scratch, from soups to dessert.

Taverner's Path. © **709/464-3269.** Main courses C$8–C$20 (US$6.40–US$16); lunch items less. MC, V. Daily 8am–9pm.

## BONAVISTA ⊛

Bonavista is a 45-minute drive from Trinity and is a strongly recommended day trip for those spending a night or two in the area.

If you're approaching Bonavista on Route 230, I'd suggest it's worth your while to detour on Route 238 through Elliston. This is a pretty coastal village and worth the few extra kilometers. More to the point, this route brings you into the town of Bonavista via a scenic road across high upland barrens. You'll get great views of the white-washed town with the expansive bay beyond as you crest the hill. This bay is noted for its icebergs, which can linger late into summer. This road provides a grand vantage point to scan the horizon for icebergs and "bergy bits" before you head down to sea level.

### EXPLORING THE TOWN

The **Ryan Premises National Historic Site** ⊛ (© **709/468-1600**) opened in 1997, with Queen Elizabeth herself presiding over the ceremonies. Located in downtown Bonavista, the new site is a very photogenic grouping of white clapboard buildings at the harbor's edge. For more than a century, this was the town's most prominent salt-fish complex, where fishermen sold their catch and bought all the sundry goods needed to keep an outport functioning. Michael Ryan opened for business here in 1857; his heirs kept the business going until 1978. (One elderly resident recalled that you could "get everything from a baby's fart to a clap of thunder" from the Ryans.) The spiffy complex today features an art gallery, local history museum, gift shop, handcrafted furniture store, and what may be the most rare and extraordinary of all: a truly fascinating exhibit on the role of the codfish industry in Newfoundland's history. An hour or two here will greatly abet you in making sense of the rest of your visit to the island.

The property is open daily mid-May through mid-October from 10am to 6pm. Admission is C$4 (US$3.20) adults, C$3.50 (US$2.80) seniors, C$2 (US$1.60) youths, and C$10 (US$8) family.

On the far side of the harbor, and across from a field of magnificent irises, is the beautiful **Mockbeggar Plantation** (© **709/468-7300**). Named after an English sea-port that shared characteristics with Bonavista, the home was occupied by prominent Newfoundland politician F. Gordon Bradley. It's been restored to how it appeared when Bradley moved here in 1940, and it features much of the original furniture. With a few telltale exceptions (note the wonderful 1940s-era carpet in the formal dining room), it shows a strong Victorian influence. The house is managed as a provincial historic site, and admission is C$2.50 (US$2) adults, free for children under 12 (also includes admission to Cape Bonavista Lighthouse, see below). It's open daily from mid-June to early October from 10am to 5:30pm.

A replica of the *Matthew* (© **877/468-1497** or 709/468-1493), the ship John Cabot sailed when he first landed in Newfoundland in 1497, floats in Bonavista's harbor. This compact ship is an exacting replica, based on plans of the original ship. (Don't confuse this ship with the other *Matthew* replica, which crossed the Atlantic and sailed around Newfoundland in 1997.) An interpretive center and occasional performances staged wharfside provide context for your tour aboard the ship, which is designed as a floating museum. Because it's an exact copy, and looks roughly as it did 500 years ago, the ship doesn't have an engine or any modern safety devices, and thus isn't allowed to leave the dock for passenger cruises. It will stay tied up along the dock in summer, and stored in an architecturally striking white clapboard boathouse in the off season.

The ship is open from June to mid-October, daily from 10am to 6pm (to 8pm in summer). Admission is C$6.50 (US$5.20) adults, C$6 (US$5) seniors, C$2.25 (US$1.80) children ages 6 to 16, C$16 (US$13) family; plan to spend an hour touring the ship.

## JUST NORTH OF TOWN

The extraordinary **Cape Bonavista Lighthouse Provincial Historic Site** *&* (*C* 709/ 468-7444) is located 6km (3½ miles) north of town on a rugged point. Built in 1843, the lighthouse is fundamentally a stone tower around which a red-and-white wood-frame house has been constructed. The keepers' quarters (the lightkeeper and his assistant both lived here) has been restored to the year 1870. You can clamber up the narrow stairs to the light itself and inspect the ingenious clockwork mechanism that kept six lanterns revolving all night long between 1895 and 1962. (With some help— it took 15 min. to wind the counterweight by hand, a job that had to be performed every 2 hr.) This light served mariners until 3 decades ago, when its role was usurped by an inelegant steel tower and beacon. Open daily in summer from 10:30am to 5:30pm; admission is C$2.50 (US$2) adult, free for under 12 (also includes admission to Mockbeggar Plantation; see above).

Below the lighthouse on a rocky promontory cleft from the mainland is a lively **puffin colony.** Dozens of these stumpy, colorful birds hop around the grassy knob and take flight into the sea winds. They're easily seen from just below the lighthouse; bring binoculars for a clearer view. Red-footed common murres dive for fish below, and whales are often sighted just offshore. This is the only place I've ever had whales and puffins in sight through my binoculars at the same time. (And there was a beautiful iceberg just off to my left.)

Also nearby is a statue of John Cabot. Although no one can prove it, long-standing tradition holds that Cape Bonavista was the first land spotted by the Italian explorer (who was working for the English) in 1497. The statue is located in handsome Landfall Municipal Park, next to the lighthouse, where you'll find picnic tables and an exceptional example of a quiggly fence, a traditional Newfoundland windbreak made of vertically woven whips or saplings.

En route to the lighthouse you'll pass a turnoff to **Dungeons Provincial Park.** It's 2km (1¼ miles) down a gravel road through coastal cow, goat, and sheep pastures. Park and follow the short trail to a punchbowl-like cavity some 50 yards across. Relentless waves carved two tunnels under the pasture, and eventually the grassy roof collapsed, leaving this gaping hole flushed by the surf. Admission is free.

## 9 The Baccalieu Trail

The Baccalieu Trail forms a loop around the long, narrow, and unnamed peninsula that separates Conception Bay from Trinity Bay. It doesn't have the distinguished 18th-century pedigree of neighboring Bonavista Peninsula, which was the region's mercantile center in the early days. But I think the history here is actually more intriguing in a quirky kind of way. Episodes here feature the mysterious Amelia Earhart, the cranky Rockwell Kent, and the pioneers of both the Arctic exploration and transatlantic communication.

Be aware that the drive isn't uninterruptedly picturesque. It's notably unscenic for a long stretch south of Carbonear on the Conception Bay side. But elsewhere you will come upon vistas that will leave you absolutely speechless.

## ESSENTIALS

**GETTING THERE**    The Baccalieu Trail is composed of Routes 80, 70, and 60. The entire detour to Bay de Verde and back from the Trans-Canada is about 250km (156 miles).

**VISITOR INFORMATION**    The **Provincial Interpretive and Information Center** (© 709/759-2170) is on the Trans-Canada Highway just west of Route 80 in Whitbourne. It's open daily in season from 8:30am to 8:30pm.

## DILDO

The picturesque fishing town of Dildo consists of homes clustered along a hilly harbor's edge and a forested prominence rising near the outer point. (It's about 12km/7½ miles north of the Trans-Canada Hwy. on Rte. 80.) While fishing has ground to a near-halt since the cod moratorium, cultural tourism has picked up some of the slack, with visitors trekking here to view traces of the once-thriving Indian culture. A highlight is a visit to an island in the mouth of the harbor, which was occupied at various times by Beothuk, Dorset Eskimo, and more modern Indians.

A good place to start a tour is the **Dildo Interpretation Centre** (© 709/582-3339), on the harbor as you come into town. (Look for the giant squid made of fiberglass in the parking lot, an actual-size model of one caught locally in 1933.) The center opened in 1997 and features displays of some of the nearly 6,000 Eskimo artifacts recovered by archaeologists on the island, including harpoon end blades, knives, soapstone bowls and lamps, and scrapers. The center also features a touch tank with crabs and starfish for kids, and exhibits on the more recent lumbering and fishing industries of the region. The center is open June through September daily from 10am to 6pm; admission is C$2 (US$1.60) adults, C$1 (US80¢) children, C$10 (US$8) family.

Oh, yes . . . the town's name. You may be wondering. The generally accepted theory is that it was named by early Spanish sailors for a person or place in Spain. Other theories: It may be from a local Indian word meaning "still waters," or, less tenably, from the chorus of an old ballad. Nobody really knows.

## HEART'S CONTENT

Heart's Content was named either after an early ship that visited here, or because of the vaguely heart-shaped harbor. In any event, this is a pleasing coastal village that claims a prominent footnote in the annals of telecommunications. In 1858 the **first trans-Atlantic telegraph cable** was brought ashore, connecting England with Newfoundland and beyond to the United States; Queen Victoria and U.S. President James Buchanan exchanged messages. After 27 days and 732 messages the cable mysteriously failed, and another cable, this one to Heart's Content, was installed in 1866. This was to blossom as a vital link between the New and the Old World. It also provided employment for 300 people in this little village and brought a measure of culture and prosperity. In the late 1800s, some 1,200 people lived here; since the 1950s, the population has hovered around 600.

You can still see rusted and frayed cables jutting from an embankment near the center of town. The brick cable station with its distinctive gingerbread trim is just across the road. At the **Cable Station Historic Site** (© **800/563-6353** or 709/583-2160), you can see the impressively bulky antique equipment and learn more about how involved this historic enterprise really was. (*A side note:* The displays and exhibits were installed in the 1970s, and will be of special interest to those who enjoy period pieces dating from the era of ABBA and platform shoes.) Open daily June through October from 10:30am to 6pm; admission is C$2.50 (US$2) adults, free for children under 12.

At the rocky point at the mouth on the north side of the harbor is a relatively modern barber-pole–striped **lighthouse** set amid impressive, rounded rocks that seem to heave up from the earth. Wonderful views of Trinity Bay can be had from here; it's a good spot for a picnic.

## BACCALIEU ISLAND

Cliff-girded **Baccalieu Island,** about 3.5km (2 miles) off the peninsula's tip, is 5km (3 miles) long and has a rich history as a fishing center and location of an important lighthouse. Today, it's better known for the vast colonies of seabirds, 11 species of which breed here. These include puffins, northern fulmar, common murre, and northern gannet. The island is also home to thick-billed murre and razorbills, and a staggering 3-million-plus Leach's storm petrels. Alas, boat tours to the island haven't been offered on a regular basis in a couple of years. Committed birders might be able to drum up a local fisherman or other boat owner who'd be willing to go out; ask at the provincial information center in Whitbourne for suggestions.

The village of **Bay de Verde** at the northern tip of the peninsula is worth an excursion even if you're not trying to visit the island. A road now reaches this remote fishing village, but it still very much has the feel of an outport untouched by modern trends. It's dominated by trim, old-fashioned houses on rocky terraces overlooking the harbor.

## HARBOUR GRACE

Harbour Grace is a historic town that sprawls along a waterfront with views out to Conception Bay. It's not a picture-perfect town—there's plenty of charmless modern architecture mixed among the historic—but you'll get a good sense of the region's rich history with an hour's poking around.

Near the **Harbour Grace Visitor Center** (© **709/596-3042**) at the south end of town are two modest memorials to transportation before the roads. The *Spirit of Harbour Grace,* a DC-3 airplane from Labrador Air, is mounted in a graceful banked turn, like a trout rising to take a fly. Just offshore and slightly out of kilter is the **SS Kyle,** a handsome coastal steamer that lies aground and listing to port. The *Kyle* was one of the last of the wood- and coal-burning coastal steamers. Launched in 1913, it plied Newfoundland's waters until 1967, when a northeaster blew her from her moorings and she came to rest on a mussel bed. A paint job in 1997 made her somewhat more festive.

Harbour Grace occupies a prominent niche in the history of **early-20th-century aviation.** A cluster of pioneer pilots used the town airfield as a jumping-off point for crossings of the Atlantic. Indeed, Newfoundland was abuzz with daring pilots during aviation's pioneer days. The first nonstop crossing of the Atlantic was by John Alcock and A. W. Brown, who flew from Newfoundland to Ireland in 1919, 8 years before

Charles Lindbergh left New York to become the first solo pilot to cross the Atlantic. In 1928, Amelia Earhart flew to Wales from Newfoundland, and 4 years later she became the first woman to solo the transatlantic trip, taking off from Harbour Grace.

You can revisit this rich history at the **Harbour Grace Airfield,** the first aerodrome in Newfoundland. It's a stunningly beautiful and pristine spot on a hillside overlooking the harbor and the town—it appears not to have changed a bit since Earhart took off for Europe more than a half-century ago. You can scramble atop the monolith at the north end of the airfield to get a sweeping view out into Conception Bay, with the lush, grassy airstrip stretching out below.

Find the airfield by driving 1.5km (1 mile) north of the information center on Route 70, and then turning left. The paved road soon stops; you don't. Continue 1.5km (1 mile) from Route 70, and turn right on another dirt road. Continue another 1.5km (1 mile), passing the end of the airstrip, and then turn right and drive to the top of the low hill. There's a small plaque commemorating the early fliers.

More local history is on view at the **Conception Bay Museum** (© 709/596-5465) on Water Street. Located on a low bluff overlooking the harbor and distant sea stacks, the museum occupies a three-story brick and granite building that was a customs station when built in 1870. Inside you'll find artifacts and costumed guides, who offer walking tours of the town's **Heritage District** by appointment. The museum is open daily from mid-June to early September, 10am to 5pm (closed daily from 1–1:30pm for lunch). Admission is C$2 (US$1.60) adults, C$1 (US80¢) seniors and children ages 10 to 18.

Boat tours of the harbor are offered by **Great Easton Boat Tours** (© 709/596-2172), a firm named after the master pirate Peter Easton. The 8m (26-ft.) fiberglass motorboat accommodates up to 12 passengers, and during a 2-hour tour you'll get a close-up view of the SS *Kyle,* and learn some of the rich folklore that's taken root in and around Conception Bay. It's best to book ahead.

## WHERE TO STAY & DINE

There are a couple of motels along the Baccalieu Trail, especially on the southern stretches of Route 70. Carbonear has two basic, serviceable motels: **Fong's Motel** (© 709/596-5114) and **Carbonear Motel** (© 877/596-5662 or 709/596-5662). Rooms at both run around C$55 to C$75 (US$44–US$60).

**NaGeira House** *(Finds)* The NaGeira House is named after an Irish princess, who was kidnapped in the 17th century and was spirited away to Carbonear, where she lived out her life. The inn opened in 1999 in a wonderful old gabled home, and the innkeepers have a good eye for detail, from the down duvets and quality linens, to the delicious breakfasts. The rooms vary widely as to size, from very small for the least expensive, to a spacious master suite with in-room Jacuzzi and fireplace. If you opt for the smallest room, you'll still have access to the comfortable common room.

7 Musgrave St. Carbonear, NF A1Y 1A4. © 800/600-7757 or 709/596-1888. Fax 709/596-4622. www.nageirahouse. com. 4 units. C$99–C$149 (US$79–US$119) double. Rates include full breakfast. Discounts available in off season. AE, MC, V **Amenities:** Restaurant. *In room:* TV (3 units).

**Rothesay House Inn B&B** *(Value)* The Queen Anne–style Rothesay House dates from 1910 and sits on a low rise looking across the street to the harbor beyond. It's well situated for exploring Harbour Grace and the Baccalieu Trail, and has four comfortable guest rooms, each with private bathroom. The inn's popular restaurant is open for three meals daily. The menu changes with the availability of goods and tends to have a number of selections for carnivores—a nice break from the more common emphasis on seafood islandwide. The menu might include pork loin chops with an apple and cream sauce, chateaubriand, or orange basil chicken. (Of course, there's also salmon or cod.)

34 Water St., Harbour Grace, NF A0A 2M0. Ⓒ **709/596-2268.** Fax 709/596-0317. www.rothesay.com. 4 units. C$95–C$125 (US$76–US$100). Rates include full breakfast. MC, V. **Amenities:** Dining room. *In room:* No phone.

## BRIGUS

The trim and tidy harbor-front village of Brigus is clustered with wood-frame homes and narrow lanes that extend out from the picturesque harbor. Brigus is remembered by some art historians as the town that gave the boot to iconoclastic American artist Rockwell Kent, who lived here, briefly, in 1914 and 1915. World War I was on, and Kent was suspected of "pro-German activities." His crime? Singing songs in Pennsylvania Dutch. Kent eventually returned to Newfoundland in 1968 as a guest of the premier and forgave the province and the people.

Near the harbor, look for the **"Brigus Tunnel,"** built in the summer of 1860 by Capt. Abraham Bartlett, whose deepwater dock was on one side of a low, rocky ridge but whose warehouses were on the other. He resolved the problem by hiring a Cornish miner to create a pathway. Although the dock and warehouses are gone, and local teens have adorned the tunnel with graffiti, you can still stroll through and be rewarded with a fine view of the harbor.

If you're in town come evening, the **Baccalieu Players** stage various shows and dinner cabarets, and host comedy nights at various venues in Brigus and beyond. For information, ask at any shop locally, or call ⒸⒸ **709/528-4817.** Performance tickets cost C$5 to C$35 (US$4–US$28).

### Hawthorne Cottage National Historic Site   This elaborate gingerbread cottage on a lovely landscaped yard in the town center was home to Capt. Bob Bartlett, who was among the support crew accompanying Robert E. Peary on his successful trip to the North Pole in 1909. (Bartlett has been lauded as the "greatest ice navigator of the century.") The cottage was originally built in 1830, was moved here from 10km (6¼ miles) away in 1833, and is now furnished much as it might have been by the local gentry at the turn of the century. Allow 2 to 3 hours if you're intrigued by Bartlett's story; otherwise, 45 minutes should be plenty of time.

Village Center (P.O. Box 5542), Brigus. Ⓒ **709/528-4004.** Admission C$3.50 (US$2.80) adults, C$3 (US$2.40) seniors, C$2 (US$1.60) children 6–16, C$8 (US$6.40) families. Mid-May to Oct daily 9am–5:30pm.

### Ye Olde Stone Barn Museum ⚜   This is one of the finest small museums in the province. Local history is the focus of this replica of an 1820 stone barn, which has been nicely curated with a limited but well-chosen selection of artifacts. These include a beautiful plate hand-painted by Rockwell Kent during his short and controversial residency here. Plan to spend 30 minutes here.

4 Magistrate's Hill. Ⓒ **709/528-4004.** Admission C$1 (US70¢) adults, C50¢ (US35¢) children. Mid-June to Labor Day daily 11am–6pm, Sept and Oct weekends only 11am–6pm. Closed Nov to mid-June.

## 10 St. John's ⭐⭐

St. John's is a world apart from the rest of Newfoundland. The island's small outports and long roads through spruce and bog are imbued with a deep melancholy. St. John's, on the other hand, is vibrant and bustling. Coming into the city after traveling the

# St. John's

*St. John's Harbour*

ⓘ Information

**ATTRACTIONS** ●
Art Gallery of Newfoundland and Labrador **6**
Commissariat House **15**
Pippy Park and Memorial University **1**
Provincial Museum of Newfoundland and Labrador **5**
Quidi Vidi **16**
Signal Hill & Cabot Tower **17**

**ACCOMMODATIONS** ■
At Wit's Inn **13**
Delta St. John's **2**
The Fairmont Newfoundland **12**
McCoubrey Manor **11**
Monkstown Manor **6**
Prescott Inn **14**
Quality Hotel Harbourview **9**
Winterholme **6**
Heritage Inn **6**

**DINING** ◆
Casa Grande **8**
The Cellar **4**
Classic Café East **3**
International Flavours **7**
Zachary's **10**

hinterlands is like stepping from Kansas into Oz—the landscape suddenly seems to burst with color and life.

This attractive port city of just over 100,000 residents crowds the steep hills around a deep harbor. Like Halifax, Nova Scotia, and Saint John, New Brunswick, St. John's also serves as a magnet for youth culture in the province, and the clubs and restaurants tend to have a more cosmopolitan feel and sharper edge. The presence of Memorial University—the province's premiere institution of higher learning less than 2 miles west of the harbor—gives the city yet another shot in the arm.

St. John's harbor is impressive, protected from the open seas by stony hills and accessible only through a pinched gap called The Narrows, a rocky defile of the sort you'd expect to see Atlas straddle. The Narrows is at the north end of the harbor and hidden from view from much of downtown, so first-time visitors may think they've stumbled upon a small lake—albeit one with tankers and other oceangoing ships.

This is very much a working harbor, the hub of much of the province's commerce. As such, don't expect quaint. Across the way are charmless oil-tank farms, along with off-loading facilities for tankers. A major container-ship wharf occupies the head of the harbor. Along the water's edge on Harbour Street downtown, you'll usually find hulking ships tied up; pedestrians are welcome to stroll and gawk, but wholesale commerce is the focus here, not boutiques.

If you can arrange it, come to St. John's after you've explored the more remote parts of Newfoundland. At that point—after a couple of weeks or even a few days of sketchy restaurant food and lackluster motel rooms—you'll really appreciate the city's urban attitude, the good choice of hotels and motels, and the varied cuisine of city restaurants.

## ESSENTIALS

**GETTING THERE**    St. John's is located 127km (79 miles) from the ferry at Argentia, 874km (543 miles) from Port aux Basques. St. John's International Airport (© **709/ 758-8500;** www.stjohnsairport.com) receives flights from Halifax, Montréal, Ottawa, Toronto, and even internationally. See "Getting There" at the beginning of this chapter for ferry and airline information. The airport is 6.5km (4 miles) from downtown; taxis from the airport to downtown hotels cost approximately C$15 (US$12), C$2 (US$1.60) for each additional traveler.

**VISITOR INFORMATION**    The city's **tourist information office** (© **709/576- 8106;** www.stjohns.ca), located at 35 New Gower St., is open year-round: from 9am to 5pm in summer, weekdays from 9am to 4:30pm in the off season.

**GETTING AROUND**    Metrobus serves much of the city. Fares are C$2 (US$1.60) for a single trip. Route information is available at the visitor information center or by calling © **709/570-2034.**

Taxis are plentiful around St. John's, and charge an initial fee of C$3 (US$2.40) plus about C$2 (US$1.60) each additional mile. One of the larger and more dependable outfits in the city is **Bugden's Taxi** (© **709/726-4400**). You can tour the city by taxi for about C$30 (US$24) per hour.

**ORIENTATION**    St. John's is built on the side of a steep hill, and the downtown is oriented along three streets—**Harbour, Water,** and **Duckworth**—that run parallel to the water's edge. These are relatively level, each following the hill's contours, one above the other. Cross streets that link these run the gamut from moderately challenging inclines to clutch-smoking vertical. Duckworth and Water Streets contain the bulk of the downtown's shops and restaurants.

Outside of downtown, St. John's is an amalgam of confusing roads that run at peculiar angles to one another and that suddenly change names as if on a whim. You can try to navigate with a map, but it's just as easy to keep an eye on a landmark—like Signal Hill—and head your car in the general direction you want to go. The city's small enough that you'll never get too lost and you'll eventually end up on the main ring road, which goes by various names, including Columbus Drive, Confederation Parkway, and Prince Philip Drive.

**SPECIAL EVENTS**  The annual **Newfoundland and Labrador Folk Festival** began in 1976. The 3-day festival is held during the first weekend in early August and includes performers from all over the province, who gather to play at Bannerman Park in downtown St. John's. (Bring a lawn chair.) Even after all these years tickets are still very affordable (it costs just C$10/US$8) for an afternoon or evening slate of performers, C$40 (US$32) for a weekend pass. Contact the festival office (✆ **709/576-8508**) for more information.

## EXPLORING ST. JOHN'S

Parking is rarely a problem in downtown St. John's. Bring loonies and quarters to feed the meters. Once you park, you can continue easily by foot; the downtown area is compact enough. In my experience St. John's drivers are uncommonly respectful of pedestrians. If you so much as take a step off the curb—or even let a look cross your face suggesting you just might, at some point, want to cross the street—drivers will slow to a halt and wave you across.

The city produces a free, informative, and helpful 40-page pocket-size brochure, entitled **"Exploring the City of Legends: Your Guide to Walking Tours and Auto Tours of St. John's."** It's a good resource for launching your visit to the city. Ask for it at the tourist information office (see above).

## DOWNTOWN ATTRACTIONS

**Anglican Cathedral of St. John the Baptist**  This impressive hillside cathedral was constructed in stages from 1843 to 1885, with additional rebuilding following the great fire of 1892. Designed in high Gothic Revival style by noted English architect Sir George Gilbert Scott, the cathedral has very fine stained glass, lavish oak carvings, and bluestone walls from nearby quarries. (The sandstone of the arches and bays was shipped from Scotland.) After you admire the historically significant architecture and the small one-room museum, stop by the crypt, where sweets and tea are served Monday through Friday from 2:30 to 4:30pm. It's an hour peacefully spent.

22 Church Hill. ✆ **709/726-5677.** Free tours June–Sept daily 10am–5pm.

**Art Gallery of Newfoundland and Labrador** ★★  This gallery recently moved downtown into The Rooms, a multi-function facility and a very appropriate home for it. Permanent and rotating exhibits in the new location mostly showcase Newfoundland talent, but the occasional touring show will also highlight other Canadian artists as well. Consult the local newspaper to see what's currently on display. Plan to spend a couple of hours here, should the current exhibitions catch your fancy.

9 Bonaventure Ave. ✆ **709/737-8209.** www.agnl.ca. C$5 (US$4) adult, C$4 (US$3.20) senior, C$3 (US$2.40) children 6–16, C$15 (US$12) family. June to mid-Oct Mon–Sat 10am–5pm (Wed–Thurs to 9pm), Sun noon–5pm; rest of year closed Mon.

**Commissariat House**    This stellar Georgian house, built in 1821, has served varied purposes over the years. Originally constructed as offices and living quarters to serve Fort William and other military installations, the home subsequently served as a rectory, nursing home, and children's hospital. Now a provincial historic site, the home has been restored to look as it would have looked in 1830, with the English china, fine paintings, and elaborate furnishings that would befit an Assistant Commissary General. Fans of historic architecture and 19th-century period furnishings could while away an enjoyable hour here.

King's Bridge Rd. © **709/729-6730**. Free admission. Mid-June to mid-Oct daily 10am–5:30pm.

**Provincial Museum of Newfoundland and Labrador** 🎯🎯 *Kids*    This downtown museum found a new home in 2005, moving to a complex known as The Rooms (the Provincial Art Gallery and Provincial Archives are also located here). It offers a good introduction to the natural and cultural history of the island, using exhibits that even kids can enjoy and understand. The second level features a lesson on canoe-building from an Innu native. The third level focuses on the process of change as glaciers retreated and native peoples settled the province; you'll learn about flora and fauna, finding out, for example, that the moose is not native to Newfoundland. The fourth level suggests how 19th-century life was lived by the province's British settlers, with a recreated fort and stories about Newfoundland's fisheries and this history of the constabulary (police). While here, watch for the delicate carvings of bear heads and the awesome power of the polar bear; special exhibitions include a Canadian heritage quilt project. Allow about an hour for a leisurely tour.

9 Bonaventure Ave. © **709/729-2329**. www.therooms.ca/museum. Admission C$5 (US$4) adults, C$4 (US$3) seniors and students, C$3 (US$2) children 6–16, family C$15 (US$12). Wed pm and 1st Sat of month free. June to mid-Oct Mon–Sat 10am–5pm (Wed–Thurs to 9pm), Sun noon–5pm; rest of the year closed Mon.

**Signal Hill** 🎯🎯 *Value*    You'll come for the history but stay for the views. Signal Hill is St. John's most visible and most visit-worthy attraction. The rugged, barren hill is the city's preeminent landmark, rising up over the entrance to the harbor and topped by a craggy castle with a flag fluttering high overhead—the signal of the name. The layers of history here are rich and complex—flags have flown atop this hill since 1704, and over the centuries a succession of military fortifications occupied these strategic slopes, as did three different hospitals. The "castle" (called Cabot Tower) dates from 1897, built in honor of Queen Victoria's Diamond Jubilee and the 400th anniversary of John Cabot's arrival in the new world.

The hill secured a spot in history in 1901, when Nobel laureate Guglielmo Marconi received the first wireless transatlantic broadcast—three short dots indicating the letter *S* in Morse code, sent from Cornwall, England—on an antenna raised 120m (400 ft.) on a kite in powerful winds.

A good place to start a tour is at the interpretive center, where you'll get a good briefing about the hill's history. Four days a week, military drills and cannon firings take place in the field next to the center (Wed and Thurs at 7pm, Sat–Sun at 3 and 7pm). From here, you can follow serpentine trails up the hill to the Cabot Tower, where you'll be rewarded with breathtaking views of the Narrows and the open ocean beyond. (Cape Spear can be seen in the distance to the south.) Look for icebergs in the early summer and whales any time. Interpretive placards, scattered about the summit, feature engaging photos from various epochs.

Atop Signal Hill at the entrance to St. John's harbor. (C) 709/772-5367. Free admission to grounds; admission to interpretive center C$4 (US$3) adults, C$3.50 (US$3) seniors, C$2 (US$1.60) children 6–16, C$10 (US$8) families. Center daily 8:30am–4:30pm (mid-June to Sept to 8pm).

## EXPLORING FARTHER AFIELD

**Fluvarium** *(R) (Finds) (Kids)*   This low, octagonal structure at the edge of Long Pond (near Memorial University, a few miles west of downtown) actually descends three stories into the earth. The second level features exhibits on river ecology, including life in the riffles (that's where trout spawn) and in shallow pools, which are rich with nutrients. On the lowest level you'll find yourself looking up into a deep pool that's located alongside the building. Watch for brown trout swimming lazily by. Plan to spend about 45 minutes here.

Pippy Park, off Allandale Rd. (C) 709/754-3474. www.fluvarium.ca. Admission C$5.50 (US$4.40) adults, C$4.50 (US$3.60) seniors and students, C$3.50 (US$2.80) children under 14. Hours variable but weekdays usually 10am–5pm, weekends noon–5pm. Closed weekends in winter. Guided tours on the half-hour in season; feeding time 4pm.

**Institute of Marine Dynamics** *(R)*   This is an oddly fascinating research facility. Work done here included engineering studies for the Hibernia oil platform (a 60-story-high drilling rig located offshore southeast of Newfoundland) and the Confederation Bridge to Prince Edward Island. On the tour you'll see three remarkable tanks, in which models of ships (as much as 3.6m/12 ft. long) and other marine structures are put through their paces. The world's longest ice tank is located here (a huge pool in a hangar-size freezer), and you'll see the 200m (600-ft.) towing tank, with wave makers and a retractable beach. Children must be 10 years or older; reservations required. Ecology buffs could easily spend an hour here.

Kerwin Place, on the campus of Memorial University. (C) 709/772-4366. Tours are free, but reservations are required. May–Aug Mon–Fri 9am–4:30pm.

**Memorial University Botanical Garden at Oxen Pond**   An abundant selection of northern plants makes this garden well worth seeking out (it's tucked over a wooded ridge on the city's western edge, behind Pippy Park). The main plots are arranged in gracious "theme gardens," including a cottage garden, a rock garden, and a peat garden. Among the most interesting is the Newfoundland Heritage Garden, with examples of 70 types of perennials traditionally found in island gardens. The floral displays aren't as ostentatious or exuberant as you'll find in other public gardens in Atlantic Canada (the gardens of Halifax and Annapolis Royal come to mind), but they will be of great interest to amateur horticulturists curious about boreal plants. Behind the gardens are winding hiking trails leading down to marshy Oxen Pond. Allow an hour for this visit.

306 Mt. Scio Rd. (C) 709/737-8590. Summer admission C$5 (US$4) adults, C$3 (US$2.40) seniors, C$1.15 (US92¢) children 6–18, C$10 (US$8) family. Spring and fall rates lower. May–Nov daily 10am–5pm. Take Thorburn Rd. past Avalon Mall; turn right on Mt. Scio Rd.

**Quidi Vidi** *(R)*   Pronounced "kitty vitty," this tiny harbor village sets new standards for the term *quaint*. The village is tucked in a narrow, rocky defile behind Signal Hill, where a narrow ocean inlet provides access to the sea. It's photogenic in the extreme and a wonderful spot to investigate by foot or bike (it's rather more difficult by car). The village consists mostly of compact homes, including the oldest home in St. John's, with very few shops. Visit here while you can; in recent years, following rancorous local debate, development plans were approved for the addition of modern housing in the area. To get to Quidi Vidi, follow Signal Hill Road to Quidi Vidi Road; turn right onto Forest Road.

From here you can easily connect to Quidi Vidi Lake, where St. John's Regatta is held the first Wednesday in August, as it has been since 1826. Look for the trail leading to the lake from near the entrance to Quidi Vidi, or ask locally.

## OUTDOOR PURSUITS

**Pippy Park** (© 709/737-3655) is on the city's hilly western side adjacent to the university and contains 1,340 hectares (3,350 acres) of developed recreation land and quiet trails. The popular park is home to the city campground and Fluvarium (see above), as well as miniature golf, picnic sites, and playgrounds.

For bike rentals, head downtown to **Canary Cycles,** 294 Water St. (© 877/4CANARY or 709/579-5972), where they offer several different types of bikes, with rates around C$30 (US$24) per day, C$10 (US$8) extra for lock and helmets.

The **Grand Concourse** (© 709/737-1077) is an ambitious project to link much of St. John's with pedestrian pathways. More than 123km (77 miles) have been completed to date, with more walkways being developed all the time;. two of the most inviting segments are the loop around Quidi Vidi Lake and the Rennie's River Trail running between Pippy Park and Quidi Vidi Lake. Bikes are not permitted on the trails. Ask at the information centers for trail status and map availability.

Another highly recommended hike is the **North Head Trail** 🎔🎔, which runs from Signal Hill to an improbable cluster of small buildings between rock face and water called the Battery. You should be reasonably fit and unafraid of heights; allow about 2 hours, assuming departure and return from near the Hotel Newfoundland.

On foot, follow Duckworth Street between the hotel and Devon House; then bear right on Battery Road. Stay on the main branch (a few smaller branches may confuse you) as it narrows, then rises, and falls while skirting a rock face to the Outer Battery. The former fishermen's homes at the Battery are literally inches from the road and not much farther from the water, and most have drop-dead views of the Narrows and the city skyline. There's a whimsical, storybook character to the place, and the real estate is now much sought after by city residents.

At the end of the Battery you'll cross right over someone's front porch (it's okay), and then the North Head Trail begins in earnest. It runs along the Narrows, past old gun emplacements, up and down heroic sets of steps, and along some narrow ledges (chains are bolted to rock as handrails for a little extra security in one spot). The trail then ascends an open headland before looping back and starting the final ascent up Signal Hill. After some time exploring here and soaking up the view, you can walk on the paved road back down Signal Hill to Duckworth Street.

## SHOPPING

A number of downtown shops tout "traditional Newfoundland" crafts and souvenirs, and the offerings range from high-quality goods to tourist-oriented schlock.

**The Bird House and Binocular Shop**    This is a recommended stop for both serious and aspiring birders. The shop has a selection of field guides, binoculars, and spotting scopes, along with backyard bird supplies. Binoculars are also available for rent, and the shop distributes a free brochure with a checklist of local species and suggested birding areas around St. John's. 166 Duckworth St. © 709/726-2473.

**Devon House Craft Center** 🎔    The nonprofit Devon House (operated by the Newfoundland and Labrador Crafts Development Association) displays the works of more than 150 of the province's artisans in an attractive old house across from the Hotel Newfoundland, specializing in works in clay. There's also a gallery of current crafts and design. 59 Duckworth St. ℂ **709/753-2749.**

**Downhome Shoppe & Gallery** This might be the best destination for standard-issue Newfoundland souvenirs. It's located at the offices of a folk-life publisher, and stocked with T-shirts, coffee mugs, postcards, dolls in tartans, and so on. 303 Water St. ℂ **888/588-6353** or 709/722-2970.

**Fred's** There's a great selection of Newfoundland and other music here on record, tape, and CD, and a knowledgeable sales staff to boot. You can sample any of the CDs on headphones before you buy. 198 Duckworth St. ℂ **709/753-9191.**

**Newfoundland Weavery** This shop started as a weaving supply store in 1972 and has since expanded to become a showcase for local arts and crafts, including pottery, oilskin coats, and pewter work. 177 Water St. ℂ **709/753-0496.**

**O'Brien's** A popular hangout for local musicians looking for equipment, O'Brien's also carries an excellent selection of local tapes and CDs, and the staff is very knowledgeable in all things musical. Music can also be ordered by mail or via the store's website at www.obriens.nf.ca. 278 Water St. ℂ **709/753-8135.**

**Wordplay** A great source for books about Newfoundland and Labrador, books by Newfoundlanders, and books by anyone else. 221 Duckworth St. ℂ **800/563-9100** or 709/726-9193.

## EXCURSIONS FROM ST. JOHN'S

Some 11km (7 miles) southeast of downtown is North America's most easterly point, home to dramatic **Cape Spear National Historic Site** (ℂ **709/772-5367**). Here you'll find a picturesque lighthouse dating from 1836, and underground passages from abandoned World War II gun batteries. A visitor center will orient you; leave plenty of time to walk the hiking trails and scout for whales surfacing out to sea. Admission to **the lighthouse,** which has been restored to its 1839 appearance and opens from 10am to 6:30pm, is C$4 (US$3.20) adults, C$3.50 (US$2.80) seniors, C$2 (US$1.60) ages 6 to 16, and C$10 (US$8) family. The lighthouse is closed mid-October to mid-May, but the grounds are open year-round.

Just 14km (8¾ miles) west of St. John's is Portugal Cove, from which frequent ferries (ℂ **709/488-2842** or 709/895-3491) depart for **Bell Island** year-round except in very stormy weather. This is a handsome and historic island, with abrupt cliffs edging the eastern shore. It was once a thriving community, early in the 20th century; an iron mine employed hundreds from 1895 to 1966, after which it no longer made economic sense to scratch ore out of the earth. Today the island is honeycombed with impressive mine shafts, many extending far out under the sea. You'll also find simple accommodations, several lowbrow seafood restaurants, and an art gallery. The ferry ride costs C$6 (US$5) per car and driver, C$3.50 (US$2.80) adult passenger, C$5.25 (US$4.20) senior driver with car, C$2 (US$1.60) children and senior passengers, and it runs every 40 minutes from about 6am until about 10:30pm. The crossing takes 20 minutes.

The No. 2 Mine has been maintained as a museum of sorts, the **Bell Island Community Museum and Mine Tour** (ℂ **709/488-2880**), where visitors can relive the life of a miner, who made his way through the perpetual underground night with a carbide lantern. During a 40-minute tour you'll descend by foot 195m (650 ft.)

underground, to where flooding now makes the mineshaft impassable. The mine actually descends 510m (1,700 ft.) into the earth, and is 2 to 3 miles long. Tours are offered frequently daily in summer; combo tickets incorporating the tour and museum admission cost C$7 (US$5.60) adults, C$5 (US$4) seniors, C$3 (US$2.40) for children under 12. Tickets for just the museum alone are cheaper. The museum is open daily from 11am to 7pm, June through September.

While on Bell Island, ask locals about the **Grebe's Nest,** a rocky point marked by an offshore sea stack. (I didn't see grebes—or any other interesting seabird life, for that matter—while I was here.) But scramble down to the shore, head south along the water, and you can make your way though a man-made tunnel about 50m (164 ft.) long, which leads to a secluded beach on the other side surrounded by towering, crumbling cliffs. Kids love the mystery and remoteness of this place.

## WHERE TO STAY

Campers should head to municipal **Pippy Park Campground** ✿ (© **877/477-3669** or 709/737-3669), just a couple miles from downtown off Allandale Road. The campground has 158 sites, most with full hookups, and a sociable tenting area. Rates range from about C$16 (US$13) for an unserviced site to C$24 (US$19) for a fully serviced site. It often books up in summer, so it's wise to call ahead for reservations. It's open from May through September.

### EXPENSIVE

**Delta St. John's Hotel** ✿✿ *Kids*    The sleek and modern Delta St. John's is located downtown near City Hall and caters largely to businesspeople. It lacks the views and the ineffable sense of class that you'll find at the Fairmont Newfoundland (see below), but it has nice touches like ship models in the lobby and a handsome pool table as the centerpiece of the lounge. It also is well located for prowling the city and features a number of amenities that choosy travelers will appreciate, such as hair dryers and coffeemakers in all rooms; management also runs a number of children's programs and offers babysitting services. The attractive restaurant off the lobby offers breakfast, lunch, and dinner daily; the dinner menu is Continental with a Mediterranean touch and features dishes such as seafood casserole, shrimp brochettes, and beef in various incarnations.

120 New Gower St., St. John's, NF A1C 6K4. © **800/268-1133** or 709/739-6404. Fax 709/570-1622. www.delta hotels.com. 276 units. C$250–C$325 (US$200–US$260) double. AE, DC, DISC, MC, V. Valet parking C$10 (US$8). Pets allowed with advance permission. **Amenities:** Restaurant; indoor pool; health club; Jacuzzi; sauna; children's program; concierge; limited room service; babysitting; laundry service; dry cleaning. *In room:* A/C, TV, minibar, fridge (some units), coffeemaker, hair dryer, iron.

**The Fairmont Newfoundland** ✿✿    The Newfoundland was built in 1982 in a starkly modern style, but it boasts a refined sensibility and attention to detail that's reminiscent of a lost era. What I like most about the hotel is how the designers and architects hid their best surprises. The lobby has one of the best views of the Narrows in the city, but you have to wander around to find it. It's a wonderful effect, and one that's used nicely throughout. (This helps compensate for the somewhat generic, conference-hotel feel of much of the decor.) The rooms themselves are standard sized and are nothing remarkable, although all have coffeemakers and bathrobes. About half have harbor views. The hotel's lobby is home to three dining establishments: The rather formal Cabot Club ranks among the best restaurants in the city and is known for tableside Caesar salads, caribou soup, and entrees like traditional pan-fried cod and halibut with a saffron truffle butter. The colorful Mediterranean-inspired Bonavista Cafe is lighter on the wallet, with lunch offerings such as burgers, generous sandwiches and dinners like Greek lamb chops, vegetable fettuccine, and poached salmon. The Narrows lounge is the spot for a nightcap.

Cavendish Sq. (P.O. Box 5637), St. John's, NF A1C 5W8. © 800/257-7544 or 709/726-4980. Fax 709/726-2025. 301 units. C$199–C$275 (US$159–US$220) double. AE, DC, DISC, MC, V. Parking C$17 (US$14). Pets C$20 (US$16) extra per night. **Amenities:** 3 restaurants; indoor pool; health club; Jacuzzi; sauna; concierge; business center; salon; 24-hr. room service; babysitting; laundry service; dry cleaning. In room: A/C, TV, minibar.

**Winterholme Heritage Inn** 🎈🎈 This stout, handsome Victorian mansion was built in 1905 and is as architecturally distinctive a place as you'll find in Newfoundland, with prominent turrets, bow-front windows, bold pediments, elaborate molded plaster ceilings, and woodwork extravagant enough to stop you in your tracks. (The oak woodwork was actually carved in England and shipped here for installation.) Room 7 is one of the most lavish; the former billiards room features a fireplace and two-person Jacuzzi, along with a plasterwork ceiling and a supple leather wing chair. Room 1 is oval-shaped and occupies one of the turrets; it also has a Jacuzzi. The attic rooms are less extraordinary, but still appealing with their odd angles and nice touches. The mansion is located a 10-minute walk from downtown.

79 Rennies Mill Rd., St. John's, NF A1C 3R1. © 800/599-7829 or 709/739-7979. Fax 709/753-9411. www.winterholme.com. 12 units. C$129–C$199 (US$103–US$159) double. AE, DC, MC, V. Free parking. In room: TV, coffeemaker, hair dryer, iron.

## MODERATE

**At Wit's Inn** 🎈🎈 *Finds* Forgive the innkeepers their pun. This lovely century-old home was wonderfully restored and opened as an inn in 1999 by a former Toronto restaurateur. It will appeal to anyone who loathes the "kountry klutter" found in establishments striving too hard for a personality. Decorated with a sure eye for bold color and simple style, this is a welcoming urban oasis just around the corner from the Fairmont Newfoundland. The rooms are not all that spacious, but neither are they too small, and each is nicely furnished with down duvets and VCRs. (The largest room is on the top floor, requiring a bit of a hike.) The beautifully refinished floors and elaborately carved banister are notable, as are many of the old fixtures (like the servant's intercom) that have been left in place. A full breakfast is served in the first floor dining room, wine and cheese are offered in the late afternoon, and there's a butler's pantry for snacking in between times. At Wit's Inn offers luxury touches at a relatively affordable price.

3 Gower St., St. John's, NF A1C 1M9. © 877/739-7420 or 709/739-7420. www.atwitsinn.ca. 4 units. C$99–C$129 (US$79–US$103) double. Rates include breakfast. Free parking. AE, MC, V. In room: VCR.

**McCoubrey Manor** 🎈🎈 *Kids* McCoubrey Manor offers the convenient location of the Fairfield Newfoundland (it's just across the street), but with Victorian charm and a more casual B&B atmosphere. The adjoining 1904 town houses are decorated in what might be called a "contemporary Victorian" style and are quite inviting, especially after a recent renovation job that increased its provincial rating to a hefty four-and-one-half stars. Upstairs rooms have private double Jacuzzis; Room 1 is brightest, and faces the street. Room 2 has a sunken Jacuzzi, an oak mantled fireplace, and lustrous trim of British Columbia fir. Just around the corner are five spacious one-, two-and three-bedroom apartments with full kitchens. What they lack in elegance they make up for in space; families take note. Evening wine and cheese get-togethers and full breakfast service (except with apartments) only add to the place's charm.

6–8 Ordnance St., St. John's, NF A1C 3K7. ℂ **888/753-7577** or 709/722-7577. Fax 709/579-7577. www.mccoubrey.com. 6 units. C$89–C$249 (US$71–US$199) double. Rates include full breakfast. AE, DC, MC, V. Free parking. **Amenities:** Coin-op washer and dryer. *In room:* A/C (4 units), TV/VCR, kitchenette (2 units), fridge (2 units), no phone (most units).

**Prescott Inn** ⟨Value⟩   The Prescott Inn is composed of an unusually attractive grouping of wood-frame town houses painted a vibrant lavender-blue. Some of the historical detailing has been restored inside, but mostly the homes have been modernized. Some rooms have carpeting; others have hardwood floors. All are furnished with eclectic antiques that rise above flea-market quality but aren't quite collectibles. The lower-priced rooms are among the city's better bargains. Room 3 might be the best of the bunch, and it is the only guest room with a private Jacuzzi. All guests are welcome to relax on the shared balcony that runs along the back of the building. If you want a room with one of the best views in the city, ask about the Battery, a scenic villagelike neighborhood perched precariously over the harbor a short drive away; the Battery units have private bathrooms and kitchens. Also note that the management owns a small tour company that both puts together self-styled itineraries and arranges car rentals.

21 Military Rd. (P.O. Box 204), St. John's, NF A1C 2C3. ℂ **888/263-3786** or 709/753-7733. Fax 709/738-7434. 6 units. Peak season C$80–C$199 (US$48–US$159) double, off season C$60–C$169 (US$48–$135) double. Rates include full breakfast. AE, DC, MC, V. Free parking. Pets allowed. *In room:* Fridge.

**Quality Hotel Harbourview**   Courteous service and a great downtown location are among the merits of this modern chain hotel, situated just down the hill from the Fairfield Newfoundland. The rooms are standard-size but comfortable and clean; they're set apart mainly by their views—ask for one overlooking the Narrows. You can walk to downtown restaurants and attractions within a few minutes. The Battery and Signal Hill are a pleasant hike in the other direction. A better-than-average restaurant serves three meals daily on the premises.

2 Hill O'Chips, St. John's, NF A1C 6B1. ℂ **800/228-5151** or 709/754-7788. Fax 709/754-5209. 160 units. C$109–C$159 (US$87–US$127) double. AE, DC, DISC, MC, V. Free parking. **Amenities:** Restaurant. *In room:* A/C, TV, coffeemaker, hair dryer, iron.

## INEXPENSIVE
**Monkstown Manor**   A stay here is like a visit with old college friends. This narrow Victorian home, a short drive or moderate walk from downtown, is run with an infectious congeniality; at times it feels more like a dormitory than an inn. More likely than not people will be playing music on the ground floor or chatting at length about bands they saw the night before. (The owners are very musical, and they run a production company that specializes in Newfoundland folk music.) The rooms in the main house have buttery wooden floors and funky decorating; the units with small kitchens are a couple of doors away. The two shared bathrooms in the main house have Jacuzzis, so at times you might have to wait your turn.

51 Monkstown Rd., St. John's, NF A1C 3T4. ℂ **888/754-7377** or 709/754-7324. Fax 709/722-8557. 4 units. C$55–C$65 (US$39–US$46) double. Rates include continental breakfast. AE, MC, V. Street parking. Pets allowed in housekeeping units. *In room:* A/C, TV/VCR.

## WHERE TO DINE
Budget travelers should wander up the city's hillside to the intersection of LaMarchant and Freshwater Streets. Within a 2-block radius, you'll find numerous options for

cheap eats at both eat-in and take-out establishments. A local favorite is **Ches's Fish and Chips,** 9 Freshwater Rd. (© **709/722-4083**), which has been serving up pleasingly unhealthy portions of fried food, chicken wings, and burgers at this location since 1958. Ches's will also deliver.

For the strongest coffee in town, head to **HavaJava** at 216 Water St. (© **709/ 753-5282**).

## EXPENSIVE

**The Cellar** ☞☞ ECLECTIC    The classy interior is a surprise here—the restaurant is located on a nondescript street and through a nondescript entrance. Inside, it's intimate and warm, not unlike an upper crust gentleman's club. The kitchen has been turning out fine meals for some time now, developing a reputation for creativity and consistency. The menu is constantly in play, but look for reliable standbys like the delicious gravlax, and the homemade bread and pastas. Fish is prepared especially well, and some cuts are paired with innovative flavors like ginger and pear butter. Lunches are the better bargain, featuring tasty offerings like baked brie in phyllo with red currant and pineapple chutney, or scallop crepes with bacon, leeks, and Swiss cheese.

152 Water St. © **709/579-8900.** Reservations recommended. Main courses C$8.50–C$21 (US$5.20–US$17) at lunch, C$7.50–C$34 (US$6–US$27) at dinner. AE, DC, DISC, MC, V. Mon–Fri 11:30am–2:30pm and 5:30–9:30pm (Fri until 10:30pm); Sat 5:30–10:30pm; Sun 5:30–9:30pm.

## MODERATE

**Casa Grande** ☞ *Value* MEXICAN    If you've developed Mexican-food withdrawal after all those outport meals of fried fish, plan to satisfy your cravings here—you won't find better Mexican food in Newfoundland, and you'd be hard-pressed to find better elsewhere in Atlantic Canada. Seating is on two floors of a narrow storefront just down the hill from the Fairfield Newfoundland. Angle for the front room of the upper level, where you'll get views of the harbor. It's often crowded and the service can be irksome; but come prepared for a wait and you'll get excellent value for your money. All the dishes are well prepared; the chile relleno has developed something of a cult following.

108 Duckworth St. © **709/753-6108.** Reservations recommended. Main courses C$7–C$8.95 (US$5.60–US$7) at lunch, C$10–C$16 (US$8–US$13) at dinner. AE, DC, MC, V. Mon–Fri 11:30am–2:30pm and 5–10pm (Fri until 11pm); Sat 5–11pm; Sun 5–9pm.

**Classic Café East** CANADIAN    This come-as-you-are spot is appropriately named—it's truly classic St. John's, and everyone seems to drop in here at one time or another. Breakfast is served 24 hours a day—but don't expect a limp croissant and tea. Macho breakfasts (for example, a sirloin with eggs, toast, home fries, and baked beans) appeal to a mixed group, from burly longshoremen to hungover musicians. Dinner entrees are equally generous and often surprisingly good.

73 Duckworth. © **709/726-4444.** Main courses C$6–C$8 (US$4–US$6) at breakfast and lunch, C$8–C$17 (US$6–US$12) at dinner. DC, MC, V. Daily 24 hr.

**Zachary's** TRADITIONAL    This informal spot with wood-slat booths offers a slew of Newfoundland favorites, like fish cakes, fried bologna, and toutons (dough fried in pork fat)—and that's just for breakfast. Dinners emphasize seafood—entrees include grilled salmon, seafood fettuccine, pan-fried cod, and lobster most of the year—but you'll also find steaks and chicken. Desserts are all homemade; especially tempting are the cheesecake, carrot cake, and date squares. You'll find more inventive spots for dinner, but you probably won't do better for reliable quality if you're on a tight budget. Breakfasts are outstanding and are served all day.

71 Duckworth St. (across from the Fairfield Newfoundland). (C) 709/579-8050. Reservations recommended. Main courses C$3.30–C$7.50 (US$2.65–US$6) at breakfast, C$6–C$9 (US$5–US$7) at lunch, C$11–C$20 (US$9–US$16) at dinner. AE, MC, V. Daily 7am–11pm.

## INEXPENSIVE

**International Flavours** *(Value)* INDIAN   This is my favorite cheap meal in St. John's. This storefront restaurant has just five tables, and all the dinners are priced at less than C$8 (US$6), which includes a decent mound of food. You'll usually have a choice of four or so dishes. Smart money gets the basic curry. Also recommended is the very satisfying mango milk shake.

124 Duckworth St. (C) 709/738-4636. Dinner plates C$6.95–C$7.95 (US$5–US$6). V. Mon–Tues and Thurs–Sat 11:30am–6:30pm; Wed 11:30am–7pm (often later).

## ST. JOHN'S AFTER DARK

The nightlife in St. John's is extraordinarily vibrant, and you'd be doing yourself an injustice if you didn't spend at least one evening on a pub crawl.

The first stop for a little local music and cordial imbibing should be **George Street,** which runs for several blocks near New Gower and Water streets, close to City Hall. Every St. John's resident confidently asserts that George Street is home to more bars per square foot than anywhere else on the planet. I have been unable to track down a global authority that verifies pubs-per-square-foot, but a walk down the street did little to rebut their claims.

George Street is packed with energetic pubs and lounges, some fueled by beer, others by testosterone, still more by lively Celtic fiddling. The best strategy for selecting a pub is a slow ramble around 10pm or later, vectoring in to spots with appealing music wafting from the door. At places with live music, cover charges are universally very nominal and rarely top C$5 (US$3).

**Trapper John's,** 2 George St. (C) 709/579-9630), is known for outstanding provincial folk music, but it tries a bit harder for that Ye Olde Newfoundland character. This is a traditional "screeching in" spot for visitors (this involves cheap Newfoundland rum and some embarrassment). For blues and traditional music, there's the lively **Fat Cat Blues Bar,** 5 George St. (C) 709/739-5554). For a more upscale spot with lower decibel levels, try **Christian's Bar,** 23 George St. (C) 709/753-9100), which offers the nonalcoholic option of specialty coffees.

If George Street's beery atmosphere reminds you of those nights in college you'd just as soon forget, a few blocks away are two pubs tucked down tiny alleys known for their genial public-house atmospheres. The **Duke of Duckworth,** 325 Duckworth St. (C) 709/739-6344), specializes in draft beers and pub lunches. **The Ship Inn,** 265 Duckworth St. (C) 709/753-3870), is a St. John's mainstay, featuring a variety of local musical acts that seem to complement rather than overwhelm the pub's cozy atmosphere.

## 11 The Southern Avalon Peninsula

The Avalon Peninsula—or just "The Avalon," as it's commonly called—is home to some of Newfoundland's most memorable and dramatic scenery, including high coastal cliffs and endless bogs. More good news: It's also relatively compact and manageable, and it can be viewed on long day trips from St. John's, or in a couple of days of scenic poking around. It's a good destination for anyone who's short on time, yet wants to get a taste of the wild. The area is especially notable for its bird colonies, as well as its herd of wild caribou. The bad news? It's out in the sea where cold and warm currents collide, resulting in legendary fogs and blustery, moist weather. Bring a rain suit and come prepared for bone-numbing dampness.

While snooping about, also listen for the distinctive Irish-influenced brogue of the residents. You'll find no more vivid testimony to the settlement of the region by Irish pioneers.

## ESSENTIALS

**GETTING THERE**   Several well-marked, well-maintained highways follow the coast of the southern Avalon Peninsula; few roads cross the damp and spongy interior. A map is essential.

**VISITOR INFORMATION**   Your best bet is to stop in the **St. John's tourist information office** (see earlier in this chapter) or at the well-marked tourist bureau just up the hill from the Argentia ferry before you begin your travels. Witless Bay has a **tourist information booth** (© 709/334-2609) at the edge of the cobblestone beach and is stocked with a handful of brochures. It's open irregularly.

## WITLESS BAY ECOLOGICAL RESERVE

The Witless Bay area, about 34km (21 miles) south of St. John's, makes an easy day trip from the city, or can serve as a launching point for an exploration of the Avalon Peninsula. The main attraction here is the **Witless Bay Ecological Reserve** *&* (© 709/635-4522), comprising four islands and the waters around them, and located a short boat ride offshore. Literally millions of seabirds nest and fish here, and it's a spectacle even if you're not a bird watcher.

On the islands you'll find the largest puffin colony in the western Atlantic Ocean, with some 60,000 puffins burrowing into the grassy slopes above the cliffs, and awkwardly launching themselves from the high rocks. The tour boats are able to edge right along the shores, about 6 or 7.5m (20 or 25 ft.) away, allowing puffin watching on even foggy days. Also on the islands is North America's second-largest murre colony.

While the islands are publicly owned and managed, access is via privately operated tour boat, several of which you'll find headquartered along Route 10 in Bay Bulls and Bauline East. It's worth shopping around since prices can vary considerably.

**Bay Bulls** is the closest town to St. John's and is home to three of the more popular tours: **Mullowney's** (© 877/783-3467 or 709/334-3666), **O'Brien's** (© 877/639-4253 or 709/753-4850), and **Gatherall's** (© 800/419-4253 or 709/334-2887). Two-and-a-half-hour tours from here range generally between C$32 and C$45 (US$26–US$36) per adult.

A quieter and more intimate way to explore the area is to sign up for a 3-hour tour with **Bay Bulls Sea Kayaking Tours** (© 709/334-3394). You'll kayak along the bay's shores, visit sea caves and small beaches, and possibly spot puffins and whales visiting the bay. The price is C$50 (US$40) per person.

## LA MANCHE PROVINCIAL PARK

La Manche means "the sleeve" in French, and the area is so named because of the long, narrow cove found here. This well-protected site was settled in 1840. Around 50 people still occupied homes on the steep hillsides flanking the cove as late as 1966, when a powerful storm all but destroyed the village. The occupants resettled elsewhere, leaving the remote village to be reclaimed by the elements.

Hikers can today follow a 30-minute pathway to the village's cove-side site, which is both melancholy and beautiful. Stone and concrete foundations can be found amid the grass and weeds. Towering gray-black cliffs rise above the cove, where a river gorge meets the sea. It's a perfect place to while away an afternoon.

The park ((C) **709/685-1823**) is well marked on Route 10, about 52km (32 miles) south of St. John's. Admission is free. The hike to the cove departs from the campground's fire exit road.

## FERRYLAND

Historic Ferryland is among the most picturesque of the Avalon villages, set at the foot of rocky hills on a harbor protected by a series of abrupt islands at its mouth.

Ferryland was among the first permanent settlements in Newfoundland. In 1621, the Colony of Avalon was established here by Sir George Calvert, First Baron of Baltimore (he was also behind the settlement of Baltimore, Maryland). Calvert sunk the equivalent of C$4 million (US$2.8 million) into the colony, which featured luxe touches like cobblestone roads, slate roofs, and fine ceramics and glassware from Europe. So up-to-date was the colony that privies featured drains leading to the shore just below the high tide mark, making these the first flush toilets in North America. (Or so the locals insist.) Later the Dutch, and then the French, sacked the colony during ongoing squabbles over territory, and eventually it was abandoned.

Recent excavations have revealed much about life here nearly 4 centuries ago. Visit the **Colony of Avalon Interpretation Centre** ⋒ ((C) **877/326-5669** or 709/432-3200) with its numerous glass-topped drawers filled with engrossing artifacts, and then ask for a tour of the six archaeological sites currently being excavated (the tour is included in the cost of admission). Other interpretive exhibits include a reproduction of a 17th-century kitchen, and three gardens of the sort you might have overseen had you lived 400 years ago. After your tour, take a walk to the lighthouse at the point (about 1 hr. round-trip), where you can scan for whales and icebergs. Ask for directions at the museum.

The site is open daily mid-May to late October from 9am to 7pm; admission is C$6 (US$5) adults, C$5 (US$4) seniors, C$4 (US$3.20) students, C$3 (US$2.40) children age 5 to 14, and C$15 (US$12) families.

### WHERE TO STAY & DINE

**The Downs Inn** Overlooking the harbor, this building served as a convent between 1914 and 1986, when it was converted to an inn. The furnishings reflect its heritage as an institution rather than a historic building—there's dated carpeting and old linoleum, and the furniture is uninspired. (Much of the religious statuary was left in place—a nice touch.) Ask for one of the two front rooms, where you can watch for whales from your windows. The front parlor has been converted to a tearoom, where you can order a nice pot of tea and a light snack such as carrot cake or a rhubarb tart. Some sandwiches are available. Innkeeper Aidan Costello also operates Southern Shore Eco Adventures and can create custom tour packages for kayaking, hiking, or whale-watching.

Irish Loop Dr., Ferryland, NF A0A 2H0. (C) **877/432-2808** or 709/432-2808. Fax 709/432-2659. acostello@nf. sympatico.ca. 4 units. C$50–C$75 (US$40–US$60) double. MC, V. Closed mid-Nov to mid-May. Small pets allowed. **Amenities:** Laundry service. *In room:* No phone.

# AVALON WILDERNESS RESERVE

Where there's bog, there's caribou. Or at least that's true in the southern part of the peninsula, which is home to the island's largest caribou herd, numbering some 13,000. You'll see signs warning you to watch for caribou along the roadway; the landscape hereabout is so misty and primeval, though, that you might feel you should also watch for druids in robes with tall walking staffs.

The caribou roam freely throughout the 1,700-sq.-km (1,054-sq.-mile) reserve, so it's largely a matter of happenstance to find them. Your best bet is to scan the high upland barrens along Route 10 between Trepassey and Peter's River (an area that's actually out of the reserve).

On Route 90 between St. Catherines and Hollyrood is the **Salmonier Nature Park** (© **709/229-7189** or 709/229-7888), where you're certain to see caribou—along with other wildlife—if you can't find the herd on the reserve. This intriguing and well-designed park is fundamentally a 2.5km (1.5 mile) nature trail, almost entirely on boardwalk, which tracks through bog and forest, and along streams and ponds. Along the route are more than a dozen unobtrusive pens, in which orphaned or injured wildlife can be observed. (It's the only such facility in the province.) Among the animals represented: arctic fox, snowy owl, moose, bald eagle, mink, otter, beaver, and lynx. It's located 11km (6¾ miles) south of the Trans-Canada Highway; admission is free. Gates are open in summer daily 10am to 5pm, and all visitors must depart by 6pm. Closed mid-October to June 1.

## WHERE TO STAY & DINE

**Trepassey Motel and Restaurant**    Trepassey is an unvarnished fishing village of 1,200 south of the reserve and near Newfoundland's southernmost tip, an area often visited by whales and unusual birds during migration. This motel's 10 rooms are clean and basic, arrayed along a single hallway that connects to the restaurant. The specialty is cod tongues, but you can find a variety of other basic dishes including pork chops, turkey, and roast beef. The view from the solarium here of the Atlantic is splendid. Most everything on the menu is under C$12 (US$10); at breakfast, try a partridge-berry muffin.

Rte. 10, Trepassey, NF A0A 4B0. © 709/438-2934. Fax 709/438-2722. 10 units. C$69 (US$55) double. AE, MC, V. **Amenities:** Restaurant. *In room:* TV/VCR.

# CAPE ST. MARY'S

**Cape St. Mary's Ecological Reserve** (see below) ranks high on my list of favorite places on Newfoundland. Granted, it's off the beaten track—some 97km (60 miles) from the Trans-Canada Highway—but it's worth every mile. A couple of notes about the surrounding area: The terrain in this southwest part of the Avalon is unique—mostly open barrens covering low, rolling hills. At times along Route 92 between North Harbour and St. Bride's, even a moderately persuasive person might convince you that you were in Oklahoma.

Also, the 46km (28½-mile) drive along Route 100 between St. Brides and Placentia is like a miniature Cabot Trail, the noted Cape Breton drive. The road climbs to open headlands, then swoops down to river valleys and through small villages. At every turn another extraordinary view of Placentia Bay unfolds. If you're arriving via Argentia ferry, the drive south is a suburban introduction to Newfoundland. Save your favorite tape or CD for the ride (Wagner's "Ride of the Valkyries" would not be a bad choice), and play it loud.

**Cape St. Mary's Ecological Reserve** 𝘨𝘨  This natural reserve is home to some 5,500 pairs of northern gannets—big, noisy, beautiful, graceful white birds with cappuccino-colored heads and black wingtips. While they can be seen wintering off the coast of Florida and elsewhere to the south, they're seldom seen in such cacophonous number as here. Most are nesting literally on top of one another on a compact, 100m (300-ft.) sea stack. At any given moment hundreds are flying above, around and below you, which is all the more impressive given their nearly 2m (6-ft.) wingspan.

You needn't take a boat ride to see this colony. Start your visit at the visitor center, which offers a quick and intriguing introduction to the indigenous bird life. Then walk 15 minutes along a grassy cliff-top pathway—through harebell, iris, and dandelion—until you arrive at an unfenced cliff just a couple of dozen yards from the sea stack (it's close enough to be impressive even in a dense fog). Also nesting on and around the island are 10,000 pairs of murre, 10,000 kittiwakes, and 100 razorbills. Note that the viewing area is not fenced, and peering down at the surging surf and hundreds of birds on the wing below is not recommended for acrophobes. Guided tours are offered twice daily (for C$7/US$5.60), and are well worthwhile; so is the summer performance series of evening concerts. Tour lengths vary, but this extensive and unique wildland is worth several hours to a half-day for die-hard shutterbugs or birders.

Off Rte. 100 (5km/3 miles east of St. Bride's). ℭ **709/635-4520.** Trail to bird rock is free; admission to interpretive center C$5 (US$4) adults, C$2 (US$1.60) children, C$10 (US$8) family. Guided tours C$7 (US$5.50; includes admission to center). Daily 9am–7pm. Closed mid-Oct to mid-May.

## WHERE TO STAY & DINE
**Atlantica Inn and Restaurant** 𝘨  The Atlantica won't win points for charm—it's a basic, aluminum-sided box among some of the newer houses in the village. But it offers great value at the price, and the five rooms are well maintained and comfortable, if a bit small. The attached restaurant is by and large the only game in town, offering three inexpensive meals daily.

Rte. 100, St. Bride's, NF A0B 2Z0. ℭ **888/999-2860** or 709/337-2860. Fax 709/337-2860. 5 units. C$45–C$55 (US$36–US$44) double. MC, V. **Amenities:** Restaurant.

**Bird Island Resort** 𝘝𝘢𝘭𝘶𝘦 𝘒𝘪𝘥𝘴  This modern, unaffected motel is located behind Manning's food market, where you'll stop to ask for a room. It's the preferred spot in town and offers some unexpected amenities including a laundry room open to guests, a tiny fitness room, and a minigolf course (all rooms come with clubs and balls). The rooms vary in size. The double efficiency units feature a separate sitting room, and several of the rooms have kitchenettes, which come in handy given the dearth of restaurants in town; families with kids will especially appreciate them. Indeed, the rooms that get snapped up first are usually 1 through 5, for that reason: All have kitchenettes, some have two bedrooms, and all face the ocean. That means great views—assuming the fog hasn't moved in.

Rte. 100, St. Bride's, NF A0B 2Z0. ℭ **888/337-2450** or 709/337-2450. Fax 709/337-2903. www.birdislandresort.com. 20 units. C$59–C$99 (US$47–US$79) double. AE, MC, V. *In room:* TV, kitchenette (some units), coffeemaker, no phone.

## PLACENTIA & ARGENTIA
Placentia was settled by the Spanish in 1662 along a cove that proved perfect as a summer fishing base. Although the town has grown and modernized, it remains small, and it requires little effort to imagine the place centuries ago, when the Spanish and

better-equipped Basque fishermen grappled for fish and drying space during the short season.

It's especially easy to let your imagination go when viewing the town from **Castle Hill National Historic Park** (© **709/227-2401**), just outside of town. This prominent hill overlooking the harbor was fortified variously by the French and English in the 17th and 18th centuries. The visitor center is expertly done, with historic maps and dioramas showing how the hilltop fortress once looked. Afterward, stroll to the summit to explore the fort's ruins and to take in the expansive views of town and sea. This is a great first stop if you're just arriving via ferry. You'll get historical background about European settlement, and learn plenty about the historical importance of the cod fisheries.

The site is open year-round; in summer (mid-June to early Sept), hours are daily from 8:30am to 8pm, in spring and fall from 8:30am to 4:30pm. The grounds are free; viewing the exhibits in the visitor center costs C$4 (US$3.20) adults, C$3.50 (US$2.80) seniors, C$2 (US$1.60) ages 6 to 16, C$10 (US$8) family.

The town of Argentia, a former military base, is on the far side of Castle Hill from Placentia. The **visitor information center** (© **709/227-5272**) on Route 100 has an informative exhibit on how a historic fishing village was displaced by the base during World War II. An instant city of some 26,000 people occupied the land, which was used by U.S. forces until 1994. In the annals of the war, the region is remembered mostly for one significant event: U.S. President Franklin D. Roosevelt and British Prime Minister Winston Churchill met on a ship just offshore as part of the Atlantic Conference, in which they hammered out their goals for the end of the war. A monument commemorating this historic meeting is located at **Ship Harbour,** about 24km (15 miles) north of Dunville, which is east of Argentia.

The sprawling former military base is mostly shuttered and melancholy these days, the buildings lonely against the scrappy hills and with only a few souls to enjoy the heartbreakingly beautiful views of Placentia Sound. As part of the conversion to civilian use, the base authority recently established the **Backland Trail,** which ascends wooded hills and passes bunkers, lookouts, and old radar sites. Ask for information on the trail at the visitor information center; the road to the trail head departs from Route 100 just downhill from the center, which is open daily from 9am to 7pm (opens at 6am to greet the incoming ferry traffic 3 days per week).

## 12 Labrador

Labrador may be far removed and remote, but it has long played an outsized role in the collective consciousness of the region. For several centuries, this deeply indented coastline was noted for its robust fisheries, and itinerant fleets plied the waters both inshore and offshore, harvesting what the sea had to offer. The empty, melancholy landscape of rolling hills along the coasts and inland serves much the same function that the American West frontier played in the United States—it's both a land of opportunity stemming from the natural resources (primarily mining these days), and a place where outdoorspeople have historically tested their mettle in a harsh environment, stalking big game and big salmon.

Although sparsely settled, people have been part of the landscape for centuries. The Innu (American Indian) culture in Labrador goes back 8,000 years, and the Inuit (Eskimo) culture 4,000 years. The Vikings sighted Labrador in 986 but didn't come ashore until 1010. Traces of the Vikings remain in the shape of "fairy holes"—deep, cylindrical holes in the rocks, angled away from the sea, where they are thought to have tied their boats.

The 16th century brought Basque whalers, as many as 2,000 of them, and they returned to Europe with 20,000 barrels of whale oil in what might be one of the globe's first oil booms. It has been said that the whale oil of Newfoundland and Labrador was as valuable to the Europeans as the gold of South America. Vestiges of a whaling station remain on Saddle Island, off the coast of Red Bay on the Labrador Straits.

Next came the British and French fishermen, fur traders, and merchants, who first came here in summers to fish, hunt, and trade, and then established permanent settlements in the 1700s. Many of the Europeans married Innu and Inuit women, but conflicts between Inuit whalers and the European settlers along the south coast prompted the Inuit communities to move to the far north, where they remain today.

Only about 30,000 people live in Labrador: 13,000 in western Labrador, 8,000 in Happy Valley–Goose Bay, with the remaining residents spread along the coast. Approximately four-fifths of those born here will remain here, with strong ties to family and neighbors. These close-knit communities typically welcome visitors warmly.

Many visitors come here for the sportfishing of brook trout, Atlantic salmon, arctic char, lake trout, white fish, and northern pike. Others come for wilderness adventure, hiking, and camping under the undulating northern lights. Still others are simply curious about a remote part of the world.

Labrador has three basic destinations, if your definition of destination includes places to stay overnight and eat. (If you come with tent and supplies, the whole, howling landmass is your destination.) Labrador West, including Labrador City and Wabush, is reached by train from Sept-Iles (pronounced "Set-*teel*"), Québec, and via Route 389, also from Québec. Central Labrador includes the commercial and industrial hub centered around Happy Valley–Goose Bay. The Labrador Straits, easily accessible from the island of Newfoundland via ferry, offer small fishing villages and glimpses of the rich history at several sites.

The most scenic route to Labrador—and the only way to visit some of the outports—is by the coastal ferry along "Iceberg Alley." The Marine Atlantic ferry that serves the coast offers cabin accommodations as well as facilities for day passengers—and it's the only means of transportation along much of the Atlantic coast of Labrador. See "Getting There," under "Exploring Newfoundland & Labrador," at the beginning of this chapter for more information.

**SPECIAL-INTEREST/ADVENTURE TOURS**   Those considering a trip to Labrador would do well to consider a packaged adventure tour. The rough terrain, limited transportation, and paucity of visitor services enhances the appeal of letting someone familiar with the land do the planning.

Labrador is considered a world-class destination among anglers. Nearly 50 fishing camps are scattered throughout the region, and many can arrange floatplane access. The **Provincial Tourism Authority** (© **800/563-6353**) can provide a list of outfitters catering to the adventure traveler and help arrange trips that match your interests and abilities.

## THE LABRADOR STRAITS ✪

The Labrador Straits are the easiest part of Labrador to explore from Newfoundland. The southeast corner of Labrador is served by ferries shuttling between St. Barbe, Newfoundland, and Blanc Sablon, Québec. (Blanc Sablon is on the Québec-Labrador

border.) From Blanc Sablon, you can travel on the one and only road, which runs 77km (48 miles) northward, dead-ending at Red Bay. (Plans call for extending this road in the future, but it may be another decade.)

Ferries are timed such that you can cross over in the morning, drive to Red Bay, and still be back for the later ferry to Newfoundland. Such a hasty trip isn't recommended, however. Better to spend a night, when you'll have a chance to meet the people, who offer the most compelling reason to visit.

The **M/V *Apollo*** (© **866/535-2567**) runs from May 1 until ice season, usually sometime in early January. The crossing takes about 1 hour and 30 minutes, and reservations are encouraged in summer (half the ferry can be reserved; the other half is first come, first served). One-way fares are C$11 (US$8.40) adults, C$5.50 (US$4.40) children ages 5 to 12, C$22 (US$17) automobile.

The terrain along the Labrador Straits is rugged, and the colors muted except for a vibrant stretch of green along the Pinware River. The few small houses are clustered close together; during the winter it's nice to have neighbors so nearby. Homes are often brightened up with "yard art"—replicas of windmills, wells, and churches.

In summer, icebergs float by the coast, and whales breach and spout offshore. The landscape is covered with cotton grass, clover, partridgeberries, bakeapples, fireweed, buttercups, and bog laurel. The fog rolls in frequently; it will either stay a while or roll right back out again. The capelin come and go as well. The tiny migrating fish crash-land on the shore by the thousands during a week in late June or early July. Local residents crowd the beach to scoop up the fish and take them home for an easy supper.

The **Visitor Information Centre** in the small, restored St. Andrews Church in L'Anse au Clair, the first town after the ferry, is open June through September. The tourist association has developed several footpaths and trails in the area, so be sure to ask about them; also ask about the "fairy holes." If you come in mid-August, plan to attend the annual Bakeapple Festival, celebrating the berry that stars in the desserts of Newfoundland and Labrador.

## EXPLORING THE LABRADOR STRAITS

Drive the "slow road" that connects the villages of the Labrador Straits. Traveling southwest to northeast, here is some of what you'll find along the way.

In L'Anse au Clair, **Moore's Handicrafts,** 8 Country Rd., just off Route 510 (© 709/931-2186), sells handmade summer and winter coats, traditional cassocks, moccasins, knitted items, handmade jewelry, and other crafts, as well as homemade jams. They also do traditional embroidery on Labrador cassocks and coats, and if you stop on the way north and choose your design, they'll finish it by the time you return to the ferry—even the same day. Prices are quite reasonable. The shop is open daily in season from 8am to 10pm.

The **Labrador Straits Crafts and Museum** ⊕ (© 709/931-2067) is just outside L'Anse-Amour (pop. 25), 19km (12 miles) from L'Anse au Clair. Two exhibit rooms focus mainly on the role of women in the history of the Labrador coast. Also you see photographs of the pilots who flew the first nonstop east-to-west transatlantic flight; they flew off course in April 1928 and landed on Greely Island, off the Labrador-Québec coast. The museum is open daily mid-July to mid-September (call for hours); admission is charged.

The **Point Amour Lighthouse** ⊕ (1858), at the western entrance to the Strait of Belle Isle, is the tallest lighthouse in the Atlantic provinces and the second tallest in all of Canada. The walls of the slightly tapered, circular tower are 2m (6½-ft.) thick at the base. You'll have to climb 122 steps for the view. The dioptric lens was imported from Europe for the princely sum of C$10,000 (US$7,000). The lighthouse, which kept watch for submarines during World War II, is still in use and was maintained by a resident lightkeeper right up until 1995. It's open to the public June to mid-October from 10am to 5:30pm (© 709/927-5825); the fee is C$2.50 (US$2) adults, free for children under 12. The lighthouse is a 3km (2-mile) drive from the main road.

After you pass the fishing settlements of **L'Anse au Loup** ("Wolf's Cove") and West St. Modeste, the road follows the scenic Pinware River, where the trees become noticeably taller. Along this stretch of road, you'll see glacial erratics—those odd boulders deposited by the melting ice cap. **Pinware Provincial Park** ⊕, 42km (26 miles) from L'Anse au Clair, has a picnic area, hiking trails, and 15 campsites. The 81km-long (50-mile) Pinware River is known for salmon fishing.

The highway ends in Red Bay. The **Red Bay National Historic Site Visitor Centre** *&&* ((C) **709/920-2051** or 709/920-2142) showcases artifacts from the late 1500s, when Basque whalers came in numbers to hunt the right and bowhead whales. Starting in 1977, excavations turned up whaling implements, pottery, glassware, and even partially preserved seamen's clothing. From here you can also arrange tours of **Saddle Island,** the home of Basque whaling stations in the 16th century. Transportation to archaeological sites on the island is available from mid-June to mid-October Monday through Saturday from 9am to 4pm. You can also opt to view **Saddle Island** *&* from the observation level on the third floor. Admission is C$7 (US$5.60) adults, C$5.50 (US$4.40) seniors, C$3.50 (US$2.80) ages 6 to 16, C$18 (US$14) family. The site is open 9am to 6pm daily. Closed early October to May.

## WHERE TO STAY

**Beachside Hospitality Home**    A stay here offers an excellent opportunity to meet a local family and learn firsthand about life in this region of Labrador. The three bed rooms have a separate entrance, and two share one of the two full bathrooms. There is a whirlpool bath, and guests have access to a telephone. Home-cooked meals are available by arrangement, or you can cook for yourself in the kitchen or outdoors on the grill; the owners also sell homemade breads, jams, and jellies, and sometimes arrange accordion-powered Newfoundland jigs at night.

9 Lodge Rd., L'Anse au Clair, Labrador, A0K 3K0. (C) **709/931-2338.** Fax 709/931-2275. 3 units, 1 with private bathroom. C$38–C$45 (US$30–US$36) double. MC, V. **Amenities:** Jacuzzi. *In room:* Kitchenette, no phone.

**Grenfell Louie A. Hall Bed & Breakfast** *(Value)*    History buffs love the Grenfell Hall—it was built in 1946 by the International Grenfell Association as a nursing station, and there's plenty of reading material about the coast's early days. The rooms are furnished with basic, contemporary-country furniture, and there's a common room with TV, VCR, and fireplace. The innkeepers can arrange to transport you to and from the ferry. (If you're just curious about the place, you're invited to stop in for C$3/US$2 per person or C$5/US$3.50 per couple.) Evening meals are available by advance arrangement, and usually feature seafood (typically cod or salmon) along with homemade bread, preserves, and dessert. Full breakfast costs extra as well.

3 Willow Ave. (P.O. Box 137), Forteau, Labrador, A0K 2P0. (C) **877/931-2916** or 709/931-2916. Fax 709/931-2189. 5 units. C$45–C$60 (US$36–US$48) double. MC, V. Rates include continental breakfast. MC, V. Closed Nov–Apr. *In room:* Iron, no phone.

**Lighthouse Cove B&B**    Hosts Cecil and Rita Davis have lived in this simple home, overlooking rocks, water, and beach, for more than 4 decades, so they can tell you much about the region. A light breakfast is included in the room rate; full breakfast and seafood supper are available on request, with dinners costing extra. From the house you can walk along a footpath to Point Amour Lighthouse.

2 Main St., L'Anse-Amour, Labrador, A0K 3J0. (C) **709/927-5690.** 3 units share 2½ bathrooms. C$40 (US$32) double. Rates include continental breakfast. MC, V. *In room:* No phone.

**Northern Light Inn** *&*    The largest and most modern hotel in the region, the Northern Light Inn has long offered comfortable, well-maintained rooms, a gift shop, a friendly staff, and a dining room. The restaurant, open from 8am to 11pm, serves soups, sandwiches, baskets of scallops, fried chicken, and pizza. In the adjacent Basque Dining Room, seafood is the specialty. The coffee shop doubles as a lounge in the evening.

58 Main St., L'Anse au Clair, Labrador, A0K 3K0. ☏ 800/563-3188 from Atlantic Canada, or 709/931-2332. Fax 709/931-2708. www.northernlightinn.com. 59 units. C$85–C$150 (US$68–US$120) double. AE, DC, MC, V. Amenities: 2 restaurants; business center; laundry service. In room: A/C, TV, hair dryer.

## WHERE TO DINE

**Seaview Restaurant** HOME COOKING    This family-style restaurant in Forteau, 13km (8 miles) northeast of L'Anse au Clair, offers eat-in or take-out meals. Seafood dishes are the specialty; the seafood basket is particularly popular. There's an adjacent grocery store and bakery, where you can buy homemade bread, peanut-butter cookies, and much more. The same management has eight basic motel rooms for C$79 to C$89 (US$56–US$63) double.

35 Main St., Forteau. ☏ 709/931-2840. Meal items C$2.20–C$20 (US$1.75–US$16). AE, MC, V. Daily 9am–11:30pm.

## LABRADOR WEST

The most affluent and industrialized part of Labrador, Labrador West lies on the Québec border and is home to the twin towns of **Wabush** and **Labrador City**, 6.5km (4 miles) apart. The two towns share many attractions, activities, and services. This region offers top-notch cross-country skiing and has hosted two World Cup events. Labrador West is also home to the largest open-pit iron ore mine in North America, which produces almost half of Canada's ore.

Labrador City or Wabush make a good base for hiking, canoeing, and birding trips. Ask for directions to **Crystal Falls,** where a short hike takes you to the falls and a view over the city. You can also play 18 holes at the **Tamarack Golf Course** (☏ 709/944-3007), open June through September, or go windsurfing, scuba diving, or sailing on one of the many surrounding lakes. And, in the winter, go cross-country skiing at **Menihek Nordic Ski Club** (☏ 709/944-5842), a complete ski center with 40km (24 miles) of groomed trails for all skill levels.

The annual **Labrador 120 Sled Dog Race,** held here in March, draws about 25 teams from North America, who match skills over vast stretches of challenging terrain.

Labrador City is a stop on the oft-overlooked **Québec North Shore and Labrador Railway** (the QNS&L), which departs from Sept-Iles, Québec, and is the only passenger train service in the entire province of Newfoundland and Labrador. The twice-weekly, 8- to 10-hour trip to Labrador City (some of the cars continue farther north to Schefferville; check when you board) covers 419km (260 miles), across 19 bridges, through 11 tunnels, along riverbanks, through forests, and past rapids, mountains, and waterfalls, and finally through subarctic vegetation. In summer a highlight is the vintage dome car (1958) with sofa seats that was once part of the Wabash Cannonball. Buy tickets from the contracted travel agency in Sept-Iles (☏ 418/968-1350). The round-trip cost is about C$150 (US$120) adults, C$75 (US$60) seniors and children 5 to 11. If you're overnighting in Sept-Iles, **Hôtel Sept-Iles** (☏ 800/463-1793 from Québec or 418/962-2581) is a decent place to stay.

For more information about activities in the area, contact **Labrador West Tourism Corporation** (☏ 709/944-7631; www.labradorwest.com).

## CENTRAL LABRADOR

From the North West River and Mud Lake to the Mealy Mountains, a visit to the interior of Labrador will bring you deep into a land of lakes, rivers, and spruce forests, where the horizon looks the same in every direction. Many believe that the Lake Melville area is "Markland, the land of forests" in the Viking sagas.

Outdoor activities include berry picking from August to the first snowfall of November, excellent sportfishing, canoeing the famed **Churchill River,** kayaking the rapid-filled Kenamou River, and snowmobiling. Look for the *Them Days* quarterly magazine (© **709/896-8531**), which chronicles the stories and memories of Labrador's people, published in Happy Valley–Goose Bay and sold everywhere.

Three displays of local history are exhibited at the local mall, the **Northern Lights Building** (© **709/896-5939**) at 170 Hamilton River Rd. You'll see examples of regional animals in the displays, including black bear, wolf, fox, lynx, otter, beaver, bald eagle, loon, duck, and the Canada goose. Also here are the **Military Museum** (uniforms, weapons, and other items from the Royal Newfoundland Regiment), and the Newfie Bullet Model Railway ("one of the largest collection of O Gauge Lionel toy trains on the east coast of Canada"). Admission to all exhibits is free; the building is open year-round.

In 1997, Labrador's first provincial museum was built near Happy Valley–Goose Bay. The **Labrador Interpretation Centre,** Hillview Drive in Northwest River (© **709/497-8566**), is home to displays of some of Labrador's finest art and is free of charge. It's open June through September Tuesday and Wednesday from 1 to 4pm, Thursday and Friday from 10am to 4pm, and weekends from 1:30 to 4:30pm.

To take a little bit of Labrador home with you, stop by **Labrador Crafts and Supplies,** 367 Hamilton River Rd. (© **709/896-8400**), in Happy Valley–Goose Bay, which sells Innu tea dolls, grass work, soapstone carvings, labradorite jewelry, hooked rugs, and parkas.

## WHERE TO STAY

Convenient to the airport, TransLab Highway, and marine dock, the full-service **Labrador Inn** ℰ (© **800/563-2763** in Atlantic Canada, or 709/896-3351) at 380 Hamilton River Rd. has 65 rooms; doubles cost from C$84 to C$120 (US$67–US$96), and a suite costs from C$105 to C$150 (US$84–US$120). The restaurant serves traditional Canadian cuisine with some local dishes, including game and seafood.

## THE NORTH COAST

The Inuit live along Labrador's North Coast, largely in Makkovik, Rigolet, Hopedale, and Nain, where they continue to fish, hunt, and carry on many aspects of their traditional culture. Though it's somewhat inaccessible, skilled outdoor enthusiasts make their ways here for the hiking, sea kayaking, camping, and climbing in the Torngat Mountains.

There's also history to be found. In 1771, a small group of Moravian missionaries began to arrive on the North Coast, bringing with them prefabricated buildings from Germany, some of which are still standing. The wood-frame structure they raised in 1782 is considered the oldest such building east of Québec City. It's located in the village of Hopedale, accessible via the ferry from Happy Valley–Goose Bay to Nain. Tours are by advance appointment only, and there's an excellent little **Moravian Museum** ℰ in one section of the mission house complex containing artifacts from both the missions and the Inuit peoples who still live here. Admission costs about C$5 (US$4) per person. Inquire about the museum and other local sights at the adjacent **Amaguk Inn** (© **709/933-3750;** www.labradoradventures.com), a suitable lodging offering the bonus of historical and fly-fishing tours of the area. Double rooms cost about C$109 (US$87). If you're in town on Sunday morning, check out the religious services, which occur twice: first in Inuit (including choral music), and then in English.

Unless you have your own cruising boat or airplane, about the only way to explore the coast in detail is aboard the M/V *Northern Ranger,* a working supply vessel operated by provincial ferry services. The excursion from Goose Bay, to Nain, Labrador—with numerous stops at tiny ports of call along the way—takes a week round-trip. The cabins are cozy but all have views; you'll eat your meals in the ship's cafeteria with the crew and local passengers. It's a unique way to experience what's arguably the last frontier left on the Atlantic seaboard.

Cruises start in mid-June and run through late November; they're not cheap. You choose between a standard or deluxe cabin, and the hefty tariff includes all meals. No autos are allowed on the boat. For the latest information on schedules and fares, contact the provincial ferry line at ℭ 800/535-2567 or check its website at www.tw.gov.nl.ca/FerryServices. (Click on "Schedules," and then locate the "H" ferry line running north along the Labrador coast on the map.)

# Index

**A**ARP, 21
Above and Beyond Tours, 20
*Acadia,* C.S.S. (Halifax), 91
Acadia Drive (St. Andrews), 150
The Acadian Coast (Nova
    Scotia), 67–69
Acadian Peninsula (New
    Brunswick), 187–191
Acadia University
    (Wolfville), 55
Access-Able Travel Source, 20
Access America, 18
Accessible Journeys, 20
Accommodations
    best, 7–8
    surfing for, 23
Active vacations, best, 2
Adventure travel, 34
Airfares, 22–23, 28
Airlines, 26, 30–31
Airport security, 26–28
Aitkens Pewter (Fredericton),
    172
Alexander Graham Bell
    National Historic Site
    (Baddeck), 128–129
Almanac Used Furniture and
    Antiques (Halifax), 95
Ambience Home Accents
    (Halifax), 95
American Airlines Vacations, 31
American Express, 37
    traveler's checks, 14
American Foundation for the
    Blind (AFB), 20
Amherst (Nova Scotia),
    107–108
Amos Pewter (Mahone Bay), 82
Anchorage Provincial Park
    (New Brunswick), 157
Anglican Cathedral of
    St. John the Baptist
    (St. John's), 277
Annapolis Royal (Nova Scotia),
    6, 58–62

Annapolis Royal Tidal Power
    Project (Nova Scotia), 59
*Anne of Green Gables*
    (Montgomery), 199
Anne of Green Gables Museum
    at Silver Bush (Prince Edward
    Island), 199
*Anne of Green Gables*
    (musical), 200, 221
Anne of Green Gables Store
    (Charlottetown), 215
Antigonish (Nova Scotia),
    113–115
Antiques
    Chester (Nova Scotia), 85
    Halifax (Nova Scotia), 95
Aquarium and Marine Centre
    (Shippagan), 188
Argentia (Newfoundland),
    290–291
Armstrong Brook (Mt. Carleton
    Provincial Park), 192
Art Gallery of Newfoundland
    and Labrador (St. John's), 277
Art Gallery of Nova Scotia
    (Halifax), 91–92
Art Gallery of Nova Scotia
    Shop (Halifax), 95
Aspenwood Tours
    (Newfoundland), 236
Atlantic Film Festival
    (Halifax), 89
Atlantic Jazz Festival (Halifax),
    88–89
Atlantic Salmon Interpretive
    Centre (near St. Andrews),
    151
Atlantic Theatre Festival
    (Wolfville), 55–56
ATMs (automated-teller
    machines), 14
The Attic (Halifax), 103
The Austrian Smokehaus
    (near Truro), 55
Avalon Peninsula
    (Newfoundland), 4

Avalon Wilderness Reserve
    (Newfoundland), 289
Avonlea (Cavendish), 200

**B**accalieu Island (Newfound-
    land), 272
Baccalieu Players (Brigus), 274
Baccalieu Trail (Newfoundland),
    270–274
Backland Trail (Newfoundland),
    291
Backpacking
    Gros Morne National Park
        (Newfoundland), 249
    New Brunswick, 143
Backroads, 34
Baddeck (Nova Scotia),
    128–131
Baker Brook Falls Trail (New-
    foundland), 249
Balancing Rock (Nova Scotia), 65
Basin Head Fisheries Museum
    (Prince Edward Island), 225
Bay Bulls (Newfoundland), 287
Bay Bulls Sea Kayaking Tours
    (Newfoundland), 287
Bay de Verde (Newfoundland),
    272
Bay Ferries, 29
Baymount Outdoor Adventures
    (New Brunswick), 145, 180
Beaches
    New Brunswick, 186–189, 191
    Newfoundland, Terra Nova
        National Park, 264
    Nova Scotia, 68, 132
    Prince Edward Island,
        5–6, 198
        Prince Edward Island
            National Park, 210
        Red Point Provincial Park,
            225
Beaconsfield (Charlottetown),
    214
Beaverbrook Art Gallery
    (Fredericton), 170

Bell, Alexander Graham, National Historic Site (Baddeck), 128–129

Bell Bay Golf Club (near Baddeck), 53

Bell Island Community Museum and Mine Tour (Newfoundland), 281–282

Bell Island (Newfoundland), 281

Berry Hill Campground (Newfoundland), 248, 249

Berry Hill (Newfoundland), 248–249

Beveridge Arts Centre (Wolfville), 55

BiddingForTravel, 22–23

Biking and mountain biking
New Brunswick, 143
    Fredericton, 169
    Fundy National Park, 178
    Fundy Trail Parkway, 165–166
    Grand Manan, 156
    Kouchibouguac National Park, 186
    Moncton, 182
    Mt. Carleton Provincial Park, 192
Newfoundland, 236
    St. John's, 280
Nova Scotia, 52
    Cabot Trail, 2, 140
    Cape Breton, 124
    Cape Breton Highlands National Park, 140
    Digby Neck, 65
    Kejimkujik National Park, 63
Prince Edward Island, 2, 196
    Prince Edward Island National Park, 210

The Bird House and Binocular Shop (St. John's), 280

Bird-watching. See also Puffins
New Brunswick
    Gagetown, 175
    Grand Manan, 143–144
Newfoundland, 236
    Baccalieu Island, 272
    Cape St. Mary's Ecological Reserve, 290
Nova Scotia, 52
    puffins, 133–134
Prince Edward Island, 223

Blomidon Provincial Park (Nova Scotia), 56

Blow Me Down Nature Trail (Newfoundland), 243

Blow Me Down Provincial Park (Newfoundland), 243

Bluenose/Bluenose II (Lunenburg), 76, 78

Bluenose Golf Club (Lunenburg), 53

Blue Rocks (near Lunenburg), 77

Boating (boat rentals). See also Canoeing; Kayaking; Sailing
    Fredericton (New Brunswick), 169–170
    Kouchibouguac National Park (New Brunswick), 186

Boat tours and cruises. See also Ferries; Whale-watching
    Labrador, 298
    New Brunswick
        Caraquet, 189
        Fredericton, 169–170
        St. Andrews, 150–151
        Saint John, 161
    Newfoundland
        Gros Morne National Park, 245, 247–248
        Harbour Grace, 273
        L'Anse aux Meadows, 252
        St. Anthony, 253
        Terra Nova National Park, 262
        Twillingate, 259
    Nova Scotia
        Cape Breton, 121, 128, 133–134
        Halifax, 90–91, 94–95
        Ovens Natural Park, 77
        Prince Edward Island (Charlottetown), 214

Bog Trail (Cape Breton), 139

Bog Trail (Kouchibouguac National Park), 187

Bohaker Trail (Nova Scotia), 60

Bonavista, 269–270

Bonavista North Regional Museum (Newfoundland), 265

Bonavista Peninsula (Newfoundland), 6, 264–270

The Bookman (Charlottetown), 215

Books, recommended, 34–36

Bore Park (Moncton), 181

Boyce Farmers' Market (Fredericton), 169

Brackley Beach (Prince Edward Island), 204

Bras d'Or Lake (Cape Breton), 128, 131–133

The Brewery (Halifax), 99

Brier Island (Nova Scotia), 66

Brigus (Newfoundland), 274

"Brigus Tunnel" (Newfoundland), 274

Brittania Hall Theatre (Tyne Valley), 231

Broad Cove Campground (Cape Breton), 140

Broom Point (Newfoundland), 248

Brudenell River Golf Course (Prince Edward Island), 197

Brudenell River Provincial Park (Prince Edward Island), 224

Buffaloland Provincial Park (Prince Edward Island), 223

Business hours, 37

Bus travel, 29, 31


CAA (Canadian Automobile Association), 37

Cable Station Historic Site (Heart's Content), 272

Cable Wharf (Halifax), 90

Cabot, John, statue of (Bonavista), 270

Cabot Trail (Cape Breton), 2, 4, 115, 119, 122, 125, 137, 140

Calithumpians of Fredericton's Outdoor Summer Theatre, 169

Callanders Beach (Kouchibouguac National Park), 187

Callefour de la Mer (Caraquet), 189

Camping
New Brunswick
    Fundy National Park, 178
    Grand Manan, 157
    Kouchibouguac National Park, 186
    Mt. Carleton Provincial Park, 192
Newfoundland, 236–237
    Gros Morne National Park, 246, 249
    St. John's, 282
    Terra Nova National Park, 263
    Twillingate area, 258–259
Nova Scotia, 53
    Annapolis Royal, 61
    Cape Breton, 123, 140
    Graves Island Provincial Park, 85

Kejimkujik National
Park, 64
Lunenburg, 78–79
Shelburne, 74
Yarmouth, 70
Prince Edward Island National
Park, 210–211
Campobello Island (New
Brunswick), 145–147
Canada Games Aquatic Centre
(Saint John), 160
Canadian Paraplegic
Association, 20
Canoeing
New Brunswick, 144
Cape Enrage, 179
Newfoundland, 237
Terra Nova National
Park, 262
Nova Scotia, 53, 63, 120
Pictou, 111
Cape Bonavista Lighthouse
Provincial Historic Site
(Newfoundland), 270
Cape Breton Clay (Margaree
Valley), 120
Cape Breton Highlands
National Park (Nova Scotia),
2, 4, 5, 137–140
Cape Breton Island (Nova
Scotia), 115–137
traveling to, 116–117
visitor information, 117
Cape Breton Miners' Museum
(Glace Bay), 134
Cape Enrage Adventures
(New Brunswick), 179
Cape Enrage (New Brunswick),
178–179
Cape Forchu (Nova Scotia), 70
Cape North (Cape Breton),
123–125
Cape St. Mary's Ecological
Reserve (Newfoundland),
289–290
Cape St. Mary's (Newfoundland),
236
Cape Spear National Historic
Site (Newfoundland), 281
Cape Split (Nova Scotia), 56
Cape Split Trail (Nova
Scotia), 56
Caraquet (New Brunswick), 189
Caribou, 289
Caribou Plain Trail (New
Brunswick), 178
Carleton, Mount (New
Brunswick), 192

Car rentals, 24
insurance, 18–19
saving money on, 30
Car travel, 28–30
Castle Hill National Historic
Park (Newfoundland), 291
Cavendish Campground (Prince
Edward Island), 211
Cavendish Cemetery (Prince
Edward Island), 200
Cavendish (Prince Edward
Island), 198–203
Cedar Trail (Kouchibouguac
National Park), 187
Cellphones, 26
Celtic Colours (Cape Breton),
117
Centers for Disease Control
and Prevention, 19
Central Labrador, 296–297
Central Newfoundland,
255–261
Charlie's Trail (Nova Scotia), 61
Charlotte County Museum
(St. Stephen), 148
Charlottetown Driving Park
(Prince Edward Island), 221
Charlottetown (Prince Edward
Island), 44, 45, 210, 212–221
accommodations, 216–218
exploring, 213–215
nightlife, 221
restaurants, 218–220
shopping, 215–216
traveling to, 212
visitor information, 212
Cheeselady's Gouda (Prince
Edward Island), 204
Chester Golf Club (Nova
Scotia), 53
Chester (Nova Scotia), 84–86
Chester Playhouse (Nova
Scotia), 85
Chéticamp Campground (Cape
Breton), 140
Chéticamp (Cape Breton),
120–122
Chignecto North Campground
(Fundy National Park), 178
Children, families with
best activities for, 5–6
information and resources,
21–22
The Chocolate Museum
(St. Stephen), 148
Christian's Bar (St. John's), 286
Churchill River (Labrador), 297
Church Point (Nova Scotia), 68

The Citadel (Halifax), 89, 91
City Cinema (Charlottetown),
221
City Hall (Halifax), 91
Clam Harbour Beach Provincial
Park (Nova Scotia), 105
Climate, 16–17
Coastal Adventures (Nova
Scotia), 34, 54, 105
Coastal Safari (Newfoundland),
238
Coastal Trail (Newfoundland),
262
Cobequid Bay (Nova Scotia),
4, 54
College of the North Atlantic
(Newfoundland), 240
Collette Vacations, 33
Colony of Avalon Interpreta-
tion Centre (Newfoundland),
288
Commissariat House
(St. John's), 278
Conception Bay Museum
(Harbour Grace), 273
Confederation Centre of the
Arts Gallery and Museum
(Charlottetown), 214–215,
221
Confederation Court Mall
(Charlottetown), 215
Confederation Landing Park
(Charlottetown), 214
Confederation Trail (Prince
Edward Island), 5, 196, 228
Consulates, 37–38
Continental Airlines
Vacations, 31
Co-operative Artisanale de
Chéticamp (Cape Breton),
121
Corner Brook (Newfoundland),
240–243
Cossit House Museum
(Sydney), 133
Côte-à-Fabien Campground
(New Brunswick), 186
Country Harbour Ferry (Nova
Scotia), 105–106
Country Walkers, 34
Cows (Charlottetown), 215
Credit cards, 15, 38
Cross-country skiing
(Labrador), 296
Cruise Manada (Prince Edward
Island), 223
Crystal Falls (Labrador), 296
Crystal Palace (near Moncton),
182

Cultures Boutique (Fredericton), 172
Cumberland County Museum (Amherst), 108
Currency and currency exchange, 13–14
Customs regulations, 12–13

**D**ark Harbour (Grand Manan), 156
Deer Lake (Newfoundland), 243–244
Delaps Cove Wilderness Trails (Nova Scotia), 60
Devon House Craft Center (St. John's), 280–281
Digby Neck (Nova Scotia), 2, 64–67
Digby (Nova Scotia), 64
Dildo Interpretation Centre (Newfoundland), 271
Dildo (Newfoundland), 271
Dildo Run Provincial Park (Newfoundland), 258
Disabilities, travelers with, 19–20
Discovery Trail Tourism Association (Newfoundland), 267
Dolan's Pub (Fredericton), 175
Dory Shop (Shelburne), 73
Downhome Shoppe & Gallery (St. John's), 281
Drala Asian Books & Gifts (Halifax), 95
Driving rules, 30
Driving tours. *See* Scenic drives
Drugstores, 37
Duke of Duckworth (St. John's), 286
Duke of York Cranberry Meadow (Cape Breton), 132
Dune de Bouctouche (New Brunswick), 184
The Dunes Studio Gallery and Café (Brackley Beach), 204
Dungeons Provincial Park (Newfoundland), 270

**E**ast Coast Outfitters (Nova Scotia), 82
Eastern Edge Outfitters (Newfoundland), 238
The Eastern Shore (Nova Scotia), 104–107
East Point Lighthouse (Prince Edward Island), 225

East Point (Prince Edward Island), 228
Economy Shoe Shop (Halifax), 103
Ecum Secum (Nova Scotia), 105
1834 Government House (Fanningbank; Charlottetown), 214
Elderhostel, 21
ElderTreks, 21
Electricity, 37
Elizabeth LeFort Gallery and Museum, 121
Embassies and consulates, 37–38
Emergencies, 38
Englishtown (Cape Breton), 127
Entry requirements, 12
Escorted tours, 32–33
*Ethie,* SS, shipwreck (Newfoundland), 248
Expedia, 22, 23
"Experience New Brunswick" campaign, 143

**F**airmont Ridge Trail (Nova Scotia), 113
Fairview Lawn Cemetery (Halifax), 93
Fallsview Park (Saint John), 161
Families with children
   best activities for, 5–6
   information and resources, 21–22
Familyhostel, 21
Family Travel Files, 21–22
Family Travel Forum, 21
Family Travel Network, 21
Farmers' Bank of Rustico (South Rustico), 203
Farmers' markets
   Boyce Farmers' Market (Fredericton), 169
   Halifax (Nova Scotia), 99
Fat Cat Blues Bar (St. John's), 286
Ferries, 28–30
   the Labrador Straits, 293
   Nova Scotia, 49, 52
   Prince Edward Island, 196
Ferryland (Newfoundland), 288
Ferry Terminal (Halifax), 89–90
Festival Antigonish, 114
Films, recommended, 36
Firefighters' Museum of Nova Scotia (Yarmouth), 70
Fire Tower Road (Nova Scotia), 63

Fisheries Museum of the Atlantic (Lunenburg), 76–77
Fisherman's Life Museum (Jeddore Oyster Pond), 104–105
Fishing
   Labrador, 292, 294
   New Brunswick, 144
   Newfoundland, 237
   Nova Scotia, 53, 128
   Prince Edward Island, 197, 204
Fishing Cove (Cape Breton), 140
Fishing Point Park (St. Anthony), 253
Fluvarium (St. John's), 279
Flying Wheels Travel, 20
Fort Anne National Historic Site (Annapolis Royal), 59
Fortress of Louisbourg National Historic Site (Cape Breton), 135–136
Fossils, 5
Fraser Cultural Centre (Tatamagouche), 109
Fredericton Lighthouse (New Brunswick), 169
Fredericton (New Brunswick), 166–175
   accommodations, 172–174
   exploring, 168–172
   nightlife, 175
   outdoor activities, 169–170
   restaurants, 174
   shopping, 172
   traveling to, 166–168
   visitor information, 168
Fred's (St. John's), 281
Freewheeling Adventures, 34, 52, 236
FreshAir Adventure (New Brunswick), 145, 177
Frommers.com, 24
Fundy Circuit (New Brunswick), 178
Fundy National Park (New Brunswick), 2, 42–43, 176–181
Fundy Trail Parkway (New Brunswick), 4, 143, 144, 165–166

**G**aelic College of Celtic Arts and Crafts (St. Ann's), 33, 127
Gagetown (New Brunswick), 175
Gallery Connexion (Fredericton), 172

Gallery 78 (Fredericton), 172
Gander (Newfoundland), 260–261
Garden tours (Shelburne), 73
Gasoline, 30
Gateway Village (Prince Edward Island), 194
Gaudreau Fine Woodworking (South Rustico), 204
Gay and lesbian travelers, 20–21
Gay.com Travel, 21
Geddes Furniture and Antiques (Halifax), 95
George Street (St. John's), 286
Giant MacAskill Museum (Englishtown), 127
Gibson Trail (Fredericton), 169
Glace Bay (Cape Breton), 134
Glasgow Lake Lookoff (Cape Breton), 139
Glenora Distillery (Cape Breton), 117
Golf
  Labrador, 296
  New Brunswick, 144
    Fredericton, 170
  Nova Scotia, 53–54, 125
  Prince Edward Island, 197
    Brudenell River Provincial Park, 224
    near Morell, 228
Golf Nova Scotia, 53–54
GoToMyPC, 25
Grafton Street Dinner Theater (Halifax), 103
Grand Concourse (St. John's), 280
Grande-Anse (New Brunswick), 190–191
Grand Falls–Windsor (Newfoundland), 255–257
Grand Manan Island (New Brunswick), 4, 5, 155–158
Grand Manan Museum (New Brunswick), 156
Grand Parade (Halifax), 91
Grand-Pré National Historic Site (Nova Scotia), 56–57
Grassy Island National Historic Site (Nova Scotia), 106
Graves Island Provincial Park (Nova Scotia), 85
Great Easton Boat Tours (Harbour Grace), 273
Great George Street (Charlottetown), 214
Great Hall of Clans (St. Ann's), 127

Great Northern Knitters (Charlottetown), 215
Great Northern Peninsula (Newfoundland), 250–255
Great Viking Feast at Leifsburdur (St. Anthony), 253
Grebe's Nest (Bell Island), 282
Green Family Forge Blacksmith Museum (Trinity), 266
The Green (Fredericton), 169
Green Gables Heritage Site (Cavendish), 200
Green Gardens Trail (Newfoundland), 5, 245–246
Green Park Provincial Park (Prince Edward Island), 231
Green Park Shipbuilding Museum (Tyne Valley), 231
Green Point campground (Newfoundland), 249
Greenwich Dunes (St. Peter's Bay), 228
Greenwich Interpretation Centre (Prince Edward Island), 228
Grenfell House Museum and Interpretation Centre (St. Anthony), 253–254
Grohmann Knives (Pictou), 111
Gros Morne Adventures (Newfoundland), 244
Gros Morne Mountain (Newfoundland), 248
Gros Morne National Park (Newfoundland), 2, 47, 237, 240, 244–250
Gros Morne Recreation Centre (Newfoundland), 248
The Gulf Museum (Port aux Basques), 239

**H**alifax Citadel National Historic Site (Nova Scotia), 92
Halifax Metro Centre (Nova Scotia), 102
Halifax (Nova Scotia), 41–42, 86–104
  accommodations, 95–98
  average monthly temperatures, 17
  exploring, 89–95
  nightlife, 102–104
  restaurants, 98–102
  special events, 88–89
  transportation, 88
  traveling to, 88
  visitor information, 88

Harbour Grace Airfield (Newfoundland), 273
Harbour Grace (Newfoundland), 272
Harbour Grace Visitor Center (Newfoundland), 272
Harbour Hopper (Halifax), 90
Harbour Station (Saint John), 165
Harmonized Sales Tax (HST), 15–16
Harvey Moore Wildlife Management Area (Prince Edward Island), 223
Hastings Auto Trail (Fundy National Park), 176–177
Hawthorne Cottage National Historic Site (Brigus), 274
Head, Mount (New Brunswick), 192
Headquarters Campground (Fundy National Park), 178
Health concerns, 19
Health insurance, 18
Heart's Content (Newfoundland), 271–272
Hector Festival (Pictou), 110
Hector Heritage Quay (Pictou), 111
Hemlocks and Hardwoods Trail (Nova Scotia), 63
Heritage Discovery Tours (St. Andrews), 149
Heritage District (Harbour Grace), 273
Herring Cove Provincial Park (New Brunswick), 146
The Highland Games (Antigonish), 114
Hiking and walking, 188–189
  best, 4–5
  New Brunswick, 144–145
    Campobello Island, 146
    Fredericton, 169
    Fundy National Park, 177–178
    Fundy Trail Parkway, 165–166
    Grand Manan, 156
    Kouchibouguac National Park, 187
    Mt. Carleton Provincial Park, 192
    Saint John, 161
  Newfoundland, 237
    Bonavista Peninsula, 267
    Gros Morne National Park, 245–246, 248–249

**Hiking and walking** *(cont.)*
La Manche Provincial
Park, 288
St. John's, 280
Salmonier Nature Park,
289
Terra Nova National Park,
262
Twillingate, 258
Nova Scotia, 54
Annapolis Royal, 59
Cape Breton, 139
Delaps Cove Wilderness
Trails, 60
Digby Neck area, 65–66
Kejimkujik National
Park, 63
Lunenburg, 76
Pleasant Bay, 123
Wolfville, 56
Prince Edward Island, 223
Orwell, 207
Prince Edward Island
National Park, 210
**Hiscock House (Trinity), 266**
**Historic Gardens (Annapolis
Royal), 60**
**Historic Properties (Halifax), 90**
**Holidays, 17**
**Homestead Trail (Prince
Edward Island), 210**
**Hopewell Rocks (New
Brunswick), 4, 145, 179–181**
**Hotels.com, 23**
**Hotwire, 22, 23**
**HST (Harmonized Sales Tax),
15–16**

**I**ceberg spotting, Twillingate
(Newfoundland), 259
**Identity theft and fraud, 38**
**Imperial Theatre (Saint John),
165**
**Ingonish (Cape Breton), 125**
**The Inside Connection (Saint
John), 159–160**
**Institute of Marine Dynamics
(St. John's), 279**
**International Association for
Medical Assistance to
Travelers (IAMAT), 19**
**International Busker Festival
(Halifax), 89**
**International Gay and Lesbian
Travel Association (IGLTA), 20**
**Internet access, 24–26**
**INTRAV, 21**

**The Inuit, 92, 291, 292, 297,
298**
**Irving Nature Park (Saint John),
161**
**Island Chocolates (Victoria),
230**
**Island Rods and Flies (Charlot-
tetown), 197**
**The Islands Provincial Park
(Nova Scotia), 74**
**Isle Madame (Cape Breton),
132**
**Itineraries, suggested, 40–47**

**J**anet Doble Pottery Studio
(Halifax), 95
**Jeremy's Bay (Nova Scotia), 64**
**Jo-Ann's Deli, Market & Bake
Shop (Mahone Bay), 82**
**Jodrey Trail (Nova Scotia), 56**
**Jost Heritage House (Sydney),
133**
**Jost Vineyards (near Malagash),
109**
**J. T. Cheeseman Provincial Park
(Newfoundland), 239**

**K**ayak.com, 22
**Kayaking**
New Brunswick, 145
Cape Enrage, 179
Fundy National Park, 177
Grand Manan, 156
Hopewell Rocks, 180
Newfoundland, 238
Red Indian Adventures,
256
Terra Nova National Park,
262
Witless Bay area, 287
Nova Scotia, 2, 54
Cape Breton, 125–127
Mahone Bay, 82
Pictou, 111
Prince Edward Island,
197–198
**Kejimkujik National Park (Nova
Scotia), 53, 62–64**
**Kellys beach (Kouchibouguac
National Park), 186**
**Kerley's Harbour Trail (New-
foundland), 267**
**Kingsbrae Garden (St.
Andrews), 151**
**King's Castle Provincial Park
(Prince Edward Island), 222**

**Kings County (Prince Edward
Island), 221–229**
**Kings Landing Historical Settle-
ment (near Fredericton),
171–172**
**King's Landing (near Frederic-
ton), 33**
**Kings Landing (New
Brunswick), 5**
**King's Theatre (Annapolis
Royal), 59**
**Kingswood golf course (Freder-
icton), 144, 170**
**The Kitchen Store (Charlotte-
town), 216**
**Kouchibouguac National Park
(New Brunswick), 185–187**
**Kouchibouguac River Trail
(New Brunswick), 187**
*Kyle,* **SS (Harbour Grace),
272, 273**

**L**abrador, 1, 11, 291–298
**Labrador City, 296**
**Labrador Crafts and Supplies
(Happy Valley–Goose Bay),
297**
**Labrador Interpretation Centre
(near Happy Valley–Goose
Bay), 297**
**Labrador 120 Sled Dog Race,
296**
**The Labrador Straits, 292–296**
**Labrador Straits Crafts and
Museum (near L'Anse-
Amour), 294**
**Labrador West, 296**
**La Dune de Bouctouche (New
Brunswick), 184**
**La Manche Provincial Park
(Newfoundland), 287–288**
**Laméque International Baroque
Music Festival (Miscou
Island), 188**
**L'Anse au Loup (Labrador), 294**
**L'Anse aux Meadows National
Historic Site, 6, 252–253**
**L'Anse aux Meadows (New-
foundland), 252**
**Lastminute.com, 22**
**Lastminutetravel.com, 22**
**La Vieille Maison (Meteghan), 68**
**Learning vacations, 33–34**
**Lester-Garland Premises
(Trinity), 266**
**Liberty Travel, 31**
**Lighthouse Point (Cape
Breton), 135**

Links at Crowbush Cove (near Morell), 228
Links at Crowbush Cove (Prince Edward Island), 197
Liquor laws, 38
Liscomb Game Sanctuary (Nova Scotia), 105
Liscomb River Trail (Nova Scotia), 105
Lobster suppers, Prince Edward Island, 206
Lomond campground (Newfoundland), 246
Lone Shieling (Cape Breton), 139
Long Point Interpretation Centre (Twillingate), 258
Long Point Lighthouse (Twillingate), 258
Long Point (Twillingate), 257
Long Range (Newfoundland), 249
Lost and found, 38
Lost-luggage insurance, 18
Louisbourg, 6, 134–137
Louisbourg Playhouse (Cape Breton), 135
Lower Deck (Halifax), 103
Loyalist House (Saint John), 160
Lucy Maud Montgomery Birthplace (New London), 200–201
Lunar Rogue (Fredericton), 175
Lunenburg Body Care, 77
Lunenburg (Nova Scotia), 1, 7, 41, 75–81
Lunenburg Whale Watching Tours (Nova Scotia), 76

Mabou (Cape Breton), 117–119
McNab's Island Ferry (Halifax), 95
McNab's Island (Nova Scotia), 93–94
Macphail, Sir Andrew, 208
    home of (near Orwell), 207
MacQueen's Island Tours & Bike Shop (Charlottetown), 197
Magdalen Islands (Les Isles de la Madeleine), 227
Magnetic Hill (Moncton), 181, 182–183
Mahone Bay (Nova Scotia), 41, 82–84
Mahone Bay Settlers Museum (Nova Scotia), 82

Mail, 38
Mail2web, 25
Maitland Bridge (Nova Scotia), 63
Malady Head campground (Newfoundland), 263
Maps, road, 30
Marble Mountain (Cape Breton), 132
Marble Mountain Museum and Library (Cape Breton), 132
Margaree River (Cape Breton), 119
Margaree Salmon Museum (Cape Breton), 119
Margaree Valley (Cape Breton), 119–120
Marine Atlantic (Newfoundland), 235–236
Marine Interpretation Centre (Terra Nova National Park), 261, 262
Mariner Cruises (Brier Island), 66
Maritime Museum of the Atlantic (Halifax), 6, 89, 90
Marquee Club (Halifax), 103
Mary March Regional Museum (Grand Falls), 256
*Mary Silliman's War* (film), 72
*Matthew*, replica of (Bonavista), 269–270
Mavilete Beach, 68
Maxwell's Plum (Halifax), 103–104
Maxxim Vacations, 33
Meat Cove Campground (Cape Breton), 123
MEDEX Assistance, 18
MedicAlert identification tag, 19
Medical insurance, 18
Memorial University Botanical Garden at Oxen Pond (St. John's), 279
Menihek Nordic Ski Club (Labrador), 296
Merrymakedge Beach Trail (Nova Scotia), 63
Middle Head (Cape Breton), 139
Military Museum (Happy Valley–Goose Bay), 297
Minas Basin (Nova Scotia), 54–58
Minchin Cove (Newfoundland), 263

Ministers Island Historic Site/Covenhoven (Chamcook), 151–152
Miramichi River (New Brunswick), 144
Miscou Centre (New Brunswick), 188
Miscou Island (New Brunswick), 188–189
Mockbeggar Plantation (Bonavista), 269
Moncton (New Brunswick), 43, 181–185
Money matters, 13–16
Montague (Prince Edward Island), 223
Montgomery, Lucy Maud
    *Anne of Green Gables*, 199
    Birthplace (New London), 200–201
    site of Cavendish home, 201
Moore's Handicrafts (L'Anse au Clair), 294
Moravian Museum (Labrador), 297
Moss-Rehab, 20
Mountain biking. *See* Biking and mountain biking
Mount Carleton Provincial Park (New Brunswick), 144
Mt. Carleton Provincial Park (New Brunswick), 191–192
Mount Stewart (Prince Edward Island), 228
Muir-Cox Shipbuilding Interpretive Centre (Shelburne), 74
Murphy's on the Water (Halifax), 90, 94–95
Murray Harbour (Prince Edward Island), 222
Murray River (Prince Edward Island), 222
Music, 36–37
Myron's (Charlottetown), 221

Nashwaak/Marysville Trail (Fredericton), 169
Naval Clock (Halifax), 89
Neil's Harbour (Cape Breton), 125
The Neptune Theatre (Halifax), 102–103
New Brunswick, 1, 141–192
    brief description of, 10
    exploring, 141–143
    outdoor activities, 143–145
    suggested itineraries, 42–43
    visitor information, 11, 142

New Brunswick Museum
(Saint John), 160
Newfoundland, 1, 233–291
brief description of, 10
exploring, 233–236
outdoor activities, 236–238
suggested itinerary, 46
visitor information, 11
Newfoundland and Labrador
Folk Festival (St. John's), 277
The Newfoundland Insectarium
(Deer Lake), 243
Newfoundland Weavery
(St. John's), 281
Newman Sound (Newfound-
land), 263
Newspapers and magazines, 39
Niger Reef Tea House
(St. Andrews), 150
North Atlantic Aviation
Museum (Gander), 260
The North Coast (Labrador),
297–298
Northern Lights Building
(Happy Valley–Goose Bay),
297
North Head Trail (Newfound-
land), 5, 280
North Hills Museum (Annapolis
Royal), 60
Northland Discovery Boat Tours
(Newfoundland), 253
North Rim (Newfoundland),
249
North River Kayak (Nova
Scotia), 54
North Rustico (Prince Edward
Island), 203–205
Northwestern Coastal Trail
(Grand Manan), 156
Nova Scotia, 1, 48–140
brief description of, 10
exploring, 48–52
outdoor activities, 52–54
suggested itineraries, 40–42
traveling to, 49, 52
visitor information, 11, 49
Nova Scotia Adventure Tourism
Association, 52
Nova Scotia Centre for Craft
and Design (Halifax), 92
Nova Scotia Doers & Dreamers
Travel Guide, 49
Nova Scotia Highland Village
Museum (near Iona), 132
Nova Scotia International
Tattoo (Halifax), 88
Nova Scotia League for Equal
Opportunities, 20

Nova Scotia Museum of Nat-
ural History (Halifax), 92–93
Nova Scotia Visitor Information
Centre (Amherst), 108
Now, Voyager, 20

O'Brien's (St. John's), 281
Ocean Explorations (Digby
Neck), 66
Ocean Watch Tours (Newfound-
land), 262
Old Burial Ground (Saint John),
159
Old Burying Ground
(Halifax), 94
Old Burying Ground Walking
Tour (Annapolis Royal), 59
Old City Market (Saint John),
160–161
Olde Dublin Pub (Charlotte-
town), 221
Old Government House (Fred-
ericton), 169, 170
The Old Trails (Newfoundland),
264
Orbitz, 22
Orwell Corner Historic Village
(Prince Edward Island), 207
Orwell (Prince Edward Island),
207–208
Osprey Ridge (near
Shelburne), 53
Outport Trail (Newfoundland),
262, 263
Outside Expeditions (Prince
Edward Island), 198, 203
Ovens Natural Park (Nova
Scotia), 77

Package tours, 31–32
Panmure Island Provincial Park
(Prince Edward Island), 222
Park Lane Shopping Centre
(Halifax), 95
Parrsboro (Nova Scotia), 5
Passamaquoddy Bay (New
Brunswick), 145–155
Peake's Wharf (Charlottetown),
213–215
Peggy's Cove Express (Halifax),
90
Peggy's Cove (Nova Scotia),
103
PEI Company Store (Charlotte-
town), 216
Perimeter Trail (Nova Scotia), 59
Petite Passage Whale Watch
(East Ferry), 66

Petit Large Campground (New
Brunswick), 186
Pets, traveling with, 39
Philip's Garden (Port au Choix),
251
Pictou (Nova Scotia), 110–113
Pier 21 (Halifax), 91
Pinware Provincial Park
(Labrador), 294
Pinware River (Labrador), 294
Pirate's Cove Whale Cruises
(Tiverton), 66
Pissing Mare Falls (Newfound-
land), 262
Placentia (Newfoundland),
290–291
Plage Grande-Anse, 191
Pleasant Bay (Cape Breton),
122–123
Point Amour Lighthouse
(Labrador), 294
Pointe-à-Maxime Campground
(New Brunswick), 186
Point Miscou Lighthouse (New
Brunswick), 188
Point Pleasant Park (Halifax),
4, 94
Point Wolfe Campground
(Fundy National Park), 178
Pokeshaw Park (Grande-Anse),
191
Police, 39
Pollett's Cove (Cape Breton),
123
Pope Museum (Grande-Anse),
191
Port au Choix National Historic
Site (Newfoundland),
251–252
Port au Choix (Newfoundland),
251–252
Port aux Basques (Newfound-
land), 238–240
Port aux Basques Railway Her-
itage Center (Newfound-
land), 239
Port Maitland Beach (Nova
Scotia), 68
Port-Royal National Historic
Site (Annapolis Royal), 60
Poverty Beach (Prince Edward
Island), 222
Prescription medications, 19
Priceline, 22, 23
Prince County (Prince Edward
Island), 229–232
Prince Edward Island,
1, 193–232
beaches, 5–6
brief description of, 10

exploring, 194–196
outdoor activities, 196–198
suggested itinerary, 44–45
visitor information, 11
Prince Edward Island Museum
and Heritage Foundation
(Orwell), 207
Prince Edward Island National
Park, 4, 208–211
Prince Edward Island Preserve
Co. (New Glasgow), 204–205
Prince William's Walk (Saint
John), 159
Privateers' Warehouse
(Halifax), 90
Province House (Charlotte-
town), 214
Province House (Halifax), 93
Province House National His-
toric Site (Charlottetown),
6, 215
Provincial Legislative Assembly
Building (Fredericton),
170–171
Provincial Museum of New-
foundland and Labrador
(St. John's), 1, 278
Public Gardens (Halifax), 94
Puffins, 52
off Bonavista (Newfound-
land), 270
tours (Cape Breton), 133–134
Pugwash (Nova Scotia),
108–110

Québec North Shore and
Labrador Railway, 296
Queens County Museum
(Gagetown), 175
Queens County (Prince Edward
Island), 198–208
traveling to, 198
visitor information, 198
Quidi Vidi (St. John's), 279–280
Quikbook.com, 23

Rappie pie, 68
Rapure Acadienne Ltd.
(Church Point), 68
Red Bay National Historic Site
Visitor Centre (Labrador),
295
Red Indian Adventures (Grand
Falls–Windsor), 256
Red Point Provincial Park
(Prince Edward Island), 225
Restaurants, best, 8–9

Reversing Falls (Saint John),
161
Ripley's Believe It or Not!
Museum (Cavendish), 201
Rising Tide Theatre (Trinity),
266
Road maps, 30
Robie Swift Park (Nova
Scotia), 56
Rock climbing, Cape Enrage
(New Brunswick), 179
Rockwood Park (Saint John),
162
Roosevelt Campobello Interna-
tional Park (New Brunswick),
146–147
Ross Memorial Museum
(St. Andrews), 149–150
Ross-Thomson House
(Shelburne), 74
Route 915 (New Brunswick),
178
Route 215 (Nova Scotia), 55
Rustico Island campground
(Prince Edward Island), 211
The Rusticos (Prince Edward
Island), 203
Ryan Building (Trinity), 266
Ryan Premises National His-
toric Site (Bonavista), 269

Sackville, HMCS (Halifax), 91
Saddle Island (Labrador), 295
Safety, 39
Sagamook, Mount (New
Brunswick), 192
Sailing, Nova Scotia, 54
Sail Mahone Bay (Nova
Scotia), 54
St. Andrews (New Brunswick),
42, 148–155
St. Ann's (Cape Breton),
127–128
St. Anthony (Newfoundland),
253–255
St. Brendan's Island (New-
foundland), 264
Saint John (New Brunswick),
42, 158–166
accommodations, 162–164
exploring, 159–161
nightlife, 165
outdoor activities, 161–162
restaurants, 164–165
traveling to, 158
visitor information, 158–159
St. John's Anglican Church
(Lunenburg), 1, 76

St. John's (Newfoundland),
46, 274–286
accommodations, 282–284
excursions from, 281–282
exploring, 277–280
nightlife, 286
orientation, 276–277
outdoor activities, 280
restaurants, 284–286
shopping, 280–281
transportation, 276
traveling to, 276
visitor information, 276
St. Mary's Church (Church
Point), 68
St. Patrick's Church Museum
(Sydney), 133
St. Paul's Anglican Church
(Halifax), 93
St. Peter's Bay (Prince Edward
Island), 227–229
St. Peter's Canal (Cape Breton),
131
St. Peters (Cape Breton), 131
St. Stephen (New Brunswick),
147–148
Salmon. See also Fishing
Atlantic Salmon Interpretive
Centre (near St. Andrews),
151
Salmonid Interpretation Cen-
tre (Grand Falls–Windsor),
255–256
Salmonid Interpretation Centre
(Grand Falls–Windsor),
255–256
Salmonier Nature Park (New-
foundland), 289
Salvage Fisherman's Museum
(Newfoundland), 264
Sandspit (Cavendish), 201
Sara Bonnyman Pottery (Tatam-
agouche), 109
SATH (Society for Accessible
Travel & Hospitality), 20
Scarlet Letter (film), 73
Scenic drives
best, 4
New Brunswick, Fundy
National Park, 176–177
Nova Scotia, 55, 70
Bras d'Or Lake, 131
Cape Breton Highlands
National Park, 139
Eastern Shore, 104–106
Lunenburg area, 77
Science East (Fredericton), 171
Scotia Trawler (Lunenburg), 77

Seabreeze Municipal Park
(Newfoundland), 258–259
Seabreeze Municipal Park
(Twillingate), 258
Seagull Pewter (Pugwash), 109
Sea kayaking
    New Brunswick, 145
        Cape Enrage, 179
        Fundy National Park, 177
        Grand Manan, 156
        Hopewell Rocks, 180
    Newfoundland, 238
        Red Indian Adventures,
        256
        Terra Nova National Park,
        262
        Witless Bay area, 287
    Nova Scotia, 2, 54
        Cape Breton, 125–127
        Mahone Bay, 82
        Pictou, 111
    Prince Edward Island,
    197–198
Sea Kayaking with Whitecap
Adventures (Newfoundland),
238
Seals, Prince Edward Island,
222, 223
Seascape Kayak Tours (Deer
Island), 145, 151
Seasons, 16–17
Seasway Hammock Shop
(North Rustico), 205
Sea Watch Tours (Grand
Manan), 157
Seniors, 21
Sensational Chocolates
(Mahone Bay), 82
Seven Day's Work (Grand
Manan), 155–156
Seven Day's Work Trail (Grand
Manan), 156
Shakespeare by the Sea
(Halifax), 102
Shallow Bay campground
(Newfoundland), 249
Sheet Harbour (Nova Scotia),
105
Shelburne County Museum
(Nova Scotia), 74
Shelburne Historic Complex
(Nova Scotia), 73–74
Shelburne (Nova Scotia), 72–75
Sherbrooke Village (Nova
Scotia), 106
Ship Harbour (Newfoundland),
291
Ship Harbour (Nova Scotia), 104
The Ship Inn (St. John's), 286

Shippagan (New Brunswick),
188–189
Shipping your luggage, 27
Shoreline Adventures (Nova
Scotia), 113
SideStep, 22
Signal Hill (St. John's), 278–279
Silent Witness Memorial
(Gander), 260
Sipu Campground (New
Brunswick), 186
Sir Wilfred Grenfell College of
Memorial University of New-
foundland, 240
Site59.com, 22
Skyline Trail (Cape Breton), 139
Small Craft Aquatic Centre
(Fredericton), 169–170
Smarter Travel, 22
Smuggler's Cove
(Meteghan), 68
Snug Harbour (Newfoundland),
249
Snug Harbour Trail (Newfound-
land), 248
Souris (Prince Edward Island),
45, 225–227
South Broad Cove (Newfound-
land), 263
Southern Avalon Peninsula
(Newfoundland), 286–291
South Kouchibouguac Camp-
ground (New Brunswick), 186
South Rustico (Prince Edward
Island), 203
South Shore (Nova Scotia),
72–86
Southwestern Newfoundland,
238–244
Special-interest trips, 33–34
Spirit of Harbour Grace
(Newfoundland), 272
Spring Garden Road
(Halifax), 89
Spry Harbour (Nova Scotia),
104
Stanhope campground (Prince
Edward Island), 211
Star Charters (Lunenburg), 76
Stonehurst (Nova Scotia), 77
Summit Place (Halifax), 89
Sunbury Shores Arts and
Nature Centre (St.
Andrews), 33
Suttles & Seawinds
(Mahone Bay), 83
Swimming
    New Brunswick, 145, 176
    Prince Edward Island, 198

Swissair Flight 111 Memorial
(Peggy's Cove), 103
Sydney and Louisbourg Rail-
way Museum (Cape Breton),
135
Sydney (Cape Breton), 133–134

T ablelands, The (Newfound-
land), 244, 246
Tablelands Trail (Newfound-
land), 245
Tamarack Golf Course
(Labrador), 296
Tancook Islands (Nova
Scotia), 85
Tatamagouche (Nova Scotia),
108–110
Taxes, 15
Telegraph cables, first trans-
Atlantic (Heart's Content),
271
Telephones, 39
Telus, 25
Terra Nova Adventures (New-
foundland), 262
Terra Nova National Park
(Newfoundland), 6, 47, 238,
261–264
Theatre New Brunswick
(Fredericton), 168
Third Vault Falls Trail (New
Brunswick), 178
Thornbloom, The Inspired
Home (Halifax), 95
Time zone, 39
Timmons Folk Art Studio
(Pleasant Bay), 123
Tipping, 39
Titanic disaster, 90, 259
    Fairview Lawn Cemetery
    (Halifax), 93
Toilets, 39
Toope, Kevin, 266
Tor Bay Provincial Park
(Nova Scotia), 106
Tours
    escorted, 32–33
    package, 31–32
T'Railway (Port aux Basques),
239
Trains and railways, 29, 31
    Port aux Basques Railway
    Heritage Center (New-
    foundland), 239
    Québec North Shore and
    Labrador Railway, 296
    Sydney and Louisbourg Rail-
    way Museum (Cape Bre-
    ton), 135

Trans-Atlantic telegraph cables (Heart's Content), 271–272
Transportation, 30–31
Trapper John's (St. John's), 286
Travel Assistance International, 18
TravelAxe, 23
Traveler's checks, 14–15
Travelex Insurance Services, 18
Travel Guard Alerts, 18
Travel Guard International, 18
Traveling Internationally with Your Kids, 21
Travel insurance, 17–19
Travel Insured International, 18
Travelocity, 22, 23
Travelweb, 23
Trinity Historical Society Museum, 266
Trinity Interpretation Centre (Newfoundland), 265–266
Trinity (Newfoundland), 7, 46, 265–269
Trinity Pageant, 266
Trip Advisor, 23
Trip-cancellation insurance, 17–18
Trout River Pond Boat Tours (Gros Morne), 245
Trout River Pond campground (Newfoundland), 246
Trout River Pond (Gros Morne), 245
Twillingate Island Boat Tours, 259
Twillingate Museum and Crafts Shop (Newfoundland), 257–258
Twillingate (Newfoundland), 7, 257–260
Tyne Valley (Prince Edward Island), 231–232

United States Tour Operators Association, 31
United Vacations, 31
Upper Clements Park (Annapolis Royal), 5, 59
Urban Cottage (Halifax), 95

VIA Rail, 1, 29
Victoria Park (Charlottetown), 214
Victoria Playhouse (Prince Edward Island), 230
Victoria (Prince Edward Island), 7, 44, 229–231
Victoria Row (Charlottetown), 221
Victoria Seaport Museum (Prince Edward Island), 230
Viking Boat Tours (Newfoundland), 252
Viking Trail (Route 430; Newfoundland), 4, 251
Village Historique Acadien (near Caraquet), 6, 33, 189–190
Visitor information, 11
Visitor Rebate Program, 16

Wabush (Labrador), 296
Washrooms, 39
Waterfront Walk (Nova Scotia), 5
Waterloo Row (Fredericton), 169
Wax World of the Stars (Cavendish), 201
Weather, 16–17
Websites
    travel-planning and booking, 22–24
    visitor information, 11

Weil Winery (Twillingate), 258
Western Brook Pond (Newfoundland), 247–248
Western Union, 38
Wet Lab (Terra Nova National Park), 262
Whales and whale-watching
    New Brunswick, 145, 150, 156–157
    Nova Scotia, 2, 54
        Cape Breton, 122–123
        Chéticamp, 121
        Digby Neck, 66
        Lunenburg, 76
White Head Island (New Brunswick), 156
White Point (Cape Breton), 125
Wi-Fi, 25
Willie Krauch & Sons Smokehouse (Tangier), 105
Witless Bay Ecological Reserve (Newfoundland), 236, 287
Wolfe Lake Campground (Fundy National Park), 178
Wolfville (Nova Scotia), 55–58
Wooden Boat Festival (Mahone Bay), 82
Wordplay (St. John's), 281

Yahoo! Mail, 25
Yarmouth Light (Nova Scotia), 70
Yarmouth (Nova Scotia), 69–72
Yarmouth Visitor Centre (Nova Scotia), 69
Ye Olde Stone Barn Museum (Brigus), 274
York-Sunbury Historical Society Museum (Fredericton), 168, 171

# *Frommer's* Complete Guides

The only guide independent travelers need to make smart choices, avoid rip-offs, get the most for their money, and travel like a pro.

Alaska
Alaska Cruises & Ports of Call
American Southwest
Amsterdam
Argentina & Chile
Arizona
Atlanta
Australia
Austria
Bahamas
Barcelona
Beijing
Belgium, Holland & Luxembourg
Bermuda
Boston
Brazil
British Columbia & the Canadian Rockies
Brussels & Bruges
Budapest & the Best of Hungary
Calgary
California
Canada
Cancún, Cozumel & the Yucatán
Cape Cod, Nantucket & Martha's Vineyard
Caribbean
Caribbean Ports of Call
Carolinas & Georgia
Chicago
China
Colorado
Costa Rica
Cruises & Ports of Call
Cuba
Denmark
Denver, Boulder & Colorado Springs

Edinburgh & Glasgow
England
Europe
Europe by Rail
European Cruises & Ports of Call
Florence, Tuscany & Umbria
Florida
France
Germany
Great Britain
Greece
Greek Islands
Halifax
Hawaii
Hong Kong
Honolulu, Waikiki & Oahu
India
Ireland
Italy
Jamaica
Japan
Kauai
Las Vegas
London
Los Angeles
Madrid
Maine Coast
Maryland & Delaware
Maui
Mexico
Montana & Wyoming
Montréal & Québec City
Munich & the Bavarian Alps
Nashville & Memphis
New England
Newfoundland & Labrador
New Mexico
New Orleans
New York City
New York State
New Zealand
Northern Italy
Norway
Nova Scotia, New Brunswick & Prince Edward Island

Oregon
Ottawa
Paris
Peru
Philadelphia & the Amish Country
Portugal
Prague & the Best of the Czech Republic
Provence & the Riviera
Puerto Rico
Rome
San Antonio & Austin
San Diego
San Francisco
Santa Fe, Taos & Albuquerque
Scandinavia
Scotland
Seattle
Seville, Granada & the Best of Andalusia
Shanghai
Sicily
Singapore & Malaysia
South Africa
South America
South Florida
South Pacific
Southeast Asia
Spain
Sweden
Switzerland
Texas
Thailand
Tokyo
Toronto
Turkey
USA
Utah
Vancouver & Victoria
Vermont, New Hampshire & Maine
Vienna & the Danube Valley
Virgin Islands
Virginia
Walt Disney World® & Orlando
Washington, D.C.
Washington State

# THE NEW TRAVELOCITY GUARANTEE

## EVERYTHING YOU BOOK WILL BE RIGHT, OR WE'LL WORK WITH OUR TRAVEL PARTNERS TO MAKE IT RIGHT, RIGHT AWAY.

*To drive home the point, we're going to use the word "right" in every single sentence.*

Let's get right to it. Right to the meat! Only Travelocity guarantees everything about your booking will be right, or we'll work with our travel partners to make it right, right away. Right on!

*Here's a picture taken smack dab right in the middle of Antigua, where the guarantee also covers you.*

*The guarantee covers all but one of the items pictured to the right.*

For example, what if the ocean view you booked actually looks out at a downright ugly parking lot? You'd be right to call – we're there for you. And no one in their right mind would be pleased to learn the rental car place has closed and left them stranded. Call Travelocity and we'll help get you back on the right track.

Now, you may be thinking, "Yeah, right, I'm so sure." That's OK; you have the right to remain skeptical. That is until we mention help is always right around the corner. Call us right off the bat, knowing that our customer service reps are there for you 24/7. Righting wrongs. Left and right.

Now if you're guessing there are some things we can't control, like the weather, well you're right. But we can help you with most things – to get all the details in righting,* visit **travelocity.com/guarantee**.

*Sorry, spelling things right is one of the few things not covered under the guarantee.

*I'd give my right arm for a guarantee like this, although I'm glad I don't have to.*

**travelocity**
*You'll never roam alone.*